CCNP Self-Study
CCNP BCMSN
Official Exam Certification Guide
Fourth Edition

David Hucaby
CCIE No. 4594

ISBN 978-81-317-0999-3

First Impression, 2007
Second Impression, 2007
Third Impression, 2007
Fourth Impression, 2008
Fifth Impression, 2008
Sixth Impression, 2008
Seventh Impression, 2009

This edition is manufactured in India and is authorized for sale only in India, Bangladesh, Bhutan, Pakistan, Nepal, Sri Lanka and the Maldives. Circulation of this edition outside of these territories is UNAUTHORIZED.

Published by Dorling Kindersley (India) Pvt. Ltd., licensees of Pearson Education in South Asia.

Head Office: 482, F.I.E., Patparganj, Delhi 110 092, India.
Registered Office: 14 Local Shopping Centre, Panchsheel Park, New Delhi 110 017, India.

Printed in India by Rahul Print O Pack.

About the Author

David Hucaby, CCIE No. 4594, is a lead network engineer for the University of Kentucky, where he works with healthcare networks based on the Cisco Catalyst, ASA, FWSM, and VPN product lines. David has a bachelor of science degree and master of science degree in electrical engineering from the University of Kentucky. He is the author of three previous books for Cisco Press, including *Cisco ASA and PIX Firewall Handbook*, *Cisco Field Manual: Router Configuration*, and *Cisco Field Manual: Catalyst Switch Configuration*.

David lives in Kentucky with his wife, Marci, and two daughters.

About the Technical Reviewers

John Tiso, CCIE No. 5162, MCSE, CCDP, holds a bachelor of science degree from Adelphi University in New York. He currently serves as a customer support engineer in the Cisco Heartland TAC. Before joining the team at Cisco, John was the lead AVVID consultant and installer for a Cisco Gold Partner. John has written and edited for Cisco Press for many years. He has also published papers in several industry publications and coauthored a book for Cisco Learning Systems. John is also a speaker at the Cisco Networkers and CIPTUG conferences.

Wayne Lewis, Ph.D., is the Cisco Academy Manager for the Pacific Center for Advanced Technology Training, based at Honolulu Community College. Since 1998, he has taught routing and switching, remote access, troubleshooting, network security, and wireless networking to instructors from universities, colleges, and high schools in Australia, Canada, Mexico, Central America, South America, China, Hong Kong, Indonesia, Korea, Singapore, Taiwan, and Japan, both onsite and at Honolulu Community College. Cisco Systems has sent Wayne to several countries to conduct inaugural Networking Academy teacher training sessions in networking to certify the initial cohorts of instructors for these countries. Before teaching networking, Wayne began teaching math at age 20 at Wichita State University, followed by the University of Hawaii and Honolulu Community College. In 1992, he received a Ph.D. in math, specializing in finite rank torsion-free modules over a Dedekind domain. He works as a contractor for Cisco Systems, performing project management for the development of network security and multilayer switching curriculum. He enjoys surfing the South Shore of Oahu in the summer and surfing big waves on the North Shore of Oahu in the winter.

Dedications

As always, this book is dedicated to the most important people in my life: my wife, Marci, and my two little daughters, Lauren and Kara. Their love, encouragement, and support carry me along. I'm so grateful to God, who gives endurance and encouragement (Romans 15:5), and has allowed me to work on projects like this.

I would also like to dedicate this book to the memory of two close relatives whom I've lost this year:

Ralph Hucaby, my uncle, a fellow EE, and a pioneer in the television industry, who always had an interest in my technical pursuits for as long as I can remember.

Phyllis Wilson, my mother in-law, who never owned a computer or touched a network, yet was genuinely interested in my writing projects. Her friendship and good cooking will always be missed.

Acknowledgments

It has been my great pleasure to work on another Cisco Press project. I enjoy the networking field very much, and technical writing even more. And more than that, I'm thankful for the joy and inner peace that Jesus Christ gives, making everything more abundant.

Technical writing may be hard work, but I'm finding that it's also quite fun because I'm working with very good friends. I can't say enough good things about Chris Cleveland. Somehow Chris is able to handle many book projects all at once, while giving each one an incredible amount of attention and improvement. Brett Bartow and Mary Beth Ray have been very helpful, as always, with their management of the book project.

I am very grateful for the insight, suggestions, and helpful comments that Wayne Lewis and John Tiso contributed. Each one offered a different perspective, which helped make this a more well-rounded book and me a more educated author. I would also like to thank my good friends Mark Macumber and Rick Herring who helped me along the way (whether they realized it or not).

Contents at a Glance

x

Contents

xvi

Icons Used in This Book

 Router

 Bridge

 Hub

 DSU/CSU

Catalyst Switch

 Modem

 ATM Switch

 ISDN/Frame Relay Switch

 Communication Server

 Gateway

 PC

 PC with Software

 Sun Workstation

 Macintosh

 Terminal

 Multilayer Switch

 Web Server

 File Server

 Laptop

Printer

 Access Server

 Cisco Works Workstation

 IBM Mainframe

 Front End Processor

Cluster Controller

 Line: Ethernet

 Line: Serial

Line: Switched Serial

Wireless Connection

 Token Ring

 FDDI

Network Cloud

 Access Point

 Lightweight Single Radio Access Point

 WLAN Controller

Command Syntax Conventions

The conventions used to present command syntax in this book are the same conventions used in the IOS Command Reference. The Command Reference describes these conventions as follows:

■ **Boldface** indicates commands and keywords that are entered literally as shown. In actual configuration examples and output (not general command syntax), boldface indicates commands that are manually input by the user (such as a **show** command).

■ *Italics* indicate arguments for which you supply actual values.

■ Vertical bars (|) separate alternative, mutually exclusive elements.

■ Square brackets [ ] indicate optional elements.

■ Braces { } indicate a required choice.

■ Braces within brackets [{ }] indicate a required choice within an optional element.

Foreword

CCNP BCMSN Exam Certification Guide, Fourth Edition, is an excellent self-study resource for the CCNP BCMSN exam. Passing the exam validates the knowledge, skills, and understanding needed to build scalable multilayer switched networks, create and deploy a global intranet, and implement basic troubleshooting techniques in environments that use Cisco multilayer switches for client hosts and services. It is one of several exams required to attain the CCNP certification.

Cisco Press Exam Certification Guide titles are designed to help educate, develop, and grow the community of Cisco networking professionals. The guides are filled with helpful features that allow you to master key concepts and assess your readiness for the certification exam. Developed in conjunction with the Cisco certifications team, Cisco Press books are the only self-study books authorized by Cisco Systems.

Most networking professionals use a variety of learning methods to gain necessary skills. Cisco Press self-study titles are a prime source of content for some individuals, and can also serve as an excellent supplement to other forms of learning. Training classes, whether delivered in a classroom or on the Internet, are a great way to quickly acquire new understanding. Hands-on practice is essential for anyone seeking to build, or hone, new skills. Authorized Cisco training classes, labs, and simulations are available exclusively from Cisco Learning Solutions Partners worldwide. Please visit www.cisco.com/go/training to learn more about Cisco Learning Solutions Partners.

I hope and expect that you'll find this guide to be an essential part of your exam preparation and a valuable addition to your personal library.

Don Field
Director, Certifications
Cisco System, Inc.
November, 2006

Introduction: Overview of Certification and How to Succeed

Professional certifications have been an important part of the computing industry for many years and will continue to become more important. Many reasons exist for these certifications, but the most popularly cited reason is that of credibility. All other considerations held equal, the certified employee/consultant/job candidate is considered more valuable than one who is not.

Objectives and Methods

The most important and somewhat obvious objective of this book is to help you pass the Cisco BCMSN exam (642-812). In fact, if the primary objective of this book were different, the book's title would be misleading; however, the methods used in this book to help you pass the BCMSN exam are designed to also make you much more knowledgeable about how to do your job. Although this book and the accompanying CD-ROM have many sample test questions, the method in which they are used is not to simply make you memorize as many questions and answers as you possibly can.

One key methodology used in this book helps you discover the exam topics about which you need more review, to help you fully understand and remember those details, and to help you prove to yourself that you have retained your knowledge of those topics. So this book helps you pass not by memorization, but by helping you truly learn and understand the topics. The BCMSN exam is just one of the foundation topics in the CCNP and CCDP certifications, and the knowledge contained within is vitally important to consider yourself a truly skilled routing and switching engineer or specialist. This book would do you a disservice if it did not attempt to help you learn the material. To that end, the book can help you pass the BCMSN exam by using the following methods:

- Helping you discover which test topics you have not mastered
- Providing explanations and information to fill in your knowledge gaps
- Supplying exercises and scenarios that enhance your ability to recall and deduce the answers to test questions
- Providing practice exercises on the topics and the testing process through test questions on the CD-ROM

Who Should Read This Book?

This book is not designed to be a general networking topics book, although it can be used for that purpose. This book is intended to tremendously increase your chances of passing the Cisco BCMSN exam. Although other objectives can be achieved from using this book, the book is written with one goal in mind: to help you pass the exam.

The BCMSN exam is primarily based on the content of the Building Converged Cisco Multilayer Switched Networks (BCMSN) 3.0 CCNP course. You should have either taken the course, read through the BCMSN coursebook or this book, or have a couple of years of LAN switching experience.

Exam Overview

Cisco offers three levels of certification, each with an increasing level of proficiency: Associate, Professional, and Expert. These are commonly known by their acronyms CCNA/CCDA (Cisco Certified Network/Design Associate), CCNP/CCDP (Cisco Certified Network/Design Professional), and CCIE (Cisco Certified Internetworking Expert). There are others as well, but this book focuses on the certifications for enterprise networks.

For the CCNP certification, you must pass a series of four core exams or pass a longer foundations exam plus one support exam. The BCMSN exam or its content is included and required for either path. For most exams, Cisco does not publish the scores needed for passing. You need to take the exam to find that out for yourself.

To see the most current requirements for the CCNP or CCDP certifications, go to cisco.com; then click Learning and Events, followed by Career Certifications and Paths.

The BCMSN exam itself is composed of 60 to 70 questions, presented in a variety of formats. You can expect to find multiple-choice, single-answer; multiple-choice, multiple-answer; drag-and-drop; fill-in-the-blank; and simulation questions. To find more specific information about the topics that can be covered on the BCMSN exam, go to cisco.com; then click Learning and Events, followed by Exam Information and then Certification Exams. The exam lasts 90 minutes and is offered through either Pearson VUE or Prometric testing centers only. See www.cisco.com/en/US/learning/le3/le11/learning_about_registering_for_exams.html for the most current information about registering for the exam.

Strategies for Exam Preparation

The strategy you use to prepare for the BCMSN exam might be slightly different than strategies used by other readers, mainly based on the skills, knowledge, and experience you already have obtained. For example, if you have attended the BCMSN course, you might take a different approach than someone who learned switching through on-the-job training.

Regardless of the strategy you use or the background you have, this book is designed to help you get to the point that you can pass the exam with the least amount of time required. For example, there is no need for you to practice or read about IP addressing and subnetting if you fully understand it already. However, many people like to make sure that they truly know a topic and read over material that they already know. Several book features help you gain the confidence that you know some material already and also help you know what topics you need to study more.

How This Book Is Organized

Although this book can be read cover to cover, it is designed to be flexible and allow you to easily move between chapters and sections of chapters to cover only the material that you need more work with. Chapters 1 through 19 are the core chapters and can be covered in any order, though some chapters are related and build upon each other. If you do intend to read them all, the order in the book is an excellent sequence to use.

When you finish with the core chapters, you have several options on how to finish your exam preparation. Chapter 20, "Scenarios for Final Preparation," provides many scenarios to help you review and refine your knowledge, without giving you a false sense of preparedness that you would get with simply reviewing a set of multiple-choice questions. You can review the questions at the end of each chapter, and you can use the CD-ROM testing software to practice the exam.

Each core chapter covers a subset of the topics on the BCMSN exam. The core chapters are organized into parts. The core chapters cover the following topics:

Part I: Overview and Design of a Campus Network

- **Chapter 1, "Campus Network Overview"**—This chapter covers the use of switches in the OSI model's various layers, the different campus network models, hierarchical network design, and how Cisco's switching products fit into a hierarchical network design.

- **Chapter 2, "Modular Network Design"**—This chapter covers how to design, size, and scale a campus network using a modular approach.

Part II: Building a Campus Network

- **Chapter 3, "Switch Operation"**—This chapter covers Layer 2 and multilayer switch operation, how various CAM and TCAM tables are used to make switching decisions, and how to monitor these tables to aid in troubleshooting.

- **Chapter 4, "Switch Port Configuration"**—This chapter covers basic Ethernet concepts, how to use scalable Ethernet, how to connect switch block devices, and how to verify switch port operation to aid in troubleshooting.

- **Chapter 5, "VLANs and Trunks"**—This chapter covers basic VLAN concepts, how to transport multiple VLANs over single links, how to configure VLAN trunks, and how to verify VLAN and trunk operation.

- **Chapter 6, "VLAN Trunking Protocol"**—This chapter covers VLAN management using VTP, VTP configuration, traffic management through VTP pruning, and how to verify VTP operation.

- **Chapter 7, "Aggregating Switch Links"**—This chapter covers switch port aggregation with EtherChannel, EtherChannel negotiation protocols, EtherChannel configuration, and how to verify EtherChannel operation.

- **Chapter 8, "Traditional Spanning Tree Protocol"**—This chapter covers IEEE 802.1D Spanning Tree Protocol (STP) and gives an overview of the other STP types that might be running on a switch.

- **Chapter 9, "Spanning Tree Configuration"**—This chapter covers the STP root bridge, how to customize the STP topology, how to tune STP convergence, redundant link convergence, and how to verify STP operation.

- **Chapter 10, "Protecting the Spanning Tree Protocol Topology"**—This chapter covers protecting the STP topology using Root Guard, BPDU Guard, and Loop Guard, and also how to use BPDU filtering and how to verify that these STP protection mechanisms are functioning properly.

- **Chapter 11, "Advanced Spanning Tree Protocol"**—This chapter covers Rapid Spanning Tree Protocol (RSTP) for Rapid PVST+ and Multiple Spanning Tree (MST) Protocol.

Part III: Layer 3 Switching

- **Chapter 12, "Multilayer Switching"**—This chapter covers interVLAN routing, multilayer switching with CEF, and how to verify that multilayer switching is functioning properly.

- **Chapter 13, "Router, Supervisor, and Power Redundancy"**—This chapter covers providing redundant router or gateway addresses on Catalyst switches and verifying that redundancy is functioning properly.

Part IV: Campus Network Services

- **Chapter 14, "IP Telephony"**—This chapter covers how a Catalyst switch can provide power to operate a Cisco IP Phone, how voice traffic can be carried over the links between an IP Phone and a Catalyst switch, QoS for voice traffic, and how to verify that IP Telephony features are functioning properly.

- **Chapter 15, "Securing Switch Access"**—This chapter covers switch Authentication, Authorization, and Accounting (AAA); port security using MAC addresses; port-based security using IEEE 802.1x; DHCP snooping; and dynamic ARP inspection.

- **Chapter 16, "Securing with VLANs"**—This chapter covers how to control traffic within a VLAN using access lists, implementing private VLANs, and monitoring traffic on switch ports for security reasons.

Part V: Wireless LANs

- **Chapter 17, "Wireless LAN Overview"**—This chapter presents an introduction to wireless LANs, radio frequency theory, and the standards that are used in a wireless LAN.

- **Chapter 18, "Wireless Architecture and Design"**—This chapter covers the operational aspects of wireless LANs, such as wireless security, wireless client mobility, and the layout of wireless devices.

- **Chapter 19, "Cisco Unified Wireless Network"**—This chapter covers the Cisco Unified Wireless Network and its components, the lightweight access points and wireless LAN controllers, and the basic configuration steps needed.

Each chapter in the book uses several features to help you make the best use of your time in that chapter. The features are as follows:

- **Assessment**—Each chapter begins with a "Do I Know This Already?" quiz that helps you determine the amount of time you need to spend studying that chapter. If you intend to read the entire chapter, you can save the quiz for later use. Questions are all multiple-choice, single-answer, to give a quick assessment of your knowledge.

- **Foundation Topics**—This is the core section of each chapter that explains the protocols, concepts, and configuration for the topics in the chapter.

- **Foundation Summary**—At the end of each chapter, a Foundation Summary collects key concepts, facts, and commands into an easy-to-review format. A more lengthy "Q&A" section follows, where many review questions are presented. Questions are mainly open-ended rather than multiple choice, as found on the exams. This is done to focus more on understanding the subject matter than on memorizing details.

- **Scenarios**—Scenarios are collected in the final chapter, Chapter 20, to allow a much more in-depth examination of a network implementation. Instead of posing a simple question asking for a single fact, the scenarios let you design, configure, and troubleshoot networks (at least on paper) without the clues inherent in a multiple-choice quiz format.

- **CD-based practice exam**—The companion CD-ROM contains two separate test banks—one composed of the questions from the book and an entirely new test bank of questions to reinforce your understanding of the book's concepts. In addition to the multiple-choice questions, you encounter some configuration simulation questions for which you actually perform configurations. This is the best tool for helping you prepare for the actual test-taking process.

How to Use This Book for Study

Retention and recall are the two features of human memory most closely related to performance on tests. This exam-preparation guide focuses on increasing both retention and recall of the topics on the exam. The other human characteristic involved in successfully passing the exam is intelligence; this book does not address that issue!

Adult retention is typically less than that of children. For example, it is common for 4-year-olds to pick up basic language skills in a new country faster than their parents. Children retain facts as an end unto itself; adults typically either need a stronger reason to remember a fact or must have a reason to think about that fact several times to retain it in memory. For these reasons, a student who attends a typical Cisco course and retains 50% of the material is actually quite an amazing student.

Memory recall is based on connectors to the information that needs to be recalled—the greater the number of connectors to a piece of information, the better chance and better speed of recall. For example, if the exam asks what VTP stands for, you automatically add information to the question. You know that the topic is switching because of the nature of the test. You might recall the term *VTP domain*, which implies that this is a type of switch domain. You might also remember that it is talking about VLANs. Having read one of the multiple-choice answers "VLAN Trunk Protocol," you might even have the infamous "a-ha" experience, in which you are then sure that your answer is correct—and possibly a brightly lit bulb is hovering over your head. All these added facts and assumptions are the connectors that eventually lead your brain to the fact that needs to be recalled. Of course, recall and retention work together. If you do not retain the knowledge, recalling it will be difficult.

This book is designed with features to help you increase retention and recall. It does this in the following ways:

- By providing succinct and complete methods of helping you decide what you recall easily and what you do not recall at all.

- By giving references to the exact passages in the book that review those concepts you did not recall, so you can quickly be reminded about a fact or concept. Repeating information that connects to another concept helps retention, and describing the same concept in several ways throughout a chapter increases the number of connectors to the same pieces of information.

- By including exercise questions that supply fewer connectors than multiple-choice questions. This helps you exercise recall and avoids giving you a false sense of confidence, as an exercise with only multiple-choice questions might do. For example, fill-in-the-blank questions require you to have better and more complete recall than multiple-choice questions.

- By pulling the entire breadth of subject matter together. A separate chapter (Chapter 20) contains scenarios and several related questions that cover every topic on the exam and gives you the chance to prove that you have gained mastery over the subject matter. This reduces the connectors implied by questions residing in a particular chapter and requires you to exercise other connectors to remember the details.

- Finally, accompanying this book is a CD-ROM that has examlike questions in a variety of formats. These are useful for you to practice taking the exam and to get accustomed to the time restrictions imposed during the exam.

In taking the "Do I Know This Already?" assessment quizzes in each chapter, make sure that you treat yourself and your knowledge fairly. If you come across a question that makes you guess at an answer, mark it wrong immediately. This forces you to read through the part of the chapter that relates to that question and forces you to learn it more thoroughly.

If you find that you do well on the assessment quizzes, it still might be wise to quickly skim through each chapter to find sections or topics that do not readily come to mind. Sometimes even reading through the detailed table of contents will reveal topics that are unfamiliar or unclear. If that happens to you, mark those chapters or topics and spend time working through those parts of the book.

Strategies for the Exam

Try to schedule the exam far enough in advance that you have ample time for study. Consider the time of day and even the day of the week so that you choose a time frame that suits your daily routine. Because the exam lasts 90 minutes, you should make sure that the exam time does not coincide with your regular lunchtime or some other part of the day when you are usually tired or trying to wake up. As for the day of the week, your work schedule might prevent you from studying a few days before the exam.

Hopefully, you can find a testing center located nearby. In any event, be sure to familiarize yourself with the driving and parking directions well ahead of time. You do not want to be frantically searching for streets or buildings a few minutes before the exam is scheduled to start. You will need at least one form of picture ID to present at the testing center.

Think about common-sense things, such as eating a nutritious meal before you leave for the exam. You need to be as comfortable as possible for the entire 90-minute exam, so it pays not to be hungry. Limiting the amount of liquids you consume right before test time might also be wise. After the exam begins, the clock does not stop for a restroom break. Also think about taking along a lightweight jacket, in case the exam room feels cold.

During the exam, try to pace yourself by knowing that there are, at most, 70 questions in a 90-minute period. That does not mean that every question should be answered in a little over a minute; it means only that you should try to move along at a regular pace. Be aware that if you are unsure about an answer, you are not allowed to mark the question and return to it later. That was allowed in exams of years past, but not anymore. This might force you into a guessing position on a question, just so you can move along to the others before the time runs out.

At the end of the exam, you receive your final score and news of your passing or failing. If you pass, congratulate yourself and breathe a sigh of relief at not having to study more!

If you fail, remind yourself that you are not a failure. It is never a disgraceful thing to fail a Cisco test, as long as you decide to try it again. Anybody who has ever taken a Cisco exam knows that to be true; just ask the people who have attempted the CCIE lab exam. As soon as you can, schedule to take the same exam again. Allow a few days so that you can study the topics that gave you trouble. The exam score should also break down the entire exam into major topics, each with its respective score. Do not be discouraged about starting over with your studies—the majority is already behind you. Just spend time brushing up on the "low spots" where you lack knowledge or confidence.

CCNP Exam Topics

Carefully consider the exam topics Cisco has posted on its website as you study, particularly for clues to how deeply you should know each topic. Beyond that, you cannot go wrong by developing a broader knowledge of the subject matter. You can do that by reading and studying the topics presented in this book. Remember that it is in your best interest to become proficient in each of the CCNP subjects. When it is time to use what you have learned, being well rounded counts more than being well tested.

Table I-1 shows the official exam topics for the BCMSN exam, as posted on Cisco.com. Note that Cisco has historically changed exam topics without changing the exam number, so do not be alarmed if small changes in the exam topics occur over time. When in doubt, go to cisco.com, click Learning and Events, and select Career Certifications and Paths.

Table I-1 *BCMSN Exam Topics*

Exam Topic	Part of This Book Where Exam Topic Is Covered
Describe the Enterprise Composite Model used for designing networks, and explain how it addresses enterprise network needs for performance, scalability, and availability*	Part I*
Describe the physical, data link, and network layer technologies used in a switched network, and identify when to use each*	Part I*
Explain the role of switches in the various modules of the Enterprise Composite Model (Campus Infrastructure, Server Farm, Enterprise Edge, Network Management)*	Part I*
Compare end-to-end and local VLANs and determine when to use each*	Part I*
Explain the functions of VLANs in a hierarchical network	Part II
Configure VLANs (native, default, static, and access)	Part II
Explain and configure VLAN trunking (i.e. IEEE 802.1Q and ISL)	Part II

Table I-1 *BCMSN Exam Topics (Continued)*

Exam Topic	Part of This Book Where Exam Topic Is Covered
Explain and configure VTP	Part II
Verify or troubleshoot VLAN configurations	Part II
Explain the functions and operations of the Spanning Tree protocols (i.e. RSTP, PVRST, and MISTP)	Part II
Configure RSTP (PVRST) and MISTP	Part II
Describe and configure STP security mechanisms (i.e. BPDU Guard, BPDU Filtering, Root Guard)	Part II
Configure and verify UDLD and Loop Guard	Part II
Verify or troubleshoot Spanning Tree protocol operations	Part II
Configure and verify link aggregation using PAgP or LACP	Part II
Explain and configure InterVLAN routing (i.e. SVI and routed ports)	Part III
Explain and enable CEF operation	Part III
Verify or troubleshoot InterVLAN routing configurations	Part III
Explain the functions and operations of gateway redundancy protocols (i.e. HSRP, VRRP, and GLBP)	Part III
Configure HSRP, VRRP, and GLBP	Part III
Verify High Availability configurations	Part III
Describe the components and operations of WLAN topologies (i.e. AP and bridge)	Part V
Describe the features of Client Devices, Network Unification, and Mobility Platforms (i.e. CCX, LWAPP)	Part V
Configure a wireless client (i.e. ADU)	Part V
Describe common Layer 2 network attacks (e.g. MAC flooding, Rogue Devices, VLAN Hopping, DHCP Spoofing, etc.)	Part IV
Explain and configure Port Security (i.e. 802.1x, VACLs, Private VLANs, DHCP Snooping, and DAI	Part IV
Verify Catalyst switch (IOS-based) security configurations (i.e. Port Security, 802.1x, VACLs, Private VLANs, DHCP Snooping, and DAI)	Part IV
Describe the characteristics of voice in the campus network	Part IV
Describe the functions of Voice VLANs and trust boundaries	Part IV
Configure and verify basic IP Phone support (i.e. Voice VLAN, Trust and CoS options, AutoQoS for voice)	Part IV

* While the topics listed here are not included in the updated list of exam topics for the 642-812 exam, you will still need to be familiar with these concepts to successfully pass the exam.

For More Information

If you have any comments about the book, you can submit those via the ciscopress.com website. Just go to the website, select Contact Us, and type in your message.

Cisco might make changes that affect the CCNP certification from time to time. You should always check cisco.com for the latest details. Also, you can look to www.ciscopress.com/title/1587201712, where we will publish any information pertinent to how you might use this book differently in light of Cisco's future changes. For example, if Cisco decided to remove a major topic from the exam, it might post that on its website; Cisco Press will make an effort to list that information as well.

This part of the book covers the following BCMSN exam topics:

- Describe the Enterprise Composite Model used for designing networks, and explain how it addresses enterprise network needs for performance, scalability, and availability

- Describe the physical, data link, and network layer technologies used in a switched network, and identify when to use each

- Explain the role of switches in the various modules of the Enterprise Composite Model (Campus Infrastructure, Server Farm, Enterprise Edge, Network Management)

- Compare end-to-end and local VLANs and determine when to use each

While the topics listed here are not included in the updated list of exam topics for the 642-812 exam, you will still need to be familiar with these concepts to successfully pass the exam.

Part I: Overview and Design of a Campus Network

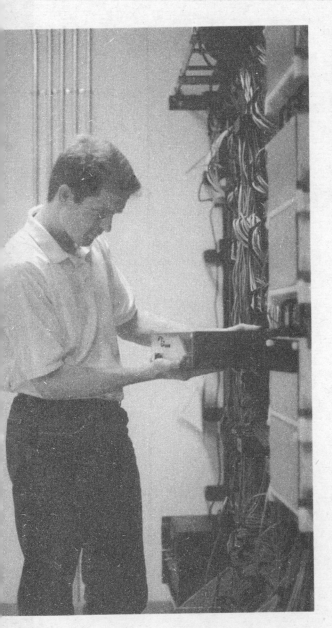

This chapter covers the following topics that you need to master for the CCNP BCMSN exam:

- **Switching Functionality**—This section covers the use of switches in the OSI model layers. You learn about the functions and application of routing and switching in Layers 2, 3, and 4, along with the concept of multilayer switching.

- **Campus Network Models**—This section presents the concept of a campus network, and describes the traditional campus model and models based on traffic patterns. This section also describes the factors that affect a campus network's design.

- **Hierarchical Network Design**—This section details a three-layer, hierarchical structure of campus network designs.

CHAPTER 1

Campus Network Overview

As campus networks have grown and technologies have matured, network engineers and architects have many more options to consider than the hubs, Ethernet switches, and routers traditionally put in place. You can use switches to improve network performance in many ways; however, simply replacing existing shared networks with switched networks is not enough. The switching function alone alleviates congestion and increases bandwidth (in addition to more complex capabilities) if properly placed and designed. Switches themselves have also improved over time. The type of switch, its capabilities, and its location within a network can greatly enhance network performance.

This chapter presents a logical design process that you can use to build a new campus network or to modify and improve an existing network.

"Do I Know This Already?" Quiz

The purpose of the "Do I Know This Already?" quiz is to help you decide whether you need to read the entire chapter. If you intend to read the entire chapter, you do not necessarily need to answer these questions now.

The 12-question quiz, derived from the major sections in the "Foundation Topics" portion of the chapter, helps you determine how to spend your limited study time.

Table 1-1 outlines the major topics discussed in this chapter and the "Do I Know This Already?" quiz questions that correspond to those topics.

Table 1-1 *"Do I Know This Already?" Foundation Topics Section-to-Question Mapping*

Foundation Topics Section	Questions Covered in This Section	Score
Switching Functionality	1–3	
Campus Networks, Traffic Pattern Models	4–7	
Hierarchical Design Model	8–12	
Total Score		

> **CAUTION**   The goal of self-assessment is to gauge your mastery of the topics in this chapter. If you do not know the answer to a question or are only partially sure of the answer, you should mark this question wrong. Giving yourself credit for an answer you correctly guess skews your self-assessment results and might provide you with a false sense of security.

You can find the answers to the quiz in Appendix A, "Answers to Chapter 'Do I Know This Already?' Quizzes and Q&A Sections." The suggested choices for your next step are as follows:

■ **6 or less overall score**—Read the entire chapter. This includes the "Foundation Topics," "Foundation Summary," and "Q&A" sections.

■ **7–9 overall score**—Begin with the "Foundation Summary" section and then follow up with the "Q&A" section at the end of the chapter.

■ **10 or more overall score**—If you want more review on these topics, skip to the "Foundation Summary" section and then go to the "Q&A" section at the end of the chapter. Otherwise, move on to Chapter 2, "Modular Network Design."

1. Layer 2 switching uses which of the following values to forward data?

   a. IP address

   b. IPX address

   c. MAC address

   d. RIP address

   e. UDP port

2. Multilayer switching (MLS) forwards packets based on what OSI layers?

   a. Layer 1

   b. Layer 2

   c. Layer 3

   d. Layer 4

   e. b, c, d

   f. a, b, c, d

3. Which of the following does a multilayer switch perform?

   a. Forwarding according to MAC address.

   b. Forwarding according to IP address.

   c. Forwarding according to UDP/TCP port numbers.

   d. All of these answers are correct.

4. What does the 20/80 rule of networking state? (Pick one.)

    a. Only 20 out of 80 packets arrive at the destination.

    b. Twenty percent of the network is used 80 percent of the time.

    c. Twenty percent of the traffic on a network segment travels across the network, whereas 80 percent of it stays local.

    d. Twenty percent of the traffic on a network segment stays local, whereas 80 percent of it travels across the network.

5. Where does a collision domain exist in a switched network?

    a. On a single switch port

    b. Across all switch ports

    c. On a single VLAN

    d. Across all VLANs

6. Where does a broadcast domain exist in a switched network?

    a. On a single switch port

    b. Across all switch ports

    c. On a single VLAN

    d. Across all VLANs

7. What is a VLAN primarily used for?

    a. To segment a collision domain

    b. To segment a broadcast domain

    c. To segment an autonomous system

    d. To segment a spanning-tree domain

8. How many layers are recommended in the hierarchical campus network design model?

    a. 1

    b. 2

    c. 3

    d. 4

    e. 7

9. End-user PCs should be connected into which of the following hierarchical layers?

    a. Distribution layer

    b. Common layer

    c. Access layer

    d. Core layer

10. In which OSI layer should devices in the distribution layer typically operate?

    a. Layer 1

    b. Layer 2

    c. Layer 3

    d. Layer 4

11. A hierarchical network's distribution layer aggregates which of the following?

    a. Core switches

    b. Broadcast domains

    c. Routing updates

    d. Access-layer switches

12. In the core layer of a hierarchical network, which of the following are aggregated?

    a. Routing tables

    b. Packet filters

    c. Distribution switches

    d. Access-layer switches

Foundation Topics

Switching Functionality

To understand how switches and routers should be chosen and placed in a network design, you should first understand how to take advantage of data communication at different layers.

The OSI reference model separates data communication into seven layers, as shown in Table 1-2. Each layer has a specific function and a specific protocol so that two devices can exchange data on the same layer. A protocol data unit (PDU) is the generic name for a block of data that a layer on one device exchanges with the same layer on a peer device. A PDU is encapsulated in a layer's protocol before it is made available to a lower-level layer, or unencapsulated before being handed to a higher-level layer.

Table 1-2 *Layers of Data Communications*

OSI Layer	Protocol Data Unit	Mechanism to Process PDU
7 (application)		
6 (presentation)		
5 (session)		
4 (transport)	TCP segment	TCP port
3 (network)	Packet	Router
2 (data link)	Frame	Switch/bridge
1 (physical)		

In Table 1-2, Layers 2, 3, and 4 are represented by the data link, network, and transport layers, respectively, with a PDU frame, packet, and TCP segment. When a TCP segment (Layer 4) needs to be transmitted to another station, the TCP segment is encapsulated as a packet (Layer 3) and further encapsulated as a frame (Layer 2). The receiving station unencapsulates Layers 2 and 3 before processing the original TCP segment.

The layered protocols also apply to networking devices. For example, a Layer 2 device transfers data by looking at the Layer 2 PDU header information. Upper-layer protocols are not looked at or even understood. Layer-specific devices are discussed in detail in the sections that follow.

Layer 2 Switching

Devices that forward frames at Layer 2 involve the following functions:

- MAC addresses are learned from the incoming frames' source addresses.

- A table of MAC addresses and their associated bridge and switch ports is built and maintained.

- Broadcast and multicast frames are flooded out to all ports (except the one that received the frame).

- Frames destined for unknown locations are flooded out to all ports (except the one that received the frame).

- Bridges and switches communicate with each other using the Spanning Tree Protocol to eliminate bridging loops.

A Layer 2 switch performs essentially the same function as a transparent bridge; however, a switch can have many ports and can perform *hardware-based bridging*. Frames are forwarded using specialized hardware, called *application-specific integrated circuits (ASIC)*. This hardware gives switching great scalability, with wire-speed performance, low latency, low cost, and high port density.

As long as Layer 2 frames are being switched between two Layer 1 interfaces of the same media type, such as two Ethernet connections or an Ethernet connection and a Fast Ethernet connection, the frames do not have to be modified. However, if the two interfaces are different media, such as Ethernet and Token Ring or Ethernet and Fiber Distributed Data Interface (FDDI), the Layer 2 switch must translate the frame contents before sending out the Layer 1 interface.

Layer 2 switching is used primarily for workgroup connectivity and network segmentation. You can contain traffic between users and servers in a workgroup within the switch. In addition, the number of stations on a network segment can be reduced with a switch, minimizing the collision domain size.

One drawback to Layer 2 switching is that it cannot be scaled effectively. Switches must forward broadcast frames to all ports, causing large switched networks to become large broadcast domains. In addition, Spanning Tree Protocol (STP) can have a slow convergence time when the switch topology changes. STP also can block certain switch ports, preventing data transfer. (Chapters 9 through 12 discuss STP and its variations in further detail.) Layer 2 switching alone cannot provide an effective, scalable network design.

Layer 3 Routing

Devices involved in Layer 3 routing perform the following functions:

- Packets are forwarded between networks based on Layer 3 addresses.

- An optimal path is determined for a packet to take through a network to the next router.

- Packet forwarding involves a table lookup of the destination network, the next-hop router address, and the router's own outbound interface.

- An optimal path can be chosen from among many possibilities.

- Routers communicate with each other using *routing protocols*.

By nature, routers do not forward broadcast packets and forward only multicast packets to segments with multicast clients. This action provides control over broadcast propagation and offers network *segmentation* into areas of common Layer 3 addressing.

Logical addressing is possible on a network with routers because the Layer 3 (network layer) address uniquely identifies a device only at the network layer of the OSI reference model. Actual frame forwarding occurs using the Layer 2, or data link, address of devices. Therefore, some method must exist to associate a device's data link layer (MAC) address with its network layer (IP) address. A router must also have addresses from both layers assigned to each of its interfaces connected to a network. This assignment gives the router the functionality to support the logical network layer addresses assigned to the physical networks.

In addition, a router must examine each packet's Layer 3 header before making a routing decision. Layer 3 security and control can be implemented on any router interface using the source and destination addresses, protocol, or other Layer 3 attribute to make decisions on whether to limit or forward the packets.

Layer 3 routing is generally performed by microprocessor-based engines, which require CPU cycles to examine each packet's network layer header. The routing table of optimal paths to Layer 3 networks can also be a large table of dynamic values, requiring a finite lookup delay. Although you can place a router anywhere in a network, the router can become a bottleneck because of a latency of packet examination and processing.

Layer 3 Switching

Devices involved in Layer 3 switching perform the following functions:

- Packets are forwarded at Layer 3, just as a router would do.

- Packets are switched using specialized hardware, ASIC, for high speed and low latency.

- Packets can be forwarded with security control and quality of service (QoS) using Layer 3 address information.

Layer 3 switches are designed to examine and forward packets in high-speed LAN environments. Whereas a router might impose a bottleneck to forwarding throughput, a Layer 3 switch can be placed anywhere in the network, with little or no performance penalty.

Layer 4 Switching

Devices involved in Layer 4 switching perform the following functions:

- Packets are forwarded using hardware switching, based on both Layer 3 addressing and Layer 4 application information. (Layer 2 addressing is also inherently used.)

- Layer 4 protocol types (UDP or TCP, for example) in packet headers are examined.

- Layer 4 segment headers are examined to determine application port numbers.

Switching at Layer 4 allows finer control over the movement of information. For example, traffic can be prioritized according to the source and destination port numbers, and QoS can be defined for end users. Therefore, video or voice data can be switched at a higher level of service, with more bandwidth availability than file transfer or HTTP traffic. Layer 4 port numbers for source and destination also can perform traffic accounting.

A Layer 4 switch also must allocate a large amount of memory to its forwarding tables. Layer 2 and Layer 3 devices have forwarding tables based on MAC and network addresses, making those tables only as large as the number of network devices. Layer 4 devices, however, must keep track of application protocols and conversations occurring in the network. Their forwarding tables become proportional to the number of network devices multiplied by the number of applications.

Multilayer Switching

Devices involved in MLS perform the following functions:

- Packets are forwarded in hardware that combines Layer 2, Layer 3, and Layer 4 switching.

- Packets are forwarded at wire speed.

- The traditional Layer 3 routing function is provided using Cisco Express Forwarding (CEF), in which a database of routes to every destination network is maintained and distributed to switching ASICs for very high forwarding performance.

Cisco switches perform multilayer switching at Layer 3 and Layer 4. At Layer 3, the Catalyst family of switches caches traffic flows based on IP addresses. At Layer 4, traffic flows are cached based on source and destination addresses, in addition to source and destination ports. All switching is performed in hardware, providing equal performance at both Layer 3 and Layer 4 switching.

Campus Network Models

A *campus network* is an enterprise network consisting of many LANs in one or more buildings, all connected and all usually in the same geographic area. A company typically owns the entire campus network as well as the physical wiring. Campus networks commonly consist of Ethernet, 802.11 wireless LANs, higher-speed Fast Ethernet, Fast EtherChannel, and Gigabit Ethernet LANs. Some campus networks also consist of legacy Token Ring and FDDI.

An understanding of traffic flow is a vital part of the campus network design. Although you can leverage high-speed LAN technologies to improve any traffic movement, the emphasis should be on providing an overall design tuned to known, studied, or predicted traffic flows. The network traffic then can be effectively moved and managed, and you can scale the campus network to support future needs.

The next sections present various network models that you can use to classify and design campus networks. Beginning with traditional shared networks, the models build on each other to leverage traffic movement and provide predictable behavior.

Shared Network Model

In the early 1990s, campus networks traditionally were constructed of a single LAN for all users to connect to and use. All devices on the LAN were forced to share the available bandwidth. LAN media such as Ethernet and Token Ring both had distance limitations and limitations on the number of devices that could be connected to a single LAN.

Network availability and performance declined as the number of connected devices increased. For example, an Ethernet LAN required all devices to share the available 10-Mbps half-duplex bandwidth. Ethernet also used the carrier sense multiple access collision detect (CSMA/CD) scheme to determine when a device could transmit data on the shared LAN. If two or more devices tried to transmit at the same time, network collisions occurred, and all devices had to become silent and wait to retransmit their data. This type of LAN is a *collision domain* because all devices are susceptible to collisions. Token Ring LANs are not susceptible to collisions because they are deterministic and allow stations to transmit only when they receive a "token" that passes around the ring.

One solution used to relieve network congestion was to segment, or divide, a LAN into discrete collision domains. This solution used transparent bridges, which forwarded only Layer 2 data frames to the network segment where the destination address was located. Bridges reduced the number of devices on a segment, lessened the probability of collisions on segments, and increased the physical distance limitations by acting as a repeater.

Bridges normally forward frames to the LAN segment where the destination address is located. However, frames containing the broadcast MAC address (ff:ff:ff:ff:ff:ff) must be flooded to all connected segments. Broadcast frames usually are associated with requests for information or services, including network service announcements. IP uses broadcasts for Address Resolution Protocol (ARP) requests to ask what MAC address is associated with a particular IP address. Other broadcast frame examples include Dynamic Host Control Protocol (DHCP) requests, IPX Get Nearest Server (GNS) requests, Service Advertising Protocol (SAP) announcements, Routing Information Protocol (RIP—both IP and IPX) advertisements, and NetBIOS name requests. A *broadcast domain* is a group of network segments where a broadcast is flooded.

Multicast traffic is traffic destined for a specific set or group of users, regardless of their location on the campus network. Multicast frames must be flooded to all segments because they are a form of broadcast. Although end users must join a multicast group to enable their applications to process and receive the multicast data, a bridge must flood the traffic to all segments because it doesn't know which stations are members of the multicast group. Multicast frames use shared bandwidth on a segment but do not force the use of CPU resources on every connected device. Only CPUs that are registered as multicast group members actually process those frames. Some multicast traffic is sporadic, as in the case of various routing protocol advertisements; other traffic, such as Cisco IP/TV multicast video, can consume most or all network resources with a steady stream of real-time data.

Broadcast traffic presents a twofold performance problem on a bridged LAN because all broadcast frames flood all bridged network segments. First, as a network grows, the broadcast traffic can grow in proportion and monopolize the available bandwidth. Second, all end-user stations must listen to, decode, and process every broadcast frame. The CPU, which performs this function, must look further into the frame to see which upper-layer protocol the broadcast is associated with. Although today's CPUs are robust and might not show a noticeable degradation from processing broadcasts, forcing unnecessary broadcast loads on every end user is not wise.

NOTE   For a discussion of the Cisco analysis performed on the effects of various protocol broadcasts on CPU performance, refer to "Broadcasts in Switched LAN Internetworks," at http://www.cisco.com/univercd/cc/td/doc/cisintwk/idg4/nd20e.htm.

LAN Segmentation Model

Referred to as *network segmentation*, localizing the traffic and effectively reducing the number of stations on a segment is necessary to prevent collisions and broadcasts from reducing a network segment's performance. By reducing the number of stations, the probability of a collision decreases because fewer stations can be transmitting at a given time. For broadcast containment, the idea is to provide a barrier at the edge of a LAN segment so that broadcasts cannot pass outward or be forwarded. The network designer can provide segmentation by using either a router or a switch.

You can use routers to connect the smaller subnetworks and either route Layer 3 packets or bridge Layer 2 packets. You can improve the effect of collisions by placing fewer stations on each segment. A router cannot propagate a collision condition from one segment to another, and broadcasts are not forwarded to other subnets by default unless bridging (or some other specialized feature) is enabled on the router. Figure 1-1 shows an example of how a router can physically segment a campus network. Although broadcasts are contained, the router becomes a potential bottleneck because it must process and route every packet leaving each subnet.

Figure 1-1   *Network Segmentation with a Router*

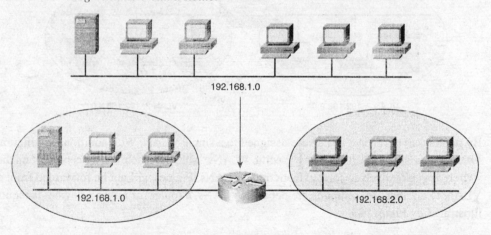

Another option is to replace shared LAN segments with switches. Switches offer greater performance with dedicated bandwidth on each port. Think of a switch as a fast multiport bridge. Each switch port becomes a separate collision domain and does not propagate collisions to any other port. However, broadcast and multicast frames are flooded out all switch ports unless more advanced switch features are invoked.

To contain broadcasts and segment a broadcast domain, you can implement virtual LANs (VLAN) within the switched network. A switch can logically divide its ports into isolated segments (broadcast domains). A VLAN is a group of switch ports (and the end devices to which they are connected) that communicate as if attached to a single shared-media LAN segment. By definition, a VLAN becomes a single broadcast domain. VLAN devices do not have to be physically located on the same switch or in the same building, as long as the VLAN itself is somehow connected between switches end to end. Figure 1-2 shows how you can segment a network into three broadcast and collision domains using three VLANs on a switch. Note that stations on a VLAN cannot communicate with stations on another VLAN in the figure—the VLANs truly are isolated.

Figure 1-2 *Segmentation Using VLANs*

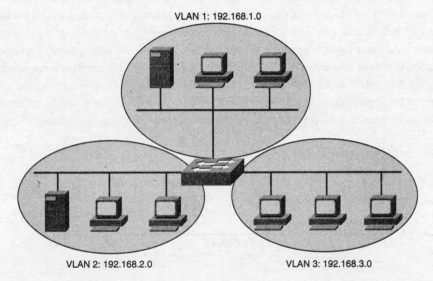

VLAN 1: 192.168.1.0

VLAN 2: 192.168.2.0   VLAN 3: 192.168.3.0

By default, all ports on a switch are assigned to a single VLAN. With additional configuration, a switch can assign its ports to many specific VLANs. Although each VLAN is present on the same switch, it is effectively separated from other VLANs. Frames will not be forwarded from one VLAN to another. To communicate between VLANs, a router (or Layer 3 device) is required, as illustrated by Figure 1-3.

Ports on each switch have been grouped and assigned to one VLAN. A port from each VLAN connects to the router. The router then forwards packets between VLANs through these ports.

To gain the most benefit from routed approaches and VLAN approaches, most campus networks now are built with a combination of Layer 2 switches and routers, or with multilayer switches. Again, the Layer 2 switches generally are placed where the small broadcast domains are located, linked by routers (or multilayer switches) that provide Layer 3 functionality. In this manner, broadcast traffic can be controlled or limited. Users also can be organized and given access to common workgroups, and traffic between workgroups can be interconnected and secured.

Figure 1-3 *Routing Traffic with VLANs*

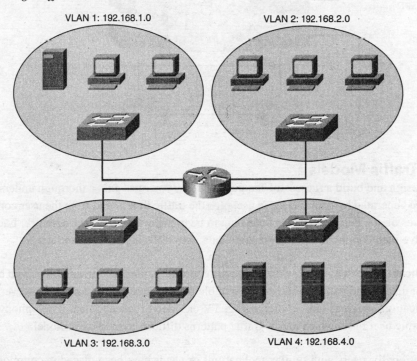

VLAN 1: 192.168.1.0   VLAN 2: 192.168.2.0

VLAN 3: 192.168.3.0   VLAN 4: 192.168.4.0

Figure 1-4 illustrates the structure of a typical routed and switched campus network. Here, the concept of Layer 2 switches and routers has been extended a bit. Each switch in the buildings supports three different VLANs for its users. A single switch port from each connects back to a router. Any switch port normally can carry only one VLAN, so something special must be occurring. These ports have been configured as *trunk links*, carrying multiple VLANs. (Trunking is discussed in Chapter 5, "VLANs and Trunks.")

Figure 1-4 *Typical Campus Network Structure*

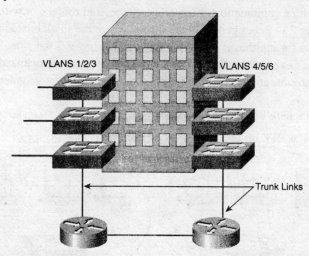

Network Traffic Models

To design and build a successful campus network, you must gain a thorough understanding of the traffic generated by applications in use, plus the traffic flow to and from the user communities. All devices on the network will produce data to be transported across the network. Each device can involve many applications that generate data with differing patterns and loads.

Applications such as email, word processing, printing, file transfer, and most web browsers bring about data traffic patterns that are predictable from source to destination. However, newer applications, such as videoconferencing, TV or video broadcasts, and IP telephony, have a more dynamic user base, which makes traffic patterns difficult to predict or model.

Traditionally, users with similar applications or needs have been placed in common workgroups, along with the servers they access most often. Whether these workgroups are logical (VLAN) or physical networks, the idea is to keep the majority of traffic between clients and servers limited to the local network segment. In the case of the switched LANs connected by routers mentioned earlier, both clients and servers would be connected to a Layer 2 switch in the workgroup's proximity. This connection provides good performance while minimizing the traffic load on the routed network backbone.

This concept of network traffic patterns is known as the 80/20 rule. In a properly designed campus network, 80% of the traffic on a given network segment is local (switched). No more than 20% of the traffic is expected to move across the network backbone (routed).

If the backbone becomes congested, the network administrator will realize that the 80/20 rule no longer is being met. What recourses are available to improve network performance again? Because of expense and complexity, upgrading the campus backbone is not a desirable option. The idea behind the 80/20 rule is to keep traffic off the backbone. Instead, the administrator can implement the following solutions:

- Reassign existing resources to bring the users and servers closer together

- Move applications and files to a different server to stay within a workgroup

- Move users logically (assigned to new VLANs) or physically to stay near their workgroups

- Add more servers, which can bring resources closer to the respective workgroups

Needless to say, conforming modern campus networks to the 80/20 rule has become difficult for the network administrator. Newer applications still use the client/server model, but the servers and their applications have been centralized in most enterprises. For example, databases, Internet access, intranet applications and resources, and email are all available from centralized servers. Not only do these applications involve larger amounts of data, but they also require a greater percentage of traffic to cross a network backbone to reach common destinations—quite a departure from the 80/20 rule.

This new model of campus traffic has become known as the 20/80 rule. Now, only 20% of the traffic is local to the workgroup, whereas at least 80% of the traffic is expected to travel off the local network and across the backbone.

This shift in traffic patterns puts a greater burden on the campus backbone's Layer 3 technology. Now, because traffic from anywhere on the network can be destined for any other part of the network, the Layer 3 performance ideally should match the Layer 2 performance. Generally, Layer 3 forwarding involves more processing resources because the data packets must be examined in greater depth. This added computation load can create bottlenecks in the campus network unless carefully designed.

Likewise, a campus network with many VLANs can become difficult to manage. In the past, VLANs were used to logically contain common workgroups and common traffic. With the 20/80 rule, end devices need to communicate with many other VLANs. Measuring traffic patterns and redesigning the campus network become too cumbersome just to keep up with the 20/80 rule model.

Predictable Network Model

Ideally, you should design a network with a predictable behavior in mind to offer low maintenance and high availability. For example, a campus network needs to recover from failures and topology changes quickly and in a predetermined manner. You should scale the network to easily support future expansions and upgrades. With a wide variety of multiprotocol and multicast traffic, the network should be capable of supporting the 20/80 rule from a traffic standpoint. In other words, design the network around traffic flows instead of a particular type of traffic.

Traffic flows in a campus network can be classified as three types, based on where the network service is located in relation to the end user. Table 1-3 lists these types, along with the extent of the campus network that is crossed.

Table 1-3 *Types of Network Services*

Service Type	Location of Service	Extent of Traffic Flow
Local	Same segment/VLAN as user	Access layer only
Remote	Different segment/VLAN as user	Access to distribution layers
Enterprise	Central to all campus users	Access to distribution to core layers

The terms *access layer*, *distribution layer*, and *core layer* are each distinct components of the hierarchical network design model. The network is divided into logical levels, or layers, according to function. These terms and the hierarchical network design are discussed in the next section.

Hierarchical Network Design

You can structure the campus network so that each of the three types of traffic flows or services outlined in Table 1-3 is best supported. Cisco has refined a hierarchical approach to network design that enables network designers to logically create a network by defining and using layers of devices. The resulting network is efficient, intelligent, scalable, and easily managed.

The hierarchical model breaks a campus network into three distinct layers, as illustrated in Figure 1-5.

Figure 1-5 *Hierarchical Network Design*

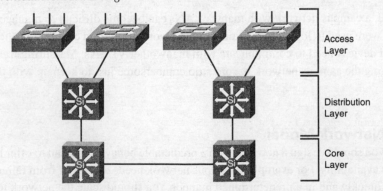

Access Layer

Distribution Layer

Core Layer

These layers are the access layer, distribution layer, and core layer. Each layer has attributes that provide both physical and logical network functions at the appropriate point in the campus network. Understanding each layer and its functions or limitations is important to properly apply the layer in the design process.

Access Layer

The access layer is present where the end users are connected to the network. Devices in this layer, sometimes called *building access switches*, should have the following capabilities:

- Low cost per switch port

- High port density

- Scalable uplinks to higher layers

- User access functions such as VLAN membership, traffic and protocol filtering, and QoS

- Resiliency through multiple uplinks

Distribution Layer

The distribution layer provides interconnection between the campus network's access and core layers. Devices in this layer, sometimes called building *distribution switches*, should have the following capabilities:

- Aggregation of multiple access-layer devices

- High Layer 3 throughput for packet handling

- Security and policy-based connectivity functions through access lists or packet filters

- QoS features

- Scalable and resilient high-speed links to the core and access layers

In the distribution layer, uplinks from all access-layer devices are aggregated, or come together. The distribution-layer switches must be capable of processing the total volume of traffic from all the connected devices. These switches should have a port density of high-speed links to support the collection of access-layer switches.

VLANs and broadcast domains converge at the distribution layer, requiring routing, filtering, and security. The switches at this layer also must be capable of performing multilayer switching with high throughput.

Core Layer

A campus network's core layer provides connectivity of all distribution-layer devices. The core, sometimes referred to as the *backbone*, must be capable of switching traffic as efficiently as possible. Core devices, sometimes called *campus backbone switches*, should have the following attributes:

■ Very high throughput at Layer 2 or Layer 3

■ No costly or unnecessary packet manipulations (access lists, packet filtering)

■ Redundancy and resilience for high availability

■ Advanced QoS functions

Devices in a campus network's core layer or backbone should be optimized for high-performance Layer 2 or Layer 3 switching. Because the core layer must handle large amounts of campuswide data (because of the new 20/80 rule of traffic flow), the core layer should be designed with simplicity and efficiency in mind.

Although campus network design is presented as a three-layer approach (access, distribution, and core layers), the hierarchy can be collapsed or simplified in certain cases. For example, small or medium-size campus networks might not have the size, multilayer switching, or volume requirements that would require the functions of all three layers. Here, you could combine the distribution and core layers for simplicity and cost savings. In this case, choose switch products based on the distribution-layer features and access-layer aggregation port densities needed.

Foundation Summary

The Foundation Summary is a collection of tables and figures that provides a convenient review of many key concepts in this chapter. If you are already comfortable with the topics in this chapter, this summary might help you recall a few details. If you just read this chapter, this review should help solidify some key facts. If you are doing your final preparation before the exam, the following tables and figures are a convenient way to review the day before the exam.

Table 1-4 *Layers of Data Communications*

OSI Layer	Protocol Data Unit	Mechanism to Process PDU
7 (application)		
6 (presentation)		
5 (session)		
4 (transport)	TCP segment	TCP port
3 (network)	Packet	Router
2 (data link)	Frame	Switch/bridge
1 (physical)		

Table 1-5 *Types of Network Services*

Service Type	Location of Service	Extent of Traffic Flow
Local	Same segment/VLAN as user	Access layer only
Remote	Different segment/VLAN as user	Access to distribution layers
Enterprise	Central to all campus users	Access to distribution to core layers

Table 1-6 *Comparison of Hierarchical Layers*

Layer	Attributes
Access	High port density to connect to end users, low cost, uplinks to higher layers of the campus network, and Layer 2 services (traffic filtering, VLAN membership, and basic QoS)
Distribution	Aggregation of access-layer devices, high Layer 3 throughput, QoS features, security- and policy-based functions, and scalable and resilient high-speed links into the core and access layers
Core	Fast data transport, no "expensive" Layer 3 processing, redundancy and resiliency for high availability, and advanced QoS

Q&A

The questions and scenarios in this book are more difficult than what you should experience on the actual exam. The questions do not attempt to cover more breadth or depth than the exam; however, they are designed to make sure that you know the answer. Rather than allowing you to derive the answers from clues hidden inside the questions themselves, the questions challenge your understanding and recall of the subject. Hopefully, these questions will help limit the number of exam questions on which you narrow your choices to two options and then guess.

You can find the answers to these questions in Appendix A.

1. For each layer of the OSI model, match the forwarding criteria used by a switch:

___ Layer 1	A. IP address
___ Layer 2	B. UDP/TCP port
___ Layer 3	C. None
___ Layer 4	D. MAC address

2. What is multilayer switching (MLS)?

3. Fill in the blanks in the following statement:

   In the 20/80 rule of networking, 20% of the traffic on a segment usually stays _____, whereas 80% travels _____.

4. What is a collision domain, and where does it exist in a switched LAN?

5. What is a broadcast domain, and where does it exist in a switched LAN?

6. What is a VLAN, and why is it used?

7. At what OSI layers do devices in the distribution layer usually operate?

8. What is network segmentation? When is it necessary, and how is it done in a campus network design?

9. Is it possible to use Layer 2 switches in the distribution layer rather than Layer 3 switches? If so, what are the limitations?

This chapter covers the following topics that you need to master for the CCNP BCMSN exam:

- **Modular Network Design**—This section covers the process of designing a campus network, based on breaking it into functional modules. You also learn how to size and scale the modules in a design.

- **Evaluating an Existing Network**—In this section, you learn about evaluating the structure and operation of an existing network, and redesigning the network according to a robust campus network model.

CHAPTER 2

Modular Network Design

This chapter presents a set of building blocks that can organize and streamline even a large, complex campus network. These building blocks then can be placed using several campus design models to provide maximum efficiency, functionality, and scalability.

"Do I Know This Already?" Quiz

The purpose of the "Do I Know This Already?" quiz is to help you decide whether you need to read the entire chapter. If you already intend to read the entire chapter, you do not necessarily need to answer these questions now.

The 14-question quiz, derived from the major sections in the "Foundation Topics" portion of the chapter, helps you determine how to spend your limited study time.

Table 2-1 outlines the major topics discussed in this chapter and the "Do I Know This Already?" quiz questions that correspond to those topics.

Table 2-1   *"Do I Know This Already?" Foundation Topics Section-to-Question Mapping*

Foundation Topics Section	Questions Covered in This Section	Score
Modular Network Design	1–12	
Evaluating an Existing Network	13–14	
Total Score		

CAUTION   The goal of self-assessment is to gauge your mastery of the topics in this chapter. If you do not know the answer to a question or are only partially sure of the answer, you should mark this question wrong. Giving yourself credit for an answer you correctly guess skews your self-assessment results and might provide you with a false sense of security.

You can find the answers to the quiz in Appendix A, "Answers to Chapter 'Do I Know This Already?' Quizzes and Q&A Sections." The suggested choices for your next step are as follows:

- **8 or less overall score**—Read the entire chapter. This includes the "Foundation Topics," "Foundation Summary," and "Q&A" sections.

- **9–10 overall score**—Begin with the "Foundation Summary" section and then follow up with the "Q&A" section at the end of the chapter.

- **12 or more overall score**—If you want more review on these topics, skip to the "Foundation Summary" section and then go to the "Q&A" section at the end of the chapter. Otherwise, move on to Chapter 3, "Switch Operation."

1. What is the purpose of breaking a campus network into a hierarchical design?

    a. To facilitate documentation

    b. To follow political or organizational policies

    c. To make the network predictable and scalable

    d. To make the network more redundant and secure

2. Which of the following are building blocks or modules used to build a scalable campus network? (Check all that apply.)

    a. Access block

    b. Distribution block

    c. Core block

    d. Server farm block

    e. Switch block

3. Which one or more of the following are the components of a typical switch block?

    a. Access-layer switches

    b. Distribution-layer switches

    c. Core-layer switches

    d. E-commerce servers

    e. Service provider switches

4. What are two types of core, or backbone, designs?

    a. Collapsed core

    b. Loop-free core

    c. Dual core

    d. Layered core

5. In a properly designed hierarchical network, a broadcast from one PC is confined to what?

   a. One access-layer switch port

   b. One access-layer switch

   c. One switch block

   d. The entire campus network

6. What is the maximum number of access-layer switches that can connect into a single distribution-layer switch?

   a. 1

   b. 2

   c. Limited only by the number of ports on the access-layer switch

   d. Limited only by the number of ports on the distribution-layer switch

   e. Unlimited

7. A switch block should be sized according to what?

   a. The number of access-layer users

   b. A maximum of 250 access-layer users

   c. A study of the traffic patterns and flows

   d. The amount of rack space available

   e. The number of servers accessed by users

8. What evidence can be seen when a switch block is too large? (Choose all that apply.)

   a. IP address space is exhausted.

   b. You run out of access-layer switch ports.

   c. Broadcast traffic becomes excessive.

   d. Traffic is throttled at the distribution-layer switches.

   e. Network congestion occurs.

9. How many distribution switches should be built into each switch block?

   a. 1

   b. 2

   c. 4

   d. 8

10. What are the most important aspects to consider when designing the core layer in a large network? (Choose all that apply.)

    a. Low cost

    b. Switches that can efficiently forward traffic, even when every uplink is at 100% capacity

    c. High port density of high-speed ports

    d. A low number of Layer 3 routing peers

11. Which services typically are located at the enterprise edge block? (Choose all that apply.)

    a. Network management

    b. Intranet server farms

    c. VPN and remote access

    d. E-commerce servers

    e. End users

12. In a server farm block, where should redundancy be provided? (Choose all that apply.)

    a. Dual connections from each distribution switch to the core.

    b. Dual connections from each access switch to the distribution switches.

    c. Dual connections from each server to the access switches.

    d. No redundancy is necessary.

13. Which of the following protocols can be used as a tool to discover a network topology?

    a. RIP

    b. CDP

    c. STP

    d. ICMP

14. Which one of the following tasks is not an appropriate strategy for migrating an existing network into the Enterprise Composite Model?

    a. Identify groups of end users as switch blocks

    b. Group common resources into switch blocks

    c. Identify distribution switches to connect the switch blocks

    d. Add redundancy between the hierarchical layers

Foundation Topics

Modular Network Design

Recall from Chapter 1, "Campus Network Overview," that a network is best constructed and maintained using a three-tiered hierarchical approach. Making a given network conform to a layered architecture might seem a little confusing.

You can design a campus network in a logical manner, using a modular approach. In this approach, each layer of the hierarchical network model can be broken into basic functional units. These units, or *modules*, then can be sized appropriately and connected, while allowing for future scalability and expansion.

You can divide enterprise campus networks into the following basic elements:

- **Switch block**—A group of access-layer switches, together with their distribution switches

- **Core block**—The campus network's backbone

Other related elements can exist. Although these elements don't contribute to the campus network's overall function, they can be designed separately and added to the network design. These elements are as follows:

- **Server farm block**—A group of enterprise servers, along with their access and distribution (layer) switches.

- **Management block**—A group of network-management resources, along with their access and distribution switches.

- **Enterprise edge block**—A collection of services related to external network access, along with their access and distribution switches.

- **Service provider edge block**—The external network services contracted or used by the enterprise network. These are the services with which the enterprise edge block interfaces.

The collection of all these elements is also known as the *Enterprise Composite Network Model*. Figure 2-1 shows a modular campus design's basic structure. Notice how each of the building-block elements can be confined to a certain area or function. Also notice how each is connected into the core block.

Figure 2-1 *Modular Approach to Campus Network Design*

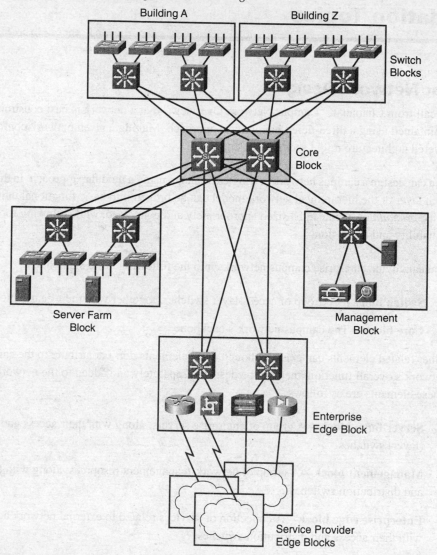

Switch Block

Recall how a campus network is divided into access, distribution, and core layers. The switch block contains switching devices from the access and distribution layers. All switch blocks then connect into the core block, providing end-to-end connectivity across the campus.

Switch blocks contain a balanced mix of Layer 2 and Layer 3 functionality, as might be present in the access and distribution layers. Layer 2 switches located in wiring closets (access layer) connect end users to the campus network. With one end user per switch port, each user receives dedicated bandwidth access.

Upstream, each access-layer switch connects to devices in the distribution layer. Here, Layer 2 functionality transports data among all connected access switches at a central connection point. Layer 3 functionality also can be provided in the form of routing and other networking services (security, quality of service [QoS], and so on). Therefore, a distribution-layer device should be a multilayer switch. Layer 3 functionality is discussed in more detail in Chapter 12, "Multilayer Switching."

The distribution layer also shields the switch block from certain failures or conditions in other parts of the network. For example, broadcasts are not propagated from the switch block into the core and other switch blocks. Therefore, the Spanning Tree Protocol (STP) is confined to each switch block, where a virtual LAN (VLAN) is bounded, keeping the spanning tree domain well defined and controlled.

Access-layer switches can support VLANs by assigning individual ports to specific VLAN numbers. In this way, stations connected to the ports configured for the same VLAN can share the same Layer 3 subnet. However, be aware that a single VLAN can support multiple subnets. Because the switch ports are configured for a VLAN number only (and not a network address), any station connected to a port can present any subnet address range. The VLAN functions as traditional network media and allows any network address to connect.

In this network design model, you should not extend VLANs beyond distribution switches. The distribution layer always should be the boundary of VLANs, subnets, and broadcasts. Although Layer 2 switches can extend VLANs to other switches and other layers of the hierarchy, this activity is discouraged. VLAN traffic should not traverse the network core. (*Trunking*, or the capability to carry many VLANs over a single connection, is discussed in Chapter 5, "VLANs and Trunks.")

Sizing a Switch Block

Containing access- and distribution-layer devices, the switch block is simple in concept. You should consider several factors, however, to determine an appropriate size for the switch block. The range of available switch devices makes the switch block size very flexible. At the access layer, switch selection usually is based on port density or the number of connected users.

The distribution layer must be sized according to the number of access-layer switches that are collapsed or brought into a distribution device. Consider the following factors:

- Traffic types and patterns

- Amount of Layer 3 switching capacity at the distribution layer

- Number of users connected to the access-layer switches

- Geographical boundaries of subnets or VLANs

- Size of spanning tree domains

Designing a switch block based solely on the number of users or stations contained within the block is usually inaccurate. Usually, no more than 2,000 users should be placed within a single switch block. Although this is useful for initially estimating a switch block's size, this idea doesn't take into account the many dynamic processes that occur on a functioning network.

Instead, switch block size should be based primarily on the following:

- Traffic types and behavior

- Size and number of common workgroups

Because of the dynamic nature of networks, you can size a switch block too large to handle the load that is placed upon it. Also, the number of users and applications on a network tends to grow over time. A provision to break up or downsize a switch block is necessary. Again, base these decisions on the actual traffic flows and patterns present in the switch block. You can estimate, model, or measure these parameters with network-analysis applications and tools.

> **NOTE** The actual network-analysis process is beyond the scope of this book. Traffic estimation, modeling, and measurement are complex procedures, each requiring its own dedicated analysis tool.

Generally, a switch block is too large if the following conditions are observed:

- The routers (multilayer switches) at the distribution layer become traffic bottlenecks. This congestion could be because of the volume of interVLAN traffic, intensive CPU processing, or switching times required by policy or security functions (access lists, queuing, and so on).

- Broadcast or multicast traffic slows the switches in the switch block. Broadcast and multicast traffic must be replicated and forwarded out many ports. This process requires some overhead in the multilayer switch, which can become too great if significant traffic volumes are present.

Access switches can have one or more redundant links to distribution-layer devices. This situation provides a fault-tolerant environment in which access layer connectivity is preserved on a secondary link if the primary link fails. In fact, because Layer 3 devices are used in the distribution layer, traffic can be load-balanced across both redundant links using redundant gateways.

Generally, you should provide two distribution switches in each switch block for redundancy, with each access-layer switch connecting to the two distribution switches. Then, each Layer 3 distribution switch can load-balance traffic over its redundant links into the core layer (also Layer 3 switches) using routing protocols.

Figure 2-2 shows a typical switch block design. At Layer 3, the two distribution switches can use one of several redundant gateway protocols to provide an active IP gateway and a standby gateway at all times. These protocols are discussed in Chapter 13, "Router, Supervisor, and Power Redundancy."

Figure 2-2 *Typical Switch Block Design*

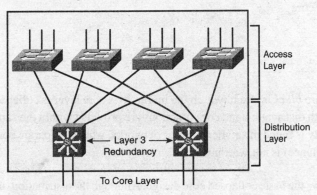

Core Block

A core block is required to connect two or more switch blocks in a campus network. Because all traffic passing to and from all switch blocks, server farm blocks, and the enterprise edge block must cross the core block, the core must be as efficient and resilient as possible. The core is the campus network's basic foundation and carries much more traffic than any other block.

A network core can use any technology (frame, cell, or packet) to transport campus data. Many campus networks use Gigabit and 10-Gigabit Ethernet as a core technology. Ethernet core blocks are reviewed at length here.

Recall that both the distribution and core layers provide Layer 3 functionality. Individual IP subnets connect all distribution and core switches. At least two subnets should be used to provide resiliency and load-balancing into the core, although you can use a single VLAN. As VLANs end at the distribution layer, they are routed into the core.

The core block might consist of a single multilayer switch, taking in the two redundant links from the distribution-layer switches. Because of the importance of the core block in a campus network, you should implement two or more identical switches in the core to provide redundancy.

The links between layers also should be designed to carry at least the amount of traffic load handled by the distribution switches. The links between core switches in the same core subnet should be of sufficient size to carry the aggregate amount of traffic coming into the core switch. Consider the average link utilization, but allow for future growth. An Ethernet core allows simple and scalable upgrades of magnitude; consider the progression from Ethernet to Fast Ethernet to Fast EtherChannel to Gigabit Ethernet to Gigabit EtherChannel, and so on.

Two basic core block designs are presented in the following sections, each designed around a campus network's size:

■   Collapsed core

■   Dual core

Collapsed Core

A *collapsed core block* is one in which the hierarchy's core layer is collapsed into the distribution layer. Here, both distribution and core functions are provided within the same switch devices. This situation usually is found in smaller campus networks, where a separate core layer (and additional cost or performance) is not warranted.

Figure 2-3 shows the basic collapsed core design. Although the distribution- and core-layer functions are performed in the same device, keeping these functions distinct and properly designed is important. Note also that the collapsed core is not an independent building block but is integrated into the distribution layer of the individual standalone switch blocks.

In the collapsed core design, each access-layer switch has a redundant link to each distribution- and core-layer switch. All Layer 3 subnets present in the access layer terminate at the distribution switches' Layer 3 ports, as in the basic switch block design. The distribution and core switches connect to each other by one or more links, completing a path to use during a redundancy failover.

Figure 2-3   *Collapsed Core Block Design*

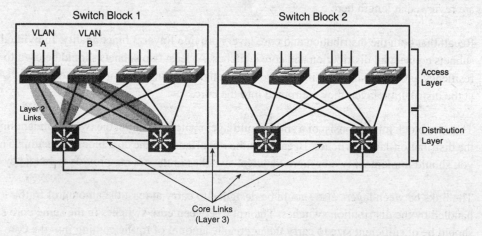

Connectivity between the distribution and core switches is accomplished using Layer 3 links (Layer 3 switch interfaces, with no inherent VLANs). The Layer 3 switches route traffic to and from each other directly. Figure 2-3 shows the extent of two VLANs. Notice that VLAN A and VLAN B each extend only from the access-layer switches, where their respective users are located, down to the distribution layer over the Layer 2 uplinks. The VLANs terminate there because the distribution layer uses Layer 3 switching. This is good because it limits the broadcast domains, removes the possibility of Layer 2 bridging loops, and provides fast failover if one uplink fails.

At Layer 3, redundancy is provided through a redundant gateway protocol for IP (covered in Chapter 13). In some of the protocols, the two distribution switches provide a common default gateway address to the access-layer switches, but only one is active at any time. In other protocols, the two switches can both be active, load-balancing traffic. If a distribution and core switch failure occurs, connectivity to the core is maintained because the redundant Layer 3 switch is always available.

Dual Core

A *dual core* connects two or more switch blocks in a redundant fashion. Although the collapsed core can connect two switch blocks with some redundancy, the core is not scalable when more switch blocks are added. Figure 2-4 illustrates the dual core. Notice that this core appears as an independent module and is not merged into any other block or layer.

Figure 2-4 *Dual Network Core Design*

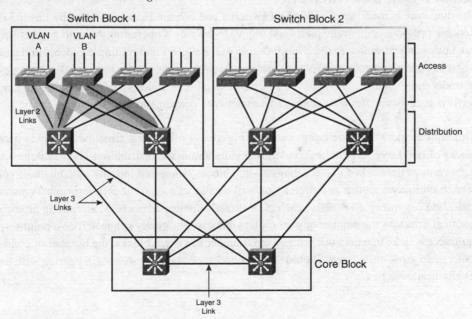

In the past, the dual core usually was built with Layer 2 switches to provide the simplest and most efficient throughput. Layer 3 switching was provided in the distribution layer. Multilayer switches now have become cost-effective and offer high switching performance. Building a dual core with multilayer switches is both possible and recommended. The dual core uses two identical switches to provide redundancy. Redundant links connect each switch block's distribution-layer portion to each of the dual core switches. The two core switches connect by a common link. In a Layer 2 core, the switches cannot be linked to avoid any bridging loops. A Layer 3 core uses routing rather than bridging, so bridging loops are not an issue.

In the dual core, each distribution switch has two equal-cost paths to the core, allowing the available bandwidth of both paths to be used simultaneously. Both paths remain active because the distribution and core layers use Layer 3 devices that can manage equal-cost paths in routing tables. The routing protocol in use determines the availability or loss of a neighboring Layer 3 device. If one switch fails, the routing protocol reroutes traffic using an alternative path through the remaining redundant switch.

Notice again in Figure 2-4 the extent of the access VLANs. Although Layer 3 devices have been added into a separate core layer, VLANs A and B still extend only from the Layer 2 access-layer switches down to the distribution layer. Although the distribution-layer switches use Layer 3 switch interfaces to provide Layer 3 functionality to the access layer, these links actually pass traffic only at Layer 2.

Core Size in a Campus Network

The dual core is made up of redundant switches and is bounded and isolated by Layer 3 devices. Routing protocols determine paths and maintain the core's operation. As with any network, you must pay some attention to the overall design of the routers and routing protocols in the network. Because routing protocols propagate updates throughout the network, network topologies might be undergoing change. The network's size (the number of routers) then affects routing protocol performance as updates are exchanged and network convergence takes place.

Although the network shown previously in Figure 2-4 might look small, with only two switch blocks of two Layer 3 switches (route processors within the distribution-layer switches) each, large campus networks can have many switch blocks connected into the core block. If you think of each multilayer switch as a router, you will recall that each route processor must communicate with and keep information about each of its directly connected peers. Most routing protocols have practical limits on the number of peer routers that can be directly connected on a point-to-point or multiaccess link. In a network with a large number of switch blocks, the number of connected routers can grow quite large. Should you be concerned about a core switch peering with too many distribution switches?

No, because the actual number of directly connected peers is quite small, regardless of the campus network size. Access-layer VLANs terminate at the distribution-layer switches. The only peering routers at that boundary are pairs of distribution switches, each providing routing redundancy for each of the access-layer VLAN subnets. At the distribution and core boundary, each distribution switch connects to only two core switches over Layer 3 switch interfaces. Therefore, only pairs of router peers are formed.

When multilayer switches are used in the distribution and core layers, the routing protocols running in both layers regard each pair of redundant links between layers as equal-cost paths. Traffic is routed across both links in a load-sharing fashion, utilizing the bandwidth of both.

One final core-layer design point is to scale the core switches to match the incoming load. At a minimum, each core switch must handle switching each of its incoming distribution links at 100% capacity.

Other Building Blocks

Other resources in the campus network can be identified and pulled into the building block model. For example, a server farm can be made up of servers running applications that users from all across the enterprise access. Most likely, those servers need to be scalable for future expansion, need to be highly accessible, and need to benefit from traffic and security policy control.

To meet these needs, you can group the resources into building blocks that are structured and placed just like regular switch block modules. These blocks should have a distribution layer of switches and redundant uplinks directly into the core layer, and should contain enterprise resources.

A list of the most common examples follows. Refer back to Figure 2-1 to see how each of these is grouped and connected into the campus network. Most of these building blocks are present in medium and large campus networks. Be familiar with the concept of pulling an enterprise function into its own switch block, as well as the structure of that block.

Server Farm Block

Any server or application accessed by most of the enterprise users usually already belongs to a server farm. The entire server farm can be identified as its own switch block and given a layer of access switches uplinked to dual distribution switches (multilayer). Connect these distribution switches into the core layer with redundant high-speed links.

Individual servers can have single network connections to one of the distribution switches. However, this presents a single point of failure. If a redundant server is used, it should connect to the alternative distribution switch. A more resilient approach is to give each server dual network connections, one going to each distribution switch. This is known as *dual-homing* the servers.

Examples of enterprise servers include corporate email, intranet services, Enterprise Resource Planning (ERP) applications, and mainframe systems. Notice that each of these is an internal resource that normally would be located inside a firewall or secured perimeter.

Network Management Block

Often campus networks must be monitored through the use of network-management tools so that performance and fault conditions can be measured and detected. You can group the entire suite of network-management applications into a single network management switch block. This is the reverse of a server farm block because the network-management tools are not enterprise resources accessed by most of the users. Instead, these tools go out to access other network devices, application servers, and user activity in all other areas of the campus network.

The network management switch block usually has a distribution layer that connects into the core switches. Because these tools are used to detect equipment and connectivity failures, availability is important. Redundant links and redundant switches should be used.

Examples of network-management resources in this switch block include the following:

- Network-monitoring applications

- System logging (syslog) servers

- Authentication, authorization, and accounting (AAA) servers

- Policy-management applications

- System administration and remote-control services

- Intrusion-detection management applications

> **NOTE**   You can easily gather network-management resources into a single switch block to centralize these functions. Each switch and router in the network must have an IP address assigned for management purposes. In the past, it was easy to "centralize" all these management addresses and traffic into a single "management" VLAN, which extended from one end of the campus to the other.
>
> The end-to-end VLAN concept is now considered a poor practice. VLANs should be isolated, as described in Chapter 1. Therefore, assigning management addresses to as many VLANs or subnets as is practical and appropriate for a campus network is now acceptable.

Enterprise Edge Block

At some point, most campus networks must connect to service providers for access to external resources. This is usually known as the *edge* of the enterprise or campus network. These resources are available to the entire campus and should be centrally accessible as an independent switch block connected to the network core.

Edge services usually are divided into these categories:

- **Internet access**—Supports outbound traffic to the Internet, as well as inbound traffic to public services, such as email and extranet web servers. This connectivity is provided by one or more Internet service providers (ISPs). Network security devices generally are placed here.

- **Remote access and VPN**—Supports inbound dialup access for external or roaming users through the Public Switched Telephone Network (PSTN). If voice traffic is supported over the campus network, Voice over IP (VoIP) gateways connect to the PSTN here. In addition, virtual private network (VPN) devices connected to the Internet support secure tunneled connections to remote locations.

- **E-commerce**—Supports all related web, application, and database servers and applications, as well as firewalls and security devices. This switch block connects to one or more ISPs.

- **WAN access**—Supports all traditional WAN connections to remote sites. This can include Frame Relay, ATM, leased line, ISDN, and so on.

Service Provider Edge Block

Each service provider that connects to an enterprise network must also have a hierarchical network design of its own. A service provider network meets an enterprise at the service provider edge, connecting to the enterprise edge block.

Studying a service provider network's structure isn't necessary because it should follow the same design principles presented here. In other words, a service provider is just another enterprise or campus network itself. Just be familiar with the fact that a campus network has an edge block, where it connects to the edge of each service provider's network.

Can I Use Layer 2 Distribution Switches?

This chapter covers the best practice design that places Layer 3 switches at both the core and distribution layers. What would happen if you could not afford Layer 3 switches at the distribution layer?

Figure 2-5 shows a dual-core campus network with Layer 2 distribution switches. Notice how each access VLAN extends not only throughout the switch block but also into the core. This is because the VLAN terminates at a Layer 3 boundary present only in the core. As an example, VLAN A's propagation is shaded in the figure.

Figure 2-5 *Design Using Layer 2 Distribution Switches*

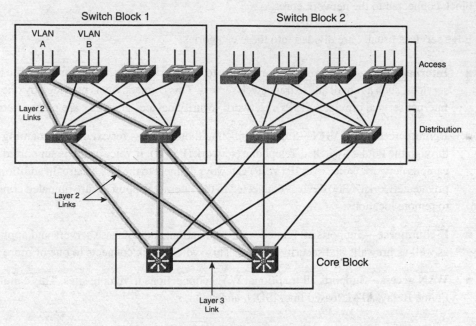

Here are some implications of this design:

■ Redundant Layer 3 gateways still can be used in the core.

■ Each VLAN propagates across the redundant trunk links from the access to the core layers. Because of this, Layer 2 bridging loops form.

■ The STP must run in all layers to prevent Layer 2 loops. This causes traffic on some links to be blocked. As a result, only one of every two access-layer switch uplinks can be used at any time.

■ When Layer 2 uplinks go down, the STP can take several seconds to unblock redundant links, causing downtime.

■ Access VLANs can propagate from one end of the campus to the other, if necessary.

■ Broadcast traffic on any access-layer VLAN also reaches into the core layer. Bandwidth on uplinks and within the core can be wasted unnecessarily.

Evaluating an Existing Network

If you are building an enterprise network from scratch, you might find that it is fairly straightforward to build it in a hierarchical fashion. After all, you can begin with switches in the core layer and fan out into lower layers to meet the users, server farms, and service providers.

In the real world, you might be more likely to find existing networks that need an overhaul to match the hierarchical model. Hopefully, if you are redesigning your own network, you already know its topology and traffic patterns. If you are working on someone else's network, you might not know about its structure.

This section provides some basic information on two tasks:

■ Discovering the existing topology

■ Planning a migration to a better campus model

Discovering the Network Topology

Whether or not a diagram of a network is available, you should consider tracing out the topology for yourself. For one thing, network documentation tends to become out-of-date or isn't drawn to show the type of information you need.

Some network administrators draw up a diagram that shows only the physical cabling between network devices. That might benefit someone who is working with the cabling, but it might not show any of the logical aspects of the network. After all, switched networks can be cabled together and then configured into many logical topologies.

As you discover or trace out a network, you might end up building several diagrams. One diagram might show all the network devices and only the physical cabling between them. Further diagrams might show Layer 2 VLANs and how they extend through the network.

To discover an existing network, you can connect a computer to any switch as a starting point and begin to "walk" the topology. Cisco devices periodically send information about themselves to any neighboring devices. This is done with the Cisco Discovery Protocol (CDP).

TIP   The information exchanged in CDP messages includes the device type, software version, links between devices, and number of ports within each device.

By default, CDP runs on each port of a Catalyst switch, and CDP advertisements occur every 60 seconds. CDP communication occurs at the data link layer so that it is independent of any network layer protocol that might be running on a network segment. This means that CDP can be sent and received using only Layer 2 functionality. CDP frames are sent as multicasts, using a destination MAC address of 01:00:0c:cc:cc:cc.

Cisco Catalyst switches regard the CDP address as a special address designating a multicast frame that should *not* be forwarded. Instead, CDP multicast frames are redirected to the switch's management port and are processed by the switch supervisor alone. Cisco switches become aware only of other directly connected Cisco devices.

CDP is enabled by default on all switch interfaces. To manually enable or disable CDP on an interface, use the following interface configuration command:

```
Switch(config-if)# [no]  cdp enable
```

If a switch port connects to a non-Cisco device or to a network outside your administrative control, consider disabling CDP on that port. Add the **no** keyword to disable CDP.

CDP is enabled by default on all Cisco switches and routers, so, chances are, you will be able to make use of it right away. With CDP, a switch becomes aware of only the devices that are directly connected to it. Therefore, you walk the topology one "hop" at a time: connect to one switch, find its neighbors, and then connect to them one at a time.

Figure 2-6 shows this process being used to discover a sample network. (The arrows in the sequence illustrated in Figure 2-6 point out where you are positioned as the topology is discovered.) A laptop PC has been connected to the console connection of an arbitrary switch, Switch-A. Here, Switch-A is a Catalyst 3550, determined either by inspection or from the **show version** command.

Figure 2-6 *Network Discovery with CDP*

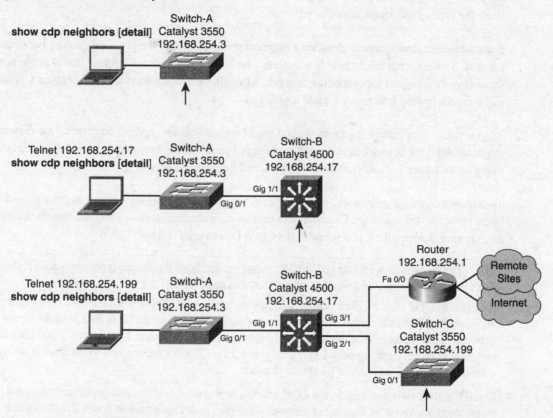

At the top of the figure, you don't know whether Switch-A is in the core, distribution, or access layer. Actually, you don't even know whether this network has been built in layers.

When you are connected and in the privileged EXEC or enable mode, you can begin looking for CDP information by using the **show cdp neighbors** command. At Switch-A, suppose the command had the output in Example 2-1.

Example 2-1   show cdp neighbors *Command Output Reveals CDP Information*

```
Switch-A# show cdp neighbors
Capability Codes: R - Router, T - Trans Bridge, B - Source Route Bridge
                  S - Switch, H - Host, I - IGMP, r - Repeater, P - Phone


Device ID        Local Intrfce    Holdtme    Capability Platform  Port ID
Switch-B         Gig 0/1            152        R S I      WS-C4506  Gig 1/1
Switch-A#
```

Based on the neighbors listed, you should be able to draw the connections to the neighboring switches and detail the names and model of those switches. Notice that the CDP neighbor information shows the local switch interface as well as the neighbor's interface for each connection. This is helpful when you move to a neighbor and need to match the connections from its viewpoint.

From the output in Example 2-1, it's apparent that Switch-A has a neighbor called Switch-B on interface GigabitEthernet 0/1. Switch-B is a Catalyst 4506.

Now you can use a variation of the command to see more detail about each neighbor. The **show cdp neighbors** [**interface** *mod/num*] **detail** command also shows the neighbor's software release, interface settings, and its IP address, as demonstrated in Example 2-2.

Example 2-2   show cdp neighbors detail *Command Output Reveals Detailed Information About Neighboring Switches*

```
Switch-A# show cdp neighbors detail

Device ID: Switch-B
Entry address(es): 192.168.254.17
Platform: cisco WS-C4506,  Capabilities: Router Switch IGMP
Interface: GigabitEthernet0/1,  Port ID (outgoing port): GigabitEthernet1/1
Holdtime : 134 sec
Version :
Cisco Internetwork Operating System Software
IOS (tm) Catalyst 4000 L3 Switch Software (cat4000-I9S-M), Version 12.2(18)EW, EARLY
DEPLOYMENT RELEASE SOFTWARE (fc1)
TAC Support: http://www.cisco.com/tac
Copyright  1986-2004 by cisco Systems, Inc.
Compiled Fri 30-Jan-04 02:04 by hqluong
advertisement version: 2
VTP Management Domain: ''
Duplex: full
Management address(es):
Switch-A#
```

When you know the IP address of a neighboring device, you can open a Telnet session from the current switch to the neighboring switch. (This assumes that the neighboring switch has been configured with an IP address and a Telnet password on its vty lines.) Choose a neighbor and use the **telnet** *ip-address* command to move to the neighbor and continue your discovery. At Switch-B (the middle of Figure 2-6), you might see the CDP neighbor output in Example 2-3.

Example 2-3 **show cdp neighbors** *Command Output Display for Switch-B*

```
Switch-B# show cdp neighbors
Capability Codes: R - Router, T - Trans Bridge, B - Source Route Bridge
                  S - Switch, H - Host, I - IGMP, r - Repeater, P - Phone
Device ID        Local Intrfce    Holdtme    Capability  Platform  Port ID
Switch-A         Gig 1/1          105          S I       WS-C3550-4Gig 0/1
Switch-C         Gig 2/1          139          S I       WS-C3550-4Gig 0/1
Router           Gig 3/1          120          R         Cisco 2610Fas 0/0
```

Next, the **show cdp neighbors detail** command reveals that Switch-C has the IP address 192.168.254.199, so you can open a Telnet session there. Switch-C might show only one neighbor (Switch-B), so you have reached the end of the switched network topology. At the bottom portion of Figure 2-6, the physical network has been discovered and drawn.

TIP You should assess the utilization or bandwidth used over various connections in the network. This is especially true of switch-to-switch links—if they are heavily used, you might want to plan for expansion. You also might want to get an idea of the total traffic being passed to and from individual server or user connections.

You can do this by using a network or protocol analyzer that is set up to monitor specific switch interfaces. However, you can get a quick snapshot of average traffic volumes with the **show interfaces** command. A switch maintains a running 5-minute average of traffic rates into and out of each interface. The output from **show interfaces** displays this information along with a host of other interface statistics.

To see only the interfaces that are in use and only the input and output data rates, you can add a filter to that command:

    show interfaces | include (is up | rate)

This produces output similar to the following:

```
Switch# show interfaces | include (is up | rate)
GigabitEthernet2/1 is up, line protocol is up (connected)
  5 minute input rate 63000 bits/sec, 34 packets/sec
  5 minute output rate 901000 bits/sec, 168 packets/sec
GigabitEthernet2/2 is up, line protocol is up (connected)
  5 minute input rate 0 bits/sec, 0 packets/sec
  5 minute output rate 194000 bits/sec, 80 packets/sec
GigabitEthernet2/3 is up, line protocol is up (connected)
  5 minute input rate 219000 bits/sec, 103 packets/sec
  5 minute output rate 1606000 bits/sec, 265 packets/sec
```

You can discover many more detailed aspects of a network. For example, you might want to know the extent of various VLANs across the switches, which interfaces are acting as trunks, the spanning tree topology for various VLANs, and so on.

These are all important things to consider in a network design and in troubleshooting a network, but they are beyond the scope of this chapter. These topics and the appropriate commands are presented in later chapters of this book.

Migrating to a Hierarchical Design

After you have discovered the topology of a network, you might find that it doesn't resemble the overall design goals that were presented earlier in this chapter. Perhaps it doesn't have a hierarchical layout with distinct layers. Or maybe you aren't able to see a modular layout with distinct switch blocks.

To move toward the campus hierarchical model, you also need to gather information about the traffic patterns crossing the network. For example, you should try to find answers to these questions:

■ Where are the enterprise resources (corporate email, web, and intranet application servers) located?

■ Where are the end user communities located?

■ Where are the service provider connections to the Internet, remote sites, and VPN users located?

Following the example of Figure 2-6, these have been identified by interviewing system administrators and network staff. Figure 2-7 shows the locations of user groups and server resources. Notice that these seem to be scattered across the entire network and that there is no clear picture of a modular network.

Figure 2-7 *Identifying User and Enterprise Resources*

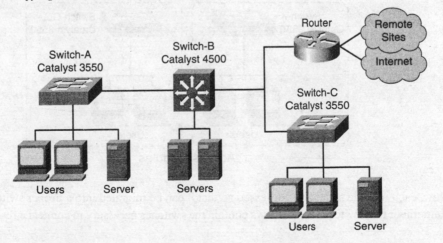

Now, you should add some structure to the design. Try to identify pieces of the network as specific modules. For example, the end user communities eventually will become switch block modules, containing both distribution- and access-layer switches. Redraw the network with the users and their switches toward the bottom.

Any resources related to connections to service providers, remote sites, or the Internet should be grouped and moved to become a service provider module or switch block. Enterprise servers, such as those in a data center, should be grouped and moved to become server farm switch blocks.

As you do this, a modular structure should begin to appear. Each module will connect into a central core layer, completing the hierarchical design. To see how the example of Figures 2-6 and 2-7 can be transformed, look at Figure 2-8. The existing switches have merely been moved so that they resemble the enterprise composite model. Without adding switches, the existing network has been migrated into the modular structure. Each module shown ultimately will become a switch block.

Figure 2-8 *Migrating an Existing Network into a Modular Structure*

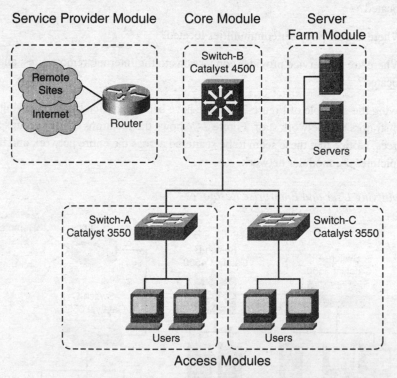

Now, each module should be addressed so that it can be migrated into a proper switch block. Remember that switch blocks always contain the switches necessary to connect a resource (users, servers, and so on) into the core layer. If this is done for the network in Figure 2-8, the network shown in Figure 2-9 might result.

Figure 2-9 *Migrating Network Modules into Switch Blocks*

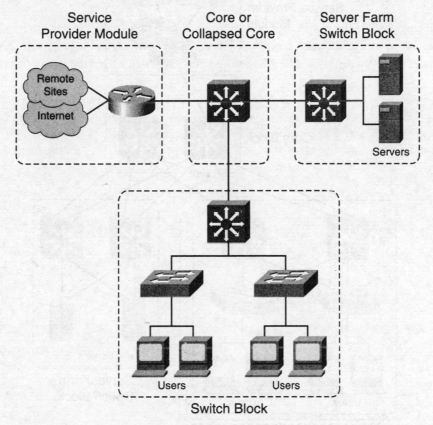

Notice that some additional switches have been added so that there is a distinct distribution layer of switches connecting into the core layer. Here, only single switches and single connections between switches have been shown. At this point, the design doesn't strictly follow the hierarchical model because there is little or no redundancy between layers.

Finally, you should add the redundant components to complete the design. The core should have dual switches. Each switch block should have dual distribution switches and dual links to both the access and core layers. These can be added now, resulting in the network shown in Figure 2-10. This might not be a practical design for a small sample network, but a full-fledged hierarchical design stages the sample network for growth and stability in the future.

Figure 2-10 *Completing the Hierarchical Campus Design*

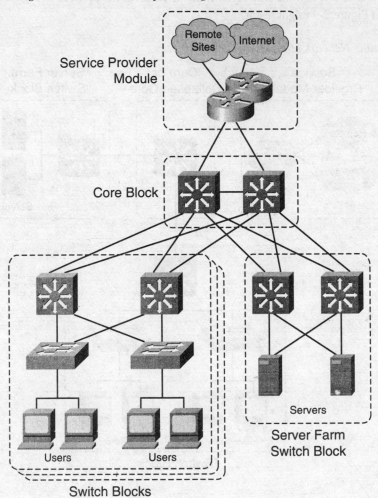

Foundation Summary

The Foundation Summary is a collection of tables, figures, lists, and other information that provides a convenient review of many key concepts in this chapter. If you are already comfortable with the topics in this chapter, this summary might help you recall a few details. If you just read this chapter, this review should help solidify some key facts. If you are doing your final preparation before the exam, the following information is a convenient way to review the day before the exam.

A campus network can be logically divided into these building blocks:

- **Switch block**—A group of access-layer switches, together with their distribution switches.

- **Core block**—The campus network's backbone.

- **Server farm block**—A group of enterprise servers, along with their access- and distribution-layer switches.

- **Management block**—A group of network-management resources, along with their access and distribution switches.

- **Enterprise edge block**—A collection of services related to external network access, along with their access and distribution switches.

- **Service provider edge block**—The external network services contracted or used by the enterprise network. These are the services with which the enterprise edge block interfaces.

Other than the core block, each switch block should have the following characteristics:

- Switches that form an access layer

- Dual distribution switches

- Redundant connections into the access and core layers

The most important factors to consider when choosing a switch block's size are as follows:

- The number of users connected to the access-layer switches

- The extent of the access VLAN or subnet

- The multilayer switching capacity of the distribution switches in the switch block

- The types, patterns, and volume of traffic passing through the switch block

The core layer in a campus network can be designed as follows:

- **Collapsed core**—The distribution- and core-layer switches are combined. This is usually acceptable in a small to medium-size network.

- **Dual core**—The distribution and core layers are separate; the core layer consists of dual or redundant multilayer switches.

Q&A

The questions and scenarios in this book are more difficult than what you should experience on the actual exam. The questions do not attempt to cover more breadth or depth than the exam; however, they are designed to make sure that you know the answer. Rather than allowing you to derive the answers from clues hidden inside the questions themselves, the questions challenge your understanding and recall of the subject. Hopefully, these questions will help limit the number of exam questions on which you narrow your choices to two options and then guess.

You can find the answers to these questions in Appendix A.

1. Where is the most appropriate place to connect a block of enterprise (internal) servers? Why?

2. How can you provide redundancy at the switch and core block layers? (Consider physical means, as well as functional methods using protocols, algorithms, and so on.)

3. What factors should you consider when sizing a switch block?

4. What are the signs of an oversized switch block?

5. What are the attributes and issues of having a collapsed core block?

6. How many switches are sufficient in a core block design?

7. What building blocks are used to build a scalable campus network?

8. What are two types of core, or backbone, designs?

9. Why should links and services provided to remote sites be grouped in a distinct building block?

10. Why should network-management applications and servers be placed in a distinct building block?

This part of the book covers the following BCMSN exam topics:

- Explain the function of the Switching Database Manager (specifically, Content Addressable Memory [CAM] and Ternary Content Addressable Memory [TCAM]) within a Catalyst switch

- Explain the functions of VLANs in a hierarchical network

- Configure VLANs (native, default, static and access)

- Explain and configure VLAN trunking (i.e., IEEE 802.1Q and ISL)

- Explain and configure VTP

- Verify or troubleshoot VLAN configurations

- Configure and verify link aggregation using PAgP or LACP

- Explain the functions and operations of the Spanning Tree Protocols (i.e., RSTP, PVRST, MISTP)

- Configure RSTP (PVRST) and MISTP

- Describe and configure STP security mechanisms (i.e., BPDU Guard, BPDU Filtering, Root Guard)

- Configure and verify UDLD and Loop Guard

- Verify or troubleshoot Spanning Tree protocol operations

Part II: Building a Campus Network

This chapter covers the following topics that you need to master for the CCNP BCMSN exam:

- **Layer 2 Switch Operation**—This section describes the functionality of a switch that forwards Ethernet frames.

- **Multilayer Switch Operation**—This section describes the mechanisms that forward packets at OSI Layers 3 and 4.

- **Tables Used in Switching**—This section explains how tables of information and computation are used to make switching decisions. Coverage focuses on the Content Addressable Memory table involved in Layer 2 forwarding, and the Ternary Content Addressable Memory used in packet-handling decisions at Layers 2 through 4.

- **Troubleshooting Switching Tables**—This section reviews the Catalyst commands that you can use to monitor the switching tables and memory. These commands can be useful when troubleshooting or tracing the sources of data or problems in a switched network.

CHAPTER 3

Switch Operation

To have a good understanding of the many features that you can configure on a Catalyst switch, you first should understand the fundamentals of the switching function itself.

This chapter serves as a primer, describing how an Ethernet switch works. It presents Layer 2 forwarding, along with the hardware functions that make forwarding possible. Multilayer switching also is explained. A considerable portion of the chapter deals with the memory architecture that performs switching at Layers 3 and 4 both flexibly and efficiently. This chapter also provides a brief overview of useful switching table–management commands.

"Do I Know This Already?" Quiz

The purpose of the "Do I Know This Already?" quiz is to help you decide whether you need to read the entire chapter. If you already intend to read the entire chapter, you do not necessarily need to answer these questions now.

The 12-question quiz, derived from the major sections in the "Foundation Topics" portion of the chapter, helps you determine how to spend your limited study time.

Table 3-1 outlines the major topics discussed in this chapter and the "Do I Know This Already?" quiz questions that correspond to those topics.

Table 3-1 *"Do I Know This Already?" Foundation Topics Section-to-Question Mapping*

Foundation Topics Section	Questions Covered in This Section	Score
Layer 2 Switch Operation	1–5	
Multilayer Switch Operation	6–9	
Switching Tables	10–11	
Troubleshooting Switching Tables	12	
Total Score		

> **CAUTION** The goal of self-assessment is to gauge your mastery of the topics in this chapter. If you do not know the answer to a question or are only partially sure of the answer, you should mark this question wrong. Giving yourself credit for an answer you correctly guess skews your self- assessment results and might provide you with a false sense of security.

You can find the answers to the quiz in Appendix A, "Answers to Chapter 'Do I Know This Already?' Quizzes and Q&A Sections." The suggested choices for your next step are as follows:

- **7 or less overall score**—Read the entire chapter. This includes the "Foundation Topics," "Foundation Summary," and "Q&A" sections.

- **8–10 overall score**—Begin with the "Foundation Summary" section and then follow up with the "Q&A" section at the end of the chapter.

- **11 or more overall score**—If you want more review on these topics, skip to the "Foundation Summary" section and then go to the "Q&A" section at the end of the chapter. Otherwise, move on to Chapter 4, "Switch Port Configuration."

1. Which of the following devices performs transparent bridging?

    a. Ethernet hub

    b. Layer 2 switch

    c. Layer 3 switch

    d. Router

2. When a PC is connected to a Layer 2 switch port, how far does the collision domain spread?

    a. No collision domain exists.

    b. One switch port.

    c. One VLAN.

    d. All ports on the switch.

3. What information is used to forward frames in a Layer 2 switch?

    a. Source MAC address

    b. Destination MAC address

    c. Source switch port

    d. IP addresses

4. What does a switch do if a MAC address cannot be found in the CAM table?

   a. The frame is forwarded to the default port.

   b. The switch generates an ARP request for the address.

   c. The switch floods the frame out all ports (except the receiving port).

   d. The switch drops the frame.

5. In the Catalyst 6500, frames can be filtered with access lists for security and QoS purposes. This filtering occurs according to which of the following?

   a. Before a CAM table lookup

   b. After a CAM table lookup

   c. Simultaneously with a CAM table lookup

   d. According to how the access lists are configured

6. Access list contents can be merged into which of the following?

   a. A CAM table

   b. A TCAM table

   c. A FIB table

   d. An ARP table

7. Multilayer switches using CEF are based on which of these techniques?

   a. Route caching

   b. Netflow switching

   c. Topology-based switching

   d. Demand-based switching

8. Which answer describes multilayer switching with CEF?

   a. The first packet is routed and then the flow is cached.

   b. The switch supervisor CPU forwards each packet.

   c. The switching hardware learns station addresses and builds a routing database.

   d. A single database of routing information is built for the switching hardware.

9. In a switch, frames are placed in which buffer after forwarding decisions are made?

    a. Ingress queues

    b. Egress queues

    c. CAM table

    d. TCAM

10. What size are the mask and pattern fields in a TCAM entry?

    a. 64 bits

    b. 128 bits

    c. 134 bits

    d. 168 bits

11. Access list rules are compiled as TCAM entries. When a packet is matched against an access list, in what order are the TCAM entries evaluated?

    a. Sequentially in the order of the original access list.

    b. Numerically by the access list number.

    c. Alphabetically by the access list name.

    d. All entries are evaluated in parallel.

12. Which Catalyst IOS command can you use to display the addresses in the CAM table?

    a. **show cam**

    b. **show mac address-table**

    c. **show mac**

    d. **show cam address-table**

Foundation Topics

Layer 2 Switch Operation

Recall that with shared Ethernet networks using hubs, many hosts are connected to a single broadcast and collision domain. In other words, shared Ethernet media operate at OSI Layer 1.

Each host must share the available bandwidth with every other connected host. When more than one host tries to talk at one time, a collision occurs, and everyone must back off and wait to talk again. This forces every host to operate in half-duplex mode, by either talking *or* listening at any given time. In addition, when one host sends a frame, all connected hosts hear it. When one host generates a frame with errors, everyone hears that, too.

At its most basic level, an Ethernet switch provides isolation from other connected hosts in several ways:

- The collision domain's scope is severely limited. On each switch port, the collision domain consists of the switch port itself and the devices directly connected to that port—either a single host or, if a shared-media hub is connected, the set of hosts connected to the hub.

- Host connections can operate in full-duplex mode because there is no contention on the media. Hosts can talk *and* listen at the same time.

- Bandwidth is no longer shared. Instead, each switch port offers dedicated bandwidth across a switching fabric to another switch port. (These connections change dynamically.)

- Errors in frames are not propagated. Each frame received on a switch port is checked for errors. Good frames are regenerated when they are forwarded or transmitted. This is known as *store-and-forward* switching technology: Packets are received, stored for inspection, and then forwarded.

- You can limit broadcast traffic to a volume threshold.

- Other types of intelligent filtering or forwarding become possible.

Transparent Bridging

A Layer 2 switch is basically a multiport transparent bridge, where each switch port is its own Ethernet LAN segment, isolated from the others. Frame forwarding is based completely on the MAC addresses contained in each frame, such that the switch will not forward a frame unless it knows the destination's location. (When the switch does not know where the destination is, it makes some safe assumptions.) Figure 3-1 shows the progression from a two-port to a multiport transparent bridge, and then to a switch.

Figure 3-1 *A Comparison of Transparent Bridges and Switches*

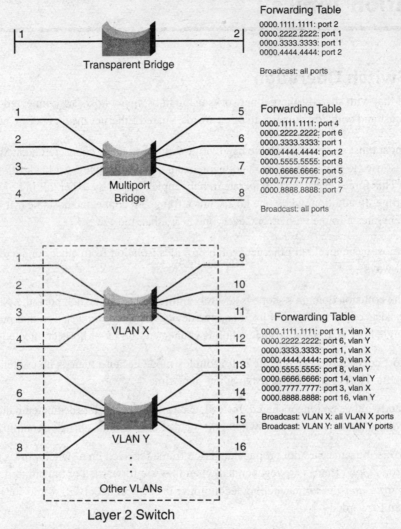

Forwarding Table

0000.1111.1111: port 2
0000.2222.2222: port 1
0000.3333.3333: port 1
0000.4444.4444: port 2

Broadcast: all ports

Transparent Bridge

Forwarding Table

0000.1111.1111: port 4
0000.2222.2222: port 6
0000.3333.3333: port 1
0000.4444.4444: port 2
0000.5555.5555: port 8
0000.6666.6666: port 5
0000.7777.7777: port 3
0000.8888.8888: port 7

Broadcast: all ports

Multiport Bridge

Forwarding Table

0000.1111.1111: port 11, vlan X
0000.2222.2222: port 6, vlan Y
0000.3333.3333: port 1, vlan X
0000.4444.4444: port 9, vlan X
0000.5555.5555: port 8, vlan Y
0000.6666.6666: port 14, vlan Y
0000.7777.7777: port 3, vlan X
0000.8888.8888: port 16, vlan Y

Broadcast: VLAN X: all VLAN X ports
Broadcast: VLAN Y: all VLAN Y ports

VLAN X

VLAN Y

Other VLANs

Layer 2 Switch

The entire process of forwarding Ethernet frames then becomes figuring out what MAC addresses connect to which switch ports. A switch either must be told explicitly where hosts are located or must learn this information for itself. You can configure MAC address locations through a switch's command-line interface, but this quickly gets out of control when there are many stations on the network or when stations move around.

To dynamically learn about station locations, a switch listens to incoming frames and keeps a table of address information. As a frame is received on a switch port, the switch inspects the source MAC address. If that address is not in the address table already, the MAC address, switch port, and virtual LAN (VLAN) on which it arrived are recorded in the table. Learning the address locations of the incoming packets is easy and straightforward.

Incoming frames also include the destination MAC address. Again, the switch looks up this address in the address table, hoping to find the switch port and VLAN where the address is attached. If it is found, the frame can be forwarded out that switch port. If the address is not found in the table, the switch must take more drastic action—the frame is forwarded in a "best effort" fashion by *flooding* it out all switch ports assigned to the source VLAN. This is known as *unknown unicast flooding*, with the unicast destination location unknown. Figure 3-2 illustrates this process, using only a single VLAN for simplification.

A switch constantly listens to incoming frames on each of its ports, learning source MAC addresses. However, be aware that the learning process is allowed only when the Spanning Tree Protocol (STP) algorithm has decided that a port is stable for normal use. STP is concerned only with maintaining a loop-free network, where frames will not be forwarded recursively. If a loop formed, a flooded frame could follow the looped path, where it would be flooded again and again.

In a similar manner, frames containing a broadcast or multicast destination address also are flooded. These destination addresses are not unknown—the switch knows them well. They are destined for multiple locations, so they must be flooded by definition. In the case of multicast addresses, flooding is performed by default.

Follow That Frame!

You should have a basic understanding of the operations that a frame undergoes as it passes through a Layer 2 switch. This helps you get a firm grasp on how to configure the switch for complex functions. Figure 3-3 shows a typical Layer 2 Catalyst switch and the decision processes that take place to forward each frame.

Figure 3-2 *Unknown Unicast Flooding*

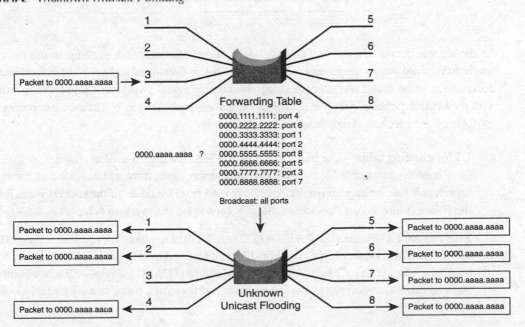

When a frame arrives at a switch port, it is placed into one of the port's ingress queues. The queues each can contain frames to be forwarded, with each queue having a different priority or service level. The switch port then can be fine-tuned so that important frames get processed and forwarded before less important frames. This can prevent time-critical data from being "lost in the shuffle" during a flurry of incoming traffic.

Figure 3-3 *Operations Within a Layer 2 Catalyst Switch*

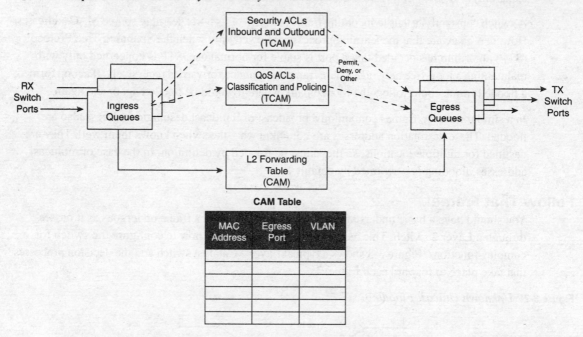

As the ingress queues are serviced and a frame is pulled off, the switch must figure out not only *where* to forward the frame, but also *whether* it should be forwarded and *how*. Three fundamental decisions must be made: one concerned with finding the egress switch port, and two concerned with forwarding policies. All these decisions are made *simultaneously* by independent portions of switching hardware and can be described as follows:

- **L2 forwarding table**—The frame's destination MAC address is used as an index, or key, into the Content Addressable Memory (CAM), or address, table. If the address is found, the egress switch port and the appropriate VLAN ID are read from the table. (If the address is not found, the frame is marked for flooding so that it is forwarded out every switch port in the VLAN.)

- **Security ACLs**—Access control lists (ACL) can be used to identify frames according to their MAC addresses, protocol types (for non-IP frames), IP addresses, protocols, and Layer 4 port numbers. The Ternary Content Addressable Memory (TCAM) contains ACLs in a compiled form so that a decision can be made on whether to forward a frame in a single table lookup.

■ **QoS ACLs**—Other ACLs can classify incoming frames according to quality of service (QoS) parameters, to police or control the rate of traffic flows, and to mark QoS parameters in outbound frames. The TCAM also is used to make these decisions in a single table lookup.

The CAM and TCAM tables are discussed in greater detail in the "Content Addressable Memory" and "Ternary Content Addressable Memory" sections, later in this chapter. After the CAM and TCAM table lookups have occurred, the frame is placed into the appropriate egress queue on the appropriate outbound switch port. The egress queue is determined by QoS values either contained in the frame or passed along with the frame. Like the ingress queues, the egress queues are serviced according to importance or time criticality; frames are sent out without being delayed by other outbound traffic.

Multilayer Switch Operation

Catalyst switches, such as the 3560 (with the appropriate Cisco IOS Software image), 4500, and 6500, also can forward frames based on Layer 3 and 4 information contained in packets. This is known as *multilayer switching (MLS)*. Naturally, Layer 2 switching is performed at the same time because even the higher-layer encapsulations still are contained in Ethernet frames.

Types of Multilayer Switching

Catalyst switches have supported two basic generations or types of MLS: route caching (first generation MLS) and topology based (second generation MLS). This section presents an overview of both, although only the second generation is supported in the Cisco IOS Software–based switch families, such as the Catalyst 3560, 4500, and 6500. You should understand the two types and the differences between them:

■ **Route caching**—The first generation of MLS, requiring a route processor (RP) and a switch engine (SE). The RP must process a traffic flow's first packet to determine the destination. The SE listens to the first packet and to the resulting destination, and sets up a "shortcut" entry in its MLS cache. The SE forwards subsequent packets in the same traffic flow based on shortcut entries in its cache.

This type of MLS also is known by the names *Netflow LAN switching*, *flow-based* or *demand-based switching*, and *"route once, switch many."* Even if this isn't used to forward packets in Cisco IOS–based Catalyst switches, the technique generates traffic flow information and statistics.

■ **Topology-based**—The second generation of MLS, utilizing specialized hardware. Layer 3 routing information builds and prepopulates a single database of the entire network topology. This database, an efficient table lookup in hardware, is consulted so that packets can be forwarded at high rates. The longest match found in the database is used as the correct Layer 3 destination. As the routing topology changes over time, the database contained in the hardware can be updated dynamically with no performance penalty.

This type of MLS is known as *Cisco Express Forwarding (CEF)*. A routing process running on the switch downloads the current routing table database into the *Forwarding Information Base (FIB)* area of hardware. CEF is discussed in greater detail in Chapter 12, "Multilayer Switching."

Follow That Packet!

The path that a Layer 3 packet follows through a multilayer switch is similar to that of a Layer 2 switch. Obviously, some means of making a Layer 3 forwarding decision must be added. Beyond that, several, sometimes unexpected, things can happen to packets as they are forwarded. Figure 3-4 shows a typical multilayer switch and the decision processes that must occur. Packets arriving on a switch port are placed in the appropriate ingress queue, just as in a Layer 2 switch.

Each packet is pulled off an ingress queue and inspected for both Layer 2 and Layer 3 destination addresses. Now, the decision of *where* to forward the packet is based on two address tables, whereas the decision of *how* to forward the packet still is based on access list results. As in Layer 2 switching, all these multilayer decisions are performed simultaneously in hardware:

- **L2 forwarding table**—The destination MAC address is used as an index to the CAM table. If the frame contains a Layer 3 packet to be forwarded, the destination MAC address is that of a Layer 3 port on the switch. In this case, the CAM table results are used only to decide that the frame should be processed at Layer 3.

- **L3 forwarding table**—The FIB table is consulted, using the destination IP address as an index. The longest match in the table is found (both address and mask), and the resulting next-hop Layer 3 address is obtained. The FIB also contains each next-hop entry's Layer 2 MAC address and the egress switch port (and VLAN ID) so that further table lookups are not necessary.

- **Security ACLs**—Inbound and outbound access lists are compiled into TCAM entries so that decisions of whether to forward a packet can be determined as a single table lookup.

- **QoS ACLs**—Packet classification, policing, and marking all can be performed as single table lookups in the QoS TCAM.

Figure 3-4 *Operations Within a Multilayer Catalyst Switch.*

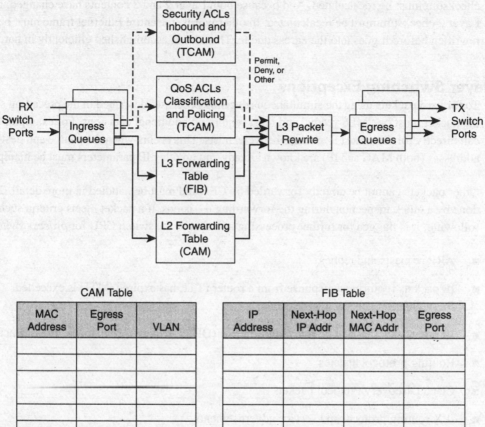

As with Layer 2 switching, the packet finally must be placed in the appropriate egress queue on the appropriate egress switch port.

However, recall that during the multilayer switching process, the next-hop destination was obtained from the FIB table, just as a router would do. The Layer 3 address identified the next hop and found its Layer 2 address. Only the Layer 2 address would be used, so the Layer 2 frames could be sent on.

The next-hop Layer 2 address must be put into the frame in place of the original destination address (the multilayer switch). The frame's Layer 2 source address also must become that of the multilayer switch before it is sent on to the next hop. As any good router must do, the Time-To-Live (TTL) value in the Layer 3 packet must be decremented by one.

Because the contents of the Layer 3 packet (the TTL value) have changed, the Layer 3 header checksum must be recalculated. And because both Layer 2 and 3 contents have changed, the Layer 2 checksum must be recalculated. In other words, the entire Ethernet frame must be rewritten before it goes into the egress queue. This also is accomplished efficiently in hardware.

Multilayer Switching Exceptions

To forward packets using the simultaneous decision processes described in the preceding section, the packet must be "MLS-ready" and must require no additional decisions. For example, CEF can directly forward most IP packets between hosts. This occurs when the source and destination addresses (both MAC and IP) are known already and no other IP parameters must be manipulated.

Other packets cannot be directly forwarded by CEF and must be handled in more detail. This is done by a quick inspection during the forwarding d   isions. If a packet meets criteria such as the following, it is flagged for further processing and sent to the switch CPU for *process switching*:

- ARP requests and replies

- IP packets requiring a response from a router (TTL has expired, MTU is exceeded, fragmentation is needed, and so on)

- IP broadcasts that will be relayed as unicast (DHCP requests, IP helper-address functions)

- Routing protocol updates

- Cisco Discovery Protocol packets

- IPX routing protocol and service advertisements

- Packets needing encryption

- Packets triggering Network Address Translation (NAT)

- Other non-IP and non-IPX protocol packets (AppleTalk, DECnet, and so on)

NOTE   On the Catalyst 6500, both IP and IPX packets are CEF-switched in hardware. All other protocols are handled by process switching on the MSFC module (the routing CPU). On the Catalyst 4500, only IP packets are CEF-switched in hardware. All other routable protocols, including IPX, are flagged for process switching by the switch CPU.

With the Catalyst 3560, only IP is CEF-switched in hardware. Other non-IP protocols are not routed at all. Instead, they are flagged for *fallback bridging*, where they are treated as transparently bridged (Layer 2 switched) packets. An external router or multilayer switch must handle any routing that still is needed during fallback bridging.

Tables Used in Switching

Catalyst switches maintain several types of tables to be used in the switching process. The tables are tailored for Layer 2 switching or MLS and are kept in very fast memory so that many fields within a frame or packet can be compared in parallel.

Content Addressable Memory

All Catalyst switch models use a CAM table for Layer 2 switching. As frames arrive on switch ports, the source MAC addresses are learned and recorded in the CAM table. The port of arrival and the VLAN both are recorded in the table, along with a time stamp. If a MAC address learned on one switch port has moved to a different port, the MAC address and time stamp are recorded for the most recent arrival port. Then, the previous entry is deleted. If a MAC address is found already present in the table for the correct arrival port, only its time stamp is updated.

Switches generally have large CAM tables so that many addresses can be looked up for frame forwarding. However, there is not enough table space to hold every possible address on large networks. To manage the CAM table space, *stale entries* (addresses that have not been heard from for a period of time) are aged out. By default, idle CAM table entries are kept for 300 seconds before they are deleted. You can change the default setting using the following configuration command:

```
Switch(config)# mac address-table aging-time seconds
```

By default, MAC addresses are learned dynamically from incoming frames. You also can configure static CAM table entries that contain MAC addresses that might not be learned otherwise. To do this, use the following configuration command:

```
Switch(config)# mac address-table static mac-address vlan vlan-id interface type
    mod/num
```

Here, the MAC address (in dotted triplet hex format) is identified with the switch port and VLAN where it appears.

> **NOTE**   You should be aware that there is a slight discrepancy in the CAM table command syntax. Until Catalyst IOS version 12.1(11)EA1, the syntax for CAM table commands used the keywords **mac-address-table**. In more recent Cisco IOS versions, the syntax has changed to use the keywords **mac address-table** (first hyphen omitted). The Catalyst 4500 and 6500 IOS Software are exceptions, however, and continue to use the **mac-address-table** keyword form.

What happens when a host's MAC address is learned on one switch port, and then the host moves so that it appears on a different switch port? Ordinarily, the host's original CAM table entry would have to age out after 300 seconds, while its address was learned on the new port. To avoid having duplicate CAM table entries, a switch purges any existing entries for a MAC address that has just been learned on a different switch port. This is a safe assumption because MAC addresses are unique, and a single host should never be seen on more than one switch port unless problems exist in the network. If a switch notices that a MAC address is being learned on alternating switch ports, it generates an error message that flags the MAC address as "flapping" between interfaces.

Ternary Content Addressable Memory

In traditional routing, ACLs can match, filter, or control specific traffic. Access lists are made up of one or more access control entities (ACE), or matching statements that are evaluated in sequential order. Evaluating an access list can take up additional time, adding to the latency of forwarding packets.

In multilayer switches, however, all the matching process that ACLs provide is implemented in hardware. TCAM allows a packet to be evaluated against an entire access list in a single table lookup. Most switches have multiple TCAMs so that both inbound and outbound security and QoS ACLs can be evaluated simultaneously, or entirely in parallel with a Layer 2 or Layer 3 forwarding decision.

The Catalyst IOS Software has two components that are part of the TCAM operation:

■ **Feature Manager (FM)**—After an access list has been created or configured, the Feature Manager software compiles, or merges, the ACEs into entries in the TCAM table. The TCAM then can be consulted at full frame-forwarding speed.

■ **Switching Database Manager (SDM)**—You can partition the TCAM on some Catalyst switches into areas for different functions. The SDM software configures or tunes the TCAM partitions, if needed. (The TCAM is fixed on Catalyst 4500 and 6500 platforms, and cannot be repartitioned.)

TCAM Structure

The TCAM is an extension of the CAM table concept. Recall that a CAM table takes in an index or key value (usually a MAC address) and looks up the resulting value (usually a switch port or VLAN ID). Table lookup is fast and always based on an exact key match consisting of two input values: 0 and 1 bits.

TCAM also uses a table-lookup operation but is greatly enhanced to allow a more abstract operation. For example, binary values (0s and 1s) make up a key into the table, but a mask value also is used to decide which bits of the key are actually relevant. This effectively makes a key consisting of three input values: 0, 1, and X (don't care) bit values—a threefold or *ternary* combination.

TCAM entries are composed of Value, Mask, and Result (VMR) combinations. Fields from frame or packet headers are fed into the TCAM, where they are matched against the value and mask pairs to yield a result. As a quick reference, these can be described as follows:

- **Values** are always 134-bit quantities, consisting of source and destination addresses and other relevant protocol information—all patterns to be matched. The information concatenated to form the value depends on the type of access list, as shown in Table 3-2. Values in the TCAM come directly from any address, port, or other protocol information given in an ACE.

- **Masks** are also 134-bit quantities, in exactly the same format, or bit order, as the values. Masks select only the value bits of interest; a mask bit is set to exactly match a value bit, or is not set for value bits that do not matter. The masks used in the TCAM stem from address or bit masks in ACEs.

- **Results** are numerical values that represent what action to take after the TCAM lookup occurs. Whereas traditional access lists offer only a *permit* or *deny* result, TCAM lookups offer a number of possible results or actions. For example, the result can be a permit or deny decision, an index value to a QoS policer, a pointer to a next-hop routing table, and so on.

Table 3-2 *TCAM Value Pattern Components*

Access List Type	Value and Mask Components, 134-Bits Wide (Number of Bits)
Ethernet	Source MAC (48), destination MAC (48), Ethertype (16)
ICMP	Source IP (32), destination IP (32), protocol (16), ICMP code (8), ICMP type (4), IP type of service (ToS) (8)
Extended IP using TCP/UDP	Source IP (32), destination IP (32), protocol (16), IP ToS (8), source port (16), source operator (4), destination port (16), destination operator (4)
Other IP	Source IP (32), destination IP (32), protocol (16), IP ToS (8)
IGMP	Source IP (32), destination IP (32), protocol (16), IP ToS (8), IGMP message type (8)
IPX	Source IPX network (32), destination IPX network (32), destination node (48), IPX packet type (16)

The TCAM always is organized by masks, where each unique mask has eight value patterns associated with it. For example, the Catalyst 6500 TCAM (one for security ACLs and one for QoS ACLs) holds up to 4,096 masks and 32,768 value patterns. The trick is that each of the mask-value pairs is evaluated *simultaneously,* or in parallel, revealing the best or longest match in a single table lookup.

TCAM Example

Figure 3-5 shows how the TCAM is built and used. This is a simple example and might or might not be identical to the results that the Feature Manager produces because the ACEs might need to be optimized or rewritten to achieve certain TCAM algorithm requirements.

Figure 3-5 *How an Access List Is Merged into TCAM*

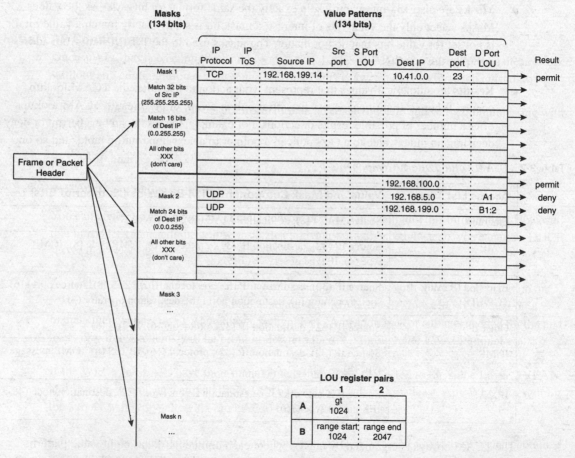

```
access-list 100 permit tcp host 192.168.199.14 10.41.0.0 0.0.255.255 eq telnet
access-list 100 permit ip any 192.168.100.0 0.0.0.255
access-list 100 deny udp any 192.168.5.0 0.0.0.255 gt 1024
access-list 100 deny udp any 192.168.199.0 0.0.0.255 range 1024 2047
```

The sample access list 100 (extended IP) is configured and merged into TCAM entries. First, the mask values must be identified in the access list. When an address value and a corresponding address mask are specified in an ACE, those mask bits must be set for matching. All other mask bits can remain in the "don't care" state. The access list contains only three unique masks: one that matches all 32 bits of the source IP address (found with an address mask of 0.0.0.0 or the keyword **host**), one that matches 16 bits of the destination address (found with an address mask of

0.0.255.255), and one that matches only 24 bits of the destination address (found with an address mask of 0.0.0.255). The keyword **any** in the ACEs means "match anything" or "don't care."

The unique masks are placed into the TCAM. Then, for each mask, all possible value patterns are identified. For example, a 32-bit source IP mask (Mask 1) can be found only in ACEs with a source IP address of 192.168.199.14 and a destination of 10.41.0.0. (The rest of Mask 1 is the destination address mask 0.0.255.255.) Those address values are placed into the first value pattern slot associated with Mask 1. Mask 2 has three value patterns: destination addresses 192.168.100.0, 192.168.5.0, and 192.168.199.0. Each of these is placed in the three pattern positions of Mask 2. This process continues until all ACEs have been merged.

When a mask's eighth pattern position has been filled, the next pattern with the same mask must be placed under a new mask. A bit of a balancing act occurs to try to fit all ACEs into the available mask and pattern entries without an overflow.

Port Operations in TCAM

You might have noticed that matching strictly based on values and masks covers only ACE statements that involve exact matches (either the **eq** port operation keyword or no Layer 4 port operations). For example, ACEs such as the following involve specific address values, address masks, and port numbers:

```
access-list test permit ip 192.168.254.0 0.0.0.255 any
access-list test permit tcp any host 192.168.199.10 eq www
```

What about ACEs that use port operators, where a comparison must be made? Consider the following:

```
access-list test permit udp any host 192.168.199.50 gt 1024
access-list test permit tcp any any range 2000 2002
```

A simple logical operation between a mask and a pattern cannot generate the desired result. The TCAM also provides a mechanism for performing a Layer 4 operation or comparison, also done during the single table lookup. If an ACE has a port operator, such as **gt**, **lt**, **neq**, or **range**, the Feature Manager software compiles the TCAM entry to include the use of the operator and the operand in a Logical Operation Unit (LOU) register. Only a limited number of LOUs are available in the TCAM. If there are more ACEs with comparison operators than there are LOUs, the Feature Manager must break up the ACEs into multiple ACEs with only regular matching (using the **eq** operator).

In Figure 3-5, two ACEs require a Layer 4 operation:

■ One that checks for UDP destination ports greater than 1024

■ One that looks for the UDP destination port range 1024 to 2047

The Feature Manager checks all ACEs for Layer 4 operation and places these into LOU register pairs. These can be loaded with operations, independent of any other ACE parameters. The LOU contents can be reused if other ACEs need the same comparisons and values. After the LOUs are loaded, they are referenced in the TCAM entries that need them. This is shown by LOUs A1 and the B1:2 pair. A finite number (actually, a rather small number) of LOUs are available in the TCAM, so the Feature Manager software must use them carefully.

Troubleshooting Switching Tables

If you see strange behavior in a Catalyst switch, it might be useful to examine the contents of the various switching tables. In any event, you might sometimes need to find out on which switch port a specific MAC address has been learned.

CAM Table Operation

To view the contents of the CAM table, you can use the following form of the **show mac address-table** EXEC command:

```
Switch# show mac address-table dynamic [address mac-address | interface type mod/num |
    vlan vlan-id]
```

The entries that have been learned dynamically will be shown. You can add the **address** keyword to specify a single MAC address, or the **interface** or **vlan** keyword to see addresses that have been learned on a specific interface or VLAN.

For example, assume that you need to find the learned location of the host with MAC address 0050.8b11.54da. The **show mac address-table dynamic address 0050.8b11.54da** command might produce the output in Example 3-1.

Example 3-1   *Determining Host Location by MAC Address*

```
Switch# show mac address-table dynamic address 0050.8b11.54da
        Mac Address Table
-------------------------------------------

Vlan    Mac Address       Type       Ports
----    -----------       ----       -----
  54    0050.8b11.54da    DYNAMIC    Fa0/1
Total Mac Addresses for this criterion: 1
Switch#
```

From this, you can see that the host somehow is connected to interface FastEthernet 0/1, on VLAN 54.

> **TIP**   If your Catalyst IOS switch is not accepting commands of the form **mac address-table**, try adding a hyphen between the keywords. For example, the Catalyst 4500 and 6500 most likely will accept **show mac-address-table** instead.

Suppose that this same command produced no output for the interface and VLAN. What might that mean? Either the host has not sent a frame that the switch can use for learning its location, or something odd is going on. Perhaps the host is using two network interface cards (NICs) to load-balance traffic; one NIC is only receiving traffic, whereas the other is only sending. Therefore, the switch never hears and learns the receiving-only NIC address.

To see the CAM table's size, use the **show mac address-table count** command. MAC address totals are shown for each active VLAN on the switch. This can give you a good idea of the size of the CAM table and how many hosts are using the network. Be aware that many MAC addresses can be learned on a switch's uplink ports.

CAM table entries can be cleared manually, if needed, by using the following EXEC command:

```
Switch# clear mac address-table dynamic [address mac-address | interface type
    mod/num | vlan vlan-id]
```

Frequently, you need to know where a user with a certain MAC address is connected. In a large network, discerning at which switch and switch port a MAC address can be found might be difficult. Start at the network's center, or core, and display the CAM table entry for the MAC address. Look at the switch port shown in the entry and move to the neighboring switch connected to that port. Then, repeat the CAM table process. Keep moving from switch to switch until you reach the edge of the network where the MAC address connects.

TCAM Operation

The TCAM in a switch is more or less self-sufficient. Access lists are compiled or merged automatically into the TCAM, so there is nothing to configure. The only concept you need to be aware of is how the TCAM resources are being used.

TCAMs have a limited number of usable mask, value pattern, and LOU entries. If access lists grow to be large or many Layer 4 operations are needed, the TCAM tables and registers can overflow. If that happens while you are configuring an ACL, the switch will generate syslog messages that flag the TCAM overflow situation as it tries to compile the ACL into TCAM entries.

Foundation Summary

The Foundation Summary is a collection of tables, lists, and other information that provides a convenient review of many key concepts in this chapter. If you are already comfortable with the topics in this chapter, this summary might help you recall a few details. If you just read this chapter, this review should help solidify some key facts. If you are doing your final prep before the exam, the following information is a convenient way to review the day before the exam:

■ Layer 2 switches learn incoming MAC addresses and record their locations based on the inbound switch ports.

■ Layer 2 switching information is stored in the Content Addressable Memory (CAM) table. The CAM is consulted to find the outbound switch port when forwarding frames.

■ Multilayer switching looks at the Layer 2 addresses, along with Layers 3 and 4 address and port information, to forward packets.

■ Multilayer switching is performed in hardware using the Cisco Express Forwarding (CEF) method.

■ CEF builds Layer 3 destination information from routing tables and Layer 2 data. This information is stored in hardware as a Forwarding Information Base (FIB) table.

■ Multilayer switches can make many policy decisions in parallel, using the Ternary Content Addressable Memory (TCAM) contents.

■ TCAM combines a 134-bit value, or pattern (made up of addresses, port numbers, or other appropriate fields), with a 134-bit mask to yield a result value. The result instructs the switch hardware on how to finish forwarding the packet.

■ Access lists for security (traditional router ACLs and VLAN ACLs) and QoS ACLs are compiled or merged into TCAM entries. These access lists then can be processed on each packet that passes through the switch, as a single table lookup.

■ As a packet exits a multilayer switch, it must be rewritten so that its header and checksum values are valid. The fields in the original packet that the switch updates are as follows:

— The source MAC address becomes the Layer 3 switch MAC address.

— The destination MAC address becomes the next-hop MAC address.

— The IP TTL value is decremented by one.

— The IP checksum is recomputed.

— The Ethernet frame checksum is recomputed.

Table 3-3 *Switching Table Commands*

Task	Command Syntax
Set the CAM table aging time.	**mac address-table aging-time** *seconds*
Configure a static CAM entry.	**mac address-table static** *mac-address* **vlan** *vlan-id* **interface** *type mod/num*
Clear a CAM table entry.	**clear mac address-table dynamic** [**address** *mac-address* | **interface** *type mod/num* | **vlan** *vlan-id*]
View the CAM table.	**show mac address-table dynamic** [**address** *mac-address* | **interface** *type mod/num* | **vlan** *vlan-id*]
View the CAM table size.	**show mac address-table count**

Q&A

The questions and scenarios in this book are more difficult than what you should experience on the actual exam. The questions do not attempt to cover more breadth or depth than the exam; however, they are designed to make sure that you know the answer. Rather than allowing you to derive the answers from clues hidden inside the questions themselves, the questions challenge your understanding and recall of the subject. Hopefully, these questions will help limit the number of exam questions on which you narrow your choices to two options and then guess.

You can find the answers to these questions in Appendix A.

1. By default, how long are CAM table entries kept before they are aged out?

2. A TCAM lookup involves which values?

3. How many table lookups are required to find a MAC address in the CAM table?

4. How many table lookups are required to match a packet against an access list that has been compiled into 10 TCAM entries?

5. How many value patterns can a TCAM store for each mask?

6. Can all packets be switched in hardware by a multilayer switch?

7. Multilayer switches must rewrite which portions of an Ethernet frame?

8. If a station receives only Ethernet frames and doesn't transmit anything, how will a switch learn of its location?

9. What is a TCAM's main purpose?

10. Why do the TCAM mask and pattern fields consist of so many bits?

11. In a multilayer switch with a TCAM, a longer access list (more ACEs or statements) takes longer to process for each frame. True or false?

12. A multilayer switch receives a packet with a certain destination IP address. Suppose that the switch has that IP address in its Layer 3 forwarding table but has no corresponding Layer 2 address. What happens to the packet next?

13. Suppose that a multilayer switch can't support a protocol with CEF, and it relies on *fallback bridging*. Can the switch still route that traffic?

14. To configure a static CAM table entry, the **mac address-table static** *mac-address* command is used. Which two other parameters also must be given?

15. As a network administrator, what aspects of a switch TCAM should you be concerned with?

16. What portion of the TCAM is used to evaluate port number comparisons in an access list?

17. Someone has asked you where the host with MAC address 00-10-20-30-40-50 is located. Assuming that you already know the switch it is connected to, what command can you use to find it?

18. Complete this command to display the size of the CAM table: **show mac** _____.

19. What protocol is used to advertise CAM table entries among neighboring switches?

20. Suppose that a host uses one MAC address to send frames and another to receive them. In other words, one address will always be the source address sent in frames, and the other will be used only as a destination address in incoming frames. Is it possible for that host to communicate with others through a Layer 2 switch? If so, how?

This chapter covers the following topics that you need to master for the CCNP BCMSN exam:

- **Ethernet Concepts**—This section discusses the concepts and technology behind various forms of Ethernet media.

- **Connectivity with Scalable Ethernet**—This section covers the configuration steps and commands needed to use Catalyst Ethernet, Fast Ethernet, and Gigabit and 10-Gigabit Ethernet switch ports in a network.

- **Connecting Switch Block Devices**—This section discusses the physical cabling and connectivity used with Catalyst switches, including console and Ethernet interfaces.

- **Troubleshooting Port Connectivity**—This section covers some of the symptoms, methods, and switch commands that you can use to diagnose problems with Ethernet switch connections.

CHAPTER 4

Switch Port Configuration

Chapters 1, "Campus Network Overview," and 2, "Modular Network Design," dealt with the logical processes that you can use to design a campus network. Connections between switch blocks were discussed so that traffic can be transported efficiently across the campus. Single connections, load balancing, and redundant paths connected switches in modular blocks for complete connectivity. However, these paths were only functional paths—no specifics were presented about how much traffic the network could handle or what physical capabilities were supported. These topics become important when you begin to size traffic loads and actually connect Cisco switch devices.

This chapter presents the various Ethernet network technologies used to establish switched connections within the campus network. The chapter also details the switch commands required for configuring and troubleshooting Ethernet LAN ports.

"Do I Know This Already?" Quiz

The purpose of the "Do I Know This Already?" quiz is to help you decide whether you need to read the entire chapter. If you already intend to read the entire chapter, you do not necessarily need to answer these questions now.

The 11-question quiz, derived from the major sections in the "Foundation Topics" portion of the chapter, helps you determine how to spend your limited study time.

Table 4-1 outlines the major topics discussed in this chapter and the "Do I Know This Already?" quiz questions that correspond to those topics.

Table 4-1   *"Do I Know This Already?" Foundation Topics Section-to-Question Mapping*

Foundation Topics Section	Questions Covered in This Section	Score
Ethernet Concepts	1–6	
Connecting Switch Block Devices	7–8	
Switch Port Configuration	9	

continues

Table 4-1 *"Do I Know This Already?" Foundation Topics Section-to-Question Mapping (Continued)*

Foundation Topics Section	Questions Covered in This Section	Score
Troubleshooting Port Connectivity	10–11	
Total Score		

> **CAUTION** The goal of self-assessment is to gauge your mastery of the topics in this chapter. If you do not know the answer to a question or are only partially sure of the answer, you should mark this question wrong. Giving yourself credit for an answer you correctly guess skews your self- assessment results and might provide you with a false sense of security.

1. What does the IEEE 802.3 standard define?

   a. Spanning Tree Protocol

   b. Token Ring

   c. Ethernet

   d. Switched Ethernet

2. At what layer are traditional 10-Mbps Ethernet, Fast Ethernet, and Gigabit Ethernet the same?

   a. Layer 1

   b. Layer 2

   c. Layer 3

   d. Layer 4

3. At what layer are traditional 10-Mbps Ethernet, Fast Ethernet, and Gigabit Ethernet different?

   a. Layer 1

   b. Layer 2

   c. Layer 3

   d. Layer 4

4. What is the maximum cable distance for a Category 5 100BASE-TX connection?

   a. 100 feet

   b. 100 m

   c. 328 m

   d. 500 m

5. Ethernet autonegotiation determines which of the following?

   a. Spanning Tree mode

   b. Duplex mode

   c. Quality of service mode

   d. Error threshold

6. Which of the following cannot be determined if the far end of a connection doesn't support autonegotiation?

   a. Link speed

   b. Link duplex mode

   c. Link media type

   d. MAC address

7. Which of these is not a standard type of Gigabit Interface Converter (GBIC) or small form factor pluggable (SFP) module?

   a. 1000BASE-LX/LH

   b. 1000BASE-T

   c. 1000BASE-FX

   d. 1000BASE-ZX

8. What type of cable should you use to connect two switches back to back using their FastEthernet 10/100 ports?

   a. Rollover cable

   b. Transfer cable

   c. Crossover cable

   d. Straight-through cable

9. Assume that you have just entered the **configure terminal** command. To configure the speed of the first FastEthernet interface on a Cisco IOS Software–based Catalyst switch to 100 Mbps, which one of these commands should you enter first?

   a. **speed 100 mbps**

   b. **speed 100**

   c. **interface fastethernet 0/1**

   d. **interface fast ethernet 0/1**

10. If a switch port is in the errdisable state, what is the first thing you should do?

    a. Reload the switch.

    b. Use the **clear errdisable port** command.

    c. Use the **shut** and **no shut** interface-configuration commands.

    d. Determine the cause of the problem.

11. Which of the following **show interface** output information can you use to diagnose a switch port problem?

    a. Port state.

    b. Port speed.

    c. Input errors.

    d. Collisions.

    e. All of these answers are correct.

You can find the answers to the quiz in Appendix A, "Answers to Chapter 'Do I Know This Already?' Quizzes and Q&A Sections." The suggested choices for your next step are as follows:

- **7 or less overall score**—Read the entire chapter. This includes the "Foundation Topics," "Foundation Summary," and "Q&A" sections.

- **8–9 overall score**—Begin with the "Foundation Summary" section and follow up with the "Q&A" section at the end of the chapter.

- **10 or more overall score**—If you want more review on these topics, skip to the "Foundation Summary" section and then go to the "Q&A" section at the end of the chapter. Otherwise, move to Chapter 5, "VLANs and Trunks."

Foundation Topics

Ethernet Concepts

This section reviews the varieties of Ethernet and their application in a campus network. Recall how the bandwidth requirements for each network segment are determined by the types of applications in use, the traffic flows within the network, and the size of the user community served. Ethernet scales to support increasing bandwidths and should be chosen to match the need at each point in the campus network. As network bandwidth requirements grow, you can scale the links between access, distribution, and core layers to match the load.

Other network media technologies available include Fiber Distribution Data Interface (FDDI), Copper Distribution Data Interface (CDDI), Token Ring, and Asynchronous Transfer Mode (ATM). Although some networks still use these media, Ethernet has emerged as the most popular choice in installed networks. Ethernet is chosen because of its low cost, market availability, and scalability to higher bandwidths.

Ethernet (10 Mbps)

Ethernet is a LAN technology based on the Institute of Electrical and Electronics Engineers (IEEE) 802.3 standard. Ethernet (in contrast to Fast Ethernet and later versions) offers a bandwidth of 10 Mbps between end users. In its most basic form, Ethernet is a shared medium that becomes both a collision and a broadcast domain. As the number of users on the shared media increases, so does the probability that a user is trying to transmit data at any given time. When one user transmits at about the same time as another, a *collision* occurs. In other words, both users can't transmit data at the same time if they both are sharing the same network media.

Ethernet is based on the *carrier sense multiple access collision detect (CSMA/CD)* technology, which requires that transmitting stations back off for a random period of time when a collision occurs. If a station must wait its turn to transmit, it cannot transmit and receive at the same time. This is called *half-duplex* operation.

The more crowded an Ethernet segment becomes, the number of stations likely to be transmitting at a given time increases. Imagine standing in a crowded room trying to tell a story. Instead of attempting to talk over the crowd, you stop and politely wait while other people talk. The more people there are in the room, the more difficult talking becomes. Likewise, as an Ethernet segment becomes more crowded, it becomes more inefficient.

Ethernet switching addresses this problem by dynamically allocating a dedicated 10-Mbps bandwidth to each of its ports. The resulting increased network performance occurs by reducing the number of users connected to an Ethernet segment. In effect, collisions are less probable and the collision domain is reduced in size.

Although switched Ethernet's job is to offer fully dedicated bandwidth to each connected device, assuming that network performance will improve across the board when switching is introduced is a common mistake. For example, consider a workgroup of users connected by a shared-media Ethernet hub. These users regularly access an enterprise server located elsewhere in the campus network. To improve performance, the decision is made to replace the hub with an Ethernet switch so that all users get dedicated 10-Mbps connections. Because the switch offers dedicated bandwidth for connections between the end-user devices connected to its ports, any user-to-user traffic probably would see improved performance. However, the enterprise server still is located elsewhere in the network, and all the switched users still must share available bandwidth across the campus to reach it. As discussed in Chapter 1, instead of throwing raw bandwidth at a problem, a design based on careful observation of traffic patterns and flows offers a better solution.

Because switched Ethernet can remove the possibility of collisions, stations do not have to listen to each other to take a turn transmitting on the wire. Instead, stations can operate in *full-duplex* mode— transmitting and receiving simultaneously. Full-duplex mode further increases network performance, with a net throughput of 10 Mbps in each direction, or 20 Mbps total throughput on each port.

Another consideration when dealing with 10-Mbps Ethernet is the physical cabling. Ethernet cabling involves the use of unshielded twisted-pair (UTP) wiring (10BASE-T Ethernet), usually restricted to an end-to-end distance of 100 m (328 feet) between active devices. Keeping cable lengths as short as possible in the wiring closet also reduces noise and crosstalk when many cables are bundled together.

In a campus network environment, Ethernet usually is used in the access layer, between end user devices and the access-layer switch. Many networks still use Ethernet to connect end users to shared-media hubs, which then connect to access-layer switches. Ethernet typically is not used at either the distribution or the core layer.

> **NOTE**   Ethernet applications (10BASE2, 10BASE5, 10BASE-F, and so on) use other cabling technologies, although they are not discussed here. For the most part, 10BASE-T with UTP wiring is the most commonly used. A useful website for further reading about Ethernet technology is Charles Spurgeon's Ethernet Web Site, at http://www.ethermanage.com/ethernet/.

Fast Ethernet

Instead of requiring campuses to invest in a completely new technology to gain increased bandwidth, the networking industry developed a higher-speed Ethernet based on existing Ethernet standards. Fast Ethernet operates at 100 Mbps and is defined in the IEEE 802.3u standard. The Ethernet cabling schemes, CSMA/CD operation, and all upper-layer protocol operations are maintained with Fast Ethernet. The net result is the same data link Media Access Control (MAC) layer merged with a new physical layer.

The campus network can use Fast Ethernet to link access- and distribution-layer switches, if no higher-speed links are available. These links can support the aggregate traffic from multiple Ethernet segments in the access layer. Fast Ethernet generally is used to connect end user workstations to the access-layer switch and to provide improved connectivity to enterprise servers.

Cabling for Fast Ethernet can involve either UTP or fiber. Table 4-2 lists the specifications for Fast Ethernet that define the media types and distances.

Table 4-2 *Cabling Specifications for Fast Ethernet*

Technology	Wiring Type	Pairs	Cable Length
100BASE-TX	EIA/TIA Category 5 UTP	2	100 m
100BASE-T2	EIA/TIA Category 3, 4, 5 UTP	2	100 m
100BASE-T4	EIA/TIA Category 3, 4, 5 UTP	4	100 m
100BASE-FX	Multimode fiber (MMF); 62.5-micron core, 125-micron outer cladding (62.5/125)	1	400 m half duplex or 2000 m full duplex
	Single-mode fiber (SMF)	1	10 km

Full-Duplex Fast Ethernet

As with traditional Ethernet, the natural progression to improve performance is to use full-duplex operation. Fast Ethernet can provide up to 100 Mbps in each direction on a switched connection, for 200 Mbps total throughput.

This maximum throughput is possible only when one device (a workstation, server, router, or another switch) is connected directly to a switch port. In addition, the devices at each end of the link must both support full-duplex operation, allowing each to transmit at will without having to detect and recover from collisions.

The Fast Ethernet specification also offers backward-compatibility to support traditional 10-Mbps Ethernet. In the case of 100BASE-TX, switch ports often are called "10/100" ports, to denote the dual speed. To provide this support, the two devices at each end of a network connection automatically can negotiate link capabilities so that they both can operate at a maximum common level. This negotiation involves detecting and selecting the highest physical layer technology (available bandwidth) and half-duplex or full-duplex operation. To properly negotiate a connection, *both* ends should be configured for autonegotiation.

The link speed is determined by electrical signaling so that either end of a link can determine what speed the other end is trying to use. If both ends of the link are configured to autonegotiate, they will use the highest speed that is common to them.

A link's duplex mode, however, is negotiated through an exchange of information. This means that for one end to successfully autonegotiate the duplex mode, the other end also must be set to autonegotiate. Otherwise, one end never will see duplex information from the other end and won't be capable of determining the correct mode to use. If duplex autonegotiation fails, a switch port always falls back to its default setting: half-duplex.

> **CAUTION**   Beware of a duplex mismatch when both ends of a link are not set for autonegotiation. During a mismatch, one end uses full duplex while the other end uses half duplex. The result is that the half-duplex station will detect a collision when both ends transmit; it will back off appropriately. The full-duplex station, however, will assume that it has the right to transmit at any time. It will not stop and wait for any reason. This can cause errors on the link and poor response times between the stations.

Autonegotiation uses the priorities shown in Table 4-3 for each mode of Ethernet to determine which technology to agree on. If both devices can support more than one technology, the technology with the highest priority is used. For example, if two devices can support both 10BASE-T and 100BASE-TX, both devices will use the higher-priority 100BASE-TX mode.

Table 4-3   *Autonegotiation Selection Priorities*

Priority	Ethernet Mode
7	100BASE-T2 (full duplex)
6	100BASE-TX (full duplex)
5	100BASE-T2 (half duplex)
4	100BASE-T4
3	100BASE-TX
2	10BASE-T (full duplex)
1	10BASE-T

To ensure proper configuration at both ends of a link, Cisco recommends that the appropriate values for transmission speed and duplex mode be configured manually on switch ports. This precludes any possibility that one end of the link will change its settings, resulting in an unusable connection. If you manually set the switch port, don't forget to manually set the device on the other end of the link accordingly. Otherwise, a speed or duplex mismatch between the two devices might occur.

Cisco provides one additional capability to Fast Ethernet, which allows several Fast Ethernet links to be bundled together for increased throughput. *Fast EtherChannel (FEC)* allows two to eight full-duplex Fast Ethernet links to act as a single physical link, for 400- to 1600-Mbps duplex bandwidth. This technology is described in greater detail in Chapter 7, "Aggregating Switch Links."

For further reading about Fast Ethernet technology, refer to the article "Fast Ethernet 100-Mbps Solutions," at Cisco.com:

> http://www.cisco.com/en/US/netsol/ns340/ns394/ns147/
> networking_solutions_white_paper09186a00800a4a29.shtml.

Gigabit Ethernet

You can scale Fast Ethernet by an additional order of magnitude with Gigabit Ethernet (which supports 1000 Mbps or 1 Gbps) using the same IEEE 802.3 Ethernet frame format as before. This scalability allows network designers and managers to leverage existing knowledge and technologies to install, migrate, manage, and maintain Gigabit Ethernet networks.

However, the physical layer has been modified to increase data-transmission speeds. Two technologies were merged to gain the benefits of each: the IEEE 802.3 Ethernet standard and the American National Standards Institute (ANSI) X3T11 FibreChannel. IEEE 802.3 provided the foundation of frame format, CSMA/CD, full duplex, and other Ethernet characteristics. FibreChannel provided a base of high-speed ASICs, optical components, and encoding/decoding and serialization mechanisms. The resulting protocol is termed IEEE 802.3z Gigabit Ethernet.

Gigabit Ethernet supports several cabling types, referred to as *1000BASE-X*. Table 4-4 lists the cabling specifications for each type.

In a campus network, you can use Gigabit Ethernet in the switch block, core block, and server block. In the switch block, it can connect access-layer switches to distribution-layer switches. In the core block, it can connect the distribution layer to the core switches and interconnects the core devices. In a server block, a Gigabit Ethernet switch can provide high-speed connections to individual servers.

Table 4-4 *Gigabit Ethernet Cabling and Distance Limitations*

GE Type	Wiring Type	Pairs	Cable Length
1000BASE-CX	Shielded twisted pair (STP)	1	25 m
1000BASE-T	EIA/TIA Category 5 UTP	4	100 m
1000BASE-SX	Multimode fiber (MMF) with 62.5-micron core; 850-nm laser	1	275 m
	MMF with 50-micron core; 850-nm laser	1	550 m

continues

Table 4-4   *Gigabit Ethernet Cabling and Distance Limitations (Continued)*

GE Type	Wiring Type	Pairs	Cable Length
1000BASE-LX/LH	MMF with 62.5-micron core; 1300-nm laser	1	550 m
	Single-mode fiber (SMF) with 50-micron core; 1300-nm laser	1	550 m
	SMF with 9-micron core; 1300-nm laser	1	10 km
1000BASE-ZX	SMF with 9-micron core; 1550-nm laser	1	70 km
	SMF with 8-micron core; 1550-nm laser	1	100 km

The "Gigabit over copper" solution that the 1000BASE-T media provides is based on the IEEE 802.3ab standard. Most Gigabit Ethernet switch ports used between switches are fixed at 1000 Mbps. However, other switch ports can support a fallback to Fast or Legacy Ethernet speeds. Here, speed can be autonegotiated between end nodes to the highest common speed—10 Mbps, 100 Mbps, or 1000 Mbps. These ports are often called "10/100/1000" ports to denote the triple speed. Here, the autonegotiation supports the same priority scheme as Fast Ethernet, although 1000BASE-T full duplex becomes the highest priority, followed by 1000BASE-T half duplex. Gigabit Ethernet's port duplex mode always is set to full duplex on Cisco switches, so duplex autonegotiation is not possible.

Finally, Cisco has extended the concept of Fast EtherChannel to bundle several Gigabit Ethernet links to act as a single physical connection. With *Gigabit EtherChannel (GEC)*, two to eight full-duplex Gigabit Ethernet connections can be aggregated, for a single logical link of up to 16 Gbps throughput. Port aggregation and the EtherChannel technology are described further in Chapter 7.

> **NOTE**   The 10-Gigabit Ethernet Alliance offers further reading about Gigabit Ethernet and its operation, migration, and standards. Refer to the "Archive White Papers" section on its website at http://www.10gea.org.

10-Gigabit Ethernet

Ethernet scales by orders of magnitude, beginning with 10 Mbps, progressing to 100 Mbps, and then to 1000 Mbps. To meet the demand for aggregating many Gigabit Ethernet links over a single connection, 10-Gigabit Ethernet was developed. Again, the Layer 2 characteristics of Ethernet have been preserved; the familiar 802.3 frame format and size, along with the MAC protocol, remain unchanged.

The 10-Gigabit Ethernet, also known as *10GbE,* and the IEEE 802.3ae standard differ from their predecessors only at the physical layer (PHY); 10GbE operates only at full duplex. The standard defines several different transceivers that can be used as Physical Media Dependent (PMD) interfaces. These are classified into the following:

- **LAN PHY**—Interconnects switches in a campus network, predominantly in the core layer

- **WAN PHY**—Interfaces with existing synchronous optical network (SONET) or synchronous digital hierarchy (SDH) networks typically found in metropolitan-area networks (MAN)

The PMD interfaces also have a common labeling scheme, much as Gigabit Ethernet does. Where Gigabit Ethernet uses 1000BASE-X to indicate the media type, 10-Gigabit Ethernet uses 10GBASE-X. Table 4-5 lists the different PMDs defined in the standard, along with the type of fiber and distance limitations. All the fiber-optic PMDs can be used as either a LAN or a WAN PHY, except for the 10GBASE-LX4, which is only a LAN PHY. Be aware that the long-wavelength PMDs carry a significantly greater expense than the others.

At press time, the Cisco Catalyst 6500, 4500 (Supervisor VI), and 3750 switches supported 10-Gigabit Ethernet PMDs in the form of XENPAK transceivers, beginning with a minimum software release.

For the most current switch compatibility listing, refer to the "Cisco 10-Gigabit Ethernet Transceiver Modules Compatibility Matrix" document at http://www.cisco.com/en/US/products/hw/modules/ps5455/products_device_support_table09186a00803857e7.html.

Table 4-5   *10-Gigabit Ethernet PMD Types and Characteristics*

PMD Type[*]	Fiber Medium	Maximum Distance
10GBASE-SR/SW (850 nm serial)	MMF: 50 micron	66 m
	MMF: 50 micron (2GHz * km modal bandwidth)	300 m
	MMF: 62.5 micron	33 m
10GBASE-LR/LW (1310 nm serial)	SMF: 9 micron	10 km
10GBASE-ER/EW (1550 nm serial)	SMF: 9 micron	40 km
10GBASE-LX4/LW4 (1310 nm WWDM)	MMF: 50 micron	300 m
	MMF: 62.5 micron	300 m
	SMF: 9 micron	10 km
10GBASE-CX4	Copper: CX4 with Infiniband connectors	15 m

[*]Transceiver types are denoted by a two-letter suffix. The first letter specifies the wavelength used: S = short, L = long, E = extra-long wavelength. The second letter specifies the PHY type: R = LAN PHY, W = WAN PHY. In the case of LX4 and LW4, L refers to a long wavelength, X and W refer to the coding used, and 4 refers to the number of wavelengths transmitted. WWDM is wide-wavelength division multiplexing.

Connecting Switch Block Devices

Switch deployment in a network involves two steps: physical connectivity and switch configuration. This section describes the connections and cabling requirements for devices in a switch block. Cable connections must be made to a switch's console port to make initial configurations. Physical connectivity between switches and end users involves cabling for the various types of LAN ports.

Console Port Cables/Connectors

A terminal-emulation program on a PC usually is required to interface with the console port on a switch. Various types of console cables and console connectors are associated with each Cisco switch family.

All Catalyst switch families use an RJ-45-to-RJ-45 *rollover cable* to make the console connection between a PC (or terminal or modem) and the console port. A rollover cable is made so that pin 1 on one RJ-45 connector goes to pin 8 on the other RJ-45 connector, pin 2 goes to pin 7, and so forth. In other words, the cable remains flat while the two RJ-45 connectors point in opposite directions.

To connect the PC end, the rollover cable plugs into an RJ-45 to DB-9 or DB-25 "terminal" adapter (or a DB-25 "modem" adapter for a modem connection). At the switch end, the rollover cable plugs directly into the console port's RJ-45 jack.

After the console port is cabled to the PC, terminal, or modem, a terminal-emulation program can be started or a user connection can be made. The console ports on all switch families require an asynchronous serial connection at 9600 baud, 8 data bits, no parity, 1 stop bit, and no flow control.

Ethernet Port Cables and Connectors

Catalyst switches support a variety of network connections, including all forms of Ethernet. In addition, Catalyst switches support several types of cabling, including UTP and optical fiber.

Fast Ethernet (100BASE-FX) ports use two-strand multimode fiber (MMF) with MT-RJ or SC connectors to provide connectivity. The MT-RJ connectors are small and modular, each containing a pair of fiber-optic strands. The connector snaps into position, but you must press a tab to remove it. The SC connectors on the fiber cables are square in shape. These connectors snap in and out of the switch port connector as the connector is pushed in or pulled out. One fiber strand is used as a transmit path and the other as a receive path. The transmit fiber on one switch device should connect to the receive fiber on the other end.

All Catalyst switch families support 10/100 autosensing (using Fast Ethernet autonegotiation) and 10/100/1000 autosensing for Gigabit Ethernet. These ports use RJ-45 connectors on Category 5 UTP cabling to complete the connections. These ports can connect to other UTP-based Ethernet autosensing devices. UTP cabling is arranged so that RJ-45 pins 1,2 and 3,6 form two twisted pairs. These pairs connect straight through to the far end.

To connect two 10/100 switch ports back to back, as in an access-layer to distribution-layer link, you must use a Category 5 UTP crossover cable. In this case, RJ-45 pins 1,2 and 3,6 are still twisted pairs, but 1,2 on one end connects to 3,6 on the other end, and 3,6 on one end connects to 1,2 on the other end.

> **NOTE**   Because UTP Ethernet connections use only pairs 1,2 and 3,6, some cable plant installers connect only these pairs and leave the remaining two pair positions empty. Although this move provides Ethernet connectivity, it is not good practice for future needs. Instead, all four RJ-45 connector pairs should be connected end to end. For example, a full four-pair UTP cable plant can be used for either Ethernet or Token Ring connectivity, without rewiring. (Token Ring UTP connections use pairs 3,6 and 4,5.)
>
> Also, to be compatible with the new IEEE 802.3ab standard for Gigabit Ethernet over copper (1000BASE-T), you must use all four pairs end to end.

Gigabit Ethernet Port Cables and Connectors

Gigabit Ethernet connections take a different approach by providing modular connectivity options. Catalyst switches with Gigabit Ethernet ports have standardized rectangular openings that can accept Gigabit Interface Converter (GBIC) or small form factor pluggable (SFP) modules. The GBIC and SFP modules provide the media personality for the port so that various cable media can connect. In this way, the switch chassis is completely modular and requires no major change to accept a new media type. Instead, the appropriate module is hot-swappable and is plugged into the switch to support the new media. GBIC modules can use SC fiber-optic and RJ-45 UTP connectors. SFP modules can use LC and MT-RJ fiber-optic and RJ-45 UTP connectors. GBIC and SFP modules are available for the following Gigabit Ethernet media:

- **1000BASE-SX**—Short-wavelength connectivity using SC fiber connectors and MMF for distances up to 550 m (1804 feet).

- **1000BASE-LX/LH**—Long-wavelength/long-haul connectivity using SC fiber connectors and either MMF or single-mode fiber (SMF); MMF can be used for distances up to 550 m (1804 feet), and SMF can be used for distances up to 10 km (32,810 feet). MMF requires a special mode-conditioning cable for fiber distances less than 100 m (328 feet) or greater than 300 m (984 feet). This keeps the GBIC from overdriving the far-end receiver on a short cable and lessens the effect of differential mode delay on a long cable.

- **1000BASE-ZX**—Extended-distance connectivity using SC fiber connectors and SMF; works for distances up to 70 km, and even to 100 km when used with premium-grade SMF.

- **GigaStack**—Uses a proprietary connector with a high-data-rate copper cable with enhanced signal integrity and electromagnetic interference (EMI) performance; provides a GBIC-to-GBIC connection between stacking Catalyst switches or between any two Gigabit switch ports over a short distance. The connection is full duplex if only one of the two stacking connectors is used; if both connectors are used, they each become half duplex over a shared bus.

- **1000BASE-T**—Sports an RJ-45 connector for four-pair UTP cabling; works for distances up to 100 m (328 feet).

NOTE You must use a four-pair Category 5 (or greater) UTP crossover cable to connect two 1000BASE-T switch ports back to back. In this case, RJ-45 pins 1,2, 3,6, 4,5, and 7,8 are still twisted pairs on one end, connecting to pins 3,6, 1,2, 7,8, and 4,5 respectively on the other end.

CAUTION The fiber-based modules always have the receive fiber on the left connector and the transmit fiber on the right connector, as you face the connectors. These modules could produce invisible laser radiation from the transmit connector. Therefore, always keep unused connectors covered with the rubber plugs, and don't ever look directly into the connectors.

Switch Port Configuration

You can configure the individual ports on a switch with various information and settings, as detailed in the following sections.

Selecting Ports to Configure

Before you can modify port settings, you must select one or more switch ports. Catalyst switches running the Catalyst operating system (CatOS) refer to these as *ports*, whereas switches running the Cisco IOS Software refer to them as *interfaces*. The BCMSN exam is based on IOS-based switches only.

To select a single switch port, enter the following command in global configuration mode:

```
Switch(config)# interface type module/number
```

The port is identified by its Ethernet type (**fastethernet**, **gigabitethernet**, **tengigabitethernet**, or **vlan**), the physical module or "blade" where it is located, and the port number within the module. Some switches, such as the Catalyst 2950 and 3560, don't have multiple modules. For those models, ports have a module number of 0 (zero). As an example, the FastEthernet 0/14 interface is selected for configuration using the following command:

```
Switch(config)# interface fastethernet 0/14
```

The Catalyst 3750 is also a fixed-configuration switch, but it can be stacked with other switches in the 3750 family. Interfaces are referenced by module and port number, where the module number represents the switch position in the stack. For example, port 24 on the switch at position 2 in the stack would be referenced as FastEthernet 2/0/24.

Naturally, you can select and configure multiple interfaces in this fashion, one at a time. If you need to make many configuration changes for each interface, however, this can get very tedious. The Catalyst IOS Software also allows multiple interfaces to be selected in a single pass, through the **interface range** configuration command. After you select the range, any interface configuration commands entered are applied to each of the interfaces in the range.

To select several arbitrary ports for a common configuration setting, you can identify them as a "range" entered as a list. All port numbers and the commas that separate them must be separated with spaces. Use the following command in global configuration mode:

```
Switch(config)# interface range type module/number [, type module/number ...]
```

For example, to select interfaces FastEthernet 0/3, 0/7, 0/9, and 0/48 for configuration, you could use this command:

```
Switch(config)# interface range fastethernet 0/3 , fastethernet 0/7 , fastethernet
    0/9 , fastethernet 0/48
```

You also can select a continuous range of ports, from a beginning interface to an ending interface. Enter the interface type and module, followed by the beginning and ending port number separated by a dash with spaces. Use this command in global configuration mode:

```
Switch(config)# interface range type module/first-number - last-number
```

For example, you could select all 48 FastEthernet interfaces on module 1 with the following command:

```
Switch(config)# interface range fastethernet 1/0 - 48
```

Finally, you sometimes need to make configuration changes to several groups or ranges of ports at the same time. You can define a macro that contains a list of interfaces or ranges of interfaces or both. Then, you can invoke the interface-range macro just before configuring the port settings. This applies the port settings to each interface that is identified by the macro. The steps for defining and applying this macro are as follows:

Step 1   Define the macro name and specify as many lists and ranges of interfaces as needed. The command syntax is open ended but follows the list and range syntax of the **interface range** commands defined previously:

```
Switch(config)# define interface-range macro-name type module/number [,
    type module/ number ...] [type module/first-number - last-number] [...]
```

Step 2   Invoke the macro called *macro-name* just as you would with a regular interface, just before entering any interface-configuration commands:

```
Switch(config)# interface range macro macro-name
```

As an example, suppose that you need to configure GigabitEthernet 2/1, 2/3 through 2/5, 3/1, 3/10, and 3/32 through 3/48 with a set of identical interface configurations. You could use the following commands to define and apply a macro, respectively:

```
Switch(config)# define interface-range MyGroup gig 2/1 , gig 2/3 - 2/5 , gig 3/1 , gig
  3/10, gig 3/32 - 3/48
Switch(config)# interface range macro MyGroup
```

Remember to surround any commas and hyphens with spaces when you enter **interface range** commands.

Identifying Ports

You can add a text description to a switch port's configuration to help identify it. This description is meant as a comment field only, as a record of port use or other unique information. The port description is included when displaying the switch configuration and interface information.

To assign a comment or description to a port, enter the following command in interface configuration mode:

```
Switch(config-if)# description description-string
```

The description string can have embedded spaces between words, if needed. To remove a description, use the **no description** interface-configuration command.

As an example, interface FastEthernet 0/11 is labeled with "Printer in Bldg A, room 213":

```
Switch(config)# interface fast 0/11
Switch(config-if)# description Printer in Bldg A, room 213
```

Port Speed

You can assign a specific speed to switch ports through switch-configuration commands. Fast Ethernet 10/100 ports can be set to speeds of 10, 100, and Auto (the default) for autonegotiate mode. Gigabit Ethernet GBIC ports always are set to a speed of 1000, whereas 1000BASE-T ports can be set to speeds of 10, 100, 1000, and Auto (the default).

NOTE   If a 10/100 or a 10/100/1000 port is assigned a speed of Auto, both its speed and duplex mode will be negotiated.

To specify the port speed on a particular Ethernet port, use the following interface-configuration command:

```
Switch(config-if)# speed {10 | 100 | 1000 | auto}
```

Port Duplex Mode

You also can assign a specific link mode to Ethernet-based switch ports. Therefore, the port operates in half-duplex, full-duplex, or autonegotiated mode. Autonegotiation is allowed only on UTP Fast Ethernet and Gigabit Ethernet ports. In this mode, the port *participates* in a negotiation by attempting full-duplex operation first and then half-duplex operation if full duplex is not successful. The autonegotiation process repeats whenever the link status changes. Be sure to set both ends of a link to the same speed and duplex settings to eliminate any chance that the two ends will be mismatched.

> **NOTE** A 10-Mbps Ethernet link (fixed speed) defaults to half duplex, whereas a 100-Mbps Fast Ethernet (dual speed 10/100) link defaults to full duplex. Multispeed links default to autonegotiate the duplex mode.

To set the link mode on a switch port, enter the following command in interface configuration mode:

```
Switch(config-if)# duplex {auto | full | half}
```

For instance, you could use the commands in Example 4-1 to configure 10/100/1000 interfaces GigabitEthernet 3/1 for autonegotiation and 3/2 for 100-Mbps full duplex (no autonegotiation).

Example 4-1 *Configuring the Link Mode on a Switch Port*

```
Switch(config)# interface gig 3/1
Switch(config-if)# speed auto
Switch(config-if)# duplex auto
Switch(config-if)# interface gig 3/2
Switch(config-if)# speed 100
Switch(config-if)# duplex full
```

Managing Error Conditions on a Switch Port

Traditionally, a network-management application was used to detect a serious error condition on a switch port. A switch periodically was polled and switch port error counters were examined to see if an error condition had occurred. If so, an alert was issued so that someone could take action to correct the problem.

Catalyst switches can detect error conditions automatically, without any further help. If a serious error occurs on a switch port, that port can be shut down automatically until someone manually enables the port again, or until a predetermined time has elapsed.

Detecting Error Conditions

By default, a Catalyst switch detects an error condition on every switch port for every possible cause. If an error condition is detected, the switch port is put into the errdisable state and is disabled. You can tune this behavior on a global basis so that only certain causes trigger any port being disabled. Use the following command in global configuration mode, where the **no** keyword is added to disable the specified cause:

```
Switch(config)# [no] errdisable detect cause [all | cause-name]
```

You can repeat this command to enable or disable more than one cause. One of the following causes triggers the errdisable state:

- **all**—Detects every possible cause

- **arp-inspection**—Detects errors with dynamic ARP inspection

- **bpduguard**—Detects when a spanning-tree bridge protocol data unit (BPDU) is received on a port configured for STP portfast

- **channel-misconfig**—Detects an error with an EtherChannel bundle

- **dhcp-rate-limit**—Detects an error with DHCP snooping

- **dtp-flap**—Detects when trunking encapsulation is changing from one type to another

- **gbic-invalid**—Detects the presence of an invalid GBIC or SFP module

- **ilpower**—Detects an error with offering inline power

- **l2ptguard**—Detects an error with Layer 2 Protocol Tunneling

- **link-flap**—Detects when the port link state is "flapping" between the up and down states

- **loopback**—Detects when an interface has been looped back

- **pagp-flap**—Detects when an EtherChannel bundle's ports no longer have consistent configurations

- **psecure-violation**—Detects conditions that trigger port security configured on a port

- **rootguard**—Detects when an STP BPDU is received from the root bridge on an unexpected port

- **security-violation**—Detects errors related to port security

- **storm-control**—Detects when a storm control threshold has been exceeded on a port

- **udld**—Detects when a link is seen to be *unidirectional* (data passing in only one direction)

- **unicast-flood**—Detects conditions that trigger unicast flood blocking on a port

- **vmps**—Detects errors when assigning a port to a dynamic VLAN through VLAN membership policy server (VMPS)

Automatically Recover from Error Conditions

By default, ports put into the errdisable state must be re-enabled manually. This is done by issuing the **shutdown** command in interface configuration mode, followed by the **no shutdown** command. Before you re-enable a port from the errdisable condition, you always should determine the cause of the problem so that the errdisable condition doesn't occur again.

You can decide to have a switch automatically re-enable an errdisabled port if it is more important to keep the link up until the problem can be resolved. To automatically re-enable an errdisabled port, you first must specify the errdisable causes that can be re-enabled. Use this command in global configuration mode, with a *cause-name* from the preceding list:

```
Switch(config)# errdisable recovery cause [all | cause-name]
```

If any errdisable causes are configured for automatic recovery, the errdisabled port stays down for 300 seconds, by default. To change the recovery timer, use the following command in global configuration mode:

```
Switch(config)# errdisable recovery interval seconds
```

You can set the interval from 30 to 86,400 seconds (24 hours).

As an example, you could use the following commands to configure all switch ports to be re-enabled automatically in 1 hour after a port security violation has been detected:

```
Switch(config)# errdisable recovery cause psecurity-violation
Switch(config)# errdisable recovery interval 3600
```

Remember that the errdisable causes and automatic recovery are configured globally—the settings apply to all switch ports.

Enable and Use the Switch Port

If the port is not enabled or activated automatically, use the **no shutdown** interface-configuration command. To view a port's current speed and duplex state, use the **show interface** command. You can see a brief summary of all interface states with the **show interfaces status** command.

Troubleshooting Port Connectivity

Suppose that you are experiencing problems with a switch port. How would you troubleshoot it? The following sections cover a few common troubleshooting techniques.

Looking for the Port State

Use the **show interfaces** EXEC command to see complete information about the switch port. The port's current state is given in the first line of output, as in Example 4-2.

Example 4-2 *Determining Port State Information*

```
Switch# show interfaces fastethernet 0/1
FastEthernet0/1 is up, line protocol is up
  Hardware is Fast Ethernet, address is 0009.b7ee.9801 (bia 0009.b7ee.9801)
  MTU 1500 bytes, BW 100000 Kbit, DLY 100 usec,
     reliability 255/255, txload 1/255, rxload 1/255
```

The first **up** tells the state of the port's physical or data link layer. If this is shown as **down**, the link is physically disconnected or a link cannot be detected. The second state, given as **line protocol is up**, shows the Layer 2 status. If the state is given as **errdisable**, the switch has detected a serious error condition on this port and has automatically disabled it.

To quickly see a list of states for all switch ports, use the **show interface status** EXEC command. Likewise, you can see a list of all ports in the errdisable state (as well as the cause) by using the **show interface status err-disabled** EXEC command.

Looking for Speed and Duplex Mismatches

If a user notices slow response time or low throughput on a 10/100 or 10/100/1000 switch port, the problem could be a mismatch of the port speed or duplex mode between the switch and the host. This is particularly common when one end of the link is set to autonegotiate the link settings and the other end is not.

Use the **show interface** command for a specific interface and look for any error counts that are greater than 0. For example, in the following output in Example 4-3, the switch port is set to autonegotiate the speed and duplex mode. It has decided on 100 Mbps at half duplex. Notice that there are many *runts* (packets that were truncated before they were fully received) and input errors. These are symptoms that a setting mismatch exists between the two ends of the link.

Example 4-3 *Determining Link Speed and Duplex Mode*

```
Switch# show interfaces fastethernet 0/13
FastEthernet0/13 is up, line protocol is up
  Hardware is Fast Ethernet, address is 00d0.589c.3e8d (bia 00d0.589c.3e8d)
  MTU 1500 bytes, BW 10000 Kbit, DLY 1000 usec,
     reliability 255/255, txload 2/255, rxload 1/255
  Encapsulation ARPA, loopback not set
  Keepalive not set
Auto-duplex (Half), Auto Speed (100), 100BASETX/FX  ARP type: ARPA, ARP
    Timeout 04:00:00
Last input never, output 00:00:01, output hang never
  Last clearing of "show interface" counters never
  Queueing strategy: fifo
  Output queue 0/40, 0 drops; input queue 0/75, 0 drops
  5 minute input rate 0 bits/sec, 0 packets/sec
  5 minute output rate 81000 bits/sec, 49 packets/sec
     500867 packets input, 89215950 bytes
     Received 12912 broadcasts, 374879 runts, 0 giants, 0 throttles
     374879 input errors, 0 CRC, 0 frame, 0 overrun, 0 ignored
     0 watchdog, 0 multicast
     0 input packets with dribble condition detected
     89672388 packets output, 2205443729 bytes, 0 underruns
     0 output errors, 0 collisions, 3 interface resets
     0 babbles, 0 late collision, 0 deferred
     0 lost carrier, 0 no carrier
     0 output buffer failures, 0 output buffers swapped out
```

Because this port is autonegotiating the link speed, it must have detected an electrical signal that indicated 100 Mbps in common with the host. However, the host most likely was configured for 100 Mbps at full duplex (not autonegotiating). The switch was incapable of exchanging duplex information, so it fell back to its default of half duplex. Again, always make sure both ends of a connection are set to the same speed and duplex.

Foundation Summary

The Foundation Summary is a collection of tables that provides a convenient review of many key concepts in this chapter. If you are already comfortable with the topics in this chapter, this summary might help you recall a few details. If you just read this chapter, this review should help solidify some key facts. If you are doing your final prep before the exam, the following tables are a convenient way to review the day before the exam.

Table 4-6 *Ethernet Standards*

Ethernet Type	Media Name	Standard Name
10-Mbps Ethernet	10BASE-X	IEEE 802.3
Fast Ethernet	100BASE-X	IEEE 802.3u
Gigabit Ethernet	1000BASE-X	IEEE 802.3z (fiber)
		IEEE 802.3ab (UTP)
10-Gigabit Ethernet	10GBASE-X	IEEE 802.3ae

Table 4-7 *Ethernet Cabling Specifications*

Technology	Wiring Type	Pairs	Cable Length
10BASE-T	EIA/TIA Category 5 UTP	2	100 m
100BASE-TX	EIA/TIA Category 5 UTP	2	100 m
100BASE-T2	EIA/TIA Category 3, 4, 5 UTP	2	100 m
100BASE-T4	EIA/TIA Category 3, 4, 5 UTP	4	100 m
100BASE-FX	Multimode fiber (MMF); 62.5-micron core, 125-micron outer cladding (62.5/125)	1	400 m half duplex / 2000 m full duplex
	Single-mode fiber (SMF)	1	10 km
1000BASE-CX	Shielded twisted pair (STP)	1	25 m
1000BASE-T	EIA/TIA Category 5 UTP	4	100 m
1000BASE-SX	MMF with 62.5-micron core; 850-nm laser	1	275 m
	MMF with 50-micron core; 850-nm laser	1	550 m

Table 4-7 *Ethernet Cabling Specifications (Continued)*

Technology	Wiring Type	Pairs	Cable Length
1000BASE-LX/LH	MMF with 62.5-micron core; 1300-nm laser	1	550 m
	SMF with 50-micron core; 1300-nm laser	1	550 m
	SMF with 9-micron core; 1300-nm laser	1	10 km
1000BASE-ZX	SMF with 9-micron core; 1550-nm laser	1	70 km
	SMF with 8-micron core; 1550-nm laser	1	100 km
10GBASE-SR/SW (850 nm serial)	MMF: 50 micron	1	66 m
	MMF: 62.5 micron	1	33 m
10GBASE-LR/LW (1310 nm serial)	SMF: 9 micron	1	10 km
10GBASE-ER/EW (1550 nm serial)	SMF: 9 micron	1	40 km
10GBASE-LX4 (1310 nm WWDM)	MMF: 50 micron	1	300 m
	MMF: 62.5 micron	1	300 m
	SMF: 9 micron	1	10 km

Table 4-8 *Switch Port Configuration Commands*

Task	Command Syntax
Select a port	**interface** *type module/number*
Select multiple ports	**interface range** *type module/number* [**,** *type module/number ...*] or **interface range** *type module/first-number – last-number*
Define an interface macro	**define interface-range** *macro-name type module/number* [**,** *type module/number ...*] [*type module/first-number – last-number*] [...] **interface range macro** *macro-name*
Identify port	**description** *description-string*

continues

Table 4-8 *Switch Port Configuration Commands (Continued)*

Task	Command Syntax
Set port speed	**speed {10 ı 100 ı 1000 ı auto}**
Set port mode	**duplex {auto ı full ı half}**
Detect port error conditions	**errdisable detect cause [all ı** *cause-name*]
Automatically recover from errdisable	**errdisable recovery cause [all ı** *cause-name*] **errdisable recovery interval** *seconds*
Manually recover from errdisable	**shutdown** **no shutdown**

Q&A

The questions and scenarios in this book are more difficult than what you should experience on the actual exam. The questions do not attempt to cover more breadth or depth than the exam; however, they are designed to make sure that you know the answer. Rather than allowing you to derive the answers from clues hidden inside the questions themselves, the questions challenge your understanding and recall of the subject. Hopefully, these questions will help limit the number of exam questions on which you narrow your choices to two options and then guess.

You can find the answers to these questions in Appendix A.

1. Put the following Ethernet standards in order of increasing bandwidth:

   a. 802.3z

   b. 802.3ae

   c. 802.3

   d. 802.3u

2. What benefits does switched Ethernet have over shared Ethernet?

3. When a 10/100 Ethernet link is autonegotiating, which will be chosen if both stations can support the same capabilities—10BASE-T full duplex, 100BASE-TX half duplex, or 100BASE-TX full duplex?

4. How many pairs of copper wires does a 1000BASE-T connection need?

5. A switch port is being configured as shown here. What command is needed next to set the port to full-duplex mode?

   ```
   Switch(config)# interface fastethernet 0/13
   Switch(config-if)#
   ```

6. If a full-duplex Gigabit Ethernet connection offers 2 Gbps throughput, can a single host send data at 2 Gbps?

7. Which GBIC would you use for a connection over multimode fiber (MMF)?

8. A Category 5 cable having only pins 1,2 and 3,6 has been installed and used for a Fast Ethernet link. Can this same cable be used for a migration to Gigabit Ethernet using 1000BASE-T GBICs, assuming that the length is less than 100 m?

9. A Catalyst 3560 switch port has been configured for 100 Mbps full-duplex mode, but a link cannot be established. What are some commands that you could use to investigate and correct the problem?

10. The 10-Gigabit Ethernet is backward-compatible with other forms of Ethernet at Layer _____ but not at Layer _____.

11. What one switch command will select Fast Ethernet interfaces 4/1 through 48 for a common configuration?

12. What is the purpose of a GBIC?

13. Suppose you need to apply several different common configurations to Fast Ethernet interfaces 3/1 through 12, 3/34, 3/48, and 5/14 through 48. What commands are needed to create an interface macro to accomplish this, and what command would apply the macro?

14. If a switch port is configured with the **speed 100** and **duplex full** commands, what will happen if the PC connected to it is set for autonegotiated speed and duplex? Now reverse the roles. (The switch will autonegotiate, but the PC won't.) What will happen?

15. By default, what will a switch do if one of its ports has a serious error condition, and how can you tell when this has happened?

16. What port speeds can you assign to a UTP Gigabit Ethernet switch port? Consider both 1000BASE-T GBIC and native RJ-45 copper switch module ports.

17. What command can you use to make sure that no switch ports automatically are shut down in an errdisable state for any reason?

18. Suppose that you commonly find that switch ports are being shut down in errdisable because users are making their connections go up and down too often. Thinking that this might be the result of odd PC behavior, you would like to visit each user to troubleshoot the problem; however, this is a minor error and you don't want to inconvenience the end users too much. What commands can you use to have the switch automatically re-enable the ports after 10 minutes? Make sure a flapping link will be recovered automatically in this time frame.

19. Look at the following **show interfaces** output. Does the high number of collisions indicate a problem? Why or why not?

```
FastEthernet0/6 is up, line protocol is up
  Hardware is Fast Ethernet, address is 000a.f4d2.5506 (bia 000a.f4d2.5506)
  Description: Front Office PC
  MTU 1500 bytes, BW 10000 Kbit, DLY 1000 usec,
     reliability 255/255, txload 1/255, rxload 1/255
  Encapsulation ARPA, loopback not set
  Keepalive set (10 sec)
  Half-duplex, 10Mb/s
  input flow-control is off, output flow-control is off
  ARP type: ARPA, ARP Timeout 04:00:00
  Last input never, output 00:00:00, output hang never
  Last clearing of "show interface" counters never
  Input queue: 0/75/0/0 (size/max/drops/flushes); Total output drops: 0
  Queueing strategy: fifo
  Output queue :0/40 (size/max)
  5 minute input rate 0 bits/sec, 0 packets/sec
  5 minute output rate 0 bits/sec, 0 packets/sec
     1321140 packets input, 227738894 bytes, 0 no buffer
     Received 13786 broadcasts, 0 runts, 0 giants, 0 throttles
     1 input errors, 1 CRC, 0 frame, 0 overrun, 0 ignored
     0 watchdog, 42 multicast, 0 pause input
     0 input packets with dribble condition detected
     87798820 packets output, 2662785561 bytes, 1316 underruns
     6 output errors, 406870 collisions, 3 interface resets
     0 babbles, 0 late collision, 19458 deferred
     0 lost carrier, 0 no carrier, 0 PAUSE output
     1316 output buffer failures, 0 output buffers swapped out
```

This chapter covers the following topics that you need to master for the CCNP BCMSN exam:

- **Virtual LANs**—This section reviews VLANs, VLAN membership, and VLAN configuration on a Catalyst switch.

- **VLAN Trunks**—This section covers transporting multiple VLANs over single links and VLAN trunking with Ethernet.

- **VLAN Trunk Configuration**—This section outlines the Catalyst switch commands that configure VLAN trunks.

- **Troubleshooting VLANs and Trunks**— This section provides commands to use when a VLAN or trunk is not operating properly.

CHAPTER 5

VLANs and Trunks

Switched campus networks can be broken up into distinct broadcast domains or virtual LANs (VLAN). A flat network topology, or a network with a single broadcast domain, can be simple to implement and manage. However, flat network topology is not scalable. Instead, the campus can be divided into segments using VLANs, while Layer 3 routing protocols manage interVLAN communication.

This chapter details the process of defining common workgroups within a group of switches. It covers switch configuration for VLANs, along with the method of identifying and transporting VLANs on various types of links.

"Do I Know This Already?" Quiz

The purpose of the "Do I Know This Already?" quiz is to help you decide whether you need to read the entire chapter. If you already intend to read the entire chapter, you do not necessarily need to answer these questions now.

The 12-question quiz, derived from the major sections in the "Foundation Topics" portion of the chapter, helps you determine how to spend your limited study time.

Table 5-1 outlines the major topics discussed in this chapter and the "Do I Know This Already?" quiz questions that correspond to those topics.

Table 5-1   *"Do I Know This Already?" Foundation Topics Section-to-Question Mapping*

Foundation Topics Section	Questions Covered in This Section	Score
Virtual LANs	1–4	
VLAN Trunks	5–12	
VLAN Trunk Configuration		
Total Score		

> **CAUTION** The goal of self-assessment is to gauge your mastery of the topics in this chapter. If you do not know the answer to a question or are only partially sure of the answer, you should mark this question wrong. Giving yourself credit for an answer you correctly guess skews your self-assessment results and might give you a false sense of security.

1. A VLAN is which of the following?

   a. Collision domain

   b. Spanning-tree domain

   c. Broadcast domain

   d. VTP domain

2. Switches provide VLAN connectivity at which layer of the OSI model?

   a. Layer 1

   b. Layer 2

   c. Layer 3

   d. Layer 4

3. Which one of the following is needed to pass data between two PCs, each connected to a different VLAN?

   a. Layer 2 switch

   b. Layer 3 switch

   c. Trunk

   d. Tunnel

4. Which Catalyst IOS switch command is used to assign a port to a VLAN?

   a. **access vlan** *vlan-id*

   b. **switchport access vlan** *vlan-id*

   c. **vlan** *vlan-id*

   d. **set port vlan** *vlan-id*

5. Which of the following is a standardized method of trunk encapsulation?

   a. 802.1d

   b. 802.1Q

   c. 802.3z

   d. 802.1a

6. What is the Cisco proprietary method for trunk encapsulation?

   a. CDP

   b. EIGRP

   c. ISL

   d. DSL

7. Which of these protocols dynamically negotiates trunking parameters?

   a. PAgP

   b. STP

   c. CDP

   d. DTP

8. How many different VLANs can an 802.1Q trunk support?

   a. 256

   b. 1024

   c. 4096

   d. 32,768

   e. 65,536

9. Which of the following incorrectly describes a native VLAN?

   a. Frames are untagged on an 802.1Q trunk.

   b. Frames are untagged on an ISL trunk.

   c. Frames can be interpreted by a nontrunking host.

   d. The native VLAN can be configured for each trunking port.

10. If two switches each support all types of trunk encapsulation on a link between them, which one will be negotiated?

    a. ISL

    b. 802.1Q

    c. DTP

    d. VTP

11. Which VLANs are allowed on a trunk link by default?

    a. None

    b. Only the native VLAN

    c. All active VLANs

    d. Only negotiated VLANs

12. Which command configures a switch port to form a trunk without using negotiation?

    a. **switch mode trunk**

    b. **switch mode trunk nonegotiate**

    c. **switch mode dynamic auto**

    d. **switch mode dynamic desirable**

The answers to the quiz are found in Appendix A, "Answers to Chapter 'Do I Know This Already?' Quizzes and Q&A Sections." The suggested choices for your next step are as follows:

- **6 or less overall score**—Read the entire chapter. This includes the "Foundation Topics," "Foundation Summary," and "Q&A" sections.

- **7–9 overall score**—Begin with the "Foundation Summary" section and then follow with the "Q&A" section at the end of the chapter.

- **10 or more overall score**—If you want more review on these topics, skip to the "Foundation Summary" section and then go to the "Q&A" section at the end of the chapter. Otherwise, move on to Chapter 6, "VLAN Trunking Protocol."

Foundation Topics

Virtual LANs

Consider a network design that consists of Layer 2 devices only. For example, this design could be a single Ethernet segment, an Ethernet switch with many ports, or a network with several interconnected Ethernet switches. A full Layer 2–only switched network is referred to as a *flat network topology*. A flat network is a single broadcast domain, such that every connected device sees every broadcast packet that is transmitted. As the number of stations on the network increases, so does the number of broadcasts.

Because of the Layer 2 foundation, flat networks cannot contain redundant paths for load balancing or fault tolerance. The reason for this is explained in Chapters 8, "Traditional Spanning Tree Protocol," through 11, "Advanced Spanning Tree Protocol." To gain any advantage from additional paths to a destination, Layer 3 routing functions must be introduced.

A switched environment offers the technology to overcome flat network limitations. Switched networks can be subdivided into VLANs. By definition, a VLAN is a single broadcast domain. All devices connected to the VLAN receive broadcasts sent by any other VLAN members. However, devices connected to a different VLAN will not receive those same broadcasts. (Naturally, VLAN members also receive unicast packets directed toward them from other VLAN members.)

A VLAN consists of hosts defined as members, communicating as a *logical* network segment. In contrast, a physical segment consists of devices that must be connected to a physical cable segment. A VLAN can have connected members located anywhere in the campus network, as long as VLAN connectivity is provided among all members. Layer 2 switches are configured with a VLAN mapping and provide the logical connectivity among the VLAN members.

Figure 5-1 shows how a VLAN can provide logical connectivity between switch ports. Two workstations on the left Catalyst switch are assigned to VLAN 1, whereas a third workstation is assigned to VLAN 100. In this example, no communication can occur between VLAN 1 and VLAN 100. Both ends of the link between the Catalysts are assigned to VLAN 1. One workstation on the right Catalyst also is assigned to VLAN 1. Because there is end-to-end connectivity of VLAN 1, any of the workstations on VLAN 1 can communicate as if they were connected to a physical network segment.

Figure 5-1 *VLAN Functionality*

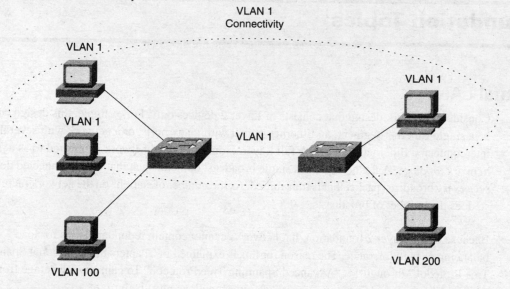

VLAN Membership

When a VLAN is provided at an access-layer switch, an end user must have some means of gaining membership to it. Two membership methods exist on Cisco Catalyst switches:

- Static VLAN configuration

- Dynamic VLAN assignment

Static VLANs

Static VLANs offer *port-based* membership, in which switch ports are assigned to specific VLANs. End user devices become members in a VLAN based on the physical switch port to which they are connected. No handshaking or unique VLAN membership protocol is needed for the end devices; they automatically assume VLAN connectivity when they connect to a port. Normally, the end device is not even aware that the VLAN exists. The switch port and its VLAN simply are viewed and used as any other network segment, with other "locally attached" members on the wire.

Switch ports are assigned to VLANs by the manual intervention of the network administrator, hence the static nature. Each port receives a Port VLAN ID (PVID) that associates it with a VLAN number. The ports on a single switch can be assigned and grouped into many VLANs. Even though two devices are connected to the same switch, traffic will not pass between them if they are connected to ports on different VLANs. To perform this function, you could use either a Layer 3 device to route packets or an external Layer 2 device to bridge packets between the two VLANs.

The static port-to-VLAN membership normally is handled in hardware with application-specific integrated circuits (ASICs) in the switch. This membership provides good performance because all port mappings are done at the hardware level, with no complex table lookups needed.

Configuring Static VLANs

This section describes the switch commands needed to configure static VLANs. By default, all switch ports are assigned to VLAN 1, are set to be a VLAN type of Ethernet, and have a maximum transmission unit (MTU) size of 1500 bytes.

First, the VLAN must be created on the switch, if it does not already exist. Then, the VLAN must be assigned to specific switch ports. VLANs always are referenced by a VLAN number, which can range from 1 to 1005. VLANs 1 and 1002 through 1005 automatically are created and are set aside for special uses. For example, VLAN 1 is the default VLAN for every switch port. VLANs 1002 to 1005 are reserved for legacy functions related to Token Ring and FDDI switching.

Catalyst IOS switches also can support extended-range VLANs, in which the VLAN number can be 1 to 4094, for compatibility with the IEEE 802.1Q standard. The extended range is enabled only when the switch is configured for VTP transparent mode with the **vtp mode transparent** global configuration command. This is because of limitations with VTP versions 1 and 2. VTP version 3 does allow extended range VLANs to be used and advertised, but this version is not available in any IOS-based Catalyst switches at press time. (VTP is covered in Chapter 6.)

> **TIP**   Although the extended range of VLAN numbers enables you to support more VLANs in your network, some limitations exist. For example, a switch normally maintains VLAN definitions in a special database file, separate from the switch configuration. The VLAN Trunking Protocol (VTP) uses the VLAN database so that VLAN definitions can be advertised and shared between switches over trunk links. When extended-range VLANs are created, they are not stored in the VLAN database file.
>
> Why does this matter? As long as the switch remains in VTP transparent mode, the extended VLANs can be used. However, if the switch is later configured to participate in VTP as either a server or a client, you must manually delete the extended VLANs. For any switch ports that were assigned to the extended VLANs, you also must reconfigure them for VLAN membership within the normal VLAN range.

To configure static VLANs, you first can define the VLAN with the following command in global configuration mode:

```
Switch(config)# vlan vlan-num
Switch(config-vlan)# name vlan-name
```

The VLAN numbered *vlan-num* immediately is created and stored in the database, along with a descriptive text string defined by *vlan-name* (up to 32 characters with no embedded spaces). The **name** command is optional; if it is not used, the default VLAN name is of the form **VLAN***XXX*, where *XXX* represents the VLAN number. If you need to include spaces to separate words in the VLAN name, use underscore characters instead.

As an example, you can use the following commands to create VLANs 2 and 101:

```
Switch(config)# vlan 2
Switch(config-vlan)# name Engineering
Switch(config-vlan)# vlan 101
Switch(config-vlan)# name Marketing
```

To delete a VLAN from the switch configuration, you can use the **no vlan** *vlan-num* command.

Next, you should assign one or more switch ports to the VLAN. Use the following configuration commands:

```
Switch(config)# interface type module/number
Switch(config-if)# switchport
Switch(config-if)# switchport mode access
Switch(config-if)# switchport access vlan vlan-num
```

The initial **switchport** command configures the port for Layer 2 operation. By default, every Catalyst IOS switch port is ready for Layer 3 operation, something that doesn't coexist with Layer 2 VLANs.

The **switchport mode access** command forces the port to be assigned to only a single VLAN, providing VLAN connectivity to the access layer or end user. The port is given a static VLAN membership by the s**witchport access vlan** command. Here, the logical VLAN is referenced by the *vlan-num* setting (1 to 1005 or 1 to 4094).

To verify VLAN configuration, use the **show vlan** command to output a list of all VLANs defined in the switch, along with the ports that are assigned to each VLAN. Example 5-1 shows some sample output from the **show vlan** command.

Example 5-1   *Verifying VLAN Configuration with* **show vlan** *Command*

```
Switch# show vlan
VLAN Name                             Status    Ports
---- -------------------------------- --------- -------------------------------
1    default                          active    Gi1/1, Gi1/2, Gi3/20, Gi4/20
2    Engineering                      active    Gi4/2, Gi4/3, Gi4/4, Gi4/5
                                                Gi4/6, Gi4/7, Gi4/8, Gi4/9
                                                Gi4/10, Gi4/11, Gi4/12
101  Marketing                        active    Gi2/5, Gi2/6, Gi2/7, Gi2/8
                                                Gi2/9, Gi2/10, Gi2/11, Gi2/12
                                                Gi2/13, Gi2/14, Gi2/15, Gi2/16
                                                Gi2/17, Gi2/18
```

Dynamic VLANs

Dynamic VLANs provide membership based on the MAC address of an end-user device. When a device is connected to a switch port, the switch must, in effect, query a database to establish VLAN membership. A network administrator also must assign the user's MAC address to a VLAN in the database of a VLAN Membership Policy Server (VMPS).

With Cisco switches, dynamic VLANs are created and managed using network-management tools such as CiscoWorks 2000. Dynamic VLANs allow a great deal of flexibility and mobility for end users but require more administrative overhead.

> **NOTE**   Dynamic VLANs are not covered in this text or in the BCMSN course or exam (at press time). For more information, refer to the "Configuring VMPS" section in a Catalyst configuration guide such as http://www.cisco.com/univercd/cc/td/doc/product/lan/cat3560/ 12225see/scg/swvlan.htm.

Deploying VLANs

To implement VLANs, you must consider the number of VLANs you need and how best to place them. As usual, the number of VLANs depends on traffic patterns, application types, segmentation of common workgroups, and network-management requirements.

An important factor to consider is the relationship between VLANs and the IP addressing schemes used. Cisco recommends a one-to-one correspondence between VLANs and IP subnets. This recommendation means that if a subnet with a 24-bit mask (255.255.255.0) is used for a VLAN, no more than 254 devices should be in the VLAN. In addition, you should not allow VLANs to extend beyond the Layer 2 domain of the distribution switch. In other words, the VLAN should not reach across a network's core and into another switch block. The idea again is to keep broadcasts and unnecessary traffic movement out of the core block.

VLANs can be scaled in the switch block by using two basic methods:

- End-to-end VLANs

- Local VLANs

End-to-End VLANs

End-to-end VLANs, also called *campus-wide VLANs*, span the entire switch fabric of a network. They are positioned to support maximum flexibility and mobility of end devices. Users can be assigned to VLANs regardless of their physical location. As a user moves around the campus, that user's VLAN membership stays the same. This means that each VLAN must be made available at the access layer in every switch block.

End-to-end VLANs should group users according to common requirements. All users in a VLAN should have roughly the same traffic flow patterns, following the 80/20 rule. Recall that this rule estimates that 80% of user traffic stays within the local workgroup, whereas 20% is destined for a remote resource in the campus network. Although only 20% of the traffic in a VLAN is expected to cross the network core, end-to-end VLANs make it possible for 100% of the traffic within a single VLAN to cross the core.

Because all VLANs must be available at each access-layer switch, VLAN trunking must be used to carry all VLANs between the access- and distribution-layer switches.

TIP   End-to-end VLANs are not recommended in an enterprise network, unless there is a good reason. In an end-to-end VLAN, broadcast traffic is carried over from one end of the network to the other, creating the possibility for a broadcast storm or Layer 2 bridging loop to spread across the whole extent of a VLAN. This can exhaust the bandwidth of distribution- and core-layer links, as well as switch CPU resources. Now the storm or loop has disrupted users on the end-to-end VLAN, in addition to users on other VLANs that might be crossing the core.

When such a problem occurs, troubleshooting becomes more difficult. In other words, the risks of end-to-end VLANs outweigh the convenience and benefits.

Local VLANs

Because most enterprise networks have moved toward the 20/80 rule (where server and intranet/Internet resources are centralized), end-to-end VLANs have become cumbersome and difficult to maintain. The 20/80 rule reverses the traffic pattern of the end-to-end VLAN: Only 20% of traffic is local, whereas 80% is destined to a remote resource across the core layer. End users usually require access to central resources outside their VLAN. Users must cross into the network core more frequently. In this type of network, VLANs should be designed to contain user communities based on geographic boundaries, with little regard to the amount of traffic leaving the VLAN.

Local or geographic VLANs range in size from a single switch in a wiring closet to an entire building. Arranging VLANs in this fashion enables the Layer 3 function in the campus network to intelligently handle the interVLAN traffic loads, where traffic passes into the core. This scenario provides maximum availability by using multiple paths to destinations, maximum scalability by keeping the VLAN within a switch block, and maximum manageability.

VLAN Trunks

At the access layer, end user devices connect to switch ports that provide simple connectivity to a single VLAN each. The attached devices are unaware of any VLAN structure and simply attach to what appears to be a normal physical network segment. Remember, sending information from an access link on one VLAN to another VLAN is not possible without the intervention of an additional device—either a Layer 3 router or an external Layer 2 bridge.

Note that a single switch port can support more than one IP subnet for the devices attached to it. For example, consider a shared Ethernet hub that is connected to a single Ethernet switch port. One user device on the hub might be configured for 192.168.1.1 255.255.255.0, whereas another is assigned 192.168.17.1 255.255.255.0. Although these subnets are discontiguous and unique, and both are communicating on one switch port, they cannot be considered separate VLANs. The switch port supports one VLAN, but multiple subnets can exist on that single VLAN.

A *trunk link*, however, can transport more than one VLAN through a single switch port. Trunk links are most beneficial when switches are connected to other switches or switches are connected to routers. A trunk link is not assigned to a specific VLAN. Instead, one, many, or all active VLANs can be transported between switches using a single physical trunk link.

Connecting two switches with separate physical links for each VLAN is possible. The top half of Figure 5-2 shows how two switches might be connected in this fashion.

Figure 5-2   *Passing VLAN Traffic Using Single Links Versus Trunk Links*

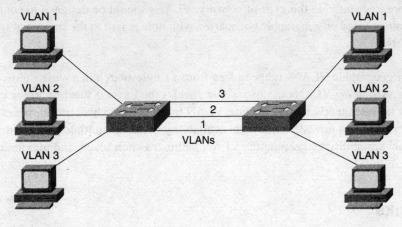

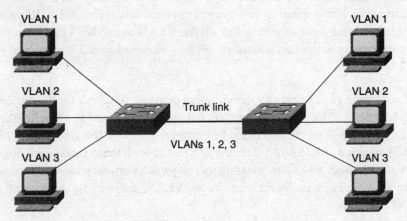

As VLANs are added to a network, the number of links can grow quickly. A more efficient use of physical interfaces and cabling involves the use of trunking. The bottom half of the figure shows how one trunk link can replace many individual VLAN links.

Cisco supports trunking on both Fast Ethernet and Gigabit Ethernet switch links, as well as aggregated Fast and Gigabit EtherChannel links. To distinguish between traffic belonging to different VLANs on a trunk link, the switch must have a method of identifying each frame with the appropriate VLAN. In fact, the switches on *each end* of a trunk link both must have the same method for correlating frames with VLAN numbers. The next section covers several available identification methods.

VLAN Frame Identification

Because a trunk link can transport many VLANs, a switch must identify frames with their respective VLANs as they are sent and received over a trunk link. Frame identification, or *tagging*, assigns a unique user-defined ID to each frame transported on a trunk link. Think of this ID as the VLAN number or VLAN "color," as if each VLAN were drawn on a network diagram in a unique color.

VLAN frame identification was developed for switched networks. As each frame is transmitted over a trunk link, a unique identifier is placed in the frame header. As each switch along the way receives these frames, the identifier is examined to determine to which VLAN the frames belong and then is removed.

If frames must be transported out another trunk link, the VLAN identifier is added back into the frame header. Otherwise, if frames are destined out an access (nontrunk) link, the switch removes the VLAN identifier before transmitting the frames to the end station. Therefore, all traces of VLAN association are hidden from the end station.

VLAN identification can be performed using two methods, each using a different frame identifier mechanism:

■   Inter-Switch Link (ISL) protocol

■   IEEE 802.1Q protocol

These methods are described in the sections that follow.

Inter-Switch Link Protocol

The Inter-Switch Link (ISL) protocol is a Cisco-proprietary method for preserving the source VLAN identification of frames passing over a trunk link. ISL performs frame identification in Layer 2 by encapsulating each frame between a header and a trailer. Any Cisco switch or router device configured for ISL can process and understand the ISL VLAN information. ISL primarily is used for Ethernet media, although Cisco has included provisions to carry Token Ring, FDDI, and ATM frames over Ethernet ISL. (A Frame-Type field in the ISL header indicates the source frame type.)

When a frame is destined out a trunk link to another switch or router, ISL adds a 26-byte header and a 4-byte trailer to the frame. The source VLAN is identified with a 15-bit VLAN ID field in the header. The trailer contains a cyclic redundancy check (CRC) value to ensure the data integrity of the new encapsulated frame. Figure 5-3 shows how Ethernet frames are encapsulated and forwarded out a trunk link. Because tagging information is added at the beginning and end of each frame, ISL sometimes is referred to as *double tagging*.

Figure 5-3 *ISL Frame Identification*

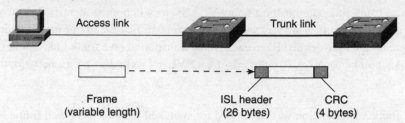

Frame	ISL header	CRC
(variable length)	(26 bytes)	(4 bytes)

If a frame is destined for an access link, the ISL encapsulation (both header and trailer) is not rewritten into the frame before transmission. This removal preserves ISL information only for trunk links and devices that can understand the protocol.

> **TIP** The ISL method of VLAN identification or trunking encapsulation no longer is supported across all Cisco Catalyst switch platforms. Even so, you should still be familiar with it and know how it compares to the standards-based IEEE 802.1Q method.

IEEE 802.1Q Protocol

The IEEE 802.1Q protocol also can carry VLAN associations over trunk links. However, this frame-identification method is standardized, allowing VLAN trunks to exist and operate between equipment from multiple vendors.

In particular, the IEEE 802.1Q standard defines an architecture for VLAN use, services provided with VLANs, and protocols and algorithms used to provide VLAN services. You can find further information about the 802.1Q standard at http://grouper.ieee.org/groups/802/1/pages/802.1Q.html.

As with Cisco ISL, IEEE 802.1Q can be used for VLAN identification with Ethernet trunks. However, instead of encapsulating each frame with a VLAN ID header and trailer, 802.1Q embeds its tagging information within the Layer 2 frame. This method is referred to as *single tagging* or *internal tagging*.

802.1Q also introduces the concept of a *native VLAN* on a trunk. Frames belonging to this VLAN are *not* encapsulated with any tagging information. If an end station is connected to an 802.1Q trunk link, the end station can receive and understand only the native VLAN frames. This provides a simple way to offer full trunk encapsulation to the devices that can understand it, while giving normal-access stations some inherent connectivity over the trunk.

In an Ethernet frame, 802.1Q adds a 4-byte tag just after the source address field, as shown in Figure 5-4.

Figure 5-4 *IEEE 802.1Q Frame-Tagging Standard*

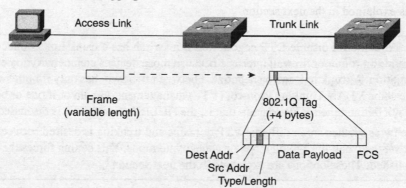

The first two bytes are used as a Tag Protocol Identifier (TPID) and always have a value of 0x8100 to signify an 802.1Q tag. The remaining two bytes are used as a Tag Control Information (TCI) field. The TCI information contains a three-bit Priority field, which is used to implement class-of-service (CoS) functions in the accompanying 802.1Q/802.1p prioritization standard. One bit of the TCI is a Canonical Format Indicator (CFI), flagging whether the MAC addresses are in Ethernet or Token Ring format. (This also is known as *canonical format*, or *little-endian* or *big-endian format*.)

The last 12 bits are used as a VLAN Identifier (VID) to indicate the source VLAN for the frame. The VID can have values from 0 to 4095, but VLANs 0, 1, and 4095 are reserved.

Note that both ISL and 802.1Q tagging methods have one implication—they add to the length of an existing Ethernet frame. ISL adds a total of 30 bytes to each frame, whereas 802.1Q adds 4 bytes. Because Ethernet frames cannot exceed 1518 bytes, the additional VLAN tagging information can cause the frame to become too large. Frames that barely exceed the MTU size are called *baby giant frames*. Switches usually report these frames as Ethernet errors or oversize frames.

> **NOTE**   Baby giant, or oversize, frames can exceed the frame size set in various standards. To properly handle and forward them anyway, Catalyst switches use proprietary hardware with the ISL encapsulation method. In the case of 802.1Q encapsulation, switches can comply with the IEEE 802.3ac standard, which extends the maximum frame length to 1522 bytes.

Dynamic Trunking Protocol

You manually can configure trunk links on Catalyst switches for either ISL or 802.1Q mode. In addition, Cisco has implemented a proprietary, point-to-point protocol called *Dynamic Trunking Protocol (DTP)* that negotiates a common trunking mode between two switches. The negotiation covers the encapsulation (ISL or 802.1Q) and whether the link becomes a trunk at all. This allows trunk links to be used without a great deal of manual configuration or administration. The use of DTP is explained in the next section.

> **TIP** You should disable DTP negotiation if a switch has a trunk link connected to a nontrunking router or firewall interface because those devices cannot participate in DTP negotiation. A trunk link can be negotiated between two switches only if both switches belong to the same VLAN Trunking Protocol (VTP) management domain or if one or both switches have not defined their VTP domain (that is, the NULL domain). VTP is discussed in Chapter 6.
>
> If the two switches are in different VTP domains and trunking is desired between them, you must set the trunk links to on mode or nonegotiate mode. This setting forces the trunk to be established. These options are explained in the next section.

VLAN Trunk Configuration

By default, all switch ports in Layer 2 mode are nontrunking and operate as access links until some intervention changes the mode. Specifically, ports actively try to become trunks as long as the far end agrees. In that case, a common encapsulation is chosen, favoring ISL if both support it. The sections that follow demonstrate the commands necessary to configure VLAN trunks.

VLAN Trunk Configuration

Use the following commands to create a VLAN trunk link:

```
Switch(config)# interface type mod/port
Switch(config-if)# switchport
Switch(config-if)# switchport trunk encapsulation {isl | dot1q | negotiate}
Switch(config-if)# switchport trunk native vlan vlan-id
Switch(config-if)# switchport trunk allowed vlan {vlan-list | all |
  {add | except | remove} vlan-list}
Switch(config-if)# switchport mode {trunk | dynamic {desirable | auto}}
```

A switch port must be in Layer 2 mode before it can support a trunk. To accomplish this, you use the **switchport** command with no other keywords. You then can configure the trunk encapsulation with the **switchport trunk encapsulation** command, as one of the following:

- **isl**—VLANs are tagged by encapsulating each frame using the Cisco ISL protocol.

- **dot1q**—VLANs are tagged in each frame using the IEEE 802.1Q standard protocol. The only exception is the native VLAN, which is sent normally and is not tagged.

- **negotiate** (the default)—The encapsulation is negotiated to select either ISL or IEEE 802.1Q, whichever both ends of the trunk support. If both ends support both types, ISL is favored. (The Catalyst 2950 switch does not support ISL encapsulation.)

In the case of an IEEE 802.1Q trunk, you should configure the native VLAN with the **switchport trunk native vlan** command, identifying the untagged or native VLAN number as *vlan-id* (1 to

4094). By default, an 802.1Q trunk uses VLAN 1 as the native VLAN. In the case of an ISL trunk, using this command has no effect because ISL doesn't support an untagged VLAN.

The last command, **switchport trunk allowed vlan**, defines which VLANs can be trunked over the link. By default, a switch transports all active VLANs (1 to 4094) over a trunk link. An active VLAN is one that has been defined on the switch and has ports assigned to carry it.

There might be times when the trunk link should not carry all VLANs. For example, broadcasts are forwarded to every switch port on a VLAN—including the trunk link because it, too, is a member of the VLAN. If the VLAN does not extend past the far end of the trunk link, propagating broadcasts across the trunk makes no sense.

You can tailor the list of allowed VLANs on the trunk by using the **switchport trunk allowed vlan** command with one of the following:

- *vlan-list*—An explicit list of VLAN numbers, separated by commas or dashes.

- **all**—All active VLANs (1 to 4094) will be allowed.

- **add** *vlan-list*—A list of VLAN numbers will be added to the already configured list; this is a shortcut to keep from typing a long list of numbers.

- **except** *vlan-list*—All VLANs (1 to 4094) will be allowed, except for the VLAN numbers listed; this is a shortcut to keep from typing a long list of numbers.

- **remove** *vlan-list*—A list of VLAN numbers will be removed from the already configured list; this is a shortcut to keep from typing a long list of numbers.

In the **switchport mode** command, you can set the trunking mode to any of the following:

- **trunk**—This setting places the port in permanent trunking mode. DTP is still operational, so if the far-end switch port is configured to trunk, dynamic desirable, or dynamic auto mode, trunking will be negotiated successfully.

  The trunk mode is usually used to establish an unconditional trunk. Therefore, the corresponding switch port at the other end of the trunk should be configured similarly. In this way, both switches always expect the trunk link to be operational without any negotiation. You also should manually configure the encapsulation mode to eliminate its negotiation.

- **dynamic desirable** (the default)—The port actively attempts to convert the link into trunking mode. In other words, it "asks" the far-end switch to bring up a trunk. If the far-end switch port is configured to trunk, dynamic desirable, or dynamic auto mode, trunking is negotiated successfully.

■ **dynamic auto**—The port can be converted into a trunk link, but only if the far-end switch actively requests it. Therefore, if the far-end switch port is configured to trunk or dynamic desirable mode, trunking is negotiated. Because of the passive negotiation behavior, the link never becomes a trunk if both ends of the link are left to the dynamic auto default.

TIP In all these modes, DTP frames are sent out every 30 seconds to keep neighboring switch ports informed of the link's mode. On critical trunk links in a network, manually configuring the trunking mode on both ends is best so that the link never can be negotiated to any other state.

If you decide to configure *both ends* of a trunk link as a fixed trunk (**switchport mode trunk**), you can disable DTP completely so that these frames are not exchanged. To do this, add the **switchport nonegotiate** command to the interface configuration. Be aware that after DTP frames are disabled, no future negotiation is possible until this configuration is reversed.

To view the trunking status on a switch port, use the **show interface** *type mod/port* **trunk** command, as demonstrated in Example 5-2.

Example 5-2 *Determining Switch Port Trunking Status*

```
Switch# show interface gigabitethernet 2/1 trunk
Port      Mode         Encapsulation Status        Native vlan
Gi2/1     on           802.1q        trunking      1


Port      Vlans allowed on trunk
Gi2/1     1-4094


Port      Vlans allowed and active in management domain
Gi2/1     1-2,526,539,998,1002-1005


Port      Vlans in spanning tree forwarding state and not pruned
Gi2/1     1-2,526,539,998,1002-1005
```

Trunk Configuration Example

As an example of trunk configuration, consider two switches, Switch-D and Switch-A, which are distribution-layer and access-layer switches, respectively. The two switches are connected by a link between their GigabitEthernet 2/1 interfaces. This link should be configured to be a trunk carrying only VLAN numbers 100 through 105, although more VLANs exist and are used.

The trunk link should use 802.1Q encapsulation, with VLAN 100 as the native VLAN. First, configure Switch-D to actively negotiate a trunk with the far-end switch. You could use the following configuration commands on Switch-D:

```
Switch-D(config)# interface gigabitethernet 2/1
Switch-D(config-if)# switchport trunk encapsulation dot1q
Switch-D(config-if)# switchport trunk native vlan 100
Switch-D(config-if)# switchport trunk allowed vlan 100-105
Switch-D(config-if)# switchport mode dynamic desirable
```

At this point, you assume that Switch-A is configured correctly, too. Now, you should try to verify that the trunk is working as expected. On Switch-D, you can view the trunk status with the following command:

```
Switch-D# show interface gigabitethernet 2/1 trunk
Port       Mode         Encapsulation Status       Native vlan
Gi1/1      desirable    802.1q        not-trunking  100
Port       Vlans allowed on trunk
Gi1/1      100
Port       Vlans allowed and active in management domain
Gi1/1      100
Port       Vlans in spanning tree forwarding state and not pruned
Gi1/1      none
```

To your surprise, the trunk's status is not-trunking. Next, you should verify that the physical link is up:

```
Switch-D# show interface status
Port    Name          Status      Vlan    Duplex  Speed Type
Gi1/1                 notconnect  1       auto    1000  1000BaseSX
Gi1/2                 notconnect  1       auto    1000  1000BaseSX
Gi2/1                 connected   100     full    1000  1000BaseSX
```

What could be preventing the trunk from being established? If Switch-D is in dynamic desirable negotiation mode, it is actively asking Switch-A to bring up a trunk. Obviously, Switch-A must not be in agreement. The desirable mode can negotiate a trunk with all other trunking modes, so Switch-A's interface must not be configured for trunking. Instead, it is most likely configured as an access port (**switchport mode access**).

Switch-A can be corrected by configuring its GigabitEthernet 2/1 interface to negotiate a trunk. Switch-D is in dynamic desirable mode, so Switch-A could use either trunk, dynamic desirable, or dynamic auto mode.

Now, suppose that you realize VLAN 103 should not be passed between these switches. You can use either of the following command sequences to manually prune VLAN 103 from the trunk:

```
Switch-D(config)# interface gigabitethernet 2/1
Switch-D(config-if)# switchport trunk allowed vlan 100-102,104-105
```

or:

```
Switch-D(config-if)# switchport trunk allowed vlan remove 103
```

In the latter case, the previous range of 100 to 105 is kept in the configuration, and only 103 automatically is removed from the list.

When you manually prune VLANs from being allowed on a trunk, the same operation should be performed at both ends of the trunk link. Otherwise, one of the two switches still could flood broadcasts from that VLAN onto the trunk, using unnecessary bandwidth in only one direction.

For completeness, the configuration of Switch-A at this point would look like the following:

```
Switch-A(config)# interface gigabitethernet 2/1
Switch-A(config-if)# switchport trunk encapsulation dot1q
Switch-A(config-if)# switchport trunk native vlan 100
Switch-A(config-if)# switchport trunk allowed vlan 100-105
Switch-A(config-if)# switchport trunk allowed vlan remove 103
Switch-A(config-if)# switchport mode dynamic desirable
```

Troubleshooting VLANs and Trunks

Remember that a VLAN is nothing more than a logical network segment that can be spread across many switches. If a PC in one location cannot communicate with a PC in another location, where both are assigned to the same IP subnet, make sure that both of their switch ports are configured for the same VLAN. If they are, examine the path between the two. Is the VLAN carried continuously along the path? If there are trunks along the way, is the VLAN being carried across the trunks?

To verify a VLAN's configuration on a switch, use the **show vlan id** *vlan-id* EXEC command, as demonstrated in Example 5-3. Make sure that the VLAN is shown to have an active status and that it has been assigned to the correct switch ports.

Example 5-3 *Verifying Switch VLAN Configuration*

```
Switch# show vlan id 2

VLAN Name                             Status    Ports
---- -------------------------------- --------- -------------------------------
2    Engineering                      active    Gi2/1, Gi2/2, Gi2/3, Gi2/4
                                                Gi4/2, Gi4/3, Gi4/4, Gi4/5
                                                Gi4/6, Gi4/7, Gi4/8, Gi4/9
                                                Gi4/10, Gi4/11, Gi4/12

VLAN Type  SAID       MTU   Parent RingNo BridgeNo Stp  BrdgMode Trans1 Trans2
---- ----- ---------- ----- ------ ------ -------- ---- -------- ------ ------
2    enet  100002     1500  -      .      .        .    .        0      0

Primary Secondary Type              Ports
------- --------- ----------------- -------------------------------------------

Switch#
```

For a trunk, these parameters must be agreeable on both ends before the trunk can operate correctly:

■ Trunking mode (unconditional trunking, negotiated, or nonnegotiated).

■ Trunk encapsulation (ISL, IEEE 802.1Q, or negotiated through DTP).

- Native VLAN. You can bring up a trunk with different native VLANs on each end; however, both switches will log error messages about the mismatch, and the potential exists that traffic will not pass correctly between the two native VLANs.

  The native VLAN mismatch is discovered through the exchange of CDP messages, not through examination of the trunk itself. Also, the native VLAN is configured independently of the trunk encapsulation, so it is possible to have a native VLAN mismatch even if the ports use ISL encapsulation. In this case, the mismatch is only cosmetic and won't cause a trunking problem.

- Allowed VLANs. By default, a trunk allows all VLANs to be transported across it. If one end of the trunk is configured to disallow a VLAN, that VLAN will not be contiguous across the trunk.

To see a comparison of how a switch port is configured for trunking versus its active state, use the **show interface** *type mod/num* **switchport** command, as demonstrated in Example 5-4. Look for the administrative versus operational values, respectively, to see if the trunk is working the way you configured it.

Notice that the port has been configured to negotiate a trunk through DTP (dynamic auto), but the port is operating in the static access (nontrunking) mode. This should tell you that both ends of the link probably are configured for the auto mode so that neither actively will request a trunk.

Example 5-4 *Comparing Switch Port Trunking Configuration and Active State*

```
Switch# show interface fastethernet 0/2 switchport
Name: Fa0/2
Switchport: Enabled
Administrative Mode: dynamic auto
Operational Mode: static access
Administrative Trunking Encapsulation: dot1q
Operational Trunking Encapsulation: native
Negotiation of Trunking: On
Access Mode VLAN: 1 (default)
Trunking Native Mode VLAN: 1 (default)
Administrative private-vlan host-association: none
Administrative private-vlan mapping: none
Operational private-vlan: none
Trunking VLANs Enabled: ALL
Pruning VLANs Enabled: 2-1001

Protected: false
Unknown unicast blocked: disabled
Unknown multicast blocked: disabled

Voice VLAN: none (Inactive)
Appliance trust: none
Switch#
```

For more concise information about a trunking port, you can use the **show interface** [*type mod/ num*] **trunk** command, as demonstrated in Example 5-5.

Example 5-5 *Viewing Concise Information About a Trunking Port*

```
Switch# show interface fastethernet 0/2 trunk

Port        Mode        Encapsulation   Status          Native vlan
Fa0/2       auto        802.1q          not-trunking    1

Port        Vlans allowed on trunk
Fa0/2       1

Port        Vlans allowed and active in management domain
Fa0/2       1

Port        Vlans in spanning tree forwarding state and not pruned
Fa0/2       1
Switch#
```

Again, notice that the port is in the auto negotiation mode, but it is currently not-trunking. Because the port is not trunking, only the access VLAN (VLAN 1 in this example) is listed as allowed and active on the trunk.

To see if and how DTP is being used on a switch, use the **show dtp** [**interface** *type mod/num*] command. Specifying an interface shows the DTP activity in greater detail.

Foundation Summary

The Foundation Summary is a collection of tables that provides a convenient review of many key concepts in this chapter. If you are already comfortable with the topics in this chapter, this summary could help you recall a few details. If you just read this chapter, this review should help solidify some key facts. If you are doing your final preparation before the exam, these tables and figures are a convenient way to review the day before the exam.

Table 5-2 *VLAN Trunk Encapsulations*

Encapsulation	Tagging Characteristics
ISL	Adds a 26-byte header and a 4-byte trailer to each frame, and includes a 15-bit VLAN ID
IEEE 802.1Q	Adds a 4-byte tag, includes a 12-bit VLAN ID

Table 5-3 *VLAN and Trunking Configuration Commands*

Task	Command Syntax
Create VLAN	`vlan vlan-num` `name vlan-name`

Assign port to VLAN	`interface type module/number`
	`switchport mode access`
	`switchport access vlan vlan-num`

Configure trunk	`interface type mod/port` `switchport trunk encapsulation {isl	dot1q	negotiate}` `switchport trunk native vlan vlan-id` `switchport trunk allowed vlan {vlan-list	all	{add	except	remove} vlan-list}` `switchport mode {trunk	dynamic {desirable	auto}}`

Table 5-4 *VLAN and Trunking Troubleshooting Commands*

Task	Command Syntax
Verify VLAN configuration	`show vlan id vlan-id`
Verify active trunk parameters	`show interface type mod/num trunk`
Compare trunk configuration and active parameters	`show interface type mod/num switchport`
Verify DTP operation	`show dtp [interface type mod/num]`

Q&A

The questions and scenarios in this book are more difficult than what you should experience on the actual exam. The questions do not attempt to cover more breadth or depth than the exam; however, they are designed to make sure that you know the answers. Instead of allowing you to derive the answers from clues hidden inside the questions themselves, the questions challenge your understanding and recall of the subject. Hopefully, these questions will help limit the number of exam questions on which you narrow your choices to two options and then guess.

The answers to these questions can be found in Appendix A.

1. What is a VLAN? When is it used?

2. When a VLAN is configured on a Catalyst switch port, in how much of the campus network will the VLAN number be unique and significant?

3. Name two types of VLANs in terms of spanning areas of the campus network.

4. What switch commands configure Fast Ethernet port 4/11 for VLAN 2?

5. Generally, what must be configured (both switch and end user device) for a port-based VLAN?

6. What is the default VLAN on all ports of a Catalyst switch?

7. What is a trunk link?

8. What methods of Ethernet VLAN frame identification can be used on a Catalyst switch trunk?

9. What is the difference between the two trunking methods? How many bytes are added to trunked frames for VLAN identification in each method?

10. What is the purpose of the Dynamic Trunking Protocol (DTP)?

11. What commands are needed to configure a Catalyst switch trunk port Gigabit 3/1 to transport only VLANs 100, 200 through 205, and 300 using IEEE 802.1Q? (Assume that trunking is enabled and active on the port already. Also assume that the **interface gigabit 3/1** command already has been entered.)

12. Two neighboring switch trunk ports are set to the auto mode with ISL trunking encapsulation mode. What will the resulting trunk mode become?

13. Complete the following command to configure the switch port to use DTP to actively ask the other end to become a trunk:

    ```
    switchport mode _____
    ```

14. Which command can set the native VLAN of a trunk port to VLAN 100 after the interface has been selected?

15. What command can configure a trunk port to stop sending and receiving DTP packets completely?

16. What command can be used on a Catalyst switch to verify exactly what VLANs will be transported over trunk link gigabitethernet 4/4?

17. Suppose that a switch port is configured with the following commands. A PC with a nontrunking NIC card is then connected to that port. What, if any, traffic will the PC successfully send and receive?

    ```
    interface fastethernet 0/12
    switchport trunk encapsulation dot1q
    switchport trunk native vlan 10
    switchport trunk allowed vlan 1-1005
    switchport mode trunk
    ```

This chapter covers the following topics that you need to master for the CCNP BCMSN exam:

- **VLAN Trunking Protocol**—This section presents Cisco VLAN Trunking Protocol (VTP) for VLAN management in a campus network.

- **VTP Configuration**—This section covers the Catalyst switch commands used to configure VTP.

- **VTP Pruning**—This section details traffic management by pruning within VTP domains, along with the commands needed for configuration.

- **Troubleshooting VTP**—This section gives a brief summary of things to consider and commands to use when VTP is not operating properly.

CHAPTER 6

VLAN Trunking Protocol

When VLANs are defined and used on switches throughout an enterprise or campus network, the administrative overhead can easily increase. Using the VLAN Trunking Protocol (VTP) makes VLAN administration more organized and manageable. This chapter covers VTP and its configuration.

A similar standards-based VLAN-management protocol for IEEE 802.1Q trunks is called *GARP VLAN Registration Protocol* (*GVRP*). The GARP and GVRP protocols are defined in the IEEE 802.1D and 802.1Q (clause 11) standards, respectively. At press time, GVRP was not supported in any of the Cisco IOS Software–based Catalyst switches. Therefore, it is not covered in this text or in the BCMSN course.

"Do I Know This Already?" Quiz

The purpose of the "Do I Know This Already?" quiz is to help you decide whether you need to read the entire chapter. If you already intend to read the entire chapter, you do not necessarily need to answer these questions now.

The 12-question quiz, derived from the major sections in the "Foundation Topics" portion of the chapter, helps you determine how to spend your limited study time.

Table 6-1 outlines the major topics discussed in this chapter and the "Do I Know This Already?" quiz questions that correspond to those topics.

Table 6-1 *"Do I Know This Already?" Foundation Topics Section-to-Question Mapping*

Foundation Topics Section	Questions Covered in This Section	Score
VTP	1–8	
VTP Configuration		
VTP Pruning	9–10	
Troubleshooting VTP	11–12	
Total Score		

> **CAUTION** The goal of self-assessment is to gauge your mastery of the topics in this chapter. If you do not know the answer to a question or are only partially sure of the answer, you should mark this question wrong. Giving yourself credit for an answer you correctly guess skews your self-assessment results and might give you a false sense of security.

1. Which of the following is not a Catalyst switch VTP mode?

   a. Server

   b. Client

   c. Designated

   d. Transparent

2. A switch in VTP transparent mode can do which one of the following?

   a. Create a new VLAN

   b. Only listen to VTP advertisements

   c. Send its own VTP advertisements

   d. Cannot make VLAN configuration changes

3. Which one of the following is a valid VTP advertisement?

   a. Triggered update

   b. VLAN database

   c. Subset

   d. Domain

4. Which one of the following is needed for VTP communication?

   a. A management VLAN

   b. A trunk link

   c. An access VLAN

   d. An IP address

5. Which one of the following VTP modes does not allow any manual VLAN configuration changes?

   a. Server

   b. Client

   c. Designated

   d. Transparent

6. Select all the parameters that decide whether to accept new VTP information:

   a. VTP priority

   b. VTP domain name

   c. Configuration revision number

   d. VTP server name

7. How many VTP management domains can a Catalyst switch participate in?

   a. 1

   b. 2

   c. Unlimited

   d. 4096

8. Which IOS command configures a Catalyst switch for VTP client mode?

   a. **set vtp mode client**

   b. **vtp client**

   c. **vtp mode client**

   d. **vtp client mode**

9. What is the purpose of VTP pruning?

   a. Limit the number of VLANs in a domain

   b. Stop unnecessary VTP advertisements

   c. Limit the extent of broadcast traffic

   d. Limit the size of the virtual tree

10. Which VLAN number is never eligible for VTP pruning?

    a. 0

    b. 1

    c. 1000

    d. 1001

11. Which of the following might present a VTP problem?

    a. Two or more VTP servers in a domain

    b. Two servers with the same configuration revision number

    c. A server in two domains

    d. A new server with a higher configuration revision number

12. If a VTP server is configured for VTP version 2, what else must happen for successful VTP communication in a domain?

    a. A VTP version 2 password must be set.

    b. All other switches in the domain must be version 2 capable.

    c. All other switches must be configured for VTP version 2.

    d. The VTP configuration revision number must be reset.

The answers to the quiz are found in Appendix A, "Answers to the Chapter 'Do I Know This Already?' Quizzes and Q&A Sections." The suggested choices for your next step are as follows:

■ **6 or less overall score**—Read the entire chapter, including the "Foundation Topics," "Foundation Summary," and "Q&A" sections.

■ **7–9 overall score**—Begin with the "Foundation Summary" section and then follow with the "Q&A" section at the end of the chapter.

■ **10 or more overall score**—If you want more review on these topics, skip to the "Foundation Summary" section and then go to the "Q&A" section at the end of the chapter. Otherwise, move on to Chapter 7, "Aggregating Switch Links."

Foundation Topics

VLAN Trunking Protocol

As the previous chapter demonstrated, VLAN configuration and trunking on a switch or a small group of switches is fairly intuitive. Campus network environments, however, usually consist of many interconnected switches. Configuring and managing a large number of switches, VLANs, and VLAN trunks quickly can get out of control.

Cisco has developed a method to manage VLANs across the campus network. The VLAN Trunking Protocol (VTP) uses Layer 2 trunk frames to communicate VLAN information among a group of switches. VTP manages the addition, deletion, and renaming of VLANs across the network from a central point of control. Any switch participating in a VTP exchange is aware of and can use any VLAN that VTP manages.

VTP Domains

VTP is organized into *management domains,* or areas with common VLAN requirements. A switch can belong to only one VTP domain, in addition to sharing VLAN information with other switches in the domain. Switches in different VTP domains, however, do not share VTP information.

Switches in a VTP domain advertise several attributes to their domain neighbors. Each advertisement contains information about the VTP management domain, VTP revision number, known VLANs, and specific VLAN parameters. When a VLAN is added to a switch in a management domain, other switches are notified of the new VLAN through *VTP advertisements*. In this way, all switches in a domain can prepare to receive traffic on their trunk ports using the new VLAN.

VTP Modes

To participate in a VTP management domain, each switch must be configured to operate in one of several modes. The VTP mode determines how the switch processes and advertises VTP information. You can use the following modes:

■ **Server mode**—VTP servers have full control over VLAN creation and modification for their domains. All VTP information is advertised to other switches in the domain, while all received VTP information is synchronized with the other switches. By default, a switch is in VTP server mode. Note that each VTP domain must have at least one server so that VLANs can be created, modified, or deleted, and VLAN information can be propagated.

■ **Client mode**—VTP clients do not allow the administrator to create, change, or delete any VLANs. Instead, they listen to VTP advertisements from other switches and modify their VLAN configurations accordingly. In effect, this is a passive listening mode. Received VTP information is forwarded out trunk links to neighboring switches in the domain, so the switch also acts as a VTP relay.

■ **Transparent mode**—VTP transparent switches do not participate in VTP. While in transparent mode, a switch does not advertise its own VLAN configuration, and a switch does not synchronize its VLAN database with received advertisements. In VTP version 1, a transparent-mode switch does not even relay VTP information it receives to other switches unless its VTP domain names and VTP version numbers match those of the other switches. In VTP version 2, transparent switches do forward received VTP advertisements out of their trunk ports, acting as VTP relays. This occurs regardless of the VTP domain name setting.

> **TIP**   While a switch is in VTP transparent mode, it can create and delete VLANs that are local only to itself. These VLAN changes, however, are not propagated to any other switch.

VTP Advertisements

Each Cisco switch participating in VTP advertises VLANs (only VLANs 1 to 1005), revision numbers, and VLAN parameters on its trunk ports to notify other switches in the management domain. VTP advertisements are sent as multicast frames. The switch intercepts frames sent to the VTP multicast address and processes them with its supervisory processor. VTP frames are forwarded out trunk links as a special case.

Because all switches in a management domain learn of new VLAN configuration changes, a VLAN must be created and configured on only one VTP server switch in the domain.

By default, management domains are set to use nonsecure advertisements without a password. You can add a password to set the domain to secure mode. The same password must be configured on every switch in the domain so that all switches exchanging VTP information use identical encryption methods.

VTP switches use an index called the *VTP configuration revision number* to keep track of the most recent information. Every switch in a VTP domain stores the configuration revision number that it last heard from a VTP advertisement. The VTP advertisement process always starts with configuration revision number 0 (zero).

When subsequent changes are made on a VTP server, the revision number is incremented before the advertisements are sent. When listening switches (configured as members of the same VTP domain as the advertising switch) receive an advertisement with a greater revision number than is stored locally, the advertisement overwrites any stored VLAN information.

Because of this, it is very important to always force any newly added network switches to have revision number 0 before being attached to the network. Otherwise, a switch might have stored a revision number that is greater than the value currently in use in the domain.

The VTP revision number is stored in NVRAM and is not altered by a power cycle of the switch. Therefore, the revision number can be initialized to 0 only by using one of the following methods:

■ Change the switch's VTP mode to transparent and then change the mode back to server.

■ Change the switch's VTP domain to a bogus name (a nonexistent VTP domain), and then change the VTP domain back to the original name.

If the VTP revision number is not reset to 0, the switch might enter the network as a VTP server and have a pre-existing revision number (from a previous life) that is higher than in previous legitimate advertisements. The new switch's VTP information would be seen as more recent, so all other switches in the VTP domain would gladly accept its database of VLANs and overwrite their good VLAN database entries with null or deleted VLAN status information.

In other words, a new server switch might inadvertently cause every other working switch to flush all records of every VLAN in production. The VLANs would be deleted from the VTP database and from the switches, causing any switch port assigned to them to become inactive. This is referred to as a *VTP synchronization problem*. For critical portions of your network, you should consider using transparent VTP mode to prevent the synchronization problem from ever becoming an issue.

TIP   It might seem intuitive that a switch acting as a VTP server could come online with a higher configuration revision number and wreak havoc on the whole domain. You should also be aware that this same thing can happen if a VTP *client* comes online with a higher revision, too!

Even though it seems as if a client should strictly listen to advertisements from servers, a client can and does send out its own advertisements. When it first powers up, a client sends a summary advertisement from its own stored database. It realizes that it has a greater revision number if it receives an inferior advertisement from a server. Therefore, it sends out a subset advertisement with the greater revision number, which VTP servers will accept as more up-to-date information.

VTP advertisements can originate as requests from client-mode switches that want to learn about the VTP database at bootup. Advertisements also can originate from server-mode switches as VLAN configuration changes occur.

VTP advertisements can occur in three forms:

■ **Summary advertisements**—VTP domain servers send summary advertisements every 300 seconds and every time a VLAN database change occurs. The summary advertisement lists information about the management domain, including VTP version, domain name, configuration revision number, time stamp, MD5 encryption hash code, and the number of subset advertisements to follow. For VLAN configuration changes, summary advertisements are followed by one or more subset advertisements with more specific VLAN configuration data. Figure 6-1 shows the summary advertisement format.

Figure 6-1   *VTP Summary Advertisement Format*

Version (1 byte)	Type (Summary Adv) (1 byte)	Number of subset advertisements to follow (1 byte)	Domain name length (1 byte)
Management Domain Name (zero-padded to 32 bytes)			
Configuration Revision Number (4 bytes)			
Updater Identity (orginating IP address: 4 bytes)			
Update Time Stamp (12 bytes)			
MD5 Digest hash code (16 bytes)			

■ **Subset advertisements**—VTP domain servers send subset advertisements after a VLAN configuration change occurs. These advertisements list the specific changes that have been performed, such as creating or deleting a VLAN, suspending or activating a VLAN, changing the name of a VLAN, and changing a VLAN's Maximum Transmission Unit (MTU). Subset advertisements can list the following VLAN parameters: status of the VLAN, VLAN type (such as Ethernet or Token Ring), MTU, length of the VLAN name, VLAN number, Security Association Identifier (SAID) value, and VLAN name. VLANs are listed individually in sequential subset advertisements. Figure 6-2 shows the VTP subset advertisement format.

Figure 6-2 *VTP Subset Advertisement and VLAN Info Field Formats*

VTP Subset Advertisement

0	1	2	3
Version (1 byte)	Type (Subset Adv) (1 byte)	Subset sequence number (1 byte)	Domain name length (1 byte)
Management Domain Name (zero-padded to 32 bytes)			
Configuration Revision Number (4 bytes)			
VLAN Info Field 1 (see below)			
VLAN Info Field ...			
VLAN Info Field N			

VTP VLAN Info Field

0	1	2	3
Info Length	VLAN Status	VLAN Type	VLAN Name Length
VLAN ID		MTU Size	
802.10 SAID			
VLAN Name (padded with zeros to multiple of 4 bytes)			

- **Advertisement requests from clients**—A VTP client can request any VLAN information it lacks. For example, a client switch might be reset and have its VLAN database cleared, and its VTP domain membership might be changed, or it might hear a VTP summary advertisement with a higher revision number than it currently has. After a client advertisement request, the VTP domain servers respond with summary and subset advertisements to bring it up-to-date. Figure 6-3 shows the advertisement request format.

Figure 6-3 *VTP Advertisement Request Format*

0	1	2	3
Version (1 byte)	Type (Adv request) (1 byte)	Reserved (1 byte)	Domain name length (1 byte)
Management Domain Name (zero-padded to 32 bytes)			
Starting advertisement to request			

Catalyst switches in server mode store VTP information separately from the switch configuration in NVRAM. VLAN and VTP data are saved in the vlan.dat file on the switch's Flash memory file system. All VTP information, including the VTP configuration revision number, is retained even when the switch power is off. In this manner, a switch can recover the last known VLAN configuration from its VTP database after it reboots.

> **TIP**   Remember that even in VTP client mode, a switch will store the last known VTP information—including the configuration revision number. Don't assume that a VTP client will start with a clean slate when it powers up.

VTP Configuration

By default, every switch operates in VTP server mode for the management domain NULL (a blank string), with no password or secure mode. If the switch hears a VTP summary advertisement on a trunk port from any other switch, it automatically learns the VTP domain name, VLANs, and the configuration revision number it hears. This makes it easy to bring up a new switch in an existing VTP domain. However, be aware that the new switch stays in VTP server mode, something that might not be desirable.

> **TIP**   You should get into the habit of double-checking the VTP configuration of any switch before you add it into your network. Make sure that the VTP configuration revision number is set to 0. You can do this by isolating the switch from the network, powering it up, and using the **show vtp status** command, as demonstrated in the following output:
>
> ```
> Switch#  show vtp status
> VTP Version                     : 2
> Configuration Revision          : 0
> Maximum VLANs supported locally : 1005
> Number of existing VLANs        : 5
> VTP Operating Mode              : Server
> VTP Domain Name                 :
> VTP Pruning Mode                : Disabled
> VTP V2 Mode                     : Disabled
> VTP Traps Generation            : Disabled
> MD5 digest                      : 0x57 0xCD 0x40 0x65 0x63 0x59 0x47 0xBD
> Configuration last modified by 0.0.0.0 at 0-0-00 00:00:00
> Local updater ID is 0.0.0.0 (no valid interface found)
> Switch#
> ```
>
> Here, the switch has a configuration revision number of 0, and is in the default state of VTP server mode with an undefined VTP domain name. This switch would be safe to add to a network.

The following sections discuss the commands and considerations that you should use to configure a switch for VTP operation.

You should be aware that there are two supported ways to configure VLAN and VTP information in Catalyst IOS switches:

■ Global conguration mode commands (for example, **vlan**, **vtp mode**, and **vtp domain**)

■ VLAN database mode commands

The **vlan database** EXEC command still is supported in Catalyst IOS Software only for backward compatibility, but this is not covered in the BCMSN course or the exam.

Configuring a VTP Management Domain

Before a switch is added into a network, the VTP management domain should be identified. If this switch is the first one on the network, the management domain must be created. Otherwise, the switch might have to join an existing management domain with other existing switches.

You can use the following global configuration command to assign a switch to a management domain, where the *domain-name* is a text string up to 32 characters long:

```
Switch(config)# vtp domain domain-name
```

Configuring the VTP Mode

Next, you need to choose the VTP mode for the new switch. The three VTP modes of operation and their guidelines for use are as follows:

■ **Server mode**—Server mode can be used on any switch in a management domain, even if other server and client switches are in use. This mode provides some redundancy in case of a server failure in the domain. Each VTP management domain should have at least one server. The first server defined in a network also defines the management domain that will be used by future VTP servers and clients. Server mode is the default VTP mode and allows VLANs to be created and deleted.

> **NOTE**   Multiple VTP servers can coexist in a domain. This usually is recommended for redundancy. The servers do not elect a primary or secondary server; they all simply function as servers. If one server is configured with a new VLAN or VTP parameter, it advertises the changes to the rest of the domain. All other servers synchronize their VTP databases to this advertisement, just as any VTP client would.

- **Client mode**—If other switches are in the management domain, you should configure a new switch for client mode operation. In this way, the switch is forced to learn any existing VTP information from a reliable existing server. After the switch has learned the current VTP information, you can reconfigure it for server mode if it will be used as a redundant server.

- **Transparent mode**—This mode is used if a switch will not share VLAN information with any other switch in the network. VLANs still can be created, deleted, and modified on the transparent switch. However, they are not advertised to other neighboring switches. VTP advertisements received by a transparent switch, however, are forwarded to other switches on trunk links.

Keeping switches in transparent mode can eliminate the chance for duplicate, overlapping VLANs in a large network with many network administrators. For example, two administrators might configure VLANs on switches in their respective areas but use the same VLAN identification or VLAN number. Even though the two VLANs have different meanings and purposes, they could overlap if both administrators advertised them using VTP servers.

You can configure the VTP mode with the following sequence of global configuration commands:

```
Switch(config)# vtp mode {server | client | transparent}
Switch(config)# vtp password password
```

If the domain is operating in secure mode, a password also can be defined. The password can be configured only on VTP servers and clients. The password itself is not sent; instead, an MD5 digest or hash code is computed and sent in VTP advertisements (servers) and is used to validate received advertisements (clients). The password is a string of 1 to 32 characters (case-sensitive).

If secure VTP is implemented using passwords, begin by configuring a password on the VTP servers. The client switches retain the last-known VTP information but cannot process received advertisements until the same password is configured on them, too.

Configuring the VTP Version

Two versions of VTP are available for use in a management domain. Catalyst switches are capable of running either VTP version 1 or VTP version 2. Within a management domain, the two versions are not interoperable. Therefore, the same VTP version must be configured on every switch in a domain. VTP version 1 is the default protocol on a switch.

If a switch is capable of running VTP version 2, however, a switch can coexist with other version 1 switches, as long as its VTP version 2 is not enabled. This situation becomes important if you want to use version 2 in a domain. Then only one server mode switch needs to have VTP version 2 enabled. The new version number is propagated to all other version 2–capable switches in the domain, causing them all to automatically enable version 2 for use.

> **TIP**   A third version of VTP addresses some of the traditional shortcomings. For example, VTP version 3 supports extended VLAN numbers (1 to 4095) that are compatible with the IEEE 802.1Q trunking standard. At press time, VTPv3 is available only on Cisco Catalyst platforms running the CatOS (non-IOS) operating system. Therefore, only VTP versions 1 and 2 are covered on the BCMSN exam and in this text.

The two versions of VTP differ in the features they support. VTP version 2 offers the following additional features over version 1:

- **Version-dependent transparent mode**—In transparent mode, VTP version 1 matches the VTP version and domain name before forwarding the information to other switches using VTP. VTP version 2 in transparent mode forwards the VTP messages without checking the version number. Because only one domain is supported in a switch, the domain name doesn't have to be checked.

- **Consistency checks**—VTP version 2 performs consistency checks on the VTP and VLAN parameters entered from the command-line interface (CLI) or by the Simple Network Management Protocol (SNMP). This checking helps prevent errors in such things as VLAN names and numbers from being propagated to other switches in the domain. However, no consistency checks are performed on VTP messages that are received on trunk links or on configuration and database data that is read from NVRAM.

- **Token Ring support**—VTP version 2 supports the use of Token Ring switching and Token Ring VLANs. (If Token Ring switching is being used, VTP version 2 must be enabled.)

- **Unrecognized Type-Length-Value (TLV) support**—VTP version 2 switches propagate received configuration change messages out other trunk links, even if the switch supervisor cannot parse or understand the message. For example, a VTP advertisement contains a Type field to denote what type of VTP message is being sent. VTP message type 1 is a summary advertisement, and message type 2 is a subset advertisement. An extension to VTP that utilizes other message types and other message length values could be in use. Instead of dropping the unrecognized VTP message, version 2 still propagates the information and keeps a copy in NVRAM.

The VTP version number is configured using the following global configuration command:

```
Switch(config)# vtp version {1 | 2}
```

By default, a switch uses VTP version 1.

VTP Configuration Example

As an example, a switch is configured as the VTP server in a domain named MyCompany. The domain will use secure VTP with the password **bigsecret**. You can use the following configuration commands to accomplish this:

```
Switch(config)#  vtp  domain  MyCompany
Switch(config)#  vtp  mode  server
Switch(config)#  vtp  password  bigsecret
```

VTP Status

The current VTP parameters for a management domain can be displayed using the **show vtp status** command. Example 6-1 demonstrates some sample output of this command from a switch acting as a VTP client in the VTP domain called CampusDomain.

Example 6-1 **show vtp status** *Reveals VTP Parameters for a Management Domain*

```
Switch# show  vtp  status
VTP Version                          : 2
Configuration Revision               : 89
Maximum VLANs supported locally : 1005
Number of existing VLANs             : 74
VTP Operating Mode                   : Client
VTP Domain Name                      : CampusDomain
VTP Pruning Mode                     : Enabled VTP V2 Mode : Disabled VTP
  Traps Generation                   : Disabled
MD5 digest                           : 0x4B 0x07 0x75 0xEC 0xB1 0x3D 0x6F 0x1F Configuration
  last modified by 192.168.199.1 at 11-19-02 09:29:56
Switch#
```

VTP message and error counters also can be displayed with the **show vtp counters** command. You can use this command for basic VTP troubleshooting to see whether the switch is interacting with other VTP nodes in the domain. Example 6-2 demonstrates some sample output from the **show vtp counters** command.

Example 6-2 **show vtp counters** *Reveals VTP Message and Error Counters*

```
Switch# show  vtp  counters
VTP statistics:
Summary advertisements received   : 1
Subset advertisements received    : 2
Request advertisements received   : 1
Summary advertisements transmitted : 1630
Subset advertisements transmitted : 0
Request advertisements transmitted : 4
Number of config revision errors  : 0
```

Example 6-2 **show vtp counters** *Reveals VTP Message and Error Counters (Continued)*

```
Number of config digest errors   : 0
Number of V1 summary errors      : 0

VTP pruning statistics:

Trunk              Join Transmitted Join Received   Summary advts received from
                                                    non-pruning-capable device
---------------- ---------------- ---------------- ----------------------------
Gi0/1                  82352           82931              0
Switch#
```

VTP Pruning

Recall that, by definition, a switch must forward broadcast frames out all available ports in the broadcast domain because broadcasts are destined everywhere there is a listener. Unless forwarded by more intelligent means, multicast frames follow the same pattern.

In addition, frames destined for an address that the switch has not yet learned or has *forgotten* (the MAC address has aged out of the address table) must be forwarded out all ports in an attempt to find the destination. These frames are referred to as *unknown unicast*.

When forwarding frames out all ports in a broadcast domain or VLAN, trunk ports are included if they transport that VLAN. By default, a trunk link transports traffic from all VLANs, unless specific VLANs are removed from the trunk. Generally, in a network with several switches, trunk links are enabled between switches, and VTP is used to manage the propagation of VLAN information. This scenario causes the trunk links between switches to carry traffic from *all* VLANs, not just from the specific VLANs created.

Consider the network shown in Figure 6-4. When end user Host PC in VLAN 3 sends a broadcast, Catalyst switch C forwards the frame out all VLAN 3 ports, including the trunk link to Catalyst A. Catalyst A, in turn, forwards the broadcast on to Catalysts B and D over those trunk links. Catalysts B and D forward the broadcast out only their access links that have been configured for VLAN 3. If Catalysts B and D do not have any active users in VLAN 3, forwarding that broadcast frame to them would consume bandwidth on the trunk links and processor resources in both switches, only to have switches B and D discard the frames.

VTP pruning makes more efficient use of trunk bandwidth by reducing unnecessary flooded traffic. Broadcast and unknown unicast frames on a VLAN are forwarded over a trunk link only if the switch on the receiving end of the trunk has ports in that VLAN.

VTP pruning occurs as an extension to VTP version 1, using an additional VTP message type. When a Catalyst switch has a port associated with a VLAN, the switch sends an advertisement to its neighbor switches that it has active ports on that VLAN. The neighbors keep this information, enabling them to decide whether flooded traffic from a VLAN should use a trunk port.

Figure 6-4 *Flooding in a Catalyst Switch Network*

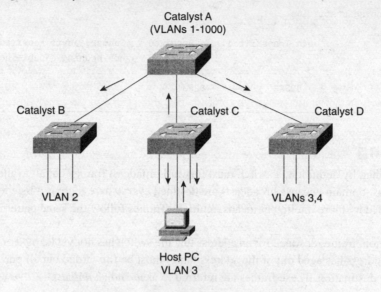

Figure 6-5 shows the network from Figure 6-4 with VTP pruning enabled. Because Catalyst B has not advertised its use of VLAN 3, Catalyst A will prune VLAN 3 from the trunk to B and will choose not to flood VLAN 3 traffic to Catalyst B over the trunk link. Catalyst D has advertised the need for VLAN 3, so traffic will be flooded to it.

Figure 6-5 *Flooding in a Catalyst Switch Network Using VTP Pruning*

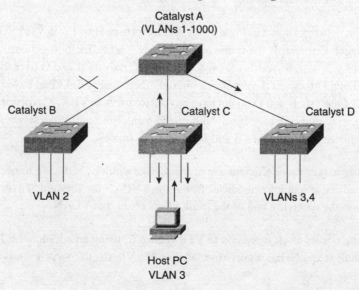

> **NOTE**   Even when VTP pruning has determined that a VLAN is not needed on a trunk, an instance of the Spanning Tree Protocol (STP) will run for every VLAN that is allowed on the trunk link. To reduce the number of STP instances, you manually should "prune" unneeded VLANs from the trunk and allow only the needed ones. Use the **switchport trunk allowed vlan** command to identify the VLANs that should be added or removed from a trunk.

Enabling VTP Pruning

By default, VTP pruning is disabled on IOS-based switches. To enable pruning, use the following global configuration command:

```
Switch(config)# vtp pruning
```

If you use this command on a VTP server, it also advertises that pruning needs to be enabled for the entire management domain. All other switches listening to that advertisement also will enable pruning.

When pruning is enabled, all general-purpose VLANs become eligible for pruning on all trunk links, if needed. However, you can modify the default list of pruning eligibility with the following interface-configuration command:

```
Switch(config)# interface type mod/num
Switch(config-if)# switchport trunk pruning vlan {add | except | none | remove}
    vlan-list
```

By default, VLANs 2 through 1001 are eligible, or "enabled," for potential pruning on every trunk. Use the following keywords with the command to tailor the list:

- *vlan-list*—An explicit list of eligible VLAN numbers (anything from 2 to 1001), separated by commas or by dashes.

- **add** *vlan-list*—A list of VLAN numbers (anything from 2 to 1001) is added to the already configured list; this is a shortcut to keep from typing a long list of numbers.

- **except** *vlan-list*—All VLANs are eligible except for the VLAN numbers listed (anything from 2 to 1001); this is a shortcut to keep from typing a long list of numbers.

- **remove** *vlan-list*—A list of VLAN numbers (anything from 2 to 1001) is removed from the already configured list; this is a shortcut to keep from typing a long list of numbers.

> **TIP** Be aware that VTP pruning has no effect on switches in the VTP transparent mode. Instead, those switches must be configured manually to "prune" VLANs from trunk links. In this case, pruning is always configured on the upstream side of a trunk. (The downstream side switch doesn't have any ports that belong to the pruned VLAN, so there is no need to prune from that end.)
>
> By default, VLANs 2 to 1001 are eligible for pruning. VLAN 1 has a special meaning because it sometimes is used for control traffic and is the default access VLAN on switch ports. Because of these historical reasons, VLAN 1 is never eligible for pruning. In addition, VLANs 1002 through 1005 are reserved for Token Ring and FDDI VLANs and are never eligible for pruning.

Troubleshooting VTP

If a switch does not seem to be receiving updated information from a VTP server, consider these possible causes:

- The switch is configured for VTP transparent mode. In this mode, incoming VTP advertisements are not processed; they are relayed only to other switches in the domain.

- If the switch is configured as a VTP client, there might not be another switch functioning as a VTP server. In this case, configure the local switch to become a VTP server itself.

- The link toward the VTP server is not in trunking mode. VTP advertisements are sent only. over trunks. Use the **show interface** *type mod/num* **switchport** to verify the operational mode as a trunk.

- Make sure the VTP domain name is configured correctly to match that of the VTP server.

- Make sure the VTP version is compatible with other switches in the VTP domain.

- Make sure the VTP password matches others in the VTP domain. If the server doesn't use a password, make sure the password is disabled or cleared on the local switch.

> **TIP** Above all else, verify a switch's VTP configuration *before* connecting it to a production network. If the switch has been configured previously or used elsewhere, it might already be in VTP server mode and have a VTP configuration revision number that is higher than that of other switches in the production VTP domain. In that case, other switches will listen and learn from the new switch because it has a higher revision number and must know more recent information. This could cause the new switch to introduce bogus VLANs into the domain or, worse yet, to cause all other switches in the domain to delete all their active VLANs.
>
> To prevent this from happening, reset the configuration revision number of every new switch before it is added to a production network.

Table 6-2 lists and describes the commands that are useful for verifying or troubleshooting VTP configuration.

Table 6-2 *VTP Configuration Troubleshooting Commands*

Function	Command syntax
Displays current VTP parameters, including the last advertising server	**show vtp status**
Displays VTP advertisement and pruning statistics	**show vtp counters**
Displays defined VLANs	**show vlan brief**
Displays trunk status, including pruning eligibility	**show interface** *type mod/num* **switchport**
Displays VTP pruning state	**show interface** *type mod/num* **pruning**

Foundation Summary

The Foundation Summary is a collection of information that provides a convenient review of many key concepts in this chapter. If you are already comfortable with the topics in this chapter, this summary can help you recall a few details. If you just read this chapter, this review should help solidify some key facts. If you are doing your final preparation before the exam, this information is a convenient way to review the day before the exam.

Table 6-3 *Catalyst VTP Modes*

VTP Mode	Characteristics
Server	All VLAN and VTP configuration changes occur here. The server advertises settings and changes to all other servers and clients in a VTP domain. (This is the default mode for Catalyst switches.)
Client	Listens to all VTP advertisements from servers in a VTP domain. Advertisements are relayed out other trunk links. No VLAN or VTP configuration changes can be made on a client.
Transparent	VLAN configuration changes are made locally, independent of any VTP domain. VTP advertisements are not received but merely are relayed out other trunk links, if possible.

Table 6-4 *Types of VTP Advertisements*

Advertisement Type	Function
Summary	Sent by server every 300 seconds and after a topology change. Contains a complete dump of all VTP domain information.
Subset	Sent by server only after a VLAN configuration change. Contains only information about the specific VLAN change.
Advertisement request	Sent by client when additional VTP information is needed. Servers send summary or subset advertisements in response.
Pruning request	Sent by clients and servers to announce VLANs that are in active use on local switch ports. These VLANs should not be pruned by neighbors. (These messages are destined for nearest-neighbor switches and are not relayed throughout the domain.)

Table 6-5 *VTP Configuration Commands*

Task	Command Syntax
Defines the VTP domain	**vtp domain** *domain-name*
Sets the VTP mode	**vtp mode** {**server**	**client**	**transparent**}
Defines an optional VTP password	**vtp password** *password*
Configures VTP version	**vtp version** {**1**	**2**}
Enables VTP pruning	**vtp pruning**
Selects VLANs eligible for pruning on a trunk interface	**interface** *type mod/num* **switchport trunk pruning vlan** {**add**	**except**	**none**	**remove**} *vlan-list*

Q&A

The questions and scenarios in this book are more difficult than what you should experience on the actual exam. The questions do not attempt to cover more breadth or depth than the exam; however, they are designed to make sure that you know the answers. Rather than allowing you to derive the answers from clues hidden inside the questions themselves, the questions challenge your understanding and recall of the subject. Hopefully, these questions will help limit the number of exam questions on which you narrow your choices to two options and then guess.

The answers to these questions can be found in Appendix A.

1. True or false: You can use VTP domains to separate broadcast domains.

2. What VTP modes can a Catalyst switch be configured for? Can VLANs be created in each of the modes?

3. How many VTP management domains can a Catalyst switch participate in? How many VTP servers can a management domain have?

4. What conditions must exist for two Catalyst switches to be in the same VTP management domain?

5. On a VTP server switch, identify what you can do to reset the VTP configuration revision number to 0.

6. How can you clear the configuration revision number on a VTP client?

7. Complete this command to make all VLANs other than 30 and 100 eligible for pruning on the trunk interface:

```
switchport trunk pruning vlan
```

8. Which VLAN numbers are never eligible for VTP pruning? Why?

9. What does the acronym VTP stand for?

10. What VTP domain name is defined on a new switch with no configuration?

11. In a network of switches, VTP domain Engineering has been configured with VLANs 1, 10 through 30, and 100. The VTP configuration revision number is currently at 23. Suppose that a new switch is connected to the network, and it has the following configuration: VTP domain Engineering, VTP server mode, only VLANs 1 and 2 defined, and configuration revision number of 30.

    What happens when the switch is connected to the network?

12. A VTP client switch has VLANs 1, 2, 3, 10, and 30 configured as part of a VTP domain; however, the switch has users connected only to access switch ports defined on VLANs 3 and 30. If VTP pruning is enabled and all VLANs are eligible, which VLANs will be pruned on the upstream switch?

13. The VTP domain Area3 consists of one server and several clients. The server's VTP configuration revision number is at 11. A new switch is added to the network. It has VTP domain name Area5 and a configuration revision number of 10. What happens when the new switch is added to the network? What happens when the VTP domain name is changed to Area3 on the new switch?

14. What command shows information about the VTP configuration on a Catalyst 3560?

This chapter covers the following topics that you need to master for the CCNP BCMSN exam:

- **Switch Port Aggregation with EtherChannel**—This section discusses the concept of aggregating, or "bundling," physical ports into a single logical link. Methods for load-balancing traffic across the physical links also are covered.

- **EtherChannel Negotiation Protocols**—This section discusses two protocols that dynamically negotiate and control EtherChannels: Port Aggregation Protocol (PAgP), a Cisco proprietary protocol, and Link Aggregation Control Protocol (LACP), a standards-based protocol.

- **EtherChannel Configuration**—This section discusses the Catalyst switch commands needed to configure EtherChannel.

- **Troubleshooting an EtherChannel**—This section gives a brief summary of things to consider and commands to use when an aggregated link is not operating properly.

CHAPTER 7

Aggregating Switch Links

In previous chapters, you learned about campus network design and connecting and organizing switches into blocks and common workgroups. Using these principles, end users can be given effective access to resources both on and off the campus network. However, today's mission-critical applications and services demand networks that provide high availability and reliability.

This chapter presents technologies that you can use in a campus network to provide higher bandwidth and reliability between switches.

"Do I Know This Already?" Quiz

The purpose of the "Do I Know This Already?" quiz is to help you decide whether you need to read the entire chapter. If you already intend to read the entire chapter, you do not necessarily need to answer these questions now.

The 13-question quiz, derived from the major sections in the "Foundation Topics" portion of the chapter, helps you determine how to spend your limited study time.

Table 7-1 outlines the major topics discussed in this chapter and the "Do I Know This Already?" quiz questions that correspond to those topics.

Table 7-1 *"Do I Know This Already?" Foundation Topics Section-to-Question Mapping*

Foundation Topics Section	Questions Covered in This Section	Score
Switch Port Aggregation with EtherChannel	1–7	
EtherChannel Negotiation	8–11	
EtherChannel Configuration	11–12	
Troubleshooting an EtherChannel	13	
Total Score		

CAUTION   The goal of self-assessment is to gauge your mastery of the topics in this chapter. If you do not know the answer to a question or are only partially sure of the answer, you should mark this question wrong. Giving yourself credit for an answer you correctly guess skews your self-assessment results and might give you a false sense of security.

1. If Fast Ethernet ports are bundled into an EtherChannel, what is the maximum throughput supported on a Catalyst switch?

   a. 100 Mbps

   b. 200 Mbps

   c. 400 Mbps

   d. 800 Mbps

   e. 1600 Mbps

2. Which of these methods distributes traffic over an EtherChannel?

   a. Round robin

   b. Least-used link

   c. A function of address

   d. A function of packet size

3. What type of interface represents an EtherChannel as a whole?

   a. Channel

   b. Port

   c. Port-channel

   d. Channel-port

4. Which of the following is not a valid method for EtherChannel load balancing?

   a. Source MAC address

   b. Source and destination MAC addresses

   c. Source IP address

   d. IP precedence

   e. UDP/TCP port

5. How can the EtherChannel load-balancing method be set?

    a. Per switch port

    b. Per EtherChannel

    c. Globally per switch

    d. Can't be configured

6. What logical operation is performed to calculate EtherChannel load balancing as a function of two addresses?

    a. OR

    b. AND

    c. XOR

    d. NOR

7. Which one of the following is a valid combination of ports for an EtherChannel?

    a. Two access links (one VLAN 5, one VLAN 5)

    b. Two access links (one VLAN 1, one VLAN 10)

    c. Two trunk links (one VLANs 1 to 10, one VLANs 1, 11 to 20)

    d. Two Fast Ethernet links (both full duplex, one 10 Mbps)

8. Which of these is a method for negotiating an EtherChannel?

    a. PAP

    b. CHAP

    c. LAPD

    d. LACP

9. Which of the following is a valid EtherChannel negotiation mode combination between two switches?

    a. PAgP auto, PAgP auto

    b. PAgP auto, PAgP desirable

    c. on, PAgP auto

    d. LACP passive, LACP passive

10. When is PagP's "desirable silent" mode useful?

    a. When the switch should not send PAgP frames

    b. When the switch should not form an EtherChannel

    c. When the switch should not expect to receive PAgP frames

    d. When the switch is using LACP mode

11. Which of the following EtherChannel modes does not send or receive any negotiation frames?

    a. **channel-group 1 mode passive**

    b. **channel-group 1 mode active**

    c. **channel-group 1 mode on**

    d. **channel-group 1 mode desirable**

    e. **channel-group 1 mode auto**

12. Two computers are the only hosts sending IP data across an EtherChannel between two switches. Several different applications are being used between them. Which of these load-balancing methods would be more likely to use the most links in the EtherChannel?

    a. Source and destination MAC addresses.

    b. Source and destination IP addresses.

    c. Source and destination TCP/UDP ports.

    d. None of the other answers is correct.

13. Which command can be used to see the status of an EtherChannel's links?

    a. **show channel link**

    b. **show etherchannel status**

    c. **show etherchannel summary**

    d. **show ether channel status**

The answers to the quiz are found in Appendix A, "Answers to Chapter 'Do I Know This Already?' Quizzes and Q&A Sections." The suggested choices for your next step are as follows:

■ **8 or less overall score**—Read the entire chapter. This includes the "Foundation Topics," "Foundation Summary," and "Q&A" sections.

■ **9–11 overall score**—Begin with the "Foundation Summary" section and then follow up with the "Q&A" section at the end of the chapter.

■ **12 or more overall score**—If you want more review on these topics, skip to the "Foundation Summary" section and then go to the "Q&A" section at the end of the chapter. Otherwise, move to Chapter 8, "Traditional Spanning Tree Protocol."

Foundation Topics

Switch Port Aggregation with EtherChannel

As discussed in Chapter 4, "Switch Port Configuration," switches can use Ethernet, Fast Ethernet, Gigabit, or 10-Gigabit Ethernet ports to scale link speeds by a factor of ten. Cisco offers another method of scaling link bandwidth by aggregating, or *bundling*, parallel links, termed the *EtherChannel* technology. Two to eight links of either Fast Ethernet (FE), Gigabit Ethernet (GE), or 10-Gigabit Ethernet (10GE) are bundled as one logical link of *Fast EtherChannel (FEC)*, *Gigabit EtherChannel (GEC)*, or *10-Gigabit Etherchannel (10GEC)*, respectively. This bundle provides a full-duplex bandwidth of up to 1600 Mbps (eight links of Fast Ethernet), 16 Gbps (eight links of Gigabit Ethernet), or 160 Gbps (eight links of 10-Gigabit Ethernet).

This also provides an easy means to "grow," or expand, a link's capacity between two switches, without having to continually purchase hardware for the next magnitude of throughput. For example, a single FastEthernet link (200 Mbps throughput) can be incrementally expanded up to eight Fast Ethernet links (1600 Mbps) as a single Fast EtherChannel. If the traffic load grows beyond that, the growth process can begin again with a single Gigabit Ethernet link (2 Gbps throughput), which can be expanded up to eight Gigabit Ethernet links as a Gigabit EtherChannel (16 Gbps). The process repeats again by moving to a single 10-Gigabit Ethernet link, and so on.

Ordinarily, having multiple or parallel links between switches creates the possibility of bridging loops, an undesirable condition. EtherChannel avoids this situation by bundling parallel links into a single, logical link, which can act as either an access or a trunk link. Switches or devices on each end of the EtherChannel link must understand and use the EtherChannel technology for proper operation.

Although an EtherChannel link is seen as a single logical link, the link doesn't necessarily have an inherent total bandwidth equal to the sum of its component physical links. For example, suppose that an FEC link is made up of four full-duplex, 100-Mbps Fast Ethernet links. Although it is possible for the FEC link to carry a total throughput of 800 Mbps (if each link becomes fully loaded), the single resulting FEC bundle does not operate at this speed.

Instead, traffic is distributed across the individual links within the EtherChannel. Each of these links operates at its inherent speed (200 Mbps full duplex for FE) but carries only the frames placed on it by the EtherChannel hardware. If one link within the bundle is favored by the load-distribution algorithm, that link will carry a disproportionate amount of traffic. In other words, the load isn't always distributed equally among the individual links. The load-balancing process is explained further in the next section.

EtherChannel also provides redundancy with several bundled physical links. If one of the links within the bundle fails, traffic sent through that link automatically is moved to an adjacent link. Failover occurs in less than a few milliseconds and is transparent to the end user. As more links fail, more traffic is moved to further adjacent links. Likewise, as links are restored, the load automatically is redistributed among the active links.

Bundling Ports with EtherChannel

EtherChannel bundles can consist of up to eight physical ports of the same Ethernet media type and speed. Some configuration restrictions exist to ensure that only similarly configured links are bundled.

Generally, all bundled ports first must belong to the same VLAN. If used as a trunk, bundled ports must be in trunking mode, have the same native VLAN, and pass the same set of VLANs. Each of the ports should have the same speed and duplex settings before being bundled. Bundled ports also must be configured with identical spanning-tree settings.

Distributing Traffic in EtherChannel

Traffic in an EtherChannel is distributed across the individual bundled links in a deterministic fashion; however, the load is not necessarily balanced equally across all the links. Instead, frames are forwarded on a specific link as a result of a hashing algorithm. The algorithm can use source IP address, destination IP address, or a combination of source and destination IP addresses, source and destination MAC addresses, or TCP/UDP port numbers. The hash algorithm computes a binary pattern that selects a link number in the bundle to carry each frame.

If only one address or port number is hashed, a switch forwards each frame by using one or more low-order bits of the hash value as an index into the bundled links. If two addresses or port numbers are hashed, a switch performs an exclusive-OR (XOR) operation on one or more low-order bits of the addresses or TCP/UDP port numbers as an index into the bundled links.

For example, an EtherChannel consisting of two links bundled together requires a 1-bit index. If the index is 0, link 0 is selected; if the index is 1, link 1 is used. Either the lowest-order address bit or the XOR of the last bit of the addresses in the frame is used as the index. A four-link bundle uses a hash of the last 2 bits. Likewise, an eight-link bundle uses a hash of the last 3 bits. The hashing operation's outcome selects the EtherChannel's outbound link. Table 7-2 shows the results of an XOR on a two-link bundle, using the source and destination addresses.

The XOR operation is performed independently on each bit position in the address value. If the two address values have the same bit value, the XOR result is always 0. If the two address bits differ, the XOR result is always 1. In this way, frames can be distributed statistically among the links with the assumption that MAC or IP addresses themselves are distributed statistically throughout the network. In a four-link EtherChannel, the XOR is performed on the lower 2 bits of the address values, resulting in a 2-bit XOR value (each bit is computed separately) or a link number from 0 to 3.

Table 7-2 *Frame Distribution on a Two-Link EtherChannel*

Binary Addresses	Two-Link EtherChannel XOR and Link Number
Addr1: ... xxxxxxx0 Addr2: ... xxxxxxx0	... xxxxxxx0: Use link 0
Addr1: ... xxxxxxx0 Addr2: ... xxxxxxx1	... xxxxxxx1: Use link 1
Addr1: ... xxxxxxx1 Addr2: ... xxxxxxx0	... xxxxxxx1: Use link 1
Addr1: ... xxxxxxx1 Addr2: ... xxxxxxx1	... xxxxxxx0: Use link 0

As an example, consider a packet being sent from IP address 192.168.1.1 to 172.31.67.46. Because EtherChannels can be built from two to eight individual links, only the rightmost (least significant) 3 bits are needed as a link index. From the source and destination addresses, these bits are 001 (1) and 110 (6), respectively. For a two-link EtherChannel, a 1-bit XOR is performed on the rightmost address bit: 1 XOR 0 = 1, causing Link 1 in the bundle to be used. A four-link EtherChannel produces a 2-bit XOR: 01 XOR 10 = 11, causing Link 3 in the bundle to be used. Finally, an eight-link EtherChannel requires a 3-bit XOR: 001 XOR 110 = 111, where Link 7 in the bundle is selected.

A conversation between two devices always is sent through the same EtherChannel link because the two endpoint addresses stay the same. However, when a device talks to several other devices, chances are that the destination addresses are distributed equally with 0s and 1s in the last bit (even and odd address values). This causes the frames to be distributed across the EtherChannel links.

Note that the load distribution is still proportional to the volume of traffic passing between pairs of hosts or link indexes. For example, suppose that there are two pairs of hosts talking across a two-link channel, and each pair of addresses results in a unique link index. Frames from one pair of hosts always travel over one link in the channel, whereas frames from the other pair travel over the other link. The links are both being used as a result of the hash algorithm, so the load is being distributed across every link in the channel.

However, if one pair of hosts has a much greater volume of traffic than the other pair, one link in the channel will be used much more than the other. This still can create a load imbalance. To remedy this condition, you should consider other methods of hashing algorithms for the channel. For example, a method that uses the source and destination addresses along with UDP or TCP port numbers can distribute traffic much differently. Then, packets are placed on links within the bundle based on the applications used within conversations between two hosts.

Configuring EtherChannel Load Balancing

The hashing operation can be performed on either MAC or IP addresses and can be based solely on source or destination addresses, or both. Use the following command to configure frame distribution for all EtherChannel switch links:

```
Switch(config)# port-channel load-balance method
```

Notice that the load-balancing method is set with a global configuration command. You must set the method globally for the switch, not on a per-port basis. Table 7-3 lists the possible values for the *method* variable, along with the hashing operation and some sample supporting switch models.

Table 7-3 *Types of EtherChannel Load-Balancing Methods*

method Value	Hash Input	Hash Operation	Switch Model
src-ip	Source IP address	bits	6500/4500/3750/3560/2970
dst-ip	Destination IP address	bits	6500/4500/3750/3560/2970
src-dst-ip	Source and destination IP address	XOR	6500/4500/3750/3560/2970
src-mac	Source MAC address	bits	6500/4500/3750/3560/2970
dst-mac	Destination MAC address	bits	6500/4500/3750/3560/2970
src-dst-mac	Source and destination MAC	XOR	6500/4500/3750/3560/2970
src-port	Source port number	bits	6500/4500
dst-port	Destination port number	bits	6500/4500
src-dst-port	Source and destination port	XOR	6500/4500

The default configuration is to use source XOR destination IP addresses, or the **src-dst-ip** method. The default for the Catalyst 2970 and 3560 is **src-mac** for Layer 2 switching. If Layer 3 switching is used on the EtherChannel, the **src-dst-ip** method will always be used, even though it is not configurable.

Normally, the default action should result in a statistical distribution of frames; however, you should determine whether the EtherChannel is imbalanced according to the traffic patterns present. For example, if a single server is receiving most of the traffic on an EtherChannel, the server's address (the destination IP address) always will remain constant in the many conversations. This can cause one link to be overused if the destination IP address is used as a component of a load-balancing method. In the case of a four-link EtherChannel, perhaps two of the four links are overused. Configuring the use of MAC addresses, or only the source IP addresses, might cause the distribution to be more balanced across all the bundled links.

> **TIP**   To verify how effectively a configured load-balancing method is performing, you can use the **show etherchannel port-channel** command. Each link in the channel is displayed, along with a hex "Load" value. Although this information is not intuitive, you can use the hex values to get an idea of each link's traffic loads relative to the others.

In some applications, EtherChannel traffic might consist of protocols other than IP. For example, IPX or SNA frames might be switched along with IP. Non-IP protocols need to be distributed according to MAC addresses because IP addresses are not applicable. Here, the switch should be configured to use MAC addresses instead of the IP default.

> **TIP**   A special case results when a router is connected to an EtherChannel. Recall that a router always uses its burned-in MAC address in Ethernet frames, even though it is forwarding packets to and from many different IP addresses. In other words, many end stations send frames to their local router address with the router's MAC address as the destination. This means that the destination MAC address is the same for all frames destined through the router.
>
> Usually, this will not present a problem because the source MAC addresses are all different. When two routers are forwarding frames to each other, however, both source and destination MAC addresses remains constant, and only one link of the EtherChannel is used. If the MAC addresses remain constant, choose IP addresses instead. Beyond that, if most of the traffic is between the same two IP addresses, as in the case of two servers talking, choose IP port numbers to disperse the frames across different links.

You should choose the load-balancing method that provides the greatest distribution or variety when the channel links are indexed. Also consider the type of addressing that is being used on the network. If most of the traffic is IP, it might make sense to load-balance according to IP addresses or TCP/UDP port numbers.

But if IP load balancing is being used, what happens to non-IP frames? If a frame can't meet the load-balancing criteria, the switch automatically falls back to the "next lowest" method. With Ethernet, MAC addresses must always be present, so the switch distributes those frames according to their MAC addresses.

A switch also provides some inherent protection against bridging loops with EtherChannels. When ports are bundled into an EtherChannel, no inbound (received) broadcasts and multicasts are sent back out over any of the remaining ports in the channel. Outbound broadcast and multicast frames are load-balanced like any other: The broadcast or multicast address becomes part of the hashing calculation to choose an outbound channel link.

EtherChannel Negotiation Protocols

EtherChannels can be negotiated between two switches to provide some dynamic link configuration. Two protocols are available to negotiate bundled links in Catalyst switches. The Port Aggregation Protocol (PAgP) is a Cisco-proprietary solution, and the Link Aggregation Control Protocol (LACP) is standards based.

Port Aggregation Protocol

To provide automatic EtherChannel configuration and negotiation between switches, Cisco developed the *Port Aggregation Protocol*. PAgP packets are exchanged between switches over EtherChannel-capable ports. Neighbors are identified and port group capabilities are learned and compared with local switch capabilities. Ports that have the same neighbor device ID and port group capability are bundled together as a bidirectional, point-to-point EtherChannel link.

PAgP forms an EtherChannel only on ports that are configured for either identical static VLANs or trunking. PAgP also dynamically modifies parameters of the EtherChannel if one of the bundled ports is modified. For example, if the configured VLAN, speed, or duplex mode of a port in an established bundle is changed, PAgP reconfigures that parameter for all ports in the bundle.

PAgP can be configured in active mode (desirable), in which a switch actively asks a far-end switch to negotiate an EtherChannel, or in passive mode (auto, the default), in which a switch negotiates an EtherChannel only if the far end initiates it.

Link Aggregation Control Protocol

LACP is a standards-based alternative to PAgP, defined in IEEE 802.3ad (also known as IEEE 802.3 Clause 43, "Link Aggregation"). LACP packets are exchanged between switches over EtherChannel-capable ports. As with PAgP, neighbors are identified and port group capabilities are learned and compared with local switch capabilities. However, LACP also assigns roles to the EtherChannel's endpoints.

The switch with the lowest *system priority* (a 2-byte priority value followed by a 6-byte switch MAC address) is allowed to make decisions about what ports actively are participating in the EtherChannel at a given time.

Ports are selected and become active according to their *port priority* value (a 2-byte priority followed by a 2-byte port number), where a low value indicates a higher priority. A set of up to 16 potential links can be defined for each EtherChannel. Through LACP, a switch selects up to eight of these having the lowest port priorities as active EtherChannel links at any given time. The other links are placed in a standby state and will be enabled in the EtherChannel if one of the active links goes down.

Like PAgP, LACP can be configured in active mode (active), in which a switch actively asks a far-end switch to negotiate an EtherChannel, or in passive mode (passive), in which a switch negotiates an EtherChannel only if the far end initiates it.

EtherChannel Configuration

For each EtherChannel on a switch, you must choose the EtherChannel negotiation protocol and assign individual switch ports to the EtherChannel. Both PAgP- and LACP-negotiated EtherChannels are described in the following sections. You also can configure an EtherChannel to use the on mode, which unconditionally bundles the links. In this case, neither PAgP nor LACP packets are sent or received.

As ports are configured to be members of an EtherChannel, the switch automatically creates a logical port-channel interface. This interface represents the channel as a whole.

Configuring a PAgP EtherChannel

To configure switch ports for PAgP negotiation (the default), use the following commands:

```
Switch(config)# interface type mod/num
Switch(config-if)# channel-protocol pagp
Switch(config-if)# channel-group number mode {on | {auto | desirable} [non-silent]}
```

On all Cisco IOS–based Catalyst models (2970, 3560, 4500, and 6500), you can select between PAgP and LACP as a channel-negotiation protocol. Older models such as the Catalyst 2950, however, offer only PAgP, so the **channel-protocol** command is not available. Each interface that will be included in a single EtherChannel bundle must be configured and assigned to the same unique channel group *number* (1 to 64). Channel negotiation must be set to on (unconditionally channel, no PAgP negotiation), auto (passively listen and wait to be asked), or desirable (actively ask).

> **TIP** IOS-based Catalyst switches do not assign interfaces to predetermined channel groups by default. In fact, the interfaces are not assigned to channel groups until you configure them manually.
>
> This is different from Catalyst OS (CatOS) switches, such as the Catalyst 4000 (Supervisors I and II), 5000, and 6500 (hybrid mode). On those platforms, Ethernet line cards are broken up into default channel groups.

By default, PAgP operates in silent submode with the desirable and auto modes, and allows ports to be added to an EtherChannel even if the other end of the link is silent and never transmits PAgP packets. This might seem to go against the idea of PAgP, in which two endpoints are supposed to negotiate a channel. After all, how can two switches negotiate anything if no PAgP packets are received?

The key is in the phrase "*if* the other end is silent." The silent submode listens for any PAgP packets from the far end, looking to negotiate a channel. If none is received, silent submode assumes that a channel should be built anyway, so no more PAgP packets are expected from the far end.

This allows a switch to form an EtherChannel with a device such as a file server or a network analyzer that doesn't participate in PAgP. In the case of a network analyzer connected to the far end, you also might want to see the PAgP packets generated by the switch, as if you were using a normal PAgP EtherChannel.

If you expect a PAgP-capable switch to be on the far end, you should add the **non-silent** keyword to the desirable or auto mode. This requires each port to receive PAgP packets before adding them to a channel. If PAgP isn't heard on an active port, the port remains in the up state, but PAgP reports to the Spanning Tree Protocol (STP) that the port is down.

> **TIP**   In practice, you might notice a delay from the time the links in a channel group are connected until the time the channel is formed and data can pass over it. You will encounter this if both switches are using the default PAgP auto mode and silent submode. Each interface waits to be asked to form a channel, and each interface waits and listens before accepting silent channel partners. The silent submode amounts to approximately a 15-second delay.
>
> Even if the two interfaces are using PAgP auto mode, the link will still eventually come up, although not as a channel. You might notice that the total delay before data can pass over the link is actually approximately 45 or 50 seconds. The first 15 seconds are the result of PAgP silent mode waiting to hear inbound PAgP messages, and the final 30 seconds are the result of the STP moving through the listening and learning stages.

As an example of PAgP configuration, suppose that you want a switch to use an EtherChannel load-balancing hash of both source and destination port numbers. A Gigabit EtherChannel will be built from interfaces GigabitEthernet 3/1 through 3/4, with the switch actively negotiating a channel. The switch should not wait to listen for silent partners. You can use the following configuration commands to accomplish this:

```
Switch(config)# port-channel load-balance src-dst-port
Switch(config)# interface range gig 3/1 - 4
Switch(config-if)# channel-protocol pagp
Switch(config-if)# channel-group 1 mode desirable non-silent
```

Configuring a LACP EtherChannel

To configure switch ports for LACP negotiation, use the following commands:

```
Switch(config)# lacp system-priority priority
Switch(config)# interface type mod/num
Switch(config-if)# channel-protocol lacp
Switch(config-if)# channel-group number mode {on | passive | active}
Switch(config-if)# lacp port-priority priority
```

First, the switch should have its LACP system priority defined (1 to 65,535; default 32,768). If desired, one switch should be assigned a lower system priority than the other so that it can make decisions about the EtherChannel's makeup. Otherwise, both switches will have the same system priority (32,768), and the one with the lower MAC address will become the decision maker.

Each interface included in a single EtherChannel bundle must be assigned to the same unique channel group *number* (1 to 64). Channel negotiation must be set to on (unconditionally channel, no LACP negotiation), passive (passively listen and wait to be asked), or active (actively ask).

You can configure more interfaces in the channel group *number* than are allowed to be active in the channel. This prepares extra standby interfaces to replace failed active ones. Use the **lacp port-priority** command to configure a lower port priority (1 to 65,535; default 32,768) for any interfaces that must be active, and a higher priority for interfaces that might be held in the standby state. Otherwise, just use the default scenario, in which all ports default to 32,768 and the lower port numbers (in interface number order) are used to select the active ports.

As an example of LACP configuration, suppose that you want to configure a switch to negotiate a Gigabit EtherChannel using interfaces GigabitEthernet 2/1 through 2/4 and 3/1 through 3/4. Interfaces GigabitEthernet 2/5 through 2/8 and 3/5 through 3/8 are also available, so these can be used as standby links to replace failed links in the channel. This switch actively should negotiate the channel and should be the decision maker about the channel operation.

You can use the following configuration commands to accomplish this:

```
Switch(config)# lacp system-priority 100
Switch(config)# interface range gig 2/1 - 4 , gig 3/1 - 4
Switch(config-if)# channel-protocol lacp
Switch(config-if)# channel-group 1 mode active
Switch(config-if)# lacp port-priority 100
Switch(config-if)# exit
Switch(config)# interface range gig 2/5 - 8 , gig 3/5 - 8
Switch(config-if)# channel-protocol lacp
Switch(config-if)# channel-group 1 mode active
```

Notice that interfaces GigabitEthernet 2/5-8 and 3/5-8 have been left to their default port priorities of 32,768. This is higher than the others, which were configured for 100, so they will be held as standby interfaces.

Troubleshooting an EtherChannel

If you find that an EtherChannel is having problems, remember that the whole concept is based on consistent configurations on *both* ends of the channel. Here are some reminders about EtherChannel operation and interaction:

- EtherChannel on mode does not send or receive PAgP or LACP packets. Therefore, both ends should be set to on mode before the channel can form.

■ EtherChannel desirable (PAgP) or active (LACP) mode attempts to ask the far end to bring up a channel. Therefore, the other end must be set to either desirable or auto mode.

■ EtherChannel auto (PAgP) or passive (LACP) mode participates in the channel protocol, but only if the far end asks for participation. Therefore, two switches in the auto or passive mode will not form an EtherChannel.

■ PAgP desirable and auto modes default to the silent submode, in which no PAgP packets are expected from the far end. If ports are set to nonsilent submode, PAgP packets must be received before a channel will form.

First, verify the EtherChannel state with the **show etherchannel summary** command. Each port in the channel is shown, along with flags indicating the port's state, as shown in Example 7-1.

Example 7-1 show etherchannel summary *Command Output*

```
Switch# show etherchannel summary
Flags:  D - down        P - in port-channel
        I - stand-alone s - suspended
        H - Hot-standby (LACP only)
        R - Layer3      S - Layer2
        u - unsuitable for bundling
        U - in use      f - failed to allocate aggregator
        d - default port
Number of channel-groups in use: 1
Number of aggregators:           1

Group  Port-channel  Protocol    Ports
------+-------------+-----------+-----------------------------------------------
1      Po1(SU)       PAgP        Fa0/41(P)  Fa0/42(P)  Fa0/43  Fa0/44(P)
                                 Fa0/45(P)  Fa0/46(P)  Fa0/47(P)  Fa0/48(P)
```

The status of the port-channel shows the EtherChannel logical interface as a whole. This should show SU (Layer 2 channel, in use) if the channel is operational. You also can examine the status of each port within the channel. Notice that most of the channel ports have flags (P), indicating that they are active in the port-channel. One port shows because it is physically not connected or down. If a port is connected but not bundled in the channel, it will have an independent, or (I), flag.

You can verify the channel negotiation mode with the **show etherchannel port** command, as shown in Example 7-2. The local switch is shown using desirable mode with PAgP (Desirable-Sl is desirable silent mode). Notice that you also can see the far end's negotiation mode under the Partner Flags heading, as A, or auto mode.

Example 7-2   **show etherchannel port** *Command Output*

```
Switch# show etherchannel port
                Channel-group listing:
                ......................

Group: 1
..........
                Ports in the group:
                ..+.................
Port: Fa0/41
...:.........

Port state    = Up Mstr In-Bndl
Channel group = 1            Mode = Desirable-Sl    Gcchange = 0
Port-channel  = Po1          GC   = 0x00010001            Pseudo port-channel = Po1
Port index    = 0            Load = 0x00          Protocol =   PAgP

Flags:  S - Device is sending Slow hello.  C - Device is in Consistent state.
        A - Device is in Auto mode.        P - Device learns on physical port.
        d - PAgP is down.
Timers: H - Hello timer is running.        Q - Quit timer is running.
        S - Switching timer is running.    I - Interface timer is running.

Local information:

                               Hello  Partner  PAgP      Learning  Group
Port       Flags State  Timers Interval Count  Priority  Method    Ifindex
Fa0/41     SC    U6/S7  H      30s      1      128       Any       55

Partner's information:

           Partner               Partner          Partner       Partner Group
Port       Name                  Device ID        Port     Age  Flags   Cap.
Fa0/41     FarEnd                00d0.5849.4100   3/1      19s  SAC     11

Age of the port in the current state: 00d:08h:05m:28s
```

Within a switch, an EtherChannel cannot form unless each of the component or member ports is configured consistently. Each must have the same switch mode (access or trunk), native VLAN, trunked VLANs, port speed, port duplex mode, and so on.

You can display a port's configuration by looking at the **show running-config interface** *type mod/num* output. Also, the **show interface** *type mod/num* **etherchannel** shows all active EtherChannel parameters for a single port. If you configure a port inconsistently with others for an EtherChannel, you see error messages from the switch.

Some messages from the switch might look like errors but are part of the normal EtherChannel process. For example, as a new port is configured as a member of an existing EtherChannel, you might see this message:

```
4d00h: %EC-5-L3DONTBNDL2: FastEthernet0/2 suspended: incompatible partner port with
    FastEthernet0/1
```

When the port first is added to the EtherChannel, it is incompatible because the STP runs on the channel and the new port. After STP takes the new port through its progression of states, the port is automatically added into the EtherChannel.

Other messages do indicate a port-compatibility error. In these cases, the cause of the error is shown. For example, the following message tells that FastEthernet0/3 has a different duplex mode than the other ports in the EtherChannel:

```
4d00h: %EC-5-CANNOT_BUNDLE2: FastEthernet0/3 is not compatible with FastEthernet0/1
    and will be suspended (duplex of Fa0/3 is full, Fa0/1 is half)
```

Finally, you can verify the EtherChannel load-balancing or hashing algorithm with the **show etherchannel load-balance** command. Remember that the switches on either end of an EtherChannel can have different load-balancing methods. The only drawback to this is that the load balancing will be asymmetric in the two directions across the channel.

Table 7-4 lists the commands useful for verifying or troubleshooting EtherChannel operation.

Table 7-4 *EtherChannel Troubleshooting Commands*

Display Function	Command Syntax
Current EtherChannel status of each member port	**show etherchannel summary** **show etherchannel port**
Time stamps of EtherChannel changes	**show etherchannel port-channel**
Detailed status about each EtherChannel component	**show etherchannel detail**
Load-balancing hashing algorithm	**show etherchannel load-balance**
Load-balancing port index used by hashing algorithm	**show etherchannel port-channel**
EtherChannel neighbors on each port	**show {pagp	lacp} neighbor**
LACP system ID	**show lacp sys-id**

Foundation Summary

The Foundation Summary is a collection of information that provides a convenient review of many key concepts in this chapter. If you are already comfortable with the topics in this chapter, this summary can help you recall a few details. If you just read this chapter, this review should help solidify some key facts. If you are doing your final preparation before the exam, this information is a convenient way to review the day before the exam.

Table 7-5 *Frame Distribution on an EtherChannel*

Channel size	A1: ... xxxxx000 A2: ... xxxxx000 (address bits the same)	A1: ... xxxxx000 A2: ... xxxxx111 (address bits differ)
2-port	Link index: 0 (0) (lowest)	Link index: 1 (1) (highest)
4-port	Link index: 00 (0) (lowest)	Link index: 11 (3) (highest)
8-port	Link index: 000 (0) (lowest)	Link index: 111 (7) (highest)

Sample address bits are shown. The XOR operation produces a 0 bit if the two input bits are the same (0,0 or 1,1) and a 1 bit if the two input bits are different (0,1 or 1,0).

Table 7-6 *EtherChannel Load-Balancing Methods*

method Value	Hash Input	Hash Operation	Switch Model
src-ip	Source IP address	bits	6500/4500/3750/3560/2970
dst-ip	Destination IP address	bits	6500/4500/3750/3560/2970
src-dst-ip	Source and destination IP address	XOR	6500/4500/3750/3560/2970
src-mac	Source MAC address	bits	6500/4500/3750/3560/2970
dst-mac	Destination MAC address	bits	6500/4500/3750/3560/2970
src-dst-mac	Source and destination MAC	XOR	6500/4500/3750/3560/2970
src-port	Source port number	bits	6500/4500
dst-port	Destination port number	bits	6500/4500
src-dst-port	Source and destination port	XOR	6500/4500

Table 7-7 *EtherChannel Negotiation Protocols*

Negotiation Mode		Negotiation Packets Sent?	Characteristics
PAgP	**LACP**		
on	on	No	All ports channeling
auto	passive	Yes	Waits to channel until asked
desirable	active	Yes	Actively asks to form a channel

Table 7-8 *EtherChannel Configuration Commands*

Task	Command Syntax
Select a load-balancing method for the switch	**port-channel load-balance** *method*
Use a PAgP mode on an interface	**channel-protocol pagp**
	channel-group *number* **mode** {**on** | {**auto** | **desirable**} [**non-silent**]}
Assign the LACP system priority	**lacp system-priority** *priority*
Use an LACP mode on an interface	**channel-protocol lacp**
	channel-group *number* **mode** {**on** | **passive** | **active**}
	lacp port-priority *priority*

Q&A

The questions in this book are more difficult than what you should experience on the actual exam. The questions do not attempt to cover more breadth or depth than the exam; however, they are designed to make sure that you know the answers. Rather than allowing you to derive the answers from clues hidden inside the questions themselves, the questions challenge your understanding and recall of the subject. Hopefully, these questions will help limit the number of exam questions on which you narrow your choices to two options and then guess.

The answers to these questions can be found in Appendix A.

1. What are some benefits of an EtherChannel?

2. How many links can be aggregated into an EtherChannel?

3. Traffic between two hosts will be distributed across all links in an EtherChannel. True or false?

4. Which methods can you use to distribute traffic in an EtherChannel?

5. How does an EtherChannel distribute broadcasts and multicasts?

6. When load balancing, what hashing functions choose a link for a frame?

7. What protocols can negotiate an EtherChannel between two switches?

8. Suppose that a switch at one end of an EtherChannel is configured to use source MAC addresses for load balancing. The switch on the other end is configured to use both source and destination IP addresses. What happens?

9. Two switches have a four-port EtherChannel between them. Both switches are load balancing using source and destination IP addresses. If a packet has the source address 192.168.15.10 and destination address 192.168.100.31, what is the EtherChannel link index?

10. What does the acronym PAgP stand for?

11. Two switches should be configured to negotiate an EtherChannel. If one switch is using PAgP auto mode, what should the other switch use?

12. What is the LACP system priority value used for?

13. Complete the following command to put an interface into EtherChannel group 3 and to use PAgP to ask the far-end switch to participate in the EtherChannel. This switch port also should require PAgP packets back from the far-end switch.

```
Switch(config-if)# channel-group _____
```

14. What interface configuration command is needed to select LACP as the EtherChannel negotiation protocol?

15. What command could you use to see the status of every port in an EtherChannel?

16. What command could you use to verify the hashing algorithm used for EtherChannel load balancing?

17. Suppose that a switch is used in a small data center where one server offers an IP-based application to many clients throughout the campus. An EtherChannel connects the data-center switch to a Layer 3 core switch, which routes traffic to all clients. What EtherChannel load-balancing method might be most appropriate at the data-center switch?

    a. Source MAC address

    b. Source IP address

    c. Destination MAC address

    d. Destination IP address

    e. Source and destination MAC address

    f. Source and destination IP address

18. Suppose that a mainframe is connected to a switch that has an EtherChannel uplink to a campus network. The EtherChannel has been configured with the **port-channel load-balance src-dst-ip** command. Most of the mainframe traffic is SNA (non-IP). What will happen to the SNA frames when they are switched? Would it be better to reconfigure the channel with **port-channel load-balance src-dst-mac**?

19. What attributes of a set of switch ports must match to form an EtherChannel?

20. What happens if one port of an EtherChannel is unplugged or goes dead? What happens when that port is reconnected?

This chapter covers the following topics that you need to master for the CCNP BCMSN exam:

- **IEEE 802.1D Overview**—This section discusses the original, or more traditional, Spanning Tree Protocol (STP). This protocol is the foundation for the default Catalyst STP and for all the enhancements that are described in Chapters 9, "Spanning Tree Configuration," through 11, "Advanced Spanning Tree Protocol."

- **Types of STP**—This section discusses other types of STP that might be running on a Catalyst switch—specifically, the Common Spanning Tree, Per-VLAN Spanning Tree (PVST), and PVST+.

CHAPTER 8

Traditional Spanning Tree Protocol

Previous chapters covered robust network designs where redundant links are used between switches. Although this increases the network availability, it also opens up the possibility for conditions that would impair the network. In a Layer 2 switched network, preventing bridging loops from forming over redundant paths is important. Spanning Tree Protocol (STP) was designed to monitor and control the Layer 2 network so that a loop-free topology is maintained.

This chapter discusses the theory and operation of the STP. More specifically, the original, or traditional, STP is covered, as defined in IEEE 802.1D. Several chapters explain STP topics in this book. Here is a brief roadmap so that you can chart a course:

- **Chapter 8, "Traditional Spanning Tree Protocol"**—Covers the theory of IEEE 802.1D

- **Chapter 9, "Spanning Tree Configuration"**—Covers the configuration commands needed for IEEE 802.1D

- **Chapter 10, "Protecting the Spanning Tree Protocol Topology"**—Covers the features and commands to filter and protect a converged STP topology from conditions that could destabilize it

- **Chapter 11, "Advanced Spanning Tree Protocol"**—Covers the newer 802.1w and 802.1s enhancements to STP, allowing more scalability and faster convergence

"Do I Know This Already?" Quiz

The purpose of the "Do I Know This Already?" quiz is to help you decide whether you need to read the entire chapter. If you already intend to read the entire chapter, you do not necessarily need to answer these questions now.

The 12-question quiz, derived from the major sections in the "Foundation Topics" portion of the chapter, helps you determine how to spend your limited study time.

Table 8-1 outlines the major topics discussed in this chapter and the "Do I Know This Already?" quiz questions that correspond to those topics.

Table 8-1   *"Do I Know This Already?" Foundation Topics Section-to-Question Mapping*

Foundation Topics Section	Questions Covered in This Section	Score
IEEE 802.1D	1–10	
Types of STP	11–12	
Total Score		

CAUTION   The goal of self-assessment is to gauge your mastery of the topics in this chapter. If you do not know the answer to a question or are only partially sure of the answer, you should mark this question wrong. Giving yourself credit for an answer you correctly guess skews your self-assessment results and might give you a false sense of security.

1. How is a bridging loop best described?

    a. A loop formed between switches for redundancy

    b. A loop formed by the Spanning Tree Protocol

    c. A loop formed between switches where frames circulate endlessly

    d. The round-trip path a frame takes from source to destination

2. Which of these is one of the parameters used to elect a Root Bridge?

    a. Root Path Cost

    b. Path Cost

    c. Bridge Priority

    d. BPDU revision number

3. If all switches in a network are left at their default STP values, which one of the following is not true?

    a. The Root Bridge will be the switch with the lowest MAC address.

    b. The Root Bridge will be the switch with the highest MAC address.

    c. One or more switches will have a Bridge Priority of 32,768.

    d. A secondary Root Bridge will be present on the network.

4. Configuration BPDUs are originated by which of the following?

    a. All switches in the STP domain

    b. Only the Root Bridge switch

    c. Only the switch that detects a topology change

    d. Only the secondary Root Bridge when it takes over

5. Which of these is the single most important design decision to be made in a network running STP?

    a. Removing any redundant links

    b. Making sure all switches run the same version of IEEE 802.1D

    c. Root Bridge placement

    d. Making sure all switches have redundant links

6. What happens to a port that is neither a Root Port nor a Designated Port?

    a. It is available for normal use.

    b. It can be used for load balancing.

    c. It is put into the Blocking state.

    d. It is disabled.

7. What is the maximum number of Root Ports that a Catalyst switch can have?

    a. 1

    b. 2

    c. Unlimited

    d. None

8. What mechanism is used to set STP timer values for all switches in a network?

    a. Configuring the timers on every switch in the network.

    b. Configuring the timers on the Root Bridge switch.

    c. Configuring the timers on both primary and secondary Root Bridge switches.

    d. The timers can't be adjusted.

9. MAC addresses can be placed into the CAM table, but no data can be sent or received if a switch port is in which of the following STP states?

    a. Blocking

    b. Forwarding

    c. Listening

    d. Learning

10. What is the default "hello" time for IEEE 802.1D?

    a. 1 second

    b. 2 seconds

    c. 30 seconds

    d. 60 seconds

11. Which of the following is the Spanning Tree Protocol defined in the IEEE 802.1Q standard?

    a. PVST

    b. CST

    c. EST

    d. MST

12. If a switch has 10 VLANs defined and active, how many instances of STP will run using PVST+ versus CST?

    a. 1 for PVST+, 1 for CST

    b. 1 for PVST+, 10 for CST

    c. 10 for PVST+, 1 for CST

    d. 10 for PVST+, 10 for CST

You can find the answers to the quiz in Appendix A, "Answers to Chapter 'Do I Know This Already?' Quizzes and Q&A Sections." The suggested choices for your next step are as follows:

■   **7 or less overall score**—Read the entire chapter. This includes the "Foundation Topics," "Foundation Summary," and "Q&A" sections.

■   **8–10 overall score**—Begin with the "Foundation Summary" section and then follow up with the "Q&A" section at the end of the chapter.

■   **11 or more overall score**—If you want more review on these topics, skip to the "Foundation Summary" section and then go to the "Q&A" section at the end of the chapter. Otherwise, move to Chapter 9.

Foundation Topics

IEEE 802.1D Overview

A robust network design not only includes efficient transfer of packets or frames, but also considers how to recover quickly from faults in the network. In a Layer 3 environment, the routing protocols in use keep track of redundant paths to a destination network so that a secondary path can be used quickly if the primary path fails. Layer 3 routing allows many paths to a destination to remain up and active, and allows load sharing across multiple paths.

In a Layer 2 environment (switching or bridging), however, no routing protocols are used, and active redundant paths are neither allowed nor desirable. Instead, some form of bridging provides data transport between networks or switch ports. The Spanning Tree Protocol (STP) provides network link redundancy so that a Layer 2 switched network can recover from failures without intervention in a timely manner. The STP is defined in the IEEE 802.1D standard.

STP is discussed in relation to the problems it solves in the sections that follow.

Bridging Loops

Recall that a Layer 2 switch mimics the function of a transparent bridge. A transparent bridge must offer segmentation between two networks while remaining transparent to all the end devices connected to it. For the purpose of this discussion, consider a two-port Ethernet switch and its similarities to a two-port transparent bridge.

A transparent bridge (and the Ethernet switch) must operate as follows:

- The bridge has no initial knowledge of any end device's location; therefore, the bridge must "listen" to frames coming into each of its ports to figure out on which network each device resides. The bridge assumes that a device using the source MAC address is located behind the port that the frame arrives on. As the listening process continues, the bridge builds a table that correlates source MAC addresses with the Bridge Port numbers where they were detected.

  The bridge can constantly update its bridging table on detecting the presence of a new MAC address or on detecting a MAC address that has changed location from one Bridge Port to another. The bridge then can forward frames by looking at the destination MAC address, looking up that address in the bridge table, and sending the frame out the port where the destination device is known to be located.

■ If a frame arrives with the broadcast address as the destination address, the bridge must forward, or flood, the frame out all available ports. However, the frame is not forwarded out the port that initially received the frame. In this way, broadcasts can reach all available Layer 2 networks. A bridge segments only collision domains—it does not segment broadcast domains.

■ If a frame arrives with a destination address that is not found in the bridge table, the bridge cannot determine which port to forward the frame to for transmission. This type of frame is known as an *unknown unicast*. In this case, the bridge treats the frame as if it were a broadcast and floods it out all remaining ports. When a reply to that frame is overheard, the bridge can learn the location of the unknown station and can add it to the bridge table for future use.

■ Frames forwarded across the bridge cannot be modified by the bridge itself. Therefore, the bridging process is effectively *transparent*.

Bridging or switching in this fashion works well. Any frame forwarded, whether to a known or unknown destination, is forwarded out the appropriate port or ports so that it is likely to be received successfully at the end device. Figure 8-1 shows a simple two-port switch functioning as a bridge, forwarding frames between two end devices. However, this network design offers no additional links or paths for redundancy if the switch or one of its links fails. In that case, the networks on either side of the bridge would become isolated from each other.

Figure 8-1 *Transparent Bridging with a Switch*

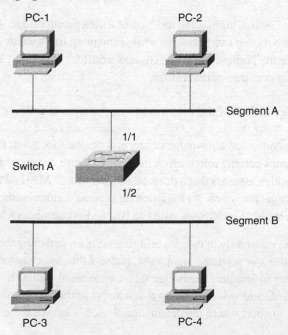

To add some redundancy, you can add a second switch between the two original network segments, as shown in Figure 8-2. Now, two switches offer the transparent bridging function in parallel. In theory, a single switch or a single link can fail without causing end-to-end connectivity to fail.

Figure 8-2   *Redundant Bridging with Two Switches*

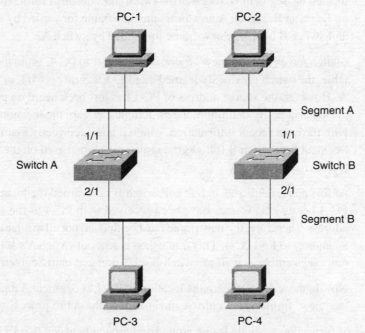

Consider what happens when PC-1 sends a frame to PC-4. For now, assume that both PC-1 and PC-4 are known to the switches and are in their address tables. PC-1 sends the frame onto network Segment A. Switch A and switch B both receive the frame on their 1/1 ports. Because PC-4 already is known to the switches, the frame is forwarded out ports 2/1 on each switch onto Segment B. The end result is that PC-4 receives two copies of the frame from PC-1. This is not ideal, but it is not disastrous, either.

Now, consider the same process of sending a frame from PC-1 to PC-4. This time, however, neither switch knows anything about the location of PC-1 or PC-4. PC-1 sends the frame to PC-4 by placing it on Segment A. The sequence of events is as follows:

Step 1   Both switch A and switch B receive the frame on their 1/1 ports. Because the MAC address of PC-1 has not yet been seen or recorded, each switch records PC-1's MAC address in its address table along with the receiving port number, 1/1. From this information, both switches infer that PC-1 must reside on Segment A.

Step 2   Because the location of PC-4 is unknown, both switches correctly decide that they must flood the frame out all available ports. This is an unknown unicast condition and is their best effort to make sure that the frame eventually reaches its destination.

Step 3   Each switch floods or copies the frame to its 2/1 port on Segment B. PC-4, located on Segment B, receives the two frames destined for it. However, on Segment B, switch A now hears the new frame forwarded by switch B, and switch B hears the new frame forwarded by switch A.

Step 4   Switch A sees that the "new" frame is from PC-1 to PC-4. From the address table, the switch previously learned that PC-1 was on port 1/1, or Segment A. However, the source address of PC-1 has just been heard on port 2/1, or Segment B. By definition, the switch must relearn the location of PC-1 with the most recent information, which it now incorrectly assumes to be Segment B. (Switch B follows the same procedure, based on the "new" frame from switch A.)

Step 5   At this point, neither switch A nor switch B has learned the location of PC-4 because no frames have been received with PC-4 as the source address. Therefore, the new frame must be flooded out all available ports in an attempt to find PC-4. This frame then is sent out switch A's 1/1 port and onto Segment A, as well as switch B's 1/1 port and onto Segment A.

Step 6   Now both switches relearn the location of PC-1 as Segment A and forward the "new" frames back onto Segment B; then the entire process repeats.

This process of forwarding a single frame around and around between two switches is known as a *bridging loop*. Neither switch is aware of the other, so each happily forwards the same frame back and forth between its segments. Also note that because two switches are involved in the loop, the original frame has been duplicated and now is sent around in two counter-rotating loops. What stops the frame from being forwarded in this fashion forever? Nothing! PC-4 begins receiving frames addressed to it as fast as the switches can forward them.

Notice how the learned location of PC-1 keeps changing as frames get looped. Even a simple unicast frame has caused a bridging loop to form, and each switch's bridge table is repeatedly corrupted with incorrect data.

What would happen if PC-1 sent a broadcast frame instead? The bridging loops (remember that two of them are produced by the two parallel switches) form exactly as before. The broadcast frames continue to circulate forever. Now, however, every end-user device located on both Segments A and B receives and processes every broadcast frame. This type of broadcast storm can easily saturate the network segments and bring every host on the segments to a halt.

The only way to end the bridging loop condition is to physically break the loop by disconnecting switch ports or shutting down a switch. Obviously, it would be better to *prevent* bridging loops than to be faced with finding and breaking them after they form.

Preventing Loops with Spanning Tree Protocol

Bridging loops form because parallel switches (or bridges) are unaware of each other. STP was developed to overcome the possibility of bridging loops so that redundant switches and switch paths could be used for their benefits. Basically, the protocol enables switches to become aware of each other so they can negotiate a loop-free path through the network.

> **NOTE**   Because STP is involved in loop detection, many people refer to the catastrophic loops as "Spanning Tree loops." This is technically incorrect because the Spanning Tree Protocol's entire function is to *prevent* bridging loops. The correct terminology for this condition is a *bridging loop*.

Loops are discovered before they are made available for use, and redundant links are effectively shut down to prevent the loops from forming. In the case of redundant links, switches can be made aware that a link shut down for loop prevention should be brought up quickly in case of a link failure. The section "Redundant Link Convergence," in Chapter 9, provides more information.

STP is communicated among all connected switches on a network. Each switch executes the Spanning Tree algorithm based on information received from other neighboring switches. The algorithm chooses a reference point in the network and calculates all the redundant paths to that reference point. When redundant paths are found, the Spanning Tree algorithm picks one path by which to forward frames and disables, or blocks, forwarding on the other redundant paths.

As its name implies, STP computes a tree structure that spans all switches in a subnet or network. Redundant paths are placed in a Blocking or Standby state to prevent frame forwarding. The switched network is then in a loop-free condition. However, if a forwarding port fails or becomes disconnected, the Spanning Tree algorithm recomputes the spanning-tree topology so that the appropriate blocked links can be reactivated.

Spanning-Tree Communication: Bridge Protocol Data Units

STP operates as switches communicate with one another. Data messages are exchanged in the form of *Bridge Protocol Data Units (BPDU)*. A switch sends a BPDU frame out a port, using the unique MAC address of the port itself as a source address. The switch is unaware of the other switches around it, so BPDU frames are sent with a destination address of the well-known STP multicast address 01-80-c2-00-00-00.

Two types of BPDU exist:

- *Configuration BPDU*, used for spanning-tree computation

- *Topology Change Notification (TCN) BPDU*, used to announce changes in the network topology

The Configuration BPDU message contains the fields shown in Table 8-2. The TCN BPDU is discussed in the "Topology Changes" section later in this chapter.

Table 8-2 *Configuration BPDU Message Content*

Field Description	Number of Bytes
Protocol ID (always 0)	2
Version (always 0)	1
Message Type (Configuration or TCN BPDU)	1
Flags	1
Root Bridge ID	8
Root Path Cost	4
Sender Bridge ID	8
Port ID	2
Message Age (in 256ths of a second)	2
Maximum Age (in 256ths of a second)	2
Hello Time (in 256ths of a second)	2
Forward Delay (in 256ths of a second)	2

The exchange of BPDU messages works toward the goal of electing reference points as a foundation for a stable spanning-tree topology. Loops also can be identified and removed by placing specific redundant ports in a Blocking or Standby state. Notice that several key fields in the BPDU are related to bridge (or switch) identification, path costs, and timer values. These all work together so that the network of switches can converge on a common spanning-tree topology and select the same reference points within the network. These reference points are defined in the sections that follow.

By default, BPDUs are sent out all switch ports every 2 seconds so that current topology information is exchanged and loops are identified quickly.

Electing a Root Bridge

For all switches in a network to agree on a loop-free topology, a common frame of reference must exist to use as a guide. This reference point is called the *Root Bridge*. (The term *bridge* continues to be used even in a switched environment because STP was developed for use in bridges. Therefore, when you see *bridge*, think *switch*.)

An election process among all connected switches chooses the Root Bridge. Each switch has a unique *Bridge ID* that identifies it to other switches. The Bridge ID is an 8-byte value consisting of the following fields:

- **Bridge Priority (2 bytes)**—The priority or weight of a switch in relation to all other switches. The priority field can have a value of 0 to 65,535 and defaults to 32,768 (or 0x8000) on every Catalyst switch.

- **MAC Address (6 bytes)**—The MAC address used by a switch can come from the Supervisor module, the backplane, or a pool of 1,024 addresses that are assigned to every Supervisor or backplane, depending on the switch model. In any event, this address is hardcoded and unique, and the user cannot change it.

When a switch first powers up, it has a narrow view of its surroundings and assumes that it is the Root Bridge itself. (This notion probably will change as other switches check in and enter the election process.) The election process then proceeds as follows: Every switch begins by sending out BPDUs with a Root Bridge ID equal to its own Bridge ID and a Sender Bridge ID that is its own Bridge ID. The Sender Bridge ID simply tells other switches who is the actual sender of the BPDU message. (After a Root Bridge is decided on, configuration BPDUs are sent only by the Root Bridge. All other bridges must forward or relay the BPDUs, adding their own Sender Bridge IDs to the message.)

Received BPDU messages are analyzed to see if a "better" Root Bridge is being announced. A Root Bridge is considered better if the Root Bridge ID value is *lower* than another. Again, think of the Root Bridge ID as being broken into Bridge Priority and MAC address fields. If two Bridge Priority values are equal, the lower MAC address makes the Bridge ID better. When a switch hears of a better Root Bridge, it replaces its own Root Bridge ID with the Root Bridge ID announced in the BPDU. The switch then is required to recommend or advertise the new Root Bridge ID in its own BPDU messages, although it still identifies itself as the Sender Bridge ID.

Sooner or later, the election converges and all switches agree on the notion that one of them is the Root Bridge. As might be expected, if a new switch with a lower Bridge Priority powers up, it begins advertising itself as the Root Bridge. Because the new switch does indeed have a lower Bridge ID, all the switches soon reconsider and record it as the new Root Bridge. This also can happen if the new switch has a Bridge Priority equal to that of the existing Root Bridge but has a lower MAC address. Root Bridge election is an ongoing process, triggered by Root Bridge ID changes in the BPDUs every 2 seconds.

As an example, consider the small network shown in Figure 8-3. For simplicity, assume that each Catalyst switch has a MAC address of all 0s, with the last hex digit equal to the switch label.

Figure 8-3 *Example of Root Bridge Election*

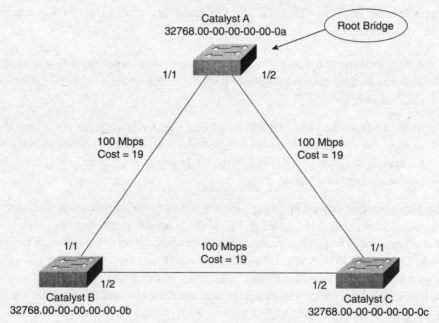

In this network, each switch has the default Bridge Priority of 32,768. The switches are interconnected with Fast Ethernet links. All three switches try to elect themselves as the Root, but all of them have equal Bridge Priority values. The election outcome produces the Root Bridge, determined by the lowest MAC address—that of Catalyst A.

Electing Root Ports

Now that a reference point has been nominated and elected for the entire switched network, each nonroot switch must figure out where it is in relation to the Root Bridge. This action can be performed by selecting only one *Root Port* on each nonroot switch. The Root Port always points toward the current Root Bridge.

STP uses the concept of cost to determine many things. Selecting a Root Port involves evaluating the *Root Path Cost*. This value is the cumulative cost of all the links leading to the Root Bridge. A particular switch link also has a cost associated with it, called the *Path Cost*. To understand the difference between these values, remember that only the Root Path Cost is carried inside the

BPDU. (Refer to Table 8-2.) As the Root Path Cost travels along, other switches can modify its value to make it cumulative. The Path Cost, however, is not contained in the BPDU. It is known only to the local switch where the port (or "path" to a neighboring switch) resides.

Path Costs are defined as a 1-byte value, with the default values shown in Table 8-3. Generally, the higher the bandwidth of a link, the lower the cost of transporting data across it. The original IEEE 802.1D standard defined Path Cost as 1000 Mbps divided by the link bandwidth in megabits per second. These values are shown in the center column of the table. Modern networks commonly use Gigabit Ethernet and OC-48 ATM, which are both either too close to or greater than the maximum scale of 1000 Mbps. The IEEE now uses a nonlinear scale for Path Cost, as shown in the right column of the table.

TIP   Be aware that there are two STP path cost scales, one that is little used with a linear scale and one commonly used that is nonlinear. If you decide to memorize some common Path Cost values, learn only the ones in the New STP Cost column of the table.

Table 8-3   *STP Path Cost*

Link Bandwidth	Old STP Cost	New STP Cost
4 Mbps	250	250
10 Mbps	100	100
16 Mbps	63	62
45 Mbps	22	39
100 Mbps	10	19
155 Mbps	6	14
622 Mbps	2	6
1 Gbps	1	4
10 Gbps	0	2

The Root Path Cost value is determined in the following manner:

1. The Root Bridge sends out a BPDU with a Root Path Cost value of 0 because its ports sit directly on the Root Bridge.

2. When the next-closest neighbor receives the BPDU, it adds the Path Cost of its own port where the BPDU arrived. (This is done as the BPDU is *received*.)

3. The neighbor sends out BPDUs with this new cumulative value as the Root Path Cost.

4. The Root Path Cost is incremented by the ingress port Path Cost as the BPDU is received at each switch down the line.

5. Notice the emphasis on incrementing the Root Path Cost as BPDUs are *received*. When computing the Spanning Tree algorithm manually, remember to compute a new Root Path Cost as BPDUs *come in* to a switch port, not as they go out.

After incrementing the Root Path Cost, a switch also records the value in its memory. When a BPDU is received on another port and the new Root Path Cost is lower than the previously recorded value, this lower value becomes the new Root Path Cost. In addition, the lower cost tells the switch that the path to the Root Bridge must be better using this port than it was on other ports. The switch has now determined which of its ports has the best path to the Root: the Root Port.

Figure 8-4 shows the same network from Figure 8-3 in the process of Root Port selection.

Figure 8-4 *Example of Root Port Selection*

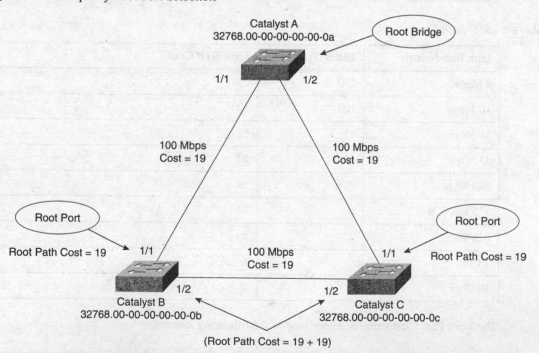

The Root Bridge, Catalyst A, already has been elected. Therefore, every other switch in the network must choose one port that has the best path to the Root Bridge. Catalyst B selects its port 1/1, with a Root Path Cost of 0 plus 19. Port 1/2 is not chosen because its Root Path Cost is 0 (BPDU from Catalyst A) plus 19 (Path Cost of A–C link), plus 19 (Path Cost of C–B link), or a total of 38. Catalyst C makes an identical choice of port 1/1.

Electing Designated Ports

By now, you should begin to see the process unfolding: A starting or reference point has been identified, and each switch "connects" itself toward the reference point with the single link that has the best path. A tree structure is beginning to emerge, but links have only been identified at this point. All links still are connected and could be active, leaving bridging loops.

To remove the possibility of bridging loops, STP makes a final computation to identify one *Designated Port* on each network segment. Suppose that two or more switches have ports connected to a single common network segment. If a frame appears on that segment, all the bridges attempt to forward it to its destination. Recall that this behavior was the basis of a bridging loop and should be avoided.

Instead, only one of the links on a segment should forward traffic to and from that segment—the one that is selected as the Designated Port. Switches choose a Designated Port based on the lowest cumulative Root Path Cost to the Root Bridge. For example, a switch always has an idea of its own Root Path Cost, which it announces in its own BPDUs. If a neighboring switch on a shared LAN segment sends a BPDU announcing a lower Root Path Cost, the neighbor must have the Designated Port. If a switch learns only of higher Root Path Costs from other BPDUs received on a port, however, it then correctly assumes that its own receiving port is the Designated Port for the segment.

Notice that the entire STP determination process has served only to identify bridges and ports. All ports are still active, and bridging loops still might lurk in the network. STP has a set of progressive states that each port must go through, regardless of the type or identification. These states actively prevent loops from forming and are described in the next section.

> **NOTE**   In each determination process discussed so far, two or more links might have identical Root Path Costs. This results in a tie condition, unless other factors are considered. All tie-breaking STP decisions are based on the following sequence of four conditions:
>
> **1.** Lowest Root Bridge ID
>
> **2.** Lowest Root Path Cost to Root Bridge
>
> **3.** Lowest Sender Bridge ID
>
> **4.** Lowest Sender Port ID

Figure 8-5 demonstrates an example of Designated Port selection. This figure is identical to Figure 8-3 and Figure 8-4, with further spanning-tree development shown. The only changes are the choices of Designated Ports, although seeing all STP decisions shown on one network diagram is handy.

Figure 8-5 *Example of Designated Port Selection*

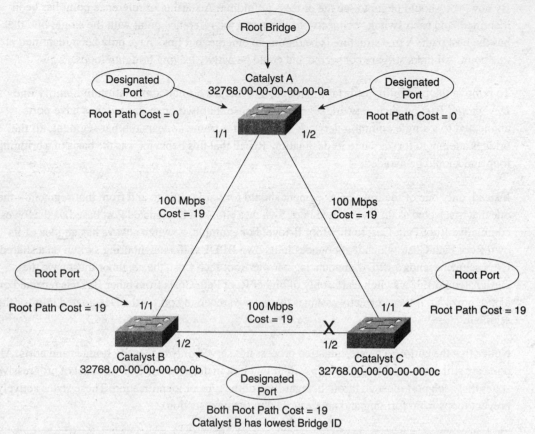

The three switches have chosen their Designated Ports (DP) for the following reasons:

- **Catalyst A**—Because this switch is the Root Bridge, all its active ports are Designated Ports, by definition. At the Root Bridge, the Root Path Cost of each port is 0.

- **Catalyst B**—Catalyst A port 1/1 is the DP for the Segment A–B because it has the lowest Root Path Cost (0). Catalyst B port 1/2 is the DP for segment B–C. The Root Path Cost for each end of this segment is 19, determined from the incoming BPDU on port 1/1. Because the Root Path Cost is equal on both ports of the segment, the DP must be chosen by the next criteria—the lowest Sender Bridge ID. When Catalyst B sends a BPDU to Catalyst C, it has the lowest MAC address in the Bridge ID. Catalyst C also sends a BPDU to Catalyst B, but its Sender Bridge ID is higher. Therefore, Catalyst B port 1/2 is selected as the segment's DP.

- **Catalyst C**—Catalyst A port 1/2 is the DP for Segment A–C because it has the lowest Root Path Cost (0). Catalyst B port 1/2 is the DP for Segment B–C. Therefore, Catalyst C port 1/2 will be neither a Root Port nor a Designated Port. As discussed in the next section, any port that is not elected to either position enters the Blocking state. Where blocking occurs, bridging loops are broken.

STP States

To participate in STP, each port of a switch must progress through several states. A port begins its life in a Disabled state, moving through several passive states and, finally, into an active state if allowed to forward traffic. The STP port states are as follows:

- **Disabled**—Ports that are administratively shut down by the network administrator, or by the system because of a fault condition, are in the Disabled state. This state is special and is not part of the normal STP progression for a port.

- **Blocking**—After a port initializes, it begins in the Blocking state so that no bridging loops can form. In the Blocking state, a port cannot receive or transmit data and cannot add MAC addresses to its address table. Instead, a port is allowed to receive only BPDUs so that the switch can hear from other neighboring switches. In addition, ports that are put into standby mode to remove a bridging loop enter the Blocking state.

- **Listening**—A port is moved from Blocking to Listening if the switch thinks that the port can be selected as a Root Port or Designated Port. In other words, the port is on its way to begin forwarding traffic.

  In the Listening state, the port still cannot send or receive data frames. However, the port is allowed to receive and send BPDUs so that it can actively participate in the Spanning Tree topology process. Here, the port finally is allowed to become a Root Port or Designated Port because the switch can advertise the port by sending BPDUs to other switches. If the port loses its Root Port or Designated Port status, it returns to the Blocking state.

- **Learning**—After a period of time called the *Forward Delay* in the Listening state, the port is allowed to move into the Learning state. The port still sends and receives BPDUs as before. In addition, the switch now can learn new MAC addresses to add to its address table. This gives the port an extra period of silent participation and allows the switch to assemble at least some address table information. The port cannot yet send any data frames, however.

- **Forwarding**—After another Forward Delay period of time in the Learning state, the port is allowed to move into the Forwarding state. The port now can send and receive data frames, collect MAC addresses in its address table, and send and receive BPDUs. The port is now a fully functioning switch port within the spanning-tree topology.

Remember that a switch port is allowed into the Forwarding state only if no redundant links (or loops) are detected and if the port has the best path to the Root Bridge as the Root Port or Designated Port.

Example 8-1 shows the output from a switch as one of its ports progresses through the STP port states.

Example 8-1 *Port Progressing Through the STP Port States*

```
*Mar 16 14:31:00 UTC: STP SW: Fa0/1 new disabled req for 1 vlans
Switch(config)# interface fastethernet 0/1
Switch(config-if)#no shutdown
Switch(config-if)#^-Z
*Mar 16 14:31:00 UTC: STP SW: Fa0/1 new blocking req for 1 vlans

Switch#show spanning interface fastethernet 0/1

Vlan            Port ID                    Designated                Port ID
Name            Prio.Nbr    Cost Sts       Cost Bridge ID            Prio.Nbr
--------------- --------  ---------  ---  --------  --------------------  --------
VLAN0001        128.1          19 LIS         0 32769 000a.f40a.2980 128.1

*Mar 16 14:31:15 UTC: STP SW: Fa0/1 new learning req for 1 vlans

Switch#show spanning interface fastethernet 0/1
Vlan            Port ID                    Designated                Port ID
Name            Prio.Nbr    Cost Sts       Cost Bridge ID            Prio.Nbr
--------------- --------  ---------  ---  --------  --------------------  --------
VLAN0001        128.1          19 LRN         0 32768 00d0.5849.4100 32.129

*Mar 16 14:31:30 UTC: STP SW: Fa0/1 new forwarding req for 1 vlans

Switch#show spanning interface fastethernet 0/1

Vlan            Port ID                    Designated                Port ID
Name            Prio.Nbr    Cost Sts       Cost Bridge ID            Prio.Nbr
--------------- --------  ---------  ---  --------  --------------------  --------
VLAN0001        128.1          19 FWD         0 32768 00d0.5849.4100 32.129
```

The example begins as the port is administratively disabled from the command line. When the port is enabled, successive **show spanning-tree interface** *type mod/port* commands display the port state as Listening, Learning, and then Forwarding. These are shown in the shaded text of the example. Notice also the time stamps and port states provided by the **debug spanning-tree switch state** command, which give a sense of the timing between port states. Because this port was eligible as a Root Port, the **show** command never could execute fast enough to show the port in the Blocking state.

STP Timers

STP operates as switches send BPDUs to each other in an effort to form a loop-free topology. The BPDUs take a finite amount of time to travel from switch to switch. In addition, news of a topology change (such as a link or Root Bridge failure) can suffer from propagation delays as the announcement travels from one side of a network to the other. Because of the possibility of these delays, keeping the spanning-tree topology from settling out or converging until all switches have had time to receive accurate information is important.

STP uses three timers to make sure that a network converges properly before a bridging loop can form. The timers and their default values are as follows:

- **Hello Time**—The time interval between Configuration BPDUs sent by the Root Bridge. The Hello Time value configured in the Root Bridge switch determines the Hello Time for all nonroot switches because they just relay the Configuration BPDUs as they are received from the root. However, all switches have a locally configured Hello Time that is used to time TCN BPDUs when they are retransmitted. The IEEE 802.1D standard specifies a default Hello Time value of 2 seconds.

- **Forward Delay**—The time interval that a switch port spends in both the Listening and Learning states. The default value is 15 seconds.

- **Max (maximum) Age**—The time interval that a switch stores a BPDU before discarding it. While executing the STP, each switch port keeps a copy of the "best" BPDU that it has heard. If the switch port loses contact with the BPDU's source (no more BPDUs are received from it), the switch assumes that a topology change must have occurred after the Max Age time elapsed and so the BPDU is aged out. The default Max Age value is 20 seconds.

The STP timers can be configured or adjusted from the switch command line. However, the timer values never should be changed from the defaults without careful consideration. Then the values should be changed only on the Root Bridge switch. Recall that the timer values are advertised in fields within the BPDU. The Root Bridge ensures that the timer values propagate to all other switches.

> **TIP** The default STP timer values are based on some assumptions about the size of the network and the length of the Hello Time. A reference model of a network having a diameter of seven switches derives these values. The diameter is measured from the Root Bridge switch outward, including the Root Bridge.
>
> In other words, if you drew the STP topology, the diameter would be the number of switches connected in series from the Root Bridge out to the end of any branch in the tree. The Hello Time is based on the time it takes for a BPDU to travel from the Root Bridge to a point seven switches away. This computation uses a Hello Time of 2 seconds.

The network diameter can be configured on the Root Bridge switch to more accurately reflect the true size of the physical network. Making that value more accurate reduces the total STP convergence time during a topology change. Cisco also recommends that if changes need to be made, only the network diameter value should be modified on the Root Bridge switch. When the diameter is changed, the switch calculates new values for all three timers automatically.

Topology Changes

To announce a change in the active network topology, switches send a TCN BPDU. Table 8-4 shows the format of these messages.

Table 8-4 *Topology Change Notification BPDU Message Content*

Field Description	# of Bytes
Protocol ID (always 0)	2
Version (always 0)	1
Message Type (Configuration or TCN BPDU)	1

A topology change occurs when a switch either moves a port into the Forwarding state or moves a port from the Forwarding or Learning states into the Blocking state. In other words, a port on an active switch comes up or goes down. The switch sends a TCN BPDU out its Root Port so that, ultimately, the Root Bridge receives news of the topology change. Notice that the TCN BPDU carries no data about the change but informs recipients only that a change has occurred. Also notice that the switch will not send TCN BPDUs if the port has been configured with PortFast enabled.

The switch continues sending TCN BPDUs every Hello Time interval until it gets an acknowledgment from its upstream neighbor. As the upstream neighbors receive the TCN BPDU, they propagate it on toward the Root Bridge and send their own acknowledgments. When the Root Bridge receives the TCN BPDU, it also sends out an acknowledgment. However, the Root Bridge sets the Topology Change flag in its Configuration BPDU, which is relayed to every other bridge in the network. This is done to signal the topology change and cause all other bridges to shorten their bridge table aging times from the default (300 seconds) to the Forward Delay value (default 15 seconds).

This condition causes the learned locations of MAC addresses to be flushed out much sooner than they normally would, easing the bridge table corruption that might occur because of the change in topology. However, any stations that are actively communicating during this time are kept in the bridge table. This condition lasts for the sum of the Forward Delay and the Max Age (default 15 + 20 seconds).

The theory behind topology changes is fairly straightforward, but it's often difficult to grasp how a working network behaves during a change. For example, suppose that you have a Layer 2 network (think of a single VLAN or a single instance of STP) that is stable and loop free. If a switch uplink suddenly failed or a new uplink was added, how would the various switches in the network react? Would users all over the network lose connectivity while the STP "recomputes" or reconverges?

Examples of different types of topology changes are presented in the following sections, along with the sequence of STP events. Each type has a different cause and a different effect. To provide continuity as the STP concepts are presented, the same network previously shown in Figures 8-3 through 8-5 is used in each of these examples.

Direct Topology Changes

A direct topology change is one that can be detected on a switch interface. For example, if a trunk link suddenly goes down, the switch on each end of the link can immediately detect a link failure. The absence of that link changes the bridging topology, so other switches should be notified.

Figure 8-6 shows a network that has converged into a stable STP topology. The VLAN is forwarding on all trunk links except port 1/2 on Catalyst C, where it is in the Blocking state.

Figure 8-6 *Effects of a Direct Topology Change*

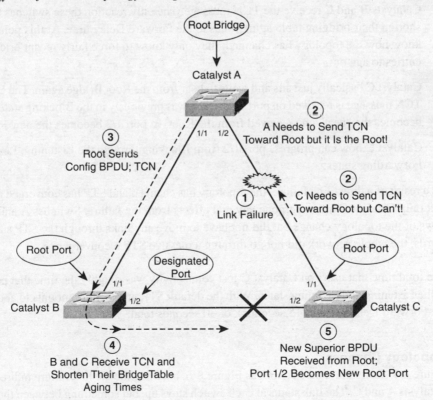

This network has just suffered a link failure between Catalyst A and Catalyst C. The sequence of events unfolds as follows:

1. Catalyst C detects a link down on its port 1/1; Catalyst A detects a link down on its port 1/2.

2. Catalyst C removes the previous "best" BPDU it had received from the Root over port 1/1. Port 1/1 is now down so that BPDU is no longer valid.

   Normally, Catalyst C would try to send a TCN message out its Root Port, to reach the Root Bridge. Here, the Root Port is broken, so that isn't possible. Without an advanced feature such as STP UplinkFast, Catalyst C isn't yet aware that another path exists to the Root.

   Also, Catalyst A is aware of the link down condition on its own port 1/2. It normally would try to send a TCN message out its Root Port to reach the Root Bridge. Here, Catalyst A *is* the Root, so that isn't really necessary.

3. The Root Bridge, Catalyst A, sends a Configuration BPDU with the TCN bit set out its port 1/1. This is received and relayed by each switch along the way, informing each one of the topology change.

4. Catalysts B and C receive the TCN message. The only reaction these switches take is to shorten their bridging table aging times to the Forward Delay time. At this point, they don't know how the topology has changed; they only know to force fairly recent bridging table entries to age out.

5. Catalyst C basically just sits and waits to hear from the Root Bridge again. The Config BPDU TCN message is received on port 1/2, which was previously in the Blocking state. This BPDU becomes the "best" one received from the Root, so port 1/2 becomes the new Root Port.

   Catalyst C now can progress port 1/2 from Blocking through the Listening, Learning, and Forwarding states.

As a result of a direct link failure, the topology has changed and STP has converged again. Notice that only Catalyst C has undergone any real effects from the failure. Switches A and B heard the news of the topology change but did not have to move any links through the STP states. In other words, the whole network did not go through a massive STP reconvergence.

The total time that users on Catalyst C lost connectivity was roughly the time that port 1/2 spent in the Listening and Learning states. With the default STP timers, this amounts to about two times the Forward Delay period (15 seconds), or 30 seconds total.

Indirect Topology Changes

Figure 8-7 shows the same network as Figure 8-6, but this time the link failure indirectly involves Catalysts A and C. The link status at each switch stays up, but something between them has failed or is filtering traffic. This could be another device, such as a service provider's switch, a firewall, and so on. As a result, no data (including BPDUs) can pass between those switches.

Figure 8-7 *Effects of a Indirect Topology Change*

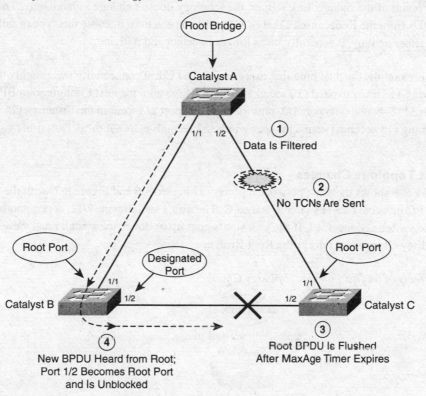

STP can detect and recover from indirect failures, thanks to timer mechanisms. The sequence of events unfolds as follows:

1. Catalysts A and C both show a link up condition; data begins to be filtered elsewhere on the link.

2. No link failure is detected, so no TCN messages are sent.

3. Catalyst C already has stored the "best" BPDU it had received from the Root over port 1/1. No further BPDUs are received from the Root over that port. After the MaxAge timer expires, no other BPDU is available to refresh the "best" entry, so it is flushed. Catalyst C now must wait to hear from the Root again on any of its ports.

4. The next Configuration BPDU from the Root is heard on Catalyst C port 1/2. This BPDU becomes the new "best" entry, and port 1/2 becomes the Root Port. Now the port is progressed from Blocking through the Listening, Learning, and finally Forwarding states.

As a result of the indirect link failure, the topology doesn't change immediately. The absence of BPDUs from the Root causes Catalyst C to take some action. Because this type of failure relies on STP timer activity, it generally takes longer to detect and mitigate.

In this example, the total time that users on Catalyst C lost connectivity was roughly the time until the MaxAge timer expired (20 seconds), plus the time until the next Configuration BPDU was received (2 seconds) on port 1/2, plus the time that port 1/2 spent in the Listening (15 seconds) and Learning (15 seconds) states. In other words, 52 seconds elapse if the default timer values are used.

Insignificant Topology Changes

Figure 8-8 shows the same network topology as Figure 8-6 and Figure 8-7, with the addition of a user PC on access-layer switch Catalyst C. The user's switch port, 2/12, is just another link as far as the switch is concerned. If the link status goes up or down, the switch must view that as a topology change and inform the Root Bridge.

Figure 8-8 *Effects of an Insignificant Topology Change*

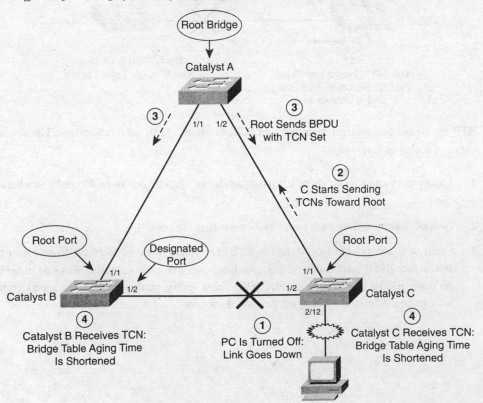

Obviously, user ports are expected to go up and down as the users reboot their machines, turn them on and off as they go to and from work, and so on. Regardless, TCN messages are sent by the switch, just as if a trunk link between switches had changed state.

To see what effect this has on the STP topology and the network, consider the following sequence of events:

1. The PC on Catalyst port 2/12 is turned off. The switch detects the link status going down.

2. Catalyst C begins sending TCN BPDUs toward the Root, over its Root Port (1/1).

3. The Root sends a TCN acknowledgment back to Catalyst C and then sends a Configuration BPDU with the TCN bit set to all downstream switches. This is done to inform every switch of a topology change somewhere in the network.

4. The TCN flag is received from the Root, and both Catalysts B and C shorten their bridge table aging times. This causes recently idle entries to be flushed, leaving only the actively transmitting stations in the table. The aging time stays short for the duration of the Forward Delay and Max Age timers.

Notice that this type of topology change is mostly cosmetic. No actual topology change occurred because none of the switches had to change port states to reach the Root Bridge. Instead, powering off the PC caused all the switches to age out entries from their bridge or CAM tables much sooner than normal.

At first, this doesn't seem like a major problem because the PC link state affects only the "newness" of the CAM table contents. If CAM table entries are flushed as a result, they probably will be learned again. This becomes a problem when every user PC is considered. Now every time *any* PC in the network powers up or down, *every* switch in the network must age out CAM table entries.

Given enough PCs, the switches could be in a constant state of flushing bridge tables. Also remember that when a switch doesn't have a CAM entry for a destination, the packet must be flooded out all its ports. Flushed tables mean more unknown unicasts, which mean more broadcasts or flooded packets throughout the network.

Fortunately, Catalyst switches have a feature that can designate a port as a special case. You can enable the STP PortFast feature on a port with a single attached PC. As a result, TCNs aren't sent when the port changes state, and the port is brought right into the Forwarding state when the link comes up. The section "Redundant Link Convergence," in Chapter 9, covers PortFast in more detail.

Types of STP

So far, this chapter has discussed STP in terms of its operation to prevent loops and to recover from topology changes in a timely manner. STP was originally developed to operate in a bridged environment, basically supporting a single LAN (or one VLAN). Implementing STP into a switched environment has required additional consideration and modification to support multiple VLANs. Because of this, the IEEE and Cisco have approached STP differently. This section reviews the three traditional types of STP that are encountered in switched networks and how they relate to one another. No specific configuration commands are associated with the various types of STP here. Instead, you need a basic understanding of how they interoperate in a network.

> **NOTE**   The IEEE has produced additional standards for spanning-tree enhancements that greatly improve on its scalability and convergence aspects. These are covered in Chapter 11. When you have a firm understanding of the more traditional forms of STP presented in this chapter, you can grasp the enhanced versions much easier.

Common Spanning Tree

The IEEE 802.1Q standard specifies how VLANs are to be trunked between switches. It also specifies only a single instance of STP that encompasses all VLANs. This instance is referred to as the *Common Spanning Tree (CST)*. All CST BPDUs are transmitted over trunk links using the native VLAN with untagged frames.

Having a single STP for many VLANs simplifies switch configuration and reduces switch CPU load during STP calculations. However, having only one STP instance can cause limitations, too. Redundant links between switches will be blocked with no capability for load balancing. Conditions also can occur that would cause CST to mistakenly enable forwarding on a link that does not carry a specific VLAN, whereas other links would be blocked.

Per-VLAN Spanning Tree

Cisco has a proprietary version of STP that offers more flexibility than the CST version. *Per-VLAN Spanning Tree (PVST)* operates a separate instance of STP for each individual VLAN. This allows the STP on each VLAN to be configured independently, offering better performance and tuning for specific conditions. Multiple spanning-trees also make load balancing possible over redundant links when the links are assigned to different VLANs. One link might forward one set of VLANs, while another redundant link might forward a different set.

Because of its proprietary nature, PVST requires the use of Cisco Inter-Switch Link (ISL) trunking encapsulation between switches. In networks where PVST and CST coexist, interoperability problems occur. Each requires a different trunking method, so BPDUs are never exchanged between STP types.

Per-VLAN Spanning Tree Plus

Cisco has a second proprietary version of STP that allows devices to interoperate with both PVST and CST. *Per-VLAN Spanning Tree Plus (PVST+)* effectively supports three groups of STP operating in the same campus network:

■ Catalyst switches running PVST

■ Catalyst switches running PVST+

■ Switches running CST over 802.1Q

To do this, PVST+ acts as a translator between groups of CST switches and groups of PVST switches. PVST+ can communicate directly with PVST by using ISL trunks. To communicate with CST, however, PVST+ exchanges BPDUs with CST as untagged frames over the native VLAN. BPDUs from other instances of STP (other VLANs) are propagated across the CST portions of the network by tunneling. PVST+ sends these BPDUs by using a unique multicast address so that the CST switches forward them on to downstream neighbors without interpreting them first. Eventually, the tunneled BPDUs reach other PVST+ switches where they are understood.

Foundation Summary

The Foundation Summary is a collection of information that provides a convenient review of many key concepts in this chapter. If you are already comfortable with the topics in this chapter, this summary can help you recall a few details. If you just read this chapter, this review should help solidify some key facts. If you are doing your final preparation before the exam, this information is a convenient way to review the day before the exam.

STP has a progression of states that each port moves through. Each state allows a port to do only certain functions, as shown in Table 8-5.

Table 8-5   *STP States and Port Activity*

STP State	The Port Can...	The Port Cannot...	Duration
Disabled		Send or receive data	
Blocking	Receive BPDUs	Send or receive data or learn MAC addresses	Indefinite if loop has been detected
Listening	Send and receive BPDUs	Send or receive data or learn MAC addresses	Forward Delay timer (15 seconds)
Learning	Send and receive BPDUs and learn MAC addresses	Send or receive data	Forward Delay timer (15 seconds)
Forwarding	Send and receive BPDUs, learn MAC addresses, and send and receive data		Indefinite as long as port is up and loop is not detected

Table 8-6   *Basic Spanning-Tree Operation*

Task	Procedure
1. Elect Root Bridge.	Lowest Bridge ID
2. Select Root Port (one per switch).	Lowest Root Path Cost; if equal, use tie-breakers
3. Select Designated Port (one per segment).	Lowest Root Path Cost; if equal, use tie-breakers
4. Block ports with loops.	Block ports that are non-Root and non–Designated Ports

To manually work out a spanning-tree topology using a network diagram, follow the basic steps in Table 8-7.

Table 8-7 *Manual STP Computation*

Task	Description
1. Identify Path Costs on links.	For each link between switches, write the Path Cost that each switch uses for the link.
2. Identify Root Bridge.	Find the switch with the lowest Bridge ID; mark it on the drawing.
3. Select Root Ports (one per switch).	For each switch, find the one port that has the best path to the Root Bridge. This is the one with the lowest Root Path Cost. Mark the port with an RP label.
4. Select Designated Ports (one per segment).	For each link between switches, identify which end of the link will be the Designated Port. This is the one with the lowest Root Path Cost; if equal on both ends, use STP tie-breakers. Mark the port with a DP label.
5. Identify the blocking ports.	Every switch port that is neither a Root nor a Designated Port will be put into the Blocking state. Mark these with an X.

Table 8-8 *Spanning-Tree Tie-Breaker Criteria*

Sequence	Criteria
1	Lowest Root Bridge ID
2	Lowest Root Path Cost
3	Lowest Sender Bridge ID
4	Lowest Sender Port ID

Table 8-9 *STP Path Cost*

Link Bandwidth	STP Cost (Nonlinear Scale)
4 Mbps	250
10 Mbps	100
16 Mbps	62
45 Mbps	39

continues

Table 8-9 *STP Path Cost (Continued)*

Link Bandwidth	STP Cost (Nonlinear Scale)
100 Mbps	19
155 Mbps	14
622 Mbps	6
1 Gbps	4
10 Gbps	2

Table 8-10 *STP Timers*

Timer	Function	Default Value
Hello	Interval between Configuration BPDUs.	2 seconds
Forward Delay	Time spent in Listening and Learning states before transitioning toward Forwarding state.	15 seconds
Max Age	Maximum length of time a BPDU can be stored without receiving an update. Timer expiration signals an indirect failure with Designated or Root Bridge.	20 seconds

Table 8-11 *Types of STP*

Type of STP	Function
CST	One instance of STP, over the native VLAN; 802.1Q based
PVST	One instance of STP per VLAN; Cisco ISL based
PVST+	Provides interoperability between CST and PVST; operates over both 802.1Q and ISL

Q&A

The questions and scenarios in this book are more difficult than what you should experience on the actual exam. The questions do not attempt to cover more breadth or depth than the exam; however, they are designed to make sure that you know the answers. Rather than allowing you to derive the answers from clues hidden inside the questions themselves, the questions challenge your understanding and recall of the subject. Hopefully, these questions will help limit the number of exam questions on which you narrow your choices to two options and then guess.

You can find the answers to these questions in Appendix A.

1. What is a bridging loop? Why is it bad?

2. Put the following STP port states in chronological order:

   a. Learning

   b. Forwarding

   c. Listening

   d. Blocking

3. Choose two types of STP messages used to communicate between bridges:

   a. Advertisement BPDU

   b. Configuration BPDU

   c. ACK BPDU

   d. TCN BPDU

4. What criteria are used to select the following?

   a. Root Bridge

   b. Root Port

   c. Designated Port

   d. Redundant (or secondary) Root Bridges

5. Which of the following switches becomes the Root Bridge, given the information in the following table? Which switch becomes the secondary Root Bridge if the Root Bridge fails?

Switch Name	Bridge Priority	MAC Address	Port Costs
Catalyst A	32,768	00-d0-10-34-26-a0	All are 19
Catalyst B	32,768	00-d0-10-34-24-a0	All are 4
Catalyst C	32,767	00-d0-10-34-27-a0	All are 19
Catalyst D	32,769	00-d0-10-34-24-a1	All are 19

6. What conditions cause an STP topology change? What effect does this have on STP and the network?

7. A Root Bridge has been elected in a switched network. Suppose that a new switch is installed with a lower Bridge ID than the existing Root Bridge. What will happen?

8. Suppose that a switch receives Configuration BPDUs on two of its ports. Both ports are assigned to the same VLAN. Each of the BPDUs announces Catalyst A as the Root Bridge. Can the switch use both of these ports as Root Ports? Why?

9. How is the Root Path Cost calculated for a switch port?

10. What conditions can cause ports on a network's Root Bridge to move into the Blocking state? (Assume that all switch connections are to other switches. No crossover cables are used to connect two ports on the same switch.)

11. What parameters can be tuned to influence the selection of a port as a Root or Designated Port?

12. After a bridging loop forms, how can you stop the endless flow of traffic?

13. In a BPDU, when can the Root Bridge ID have the same value as the Sender Bridge ID?

14. Which of these is true about the Root Path Cost?

    a. It is a value sent by the Root Bridge that cannot be changed along the way.

    b. It is incremented as a switch receives a BPDU.

    c. It is incremented as a switch sends a BPDU.

    d. It is incremented by the Path Cost of a port.

15. Suppose that two switches are connected by a common link. Each must decide which one will have the Designated Port on the link. Which switch takes on this role if these STP advertisements occur?

    a. The link is on switch A's port number 12 and on switch B's port number 5.

    b. Switch A has a Bridge ID of 32,768:0000.1111.2222, and switch B has 8192:0000.5555.6666.

    c. Switch A advertises a Root Path Cost of 8, whereas B advertises 12.

16. Using the default STP timers, how long does it take for a port to move from the Blocking state to the Forwarding state?

17. If the Root Bridge sets the Topology Change flag in the BPDU, what must the other switches in the network do?

18. Over what VLANs does the CST form of STP run?

19. What is the major difference between PVST and PVST+?

20. Two switches are connected by a common active link. When might neither switch have a Designated Port on the link?

This chapter covers the following topics that you need to master for the CCNP BCMSN exam:

- **STP Root Bridge**—This section discusses the importance of identifying a Root Bridge, as well as suggestions for its placement in the network. This section also presents the Root Bridge configuration commands.

- **Spanning-Tree Customization**—This section covers the configuration commands that enable you to alter the spanning-tree topology.

- **Tuning Spanning-Tree Convergence**—This section discusses how to alter, or tune, the STP timers to achieve optimum convergence times in a network.

- **Redundant Link Convergence**—This section describes the methods that cause a network to converge more quickly after a topology change.

- **Troubleshooting STP**—This section offers a brief summary of the commands you can use to verify that an STP instance is working properly.

CHAPTER 9

Spanning Tree Configuration

This chapter presents the design and configuration considerations necessary to implement the IEEE 802.1D Spanning Tree Protocol (STP) in a campus network. This chapter also discusses the commands needed to configure the STP features, previously described in Chapter 8, "Traditional Spanning Tree Protocol."

You can also tune STP or make it converge more efficiently in a given network. This chapter presents the theory and commands needed to accomplish this.

"Do I Know This Already?" Quiz

The purpose of the "Do I Know This Already?" quiz is to help you decide what parts of this chapter to use. If you already intend to read the entire chapter, you do not necessarily need to answer these questions now.

The quiz, derived from the major sections in the "Foundation Topics" portion of the chapter, helps you determine how to spend your limited study time.

Table 9-1 outlines the major topics discussed in this chapter and the "Do I Know This Already?" quiz questions that correspond to those topics.

Table 9-1 *"Do I Know This Already?" Foundation Topics Section-to-Question Mapping*

Foundation Topics Section	Questions Covered in This Section	Score
STP Root Bridge	1–5	
Spanning-Tree Customization	6–7	
Tuning Spanning-Tree Convergence	8–9	
Redundant Link Convergence	10–12	
Total Score		

> **CAUTION** The goal of self-assessment is to gauge your mastery of the topics in this chapter. If you do not know the answer to a question or are only partially sure of the answer, you should mark this question wrong. Giving yourself credit for an answer you correctly guess skews your self-assessment results and might give you a false sense of security.

1. Where should the Root Bridge be placed on a network?

   a. On the fastest switch

   b. Closest to the most users

   c. Closest to the center of the network

   d. On the least-used switch

2. Which of the following is a result of a poorly placed Root Bridge in a network?

   a. Bridging loops form.

   b. STP topology can't be resolved.

   c. STP topology can take unexpected paths.

   d. Root Bridge election flapping occurs.

3. Which of these parameters should you change to make a switch become a Root Bridge?

   a. Switch MAC address

   b. Path cost

   c. Port priority

   d. Bridge priority

4. What is the default 802.1D STP bridge priority on a Catalyst switch?

   a. 0

   b. 1

   c. 32,768

   d. 65,535

5. Which of the following commands is most likely to make a switch become the Root Bridge for VLAN 5, assuming that all switches have the default STP parameters?

   a. **spanning-tree root**

   b. **spanning-tree root vlan 5**

   c. **spanning-tree vlan 5 priority 100**

   d. **spanning-tree vlan 5 root**

6. What is the default path cost of a Gigabit Ethernet switch port?

    a. 1

    b. 2

    c. 4

    d. 19

    e. 1000

7. What command can change the path cost of interface Gigabit Ethernet 3/1 to a value of 8?

    a. **spanning-tree path-cost 8**

    b. **spanning-tree cost 8**

    c. **spanning-tree port-cost 8**

    d. **spanning-tree gig 3/1 cost 8**

8. What happens if the Root Bridge switch and another switch are configured with different STP hello timer values?

    a. Nothing—each sends hellos at different times.

    b. A bridging loop could form because the two switches are out of sync.

    c. The switch with the lower Hello timer becomes the Root Bridge.

    d. The other switch changes its Hello timer to match the Root Bridge.

9. What network diameter value is the basis for the default STP timer calculations?

    a. 1

    b. 3

    c. 7

    d. 9

    e. 15

10. Where should the STP PortFast feature be used?

    a. An access-layer switch port connected to a PC

    b. An access-layer switch port connected to a hub

    c. A distribution-layer switch port connected to an access layer switch

    d. A core-layer switch port

11. Where should the STP UplinkFast feature be enabled?

   a. An access-layer switch

   b. A distribution-layer switch

   c. A core-layer switch

   d. All of these answers are correct

12. If used, the STP BackboneFast feature should be enabled on which of these?

   a. All backbone- or core-layer switches

   b. All backbone- and distribution-layer switches

   c. All access-layer switches

   d. All switches in the network

The answers to the "Do I Know This Already?" quiz are found in Appendix A, "Answers to Chapter 'Do I Know This Already?' Quizzes and Q&A Sections." The suggested choices for your next step are as follows:

■ **10 or less overall score**—Read the entire chapter. This includes the "Foundation Topics," "Foundation Summary," and "Q&A" sections.

■ **11 or 12 overall score**—If you want more review on these topics, skip to the "Foundation Summary" section and then go to the "Q&A" section at the end of the chapter. Otherwise, move to Chapter 10, "Protecting the Spanning Tree Protocol Topology."

Foundation Topics

STP Root Bridge

STP and its computations are predictable; however, other factors might subtly influence STP decisions, making the resulting tree structure neither expected nor ideal.

As the network administrator, you can make adjustments to the spanning-tree operation to control its behavior. The location of the Root Bridge should be determined as part of the design process. You can use redundant links for load balancing in parallel, if configured correctly. You can also configure Spanning Tree Protocol (STP) to converge quickly and predictably in the event of a major topology change.

> **TIP** By default, STP is enabled for all active VLANs and on all ports of a switch. STP should remain enabled in a network to prevent bridging loops from forming. However, you might find that STP has been disabled in some way.
>
> If an entire instance of STP has been disabled, you can re-enable it with the following global configuration command:
>
> ```
> Switch(config)# spanning-tree vlan vlan-id
> ```
>
> If STP has been disabled for a specific VLAN on a specific port, you can re-enable it with the following interface configuration command:
>
> ```
> Switch (config-if)# spanning-tree vlan vlan-id
> ```

Root Bridge Placement

Although STP is wonderfully automatic with its default values and election processes, the resulting tree structure might perform quite differently than expected. The Root Bridge election is based on the idea that one switch is chosen as a common reference point, and all other switches choose ports that have the best-cost path to the root. The Root Bridge election is also based on the idea that the Root Bridge can become a central hub that interconnects other legs of the network. Therefore, the Root Bridge can be faced with heavy switching loads in its central location.

If the Root Bridge election is left to its default state, several things can occur to result in a poor choice. For example, the *slowest* switch (or bridge) could be elected as the Root Bridge. If heavy traffic loads are expected to pass through the Root Bridge, the slowest switch is not the ideal candidate. Recall that the only criteria for Root Bridge election is that the switch must have the lowest Bridge ID (bridge priority and MAC address), which is not necessarily the best choice to ensure optimal performance. If the slowest switch has the same bridge priority as the others and has the lowest MAC address, the slowest switch will be chosen as the Root.

A second factor to consider relates to redundancy. If all switches are left at their default states, only one Root Bridge is elected, with no clear choice for a backup. What happens if that switch fails? Another Root Bridge election occurs, but again, the choice might not be the ideal switch or the ideal location.

The final consideration is the location of the Root Bridge switch. As before, an election with default switch values could place the Root Bridge in an unexpected location in the network. More important, an inefficient spanning-tree structure could result, causing traffic from a large portion of the network to take a long and winding path just to pass through the Root Bridge.

Figure 9-1 shows a portion of a real-world hierarchical campus network.

Figure 9-1 *Campus Network with an Inefficient Root Bridge Election*

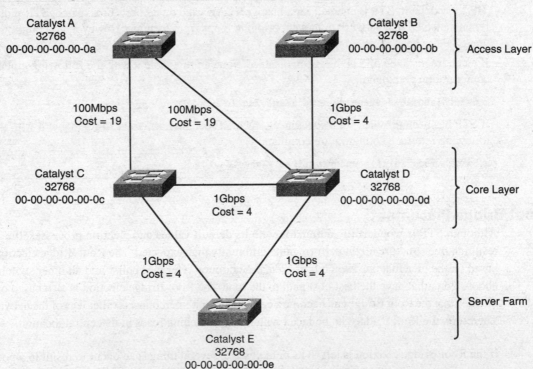

Catalyst switches A and B are two access-layer devices; Catalysts C and D form the core layer, and Catalyst E connects a server farm into the network core. Notice that most of the switches use redundant links to other layers of the hierarchy, as suggested in Chapter 2, "Modular Network

Design." At the time of this example, however, many switches, such as Catalyst B, still have only a single connection into the core. These switches are slated for an "upgrade," in which a redundant link will be added to the other half of the core.

As you will see, Catalyst A will become the Root Bridge because of its low MAC address. All switches have been left to their default STP states—the bridge priority of each is 32,768 (or 32,768 plus the VLAN ID, if the extended system ID is enabled). Figure 9-2 shows the converged state of STP. For the purposes of this discussion, the Root Ports and Designated Ports are simply shown on the network diagram. As an exercise, you should work through the spanning-tree process yourself, based on the information shown in the figure. The more examples you can work out by hand, the better you will understand the entire spanning-tree process.

Figure 9-2 *Campus Network with STP Converged*

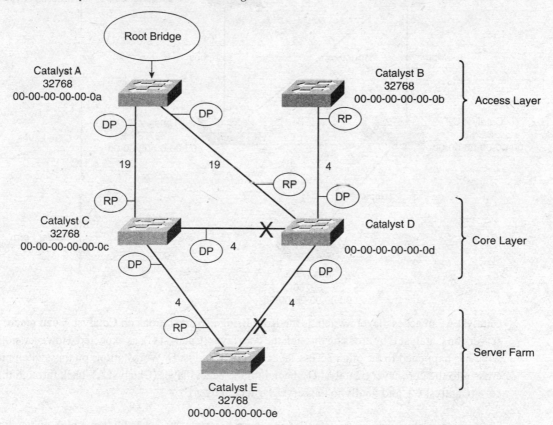

Notice that Catalyst A, one of the access-layer switches, has been elected the Root Bridge. Unfortunately, Catalyst A cannot take advantage of the 1-Gbps links, unlike the other switches.

Also note the location of the X symbols over the ports that are neither Root Ports nor Designated Ports. These ports will enter the Blocking state, and no data packets will pass through them.

Finally, Figure 9-3 shows the same network with the blocking links removed. Now you can see the true structure of the final spanning tree.

Figure 9-3   *Final Spanning-Tree Structure for the Campus Network*

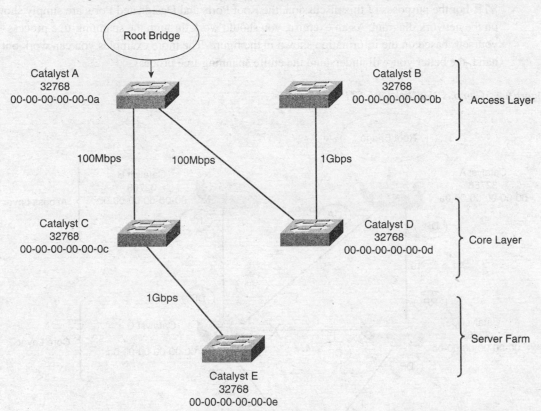

Catalyst A, an access-layer switch, is the Root Bridge. Workstations on Catalyst A can reach servers on Catalyst E by crossing through the core layer (Catalyst C), as expected. However, notice what has happened to the other access-layer switch, Catalyst B. Workstations on this switch must cross into the core layer (Catalyst D), back into the access layer (Catalyst A), back through the core (Catalyst C), and finally to the server farm (Catalyst E).

This action is obviously inefficient. For one thing, Catalyst A is probably not a high-end switch because it is used in the access layer. However, the biggest issue is that other access-layer areas are forced to thread through the relatively slow uplinks on Catalyst A. This winding path will become a major bottleneck to the users.

Root Bridge Configuration

To prevent the surprises outlined in the previous section, you should *always* do two things:

- Configure one switch as a Root Bridge in a determined fashion.

- Configure another switch as a secondary Root Bridge, in case of a primary Root Bridge failure.

As the common reference point, the Root Bridge (and the secondary) should be placed near the center of the Layer 2 network. For example, a switch in the distribution layer would make a better Root Bridge choice than one in the access layer because more traffic is expected to pass through the distribution-layer devices. In a flat switched network (no Layer 3 devices), a switch near a server farm would be a more efficient Root Bridge than switches elsewhere. Most traffic will be destined to and from the server farm and will benefit from a predetermined, direct path.

TIP   A Catalyst switch can be configured to use one of the following formats for its STP Bridge ID:

- Traditional 802.1D bridge priority value (16 bits), followed by the unique switch MAC address for the VLAN

- The 802.1t extended system ID (4-bit priority multiplier, plus a 12-bit VLAN ID), followed by a nonunique switch MAC address for the VLAN

If the switch can't support 1,024 unique MAC addresses for its own use, the extended system ID is always enabled by default. Otherwise, the traditional method is enabled by default.

To begin using the extended system ID method, you can uses the following global configuration command:

```
Switch(config)# spanning-tree extend system-id
```

Otherwise, you can use the traditional method by beginning the command with the **no** keyword.

You can configure a Catalyst switch to become the Root Bridge using one of two methods, which are configured as follows:

- Manually setting the bridge priority value so that a switch is given a lower-than-default Bridge ID value to win a Root Bridge election. You must know the bridge priorities of every other switch in a VLAN so that you can choose a value that is less than all the others. The command to accomplish this is as follows:

```
Switch(config)# spanning-tree vlan vlan-list priority bridge-priority
```

The *bridge-priority* value defaults to 32,768, but you can also assign a value of 0 to 65,535. If STP extended system ID is enabled, the default *bridge-priority* is 32,768 plus the VLAN number. In that case, the value can range from 0 to 61,440, but only as multiples of 4,096. A lower bridge priority is preferable.

Remember that Catalyst switches run one instance of STP for each VLAN (PVST+), so the VLAN ID must always be given. You should designate an appropriate Root Bridge for each VLAN. For example, you could use the following command to set the bridge priority for VLAN 5 and VLANs 100 through 200 to 4096:

```
Switch(config)# spanning-tree vlan 5,100-200 priority 4096
```

■ Causing the would-be Root Bridge switch to choose its own priority, based on some assumptions about other switches in the network. You can accomplish this with the following command:

```
Switch(config)# spanning-tree vlan vlan-id root {primary | secondary} [diameter
    diameter]
```

This command is actually a macro on the Catalyst that executes several other commands. The result is a more direct and automatic way to force one switch to become the Root Bridge. Notice that the actual bridge priorities are not given in the command. Instead, the switch modifies its STP values according to the current values in use within the active network. *These values are modified only once, when the macro command is issued.* Use the **primary** keyword to make the switch attempt to become the primary Root Bridge. This command modifies the switch's bridge priority value to become less than the bridge priority of the current Root Bridge. If the current root priority is more than 24,576, the local switch sets its priority to 24,576. If the current root priority is less than that, the local switch sets its priority to 4096 less than the current root.

For the **secondary** Root Bridge, the root priority is set to an artificially low value of 28,672. There is no way to query or listen to the network to find another potential secondary root simply because there are no advertisements or elections of secondary Root Bridges. Instead, the fixed secondary priority is used under the assumption that it will be less than the default priorities (32,768) that might be used on switches elsewhere. You can also modify the network diameter by adding the **diameter** keyword to this command. This modification is discussed further in the "Tuning Spanning-Tree Convergence" section later in the chapter.

As a final example, consider a switch that is currently using its default bridge priority for VLAN 100. In the extended system-id mode, the default priority is 32,768 plus 100 (the VLAN number). The output in Example 9-1 demonstrates this under the Bridge ID information. The default priority is greater than the current Root Bridge priority of 4200, so the local switch cannot become the root.

Example 9-1 *Displaying the STP Bridge Priority Values*

```
Switch# show spanning-tree vlan 100
VLAN0100
  Spanning tree enabled protocol ieee
  Root ID    Priority    4200
             Address     000b.5f65.1f80
```

Example 9-1 *Displaying the STP Bridge Priority Values (Continued)*

```
                Cost       4
                Port       1 (GigabitEthernet0/1)
                Hello Time  2 sec  Max Age 20 sec  Forward Delay 15 sec

  Bridge ID  Priority     32868  (priority 32768 sys-id-ext 100)
             Address      000c.8554.9a80
             Hello Time   2 sec  Max Age 20 sec  Forward Delay 15 sec
             Aging Time 300
[output omitted]
```

Now, the automatic method is used to attempt to make the switch become root for VLAN 100, using the command demonstrated in Example 9-2.

Example 9-2 *Using a Macro Command to Configure a Root Bridge*

```
Switch(config)# spanning-tree vlan 100 root primary
% Failed to make the bridge root for vlan 100
% It may be possible to make the bridge root by setting the priority
% for some (or all) of these instances to zero.
Switch(config)#
```

Why did this method fail? The current Root Bridge has a bridge priority of 4200. Because that priority is less than 24,576, the local switch will try to set its priority to 4,096 less than the current root. Although the resulting priority would be 104, the local switch is using an extended system ID, which requires bridge priority values that are multiples of 4,096. The only value that would work is 0, but the automatic method will not use it. Instead, the only other option is to manually configure the bridge priority to 0 with the following command:

```
Switch(config)# spanning-tree vlan 100 priority 0
```

Remember that on switches that use an extended system ID, the bridge priority is the configured priority (multiple of 4,096) plus the VLAN number. Even though the priority was set to 0 with the previous command, the switch is actually using a value of 100—priority 0 plus VLAN number 100, as the output in Example 9-3 reveals.

Example 9-3 *Displaying Bridge Priorities with Extended System IDs*

```
Switch# show spanning-tree vlan 100
VLAN0100
  Spanning tree enabled protocol ieee
  Root ID    Priority    100
             Address     000c.8554.9a80
             This bridge is the root
             Hello Time   2 sec  Max Age 20 sec  Forward Delay 15 sec
```

continues

Example 9-3 *Displaying Bridge Priorities with Extended System IDs (Continued)*

```
 Bridge ID  Priority    100    (priority 0 sys-id-ext 100)
            Address     000c.8554.9a80
            Hello Time   2 sec  Max Age 20 sec  Forward Delay 15 sec
            Aging Time 300
[output omitted]
```

> **NOTE** The **spanning-tree vlan** *vlan-id* **root** command will not be shown in a Catalyst switch configuration because the command is actually a macro executing other switch commands. The actual commands and values produced by the macro will be shown, however. For example, the macro can potentially adjust the four STP values as follows:
>
> ```
> Switch(config)# spanning-tree vlan 1 root primary
>   vlan 1 bridge priority set to 24576
>   vlan 1 bridge max aging time unchanged at 20
>   vlan 1 bridge hello time unchanged at 2
>   vlan 1 bridge forward delay unchanged at 15
> ```
>
> Be aware that this macro doesn't guarantee that the switch will become the root and maintain that status. After the macro is used, it is entirely possible for another switch in the network to have its bridge priority configured to a lower value. The other switch would become the new root, displacing the switch that ran the macro.
>
> On the root, it is usually good practice to directly modify the bridge priority to an artificially low value (even priority 1 or 0) with the **spanning-tree vlan** *vlan-id* **priority** *bridge-priority* command. This makes it more difficult for another switch in the network to win the Root Bridge election, unless it is manually configured with a priority that is even lower.

Spanning-Tree Customization

The most important decision you can make when designing your spanning-tree topology is the placement of the Root Bridge. Other decisions, such as the exact loop-free path structure, will occur automatically as a result of the Spanning Tree Algorithm (STA). Occasionally, the path might need additional tuning, but only under special circumstances and after careful consideration.

Recall the sequence of four criteria that STP uses to choose a path:

1. Lowest Bridge ID

2. Lowest Root Path Cost

3. Lowest sender Bridge ID

4. Lowest sender port ID

The previous section discussed how to tune a switch's Bridge ID to force it to become the Root Bridge in a network. You can also change the bridge priority on a switch to influence the value it uses in the sender Bridge ID that it announced as it relays BPDUs to other neighboring switches.

Only the automatic STP computation has been discussed, using the default switch port costs to make specific path decisions. The following sections discuss ways you can influence the exact topology that results.

Tuning the Root Path Cost

The Root Path Cost for each active port of a switch is determined by the cumulative cost as a BPDU travels along. As a switch *receives* a BPDU, the port cost of the receiving port is added to the root path cost in the BPDU. The port or port path cost is inversely proportional to the port's bandwidth. If desired, a port's cost can be modified from the default value.

NOTE   Before modifying a switch port's path cost, you should always calculate the Root Path Costs of other alternative paths through the network. Changing one port's cost might influence STP to choose that port as a Root Port, but other paths still could be preferred. You also should calculate a port's existing path cost to determine what the new cost value should be. Careful calculation will ensure that the desired path indeed will be chosen.

Use the following interface configuration command to set a switch port's path cost:

```
Switch (config-if)# spanning-tree [vlan vlan-id] cost cost
```

If the **vlan** parameter is given, the port cost is modified only for the specified VLAN. Otherwise, the cost is modified for the port as a whole (all active VLANs). The *cost* value can range from 1 to 65,535. There are standard or default values that correspond to port bandwidth, as shown in Table 9-2.

Table 9-2 *STP Port Cost*

Link Bandwidth	STP Cost
4 Mbps	250
10 Mbps	100
16 Mbps	62
45 Mbps	39
100 Mbps	19
155 Mbps	14
622 Mbps	6
1 Gbps	4
10 Gbps	2

For example, a Gigabit Ethernet interface has a default port cost of 4. You can use the following command to change the cost to 2, but only for VLAN 10:

```
Switch(config-if)# spanning-tree vlan 10 cost 2
```

You can see the port cost of an interface by using the following command:

```
Switch# show spanning-tree interface type mod/num [cost]
```

As an example, GigabitEthernet 0/1 is configured as a trunk port, carrying VLANs 1, 10, and 20. Example 9-4 shows the port cost for each of the VLANs.

Example 9-4 *Displaying STP Port Cost Values on an Interface*

```
Switch# show spanning-tree interface gigabitEthernet 0/1
Vlan            Role Sts Cost      Prio.Nbr Type
--------------- ---- --- --------- -------- --------------------------------
VLAN0001        Root FWD 4         128.1    P2p
VLAN0010        Desg FWD 2         128.1    P2p
VLAN0020        Root FWD 4         128.1    P2p
```

Tuning the Port ID

The fourth criteria of an STP decision is the port ID. The port ID value that a switch uses is actually a 16-bit quantity: 8 bits for the port priority and 8 bits for the port number. The port priority is a value from 0 to 255 and defaults to 128 for all ports. The port number can range from 0 to 255 and represents the port's actual physical mapping. Port numbers begin with 1 at port 0/1 and increment across each module. (The numbers might not be consecutive because each module is assigned a particular range of numbers.)

> **TIP** Port numbers are usually intuitive on a fixed configuration switch, such as a 48-port Catalyst 3560. The STP port number is simply the interface number, from 1 to 48.
>
> However, it is not easy to find the STP port number in a switch with many modules and many ports. Notice how GigabitEthernet 3/16 is also known as port number 144 in the following example:
>
> ```
> Switch# show spanning-tree interface gigabitEthernet 3/16
> Vlan            Role Sts Cost      Prio.Nbr Type
> --------------- ---- --- --------- -------- --------------------------------
> VLAN0010        Desg FWD 4         128.144  Edge P2p
> VLAN0100        Desg FWD 4         128.144  Edge P2p
> VLAN0200        Desg FWD 4         128.144  Edge P2p
> Switch#
> ```
>
> The entire port ID consists of the port priority followed by the port number. In the preceding example output, the port ID is 128.144. As a 16-bit quantity in hex, it is 8090. In addition, ports that are bundled into an EtherChannel or Port-channel interface always have a higher port ID than they would if they were not bundled.

Obviously, a switch port's port number is fixed because it is based only on its hardware location or index. The port ID, however, can be modified to influence an STP decision by using the port priority. You can configure the port priority with this interface-configuration command:

```
Switch(config-if)# spanning-tree [vlan vlan-list] port-priority port-priority
```

You can modify the port priority for one or more VLANs by using the **vlan** parameter. The VLAN numbers are given as *vlan-list*, a list of single values or ranges of values separated by commas. Otherwise, the port priority is set for the port as a whole (all active VLANs). The value of *port-priority* can range from 0 to 255 and defaults to 128. A lower port priority value indicates a more preferred path toward the Root Bridge.

As an example, you can use the following command sequence to change the port priority of GigabitEthernet 3/16 from 128 (the default) to 64 for VLANs 10 and 100:

```
Switch(config)# interface gigabitethernet 3/16
Switch(config-if)# spanning-tree vlan 10,100 port-priority 64
```

You can confirm the changes with the **show spanning-tree interface** command, as demonstrated in Example 9-5.

Example 9-5 *Confirming STP Port Priority Values After Configuration*

```
Switch# show spanning-tree interface gigabitEthernet 3/16
Vlan              Role Sts Cost      Prio.Nbr Type
---------------- ---- --- --------- -------- --------------------------------
VLAN0010          Desg FWD 4         64.144   Edge P2p
VLAN0100          Desg FWD 4         64.144   Edge P2p
VLAN0200          Desg FWD 4         128.144  Edge P2p
Switch#
```

Tuning Spanning-Tree Convergence

STP uses several timers, a sequence of states that ports must move through, and specific topology change conditions to prevent bridging loops from forming in a complex network. Each of these parameters or requirements is based on certain default values for a typical network size and function. For the majority of cases, the default STP operation is sufficient to keep the network loop free and enable users to communicate.

However, in certain situations, the default STP can cause network access to be delayed while timers expire and while preventing loops on links where loops are not possible. For example, when a single PC is connected to a switch port, a bridging loop is simply not possible. Another situation relates to the size of a Layer 2 switched network: The default STP timers are based on a benchmark network size.

In a network that is smaller, waiting until the default timer values expire might not make sense when they could be safely set to shorter values. In situations like this, you can safely make adjustments to the STP convergence process for more efficiency.

Modifying STP Timers

Recall that STP uses three timers to keep track of various port operation states and communication between bridges. The three STP timers can be adjusted by using the commands documented in the sections that follow. Remember that the timers need to be modified only on the Root Bridge because the Root Bridge propagates all three timer values throughout the network as fields in the configuration BPDU.

Manually Configuring STP Timers

Use one or more of the following global configuration commands to modify STP timers:

```
Switch(config)# spanning-tree [vlan vlan-id] hello-time seconds
Switch(config)# spanning-tree [vlan vlan-id] forward-time seconds
Switch(config)# spanning-tree [vlan vlan-id] max-age seconds
```

Notice that the timers can be changed for a single instance (VLAN) of STP on the switch by using the **vlan** *vlan-id* parameters. If you omit the **vlan** keyword, the timer values are configured for *all* instances (all VLANs) of STP on the switch.

The *Hello timer* triggers periodic "hello" (actually, the configuration BPDU) messages that are sent from the root to other bridges in the network. This timer also sets the interval in which a bridge expects to hear a hello relayed from its neighboring bridges. Configuration BPDUs are sent every 2 seconds, by default. You can modify the Hello timer with the **hello-time** keyword, along with a value of 1 to 10 seconds, as in the following command:

```
Switch(config)# spanning-tree hello-time 1
```

The *Forward Delay timer* determines the amount of time a port stays in the Listening state before moving into the Learning state, and how long it stays in the Learning state before moving to the Forwarding state. You can modify the Forward Delay timer with the **forward-time** keyword. The default value is 15 seconds, but this can be set to a value of 4 to 30 seconds. This timer should be modified only under careful consideration because the value depends on the diameter of the network and the propagation of BPDUs across all switches. A value that is too low allows loops to form, possibly crippling a network.

The *Max Age timer* specifies a stored BPDU's lifetime that has been received from a neighboring switch with a designated port. Suppose that BPDUs are being received on a nondesignated switch port every 2 seconds, as expected. Then an *indirect failure*, or one that doesn't involve a physical link going down, occurs that prevents BPDUs from being sent. The receiving switch waits until the Max Age timer expires to listen for further BPDUs. If none is received, the nondesignated port moves into the Listening state, and the receiving switch generates configuration BPDUs. This port then becomes the Designated Port to restore connectivity on the segment.

To modify the Max Age timer, use the **max-age** keyword. The timer value defaults to 20 seconds but can be set from 6 to 40 seconds.

Automatically Configuring STP Timers

Modifying STP timers can be tricky, given the conservative nature of the default values and the calculations needed to derive proper STP operation. Timer values are basically dependent on the Hello Time and the switched network's diameter, in terms of switch hops. Catalyst switches offer a single command that can change the timer values in a more controlled fashion. Although described earlier, the **spanning-tree vlan** *vlan-list* **root** macro command is a better tool to use than setting the timers with the individual commands. This global configuration command has the following syntax:

```
Switch(config)# spanning-tree vlan vlan-list root {primary | secondary} [diameter
    diameter [hello-time hello-time]]
```

Here, STP timers will be adjusted according to the formulas specified in the 802.1D standard by giving only the network's diameter (the maximum number of switches that traffic will traverse across a Layer 2 network) and an optional *hello-time*. If you do not specify a Hello Time, the default value of 2 seconds is assumed.

This command can be used only on a per-VLAN basis, to modify the timers for a particular VLAN's spanning tree instance. The network diameter can be a value from one to seven switch hops. Because this command makes a switch become the Root Bridge, all the modified timer values resulting from this command will be propagated to other switches through the configuration BPDU.

As an example, suppose that a small network consists of three switches connected in a triangle fashion. The command output in Example 9-6 shows the current (default) STP timer values that are in use for VLAN 100.

Example 9-6 *Displaying the STP Timer Values in Use*

```
Switch# show spanning-tree vlan 100
VLAN0100
  Spanning tree enabled protocol ieee
  Root ID    Priority    100
             Address     000c.8554.9a80
             This bridge is the root
             Hello Time   2 sec  Max Age 20 sec  Forward Delay 15 sec

  Bridge ID  Priority    100    (priority 0 sys-id-ext 100)
             Address     000c.8554.9a80
             Hello Time   2 sec  Max Age 20 sec  Forward Delay 15 sec
             Aging Time 300
[output omitted]
```

The longest path that a packet can take through the sample network is three switches. This is considerably less than the reference diameter of seven that is used to calculate the default timer values. Therefore, you can safely assume that this network diameter is three, provided that no additional switches will be added to lengthen the longest path. Suppose that a Hello Time of 1 second is also desired, to shorten the time needed to detect a dead neighbor. The following command attempts to make the local switch become the Root Bridge and automatically adjusts the STP timers:

```
Switch(config)# spanning-tree vlan 100 root primary diameter 3 hello-time 1
```

You can confirm the new timer values with the **show spanning-tree vlan** *vlan-id* command, as demonstrated in Example 9-7.

Example 9-7 *Confirming STP Timer Configuration Changes*

```
Switch# show spanning-tree vlan 100
VLAN0100
  Spanning tree enabled protocol ieee
  Root ID    Priority    100
             Address     000c.8554.9a80
             This bridge is the root
             Hello Time   1 sec  Max Age  7 sec  Forward Delay  5 sec

  Bridge ID  Priority    100    (priority 0 sys-id-ext 100)
             Address     000c.8554.9a80
             Hello Time   1 sec  Max Age  7 sec  Forward Delay  5 sec
             Aging Time 300
```

Redundant Link Convergence

Some additional methods allow faster STP convergence in the event of a link failure:

- **PortFast**—Enables fast connectivity to be established on access-layer switch ports to workstations that are booting up

- **UplinkFast**—Enables fast-uplink failover on an access-layer switch when dual uplinks are connected into the distribution layer

- **BackboneFast**—Enables fast convergence in the network backbone (core) after a spanning-tree topology change occurs

Instead of modifying timer values, these methods work by controlling convergence on specifically located ports within the network hierarchy.

> **TIP** The STP has been enhanced to allow almost instantaneous topology changes instead of having to rely on these Cisco-proprietary extensions. This enhancement is known as the Rapid Spanning Tree Protocol, or IEEE 802.1w, and is covered in Chapter 11, "Advanced Spanning Tree Protocol." You should become familiar with the topics in this chapter first because they provide the basis for the concepts in Chapter 11.

PortFast: Access-Layer Nodes

An end-user workstation is usually connected to a switch port in the access layer. If the workstation is powered off and then turned on, the switch will sense that the port link status has gone down and back up. The port will not be in a usable state until STP cycles from the Blocking state to the Forwarding state. With the default STP timers, this transition takes at least 30 seconds (15 seconds for Listening to Learning, and 15 seconds for Learning to Forwarding). Therefore, the workstation cannot transmit or receive any useful data until the Forwarding state finally is reached on the port.

> **TIP**   Port initialization delays of up to 50 seconds can be observed. As discussed, 30 of these seconds are due to the STP state transitions. If a switch port is running Port Aggregation Protocol (PAgP) to negotiate EtherChannel configuration, an additional 20-second delay can occur.

On switch ports that connect only to single workstations or specific devices, bridging loops never should be possible. The potential for a loop exists only if the workstation had additional connections back into the network and if it was bridging traffic itself. For example, this can happen on PCs that are running Windows XP when network bridging has been enabled. In most situations, this is not very likely to happen.

Catalyst switches offer the PortFast feature, which shortens the Listening and Learning states to a negligible amount of time. When a workstation link comes up, the switch immediately moves the PortFast port into the Forwarding state. Spanning-tree loop detection is still in operation, however, and the port moves into the Blocking state if a loop is ever detected on the port.

By default, PortFast is disabled on all switch ports. You can configure PortFast as a global default, affecting all switch ports with a single command. All ports that are configured for access mode (nontrunking) will have PortFast automatically enabled. You can use the following global configuration command to enable PortFast as the default:

```
Switch(config)# spanning-tree portfast default
```

You can also enable or disable the PortFast feature on specific switch ports by using the following interface-configuration command:

```
Switch(config-if)# [no] spanning-tree portfast
```

Obviously, you should not enable PortFast on a switch port that is connected to a hub or another switch because bridging loops could form. One other benefit of PortFast is that topology change notification (TCN) BPDUs are not sent when a switch port in PortFast mode goes up or down. This simplifies the TCN transmission on a large network when end-user workstations are coming up or shutting down.

> **TIP** You can also use a macro configuration command to force a switch port to support a single host. The following command enables STP PortFast, sets the port to access (nontrunking) mode, and disables PAgP to prevent the port from participating in an EtherChannel:
>
> ```
> Switch(config)# interface type mod/num
> Switch(config-if)# switchport host
> switchport mode will be set to access
> spanning-tree portfast will be enabled
> channel group will be disabled
> ```

You can display the current PortFast status with the following command:

```
Switch# show spanning-tree interface type mod/num portfast
```

For example, the following output shows that port FastEthernet 0/1 supports only access VLAN 10 and has PortFast enabled:

```
Switch# show spanning-tree interface fastethernet 0/1 portfast
VLAN0010        enabled
Switch#
```

UplinkFast: Access-Layer Uplinks

Consider an access-layer switch that has redundant uplink connections to two distribution-layer switches. Normally, one uplink would be in the Forwarding state and the other would be in the Blocking state. If the primary uplink went down, up to 50 seconds could elapse before the redundant uplink could be used.

The UplinkFast feature on Catalyst switches enables leaf-node switches or switches at the ends of the spanning-tree branches to have a functioning root port while keeping *one or more* redundant or potential root ports in Blocking mode. When the primary Root Port uplink fails, another blocked uplink immediately can be brought up for use.

> **TIP** Many Catalyst switches have two built-in, high-speed uplink ports (Gigabit Ethernet, for example). You might get the idea that UplinkFast can only toggle between two leaf-node uplink ports. This is entirely untrue. UplinkFast keeps a record of *all* parallel paths to the Root Bridge. All uplink ports but one are kept in the Blocking state. If the Root Port fails, the uplink with the next-lowest Root Path Cost is unblocked and used without delay.

To enable the UplinkFast feature, use the following global configuration command:

```
Switch(config)# spanning-tree uplinkfast [max-update-rate pkts-per-second]
```

When UplinkFast is enabled, it is enabled for the entire switch and all VLANs. UplinkFast works by keeping track of possible paths to the Root Bridge. Therefore, the command *is not allowed on the Root Bridge switch*. UplinkFast also makes some modifications to the local switch to ensure that it does not become the Root Bridge and that the switch is not used as a transit switch to get to the Root Bridge. In other words, the goal is to keep UplinkFast limited to leaf-node switches that are farthest from the Root.

First, the switch's bridge priority is raised to 49,152, making it unlikely that the switch will be elected to Root Bridge status. The port cost of all local switch ports is incremented by 3,000, making the ports undesirable as paths to the root for any downstream switches.

The command also includes a **max-update-rate** parameter. When an uplink on a switch goes down, UplinkFast makes it easy for the local switch to update its bridging table of MAC addresses to point to the new uplink. However, UplinkFast also provides a mechanism for the local switch to notify other upstream switches that stations downstream (or within the access layer) can be reached over the newly activated uplink.

The switch accomplishes this by sending dummy multicast frames to destination 0100.0ccd.cdcd on behalf of the stations contained in its Content-Addressable Memory (CAM) table. The MAC addresses are used as the source addresses in the dummy frames, as if the stations actually had sent them. The idea is to quickly send the multicast frames over the new uplink, giving upstream hosts a chance to receive the frames and learn of the new path to those source addresses.

These multicast frames are sent out at a rate specified by the **max-update-rate** parameter in packets per second. This limits the amount of bandwidth used for the dummy multicasts if the CAM table is quite large. The default is 150 packets per second (pps), but the rate can range from 0 to 65,535 pps. If the value is 0, no dummy multicasts are sent.

TIP   You can use the following command to display the current status of STP UplinkFast:

```
Switch# show spanning-tree uplinkfast
UplinkFast is enabled
Station update rate set to 150 packets/sec.
UplinkFast statistics
-----------------------
Number of transitions via uplinkFast (all VLANs)            : 2
Number of proxy multicast addresses transmitted (all VLANs) : 52
Name                    Interface List
--------------------    ------------------------------------
VLAN0001                Gi0/1(fwd)
VLAN0010                Gi0/1(fwd)
VLAN0100                Gi0/1(fwd)
Switch#
```

BackboneFast: Redundant Backbone Paths

In the network backbone, or core layer, a different method is used to shorten STP convergence. BackboneFast works by having a switch actively determine whether alternative paths exist to the Root Bridge, in case the switch detects an *indirect link failure*. Indirect link failures occur when a link that is not directly connected to a switch fails.

A switch detects an indirect link failure when it receives inferior BPDUs from its designated bridge on either its Root Port or a blocked port. (Inferior BPDUs are sent from a designated bridge that has lost its connection to the Root Bridge, making it announce itself as the new Root.)

Normally, a switch must wait for the Max Age timer to expire before responding to the inferior BPDUs. However, BackboneFast begins to determine whether other alternative paths to the Root Bridge exist according to the following port types that received the inferior BPDU:

- If the inferior BPDU arrives on a port in the Blocking state, the switch considers the Root Port and all other blocked ports to be alternate paths to the Root Bridge.

- If the inferior BPDU arrives on the Root Port itself, the switch considers all blocked ports to be alternate paths to the Root Bridge.

- If the inferior BPDU arrives on the Root Port and no ports are blocked, however, the switch assumes that it has lost connectivity with the Root Bridge. In this case, the switch assumes that it has become the Root Bridge, and BackboneFast allows it to do so before the Max Age timer expires.

Detecting alternative paths to the Root Bridge also involves an interactive process with other bridges. If the local switch has blocked ports, BackboneFast begins to use the *Root Link Query (RLQ)* protocol to see if upstream switches have stable connections to the Root Bridge.

First, RLQ Requests are sent out. If a switch receives an RLQ Request and either is the Root Bridge or has lost connection to the Root, it sends an RLQ Reply. Otherwise, the RLQ Request is propagated on to other switches until an RLQ Reply can be generated. On the local switch, if an RLQ Reply is received on its current Root Port, the path to the Root Bridge is intact and stable. If it is received on a nonroot port, an alternative Root Path must be chosen. The Max Age timer immediately is expired so that a new Root Port can be found.

BackboneFast is simple to configure and operates by short-circuiting the Max Age timer when needed. Although this function shortens the time a switch waits to detect a Root Path failure, ports still must go through full-length Forward Delay timer intervals during the Listening and Learning states. Where PortFast and UplinkFast enable immediate transitions, BackboneFast can reduce the maximum convergence delay only from 50 to 30 seconds.

To configure BackboneFast, use the following global configuration command:

```
Switch(config)# spanning-tree backbonefast
```

When used, BackboneFast should be enabled on *all* switches in the network because BackboneFast requires the use of the RLQ Request and Reply mechanism to inform switches of Root Path stability. The RLQ protocol is active only when BackboneFast is enabled on a switch. By default, BackboneFast is disabled.

> **TIP**   You can verify the current BackboneFast state with the following command:
>
> ```
> Switch# show spanning-tree backbonefast
> BackboneFast is enabled
> Switch#
> ```

Troubleshooting STP

Because the STP running in a network uses several timers, costs, and dynamic calculations, predicting the current state is difficult. You can use a network diagram and work out the STP topology by hand, but any change on the network could produce an entirely different outcome. Then, figure in something like PVST+, in which you have one instance of STP running for each VLAN present. Obviously, simply viewing the STP status on the active network devices would be better.

You can display information about many aspects of the STP from a Catalyst switch command-line interface (CLI). Specifically, you need to find out the current Root Bridge and its location in the network. You also might want to see the Bridge ID of the switch where you are connected, to see how it participates in STP. Use the information in Table 9-3 to determine what command is useful for what situation.

Table 9-3 *Commands for Displaying Spanning Tree Information*

Task	Command Syntax
View all possible STP parameters for all VLANs. Port information is summarized.	Switch# **show spanning-tree**
View all possible STP information for all VLANs. Port information is very detailed.	Switch# **show spanning-tree detail**
View the total number of switch ports currently in each of the STP states.	Switch# **show spanning-tree** [**vlan** *vlan-id*] **summary**
Find the Root Bridge ID, the Root Port, and the Root Path Cost.	Switch# **show spanning-tree** [**vlan** *vlan-id*] **root**
Show the Bridge ID and STP timers for the local switch.	Switch# **show spanning-tree** [**vlan** *vlan-id*] **bridge**
Show the STP UplinkFast status.	Switch# **show spanning-tree uplinkfast**
Show the STP BackboneFast status.	Switch# **show spanning-tree backbonefast**

Foundation Summary

The Foundation Summary is a collection of information that provides a convenient review of many key concepts in this chapter. If you are already comfortable with the topics in this chapter, this summary can help you recall a few details. If you just read this chapter, this review should help solidify some key facts. If you are doing your final preparation before the exam, these tables and figures are a convenient way to review the day before the exam.

Table 9-4   *STP Configuration Commands*

Task	Command Syntax
Enable STP	Switch(config)# **spanning-tree** *vlan-id*
Set bridge priority	Switch(config)# **spanning-tree vlan** *vlan-id* **priority** *bridge-priority*
Set Root Bridge (macro)	Switch(config)# **spanning-tree vlan** *vlan-id* **root {primary | secondary}** [**diameter** *diameter*]
Set port cost	Switch(config)# **spanning-tree** [**vlan** *vlan-id*] **cost** *cost*
Set port priority	Switch(config)# **spanning-tree** [**vlan** *vlan-id*] **port-priority** *port-priority*
Set STP timers	Switch(config)# **spanning-tree** [**vlan** *vlan-id*] **hello-time** *seconds* Switch(config)# **spanning-tree** [**vlan** *vlan-id*] **forward-time** *seconds* Switch(config)# **spanning-tree** [**vlan** *vlan-id*] **max-age** *seconds*
Set PortFast on an interface	Switch(config)# **spanning-tree portfast**
Set UplinkFast on a switch	Switch(config)# **spanning-tree uplinkfast** [**max-update-rate** *pkts-per-second*]
Set BackboneFast on a switch	Switch(config)# **spanning-tree backbonefast**

Q&A

The questions and scenarios in this book are more difficult than what you should experience on the actual exam. The questions do not attempt to cover more breadth or depth than the exam; however, they are designed to make sure that you know the answers. Rather than allowing you to derive the answers from clues hidden inside the questions themselves, the questions challenge your understanding and recall of the subject. Hopefully, these questions will help limit the number of exam questions on which you narrow your choices to two options and then guess.

You can find the answers to these questions in Appendix A.

1. What commands can configure a Catalyst 4500 switch as the Root Bridge on VLAN 10, assuming that the other switches are using the default STP values?

2. Using your Root Bridge answer from question 1, what commands can configure a Catalyst 3560 switch as a secondary or backup Root Bridge on VLAN 10?

3. Which of the following switches will become the Root Bridge, given the information in the following table? Which switch will become the secondary Root Bridge if the Root Bridge fails?

Switch Name	Bridge Priority	MAC Address	Port Costs
Catalyst A	32,768	00-d0-10-34-26-a0	All are 19.
Catalyst B	32,768	00-d0-10-34-24-a0	All are 4.
Catalyst C	32,767	00-d0-10-34-27-a0	All are 19.
Catalyst D	32,769	00-d0-10-34-24-a1	All are 19.

Questions 4 through 7 are based on a network that contains two switches, Catalyst A and B. Their bridge priorities and MAC addresses are 32,768:0000.aaaa.aaaa and 32,768:0000.bbbb.bbbb, respectively.

4. Which switch will become the Root Bridge?

5. If switch B's bridge priority is changed to 10,000, which one will be Root?

6. If switch B's bridge priority is changed to 32,769, which one will be Root?

7. If switch C is introduced with 40000:0000.0000.cccc, which will be the secondary Root?

8. Suppose that a switch is configured with the **spanning-tree vlan 10 root primary** command. Then, another switch is connected to the network. The new switch has a bridge priority of 8,192. Which one of the following happens?

   a. When the new switch advertises itself, the original Root Bridge detects it and lower its bridge priority to 4,096 less than the new switch.

   b. The new switch becomes and stays the Root Bridge (bridge priority 8,192).

   c. No change; both switches keep their current bridge priorities.

   d. The new switch detects that a Root Bridge already exists and raises its own bridge priority to 32,768.

9. Three switches in a network have the following bridge priorities: 32,768, 16,384, and 8,192. If a fourth switch is configured with **spanning-tree vlan 1 root secondary**, what is the bridge priority of the switches that become the primary and secondary Root Bridges?

10. What STP timer values automatically can be modified by setting the network diameter?

11. Which STP timer determines how long a port stays in the Listening state? What is its default value?

12. What is the purpose of the Max Age timer?

13. Three switches are connected to each other, forming a triangle shape. STP prevents a loop from forming. What is the most accurate value that could be used for the network diameter?

14. Which of the following will not benefit from STP UplinkFast?

   a. An access-layer switch with one uplink port

   b. An access-layer switch with two uplink ports

   c. An access-layer switch with three uplink ports

   d. An access-layer switch with four uplink ports

15. What command can enable the STP PortFast feature on a switch? What configuration mode must you enter first?

16. What happens if the STP Hello Time is decreased to 1 second in an effort to speed up STP convergence? What happens if the Hello Time is increased to 10 seconds?

17. What switch command safely can adjust the STP timers on the Root Bridge in VLAN 7? Assume that the network consists of Catalysts A, B, and C, all connected to each other in a triangle fashion.

For questions 18 and 19, refer to the following output:

```
Switch# show spanning-tree vlan 50
VLAN50
  Spanning tree enabled protocol ieee
  Root ID    Priority    8000
             Address     00d0.0457.3831
             Cost        12
             Port        49 (GigabitEthernet0/1)
             Hello Time   2 sec  Max Age 20 sec  Forward Delay 15 sec

  Bridge ID  Priority    32818  (priority 32768 sys-id-ext 50)
             Address     0009.b7ee.9800
             Hello Time   2 sec  Max Age 20 sec  Forward Delay 15 sec
             Aging Time 300

Interface                                Designated
Name             Port ID Prio  Cost Sts  Cost Bridge ID             Port ID
---------------- ------- ---  ------ ---  ---- ------------------    -------
FastEthernet0/1  128.1   128      19 FWD  12 32818 0009.b7ee.9800 128.1
FastEthernet0/2  128.2   128      19 FWD  12 32818 0009.b7ee.9800 128.2
FastEthernet0/4  128.4   128     100 FWD  12 32818 0009.b7ee.9800 128.4
FastEthernet0/7  128.7   128      19 FWD  12 32818 0009.b7ee.9800 128.7
FastEthernet0/8  128.8   128      19 FWD  12 32818 0009.b7ee.9800 128.8
FastEthernet0/9  128.9   128      19 FWD  12 32818 0009.b7ee.9800 128.9
FastEthernet0/10 128.10  128      19 FWD  12 32818 0009.b7ee.9800 128.10
FastEthernet0/11 128.11  128      19 FWD  12 32818 0009.b7ee.9800 128.11
FastEthernet0/12 128.12  128      19 FWD  12 32818 0009.b7ee.9800 128.12
FastEthernet0/17 128.13  128      19 FWD  12 32818 0009.b7ee.9800 128.13
FastEthernet0/20 128.16  128      19 FWD  12 32818 0009.b7ee.9800 128.16
FastEthernet0/21 128.17  128      19 FWD  12 32818 0009.b7ee.9800 128.17
FastEthernet0/23 128.19  128      19 FWD  12 32818 0009.b7ee.9800 128.19
FastEthernet0/24 128.20  128      19 FWD  12 32818 0009.b7ee.9800 128.20
```

18. What is the Bridge ID for the current Root Bridge? Is the switch that produced this output the actual Root Bridge?

19. What is the path cost of interface FastEthernet 0/4, and why is it different from the others?

20. Why does the column marked "Designated Bridge ID" have the same value for every switch port?

21. Suppose that you need to troubleshoot your spanning-tree topology and operation. What commands and information can you use on a switch to find information about the current STP topology in VLAN 39?

This chapter covers the following topics that you need to master for the CCNP BCMSN exam:

- **Root Guard**—This section discusses how to protect the STP topology against unexpected switches advertising to become the Root Bridge.

- **BPDU Guard**—This section covers unexpected STP advertisements on switch ports configured for PortFast, where single hosts connect.

- **Loop Guard**—This section discusses how to protect the STP topology against the loss of BPDUs from the Root Bridge on a switch port.

- **UDLD**—This section presents a feature to detect and protect against unidirectional, switch-to-switch links.

- **BPDU Filtering**—This section explains how to filter BPDUs on a switch port to prevent the port from participating in STP altogether. Bridging loops are neither detected nor prevented.

- **Troubleshooting STP Protection**—This section summarizes the commands that diagnose or verify actions to protect the topology.

CHAPTER 10

Protecting the Spanning Tree Protocol Topology

Achieving and maintaining a loop-free Spanning Tree Protocol (STP) topology revolves around the simple process of sending and receiving bridge protocol data units (BPDU). Under normal conditions, with all switches playing fairly and according to the rules, a loop-free topology is determined dynamically.

This chapter discusses two basic conditions that can occur to disrupt the loop-free topology (even while STP is running):

- On a port that has not been receiving BPDUs, BPDUs are not expected. When BPDUs suddenly appear for some reason, the STP topology can reconverge to give unexpected results.

- On a port that normally receives BPDUs, BPDUs always are expected. When BPDUs suddenly disappear for some reason, a switch can make incorrect assumptions about the topology and unintentionally create loops.

"Do I Know This Already?" Quiz

The purpose of the "Do I Know This Already?" quiz is to help you decide what parts of this chapter to use. If you intend to read the entire chapter, you do not necessarily need to answer these questions now.

The quiz, derived from the major sections in the "Foundation Topics" portion of the chapter, helps you determine how to spend your limited study time.

Table 10-1 outlines the major topics discussed in this chapter and the "Do I Know This Already?" quiz questions that correspond to those topics.

Table 10-1 *"Do I Know This Already?" Foundation Topics Section-to-Question Mapping*

Foundation Topics Section	Questions Covered in This Section	Score
Root Guard	1–4	
BPDU Guard	5	
Loop Guard	6–8	
UDLD	9–11	
BPDU Filtering	12	
Total Score		

> **CAUTION**   The goal of self-assessment is to gauge your mastery of the topics in this chapter. If you do not know the answer to a question or are only partially sure of the answer, you should mark this question wrong. Giving yourself credit for an answer you correctly guess skews your self-assessment results and might give you a false sense of security.

1. Why is it important to protect the placement of the Root Bridge?

   a. To keep two Root Bridges from becoming active

   b. To keep the STP topology stable

   c. So all hosts have the correct gateway

   d. So the Root Bridge can have complete knowledge of the STP topology

2. Which of the following features protects a switch port from accepting superior BPDUs?

   a. STP loop guard

   b. STP BPDU guard

   c. STP root guard

   d. UDLD

3. Which of the following commands can you use to enable STP root guard on a switch port?

   a. **spanning-tree root guard**

   b. **spanning-tree root-guard**

   c. **spanning-tree guard root**

   d. **spanning-tree rootguard enable**

4. Where should the STP root guard feature be enabled on a switch?

   a. All ports

   b. Only ports where the Root Bridge should never appear

   c. Only ports where the Root Bridge should be located

   d. Only ports with PortFast enabled

5. Which of the following features protects a switch port from accepting BPDUs when PortFast is enabled?

   a. STP loop guard

   b. STP BPDU guard

   c. STP root guard

   d. UDLD

6. To maintain a loop-free STP topology, which one of the following should a switch uplink be protected against?

   a. A sudden loss of BPDUs

   b. Too many BPDUs

   c. The wrong version of BPDUs

   d. BPDUs relayed from the Root Bridge

7. Which of the following commands can enable STP loop guard on a switch port?

   a. **spanning-tree loop guard**

   b. **spanning-tree guard loop**

   c. **spanning-tree loop-guard**

   d. **spanning-tree loopguard enable**

8. STP loop guard detects which of the following conditions?

   a. The sudden appearance of superior BPDUs

   b. The sudden lack of BPDUs

   c. The appearance of duplicate BPDUs

   d. The appearance of two Root Bridges

9. Which of the following features can actively test for the loss of the receive side of a link between switches?

    a. POST

    b. BPDU

    c. UDLD

    d. STP

10. UDLD must detect a unidirectional link before which of the following?

    a. The Max Age timer expires

    b. STP moves the link to the Blocking state

    c. STP moves the link to the Forwarding state

    d. STP moves the link to the Listening state

11. What must a switch do when it receives a UDLD message on a link?

    a. Relay the message on to other switches

    b. Send a UDLD acknowledgment

    c. Echo the message back across the link

    d. Drop the message

12. Which of the following features effectively disables spanning-tree operation on a switch port?

    a. STP PortFast

    b. STP BPDU filtering

    c. STP BPDU guard

    d. STP root guard

You can find the answers to the "Do I Know This Already?" quiz in Appendix A, "Answers to Chapter 'Do I Know This Already?' Quizzes and Q&A Sections." The suggested choices for your next step are as follows:

- **10 or less overall score**—Read the entire chapter. This includes the "Foundation Topics," "Foundation Summary," and "Q&A" sections.

- **11 or 12 overall score**—If you want more review on these topics, skip to the "Foundation Summary" section, and then go to the "Q&A" section at the end of the chapter. Otherwise, move to Chapter 11, "Advanced Spanning Tree Protocol."

Foundation Topics

Protecting Against Unexpected BPDUs

A network running STP uses BPDUs to communicate between switches (bridges). Switches become aware of each other and of the topology that interconnects them. After a Root Bridge is elected, BPDUs are generated by the root and are relayed down through the spanning-tree topology. Eventually, all switches in the STP domain receive the root's BPDUs so that the network converges and a stable loop-free topology forms.

To maintain an efficient topology, the placement of the Root Bridge must be predictable. Hopefully, you configured one switch to become the Root Bridge and a second one to be the secondary root. What happens when a "foreign" or rogue switch is connected to the network, and that switch suddenly is capable of becoming the Root Bridge? Cisco added two STP features that help prevent the unexpected: root guard and BPDU guard.

Root Guard

After an STP topology has converged and becomes loop free, switch ports are assigned the following roles:

- **Root port**—The one port on a switch that is closest (with the lowest root path cost) to the Root Bridge.

- **Designated port**—The port on a LAN segment that is closest to the root. This port relays, or transmits, BPDUs down the tree.

- **Blocking port**—Ports that are neither root nor designated ports.

- **Alternate port**—Ports that are candidate root ports (they are also close to the Root Bridge) but are in the Blocking state. These ports are identified for quick use by the STP UplinkFast feature.

- **Forwarding port**—Ports where no other STP activity is detected or expected. These are ports with normal end-user connections.

The Root Bridge always is expected to be seen on the root port and the alternate ports because these are "closest" (have the best-cost path) to it.

Suppose that another switch is introduced into the network with a bridge priority that is more desirable (lower) than that of the current Root Bridge. The new switch then would become the Root Bridge, and the STP topology might reconverge to a new shape. This is entirely permissible by the STP because the switch with the lowest Bridge ID always wins the root election.

However, this is not always desirable for you, the network administrator, because the new STP topology might be something totally unacceptable. In addition, while the topology is reconverging, your production network might become unavailable.

The root guard feature was developed as a means to control where candidate Root Bridges can be connected and found on a network. Basically, a switch learns the current Root Bridge's Bridge ID. If another switch advertises a *superior BPDU*, or one with a better Bridge ID, on a port where root guard is enabled, the local switch will not allow the new switch to become the root. As long as the superior BPDUs are being received on the port, the port will be kept in the *root-inconsistent* STP state. No data can be sent or received in that state, but the switch can listen to BPDUs received on the port to detect a new root advertising itself.

In essence, root guard designates that a port can only forward or relay BPDUs; the port can't be used to receive BPDUs. Root guard prevents the port from ever becoming a root port where BPDUs normally would be received from the Root Bridge.

You can enable root guard only on a per-port basis. By default, it is disabled on all switch ports. To enable it, use the following interface configuration command:

```
Switch(config-if)# spanning-tree guard root
```

When the superior BPDUs no longer are received, the port is cycled through the normal STP states to return to normal use.

Use root guard on switch ports where you never expect to find the Root Bridge for a VLAN. In fact, root guard affects the entire port so that a Root Bridge never can be allowed on *any* VLAN on the port. When a superior BPDU is heard on the port, the entire port, in effect, becomes blocked.

> **TIP**   You can display switch ports that root guard has put into the root-inconsistent state with the following command:
>
> ```
> Switch# show spanning-tree inconsistentports
> ```

BPDU Guard

Recall that the traditional STP offers the PortFast feature, in which switch ports are allowed to immediately enter the Forwarding state as soon as the link comes up. Normally, PortFast provides quick network access to end-user devices, where bridging loops never are expected to form. Even while PortFast is enabled on a port, STP still is running and can detect a bridging loop. However, a loop can be detected only in a finite amount of time—the length of time required to move the port through the normal STP states.

> **NOTE**   Remember that enabling PortFast on a port is not the same as disabling the STP on it.

By definition, if you enable PortFast, you do not expect to find anything that can cause a bridging loop—especially another switch or device that produces BPDUs. Suppose that a switch is connected by mistake to a port where PortFast is enabled. Now there is a potential for a bridging loop to form. An even greater consequence is that the potential now exists for the newly connected device to advertise itself and become the new Root Bridge.

The BPDU guard feature was developed to further protect the integrity of switch ports that have PortFast enabled. If any BPDU (whether superior to the current root or not) is received on a port where BPDU guard is enabled, that port immediately is put into the errdisable state. The port is shut down in an error condition and must be either manually re-enabled or automatically recovered through the errdisable timeout function.

By default, BPDU guard is disabled on all switch ports. You can configure BPDU guard as a global default, affecting all switch ports with a single command. All ports that have PortFast enabled also have BPDU guard automatically enabled. You can use the following global configuration command to enable BPDU guard as the default:

```
Switch(config)# spanning-tree portfast bpduguard default
```

You also can enable or disable BPDU guard on a per-port basis, using the following interface configuration command:

```
Switch(config-if)# [no] spanning-tree bpduguard enable
```

When the BPDUs no longer are received, the port still remains in the errdisable state. See Chapter 4, "Switch Port Configuration," for more information about recovering from the errdisable state.

You should use BPDU guard on all switch ports where STP PortFast is enabled. This prevents any possibility that a switch will be added to the port, either intentionally or by mistake. An obvious application for BPDU guard is on access-layer switch ports where users and end devices connect. BPDUs normally would not be expected there and would be detected if a switch or hub inadvertently was connected.

Naturally, BPDU guard does not prevent a bridging loop from forming if an Ethernet hub is connected to the PortFast port. This is because a hub doesn't transmit BPDUs itself; it merely repeats Ethernet frames from its other ports. A loop could form if the hub became connected to two locations in the network, providing a path for frames to be looped without any STP activity.

You never should enable BPDU guard on any switch uplink where the Root Bridge is located. If a switch has multiple uplinks, any of those ports could receive legitimate BPDUs from the root— even if they are in the Blocking state as a result of the UplinkFast feature. If BPDU guard is enabled on an uplink port, BPDUs will be detected and the uplink will be put into the errdisable state. This will preclude that uplink port from being used as an uplink into the network.

Protecting Against Sudden Loss of BPDUs

STP BPDUs are used as probes to learn about a network topology. When the switches participating in STP converge on a common and consistent loop-free topology, BPDUs still must be sent by the Root Bridge and must be relayed by every other switch in the STP domain. The STP topology's integrity then depends on a continuous and regular flow of BPDUs from the root.

What happens if a switch doesn't receive BPDUs in a timely manner or when it doesn't receive any? The switch can view that condition as acceptable—perhaps an upstream switch or an upstream link is dead. In that case, the topology must have changed, so blocked ports eventually can be unblocked again.

However, if the absence of BPDUs is actually a mistake and BPDUs are not being received even though there is no topology change, bridging loops easily can form.

Cisco has added two STP features that help detect or prevent the unexpected loss of BPDUs:

- Loop guard

- Unidirectional Link Detection (UDLD)

Loop Guard

Suppose that a switch port is receiving BPDUs and the switch port is in the Blocking state. The port makes up a redundant path; it is blocking because it is neither a root port nor a designated port. It will remain in the Blocking state as long as a steady flow of BPDUs is received.

If BPDUs are being sent over a link but the flow of BPDUs stops for some reason, the last-known BPDU is kept until the Max Age timer expires. Then that BPDU is flushed, and the switch thinks there is no longer a need to block the port. After all, if no BPDUs are received, there must not be another STP device connected there.

The switch then moves the port through the STP states until it begins to forward traffic—and forms a bridging loop. In its final state, the port becomes a designated port where it begins to relay or send BPDUs downstream, when it actually should be receiving BPDUs from upstream.

To prevent this situation, you can use the loop guard STP feature. When enabled, loop guard keeps track of the BPDU activity on nondesignated ports. While BPDUs are received, the port is allowed to behave normally. When BPDUs go missing, loop guard moves the port into the loop-inconsistent state. The port is effectively blocking at this point to prevent a loop from forming and to keep it in the nondesignated role.

When BPDUs are received on the port again, loop guard allows the port to move through the normal STP states and become active. In this fashion, loop guard automatically governs ports without the need for manual intervention.

By default, loop guard is disabled on all switch ports. You can enable loop guard as a global default, affecting all switch ports, with the following global configuration command:

```
Switch(config)# spanning-tree loopguard default
```

You also can enable or disable loop guard on a specific switch port by using the following interface-configuration command:

```
Switch(config-if)# [no] spanning-tree guard loop
```

Although loop guard is configured on a switch port, its corrective blocking action is taken on a per-VLAN basis. In other words, loop guard doesn't block the entire port; only the offending VLANs are blocked.

You can enable loop guard on all switch ports, regardless of their functions. The switch figures out which ports are nondesignated and monitors the BPDU activity to keep them nondesignated. Nondesignated ports are generally the root port, alternate root ports, and ports that normally are blocking.

UDLD

In a campus network, switches are connected by bidirectional links, where traffic can flow in two directions. Clearly, if a link has a physical layer problem, the two switches it connects detect a problem and the link is shown as not connected.

What would happen if just one side of the link (receive or transmit) had an odd failure, such as malfunctioning transmit circuitry in a gigabit interface converter (GBIC) or Small Form-Factor Pluggable (SFP) modules? In some cases, the two switches still might see a functional bidirectional link, although traffic actually would be delivered in only one direction. This is known as a *unidirectional link*.

A unidirectional link poses a potential danger to STP topologies because BPDUs will not be received on one end of the link. If that end of the link normally would be in the Blocking state, it will not be that way for long. A switch interprets the absence of BPDUs to mean that the port can be moved safely through the STP states so that traffic can be forwarded. However, if that is done on a unidirectional link, a bridging loop forms and the switch never realizes the mistake.

To prevent this situation, you can use the Cisco-proprietary UniDirectional Link Detection (UDLD) STP feature. When enabled, UDLD interactively monitors a port to see if the link is truly bidirectional. A switch sends special Layer 2 UDLD frames identifying its switch port at regular intervals. UDLD expects the far-end switch to echo those frames back across the same link, with the far-end switch port's identification added.

If a UDLD frame is received in return and both neighboring ports are identified in the frame, the link must be bidirectional. However, if the echoed frames are not seen, the link must be unidirectional for some reason.

Naturally, an echo process such as this requires *both ends* of the link to be configured for UDLD. Otherwise, one end of the link will not echo the frames back to the originator. In addition, each switch at the end of a link sends its own UDLD messages independently, expecting echoes from the far end. This means that two echo processes are occurring on any given link.

UDLD messages are sent at regular intervals, as long as the link is active. You can configure the message interval UDLD uses (the default is 15 seconds). The objective behind UDLD is to detect a unidirectional link condition before STP has time to move a blocked port into the Forwarding state. To do this, the target time must be less than the Max Age timer plus two intervals of the Forward Delay timer, or 50 seconds. UDLD can detect a unidirectional link after about three times the UDLD message interval (45 seconds total, using the default).

UDLD has two modes of operation:

■ **Normal mode**—When a unidirectional link condition is detected, the port is allowed to continue its operation. UDLD merely marks the port as having an undetermined state and generates a syslog message.

■ **Aggressive mode**—When a unidirectional link condition is detected, the switch takes action to re-establish the link. UDLD messages are sent out once a second for 8 seconds. If none of those messages is echoed back, the port is placed in the errdisable state so that it cannot be used.

You configure UDLD on a per-port basis, although you can enable it globally for all fiber-optic switch ports (either native fiber or fiber-based GBIC or SFP modules). By default, UDLD is disabled on all switch ports. To enable it globally, use the following global configuration command:

```
Switch(config)# udld {enable | aggressive | message time seconds}
```

For normal mode, use the **enable** keyword; for aggressive mode, use the **aggressive** keyword. You can use the **message time** keywords to set the message interval to *seconds*, ranging from 7 to 90 seconds. (The default interval varies according to switch platform. For example, the Catalyst 3550 default is 7 seconds; the Catalyst 4500 and 6500 default is 15 seconds.)

You also can enable or disable UDLD on individual switch ports, if needed, using the following interface configuration command:

```
Switch(config-if)# udld {enable | aggressive | disable}
```

Here, you can use the **disable** keyword to completely disable UDLD on a fiber-optic interface.

> **NOTE**   The default UDLD message interval times differ among Catalyst switch platforms. Although two neighbors might have mismatched message time values, UDLD still works correctly. This is because each of the two neighbors simply echoes UDLD messages back as they are received, without knowledge of their neighbor's own time interval. The time interval is used only to decide when to send UDLD messages and as a basis for detecting a unidirectional link from the absence of echoed messages.
>
> If you decide to change the default message time, make sure that UDLD still can detect a fault *before* STP decides to move a link to the Forwarding state.

You safely can enable UDLD on all switch ports. The switch globally enables UDLD only on ports that use fiber-optic media. Twisted-pair or copper media does not suffer from the physical layer conditions that allow a unidirectional link to form. However, you can enable UDLD on nonfiber links individually, if you want.

At this point, you might be wondering how UDLD can be enabled gracefully on the two end switches. Recall that in aggressive mode, UDLD disables the link if the neighbor does not reflect the messages back within a certain time period. If you are enabling UDLD on a production network, is there a chance that UDLD will disable working links before you can get the far end configured?

The answer is no. UDLD makes some intelligent assumptions when it is enabled on a link for the first time. First, UDLD has no record of any neighbor on the link. It starts sending out messages, hoping that a neighboring switch will hear them and echo them back. Obviously, the device at the far end also must support UDLD so that the messages will be echoed back.

If the neighboring switch does not yet have UDLD enabled, no messages will be echoed. UDLD will keep trying (indefinitely) to detect a neighbor and will not disable the link. After the neighbor has UDLD configured also, both switches become aware of each other and the bidirectional state of the link through their UDLD message exchanges. From then on, if messages are not echoed, the link can accurately be labeled as unidirectional.

Finally, be aware that if UDLD detects a unidirectional condition on a link, it takes action on only that link. This becomes important in an EtherChannel: If one link within the channel becomes unidirectional, UDLD flags or disables only the offending link in the bundle, not the entire EtherChannel. UDLD sends and echoes its messages on each link within an EtherChannel channel independently.

Using BPDU Filtering to Disable STP on a Port

Ordinarily, STP operates on all switch ports in an effort to eliminate bridging loops before they can form. BPDUs are sent on all switch ports—even ports where PortFast has been enabled. BPDUs also can be received and processed if any are sent by neighboring switches.

You always should allow STP to run on a switch to prevent loops. However, in special cases when you need to prevent BPDUs from being sent or processed on one or more switch ports, you can use BPDU filtering to effectively disable STP on those ports.

By default, BPDU filtering is disabled on all switch ports. You can configure BPDU filtering as a global default, affecting all switch ports with the following global configuration command:

```
Switch(config)# spanning-tree portfast bpdufilter default
```

All ports that have PortFast enabled also have BPDU filtering automatically enabled.

You also can enable or disable BPDU filtering on specific switch ports by using the following interface configuration command:

```
Switch(config-if)# spanning-tree bpdufilter {enable | disable}
```

Be very careful to enable BPDU filtering only under controlled circumstances in which you are absolutely sure that a switch port will have a single host connected and that a loop will be impossible. Enable BPDU filtering only if the connected device cannot allow BPDUs to be accepted or sent. Otherwise, you should permit STP to operate on the switch ports as a precaution.

Troubleshooting STP Protection

With several different types of STP protection features available, you might need to know which (if any) has been configured on a switch port. Table 10-2 lists and describes the EXEC commands useful for verifying the features presented in this chapter.

Table 10-2 *Commands for Verifying and Troubleshooting STP Protection Features*

Display Function	Command Syntax
List the ports that have been labeled in an inconsistent state	Switch# **show spanning-tree inconsistentports**
Look for detailed reasons for inconsistencies	Switch# **show spanning-tree interface** *type mod/num* [**detail**]
Display the global BPDU guard, BPDU filter, and loop guard states	Switch# **show spanning-tree summary**
Display the UDLD status on one or all ports	Switch# **show udld** [*type mod/num*]
Re-enable ports that UDLD aggressive mode has errdisabled	Switch# **udld reset**

Foundation Summary

The Foundation Summary is a collection of information that provides a convenient review of many key concepts in this chapter. If you are already comfortable with the topics in this chapter, this summary could help you recall a few details. If you just read this chapter, this review can help solidify some key facts. If you are doing your final preparation before the exam, these tables and figures are a convenient way to review the day before the exam.

With so many similar and mutually exclusive STP protection features available, you might have a hard time remembering which ones to use where. Use Figure 10-1 as a quick reference.

Figure 10-1 *Guidelines for Applying STP Protection Features in a Network*

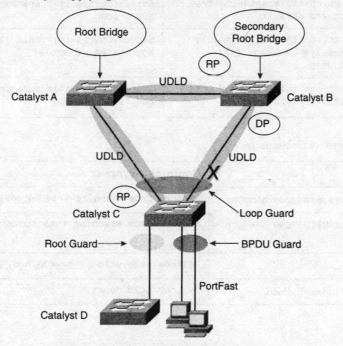

Root guard: Apply to ports where root is never expected.

BPDU guard: Apply to all user ports where PortFast is enabled.

Loop guard: Apply to nondesignated ports but okay to apply to all ports.

UDLD: Apply to all fiber-optic links between switches (must be enabled on both ends).

Permissible combinations on a switch port:
  Loop guard and UDLD
  Root guard and UDLD

Not permissible on a switch port:

  Root guard and Loop guard
  Root guard and BPDU guard

Figure 10-1 shows two backbone switches (Catalyst A and B), along with an access-layer switch (Catalyst C), with redundant uplinks. Users are connected to the access switch, where PortFast is in use. An additional access switch (Catalyst D) has an uplink to access-layer switch C. All switch-to-switch links are fiber-based Gigabit Ethernet. Obviously, a Root Bridge never should appear out of Catalyst D.

Table 10-3   *STP Protection Configuration Commands*

Task	Global Command Syntax	Interface Command Syntax
Enable root guard	—	`Switch(config-if)# `**`spanning-tree`** **`guard root`**
Enable BPDU guard	`Switch(config)# `**`spanning-tree`** **`portfast bpduguard default`**	`Switch(config-if)# `**`spanning-tree`** **`bpduguard enable`**
Enable loop guard	`Switch(config)# `**`spanning-tree`** **`loopguard default`**	`Switch(config-if)# `**`spanning-tree`** **`guard loop`**
Enable UDLD	`Switch(config)# `**`udld {enable |`** **`aggressive	message time`** *`seconds`*`}`	`Switch(config-if)# `**`udld {enable |`** **`aggressive	disable}`**
Enable BPDU filtering	`Switch(config)# `**`spanning-tree`** **`bpdufilter default`**	`Switch(config-if)# `**`spanning-tree`** **`bpdufilter enable`**

Table 10-4   *STP Protection Activity Commands*

Task	Command Syntax
Look for ports that have been put in an inconsistent state	`Switch# `**`show spanning-tree inconsistentports`**
Display the global BPDU guard, BPDU filter, and loop guard states	`Switch# `**`show spanning-tree summary`**
Show UDLD status	`Switch# `**`show udld`** `[`*`type mod/num`*`]`
Re-enable all ports that UDLD has errdisabled	`Switch# `**`udld reset`**

Q&A

The questions and scenarios in this book are more difficult than what you should experience on the actual exam. The questions do not attempt to cover more breadth or depth than the exam; however, they are designed to make sure that you know the answers. Rather than allowing you to derive the answers from clues hidden inside the questions themselves, the questions challenge your understanding and recall of the subject. Hopefully, these questions will help limit the number of exam questions on which you narrow your choices to two options and then guess.

The answers to these questions can be found in Appendix A.

1. Why would a unidirectional link be bad?

2. What condition must be met to keep a switch port in the Blocking state?

3. If a switch port is shown to be in the root-inconsistent state, what has happened on it?

4. When root guard has been triggered on a switch port, what must be done to enable the port for use again?

5. When BPDU guard is enabled on a switch port, what state will the port be put in if a BPDU is received on it?

6. When BPDU guard has been triggered on a switch port, what must be done to enable the port for use again?

7. When loop guard is enabled on a switch port, what state will the port be put in if BPDUs are noted to be missing?

8. Can STP loop guard be enabled on all switch ports?

9. When UDLD is enabled on a switch port, what else must be done to detect a unidirectional link on the port?

10. What is the difference between the UDLD normal and aggressive modes?

11. What command enables UDLD aggressive mode on a switch interface?

12. If two switches enable UDLD on the ports that have a common link, do their UDLD message times have to agree?

13. UDLD should be used on switch ports with what type of media?

14. Can UDLD be used on all switch ports without causing problems?

15. Is it possible to disable STP on a single switch port without disabling the whole STP instance? If so, how can you do that?

16. Complete the following command to display all ports that are disabled because of STP protection features:

```
show spanning-tree _____
```

This chapter covers the following topics that you need to master for the CCNP BCMSN exam:

- **Rapid Spanning Tree Protocol (RSTP)**— This section discusses the enhancements that allow switches to run STP efficiently, offering fast convergence.

- **Multiple Spanning Tree (MST) Protocol**— This section discusses the latest IEEE standard that supports a reduced number of STP instances for a campus network while using RSTP for efficient operation.

CHAPTER 11

Advanced Spanning Tree Protocol

Familiarity with the IEEE 802.1D STP standard is essential because that protocol is used universally to maintain loop-free bridged and switched networks. However, it now is considered a legacy protocol, offering topology change and convergence times that are not as acceptable as they once were.

This chapter discusses the many STP enhancements that are available in new standards. Rapid STP (RSTP) is presented first because it provides the foundation for efficient STP activity. RSTP can be coupled with either per-VLAN STP (PVST+) or Multiple STP modes. This allows a Layer 2 campus network to undergo change quickly and efficiently, with little downtime for today's applications.

This chapter also covers Multiple STP (MST or MSTP). MST allows VLANs to be individually mapped into arbitrary STP instances while RSTP operates in the background. You can use MST to greatly simplify the Layer 2 topologies and STP operations when many VLANs (and many instances of STP) are present in a network.

"Do I Know This Already?" Quiz

The purpose of the "Do I Know This Already?" quiz is to help you decide whether you need to read the entire chapter. If you already intend to read the entire chapter, you do not necessarily need to answer these questions now.

The quiz, derived from the major sections in the "Foundation Topics" portion of the chapter, helps you determine how to spend your limited study time.

Table 11-1 outlines the major topics discussed in this chapter and the "Do I Know This Already?" quiz questions that correspond to those topics.

Table 11-1 *"Do I Know This Already?" Foundation Topics Section-to-Question Mapping*

Foundation Topics Section	Questions Covered in This Section	Score
Rapid STP	1–8	
Multiple STP (MST)	9–12	
Total Score		

CAUTION The goal of self-assessment is to gauge your mastery of the topics in this chapter. If you do not know the answer to a question or are only partially sure of the answer, you should mark this question wrong. Giving yourself credit for an answer you correctly guess skews your self-assessment results and might give you a false sense of security.

1. Which one of the following enables the use of RSTP?

   a. PVST+

   b. RPVST+

   c. 802.1D

   d. CST

   e. MST

2. On which standard is RSTP based?

   a. 802.1Q

   b. 802.1D

   c. 802.1w

   d. 802.1s

3. Which of the following is not a port state in RSTP?

   a. Listening

   b. Learning

   c. Discarding

   d. Forwarding

4. When a switch running RSTP receives an 802.1D BPDU, what happens?

    a. The BPDU is discarded or dropped.

    b. An ICMP message is returned.

    c. The switch begins to use 802.1D rules on that port.

    d. The switch disables RSTP.

5. When does an RSTP switch consider a neighbor to be down?

    a. After three BPDUs are missed

    b. After six BPDUs are missed

    c. After the Max Age timer expires

    d. After the Forward timer expires

6. Which process is used during RSTP convergence?

    a. BPDU propagation

    b. Synchronization

    c. Forward timer expiration

    d. BPDU acknowledgments

7. What causes RSTP to view a port as a point-to-point port?

    a. Port speed

    b. Port media

    c. Port duplex

    d. Port priority

8. Which of the following events triggers a topology change with RSTP on a nonedge port?

    a. A port comes up or goes down.

    b. A port comes up.

    c. A port goes down.

    d. A port moves to the Forwarding state.

9. Which of the following is *not* a characteristic of MST?

   a. A reduced number of STP instances

   b. Fast STP convergence

   c. Eliminated need for CST

   d. Interoperability with PVST+

10. Which of the following standards defines the MST protocol?

    a. 802.1Q

    b. 802.1D

    c. 802.1w

    d. 802.1s

11. How many instances of STP are supported in the Cisco implementation of MST?

    a. 1

    b. 16

    c. 256

    d. 4096

12. What switch command can be used to change from PVST+ to MST?

    a. **spanning-tree mst enable**

    b. **no spanning-tree pvst+**

    c. **spanning-tree mode mst**

    d. **spanning-tree mst**

You can find the answers to the "Do I Know This Already?" quiz in Appendix A, "Answers to Chapter 'Do I Know This Already?' Quizzes and Q&A Sections." The suggested choices for your next step are as follows:

■ **10 or less overall score**—Read the entire chapter. This includes the "Foundation Topics," "Foundation Summary," and "Q&A" sections.

■ **11 or 12 overall score**—If you want more review on these topics, skip to the "Foundation Summary" section and then go to the "Q&A" section at the end of the chapter. Otherwise, move to Chapter 12, "Multilayer Switching."

Foundation Topics

Rapid Spanning Tree Protocol

The IEEE 802.1D Spanning Tree Protocol was designed to keep a switched or bridged network loop free, with adjustments made to the network topology dynamically. A topology change typically takes 30 seconds, with a port moving from the Blocking state to the Forwarding state after two intervals of the Forward Delay timer. As technology has improved, 30 seconds has become an unbearable length of time to wait for a production network to fail over or "heal" itself during a problem.

The IEEE 802.1w standard was developed to use 802.1D's principal concepts and make the resulting convergence much faster. This is also known as the Rapid Spanning Tree Protocol (RSTP), which defines how switches must interact with each other to keep the network topology loop free, in a very efficient manner.

As with 802.1D, RSTP's basic functionality can be applied as a single instance or multiple instances. This can be done by using RSTP as the underlying mechanism for the Cisco-proprietary Per-VLAN Spanning Tree Protocol (PVST+). The resulting combination is called *Rapid PVST+* (RPVST+). RSTP also is used as part of the IEEE 802.1s Multiple Spanning Tree (MST) operation. RSTP operates consistently in each, but replicating RSTP as multiple instances requires different approaches.

RSTP Port Behavior

In 802.1D, each switch port is assigned a role and a state at any given time. Depending on the port's proximity to the Root Bridge, it takes on one of the following roles:

- Root port

- Designated port

- Blocking port (neither root nor designated)

The Cisco-proprietary UplinkFast feature also reserved a hidden alternate port role for ports that offered parallel paths to the root but were in the Blocking state.

Recall that each switch port also is assigned one of five possible states:

- Disabled

- Blocking

- Listening

- Learning

- Forwarding

Only the Forwarding state allows data to be sent and received. A port's state is somewhat tied to its role. For example, a blocking port cannot be a root port or a designated port.

RSTP achieves its rapid nature by letting each switch interact with its neighbors through each port. This interaction is performed based on a port's role, not strictly on the BPDUs that are relayed from the Root Bridge. After the role is determined, each port can be given a state that determines what it does with incoming data.

The Root Bridge in a network using RSTP is elected just as with 802.1D—by the lowest Bridge ID. After all switches agree on the identity of the root, the following port roles are determined:

- **Root port**—The one switch port on each switch that has the best root path cost to the root. This is identical to 802.1D. (By definition, the Root Bridge has no root ports.)

- **Designated port**—The switch port on a network segment that has the best root path cost to the root.

- **Alternate port**—A port that has an alternative path to the root, different than the path the root port takes. This path is less desirable than that of the root port. (An example of this is an access-layer switch with two uplink ports; one becomes the root port, and the other is an alternate port.)

- **Backup port**—A port that provides a redundant (but less desirable) connection to a segment where another switch port already connects. If that common segment is lost, the switch might or might not have a path back to the root.

RSTP defines port states only according to what the port does with incoming frames. (Naturally, if incoming frames are ignored or dropped, so are outgoing frames.) Any port role can have any of these port states:

- **Discarding**—Incoming frames simply are dropped; no MAC addresses are learned. (This state combines the 802.1D Disabled, Blocking, and Listening states because all three did not effectively forward anything. The Listening state is not needed because RSTP quickly can negotiate a state change without listening for BPDUs first.)

- **Learning**—Incoming frames are dropped, but MAC addresses are learned.

- **Forwarding**—Incoming frames are forwarded according to MAC addresses that have been (and are being) learned.

BPDUs in RSTP

In 802.1D, BPDUs basically originate from the Root Bridge and are relayed by all switches down through the tree. Because of this propagation of BPDUs, 802.1D convergence must wait for steady-state conditions before proceeding.

RSTP uses the 802.1D BPDU format for backward compatibility. However, some previously unused bits in the Message Type field are used. The sending switch port identifies itself by its RSTP role and state. The BPDU version also is set to 2 to distinguish RSTP BPDUs from 802.1D BPDUs. In addition, RSTP uses an interactive process so that two neighboring switches can negotiate state changes. Some BPDU bits are used to flag messages during this negotiation.

BPDUs are sent out every switch port at Hello Time intervals, regardless of whether BPDUs are received from the root. In this way, any switch anywhere in the network can play an active role in maintaining the topology. Switches also can expect to receive regular BPDUs from their neighbors. When three BPDUs are missed in a row, that neighbor is presumed to be down, and all information related to the port leading to the neighbor immediately is aged out. This means that a switch can detect a neighbor failure in three Hello intervals (default 6 seconds), versus the Max Age timer interval (default 20 seconds) for 802.1D.

Because RSTP distinguishes its BPDUs from 802.1D BPDUs, it can coexist with switches still using 802.1D. Each port attempts to operate according to the STP BPDU that is received. For example, when an 802.1D BPDU (version 0) is received on a port, that port begins to operate according to the 802.1D rules.

However, each port has a measure that locks the protocol in use, in case BPDUs from both 802.1D and RSTP are received within a short time frame. This can occur if the switches in a network are being migrated from one STP type to another. Instead of flapping or toggling the STP type during a migration, the switch holds the protocol type for the duration of a migration delay timer. After this timer expires, the port is free to change protocols if needed.

RSTP Convergence

The convergence of STP in a network is the process that takes all switches from a state of independence (each thinks it must be the STP root) to one of uniformity, in which each switch has a place in a loop-free tree topology. You can think of convergence as a two-stage process:

1. One common Root Bridge must be "elected," and all switches must know about it.

2. The state of every switch port in the STP domain must be brought from a Blocking state to the appropriate state to prevent loops.

Convergence generally takes time because messages are propagated from switch to switch. The traditional 802.1D STP also requires the expiration of several timers before switch ports can safely be allowed to forward data.

RSTP takes a different approach when a switch needs to decide how to participate in the tree topology. When a switch first joins the topology (perhaps it was just powered up) or has detected a failure in the existing topology, RSTP requires it to base its forwarding decisions on the type of port.

Port Types

Every switch port can be considered one of the following types:

- **Edge port**—A port at the "edge" of the network, where only a single host connects. Traditionally, this has been identified by enabling the STP PortFast feature. RSTP keeps the PortFast concept for familiarity. By definition, the port cannot form a loop as it connects to one host, so it can be placed immediately in the Forwarding state. However, if a BPDU ever is received on an edge port, the port immediately loses its edge port status.

- **Root port**—The port that has the best cost to the root of the STP instance. Only one root port can be selected and active at any time, although alternative paths to the root can exist through other ports. If alternative paths are detected, those ports are identified as alternate root ports and immediately can be placed in the Forwarding state when the existing root port fails.

- **Point-to-point port**—Any port that connects to another switch and becomes a designated port. A quick handshake with the neighboring switch, rather than a timer expiration, decides the port state. BPDUs are exchanged back and forth in the form of a proposal and an agreement. One switch proposes that its port becomes a designated port; if the other switch agrees, it replies with an agreement message.

Point-to-point ports automatically are determined by the duplex mode in use. Full-duplex ports are considered point to point because only two switches can be present on the link. STP convergence can occur quickly over a point-to-point link through RSTP handshake messages.

Half-duplex ports, on the other hand, are considered to be on a shared medium with possibly more than two switches present. They are not point-to-point ports. STP convergence on a half-duplex port must occur between several directly connected switches. Therefore, the traditional 802.1D style convergence must be used. This results in a slower response because the shared-medium ports must go through the fixed Listening and Learning state time periods.

It's easy to see how two switches quickly can converge to a common idea of which one is the root and which one will have the designated port after just a single exchange of BPDUs. What about a larger network, where 802.1D BPDUs normally would have to be relayed from switch to switch?

RSTP handles the complete STP convergence of the network as a propagation of handshakes over point-to-point links. When a switch needs to make an STP decision, a handshake is made with the nearest neighbor. When that is successful, the handshake sequence is moved to the next switch and the next, as an ever-expanding wave moving toward the network's edges.

During each handshake sequence, a switch must take measures to completely ensure that it will not introduce a bridging loop before moving the handshake outward. This is done through a synchronization process.

Synchronization

To participate in RSTP convergence, a switch must decide the state of each of its ports. Nonedge ports begin in the Discarding state. After BPDUs are exchanged between the switch and its neighbor, the Root Bridge can be identified. If a port receives a superior BPDU from a neighbor, that port becomes the root port.

For each nonedge port, the switch exchanges a proposal-agreement handshake to decide the state of each end of the link. Each switch assumes that its port should become the designated port for the segment, and a proposal message (a configuration BPDU) is sent to the neighbor suggesting this.

When a switch receives a proposal message on a port, the following sequence of events occurs Figure 11-1 shows the sequence, based on the center Catalyst switch:

1. If the proposal's sender has a superior BPDU, the local switch realizes that the sender should be the designated switch (having the designated port) and that its own port must become the new root port.

2. Before the switch agrees to anything, it must synchronize itself with the topology.

3. All nonedge ports immediately are moved into the Discarding (blocking) state so that no bridging loops can form.

4. An agreement message (a configuration BPDU) is sent back to the sender, indicating that the switch is in agreement with the new designated port choice. This also tells the sender that the switch is in the process of synchronizing itself.

5. The root port immediately is moved to the Forwarding state. The sender's port also immediately can begin forwarding.

6. For each nonedge port that is currently in the Discarding state, a proposal message is sent to the respective neighbor.

7. An agreement message is expected and received from a neighbor on a nonedge port.

8. The nonedge port immediately is moved to the Forwarding state.

Figure 11-1 *Sequence of Events During RSTP Convergence*

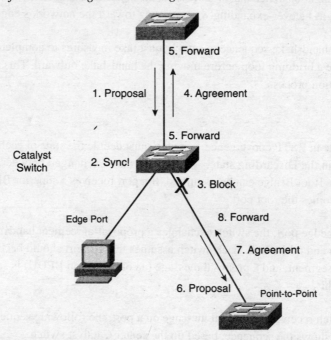

Notice that the RSTP convergence begins with a switch sending a proposal message. The recipient of the proposal must synchronize itself by effectively isolating itself from the rest of the topology. All nonedge ports are blocked until a proposal message can be sent, causing the nearest neighbors to synchronize themselves. This creates a moving "wave" of synchronizing switches, which quickly can decide to start forwarding on their links only if their neighbors agree. Figure 11-2 shows how the synchronization wave travels through a network at three successive time intervals. Isolating the switches along the traveling wave inherently prevents bridging loops.

The entire convergence process happens quickly, at the speed of BPDU transmission, without the use of any timers. However, a designated port that sends a proposal message might not receive an agreement message reply. Suppose that the neighboring switch does not understand RSTP or has a problem replying. The sending switch then must become overly cautious and must begin playing by the 802.1D rules—the port must be moved through the legacy Listening and Learning states (using the Forward Delay timer) before moving to the Forwarding state.

Figure 11-2 *RSTP Synchronization Traveling Through a Network*

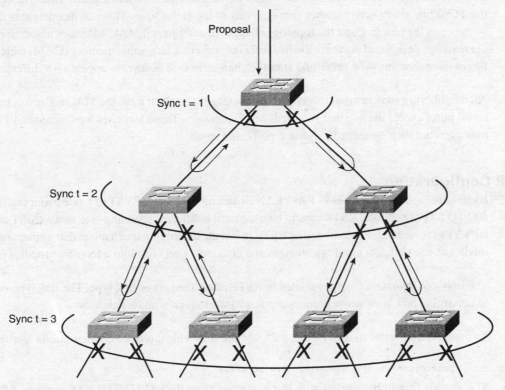

Topology Changes and RSTP

Recall that when an 802.1D switch detects a port state change (either up or down), it signals the Root Bridge by sending topology change notification (TCN) BPDUs. The Root Bridge, in turn, must signal the topology change by sending out a TCN message that is relayed to all switches in the STP domain.

RSTP detects a topology change only when a nonedge port transitions to the Forwarding state. This might seem odd because a link failure is not used as a trigger. RSTP uses all of its rapid convergence mechanisms to prevent bridging loops from forming. Therefore, topology changes are detected only so that bridging tables can be updated and corrected as hosts appear first on a failed port and then on a different functioning port.

When a topology change is detected, a switch must propagate news of the change to other switches in the network so that they can correct their bridging tables, too. This process is similar to the convergence and synchronization mechanism; topology change (TC) messages propagate through the network in an ever-expanding wave.

BPDUs, with their TC bit set, are sent out all of the nonedge designated ports. This is done until the TC While timer expires, after two intervals of the Hello time. This notifies neighboring switches of the new link and the topology change. In addition, all MAC addresses associated with the nonedge designated ports are flushed from the content-addressable memory (CAM) table. This forces the addresses to be relearned after the change, in case hosts now appear on a different link.

All neighboring switches that receive the TC messages also must flush the MAC addresses learned on all ports except the one that received the TC message. Those switches then must send TC messages out their nonedge designated ports, and so on.

RSTP Configuration

By default, a switch operates in Per-VLAN Spanning Tree Plus (PVST+) mode using traditional 802.1D STP. Therefore, RSTP cannot be used until a different spanning-tree mode (MST or RPVST+) is enabled. Remember that RSTP is just the underlying mechanism that a spanning-tree mode can use to detect topology changes and converge a network into a loop-free topology.

The only configuration changes related to RSTP affect the port or link type. The link type is used to determine how a switch negotiates topology information with its neighbors.

To configure a port as an RSTP edge port, use the following interface configuration command:

```
Switch(config-if)# spanning-tree portfast
```

You already should be familiar with this command from the 802.1D STP configuration. After PortFast is enabled, the port is considered to have only one host and is positioned at the edge of the network.

By default, RSTP automatically decides that a port is a point-to-point link if it is operating in full-duplex mode. Ports connecting to other switches are usually full duplex because there are only two switches on the link. However, you can override the automatic determination, if needed. For example, a port connecting to one other switch might be operating at half duplex, for some reason. To force the port to act as a point-to-point link, use the following interface configuration command:

```
Switch(config-if)# spanning-tree link-type point-to-point
```

Rapid Per-VLAN Spanning Tree Protocol

Chapter 8, "Traditional Spanning Tree Protocol," described PVST+ as the default STP mode on Catalyst switches. In PVST+, one spanning tree instance is created and used for each active VLAN that is defined on the switch. Each STP instance behaves according to the traditional 802.1D STP rules.

You can improve the efficiency of each STP instance by configuring a switch to begin using RSTP instead. This means that each VLAN will have its own independent instance of RSTP running on the switch. This mode is known as *Rapid PVST+ (RPVST+)*.

You need only one configuration step to change the STP mode and begin using RPVST+. You can use the following global configuration command to accomplish this:

```
Switch(config)# spanning-tree mode rapid-pvst
```

Be careful when you use this command on a production network because any STP process that is currently running must be restarted. This can cause functioning links to move through the traditional STP states, preventing data from flowing for a short time.

> **TIP**   To revert back to the default PVST+ mode, using traditional 802.1D STP, you can use the following command:
>
> ```
> Switch(config)# spanning-tree mode pvst
> ```

After you enable the RPVST+ mode, the switch must support both RSTP and 802.1D STP neighbors. The switch can detect the neighbor's STP type by the BPDU version that is received. You can see the neighbor type in the output of the **show spanning-tree vlan** *vlan-id* command, as demonstrated in Example 11-1.

Example 11-1   *Detecting a Neighboring Switch's STP Type*

```
Switch# show spanning-tree vlan 171
VLAN0171
  Spanning tree enabled protocol rstp
  Root ID    Priority    4267
             Address     00d0.0457.38aa
             Cost        3
             Port        833 (Port-channel1)
             Hello Time   2 sec  Max Age 20 sec  Forward Delay 15 sec

  Bridge ID  Priority    32939  (priority 32768 sys-id-ext 171)
             Address     0007.0d55.a800
             Hello Time   2 sec  Max Age 20 sec  Forward Delay 15 sec
             Aging Time 300

Interface        Role Sts Cost      Prio.Nbr Type
---------------- ---- --- --------- -------- --------------------------------
Gi7/8            Desg FWD 4         128.392  P2p
Gi9/6            Altn BLK 4         128.518  P2p Peer(STP)
Po1              Root FWD 3         128.833  P2p
Po2              Desg FWD 3         128.834  P2p
Po3              Desg FWD 3         128.835  P2p
Switch#
```

The output in Example 11-1 shows information about the RSTP instance for VLAN 171. The first shaded line confirms that the local switch indeed is running RSTP. (The only other way to confirm the STP mode is to locate the **spanning-tree mode** command in the running configuration.)

In addition, this output displays all the active ports participating in the VLAN 171 instance of RSTP, along with their port types. The string **P2p** denotes a point-to-point RSTP port type in which a full-duplex link connects two neighboring switches that both are running RSTP. If you see **P2p Peer(STP)**, the port is a point-to-point type but the neighboring device is running traditional 802.1D STP.

Multiple Spanning Tree Protocol

Chapter 8 covered two "flavors" of spanning-tree implementations—IEEE 802.1Q and PVST+—both based on the 802.1D STP. These also represent the two extremes of STP operation in a network:

- **802.1Q**—Only a single instance of STP is used for all VLANs. If there are 500 VLANs, only one instance of STP will be running. This is called the Common Spanning Tree (CST) and operates over the trunk's native VLAN.

- **PVST+**—One instance of STP is used for each active VLAN in the network. If there are 500 VLANs, 500 independent instances of STP will be running.

In most networks, each switch has a redundant path to another switch. For example, an access-layer switch usually has two uplinks, each connecting to a different distribution- or core-layer switch. If 802.1Q's CST is used, only one STP instance will run. This means that there is only one loop-free topology at any given time and that only one of the two uplinks in the access-layer switch will be forwarding. The other uplink always will be blocking.

Obviously, arranging the network so that both uplinks can be used simultaneously would be best. One uplink should carry one set of VLANs, whereas the other should carry a different set as a type of load balancing.

PVST+ seems more attractive to meet that goal because it allows different VLANs to have different topologies so that each uplink can be forwarding. But think of the consequences: As the number of VLANs increases, so does the number of independent STP instances. Each instance uses some amount of the switch CPU and memory resources. The more instances that are in use, the fewer CPU resources will be available for switching.

Beyond that, what is the real benefit of having 500 STP topologies for 500 VLANs, when only a small number of possible topologies exist for a switch with two uplinks? Figure 11-3 shows a typical network with an access-layer switch connecting to a pair of core switches. Two VLANs are in use, with the Root Bridges configured to support load balancing across the two uplinks. The right portion of the figure shows every possible topology for VLANs A and B. Notice that because the access-layer switch has only two uplinks, only two topologies actually matter—one in which the left uplink forwards, and one in which the right uplink forwards.

Figure 11-3 *Possible STP Topologies for Two VLANs*

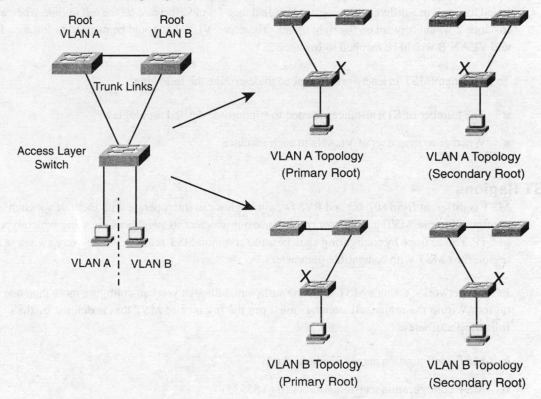

Notice also that the number of useful topologies is independent of the number of VLANs. If 10 or 100 VLANs were used in the figure, there would still be only two possible outcomes at the access-layer switch. Therefore, running 10 or 100 instances of STP when only a couple would suffice is rather wasteful.

The Multiple Spanning Tree Protocol was developed to address the lack of and surplus of STP instances. As a result, the network administrator can configure exactly the number of STP instances that makes sense for the enterprise network, no matter how many VLANs are in use. MST is defined in the IEEE 802.1s standard.

MST Overview

MST is built on the concept of mapping one or more VLANs to a single STP instance. Multiple instances of STP can be used (hence the name MST), with each instance supporting a different group of VLANs.

For the network shown in Figure 11-3, only two MST instances would be needed. Each could be tuned to result in a different topology so that Instance 1 would forward on the left uplink, whereas Instance 2 would forward on the right uplink. Therefore, VLAN A would be mapped to Instance 1, and VLAN B would be mapped to Instance 2.

To implement MST in a network, you need to determine the following:

- The number of STP instances needed to support the desired topologies

- Whether to map a set of VLANs to each instance

MST Regions

MST is different from 802.1Q and PVST+, although it can interoperate with them. If a switch is configured to use MST, it somehow must figure out which of its neighbors are using which type of STP. This is done by configuring switches into common MST regions, where every switch in a region runs MST with compatible parameters.

In most networks, a single MST region is sufficient, although you can configure more than one region. Within the region, all switches must run the instance of MST that is defined by the following attributes:

- MST configuration name (32 characters)

- MST configuration revision number (0 to 65535)

- MST instance-to-VLAN mapping table (4,096 entries)

If two switches have the same set of attributes, they belong to the same MST region. If not, they belong to two independent regions.

MST BPDUs contain configuration attributes so that switches receiving BPDUs can compare them against their local MST configurations. If the attributes match, the STP instances within MST can be shared as part of the same region. If not, a switch is seen to be at the MST region boundary, where one region meets another or one region meets traditional 802.1D STP.

> **NOTE**   The entire MST instance-to-VLAN mapping table is not sent in the BPDUs because the instance mappings must be configured on each switch. Instead, a digest, or a hash code computed from the table contents, is sent. As the contents of the table change, the digest value will be different. Therefore, a switch quickly can compare a received digest to its own to see if the advertised table is the same.

Spanning Tree Instances Within MST

MST was designed to interoperate with all other forms of STP. Therefore, it also must support STP instances from each. This is where MST can get confusing. Think of the entire enterprise network as having a single CST topology so that one instance of STP represents any and all VLANs and MST regions present. The CST maintains a common loop-free topology while integrating all forms of STP that might be in use.

To do this, CST must regard each MST region as a single "black box" bridge because it has no idea what is inside the region, nor does it care. CST maintains a loop-free topology only with the links that connect the regions to each other and to standalone switches running 802.1Q CST.

IST Instances

Something other than CST must work out a loop-free topology inside each MST region. Within a single MST region, an Internal Spanning Tree (IST) instance runs to work out a loop-free topology between the links where CST meets the region boundary and all switches inside the region. Think of the IST instance as a locally significant CST, bounded by the edges of the region.

The IST presents the entire region as a single virtual bridge to the CST outside. BPDUs are exchanged at the region boundary only over the native VLAN of trunks, as if a single CST were in operation. And, indeed, it is.

Figure 11-4 shows the basic concept behind the IST instance. The network at the left has an MST region, where several switches are running compatible MST configurations. Another switch is outside the region because it is running only the CST from 802.1Q.

The same network is shown at the right, where the IST has produced a loop-free topology for the network inside the region. The IST makes the internal network look like a single bridge (the "big switch" in the cloud) that can interface with the CST running outside the region.

MST Instances

Recall that the whole idea behind MST is the capability to map multiple VLANs to a smaller number of STP instances. Inside a region, the actual MST instances (MSTIs) exist alongside the IST. Cisco supports a maximum of 16 MSTIs in each region. IST always exists as MSTI number 0, leaving MSTIs 1 through 15 available for use.

Figure 11-4 *Concepts Behind the IST Instance*

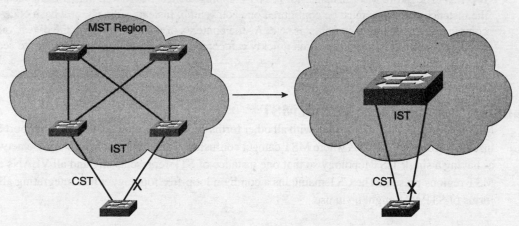

Figure 11-5 shows how different MSTIs can exist within a single MST region. The left portion of the figure is identical to that of Figure 11-4. In this network, two MST instances, MSTI 1 and MSTI 2, are configured with different VLANs mapped to each. Their topologies follow the same structure as the network on the left side of the figure, but each has converged differently.

Figure 11-5 *Concepts Behind MST Instances*

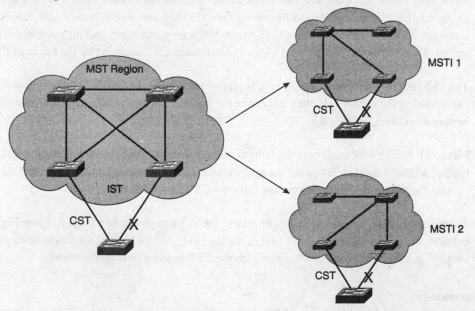

Notice that within the MST cloud, there are now three independent STP instances coexisting: MSTI1, MSTI 2, and the IST.

Only the IST (MSTI 0) is allowed to send and receive MST BPDUs. Information about each of the other MSTIs is appended to the MST BPDU as an M-record. Therefore, even if a region has all 16 instances active, only one BPDU is needed to convey STP information about them all.

Each of the MSTIs is significant only within a region, even if an adjacent region has the same MSTIs in use. In other words, the MSTIs combine with the IST only at the region boundary to form a subtree of the CST. That means only IST BPDUs are sent into and out of a region.

What if an MST region connects with a switch running traditional PVST+? MST can detect this situation by listening to the received BPDUs. If BPDUs are heard from more than one VLAN (the CST), PVST+ must be in use. When the MST region sends a BPDU toward the PVST+ switch, the IST BPDUs are replicated into all of the VLANs on the PVST+ switch trunk.

> **TIP**   Keep in mind that the IST instance is active on *every* port on a switch. Even if a port does not carry VLANs that have been mapped to the IST, IST must be running on the port. Also, by default, all VLANs are mapped to the IST instance. You must explicitly map them to other instances, if needed.

MST Configuration

You must manually configure the MST configuration attributes on each switch in a region. There is currently no method to propagate this information from one switch to another, as is done with a protocol such as VLAN Trunking Protocol (VTP). To define the MST region, use the following configuration commands in the order shown:

Step 1   Enable MST on the switch:

```
Switch(config)# spanning-tree mode mst
```

Step 2   Enter the MST configuration mode:

```
Switch(config)# spanning-tree mst configuration
```

Step 3   Assign a region configuration name (up to 32 characters):

```
Switch(config-mst)# name name
```

Step 4   Assign a region configuration revision number (0 to 65,535):

```
Switch(config-mst)# revision version
```

The configuration revision number gives you a means of tracking changes to the MST region configuration. Each time you make changes to the configuration, you should increase the number by one. Remember that the region configuration (including the revision number) must match on all switches in the region. Therefore, you also need to update the revision numbers on the other switches to match.

Step 5   Map VLANs to an MST instance:

```
Switch(config-mst)# instance instance-id vlan vlan-list
```

The *instance-id* (0 to 15) carries topology information for the VLANs listed in *vlan-list*. The list can contain one or more VLANs separated by commas. You also can add a range of VLANs to the list by separating numbers with a hyphen. VLAN numbers can range from 1 to 4,094. (Remember that, by default, all VLANs are mapped to instance 0, the IST.)

Step 6   Show the pending changes you have made:

```
Switch(config-mst)# show pending
```

Step 7   Exit the MST configuration mode; commit the changes to the active MST region configuration:

```
Switch(config-mst)# exit
```

After MST is enabled and configured, PVST+ operation stops and the switch changes to RSTP operation. A switch cannot run both MST and PVST+ at the same time.

You also can tune the parameters that MST uses when it interacts with CST or traditional 802.1D. The parameters and timers are identical to those discussed in Chapter 9, "Spanning Tree Configuration." In fact, the commands are very similar except for the addition of the **mst** keyword and the *instance-id*. Instead of tuning STP for a VLAN instance, you use an MST instance.

Table 11-2 summarizes the commands as a quick reference. Notice that the timer configurations are applied to MST as a whole, not to a specific MST instance. This is because all instance timers are defined through the IST instance and BPDUs.

Table 11-2 *MST Configuration Commands*

Task	Command Syntax
Set Root Bridge (macro)	`Switch(config)# spanning-tree mst instance-id root {primary	secondary} [diameter diameter]`
Set bridge priority	`Switch(config)# spanning-tree mst instance-id priority bridge-priority`
Set port cost	`Switch(config)# spanning-tree mst instance-id cost cost`
Set port priority	`Switch(config)# spanning-tree mst instance-id port-priority port-priority`

Set STP timers	`Switch(config)# spanning-tree mst hello-time seconds`
	`Switch(config)# spanning-tree mst forward-time seconds`
	`Switch(config)# spanning-tree mst max-age seconds`

Foundation Summary

The Foundation Summary is a collection of information that provides a convenient review of many key concepts in this chapter. If you are already comfortable with the topics in this chapter, this summary can help you recall a few details. If you just read this chapter, this review should help solidify some key facts. If you are doing your final preparation before the exam, this information is a convenient way to review the day before the exam.

RSTP port roles:

■ Root port

■ Designated port

■ Alternate port

■ Backup port

RSTP port states:

■ Discarding

■ Learning

■ Forwarding

Table 11-3 *RSTP Configuration Commands*

Task	Command Syntax
Define an edge port	Switch(config-if)# **spanning-tree portfast**
Override a port type	Switch(config-if)# **spanning-tree link-type point-to-point**

STP instances involved with MST:

■ **Common Spanning Tree (CST)**—Used to maintain a single loop-free topology for the entire network

■ **Internal Spanning Tree (IST)**—Used like CST, to maintain a single, loop-free topology *inside* an MST region

■ **MST instances (MSTIs)**—Used inside an MST region to maintain loop-free topologies for sets of mapped VLANs

Table 11-4 *MST Region Configuration Commands*

Task	Command Syntax
Enable MST on a switch	Switch(config)# **spanning-tree mode mst**
Enter MST configuration mode	Switch(config)# **spanning-tree mst configuration**
Name the MST region	Switch(config-mst)# **name** *name*
Set the configuration revision number	Switch(config-mst)# **revision** *version*
Map VLANs to an MST instance	Switch(config-mst)# **instance** *instance-id* **vlan** *vlan-list*
Confirm new MST configuration changes	Switch(config-mst)# **show pending**
Commit new MST changes	Switch(config-mst)# **exit**

Table 11-5 *MST Tuning Configuration Commands*

Task	Command Syntax
Set the Root Bridge	Switch(config)# **spanning-tree mst** *instance-id* **root {primary | secondary} [diameter** *diameter*]
Set bridge priority	Switch(config)# **spanning-tree mst** *instance-id* **priority** *bridge-priority*
Set port cost	Switch(config)# **spanning-tree mst** *instance-id* **cost** *cost*
Set port priority	Switch(config)# **spanning-tree mst** *instance-id* **port-priority** *port-priority*
Set STP timers	Switch(config)# **spanning-tree mst hello-time** *seconds* Switch(config)# **spanning-tree mst forward-time** *seconds* Switch(config)# **spanning-tree mst max-age** *seconds*

Q&A

The questions and scenarios in this book are more difficult than what you should experience on the actual exam. The questions do not attempt to cover more breadth or depth than the exam; however, they are designed to make sure that you know the answers. Rather than allowing you to derive the answers from clues hidden inside the questions themselves, the questions challenge your understanding and recall of the subject. Hopefully, these questions will help limit the number of exam questions on which you narrow your choices to two options and then guess.

You can find the answers to these questions in Appendix A.

1. What is synchronization in RSTP?

2. What is an alternate port?

3. What is the difference between an alternate port and a backup port?

4. Can a switch port be a designated port and be in the Discarding state?

5. Which port type *cannot* participate in RSTP synchronization?

6. What two messages must be exchanged during RSTP synchronization?

7. After an agreement message is received from a neighboring switch, how much time elapses before the port can begin forwarding? (Consider any timers that must expire or other conditions that must be met.)

8. After a switch receives news of a topology change, how long does it wait to flush entries from its CAM table?

9. What command configures a port as an RSTP edge port?

10. Suppose interface FastEthernet 0/1 is in half-duplex mode, but you want it to be considered a point-to-point link for RSTP. What command can accomplish this?

11. Put the following in order of the number of supported STP instances, from lowest to highest:

    a. MST

    b. PVST+

    c. CST

    d. 802.1D

12. What three parameters must be configured to uniquely define an MST region?

13. What parameter does a switch examine to see if its neighbors have the same VLAN-to-MST instance mappings? How is that information passed among switches?

14. Which MST instance in a region corresponds to the CST of 802.1Q?

15. Which MST instance is the IST?

16. When an MST region meets a PVST+ domain, how is each MST instance propagated into PVST+?

17. Is it wise to assign VLANs to MST instance 0? Why or why not?

18. The commands have just been entered to define an MST region on a switch. You are still at the MST configuration prompt. What command must you enter to commit the MST changes on the switch?

19. How can MST configuration information be propagated to other Cisco switches?

20. A switch can interact with both 802.1D and RSTP. Can it run both PVST+ and MST simultaneously?

This part of the book covers the following BCMSN exam topics:

- Explain and configure InterVLAN routing (i.e., SVI and routed ports)
- Explain and enable CEF operation
- Verify or troubleshoot InterLAN routing configurations
- Explain the functions and operations of gateway redundancy protocols (HSRP, VRRP, and GLBP)
- Configure HSRP, VRRP, and GLBP
- Verify High Availability configurations

Part III: Layer 3 Switching

This chapter covers the following topics that you need to master for the CCNP BCMSN exam:

- **InterVLAN Routing**—This section discusses how you can use a routing function with a switch to forward packets between VLANs.

- **Multilayer Switching with CEF**—This section discusses Cisco Express Forwarding (CEF) and how it is implemented on Catalyst switches. CEF forwards or routes packets in hardware at a high throughput.

- **Troubleshooting Multilayer Switching**—This section provides a brief summary of the commands that can verify the configuration and operation of InterVLAN routing, CEF, and fallback bridging.

CHAPTER 12

Multilayer Switching

Chapter 3, "Switch Operation," presents a functional overview of how multilayer switching (MLS) is performed at Layers 3 and 4. The actual MLS process can take two forms: InterVLAN routing and Cisco Express Forwarding (CEF). This chapter expands on multilayer switch operation by discussing both of these topics in greater detail.

"Do I Know This Already?" Quiz

The purpose of the "Do I Know This Already?" quiz is to help you decide what parts of this chapter to use. If you already intend to read the entire chapter, you do not necessarily need to answer these questions now.

The quiz, derived from the major sections in the "Foundation Topics" portion of the chapter, helps you determine how to spend your limited study time.

Table 12-1 outlines the major topics discussed in this chapter and the "Do I Know This Already?" quiz questions that correspond to those topics.

Table 12-1 *"Do I Know This Already?" Foundation Topics Section-to-Question Mapping*

Foundation Topics Section	Questions Covered in This Section	Score
InterVLAN Routing	1–5	
Multilayer Switching with CEF	6–11	
Troubleshooting Multilayer Switching	12	
Total Score		

CAUTION   The goal of self-assessment is to gauge your mastery of the topics in this chapter. If you do not know the answer to a question or are only partially sure of the answer, you should mark this question wrong. Giving yourself credit for an answer you correctly guess skews your self-assessment results and might give you a false sense of security.

1. Which of the following arrangements can be considered InterVLAN routing?

   a. One switch, two VLANs, one connection to a router

   b. One switch, two VLANs, two connections to a router

   c. Two switches, two VLANs, two connections to a router

   d. All of these answers are correct

2. How many interfaces are needed in a "router on a stick" implementation for InterVLAN routing among four VLANs?

   a. 1

   b. 2

   c. 4

   d. Cannot be determined

3. Which of the following commands configures a switch port for Layer 2 operation?

   a. **switchport**

   b. **no switchport**

   c. **ip address 192.168.199.1 255.255.255.0**

   d. **no ip address**

4. Which of the following commands configures a switch port for Layer 3 operation?

   a. **switchport**

   b. **no switchport**

   c. **ip address 192.168.199.1 255.255.255.0**

   d. **no ip address**

5. Which one of the following interfaces is an SVI?

   a. **interface fastethernet 0/1**

   b. **interface gigabit 0/1**

   c. **interface vlan 1**

   d. **interface svi 1**

6. What information must be learned before CEF can forward packets?

   a. The source and destination of the first packet in a traffic flow

   b. The MAC addresses of both the source and destination

   c. The contents of the routing table

   d. The outbound port of the first packet in a flow

7. Which of the following best defines an adjacency?

   a. Two switches connected by a common link

   b. Two contiguous routes in the FIB

   c. Two multilayer switches connected by a common link

   d. The MAC address of a host is known

8. Assume that CEF is active on a switch. What happens to a packet that arrives needing fragmentation?

   a. The packet is switched by CEF and kept intact.

   b. The packet is fragmented by CEF.

   c. The packet is dropped.

   d. The packet is sent to the Layer 3 engine.

9. Suppose that a host sends a packet to a destination IP address and that the CEF-based switch does not yet have a valid MAC address for the destination. How is the ARP entry (MAC address) of the next-hop destination in the FIB obtained?

   a. The sending host must send an ARP request for it.

   b. The Layer 3 forwarding engine (CEF hardware) must send an ARP request for it.

   c. CEF must wait until the Layer 3 engine sends an ARP request for it.

   d. All packets to the destination are dropped.

10. During a packet rewrite, what happens to the source MAC address?

   a. There is no change.

   b. It is changed to the destination MAC address.

   c. It is changed to the MAC address of the outbound Layer 3 switch interface.

   d. It is changed to the MAC address of the next-hop destination.

11. What Spanning Tree Protocol is used for fallback bridging?

    a. 802.1D

    b. IBM STP

    c. PVST+

    d. VLAN-bridge

12. What command can you use to view the CEF FIB table contents?

    a. **show fib**

    b. **show ip cef fib**

    c. **show ip cef**

    d. **show fib-table**

You can find the answers to the "Do I Know This Already?" quiz in Appendix A, "Answers to Chapter 'Do I Know This Already?' Quizzes and Q&A Sections." The suggested choices for your next step are as follows:

- **10 or less overall score**—Read the entire chapter. This includes the "Foundation Topics," "Foundation Summary," and "Q&A" sections.

- **11 or 12 overall score**—If you want more review on these topics, skip to the "Foundation Summary" section and then go to the "Q&A" section at the end of the chapter. Otherwise, move to Chapter 13, "Router, Supervisor, and Power Redundancy."

Foundation Topics

InterVLAN Routing

Recall that a Layer 2 network is defined as a broadcast domain. A Layer 2 network also can exist as a VLAN inside one or more switches. VLANs essentially are isolated from each other so that packets in one VLAN cannot cross into another VLAN.

To transport packets between VLANs, you must use a Layer 3 device. Traditionally, this has been a router's function. The router must have a physical or logical connection to each VLAN so that it can forward packets between them. This is known as *interVLAN routing*.

InterVLAN routing can be performed by an external router that connects to each of the VLANs on a switch. Separate physical connections can be used, or the router can access each of the VLANs through a single trunk link. Part A of Figure 12-1 illustrates this concept. The external router also can connect to the switch through a single trunk link, carrying all the necessary VLANs, as illustrated in Part B of Figure 12-1. Part B illustrates what commonly is referred to as a "router on a stick" or a "one-armed router" because the router needs only a single interface to do its job.

Finally, Part C of Figure 12-1 shows how the routing and switching functions can be combined into one device: a multilayer switch. No external router is needed.

Figure 12-1 *Examples of InterVLAN Routing Connections*

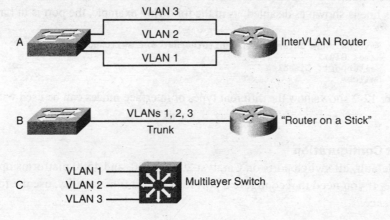

Types of Interfaces

Multilayer switches can perform both Layer 2 switching and interVLAN routing, as appropriate. Layer 2 switching occurs between interfaces that are assigned to Layer 2 VLANs or Layer 2 trunks. Layer 3 switching can occur between any type of interface, as long as the interface can have a Layer 3 address assigned to it.

As with a router, a multilayer switch can assign a Layer 3 address to a physical interface. It also can assign a Layer 3 address to a logical interface that represents an entire VLAN. This is known as a *switched virtual interface (SVI)*.

Configuring InterVLAN Routing

InterVLAN routing first requires that routing be enabled for the Layer 3 protocol. In addition, you must configure static routes or a dynamic routing protocol. These topics are covered fully in the BSCI course.

Because a multilayer switch supports many different types of interfaces for Layer 2 or Layer 3 switching, you must define each interface on a switch that will be used. By default, every switch port on platforms such as the Catalyst 2950, 3560, or 4500 is a Layer 2 interface, whereas every switch port on a Catalyst 6500 (native IOS) is a Layer 3 interface. If another type or mode is needed, you must explicitly configure it.

A port is either in Layer 2 or Layer 3 mode, depending on the use of the **switchport** configuration command. You can display a port's current mode with the following command:

```
Switch# show interface type mod/num switchport
```

If the **Switchport:** line in the command output is shown as enabled, the port is in Layer 2 mode. If this line is shown as disabled, as in the following example, the port is in Layer 3 mode:

```
Switch# show interface gigabitethernet 0/1 switchport
Name: Gi0/1
Switchport: Disabled
Switch#
```

Figure 12-2 shows how the different types of interface modes can be used within a single switch.

Layer 2 Port Configuration

By default, all switch ports on Catalyst 2950, 3560, and 4500 platforms operate in Layer 2 mode. If you need to reconfigure a port for Layer 2 functionality, use the following command sequence:

```
Switch(config)# interface type mod/num
Switch(config-if)# switchport
```

Figure 12-2 *Catalyst Switch with Various Types of Ports*

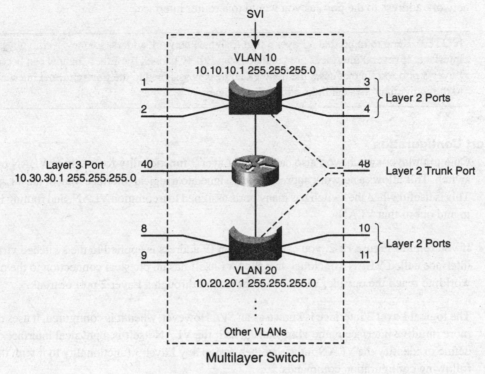

The **switchport** command puts the port in Layer 2 mode. Then you can use other **switchport** command keywords to configure trunking, access VLANs, and so on. As displayed in Figure 12-2, several Layer 2 ports exist, each assigned to a specific VLAN. A Layer 2 port also can act as a trunk, transporting multiple VLANs.

Layer 3 Port Configuration

Physical switch ports also can operate as Layer 3 interfaces, where a Layer 3 network address is assigned and routing can occur, as shown previously in Figure 12-2. By default, all switch ports on the Catalyst 6500 platform (native IOS) operate in the Layer 3 mode. For Layer 3 functionality, you must explicitly configure switch ports with the following command sequence:

```
Switch(config)# interface type mod/num
Switch(config-if)# no switchport
Switch(config-if)# ip address ip-address mask [secondary]
```

The **no switchport** command takes the port out of Layer 2 operation. You then can assign a network address to the port, as you would to a router interface.

> **NOTE** Keep in mind that a Layer 3 port assigns a network address to one specific physical interface. If several interfaces are bundled as an EtherChannel, the EtherChannel can become a Layer 3 port too. In that case, the network address is assigned to the **port-channel** interface—not to the individual physical links within the channel.

SVI Port Configuration

On a multilayer switch, you also can enable Layer 3 functionality for an entire VLAN on the switch. This allows a network address to be assigned to a logical interface: that of the VLAN itself. This is useful when the switch has many ports assigned to a common VLAN, and routing is needed in and out of that VLAN.

If you refer to Figure 12-2, you can see how an IP address is applied to the switched virtual interface called VLAN 10. Notice that the SVI itself has no physical connection to the outside world; to reach the outside, VLAN 10 must extend through a Layer 2 port or trunk.

The logical Layer 3 interface is known as an *SVI*. However, when it is configured, it uses the much more intuitive interface name **vlan** *vlan-id*, as if the VLAN itself is a physical interface. First, define or identify the VLAN interface; then assign any Layer 3 functionality to it with the following configuration commands:

```
Switch(config)# interface vlan vlan-id
Switch(config-if)# ip address ip-address mask [secondary]
```

The VLAN must be defined and active on the switch before the SVI can be used. Make sure that the new VLAN interface also is enabled with the **no shutdown** interface configuration command.

> **NOTE** The VLAN and the SVI are configured separately, even though they interoperate. Creating or configuring the SVI doesn't create or configure the VLAN; you still must define each one independently.
>
> As an example, the following commands show how VLAN 100 is created and then defined as a Layer 3 SVI:
>
> ```
> Switch(config)# vlan 100
> Switch(config-vlan)# name Example_VLAN
> Switch(config-vlan)# exit
> Switch(config)# interface vlan 100
> Switch(config-if)# ip address 192.168.100.1 255.255.255.0
> Switch(config-if)# no shutdown
> ```

Multilayer Switching with CEF

Catalyst switches can use several methods to forward packets based on Layer 3 and Layer 4 information. The current generation of Catalyst multilayer switches uses the efficient Cisco Express Forwarding (CEF) method. This section describes the evolution of multilayer switching and discusses CEF in detail. Although CEF is easy to configure and use, the underlying switching mechanisms are more involved and should be understood.

Traditional MLS Overview

Multilayer switching began as a dual effort between a route processor (RP) and a switching engine (SE). The basic idea is to "route once and switch many." The RP receives the first packet of a new traffic flow between two hosts, as usual. A routing decision is made, and the packet is forwarded toward the destination.

To participate in multilayer switching, the SE must know the identity of each RP. The SE then can listen in to the first packet going to the router and also going away from the router. If the SE can switch the packet in both directions, it can learn a "shortcut path" so that subsequent packets of the same flow can be switched directly to the destination port without passing through the RP.

This technique also is known as *NetFlow switching* or *route cache switching*. Traditionally, NetFlow switching was performed on Cisco hardware, such as the Catalyst 6000 Supervisor 1/1a and Multilayer Switch Feature Card (MSFC), Catalyst 5500 with a Route Switch Module (RSM), Route Switch Feature Card (RSFC), or external router. Basically, the hardware consisted of an independent RP component and a NetFlow-capable SE component.

CEF Overview

NetFlow switching has given way to a more efficient form of multilayer switching: Cisco Express Forwarding. Cisco developed CEF for its line of routers, offering high-performance packet forwarding through the use of dynamic lookup tables.

CEF also has been carried over to the Catalyst switching platforms. The following platforms all perform CEF in hardware:

- Catalyst 6500 Supervisor 720 (with an integrated MSFC3)

- Catalyst 6500 Supervisor 2/MSFC2 combination

- Catalyst 4500 Supervisor III, IV, and V

- Fixed-configuration switches, such as the Catalyst 3750, 3560, 3550, and 2950

CEF runs by default, taking advantage of the specialized hardware.

A CEF-based multilayer switch consists of two basic functional blocks, as shown in Figure 12-3: The Layer 3 Engine is involved in building routing information that the Layer 3 Forwarding Engine can use to switch packets in hardware.

Figure 12-3 *Packet Flow Through a CEF-Based Multilayer Switch*

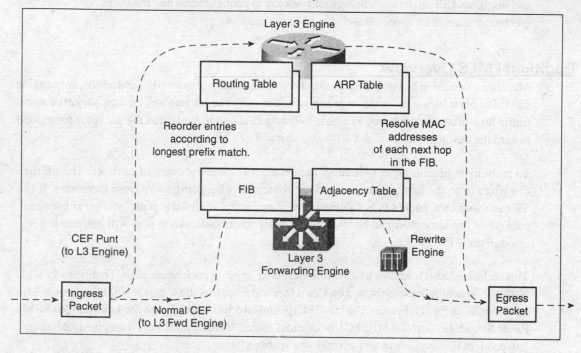

Forwarding Information Base

The Layer 3 engine (essentially a router) maintains routing information, whether from static routes or dynamic routing protocols. Basically, the routing table is reformatted into an ordered list with the most specific route first, for each IP destination subnet in the table. The new format is called a Forwarding Information Base (FIB) and contains routing or forwarding information that the network prefix can reference.

In other words, a route to 10.1.0.0/16 might be contained in the FIB along with routes to 10.1.1.0/24 and 10.1.1.128/25, if those exist. Notice that these examples are increasingly more specific subnets, as designated by the longer subnet masks. In the FIB, these would be ordered with the most specific, or longest match, first, followed by less specific subnets. When the switch receives a packet, it easily can examine the destination address and find the longest-match destination route entry in the FIB.

The FIB also contains the next-hop address for each entry. When a longest-match entry is found in the FIB, the Layer 3 next-hop address is found, too.

You might be surprised to know that the FIB also contains host route (subnet mask 255.255.255.255) entries. These normally are not found in the routing table unless they are advertised or manually configured. Host routes are maintained in the FIB for the most efficient routing lookup to directly connected or adjacent hosts.

As with a routing table, the FIB is dynamic in nature. When the Layer 3 engine sees a change in the routing topology, it sends an update to the FIB. Anytime the routing table receives a change to a route prefix or the next-hop address, the FIB receives the same change. Also, if a next-hop address is changed or aged out of the Address Resolution Protocol (ARP) table, the FIB must reflect the same change.

You can display FIB table entries related to a specific interface or VLAN with the following form of the **show ip cef** command:

```
Switch# show ip cef [type mod/num | vlan vlan-id] [detail]
```

The FIB entries corresponding to the VLAN 101 switched virtual interface might be shown as demonstrated in Example 12-1.

Example 12-1 *Displaying FIB Table Entries for a Specified VLAN*

```
Switch# show ip cef vlan 101
Prefix            Next Hop          Interface
10.1.1.0/24       attached          Vlan101
10.1.1.2/32       10.1.1.2          Vlan101
10.1.1.3/32       10.1.1.3          Vlan101
Switch#
```

You also can view FIB entries by specifying an IP prefix address and mask, using the following form of the **show ip cef** command:

```
Switch# show ip cef [prefix-ip prefix-mask] [longer-prefixes] [detail]
```

The output in Example 12-2 displays any subnet within 10.1.0.0/16 that is known by the switch, regardless of the prefix or mask length. Normally, only an exact match of the IP prefix and mask will be displayed if it exists in the CEF table. To see other longer match entries, you can add the **longer-prefixes** keyword.

Example 12-2 *Displaying FIB Table Entries for a Specified IP Prefix Address/Mask*

```
Switch# show ip cef 10.1.0.0 255.255.0.0 longer-prefixes
Prefix            Next Hop          Interface
10.1.1.0/24       attached          Vlan101
10.1.1.2/32       10.1.1.2          Vlan101
10.1.1.3/32       10.1.1.3          Vlan101
10.1.2.0/24       attached          Vlan102
10.1.3.0/26       192.168.1.2       Vlan99
```

continues

Example 12-2 *Displaying FIB Table Entries for a Specified IP Prefix Address/Mask (Continued)*

```
                    192.168.1.3              Vlan99
10.1.3.64/26        192.168.1.2              Vlan99
                    192.168.1.3              Vlan99
10.1.3.128/26       192.168.1.4              Vlan99
                    192.168.1.3              Vlan99
[output omitted]
Switch#
```

Notice that the first three entries are the same ones listed in Example 12-1. Other subnets also are displayed, along with their next-hop router addresses and switch interfaces.

You can add the **detail** keyword to see more information about each FIB table entry for CEF, as demonstrated in Example 12-3.

Example 12-3 *Displaying Detailed CEF Entry Information*

```
Switch# show ip cef 10.1.3.0 255.255.255.192 detail
10.1.3.0/26, version 270, epoch 0, per-destination sharing
0 packets, 0 bytes
  via 192.168.1.2, Vlan99, 0 dependencies
    traffic share 1
    next hop 192.168.1.2, Vlan99
    valid adjacency
  via 192.168.1.3, Vlan99, 0 dependencies
    traffic share 1
    next hop 192.168.1.3, Vlan99
    valid adjacency
  0 packets, 0 bytes switched through the prefix
  tmstats: external 0 packets, 0 bytes
           internal 0 packets, 0 bytes
Switch#
```

The version number describes the number of times the CEF entry has been updated since the table was generated. The epoch number denotes the number of times the CEF table has been flushed and regenerated as a whole. The 10.1.3.0/26 subnet has two next-hop router addresses, so the local switch is using per-destination load sharing between the two routers.

After the FIB is built, packets can be forwarded along the bottom dashed path in Figure 12-3. This follows the hardware switching process, in which no "expensive" or time-consuming operations are needed. At times, however, a packet cannot be switched in hardware, according to the FIB. Packets then are marked as "CEF punt" and immediately are sent to the Layer 3 engine for further processing, as shown in the top dashed path in Figure 12-3. Some of the conditions that can cause this are as follows:

■   An entry cannot be located in the FIB

■   The FIB table is full

- The IP Time To Live (TTL) has expired

- The maximum transmission unit (MTU) is exceeded, and the packet must be fragmented

- An Internet Control Message Protocol (ICMP) redirect is involved

- The encapsulation type is not supported

- Packets are tunneled, requiring a compression or encryption operation

- An access list with the **log** option is triggered

- A Network Address Translation (NAT) operation must be performed (except on the Catalyst 6500 Supervisor 720, which can handle NAT in hardware)

CEF operations can be handled on a single hardware platform, such as the Catalyst 3560 and 3750 switches. The FIB is generated and contained centrally in the switch. CEF also can be optimized through the use of specialized forwarding hardware, using the following techniques:

- **Accelerated CEF (aCEF)**—CEF is distributed across multiple Layer 3 forwarding engines, typically located on Catalyst 6500 line cards. These engines do not have the capability to store and use the entire FIB, so only a portion of the FIB is downloaded to them at any time. This functions as an FIB "cache," containing entries that are likely to be used again. If FIB entries are not found in the cache, requests are sent to the Layer 3 engine for more FIB information. The net result is that CEF is accelerated on the line cards, but not necessarily at a sustained wire-speed rate.

- **Distributed CEF (dCEF)**—CEF can be distributed completely among multiple Layer 3 forwarding engines for even greater performance. Because the FIB is self-contained for complete Layer 3 forwarding, it can be replicated across any number of independent Layer 3 forwarding engines. The Catalyst 6500 has line cards that support dCEF, each with its own FIB table and forwarding engine. A central Layer 3 engine (the MSFC3, for example) maintains the routing table and generates the FIB, which is then dynamically downloaded in full to each of the line cards.

Adjacency Table

A router normally maintains a routing table containing Layer 3 network and next-hop information, and an ARP table containing Layer 3 to Layer 2 address mapping. These tables are kept independently.

Recall that the FIB keeps the Layer 3 next-hop address for each entry. To streamline packet forwarding even more, the FIB has corresponding Layer 2 information for every next-hop entry. This portion of the FIB is called the *adjacency table*, consisting of the MAC addresses of nodes that can be reached in a single Layer 2 hop.

You can display the adjacency table's contents with the following command:

```
Switch# show adjacency [type mod/num | vlan vlan-id] [summary | detail]
```

As an example, the total number of adjacencies known on each physical or VLAN interface can be displayed with the **show adjacency summary** command, as demonstrated in Example 12-4.

Example 12-4 *Displaying the Total Number of Known Adjacencies*

```
Switch# show adjacency summary
Adjacency Table has 106 adjacencies
  Table epoch: 0 (106 entries at this epoch)
  Interface                Adjacency Count
  Vlan99                   21
  Vlan101                  3
  Vlan102                  1
  Vlan103                  47
  Vlan104                  7
  Vlan105                  27
Switch#
```

Adjacencies are kept for each next-hop router and each host that is connected directly to the local switch. You can see more detailed information about the adjacencies by using the **detail** keyword, as demonstrated in Example 12-5.

Example 12-5 *Displaying Detailed Information About Adjacencies*

```
Switch# show adjacency vlan 99 detail
Protocol Interface              Address
IP      Vlan99                  192.168.1.2(5)
                                0 packets, 0 bytes
                                000A5E45B145000E387D51000800
                                ARP        01:52:50
                                Epoch: 0
IP      Vlan99                  192.168.1.3(5)
                                1 packets, 104 bytes
                                000CF1C909A0000E387D51000800
                                ARP        04:02:11
                                Epoch: 0
```

Notice that the adjacency entries include both the IP address (Layer 3) and the MAC address (Layer 2) of the directly attached host. The MAC address could be shown as the first six octets of the long string of hex digits (as shaded in the previous output) or on a line by itself. The remainder of the string of hex digits contains the MAC address of the Layer 3 engine's interface (six octets, corresponding to the Vlan99 interface in the example) and the EtherType value (two octets, where 0800 denotes IP).

The adjacency table information is built from the ARP table. Example 12-5 shows adjacency with the age of its ARP entry. As a next-hop address receives a valid ARP entry, the adjacency table is updated. If an ARP entry does not exist, the FIB entry is marked as "CEF glean." This means that the Layer 3 forwarding engine can't forward the packet in hardware because of the missing Layer 2 next-hop address. The packet is sent to the Layer 3 engine so that it can generate an ARP request and receive an ARP reply. This is known as the *CEF glean* state, in which the Layer 3 engine must glean the next-hop destination's MAC address.

The glean state can be demonstrated in several ways, as demonstrated in Example 12-6.

Example 12-6 *Displaying Adjacencies in the CEF Glean State*

```
Switch# show ip cef adjacency glean
Prefix                 Next Hop              Interface
10.1.1.2/32            attached              Vlan101
127.0.0.0/8            attached              EOBC0/0
[output omitted]
Switch# show ip arp 10.1.1.2

Switch# show ip cef 10.1.1.2 255.255.255.255 detail
10.1.1.2/32, version 688, epoch 0, attached, connected
0 packets, 0 bytes
  via Vlan101, 0 dependencies
    valid glean adjacency
Switch#
```

Notice that the FIB entry for directly connected host 10.1.1.2/32 is present but listed in the glean state. The **show ip arp** command shows that there is no valid ARP entry for the IP address.

During the time that an FIB entry is in the CEF glean state waiting for the ARP resolution, subsequent packets to that host are immediately dropped so that the input queues do not fill and the Layer 3 engine does not become too busy worrying about the need for duplicate ARP requests. This is called *ARP throttling* or *throttling adjacency.* If an ARP reply is not received in 2 seconds, the throttling is released so that another ARP request can be triggered. Otherwise, after an ARP reply is received, the throttling is released, the FIB entry can be completed, and packets can be forwarded completely in hardware.

The adjacency table also can contain other types of entries so that packets can be handled efficiently. For example, you might see the following adjacency types listed:

■   **Null adjacency**—Used to switch packets destined for the null interface. The null interface always is defined on a router or switch; it represents a logical interface that silently absorbs packets without actually forwarding them.

■ **Drop adjacency**—Used to switch packets that can't be forwarded normally. In effect, these packets are dropped without being forwarded. Packets can be dropped because of an encapsulation failure, an unresolved address, an unsupported protocol, no valid route present, no valid adjacency, or a checksum error. You can gauge drop adjacency activity with the following command:

```
Switch# show cef drop
CEF Drop Statistics
Slot  Encap_fail  Unresolved Unsupported    No_route    No_adj  ChkSum_Err
RP       8799327           1       45827     5089667        32           0
Switch#
```

■ **Discard adjacency**—Used when packets must be discarded because of an access list or other policy action.

■ **Punt adjacency**—Used when packets must be sent to the Layer 3 engine for further processing. You can gauge the CEF punt activity by looking at the various punt adjacency reasons listed by the **show cef not-cef-switched** command:

```
Switch# show cef not-cef-switched
CEF Packets passed on to next switching layer
Slot  No_adj No_encap Unsupp'ted Redirect  Receive  Options   Access    Frag
RP   3579706        0          0        0 41258564        0        0       0
Switch#
```

The reasons shown are as follows:

— **No_adj**—An incomplete adjacency

— **No_encap**—An incomplete ARP resolution

— **Unsupp'ted**—Unsupported packet features

— **Redirect**—ICMP redirect

— **Receive**—Layer 3 engine interfaces; includes packets destined for IP addresses that are assigned to interfaces on the Layer 3 engine, IP network addresses, and IP broadcast addresses

— **Options**—IP options present

— **Access**—Access list evaluation failure

— **Frag**—Fragmentation failure

Packet Rewrite

When a multilayer switch finds valid entries in the FIB and adjacency tables, a packet is almost ready to be forwarded. One step remains: The packet header information must be rewritten. Keep in mind that multilayer switching occurs as quick table lookups to find the next-hop address and the outbound switch port. The packet is untouched and still has the original destination MAC address of the switch itself. The IP header also must be adjusted, as if a traditional router had done the forwarding.

The switch has an additional functional block that performs a packet rewrite in real time. The packet rewrite engine (shown in Figure 12-3) makes the following changes to the packet just before forwarding:

■ **Layer 2 destination address**—Changed to the next-hop device's MAC address

■ **Layer 2 source address**—Changed to the outbound Layer 3 switch interface's MAC address

■ **Layer 3 IP Time To Live (TTL)**—Decremented by one because one router hop has just occurred

■ **Layer 3 IP checksum**—Recalculated to include changes to the IP header

■ **Layer 2 frame checksum**—Recalculated to include changes to the Layer 2 and Layer 3 headers

A traditional router normally would make the same changes to each packet. The multilayer switch must act as if a traditional router were being used, making identical changes. However, the multilayer switch can do this very efficiently with dedicated packet-rewrite hardware and address information obtained from table lookups.

Configuring CEF

CEF is enabled on all CEF-capable Catalyst switches by default. In fact, the Catalyst 6500 (with a Supervisor 720 and its integrated MSFC3, or a Supervisor 2 and MSFC2 combination) runs CEF inherently, so CEF never can be disabled.

> **TIP** Switches such as the Catalyst 3750 and 4500 run CEF by default, but you can disable CEF on a per-interface basis. You can use the **no ip route-cache cef** and **no ip cef** interface configuration commands to disable CEF on the Catalyst 3750 and 4500, respectively.
>
> You should always keep CEF enabled whenever possible, except when you need to disable it for debugging purposes.

Fallback Bridging

For protocols that CEF can't route or switch, a technique known as *fallback bridging* is used. Sample protocols are IPX and AppleTalk, which are routable but not supported by CEF, as well as SNA and LAT, which are not routable. To summarize fallback bridging operation, each SVI associated with a VLAN in which nonroutable protocols are being used is assigned to a bridge group. Packets that cannot be routed from one VLAN to another are bridged transparently instead, as long as the two VLANs belong to the same bridge group.

> **NOTE** Only the Catalyst 3560 and 3750 offer fallback bridging; these platforms can CEF-switch IP packets, but no others. The Catalyst 4500 and 6500 (all Supervisor models running Cisco IOS Software) also can CEF-switch IP but can handle other routable protocols more slowly with their Layer 3 engines. Those two platforms have no need for fallback bridging.

Bridge groups used in fallback bridging do not interact with normal Layer 2 switching (also using bridging). They do use a special Spanning Tree Protocol to maintain loop-free fallback bridging, but these bridge protocol data units (BPDU) are not exchanged with other 802.1D, Rapid Spanning Tree Protocol (RSTP), or Multiple Spanning Tree (MST) BPDUs on VLANs. Instead, the VLAN-bridge STP is used, with one instance per fallback bridge group.

To configure fallback bridging, first decide which VLANs have traffic that CEF cannot route. Begin by enabling a fallback bridge group and its instance of the VLAN-bridge STP:

```
Switch(config)# bridge-group bridge-group protocol vlan-bridge
```

Next, for each VLAN SVI in which nonroutable traffic will be bridged, assign it to the appropriate bridge group:

```
Switch(config)# interface vlan vlan-id
Switch(config-if)# bridge-group bridge-group
```

You can configure up to 31 different fallback bridge groups on a switch. Although the VLAN bridge STP instance running on each bridge group does not interact with normal 802.1D STP, it does behave similarly. For example, you can configure the bridge priority, port priority and cost, Hello timer, Forward Delay timer, and Max Age timer. These parameters all should look familiar because they are used in the 802.1D STP. Rather than using the **spanning-tree** command to adjust the parameter values, you must adjust them according to the bridge group number with the **bridge-group** *bridge-group* command keywords.

Verifying Multilayer Switching

The multilayer switching topics presented in this chapter are not difficult to configure; however, you might need to verify how a switch is forwarding packets. In particular, the following sections discuss the commands that you can use to verify the operation of InterVLAN routing, CEF, and fallback bridging.

Verifying InterVLAN Routing

To verify the configuration of a Layer 2 port, you can use the following EXEC command:

```
Switch# show interface type mod/num switchport
```

The output from this command displays the access VLAN or the trunking mode and native VLAN. The administrative modes reflect what has been configured for the port, whereas the operational modes show the port's active status.

You can use this same command to verify the configuration of a Layer 3 or routed port. In this case, you should see the switchport (Layer 2) mode disabled, as in Example 12-7.

Example 12-7   *Verifying Configuration of a Layer 3 Switch Port*

```
Switch# show interface fastethernet 0/16 switchport
Name: Fa0/16
Switchport: Disabled
Switch#
```

To see the physical interface's status and counters, use the command without the **switchport** keyword. To see a summary listing of all interfaces, you can use the **show interface status** command.

To verify the configuration of an SVI, you can use the following EXEC command:

```
Switch# show interface vlan vlan-id
```

The VLAN interface should be up, with the line protocol also up. If this is not true, either the interface is disabled with the **shutdown** command or the VLAN itself has not been defined on the switch. Use the **show vlan** command to see a list of configured VLANs.

Example 12-8 shows the output produced from the **show vlan** command. Notice that each defined VLAN is shown, along with the switch ports that are assigned to it.

Example 12-8   *Displaying a List of Configured VLANs*

```
Switch# show vlan

VLAN Name                             Status    Ports
---- -------------------------------- --------- -------------------------------
1    default                          active    Fa0/5, Fa0/6, Fa0/7, Fa0/8
                                                Fa0/9, Fa0/10, Fa0/11, Fa0/12
                                                Fa0/13, Fa0/14, Fa0/15, Fa0/17
                                                Fa0/18, Fa0/19, Fa0/20, Fa0/21
                                                Fa0/22, Fa0/23, Fa0/24, Fa0/25
                                                Fa0/26, Fa0/27, Fa0/28, Fa0/29
                                                Fa0/30, Fa0/32, Fa0/33, Fa0/34
                                                Fa0/36, Fa0/37, Fa0/38, Fa0/39
                                                Fa0/41, Fa0/42, Fa0/43, Fa0/44
                                                Fa0/45, Fa0/46, Fa0/47, Gi0/1
                                                Gi0/2
2    VLAN0002                         active    Fa0/40
5    VLAN0005                         active
```

continues

Example 12-8 *Displaying a List of Configured VLANs (Continued)*

```
10   VLAN0010                        active
11   VLAN0011                        active    Fa0/31
12   VLAN0012                        active
99   VLAN0099                        active    Fa0/35
Switch#
```

You also can display the IP-related information about a switch interface with the **show ip interface** command, as demonstrated in Example 12-9.

Example 12-9 *Displaying IP-Related Information About a Switch Interface*

```
Switch# show ip interface vlan 101
Vlan101 is up, line protocol is up
  Internet address is 10.1.1.1/24
  Broadcast address is 255.255.255.255
  Address determined by setup command
  MTU is 1500 bytes
  Helper address is not set
  Directed broadcast forwarding is disabled
  Outgoing access list is not set
  Inbound  access list is not set
  Proxy ARP is enabled
  Local Proxy ARP is disabled
  Security level is default
  Split horizon is enabled
  ICMP redirects are always sent
  ICMP unreachables are always sent
  ICMP mask replies are never sent
  IP fast switching is enabled
  IP fast switching on the same interface is disabled
  IP Flow switching is disabled
  IP CEF switching is enabled
  IP Feature Fast switching turbo vector
  IP Feature CEF switching turbo vector
  IP multicast fast switching is enabled
  IP multicast distributed fast switching is disabled
  IP route-cache flags are Fast, Distributed, CEF
  Router Discovery is disabled
  IP output packet accounting is disabled
  IP access violation accounting is disabled
  TCP/IP header compression is disabled
  RTP/IP header compression is disabled
  Probe proxy name replies are disabled
  Policy routing is disabled
  Network address translation is disabled
  WCCP Redirect outbound is disabled
  WCCP Redirect inbound is disabled
```

Example 12-9 *Displaying IP-Related Information About a Switch Interface (Continued)*

```
    WCCP Redirect exclude is disabled
    BGP Policy Mapping is disabled
    Sampled Netflow is disabled
    IP multicast multilayer switching is disabled
Switch#
```

You can use the **show ip interface brief** command to see a summary listing of the interfaces involved in routing IP traffic, as demonstrated in Example 12-10.

Example 12-10 *Displaying a Summary Listing of Interfaces Routing IP Traffic*

```
Switch# show ip interface brief
Interface            IP-Address      OK? Method Status                Protocol
Vlan1                unassigned      YES NVRAM  administratively down down
Vlan54               10.3.1.6        YES manual up                    up
Vlan101              10.1.1.1        YES manual up                    up
GigabitEthernet1/1   10.1.5.1        YES manual up                    up
[output omitted]
Switch#
```

Verifying CEF

CEF operation depends on the correct routing information being generated and downloaded to the Layer 3 forwarding engine hardware. This information is contained in the FIB and is maintained dynamically. To view the entire FIB, use the following EXEC command:

    Switch# **show ip cef**

Example 12-11 shows sample output from this command.

Example 12-11 *Displaying the FIB Contents for a Switch*

```
Switch# show ip cef
Prefix               Next Hop         Interface
0.0.0.0/32           receive
192.168.199.0/24     attached         Vlan1
192.168.199.0/32     receive
192.168.199.1/32     receive
192.168.199.2/32     192.168.199.2    Vlan1
192.168.199.255/32   receive
Switch#
```

On this switch, only VLAN 1 has been configured with the IP address 192.168.199.1 255.255.255.0. Notice several things about the FIB for such a small configuration:

- **0.0.0.0/32**—An FIB entry has been reserved for the default route. No next hop is defined, so the entry is marked "receive" so that packets will be sent to the Layer 3 engine for further processing.

- **192.168.199.0/24**—The subnet assigned to the VLAN 1 interface is given its own entry. This is marked "attached" because it is connected directly to an SVI, VLAN 1.

- **192.168.199.0/32**—An FIB entry has been reserved for the exact network address. This is used to contain an adjacency for packets sent to the network address, if the network is not directly connected. In this case, there is no adjacency, and the entry is marked "receive."

- **192.168.199.1/32**—An entry has been reserved for the VLAN 1 SVI's IP address. Notice that this is a host route (/32). Packets destined for the VLAN 1 interface must be dealt with internally, so the entry is marked "receive."

- **192.168.199.2/32**—This is an entry for a neighboring multilayer switch, found on the VLAN 1 interface. The next-hop field has been filled in with the same IP address, denoting that an adjacency is available.

- **192.168.199.255/32**—An FIB entry has been reserved for the 192.168.199.0 subnet's broadcast address. The route processor (Layer 3 engine) handles all directed broadcasts, so the entry is marked "receive."

To see complete FIB table information for a specific interface, use the following EXEC command:

```
Switch# show ip cef type mod/num [detail]
```

Verifying Fallback Bridging

To verify the operation of fallback bridging, you can use the following EXEC commands:

```
Switch# show bridge group
Switch# show bridge bridge-group [verbose]
```

The first command shows a summary of all active fallback bridge groups, along with their STP states. The second command displays the bridging table contents for a specific fallback bridge group.

Foundation Summary

The Foundation Summary is a collection of information that provides a convenient review of many key concepts in this chapter. If you are already comfortable with the topics in this chapter, this summary can help you recall a few details. If you just read this chapter, this review should help solidify some key facts. If you are doing your final preparation before the exam, this information is a convenient way to review the day before the exam.

Table 12-2 *InterVLAN Routing Configuration Commands*

Task	Command Syntax
Put a port into Layer 2 mode	Switch(config-if)# **switchport**
Put a port into Layer 3 mode	Switch(config-if)# **no switchport**
Define an SVI	Switch(config)# **interface vlan** *vlan-id*

Components of CEF:

■ **Forwarding Information Base (FIB)**—Contains routing and next-hop information. Lookups are performed according to longest-match IP prefix.

■ **Adjacency table**—Contains Layer 2 address information for next-hop FIB entries that are one hop away.

■ **Packet rewrite**—Hardware dedicated to rewriting the Layer 2 and Layer 3 header information of outbound packets after the forwarding decisions have been made.

Table 12-3 *Fallback Bridging Configuration Commands*

Task	Command Syntax
Define a fallback bridge group	Switch(config)# **bridge-group** *bridge-group* **protocol vlan-bridge**
Assign an interface to a bridge group	Switch(config)# **interface vlan** *vlan-id* Switch(config-if)# **bridge-group** *bridge-group*

Table 12-4 *Multilayer Switching Verification Commands*

Task	Command Syntax
Show a Layer 2 port status	Switch# **show interface** *type mod/num* **switchport**
Show a Layer 3 port status	Switch# **show interface** *type mod/num*
Show an SVI status	Switch# **show interface vlan** *vlan-id*
View the FIB contents	Switch# **show ip cef**
View FIB information for an interface	Switch# **show ip cef** [*type mod/num* | **vlan** *vlan-id*] [**detail**]
View FIB information for an IP prefix	Switch# **show ip cef** [*prefix-ip prefix-mask*] [**longer-prefixes**] [**detail**]
View FIB adjacency information	Switch# **show adjacency** [*type mod/num* | **vlan** *vlan-id*] [**summary** | **detail**]
View counters for packets not switched by CEF	Switch# **show cef not-cef-switched**
Show fallback bridge group status	Switch# **show bridge group**
Show fallback bridging table contents	Switch# **show bridge** *bridge-group*

Q&A

The questions and scenarios in this book are more difficult than what you should experience on the actual exam. The questions do not attempt to cover more breadth or depth than the exam; however, they are designed to make sure that you know the answers. Rather than allowing you to derive the answers from clues hidden inside the questions themselves, the questions challenge your understanding and recall of the subject. Hopefully, these questions will help limit the number of exam questions on which you narrow your choices to two options and then guess.

You can find the answers to these questions in Appendix A.

1. What might you need to implement interVLAN routing?

2. Can interVLAN routing be performed over a single trunk link?

3. To configure an SVI, what commands are needed?

4. What command can verify the VLAN assignments on a Layer 2 port?

5. A switch has the following interface configurations in its running configuration:

```
interface fastethernet 0/1
 switchport access vlan 5
!
interface vlan 5
 ip address 192.168.10.1 255.255.255.0
 no shutdown
```

What is necessary for packets to get from the FastEthernet interface to the VLAN 5 SVI?

6. What is the source of FIB information?

7. How often is the FIB updated?

8. What is meant by the term *CEF punt*?

9. What happens to the FIB when distributed CEF (dCEF) is used?

10. What happens during a CEF glean process?

11. What does a multilayer switch do to the IP TTL value just before a packet is forwarded?

12. What is fallback bridging?

13. Is it possible for an SVI to go down? If so, for what reasons?

This chapter covers the following topics that you need to master for the CCNP BCMSN exam:

- **Router Redundancy**—This section discusses three protocols that are available on Catalyst switches to provide redundant router or gateway addresses. The protocols include Hot Standby Routing Protocol (HSRP), Virtual Router Redundancy Protocol (VRRP), and Gateway Load Balancing Protocol (GLBP).

- **Supervisor and Route Processor Redundancy**—This section covers the methods that can be used on some Catalyst switch platforms to operate an active-standby pair of hardware modules in one chassis. The redundancy modes include Route Processor Redundancy (RPR), RPR+, Stateful Switchover (SSO), and Non-Stop Forwarding (NSF).

- **Power Supply Redundancy**—This section explains how two power supplies can be used in a Catalyst 4500R or 6500 chassis. Both power supplies can be active; you can configure whether one supply provides the total chassis load or whether both supplies share the total load.

CHAPTER 13

Router, Supervisor, and Power Redundancy

A multilayer switch can provide routing functions for devices on a network, as described in Chapter 12, "Multilayer Switching." If that switch happens to fail, clients have no way of having their traffic forwarded; their gateway has gone away.

Other multilayer switches can be added into the network to provide redundancy in the form of redundant router or gateway addresses. This chapter describes the protocols that can be used for redundant router addresses, load balancing across multiple routers, and load balancing into a server farm.

This chapter also describes the features that support redundancy in hardware. Within a single multilayer switch chassis, two supervisor modules with integrated route processors can be used to provide hardware redundancy. If an entire supervisor module fails, the other module can pick up the pieces and continue operating the switch. The same is true for redundant power supplies within a single chassis.

"Do I Know This Already?" Quiz

The purpose of the "Do I Know This Already?" quiz is to help you decide what parts of this chapter to use. If you already intend to read the entire chapter, you do not necessarily need to answer these questions now.

The quiz, derived from the major sections in the "Foundation Topics" portion of the chapter, helps you determine how to spend your limited study time.

Table 13-1 outlines the major topics discussed in this chapter and the "Do I Know This Already?" quiz questions that correspond to those topics.

Table 13-1 *"Do I Know This Already?" Foundation Topics Section-to-Question Mapping*

Foundation Topics Section	Questions Covered in This Section	Score
Router Redundancy: HSRP	1–5	
Router Redundancy: VRRP	6–7	
Router Redundancy: GLBP	8–10	
Hardware Redundancy	11–12	
Total Score		

> **CAUTION** The goal of self-assessment is to gauge your mastery of the topics in this chapter. If you do not know the answer to a question or are only partially sure of the answer, you should mark this question wrong. Giving yourself credit for an answer you correctly guess skews your self-assessment results and might give you a false sense of security.

1. Which one of the following do multilayer switches share when running HSRP?

    a. Routing tables

    b. ARP cache

    c. CAM table

    d. IP address

2. What HSRP group uses the MAC address 0000.0c07.ac11?

    a. Group 0

    b. Group 7

    c. Group 11

    d. Group 17

3. Two routers are configured for an HSRP group. One router uses the default HSRP priority. What priority should be assigned to the other router to make it more likely to be the active router?

    a. 1

    b. 100

    c. 200

    d. 500

4. How many routers are in the Standby state in an HSRP group?

    a. 0

    b. 1

    c. 2

    d. All but the active router

5. A multilayer switch is configured as follows:

```
interface fastethernet 1/1
no switchport
ip address 192.168.199.3 255.255.255.0
standby 1 ip 192.168.199.2
```

Which IP address should a client PC use as its default gateway?

   a. 192.168.199.1

   b. 192.168.199.2

   c. 192.168.199.3

   d. Any of these answers is correct

6. Which one of the following is based on an IETF RFC standard?

   a. HSRP

   b. VRRP

   c. GLBP

   d. STP

7. What VRRP group uses the virtual MAC address 0000.5e00.01ff?

   a. Group 0

   b. Group 1

   c. Group 255

   d. Group 94

8. Which one of the following protocols is the best choice for load-balancing redundant gateways?

   a. HSRP

   b. VRRP

   c. GLBP

   d. GVRP

9. Which one of the following GLBP functions answers ARP requests?

   a. AVF

   b. VARP

   c. AVG

   d. MVR

10. By default, which of the following virtual MAC addresses will be sent to the next client that looks for the virtual gateway?

    a. The GLBP interface's MAC address

    b. The next virtual MAC address in the sequence

    c. The virtual MAC address of the least-used router

    d. 0000.0c07.ac00

11. Which one of these features is used to reduce the amount of time needed to rebuild the routing information after a supervisor module failure?

    a. NFS

    b. NSF

    c. RPR+

    d. SSO

12. Which one of the following features provides the fastest failover for supervisor or route processor redundancy?

    a. SSL

    b. SSO

    c. RPR+

    d. RPR

The answers to the "Do I Know This Already?" quiz are found in Appendix A, "Answers to Chapter 'Do I Know This Already?' Quizzes and Q&A Sections." The suggested choices for your next step are as follows:

■ **10 or less overall score**—Read the entire chapter. This includes the "Foundation Topics," "Foundation Summary," and "Q&A" sections.

■ **11 or 12 overall score**—If you want more review on these topics, skip to the "Foundation Summary" section and then go to the "Q&A" section at the end of the chapter. Otherwise, move to Chapter 14, "IP Telephony."

Foundation Topics

Router Redundancy in Multilayer Switching

Multilayer switches can act as IP gateways for connected hosts by providing gateway addresses at VLAN SVIs and Layer 3 physical interfaces. These switches can also participate in routing protocols, just as traditional routers do.

For high availability, multilayer switches should offer a means of preventing one switch (gateway) failure from isolating an entire VLAN. This chapter discusses several approaches to providing router redundancy, including the following:

- Hot Standby Router Protocol (HSRP)

- Virtual Router Redundancy Protocol (VRRP)

- Gateway Load Balancing Protocol (GLBP)

Packet Forwarding Review

When a host must communicate with a device on its local subnet, it can generate an Address Resolution Protocol (ARP) request, wait for the ARP reply, and exchange packets directly. However, if the far end is located on a different subnet, the host must rely on an intermediate system (a router, for example) to relay packets to and from that subnet.

A host identifies its nearest router, also known as the *default gateway* or *next hop*, by its IP address. If the host understands something about routing, it recognizes that all packets destined off-net must be sent to the gateway's MAC address rather than the far end's MAC address. Therefore, the host first sends an ARP request to find the gateway's MAC address. Then packets can be relayed to the gateway directly without having to look for ARP entries for individual destinations.

If the host is not so savvy about routing, it might still generate ARP requests for every off-net destination, hoping that someone will answer. Obviously, the off-net destinations cannot answer because they never receive the ARP request broadcasts; these requests are not forwarded across subnets. Instead, you can configure the gateway to provide a proxy ARP function so that it will reply to ARP requests with its own MAC address, as if the destination itself had responded.

Now the issue of gateway availability becomes important. If the gateway router for a subnet or VLAN goes down, packets have no way of being forwarded off the local subnet. Several protocols are available that allow multiple routing devices to share a common gateway address so that if one goes down, another automatically can pick up the active gateway role. The sections that follow describe these protocols.

Hot Standby Router Protocol

HSRP is a Cisco-proprietary protocol developed to allow several routers (or multilayer switches) to appear as a single gateway IP address. RFC 2281 describes this protocol in more detail.

Basically, each of the routers that provides redundancy for a given gateway address is assigned to a common HSRP group. One router is elected as the primary, or *active,* HSRP router; another is elected as the *standby* HSRP router; and all the others remain in the *listen* HSRP state. The routers exchange HSRP hello messages at regular intervals so that they can remain aware of each other's existence and that of the active router.

> **NOTE**   HSRP sends its hello messages to the multicast destination 224.0.0.2 ("all routers") using UDP port 1985.

An HSRP group can be assigned an arbitrary group number, from 0 to 255. If you configure HSRP groups on several VLAN interfaces, it can be handy to make the group number the same as the VLAN number. However, most Catalyst switches support only up to 16 unique HSRP group numbers. If you have more than 16 VLANs, you will quickly run out of group numbers. An alternative is to make the group number the same (that is, 1) for every VLAN interface. This is perfectly valid because the HSRP groups are only locally significant on an interface. In other words, HSRP Group 1 on interface VLAN 10 is unique and independent from HSRP Group 1 on interface VLAN 11.

HSRP Router Election

HSRP election is based on a priority value (0 to 255) that is configured on each router in the group. By default, the priority is 100. The router with the highest priority value (255 is highest) becomes the active router for the group. If all router priorities are equal or set to the default value, the router with the highest IP address on the HSRP interface becomes the active router. To set the priority, use the following interface configuration command:

```
Switch(config-if)# standby group priority priority
```

For example, suppose that one switch is left at its default priority of 100, while the local switch is intended to win the active role election. You can use the following command to set the HSRP priority to 200:

```
Switch(config-if)# standby 1 priority 200
```

When HSRP is configured on an interface, the router progresses through a series of states before becoming active. This forces a router to listen for others in a group and see where it fits into the pecking order. Devices participating in HSRP must progress their interfaces through the following state sequence:

1. Disabled

2. Init

3. Listen

4. Speak

5. Standby

6. Active

Only the standby (the one with the second-highest priority) router monitors the hello messages from the active router. By default, hellos are sent every 3 seconds. If hellos are missed for the duration of the holdtime timer (default 10 seconds, or three times the hello timer), the active router is presumed to be down. The standby router is then clear to assume the active role.

At that point, if other routers are sitting in the Listen state, the next-highest priority router is allowed to become the new standby router.

If you need to change the timer values, use the following interface configuration command. If you decide to change the timers on a router, you should change them identically on all routers in the HSRP group.

```
Switch(config-if)# standby group timers [msec] hello [msec] holdtime
```

The hello and holdtime values can be given in seconds or in milliseconds, if the **msec** keyword precedes a value. The hello time can range from 1 to 254 seconds or from 15 to 999 milliseconds. The holdtime always should be at least three times the hello timer, and can range from 1 to 255 seconds or 50 to 3000 milliseconds.

As an example, the following command can be used to set the hello time at 100 milliseconds and the holdtime to 300 milliseconds:

```
Switch(config-if)# standby 1 timers msec 100 msec 300
```

NOTE   Be aware that decreasing the HSRP hello time allows a router failure to be detected more quickly. At the same time, HSRP hellos will be sent more often, increasing the amount of traffic on the interface.

Normally, after the active router fails and the standby becomes active, the original active router cannot immediately become active when it is restored. In other words, if a router is not already active, it cannot become active again until the current active router fails—even if its priority is higher than that of the active router. An interesting case arises when routers are just being powered up or added to a network. The first router to bring up its interface becomes the HSRP active router, even if it has the lowest priority of all.

You can configure a router to pre-empt or immediately take over the active role if its priority is the highest *at any time*. Use the following interface-configuration command to allow pre-emption:

```
Switch(config-if)# standby group preempt [delay [minimum seconds] [reload seconds]]
```

By default, the local router immediately can pre-empt another router that has the active role. To delay the pre-emption, use the **delay** keyword followed by one or both of the following parameters:

- Add the **minimum** keyword to force the router to wait for *seconds* (0 to 3,600 seconds) before attempting to overthrow an active router with a lower priority. This delay time begins as soon as the router is capable of assuming the active role, such as after an interface comes up or after HSRP is configured.

- Add the **reload** keyword to force the router to wait for *seconds* (0 to 3,600 seconds) after it has been reloaded or restarted. This is handy if there are routing protocols that need time to converge. The local router should not become the active gateway before its routing table is fully populated; otherwise, it might not be capable of routing traffic properly.

HSRP also can use an authentication method to prevent unexpected devices from spoofing or participating in HSRP. All routers in the same standby group must have an identical authentication method and key. You can use either plain-text or MD5 authentication, as described in the following sections.

Plain-Text HSRP Authentication

HSRP messages are sent with a plain-text key string (up to eight characters), as a simple method to authenticate HSRP peers. If the key string in a message matches the key configured on an HSRP peer, the message is accepted.

When keys are sent in the clear, they can be easily intercepted and used to impersonate legitimate peers. Plain-text authentication is intended only to prevent peers with a default configuration from participating in HSRP. Cisco devices use "cisco" as the default key string.

You can configure a plain-text authentication key for an HSRP group with the following interface configuration command:

```
Switch(config-if)# standby group authentication string
```

MD5 Authentication

A Message Digest 5 (MD5) hash is computed on a portion of each HSRP message and a secret key known only to legitimate HSRP group peers. The MD5 hash value is sent along with HSRP messages. As a message is received, the peer recomputes the hash of the expected message contents and its own secret key; if the hash values are identical, the message is accepted.

MD5 authentication is more secure than plain-text authentication because the hash value contained in the HSRP messages is extremely difficult (if not impossible) to reverse. The hash value itself is not used as a key; instead, the hash is used to validate the message contents.

You can configure MD5 authentication by associating a key string with an interface, using the following interface-configuration command:

```
Switch(config-if)# standby group authentication md5 key-string [0 | 7] string
```

By default, the key *string* (up to 64 characters) is given as plain text. This is the same as specifying the **0** keyword. After the key string is entered, it is shown as an encrypted value in the switch configuration. You also can copy and paste an encrypted key string value into this command by preceding the string with the **7** keyword.

Alternatively, you can define an MD5 key string as a key on a key chain. This method is more flexible, enabling you to define more than one key on the switch. Any of the keys then can be associated with HSRP on any interface. If a key needs to be changed, you simply add a new key to the key chain and retire (delete) an old key.

First define the key chain globally with the **key chain** command; then add one key at a time with the **key** and **key-string** commands. The *key-number* index is arbitrary, but keys are tried in sequential order. Finally, associate the key chain with HSRP on an interface by referencing its *chain-name*. You can use the following commands to configure HSRP MD5 authentication:

```
Switch(config)# key chain chain-name
Switch(config-keychain)# key key-number
Switch(config-keychain-key)# key-string [0 | 7] string
Switch(config)# interface type mod/num
Switch(config-if)# standby group authentication md5 key-chain chain-name
```

TIP   HSRP MD5 authentication was introduced into some Catalyst switch platforms with Cisco IOS Software Release 12.2(25)S. At press time, this feature was available only on the Catalyst 3560 and 3750.

Conceding the Election

Consider an active router in an HSRP group: A group of clients sends packets to it for forwarding, and it has one or more links to the rest of the world. If one of those links fails, the router remains active. If all of those links fail, the router still remains active. But sooner or later, the path to the rest of the world is either crippled or removed, and packets from the clients no longer can be forwarded.

HSRP has a mechanism for detecting link failures and swaying the election, giving another router an opportunity to take over the active role. When a specific interface is tracked, HSRP reduces the router's priority by a configurable amount as soon as the interface goes down. If more than one interface is tracked, the priority is reduced even more with each failed interface. The priority is incremented by the same amount as interfaces come back up.

This is particularly useful when a switch has several paths out of a VLAN or subnet; as more interfaces fail and remove the possible paths, other HSRP peers should appear to be more desirable and take over the active role. To configure interface tracking, use the following interface configuration command:

```
Switch(config-if)# standby group track type mod/num [decrementvalue]
```

By default, the *decrementvalue* for an interface is 10. Keep in mind that interface tracking doesn't involve the state of the HSRP interface itself. Instead, the state of other specific interfaces affects the usefulness of the local router as a gateway. You also should be aware that the only way another router can take over the active role after interface tracking reduces the priority is if the following two conditions are met:

- Another router now has a higher HSRP priority.

- That same router is using **preempt** in its HSRP configuration.

Without pre-emption, the active role cannot be given to any other router.

HSRP Gateway Addressing

Each router in an HSRP group has its own unique IP address assigned to an interface. This address is used for all routing protocol and management traffic initiated by or destined to the router. In addition, each router has a common gateway IP address, the virtual router address, which is kept alive by HSRP. This address also is referred to as the *HSRP address* or the *standby address*. Clients can point to that virtual router address as their default gateway, knowing that a router always keeps that address active. Keep in mind that the actual interface address and the virtual (standby) address must be configured to be in the same IP subnet.

You can assign the HSRP address with the following interface command:

```
Switch(config-if)# standby group ip ip-address [secondary]
```

When HSRP is used on an interface that has secondary IP addresses, you can add the **secondary** keyword so that HSRP can provide a redundant secondary gateway address.

Naturally, each router keeps a unique MAC address for its interface. This MAC address is always associated with the unique IP address configured on the interface. For the virtual router address, HSRP defines a special MAC address of the form 0000.0c07.ac*xx*, where *xx* represents the HSRP group number as a two-digit hex value. For example, HSRP Group 1 appears as 0000.0c07.ac01, HSRP Group 16 appears as 0000.0c07.ac10, and so on.

Figure 13-1 shows a simple network in which two multilayer switches use HSRP Group 1 to provide the redundant gateway address 192.168.1.1. CatalystA is the active router, with priority 200, and answers the ARP request for the gateway address. Because CatalystB is in the Standby state, it never is used for traffic sent to 192.168.1.1. Instead, only CatalystA performs the gateway routing function, and only its uplink to the access layer is utilized.

Figure 13-1 *Typical HSRP Scenario with One HSRP Group*

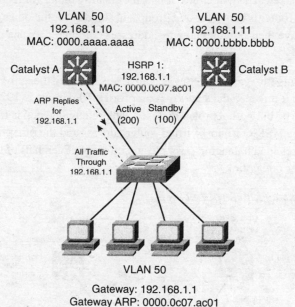

Example 13-1 shows the configuration commands you can use on CatalystA. CatalystB would be configured similarly, except that its HSRP priority would use the default value of 100.

Example 13-1 *Configuring an HSRP Group on a Switch*

```
CatalystA(config)# interface vlan 50
CatalystA(config-if)# ip address 192.168.1.10 255.255.255.0
CatalystA(config-if)# standby 1 priority 200
CatalystA(config-if)# standby 1 preempt
CatalystA(config-if)# standby 1 ip 192.168.1.1
```

Load Balancing with HSRP

Consider a network in which HSRP is used on two distribution switches to provide a redundant gateway address for access-layer users. Only one of the two becomes the active HSRP router; the other remains in standby. All the users send their traffic to the active router over the uplink to the active router. The standby router and its uplink essentially sit idle until a router failure occurs.

Load balancing traffic across two uplinks to two HSRP routers with a single HSRP group is not possible. Then how is it possible to load balance with HSRP? The trick is to use two HSRP groups:

- One group assigns an active router to one switch.

- The other group assigns another active router to the other switch.

In this way, two different virtual router or gateway addresses can be used simultaneously. The rest of the trick is to make each switch function as the standby router for its partner's HSRP group. In other words, each router is active for one group and standby for the other group. The clients or end users also must have their default gateway addresses configured as one of the two virtual HSRP group addresses.

Figure 13-2 presents this scenario. Now, CatalystA is not only the active router for HSRP Group 1 (192.168.1.1), but it is also the standby router for HSRP Group 2 (192.168.1.2). CatalystB is configured similarly, but with its roles reversed. The remaining step is to configure half of the client PCs with the HSRP Group 1 virtual router address and the other half with the Group 2 address. This makes load balancing possible and effective. Each half of the hosts uses one switch as its gateway over one uplink.

Figure 13-2 *Load Balancing with Two HSRP Groups*

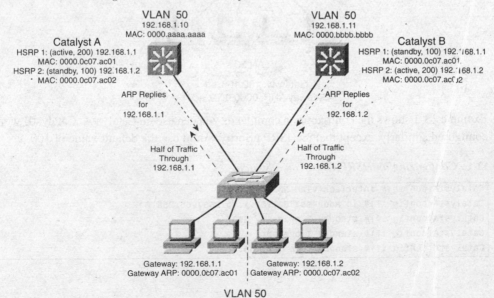

Example 13-2 shows the configuration commands you can use for the scenario shown in Figure 13-2.

Example 13-2 *Configuring Load Balancing Between HSRP Groups*

```
CatalystA(config)# interface vlan 50
CatalystA(config-if)# ip address 192.168.1.10 255.255.255.0
CatalystA(config-if)# standby 1 priority 200
CatalystA(config-if)# standby 1 preempt
CatalystA(config-if)# standby 1 ip 192.168.1.1
CatalystA(config-if)# standby 1 authentication MyKey
CatalystA(config-if)# standby 2 priority 100
CatalystA(config-if)# standby 2 ip 192.168.1.2
CatalystA(config-if)# standby 2 authentication MyKey

CatalystB(config)# interface vlan 50
CatalystB(config-if)# ip address 192.168.1.11 255.255.255.0
CatalystB(config-if)# standby 1 priority 100
CatalystB(config-if)# standby 1 ip 192.168.1.1
CatalystB(config-if)# standby 1 authentication MyKey
CatalystB(config-if)# standby 2 priority 200
CatalystB(config-if)# standby 2 preempt
CatalystB(config-if)# standby 2 ip 192.168.1.2
CatalystB(config-if)# standby 2 authentication MyKey
```

You can use the following command to display information about the status of one or more HSRP groups and interfaces:

```
Router# show standby [brief] [vlan vlan-id | type mod/num]
```

Based on the configuration in Example 13-2, the output in Example 13-3 shows that the CatalystA switch is the active router for HSRP group 1 and the standby router for HSRP group 2 on interface VLAN 50.

Example 13-3 *Displaying the HSRP Router Role of a Switch: CatalystA*

```
CatalystA# show standby vlan 50 brief
                   P indicates configured to preempt.
                   |
Interface  Grp Prio P State   Active addr    Standby addr   Group addr
Vl50        1  200  P Active  local          192.168.1.11   192.168.1.1
Vl50        2  100    Standby 192.168.1.11   local          192.168.1.2
CatalystA#
CatalystA# show standby vlan 50
Vlan50 - Group 1
  Local state is Active, priority 200, may preempt
  Hellotime 3 sec, holdtime 10 sec
  Next hello sent in 2.248
```

continues

Example 13-3   *Displaying the HSRP Router Role of a Switch: CatalystA (Continued)*

```
    Virtual IP address is 192.168.1.1 configured
    Active router is local
    Standby router is 192.168.1.11 expires in 9.860
    Virtual mac address is 0000.0c07.ac01
    Authentication text "MyKey"
    2 state changes, last state change 00:11:58
    IP redundancy name is "hsrp-Vl50-1" (default)
  Vlan50 - Group 2
    Local state is Standby, priority 100
    Hellotime 3 sec, holdtime 10 sec
    Next hello sent in 1.302
    Virtual IP address is 192.168.1.2 configured
    Active router is 192.168.1.11, priority 200 expires in 7.812
    Standby router is local
    Authentication text "MyKey"
    4 state changes, last state change 00:10:04
    IP redundancy name is "hsrp-Vl50-2" (default)
CatalystA#
```

The output from CatalystB in Example 13-4 shows that it has inverted roles from CatalystA for HSRP groups 1 and 2.

Example 13-4   *Displaying the HSRP Router Role of a Switch: CatalystB*

```
CatalystB#show standby vlan 50 brief
                     P indicates configured to preempt.
                     |
Interface  Grp Prio P State   Active addr    Standby addr   Group addr
Vl50        1  100    Standby 192.168.1.10   local          192.168.1.1
Vl50        2  200  P Active  local          192.168.1.10   192.168.1.2
CatalystB#
CatalystB#show standby vlan 50
Vlan50 - Group 1
  Local state is Standby, priority 100
  Hellotime 3 sec, holdtime 10 sec
  Next hello sent in 0.980
  Virtual IP address is 192.168.1.1 configured
  Active router is 192.168.1.10, priority 200 expires in 8.128
  Standby router is local
  Authentication text "MyKey"
  1 state changes, last state change 00:01:12
  IP redundancy name is "hsrp-Vl50-1" (default)
Vlan50 - Group 2
  Local state is Active, priority 200, may preempt
  Hellotime 3 sec, holdtime 10 sec
  Next hello sent in 2.888
```

Example 13-4 *Displaying the HSRP Router Role of a Switch: CatalystB (Continued)*

```
   Virtual IP address is 192.168.1.2 configured
   Active router is local
   Standby router is 192.168.1.10 expires in 8.500
   Virtual mac address is 0000.0c07.ac02
   Authentication text "MyKey"
   1 state changes, last state change 00:01:16
CatalystB#
```

Virtual Router Redundancy Protocol

The Virtual Router Redundancy Protocol (VRRP) is a standards-based alternative to HSRP, defined in IETF standard RFC 2338. VRRP is so similar to HSRP that you need to learn only slightly different terminology and a couple of slight functional differences. When you understand HSRP operation and configuration, you will also understand VRRP. This section is brief, highlighting only the differences between HSRP and VRRP.

■ VRRP provides one redundant gateway address from a group of routers. The active router is called the *master router*, whereas all others are in the *backup state*. The master router is the one with the highest router priority in the VRRP group.

■ VRRP group numbers range from 0 to 255; router priorities range from 1 to 254 (254 is the highest, 100 is the default).

■ The virtual router MAC address is of the form 0000.5e00.01xx, where xx is a two-digit hex VRRP group number.

■ VRRP advertisements are sent at 1-second intervals. Backup routers optionally can learn the advertisement interval from the master router.

■ By default, all VRRP routers are configured to pre-empt the current master router if their priorities are greater.

■ VRRP has no mechanism for tracking interfaces to allow more capable routers to take over the master role.

NOTE   VRRP sends its advertisements to the multicast destination address 224.0.0.18 (VRRP), using IP protocol 112. VRRP was introduced in Cisco IOS Software Release 12.0(18)ST for routers. At press time, VRRP is available only for the Catalyst 4500 (Cisco IOS Release 12.2[31]SG), Catalyst 6500 Supervisor 2 (Cisco IOS Software Release 12.2[9]ZA or later) and Catalyst 6500 Supervisor 720 (Cisco IOS Software Release 12.2[17a]SX4 or later).

To configure VRRP, use the interface-configuration commands documented in Table 13-2.

Table 13-2   *VRRP Configuration Commands*

Task	Command Syntax
Assign a VRRP router priority (default 100)	**vrrp** *group* **priority** *level*
Alter the advertisement timer (default 1 second)	**vrrp** *group* **timers advertise** [*msec*] *interval*
Learn the advertisement interval from the master router	**vrrp** *group* **timers learn**
Disable pre-empting (default is to preempt)	**no vrrp** *group* **preempt**
Change the pre-empt delay (default 0 seconds)	**vrrp** *group* **preempt** [**delay** *seconds*]
Use authentication for advertisements	**vrrp** *group* **authentication** *string*
Assign a virtual IP address	**vrrp** *group* **ip** *ip-address* [**secondary**]

As an example, the load-balancing scenario shown in Figure 13-2 is implemented using VRRP. You would use the configuration commands in Example 13-5 on the two Catalyst switches.

Example 13-5   *Configuring Load Balancing with VRRP*

```
CatalystA(config)# interface vlan 50
CatalystA(config-if)# ip address 192.168.1.10 255.255.255.0
CatalystA(config-if)# vrrp 1 priority 200
CatalystA(config-if)# vrrp 1 ip 192.168.1.1
CatalystA(config-if)# vrrp 2 priority 100
CatalystA(config-if)# no vrrp 2 preempt
CatalystA(config-if)# vrrp 2 ip 192.168.1.2
CatalystB(config)# interface vlan 50
CatalystB(config-if)# ip address 192.168.1.11 255.255.255.0
CatalystB(config-if)# vrrp 1 priority 100
CatalystA(config-if)# no vrrp 1 preempt
CatalystB(config-if)# vrrp 1 ip 192.168.1.1
CatalystB(config-if)# vrrp 2 priority 200
CatalystB(config-if)# vrrp 2 ip 192.168.1.2
```

You can use the following command to display information about VRRP status on one or more interfaces:

```
Switch# show vrrp [brief]
```

Example 13-6 shows this command executed on both CatalystA and CatalystB, with the output showing the alternating roles for the two VRRP groups configured in Example 13-5.

Example 13-6 *Displaying Switch Roles for VRRP Load Balancing*

```
CatalystA# show vrrp brief
Interface       Grp Pri Time  Own Pre State   Master addr      Group addr
Vlan50          1   200 3218      Y   Master  192.168.1.10     192.168.1.1
Vlan50          2   100 3609          Backup  192.168.1.11     192.168.1.2
CatalystA#
```
```
CatalystB# show vrrp brief
Interface       Grp Pri Time  Own Pre State   Master addr      Group addr
Vlan50          1   100 3609          Backup  192.168.1.10     192.168.1.1
Vlan50          2   200 3218      Y   Master  192.168.1.11     192.168.1.2
CatalystB#
```

Table 13-3 compares the detailed VRRP status between the CatalystA and CatalystB switches.

Table 13-3 *Verifying VRRP Status for Multiple VRRP Groups*

CatalystA	CatalystB

CatalystA# **show vrrp**
Vlan50 - Group 1
  State is Master
  Virtual IP address is 192.168.1.1
  Virtual MAC address is 0000.5e00.0101
  Advertisement interval is 1.000 sec
  Preemption is enabled
    min delay is 0.000 sec
  Priority is 200
  Authentication is enabled
  Master Router is 192.168.1.10 (local),
priority is 200
  Master Advertisement interval is
1.000 sec
  Master Down interval is 3.218 sec
 	
Vlan50 - Group 2
  State is Backup
  Virtual IP address is 192.168.1.2
  Virtual MAC address is 0000.5e00.0102
  Advertisement interval is 1.000 sec
  Preemption is disabled
  Priority is 100
  Authentication is enabled
  Master Router is 192.168.1.11, priority
is 200
  Master Advertisement interval is
1.000 sec
  Master Down interval is 3.609 sec
(expires in 2.977 sec)
CatalystA#
	CatalystB# **show vrrp**
	Vlan50 - Group 1
	  State is Backup
	  Virtual IP address is 192.168.1.1
	  Virtual MAC address is 0000.5e00.0101
	  Advertisement interval is 1.000 sec
	  Preemption is disabled
	  Priority is 100
	  Authentication is enabled
	  Master Router is 192.168.1.10, priority
	is 200
	  Master Advertisement interval is
	1.000 sec
	  Master Down interval is 3.609 sec
	(expires in 2.833 sec)
	
	Vlan50 - Group 2
	  State is Master
	  Virtual IP address is 192.168.1.2
	  Virtual MAC address is 0000.5e00.0102
	  Advertisement interval is 1.000 sec
	  Preemption is enabled
	    min delay is 0.000 sec
	  Priority is 200
	  Authentication is enabled
	  Master Router is 192.168.1.11 (local),
	priority is 200
	  Master Advertisement interval is
	1.000 sec
	  Master Down interval is 3.218 sec
	CatalystB#

Gateway Load Balancing Protocol

You should now know how both HSRP and VRRP can effectively provide a redundant gateway (virtual router) address. You can accomplish load balancing by configuring only multiple HSRP/VRRP groups to have multiple virtual router addresses. More manual configuration is needed so that the client machines are divided among the virtual routers. Each group of clients must point to the appropriate virtual router. This makes load balancing somewhat labor-intensive, having a more or less fixed, or static, behavior.

The Gateway Load Balancing Protocol (GLBP) is a Cisco-proprietary protocol designed to overcome the limitations of existing redundant router protocols. Some of the concepts are the same as with HSRP/VRRP, but the terminology is different and the behavior is much more dynamic and robust.

> **NOTE** GLBP was introduced in Cisco IOS Software Release 12.2(14)S for routers. At press time, GLBP is available only for the Catalyst 6500 Supervisor 2 with IOS Release 12.2(14)SY4 or later, and Supervisor 720 with IOS Release 12.2(17a)SX4 switch platforms.

To provide a virtual router, multiple switches (routers) are assigned to a common GLBP group. Instead of having just one active router performing forwarding for the virtual router address, *all* routers in the group can participate and offer load balancing by forwarding a portion of the overall traffic.

The advantage is that none of the clients has to be pointed toward a specific gateway address; they can all have the same default gateway set to the virtual router IP address. The load balancing is provided completely through the use of virtual router MAC addresses in ARP replies returned to the clients. As a client sends an ARP request looking for the virtual router address, GLBP sends back an ARP reply with the virtual MAC address of a selected router in the group. The result is that all clients use the same gateway address but have differing MAC addresses for it.

Active Virtual Gateway

The trick behind this load balancing lies in the GLBP group. One router is elected the *active virtual gateway (AVG)*. This router has the highest priority value, or the highest IP address in the group, if there is no highest priority. The AVG answers all ARP requests for the virtual router address. Which MAC address it returns depends on which load-balancing algorithm it is configured to use. In any event, the virtual MAC address supported by one of the routers in the group is returned.

The AVG also assigns the necessary virtual MAC addresses to each of the routers participating in the GLBP group. Up to four virtual MAC addresses can be used in any group. Each of these routers is referred to as an *active virtual forwarder (AVF)*, forwarding traffic received on its virtual MAC address. Other routers in the group serve as backup or secondary virtual forwarders, in case the AVF fails. The AVG also assigns secondary roles.

Assign the GLBP priority to a router with the following interface configuration command:

```
Switch(config-if)# glbp group priority level
```

GLBP group numbers range from 0 to 1023. The router priority can be 1 to 255 (255 is the highest priority), defaulting to 100.

As with HSRP, another router cannot take over an active role until the current active router fails. GLBP does allow a router to pre-empt and become the AVG if it has a higher priority than the current AVG. Use the following command to enable pre-empting and to set a time delay before pre-empting begins:

```
Switch(config-if)# glbp group preempt [delay minimum seconds]
```

Routers participating in GLBP must monitor each other's presence so that another router can assume the role of a failed router. To do this, the AVG sends periodic hello messages to each of the other GLBP peers. In addition, it expects to receive hello messages from each of them.

Hello messages are sent at *hellotime* intervals, with a default of 3 seconds. If hellos aren't received from a peer within a *holdtime*, defaulting to 10 seconds, that peer is presumed to have failed. You can adjust the GLBP timers with the following interface-configuration command:

```
Switch(config-if)# glbp group timers [msec] hellotime [msec] holdtime
```

The timer values normally are given in seconds, unless they are preceded by the **msec** keyword, to indicate milliseconds. The *hellotime* can range from 1 to 60 seconds or from 50 to 60,000 milliseconds. The *holdtime* must be greater than the *hellotime* and can go up to 180 seconds or 180,000 milliseconds. You always should make the *holdtime* at least three times greater than the *hellotime* to give some tolerance to missed or delayed hellos from a functional peer.

> **TIP**   Although you can use the previous command to configure the GLBP timers on each peer router, it isn't necessary. Instead, just configure the timers on the router you have identified as the AVG. The AVG will advertise the timer values it is using, and every other peer will learn those values if they have not already been explicitly set.

Active Virtual Forwarder

By default, GLBP uses the periodic hello messages to detect AVF failures, too. Each router within a GLBP group must send hellos to every other GLBP peer. Hellos also are expected from every other peer. For example, if hellos from the AVF are not received by the AVG before its holdtime timer expires, the AVG assumes that the current AVF has failed. The AVG then assigns the AVF role to another router.

Naturally, the router that is given the new AVF role might already be an AVF for a different virtual MAC address. Although a router can masquerade as two different virtual MAC addresses to support the two AVF functions, it doesn't make much sense to continue doing that for a long period of time. The AVG maintains two timers that help resolve this condition.

The *redirect* timer is used to determine when the AVG will stop using the old virtual MAC address in ARP replies. The AVF corresponding to the old address continues to act as a gateway for any clients that try to use it.

When the *timeout* timer expires, the old MAC address and the virtual forwarder using it are flushed from all the GLBP peers. The AVG assumes that the previously failed AVF will not return to service, so the resources assigned to it must be reclaimed. At this point, clients still using the old MAC address in their ARP caches must refresh the entry to obtain the new virtual MAC address.

The *redirect* timer defaults to 600 seconds (10 minutes) and can range from 0 to 3,600 seconds (1 hour). The *timeout* timer defaults to 14,400 seconds (4 hours) and can range from 700 to 64,800 seconds (18 hours). You can adjust these timers with the following interface-configuration command:

```
Switch(config-if)# glbp group timers redirect redirect timeout
```

GLBP also can use a weighting function to determine which router becomes the AVF for a virtual MAC address in a group. Each router begins with a maximum weight value (1 to 254). As specific interfaces go down, the weight is decreased by a configured amount. GLBP uses thresholds to determine when a router can and cannot be the AVF. If the weight falls below the lower threshold, the router must give up its AVF role. When the weight rises above the upper threshold, the router can resume its AVF role.

By default, a router receives a maximum weight of 100. If you want to make a dynamic weighting adjustment, GLBP must know which interfaces to track and how to adjust the weight. You first must define an interface as a tracked object with the following global configuration command:

```
Switch(config)# track object-number interface type mod/num {line-protocol | ip routing}
```

The *object-number* is an arbitrary index (1 to 500) that is used for weight adjustment. The condition that triggers an adjustment can be **line-protocol** (the interface line protocol is up) or **ip routing** (IP routing is enabled, the interface has an IP address, and the interface is up).

Next, you must define the weighting thresholds for the interface with the following interface configuration command:

```
Switch(config-if)# glbp group weighting maximum [lower lower] [upper upper]
```

The maximum weight can range from 1 to 254 (default 100). The upper (default *maximum*) and lower (default 1) thresholds define when the router can and cannot be the AVF, respectively.

Finally, you must configure GLBP to know which objects to track so that the weighting can be adjusted with the following interface configuration command:

```
Switch(config-if)# glbp group weighting track object-number [decrement value]
```

When the tracked object fails, the weighting is decremented by *value* (1 to 254, default 10).

Likewise, a router that might serve as an AVF cannot pre-empt another when it has a higher weight value.

GLBP Load Balancing

The AVG establishes load balancing by handing out virtual router MAC addresses to clients in a deterministic fashion. Naturally, the AVG first must inform the AVFs in the group of the virtual MAC address that each should use. Up to four virtual MAC addresses, assigned in sequential order, can be used in a group.

You can use one of the following load-balancing methods in a GLBP group:

- **Round robin**—Each new ARP request for the virtual router address receives the next available virtual MAC address in reply. Traffic load is distributed evenly across all routers participating as AVFs in the group, assuming that each of the clients sends and receives the same amount of traffic. This is the default method used by GLBP.

- **Weighted**—The GLBP group interface's weighting value determines the proportion of traffic that should be sent to that AVF. A higher weighting results in more frequent ARP replies containing the virtual MAC address of that router. If interface tracking is not configured, the maximum weighting value configured is used to set the relative proportions among AVFs.

- **Host-dependent**—Each client that generates an ARP request for the virtual router address always receives the same virtual MAC address in reply. This method is used if the clients have a need for a consistent gateway MAC address. (Otherwise, a client could receive replies with different MAC addresses for the router over time, depending on the load-balancing method in use.)

On the AVG router (or its successors), use the following interface configuration command to define the method:

```
Switch(config-if)# glbp group load-balancing [round-robin | weighted | host-dependent]
```

Enabling GLBP

To enable GLBP, you must assign a virtual IP address to the group by using the following interface configuration command:

```
Switch(config-if)# glbp group ip [ip-address [secondary]]
```

If the *ip-address* is not given in the command, it is learned from another router in the group. However, if this router is to be the AVG, you must explicitly configure the IP address; otherwise, no other router knows what the value should be.

Figure 13-3 shows a typical network in which three multilayer switches are participating in a common GLBP group. CatalystA is elected the AVG, so it coordinates the entire GLBP process. The AVG answers all ARP requests for the virtual router 192.168.1.1. It has identified itself, CatalystB, and CatalystC as AVFs for the group.

Figure 13-3 *Multilayer Switches in a GLBP Group*

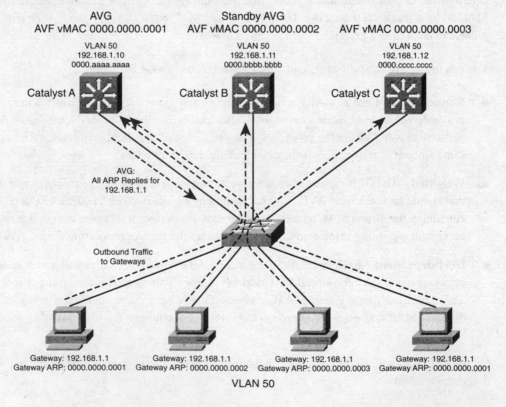

In this figure, round-robin load balancing is being used. Each of the client PCs looks for the virtual router address in turn, from left to right. Each time the AVG replies, the next sequential virtual MAC address is sent back to a client. After the fourth PC sends a request, all three virtual MAC addresses (and AVF routers) have been used, so the AVG cycles back to the first virtual MAC address.

Notice that only one GLBP group has been configured, and all clients know of only one gateway IP address: 192.168.1.1. However, all uplinks are being utilized, and all routers are proportionately forwarding traffic.

Redundancy is also inherent in the GLBP group: CatalystA is the AVG, but the next-highest priority router can take over if the AVG fails. All routers have been given an AVF role for a unique virtual MAC address in the group. If one AVF fails, some clients remember the last-known virtual MAC address that was handed out. Therefore, another of the routers also takes over the AVF role for the failed router, causing the virtual MAC address to remain alive at all times.

Figure 13-4 shows how these redundancy features react when the current active AVG fails. Before its failure, CatalystA was the AVG because of its higher GLBP priority. After it failed, CatalystB became the AVG, answering ARP requests with the appropriate virtual MAC address for gateway 192.168.1.1. CatalystA also had been acting as an AVF, participating in the gateway load balancing. CatalystB also picks up this responsibility, using its virtual MAC address 0000.0000.0002 along with the one CatalystA had been using, 000.0000.0001. Therefore, any hosts that know the gateway by any of its virtual MAC addresses still can reach a live gateway or AVF.

You can implement the scenario shown in Figures 13-3 and 13-4 with the configuration commands in Example 13-7 for CatalystA, CatalystB, and CatalystC, respectively.

Example 13-7 *Configuring GLBP Load Balancing*

```
CatalystA(config)# interface vlan 50
CatalystA(config-if)# ip address 192.168.1.10 255.255.255.0
CatalystA(config-if)# glbp 1 priority 200
CatalystA(config-if)# glbp 1 preempt
CatalystA(config-if)# glbp 1 ip 192.168.1.1
CatalystB(config)# interface vlan 50
CatalystB(config-if)# ip address 192.168.1.11 255.255.255.0
CatalystB(config-if)# glbp 1 priority 150
CatalystB(config-if)# glbp 1 preempt
CatalystB(config-if)# glbp 1 ip 192.168.1.1
CatalystC(config)# interface vlan 50
CatalystC(config-if)# ip address 192.168.1.12 255.255.255.0
CatalystC(config-if)# glbp 1 priority 100
CatalystC(config-if)# glbp 1 ip 192.168.1.1
```

Figure 13-4 *How GLBP Reacts to a Component Failure*

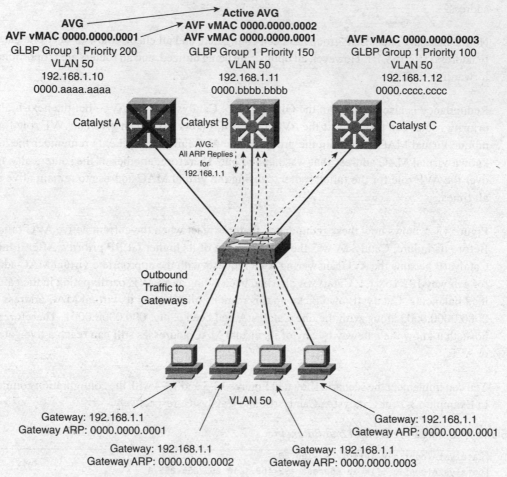

You can verify GLBP operation with the **show glbp [brief]** command, as demonstrated in Example 13-8. With the **brief** keyword, the GLBP roles are summarized showing the interface, GLBP group number (Grp), virtual forwarder number (Fwd), GLBP priority (Pri), state, and addresses.

Example 13-8 *Verifying GLBP Operation*

```
CatalystA# show glbp brief
Interface   Grp  Fwd  Pri  State   Address          Active router     Standby router
V150        1    -    200  Active  192.168.1.1      local             192.168.1.11
V150        1    1    7    Active  0007.b400.0101   local             -
V150        1    2    7    Listen  0007.b400.0102   192.168.1.11      -
V150        1    3    7    Listen  0007.b400.0103   192.168.1.13      -
CatalystA#
```
```
CatalystB# show glbp brief
Interface   Grp  Fwd  Pri  State   Address          Active router     Standby router
```

Example 13-8 *Verifying GLBP Operation (Continued)*

```
V150        1   -   150 Standby  192.168.1.1     192.168.1.10    local
V150        1   1   7   Listen   0007.b400.0101  192.168.1.10    -
V150        1   2   7   Active   0007.b400.0102  local           -
V150        1   3   7   Listen   0007.b400.0103  192.168.1.13    -
CatalystB#
CatalystC# show glbp brief
Interface  Grp Fwd Pri State    Address         Active router   Standby router
V150        1   -   100 Listen   192.168.1.1     192.168.1.10    192.168.1.11
V150        1   1   7   Listen   0007.b400.0101  192.168.1.10    -
V150        1   2   7   Listen   0007.b400.0102  192.168.1.11    -
V150        1   3   7   Active   0007.b400.0103  local           -
CatalystC#
```

Notice that CatalystA is shown to be the AVG because it has a dash in the Fwd column and is in the Active state. It also is acting as AVF for virtual forwarder number 1. Because the GLBP group has three routers, there are three virtual forwarders and virtual MAC addresses. CatalystA is in the Listen state for forwarders number 2 and 3, waiting to be given an active role in case one of those AVFs fails.

CatalystB is shown to have the Standby role, waiting to take over in case the AVG fails. It is the AVF for virtual forwarder number 2.

Finally, CatalystC has the lowest GLBP priority, so it stays in the Listen state, waiting for the active or standby AVG to fail. It is also the AVF for virtual forwarder number 3.

You also can display more detailed information about the GLBP configuration and status by omitting the **brief** keyword. Example 13-9 shows this output on the AVG router. Because this is the AVG, the virtual forwarder roles it has assigned to each of the routers in the GLBP group also are shown.

Example 13-9 *Displaying Detailed GLBP Configuration and Status Information*

```
CatalystA# show glbp
Vlan50 - Group 1
  State is Active
    7 state changes, last state change 03:28:05
  Virtual IP address is 192.168.1.1
  Hello time 3 sec, hold time 10 sec
    Next hello sent in 1.672 secs
  Redirect time 600 sec, forwarder time-out 14400 sec
  Preemption enabled, min delay 0 sec
  Active is local
  Standby is 192.168.1.11, priority 150 (expires in 9.632 sec)
  Priority 200 (configured)
  Weighting 100 (default 100), thresholds: lower 1, upper 100
```

continues

Example 13-9   *Displaying Detailed GLBP Configuration and Status Information (Continued)*

```
Load balancing: round-robin
There are 3 forwarders (1 active)
Forwarder 1
  State is Active
    3 state changes, last state change 03:27:37
  MAC address is 0007.b400.0101 (default)
  Owner ID is 00d0.0229.b80a
  Redirection enabled
  Preemption enabled, min delay 30 sec
  Active is local, weighting 100
Forwarder 2
  State is Listen
  MAC address is 0007.b400.0102 (learnt)
  Owner ID is 0007.b372.dc4a
  Redirection enabled, 598.308 sec remaining (maximum 600 sec)
  Time to live: 14398.308 sec (maximum 14400 sec)
  Preemption enabled, min delay 30 sec
  Active is 192.168.1.11 (primary), weighting 100 (expires in 8.308 sec)
Forwarder 3
  State is Listen
  MAC address is 0007.b400.0103 (learnt)
  Owner ID is 00d0.ff8a.2c0a
  Redirection enabled, 599.892 sec remaining (maximum 600 sec)
  Time to live: 14399.892 sec (maximum 14400 sec)
  Preemption enabled, min delay 30 sec
  Active is 192.168.1.13 (primary), weighting 100 (expires in 9.892 sec)
CatalystA#
```

Verifying Gateway Redundancy

To verify the operation of the features discussed in this chapter, you can use the commands listed in Table 13-4. In particular, look for the active, standby, or backup routers in use.

Table 13-4   *Gateway Redundancy Verification Commands*

Task	Command Syntax
HSRP and VRRP	
Display HSRP status	**show standby brief**
Display HSRP on an interface	**show standby** *type mod/num*
Display VRRP status	**show vrrp brief all**
Display VRRP on an interface	**show vrrp interface** *type mod/num*
GLBP	
Display status of a GLBP group	**show glbp** [*group*] [**brief**]

Redundancy Within a Switch Chassis

The router or gateway redundancy protocols, such as HSRP, VRRP, and GLBP, can provide high availability only for the default gateway addresses. If one of the redundant gateway routers fails, another can pick up the pieces and appear to be the same gateway address.

But what happens to the devices that are connected directly to the router that fails? If the switching or routing engine fails, packets probably will not get routed and interfaces will go down. Some Cisco switches have the capability to provide redundancy for the supervisor engine itself. This is accomplished by having redundant hardware in place within a switch chassis, ready to take over during a failure.

You also should consider switch power as a vital part of achieving high availability. For example, if a switch has a single power supply and a single power cord, the whole switch will fail if the power supply fails or if the power cord is accidentally unplugged. Some switch platforms can have multiple power supplies; if one power supply fails, another immediately takes over the load.

Redundant Switch Supervisors

Modular switch platforms such as the Catalyst 4500R and 6500 can accept two supervisor modules installed in a single chassis. The first supervisor module to successfully boot up becomes the active supervisor for the chassis. The other supervisor remains in a standby role, waiting for the active supervisor to fail.

The active supervisor always is allowed to boot up and become fully initialized and operational. All switching functions are provided by the active supervisor. The standby supervisor, however, is allowed to boot up and initialize only to a certain level. When the active module fails, the standby module can proceed to initialize any remaining functions and take over the active role.

Redundant supervisor modules can be configured in several modes. The redundancy mode affects how the two supervisors handshake and synchronize information. In addition, the mode limits the standby supervisor's state of readiness. The more ready the standby module is allowed to become, the less initialization and failover time will be required.

You can use the following redundancy modes on Catalyst switches:

- **Route Processor Redundancy (RPR)**—The redundant supervisor is only partially booted and initialized. When the active module fails, the standby module must reload every other module in the switch and then initialize all the supervisor functions.

- **Route Processor Redundancy Plus (RPR+)**—The redundant supervisor is booted, allowing the supervisor and route engine to initialize. No Layer 2 or Layer 3 functions are started, however. When the active module fails, the standby module finishes initializing without reloading other switch modules. This allows switch ports to retain their state.

- **Stateful Switchover (SSO)**—The redundant supervisor is fully booted and initialized. Both the startup and running configuration contents are synchronized between the supervisor modules. Layer 2 information is maintained on both supervisors so that hardware switching can continue during a failover. The state of the switch interfaces is also maintained on both supervisors so that links don't flap during a failover.

> **TIP** Sometimes the redundancy mode terminology can be confusing. In addition to the RPR, RPR+, and SSO terms, you might see Single Router Mode (SRM) and Dual Router Mode (DRM).
>
> SRM simply means that two route processors (integrated into the supervisors) are being used, but only one of them is active at any time. In DRM, two route processors are active at all times. HSRP usually is used to provide redundancy in DRM.
>
> Although RPR and RPR+ have only one active supervisor, the route processor portion is not initialized on the standby unit. Therefore, SRM is not compatible with RPR or RPR+.
>
> SRM is inherent with SSO, which brings up the standby route processor. You usually will find the two redundancy terms together, as "SRM with SSO."

Configuring the Redundancy Mode

Table 13-5 details the redundancy modes you can configure on supported switch platforms.

Table 13-5 *Redundancy Modes, Platform Support, and Failover Time*

Redundancy Mode	Supported Platforms	Failover Time
RPR	Catalyst 6500 Supervisors 2 and 720, Catalyst 4500R Supervisors IV and V	Good (> 2 minutes)
Route Processor Redundancy Plus (RPR+)	Catalyst 6500 Supervisors 2 and 720	Better (> 30 seconds)
Stateful Switchover (SSO)	Catalyst 6500 Supervisor 720, Catalyst 4500R Supervisors IV and V	Best (> 1 second)

Figure 13-5 shows how the supervisor redundancy modes compare with respect to the functions they perform. The shaded functions are performed as the standby supervisor initializes and then waits for the active supervisor to fail. When a failure is detected, the remaining functions must be performed in sequence before the standby supervisor can become fully active. Notice how the redundancy modes get progressively more initialized and ready to become active.

Figure 13-5   *Standby Supervisor Readiness as a Function of Redundancy Mode*

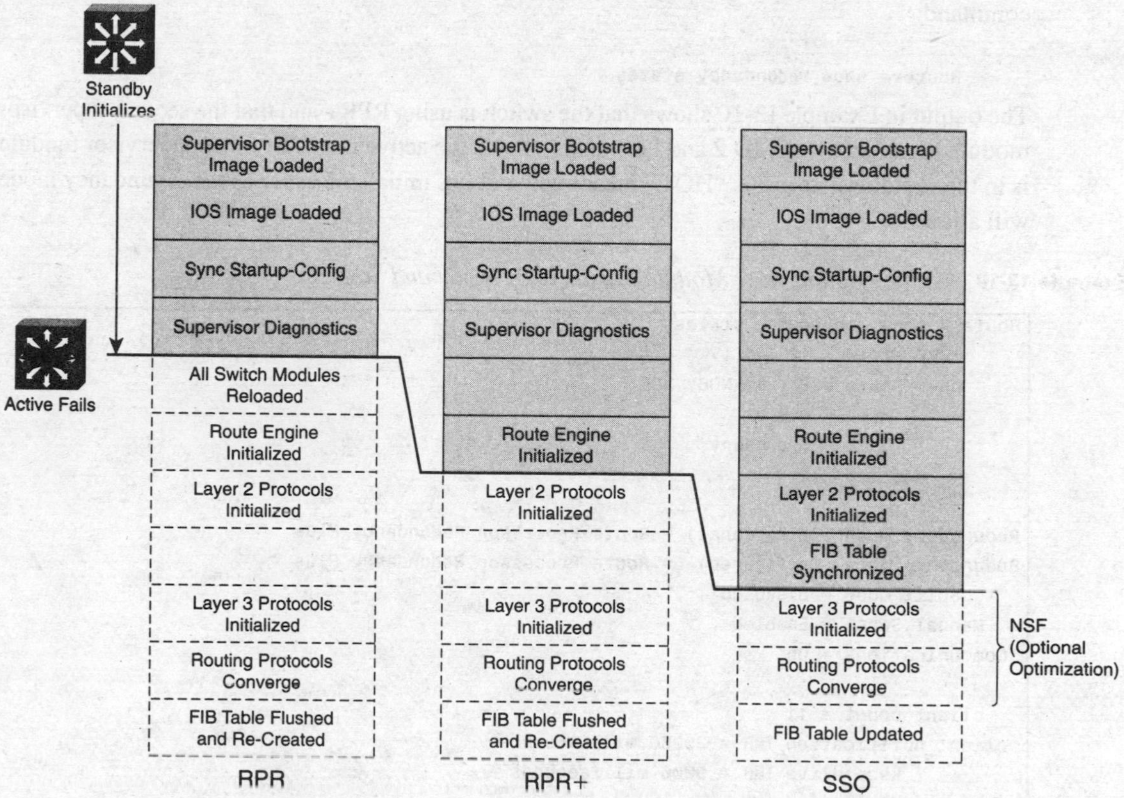

You can configure the supervisor redundancy mode by entering the redundancy-configuration mode with the following command:

```
Router(config)# redundancy
```

Next, select the redundancy mode with one of the following commands:

```
Router(config-red)# mode {rpr | rpr-plus | sso}
```

If you are configuring redundancy for the first time on the switch, you must enter the previous commands on both supervisor modules. When the redundancy mode is enabled, you will make all configuration changes on the active supervisor only. The running configuration is synchronized automatically from the active to the standby module.

TIP   If you configure RPR+ with the **rpr-plus** keyword, the supervisor attempts to bring up RPR+ with its peer module. The IOS images must be of exactly the same release before RPR+ will work. If the images differ, the supervisor automatically falls back to RPR mode instead.

You can verify the redundancy mode and state of the supervisor modules by using the following command:

```
Router# show redundancy states
```

The output in Example 13-10 shows that the switch is using RPR+ and that the second supervisor module (denoted by unit ID 2 and "my state") holds the active role. The other supervisor module is in the standby state and is "HOT," meaning that it has initialized as far as the redundancy mode will allow.

Example 13-10 *Verifying Supervisor Module Redundancy Mode and State*

```
Router# show redundancy states
       my state = 13 -ACTIVE
     peer state = 8   -STANDBY HOT
           Mode = Duplex
           Unit = Secondary
        Unit ID = 2

Redundancy Mode (Operational) = Route Processor Redundancy Plus
Redundancy Mode (Configured)  = Route Processor Redundancy Plus
     Split Mode = Disabled
   Manual Swact = Enabled
 Communications = Up

   client count = 11
client_notification_TMR = 30000 milliseconds
         keep_alive TMR = 9000 milliseconds
       keep_alive count = 1
   keep_alive threshold = 18
           RF debug mask = 0x0
Router#
```

Configuring Supervisor Synchronization

By default, the active supervisor synchronizes its startup configuration and configuration register values with the standby supervisor. You also can specify other information that should be synchronized.

First, use the following commands to enter the main-cpu configuration mode:

```
Router(config)# redundancy
Router(config-red)# main-cpu
```

Then use the following command to specify the information that will be synchronized:

```
Router(config-r-mc)# auto-sync {startup-config | config-register | bootvar}
```

You can repeat the command if you need to use more than one of the keywords. To return to the default, use the **auto-sync standard** command.

Non-Stop Forwarding

You can enable another redundancy feature along with SSO on the Catalyst 4500R and 6500 (Supervisor 720 only). Non-Stop Forwarding (NSF) is an interactive method that focuses on quickly rebuilding the routing information base (RIB) table after a supervisor switchover. The RIB is used to generate the FIB table for CEF, which is downloaded to any switch modules or hardware that can perform CEF.

Instead of waiting on any configured Layer 3 routing protocols to converge and rebuild the FIB, a router can use NSF to get assistance from other NSF-aware neighbors. The neighbors then can provide routing information to the standby supervisor, allowing the routing tables to be assembled quickly. In a nutshell, the Cisco-proprietary NSF functions must be built into the routing protocols on both the router that will need assistance and the router that will provide assistance.

NSF is supported by the BGP, EIGRP, OSPF, and IS-IS routing protocols. NSF is available on the Catalyst 6500 Supervisor 720 (with the integrated MSFC3) and on the Catalyst 4500R Supervisor III, IV, and V running IOS Software Release 12.2(20)EWA or later.

To configure NSF, you must add the commands in Table 13-6 to any routing protocol configuration on the switch.

Table 13-6 *Configuring NSF (by Routing Protocol)*

Routing Protocol	Configuration Commands
BGP	Router(config)# **router bgp** *as-number* Router(config-router)# **bgp graceful-restart**
EIGRP	Router(config)# **router eigrp** *as-number* Router(config-router)# **nsf**
OSPF	Router(config)# **router ospf** *process-id* Router(config-router)# **nsf**
IS-IS	Router(config)# **router isis** [*tag*] Router(config-router)# **nsf** [**cisco** ι **ietf**] Router(config-router)# **nsf interval** [*minutes*] Router(config-router)# **nsf t3** {**manual** [*seconds*] ι **adjacency**} Router(config-router)# **nsf interface wait** *seconds*

Redundant Power Supplies

The Cisco Catalyst 6500 and 4500R platforms can accept two power supply modules in a single chassis. The power supplies must be identical, having the same power input and maximum power output ratings. The switch can be configured to operate in one of two possible power modes:

- **Combined mode**—Both power supplies work together to share the total power load for all modules that are installed in the switch chassis. The total load required can exceed the maximum power output rating of one power supply but must not exceed the sum of both supplies.

  Combined mode is useful for meeting large power requirements if many switch modules are installed or if Power over Ethernet (PoE) is being used to supply power to end devices such as IP telephones. However, combined mode *does not* provide power redundancy. If one power supply fails, the switch powers down some of its modules until the required power load can be met by the one functioning power supply.

- **Redundant mode**—Each of the installed power supplies can supply the total power load that is required by the whole switch chassis. If one power supply fails, the other immediately can carry the total power load of the switch without powering down any modules.

By default, a switch is configured for redundant mode. If two power supplies are installed and functioning, they are managed as redundant replacements for each other. Both supplies are enabled and active, as if they were both supplying power. In fact, you probably won't be able to tell which supply is actually powering the switch until one of them is turned off or fails.

You can display the current power configuration and status of a switch with the following command:

Switch# **show power** [**redundancy-mode** | **status** | **available** | **used** | **total**]

If you don't use any of the optional keywords, the resulting output yields all information about the system power. For instance, notice that the switch in Example 13-11 is in redundant mode and that both power supplies are operational.

Example 13-11 *Verifying Switch Redundant Mode and Power Supply Operational Status*

```
Switch# show power
system power redundancy mode = redundant
system power total =     1153.32 Watts (27.46 Amps @ 42V)
system power used =       693.42 Watts (16.51 Amps @ 42V)
system power available =  459.90 Watts (10.95 Amps @ 42V)
                    Power-Capacity PS-Fan Output Oper
PS   Type           Watts   A @42V Status Status State
---- ----------------- ------- ------ ------ ------ -----
1    WS-CAC-1300W   1153.32 27.46  OK     OK     on
2    WS-CAC-1300W   1153.32 27.46  OK     OK     on
                    Pwr-Requested  Pwr-Allocated  Admin Oper
Slot Card-Type      Watts   A @42V Watts   A @42V State State
---- ----------------- ------- ------ ------- ------ ----- -----
1    WS-X6K-SUP2-2GE 145.32 3.46   145.32 3.46   on    on
2                    -      -      145.32 3.46   -     -
3    WS-X6348-RJ45  100.38 2.39   100.38 2.39   on    on
4    WS-X6516-GBIC  142.80 3.40   142.80 3.40   on    on
5    WS-C6500-SFM   117.18 2.79   117.18 2.79   on    on
Switch#
```

The **show power** command also displays information about the status of each switch module, the amount of power it has requested to receive, and the amount of power it is actually being budgeted. Most switch modules have a fixed power requirement, so the power requested and allocated values are equal.

One important exception is any switch module that supplies inline power or PoE to end devices. These end devices can request a power budget when they initialize and can request a different budget at any later time. Cisco IP telephones and wireless access points are good examples of this. Power requests are handled through Cisco Discovery Protocol (CDP) exchanges between the device and the switch. You can display the current power status of inline power switch ports with the **show power inline** command, as demonstrated in Example 13-12.

Example 13-12 *Verifying Inline Power Switch Port Status*

```
Switch# show power inline
Interface  Admin  Oper   Power    Device
                         (Watts)
.........  .....  .....  .......  ....................
Fa3/1      auto   off          0  n/a
Fa3/2      auto   on         6.2  cisco AIR-AP1230B-A
Fa3/3      auto   on         6.2  cisco AIR-AP1230B-A
Fa3/4      auto   on         5.6  Cisco IP Phone 7905
Fa3/5      auto   on         5.6  Cisco IP Phone 7905
Fa3/6      auto   on         6.3  Cisco IP Phone 7940
Fa3/7      auto   on         6.3  Cisco IP Phone 7940
Fa3/8      auto   on         6.3  Cisco IP Phone 7940
Fa3/9      auto   off          0  n/a
Fa3/10     auto   on         6.3  Cisco IP Phone 7912
Fa3/11     auto   off          0  n/a
Fa3/12     auto   on         6.3  Cisco IP Phone 7940
Fa3/13     auto   on         6.3  Cisco IP Phone 7940
Fa3/14     auto   on         6.3  Cisco IP Phone 7940
[output omitted]
```

You can change the power supply mode by using the following command:

```
Switch(config)# power redundancy-mode {redundant | combined}
```

You also can control the power that is being supplied to a switch module. For example, if you want to remove a module for repair or relocation, you can disable its power before it is pulled out of the chassis. Use the following command to control the power to the module in chassis slot number *slot*:

```
Switch(config)# [no] power enable module slot
```

Without the **no** keyword, the module is powered on; include the **no** keyword to remove power from the module.

Foundation Summary

The Foundation Summary is a collection of information that provides a convenient review of many key concepts in this chapter. If you are already comfortable with the topics in this chapter, this summary can help you recall a few details. If you just read this chapter, this review should help solidify some key facts. If you are doing your final preparation before the exam, this information is a convenient way to review the day before the exam.

Table 13-7   *Comparison of Router Redundancy Protocols*

	HSRP	**VRRP**	**GLBP**
Standardized	No; Cisco-proprietary, RFC 2281	Yes; RFC 2338	No; Cisco-proprietary
Router roles	Active router, standby router	Master router, backup router	AVG, AVF
Load balancing	Only through multiple HSRP groups, different client gateways	Only through multiple VRRP groups, different client gateways	Inherent with one GLBP group; all clients use same gateway; several methods available
Interface tracking	Yes	No	Yes
Virtual router MAC address	0000.0c07.acxx	0000.5e00.01xx	Assigned by AVG

Table 13-8   *HSRP Configuration Commands*

Task	**Command Syntax**
Set the HSRP priority	**standby** *group* **priority** *priority*
Set the HSRP timers	**standby** *group* **timer**s *hello holdtime*
Allow router pre-emption	**standby** *group* **preempt** [**delay** *seconds*]
Use group authentication	**standby** *group* **authentication** *string*
Adjust priority by tracking an interface	**standby** *group* **track** *type mod/num decrementvalue*
Assign the virtual router address	**standby** *group* **ip** *ip-address* [**secondary**]

Table 13-9 *VRRP Configuration Commands*

Task	Command Syntax
Assign a VRRP router priority (default 100)	**vrrp** *group* **priority** *level*
Alter the advertisement timer (default 1 second)	**vrrp** *group* **timers advertise** [**msec**] *interval*
Learn the advertisement interval from the master router	**vrrp** *group* **timers learn**
Disable pre-empting (default is to pre-empt)	**no vrrp** *group* **preempt**
Change the pre-empt delay (default 0 seconds)	**vrrp** *group* **preempt** [**delay** *seconds*]
Use authentication for advertisements	**vrrp** *group* **authentication** *string*
Assign a virtual IP address	**vrrp** *group* **ip** *ip-address* [**secondary**]

Table 13-10 *GLBP Configuration Commands*

Task	Command Syntax
Assign a GLBP priority	**glbp** *group* **priority** *level*
Allow GLBP pre-emption	**glbp** *group* **preempt** [**delay minimum** *seconds*]
Define an object to be tracked	**track** *object-number* **interface** *type mod/num* {**line-protocol** ı **ip routing**}
Define the weighting thresholds	**glbp** *group* **weighting** *maximum* [**lower** *lower*] [**upper** *upper*]
Track an object	**glbp** *group* **weighting track** *object-number* [**decrement** *value*]
Choose the load-balancing method	**glbp** *group* **load-balancing** [**round-robin** ı **weighted** ı **host-dependent**]
Assign a virtual router address	**glbp** *group* **ip** [*ip-address* [**secondary**]]

Q&A

The questions and scenarios in this book are more difficult than what you should experience on the actual exam. The questions do not attempt to cover more breadth or depth than the exam; however, they are designed to make sure that you know the answer. Rather than allowing you to derive the answers from clues hidden inside the questions themselves, the questions challenge your understanding and recall of the subject. Hopefully, these questions will help limit the number of exam questions on which you narrow your choices to two options and then guess.

You can find the answers to these questions in Appendix A.

1. A multilayer switch has been configured with the command **standby 5 priority 120**. What router-redundancy protocol is being used?

2. What feature can you use to prevent other routers from accidentally participating in an HSRP group?

3. What command can configure an HSRP group to use a virtual router address of 192.168.222.100?

4. The **show standby vlan 271** command produces the following output:

```
Vlan271 - Group 1
  Local state is Active, priority 210, may preempt
  Hellotime 3 holdtime 40 configured hellotime 3 sec holdtime 40 sec
  Next hello sent in 00:00:00.594
  Virtual IP address is 192.168.111.1 configured
    Secondary virtual IP address 10.1.111.1
    Secondary virtual IP address 172.21.111.1
  Active router is local
  Standby router is unknown expires in 00:00:37
  Standby virtual mac address is 0000.0c07.ac01
  2 state changes, last state change 5d17h
```

If the local router fails, which router takes over the active role for the virtual router address 192.168.111.1?

5. What is meant by pre-empting in HSRP?

6. What protocols discussed in this chapter support interface tracking?

7. The **show standby brief** command has been used to check the status of all HSRP groups on the local router. The output from this command is as follows:

```
Switch# show standby brief
                     P indicates configured to preempt.
                     |
    Interface Grp Prio  P   State   Active addr  Standby addr   Group addr
    Vl100      1   210  P   Active  local        192.168.75.2   192.168.75.1
    Vl101      1   210  P   Active  local        192.168.107.2  192.168.107.1
    Vl102      1   210  P   Active  local        192.168.71.2   192.168.71.1
```

Each interface is shown to have Group 1. Is this a problem?

8. How many HSRP groups are needed to load-balance traffic over two routers?

9. What load-balancing methods can GLBP use?

10. What command can you use to see the status of the active and standby routers on the VLAN 171 interface?

11. How many GLBP groups are needed to load-balance traffic over four routers?

12. To use NSF on a multilayer switch with redundant supervisor modules, what must be configured in addition to the redundancy mode? What else must be present in the network?

13. How is SSO different from SRM with SSO redundancy mode?

14. If two Catalyst 6500 power supplies are configured with the **power redundancy-mode combined**, what will happen if one of them fails?

This part of the book covers the following BCMSN exam topics:

- Describe the characteristics of voice in the campus network

- Describe the functions of Voice VLANs and trust boundaries

- Configure and verify basic IP Phone support (Voice VLAN, trust and CoS options, AutoQoS for voice)

- Describe common Layer 2 network attacks (MAC flooding, rogue devices, VLAN hopping, DHCP spoofing, and so on)

- Explain and configure Port Security, 802.1x, VACLs, Private VLANs, DHCP Snooping, and DAI

- Verify Catalyst switch (IOS-based) security configurations (Port Security, 802.1x, VACLs, Private VLANs, DHCP Snooping, and DAI)

Part IV: Campus Network Services

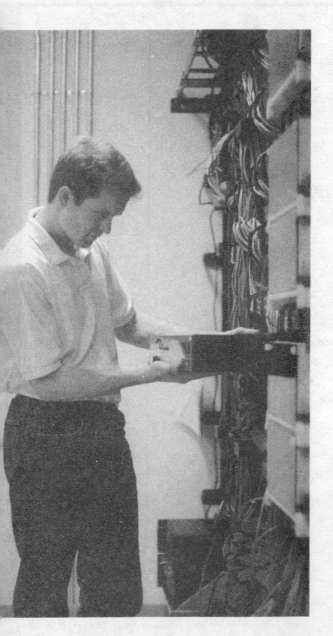

Part IV: Campus Network Services

This chapter covers the following topics that you need to master for the CCNP BCMSN exam:

- **Power over Ethernet**—This section discusses how a Catalyst switch can provide power to operate devices such as Cisco IP Phones.

- **Voice VLANs**—This section explains how voice traffic can be carried over the links between an IP Phone and a Catalyst switch.

- **Voice QoS**—This section provides an overview of the mechanisms that provide premium quality of service (QoS) for voice traffic.

CHAPTER 14

IP Telephony

In addition to carrying regular data, switched campus networks can carry packets that are related to telephone calls. Voice over IP (VoIP), otherwise known as *IP Telephony* (*IPT*), uses IP Phones that are connected to switched Ethernet ports.

To properly and effectively carry the traffic for a successful phone call, a combination of many switching features must be used. For example, the Catalyst switches can provide power to IP Phones, form trunk links with IP Phones, and provide the proper level of QoS for voice packet delivery. This chapter covers all these topics as related to the Cisco IP Phone.

"Do I Know This Already?" Quiz

The purpose of the "Do I Know This Already?" quiz is to help you decide what parts of this chapter to use. If you already intend to read the entire chapter, you do not necessarily need to answer these questions now.

The quiz, derived from the major sections in the "Foundation Topics" portion of the chapter, helps you determine how to spend your limited study time.

Table 14-1 outlines the major topics discussed in this chapter and the "Do I Know This Already?" quiz questions that correspond to those topics.

Table 14-1 *"Do I Know This Already?" Foundation Topics Section-to-Question Mapping*

Foundation Topics Section	Questions Covered in This Section	Score
Power over Ethernet	1–2	
Voice VLANs	3–7	
Voice QoS	8–10	
Verifying IP Telephony	11–12	
Total Score		

> **CAUTION** The goal of self-assessment is to gauge your mastery of the topics in this chapter. If you do not know the answer to a question or are only partially sure of the answer, you should mark this question wrong. Giving yourself credit for an answer you correctly guess skews your self-assessment results and might give you a false sense of security.

1. For a Catalyst switch to offer Power over Ethernet to a device, what must occur?

    a. Nothing; power always is enabled on a port.

    b. The switch must detect that the device needs inline power.

    c. The device must send a CDP message asking for power.

    d. The switch is configured to turn on power to the port.

2. Which one of these commands can enable Power over Ethernet to a switch interface?

    a. **inline power enable**

    b. **inline power on**

    c. **power inline on**

    d. **power inline auto**

3. What does a Cisco IP Phone contain to allow it to pass both voice and data packets?

    a. An internal Ethernet hub

    b. An internal two-port switch

    c. An internal three-port switch

    d. An internal four-port switch

4. How can voice traffic be kept separate from any other data traffic through an IP Phone?

    a. Voice and data travel over separate links.

    b. A special-case 802.1Q trunk is used to connect to the switch.

    c. Voice and data can't be separated; they must intermingle on the link.

    d. Voice and data packets both are encapsulated over an ISL trunk.

5. What command configures an IP Phone to use VLAN 9 for voice traffic?

    a. **switchport voice vlan 9**

    b. **switchport voice-vlan 9**

    c. **switchport voice 9**

    d. **switchport voip 9**

6. What is the default voice VLAN condition for a switch port?

    a. **switchport voice vlan 1**

    b. **switchport voice vlan dot1p**

    c. **switchport voice vlan untagged**

    d. **switchport voice vlan none**

7. If the **switchport voice vlan 50** command has been used, what VLAN numbers will the voice and PC data be carried over, respectively?

    a. VLAN 50, native VLAN

    b. VLAN 50, VLAN 1

    c. VLAN 1, VLAN 50

    d. native VLAN, VLAN 50

8. When a PC is connected to the PC switch port on an IP Phone, how is QoS trust handled?

    a. The IP Phone always trusts the class of service (CoS) information coming from the PC.

    b. The IP Phone never trusts the PC and always overwrites the CoS bits.

    c. QoS trust for the PC data is handled at the Catalyst switch port, not the IP Phone.

    d. The Catalyst switch instructs the IP Phone how to trust the PC QoS information.

9. An IP Phone should mark all incoming traffic from an attached PC to have CoS 1. Complete the following switch command to make that happen:

```
switchport priority extend _____
```

    a. **untrusted**

    b. **1**

    c. **cos 1**

    d. **overwrite 1**

10. What command can verify the Power over Ethernet status of each switch port?

    a. **show inline power**

    b. **show power inline**

    c. **show interface**

    d. **show running-config**

11. What command can verify the voice VLAN used by a Cisco IP Phone?

    a. **show cdp neighbor**

    b. **show interface switchport**

    c. **show vlan**

    d. **show trunk**

12. Which DSCP codepoint name usually is used for time-critical packets containing voice data?

    a. 7

    b. Critical

    c. AF

    d. EF

The answers to the "Do I Know This Already?" quiz are found in Appendix A, "Answers to Chapter 'Do I Know This Already?' Quizzes and Q&A Sections." The suggested choices for your next step are as follows:

■ **10 or less overall score**—Read the entire chapter. This includes the "Foundation Topics," "Foundation Summary," and "Q&A" sections.

■ **11 or 12 overall score**—If you want more review on these topics, skip to the "Foundation Summary" section and then go to the "Q&A" section at the end of the chapter. Otherwise, move to Chapter 15, "Securing Switch Access."

Foundation Topics

Power over Ethernet (PoE)

A Cisco IP Phone is like any other node on the network—it must have power to operate. Power can come from two sources:

- An external AC adapter

- Power over Ethernet (DC) over the network data cable

The external AC adapter plugs into a normal AC wall outlet and provides 48V DC to the phone. These adapters, commonly called *wall warts*, are handy if no other power source is available. However, if a power failure occurs to the room or outlet where the adapter is located, the IP Phone will fail.

A more elegant solution is available as *inline power* or *Power over Ethernet (PoE)*. Here, the same 48V DC supply is provided to an IP Phone over the same unshielded twisted-pair cable that is used for Ethernet connectivity. The DC power's source is the Catalyst switch itself. No other power source is needed, unless an AC adapter is required as a redundant source.

PoE has the benefit that it can be managed, monitored, and offered only to an IP Phone. In fact, this capability isn't limited to Cisco IP Phones—any device that can request and use inline power in a compatible manner can be used. Otherwise, if a nonpowered device such as a normal PC is plugged into the same switch port, the switch will not offer power to it.

The Catalyst switch also can be connected to an uninterruptible power supply (UPS) so that it continues to receive and offer power even if the regular AC source fails. This allows an IP Phone or other powered device to be available for use even across a power failure.

How Power over Ethernet Works

A Catalyst switch can offer power over its Ethernet ports only if it is designed to do so. It must have one or more power supplies that are rated for the additional load that will be offered to the connected devices. PoE is available on many platforms, including the Catalyst 3750-PWR, Catalyst 4500, and Catalyst 6500.

Two methods provide PoE to connected devices:

- **Cisco Inline Power (ILP)**—A Cisco-proprietary method developed before the IEEE 802.3af standard

- **IEEE 802.3af**—A standards-based method that offers vendor interoperability (see http://standards.ieee.org/getieee802/download/802.3af-2003.pdf)

Detecting a Powered Device

The switch always keeps the power disabled when a switch port is down. However, the switch must continually try to detect whether a powered device is connected to a port. If it is, the switch must begin providing power so that the device can initialize and become operational. Only then will the Ethernet link be established.

Because there are two PoE methods, a Catalyst switch tries both to detect a powered device. For IEEE 802.3af, the switch begins by supplying a small voltage across the transmit and receive pairs of the copper twisted-pair connection. It then can measure the resistance across the pairs to detect whether current is being drawn by the device. If 25K Ohm resistance is measured, a powered device is indeed present.

The switch also can apply several predetermined voltages to test for corresponding resistance values. These values are applied by the powered device to indicate which of the five IEEE 802.3af power classes it belongs to. Knowing this, the switch can begin allocating the appropriate maximum power needed by the device. Table 14-2 defines the power classes.

Table 14-2   *IEEE 802.3af Power Classes*

Power Class	Maximum Power Offered at 48V DC	Notes
0	15.4W	Default class
1	4.0W	Optional class
2	7.0W	Optional class
3	15.4W	Optional class
4	—	Reserved for future use

The default class is used if either the switch or the powered device doesn't support or doesn't attempt the optional power class discovery. At press time, class 4 is not used; it holds a place for future devices that will require a greater power budget than the current Catalyst switches can supply.

Cisco inline power device discovery takes a totally different approach than IEEE 802.3af. Instead of offering voltage and checking resistance, the switch sends out a 340kHz test tone on the transmit pair of the twisted-pair Ethernet cable. A tone is transmitted instead of DC power because the switch first must detect an inline power-capable device before offering it power. Otherwise, other types of devices (normal PCs, for example) could be damaged.

A powered device such as a Cisco IP Phone loops the transmit and receives pairs of its Ethernet connection while it is powered off. When it is connected to an inline power switch port, the switch can "hear" its test tone looped back. Then it safely assumes that a known powered device is present, and power can be applied to it.

Supplying Power to a Device

A switch first offers a default power allocation to the powered device. On a Catalyst 3750-24-PWR, for example, an IP Phone first receives 15.4W (0.32 amps at 48V DC).

Power can be supplied in two ways:

■ For Cisco ILP, inline power is provided over data pairs 2 and 3 (RJ-45 pins 1,2 and 3,6) at 48V DC.

■ For IEEE 802.3af, power can be supplied in the same fashion (pins 1,2 and 3,6) or over pairs 1 and 4 (RJ-45 pins 4,5 and 7,8).

Now the device has a chance to power up and bring up its Ethernet link, too. The power budget offered to the device can be changed from the default to a more appropriate value. This can help prevent the switch from wasting its total power budget on devices that use far less power than the per-port default. With IEEE 802.3af, the power budget can be changed by detecting the device's power class.

For Cisco ILP, the switch can attempt a Cisco Discovery Protocol (CDP) message exchange with the device. If CDP information is returned, the switch can discover the device type (Cisco IP Phone, for example) and the device's actual power requirements. The switch then can reduce the inline power to the amount requested by the device.

To see this in operation, look at Example 14-1. Here, the power was reduced from 15,000 mW to 6300 mW. This output was produced by the **debug ilpower controller** and **debug cdp packets** commands.

Example 14-1 *Displaying Inline Power Adjustment*

```
00:58:46: ILP uses AC Disconnect(Fa1/0/47): state= ILP_DETECTING_S, event=
  PHY_CSCO_DETECTED_EV
00:58:46: %ILPOWER-7-DETECT: Interface Fa1/0/47: Power Device detected: Cisco PD
00:58:46: Ilpower PD device 1 class 2 from interface (Fa1/0/47)
00:58:46: ilpower new power from pd discovery Fa1/0/47, power_status ok
00:58:46: Ilpower interface (Fa1/0/47) power status change, allocated power 15400
00:58:46: ILP Power apply to ( Fa1/0/47 ) Okay
00:58:46: ILP Start PHY Cisco IP phone detection ( Fa1/0/47 ) Okay
00:58:46: %ILPOWER-5-POWER_GRANTED: Interface Fa1/0/47: Power granted
00:58:46: ILP uses AC Disconnect(Fa1/0/47): state= ILP_CSCO_PD_DETECTED_S, event=
  IEEE_PWR_GOOD_EV
00:58:48: ILP State_Machine ( Fa1/0/47 ): State= ILP_PWR_GOOD_USE_IEEE_DISC_S, Event=
  PHY_LINK_UP_EV
```

continues

Example 14-1 *Displaying Inline Power Adjustment (Continued)*

```
00:58:48: ILP uses AC Disconnect(Fa1/0/47): state= ILP_PWR_GOOD_USE_IEEE_DISC_S, event=
    PHY_LINK_UP_EV
00:58:50: %LINK-3-UPDOWN: Interface FastEthernet1/0/47, changed state to up
00:58:50: CDP-AD: Interface FastEthernet1/0/47 coming up
00:58:50: ilpower_powerman_power_available_tlv: about sending patlv on Fa1/0/47
00:58:50:     req id 0, man id 1, pwr avail 15400, pwr man -1
00:58:50: CDP-PA: version 2 packet sent out on FastEthernet1/0/47
00:58:51: %LINEPROTO-5-UPDOWN: Line protocol on Interface FastEthernet1/0/47, changed state
    to up
00:58:54: CDP-PA: Packet received from SIP0012435D594D on interface FastEthernet1/0/47
00:58:54: **Entry NOT found in cache**
00:58:54: Interface(Fa1/0/47) - processing old tlv from cdp, request 6300, current
    allocated 15400
00:58:54: Interface (Fa1/0/47) efficiency is 100
00:58:54: ilpower_powerman_power_available_tlv: about sending patlv on Fa1/0/47
00:58:54:     req id 0, man id 1, pwr avail 6300, pwr man -1
00:58:54: CDP-PA: version 2 packet sent out on FastEthernet1/0/47
```

Configuring Power over Ethernet

PoE or inline power configuration is simple. Each switch port can automatically detect the presence of an inline power-capable device before applying power, or the feature can be disabled to ensure that the port can never detect or offer inline power. By default, every switch port attempts to discover an inline-powered device. To change this behavior, use the following interface-configuration commands:

```
Switch(config)# interface type mod/num
Switch(config-if)# power inline {auto [max milli-watts] | static
    [max milli-watts] | never}
```

By default, every switch interface is configured for **auto** mode, where the device and power budget automatically is discovered. In addition, the default power budget is 15.4W. You can change the maximum power offered as **max** *milli-watts* (4000 to 15400).

You can configure a **static** power budget for a switch port if you have a device that can't interact with either of the powered device-discovery methods. Again, you can set the maximum power offered to the device with **max** *milli-watts*. Otherwise, the default value of 15.4W is used.

If you want to disable PoE on a switch port, use the **never** keyword. Power never will be offered and powered devices never will be detected on that port.

Verifying Power over Ethernet

You can verify the power status for a switch port with the following EXEC command:

```
Switch# show power inline [type mod/num]
```

Example 14-2 provides some sample output from this command. If the class is shown as **n/a**, Cisco ILP has been used to supply power. Otherwise, the IEEE 802.3af power class (0 through 4) is shown.

Example 14-2 *Displaying PoE Status for Switch Ports*

```
Switch# show power inline
Module  Available  Used     Remaining
        (Watts)    (Watts)  (Watts)
------  ---------  -------  ---------
1          370.0     39.0      331.0
Interface Admin  Oper      Power  Device               Class Max
                           (Watts)
--------- ------ --------- ------- -------------------- ----- ----
Fa1/0/1   auto   on         6.5    AIR-AP1231G-A-K9      n/a  15.4
Fa1/0/2   auto   on         6.3    IP Phone 7940         n/a  15.4
Fa1/0/3   auto   on         6.3    IP Phone 7960         n/a  15.4
Fa1/0/4   auto   on        15.4    Ieee PD               0    15.4
Fa1/0/5   auto   on         4.5    Ieee PD               1    15.4
Fa1/0/6   static on        15.4    n/a                   n/a  15.4
Fa1/0/7   auto   off        0.0    n/a                   n/a  15.4
[output omitted]
```

CAUTION   A Catalyst switch waits for 4 seconds after inline power is applied to a port to see whether an IP Phone comes alive. If not, the power is removed from the port.

Be careful if you plug an IP phone into a switch port, and then remove it and plug in a normal Ethernet device. The inline power still could be applied during the 4-second interval, damaging a nonpowered device. Wait 10 seconds after unplugging an IP Phone before plugging anything back into the same port.

Voice VLANs

A Cisco IP Phone provides a data connection for a user's PC, in addition to its own voice data stream. This allows a single Ethernet drop to be installed per user. The IP Phone also can control some aspects of how the packets (both voice and user data) are presented to the switch.

Most Cisco IP Phone models contain a three-port switch, connecting to the upstream switch, the user's PC, and the internal VoIP data stream, as illustrated in Figure 14-1. The voice and user PC ports always function as access-mode switch ports. The port that connects to the upstream switch, however, can operate as an 802.1Q trunk or as an access-mode (single VLAN) port.

Figure 14-1 *Basic Connections to a Cisco IP Phone*

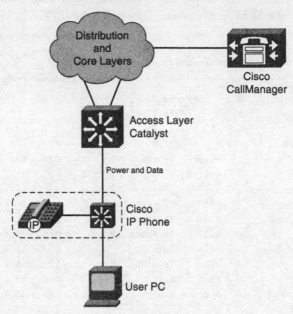

The link mode between the IP Phone and the switch is negotiated; you can configure the switch to instruct the phone to use a special-case 802.1Q trunk or a single VLAN access link. With a trunk, the voice traffic can be isolated from other user data, providing security and QoS capabilities.

As an access link, both voice and data must be combined over the single VLAN. This simplifies other aspects of the switch configuration because a separate voice VLAN is not needed, but it could compromise the voice quality, depending on the PC application mix and traffic load.

Voice VLAN Configuration

Although you can configure the IP Phone uplink as a trunk or nontrunk, the real consideration pertains to how the voice traffic will be encapsulated. The voice packets must be carried over a unique voice VLAN (known as the *voice VLAN ID* or *VVID*) or over the regular data VLAN (known as the *native VLAN* or the *port VLAN ID, PVID*). The QoS information from the voice packets also must be carried.

To configure the IP Phone uplink, just configure the switch port where it connects. The switch instructs the phone to follow the mode that is selected. In addition, the switch port does not need any special trunking configuration commands if a trunk is wanted. If an 802.1Q trunk is needed, a special-case trunk automatically is negotiated by the Dynamic Trunking Protocol (DTP) and CDP.

Use the following interface configuration command to select the voice VLAN mode that will be used:

```
Switch(config-if)# switchport voice vlan {vlan-id | dot1p | untagged | none}
```

Figure 14-2 shows the four different voice VLAN configurations. Pay particular attention to the link between the IP Phone and the switch.

Table 14-3 documents the four different voice VLAN configurations.

Table 14-3 *Trunking Modes with a Cisco IP Phone*

Keyword	Representation in Figure 14-2	Native VLAN (Untagged)	Voice VLAN	Voice QoS (CoS bits)
vlan-id	A	PC data	VLAN *vlan-id*	802.1p
dot1p	B	PC data	VLAN 0	802.1p
untagged	C	PC data/voice	—	—
none (default)	D	PC data/voice	—	—

The default condition for every switch port is **none**, where a trunk is not used. All modes except for **none** use the special-case 802.1Q trunk. The only difference between the **dot1p** and **untagged** modes is the encapsulation of voice traffic. The **dot1p** mode puts the voice packets on VLAN 0, which requires a VLAN ID (not the native VLAN) but doesn't require a unique voice VLAN to be created. The **untagged** mode puts voice packets in the native VLAN, requiring neither a VLAN ID nor a unique voice VLAN.

The most versatile mode uses the *vlan-id*, as shown in case A in Figure 14-2. Here, voice and user data are carried over separate VLANs. VoIP packets in the voice VLAN also carry the CoS bits in the 802.1p trunk encapsulation field.

Be aware that the special-case 802.1Q trunk automatically is enabled through a CDP information exchange between the switch and the IP Phone. The trunk contains only two VLANs—a voice VLAN (tagged VVID) and the data VLAN. The switch port's access VLAN is used as the data VLAN that carries packets to and from a PC that is connected to the phone's PC port.

If an IP Phone is removed and a PC is connected to the same switch port, the PC still will be capable of operating because the data VLAN still will appear as the access VLAN—even though the special trunk no longer is enabled.

Figure 14-2 *Trunking Modes for Voice VLANs with a Cisco IP Phone*

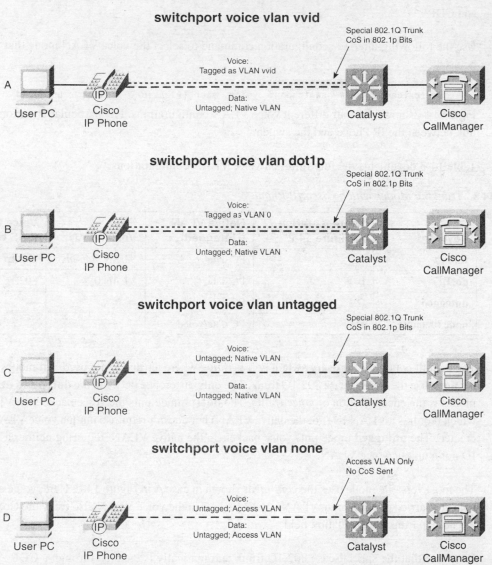

Verifying Voice VLAN Operation

You can verify the switch port mode (access or trunk) and the voice VLAN by using the **show interface switchport** command. As demonstrated in Example 14-3, the port is in access mode and uses access VLAN 10 and voice VLAN 110.

Example 14-3 *Verifying Switch Port Mode and Voice VLAN*

```
Switch# show interfaces fastEthernet 1/0/1 switchport
Name: Fa1/0/1
Switchport: Enabled
Administrative Mode: dynamic auto
Operational Mode: static access
Administrative Trunking Encapsulation: negotiate
Operational Trunking Encapsulation: native
Negotiation of Trunking: On
Access Mode VLAN: 10 (VLAN0010)
Trunking Native Mode VLAN: 1 (default)
Administrative Native VLAN tagging: enabled
Voice VLAN: 110 (VoIP)
Administrative private-vlan host-association: none
Administrative private-vlan mapping: none
Administrative private-vlan trunk native VLAN: none
Administrative private-vlan trunk Native VLAN tagging: enabled
Administrative private-vlan trunk encapsulation: dot1q
Administrative private-vlan trunk normal VLANs: none
Administrative private-vlan trunk private VLANs: none
Operational private-vlan: none
Trunking VLANs Enabled: ALL
Pruning VLANs Enabled: 2-1001
Capture Mode Disabled
Capture VLANs Allowed: ALL
Protected: false
Unknown unicast blocked: disabled
Unknown multicast blocked: disabled
Appliance trust: none
Switch#
```

When the IP Phone trunk is active, it is not shown in the trunking mode from any Cisco IOS Software **show** command. However, you can verify the VLANs being carried over the trunk link by looking at the Spanning Tree Protocol (STP) activity. STP runs with two instances—one for the voice VLAN and one for the data VLAN, which can be seen with the **show spanning-tree interface** command.

For example, suppose that a switch port is configured with access VLAN 10, voice VLAN 110, and native VLAN 99. Example 14-4 shows the switch port configuration and STP information when the switch port is in access mode.

Example 14-4 *IP Phone Trunk Configuration and STP Information*

```
Switch# show running-config interface fastethernet 1/0/1
interface FastEthernet1/0/1
 switchport trunk native vlan 99
```

continues

Example 14-4 *IP Phone Trunk Configuration and STP Information (Continued)*

```
 switchport access vlan 63
 switchport voice vlan 306
Switch# show  spanning-tree  interface  fastethernet  1/0/1
Vlan            Role Sts Cost      Prio.Nbr Type
---------------- ---- --- --------- -------- --------------------------------
VLAN0010        Desg FWD 19        128.51   P2p
VLAN0110        Desg FWD 19        128.51   P2p
Switch#
```

The access VLAN (10) is being used as the data VLAN from the IP Phone.

Voice QoS

On a quiet, underutilized network, a switch generally can forward packets as soon as they are received. However, if a network is congested, packets can't always be delivered in a timely manner. Traditionally, network congestion has been handled by increasing link bandwidths and switching hardware performance. This does little to address how one type of traffic can be preferred or delivered ahead of another.

Quality of service (QoS) is the overall method used in a network to protect and prioritize time-critical or important traffic. The most important aspect of transporting voice traffic across a switched campus network is maintaining the proper QoS level. Voice packets must be delivered in the most timely fashion possible, with little jitter, little loss, and little delay.

Remember, a user expects to receive a dial tone, a call to go through, and a good-quality audio connection with the far end when an IP Phone is used. Above that, any call that is made could be an emergency 911 call. It is then very important that QoS be implemented properly.

QoS Overview

The majority of this book has discussed how Layer 2 and Layer 3 Catalyst switches forward packets from one switch port to another. On the surface, it might seem that there is only one way to forward packets—just look up the next packet's destination in a Content Addressable Memory (CAM) or Cisco Express Forwarding (CEF) table and send it on its way. But that addresses only *whether* the packet can be forwarded, not *how* it can be forwarded.

Different types of applications have different requirements for how their data should be sent end to end. For example, it might be acceptable to wait a short time for a web page to be displayed after a user requests it. That same user probably cannot tolerate the same delays in receiving packets that belong to a streaming video presentation or an audio telephone call. Any loss or delay in packet delivery could ruin the purpose of the application.

Three basic things can happen to packets as they are sent from one host to another across a network:

- **Delay**—As a packet is sent from one network device to another, its delivery is delayed by some amount of time. This can be caused by the time required to send the packet serially across a wire, the time required for a router or switch to perform table lookups or make decisions, the time required for the data to travel over a geographically long path, and so on. The total delay from start to finish is called the *latency*. This is seen most easily as the time from when a user presses a key until the time the character is echoed and displayed in a terminal session.

- **Jitter**—Some applications involve the delivery of a stream of related data. As these packets are delivered, variations can occur in the amount of delay so that they do not all arrive at predictable times. The variation in delay is called *jitter*. Audio streams are particularly susceptible to jitter; if the audio data is not played back at a constant rate, the resulting speech or music sounds choppy.

- **Loss**—In extreme cases, packets that enter a congested or error-prone part of the network are simply dropped without delivery. Some amount of packet loss is acceptable and recoverable by applications that use a reliable, connection-oriented protocol such as TCP. Other application protocols are not as tolerant, and dropped packets mean data is missing.

To address and alleviate these conditions, a network can employ three basic types of QoS:

- Best-effort delivery
- Integrated Services model
- Differentiated Services model

Keep in mind that QoS works toward making policies or promises to improve packet delivery from a sender to a receiver. The same QoS policies should be used on *every* network device that connects the sender to the receiver. QoS must be implemented end to end before it can be totally effective.

Best-Effort Delivery

A network that simply forwards packets in the order they were received has no real QoS. Switches and routers then make their "best effort" to deliver packets as quickly as possible, with no regard for the type of traffic or the need for priority service.

To get an idea of how QoS operates in a network, consider a fire truck or an ambulance trying to quickly work its way through a crowded city. The lights are flashing and the siren is sounding to signal that this is a "priority" vehicle needing to get through ahead of everyone else. The priority vehicle does not need to obey normal traffic rules.

However, the best effort scenario says that the fire truck must stay within the normal flow of traffic. At an intersection, it must wait in the line or queue of traffic like any other vehicle—even if its lights and siren are on. It might arrive on time or too late to help, depending on the conditions along the road.

Integrated Services Model

One approach to QoS is the Integrated Services (IntServ) model. The basic idea is to prearrange a path for priority data along the complete path, from source to destination. Beginning with RFC 1633, the Resource Reservation Protocol (RSVP) was developed as the mechanism for scheduling and reserving adequate path bandwidth for an application.

The source application itself is involved by requesting QoS parameters through RSVP. Each network device along the way must check to see whether it can support the request. When a complete path meeting the minimum requirements is made, the source is signaled with a confirmation. Then the source application can begin using the path.

Applying the fire truck example to the IntServ model, a fire truck would radio ahead to the nearest intersection before it left the firehouse. Police stationed at each intersection would contact each other in turn, to announce that the fire truck was coming and to assess the traffic conditions. The police might reserve a special lane so that the fire truck could move at full speed toward the destination, regardless of what other traffic might be present.

Differentiated Services Model

As you might imagine, the IntServ model does not scale very well when many sources are trying to compete with each other to reserve end-to-end bandwidth. Another approach is the Differentiated Services (DiffServ) model, which permits each network device to handle packets on an individual basis. Each router or switch can be configured with QoS policies to follow, and forwarding decisions are made accordingly.

DiffServ requires no advance reservations; QoS is handled dynamically, in a distributed fashion. In other words, whereas IntServ applies QoS on a per-flow basis, DiffServ applies it on a per-hop basis to a whole group of similar flows. DiffServ also bases its QoS decisions on information contained in each packet header.

Continuing with the emergency vehicle analogy, here police are stationed at every intersection, as before. However, none of them knows a fire truck is coming until they see the lights or hear the siren. At each intersection, a decision is made as to how to handle the approaching fire truck. Other traffic can be held back, if needed, so that the fire truck can go right through.

Giving premium service to voice traffic focuses almost entirely on the DiffServ model. QoS is a complex and intricate topic in itself. The BCMSN course and exam cover only the theory behind DiffServ QoS, along with the features and commands that address voice QoS specifically.

DiffServ QoS

DiffServ is a per-hop behavior, with each router or switch inspecting each packet's header to decide how to go about forwarding that packet. All the information needed for this decision is carried along with each packet in the header. The packet itself cannot affect how it will be handled. Instead, it merely presents some flags, classifications, or markings that can be used to make a forwarding decision based on QoS policies that are configured into each switch or router along the path.

Layer 2 QoS Classification

Layer 2 frames themselves have no mechanism to indicate the priority or importance of their contents. One frame looks just as important as another. Therefore, a Layer 2 switch can forward frames only according to a best-effort delivery.

When frames are carried from switch to switch, however, an opportunity for classification occurs. Recall that a trunk is used to carry frames from multiple VLANs between switches. The trunk does this by encapsulating the frames and adding a tag indicating the source VLAN number. The encapsulation also includes a field that can mark the class of service (CoS) of each frame. This can be used at switch boundaries to make some QoS decisions. After a trunk is unencapsulated at the far-end switch, the CoS information is removed and lost.

The two trunk encapsulations handle CoS differently:

- **IEEE 802.1Q**—Each frame is tagged with a 12-bit VLAN ID and a User field. The User field contains three 802.1p priority bits that indicate the frame CoS, a unitless value ranging from 0 (lowest-priority delivery) to 7 (highest-priority delivery). Frames from the native VLAN are not tagged (no VLAN ID or User field), so they receive a default CoS that is configured on the receiving switch.

- **Inter-Switch Link (ISL)**—Each frame is tagged with a 15-bit VLAN ID. In addition, next to the frame Type field is a 4-bit User field. The lower 3 bits of the User field are used as a CoS value. Although ISL is not standards based, Catalyst switches make CoS seamless by copying the 802.1p CoS bits from an 802.1Q trunk into the User CoS bits of an ISL trunk. This allows CoS information to propagate along trunks of differing encapsulations.

Layer 3 QoS Classification with DSCP

From the beginning, IP packets have always had a type of service (ToS) byte that can be used to mark packets. This byte is divided into a 3-bit IP Precedence value and a 4-bit ToS value. This offers a rather limited mechanism for QoS because only the 3 bits of IP Precedence are used to describe the per-hop QoS behavior.

The DiffServ model keeps the existing IP ToS byte but uses it in a more scalable fashion. This byte also is referred to as the *Differentiated Services (DS)* field, with a different format, as shown in Figure 14-3. The 6-bit DS value is known as the *Differentiated Service Code Point (DSCP)* and is the one value that is examined by any DiffServ network device.

Don't be confused by the dual QoS terminology—the ToS and DS bytes are the same, occupying the same location in the IP header. Only the names are different, along with the way the value is interpreted. In fact, the DSCP bits have been arranged to be backward compatible with the IP precedence bits so that a non-DiffServ device still can interpret some QoS information.

Figure 14-3 *ToS and DSCP Byte Formats*

ToS Byte:	P2	P1	P0	T3	T2	T1	T0	Zero
DS Byte:	DS5	DS4	DS3	DS2	DS1	DS0	ECN1	ECN0
	(Class Selector)			(Drop Precedence)				

The DSCP value is divided into a 3-bit class selector and a 3-bit Drop Precedence value. Refer to Table 14-4 to see how the IP precedence, DSCP per-hop behavior, and DSCP codepoint names and numbers relate.

Table 14-4 *Mapping of IP Precedence and DSCP Fields*

IP Precedence (3 Bits)			DSCP (6 Bits)					
Name	Value	Bits	Per-Hop Behavior	Class Selector	Drop Precedence	Codepoint Name	DSCP Bits (Decimal)
Routine	0	000	Default			Default	000 000 (0)
Priority	1	001	AF	1	1: Low	AF11	001 010 (10)
					2: Medium	AF12	001 100 (12)
					3: High	AF13	001 110 (14)
Immediate	2	010	AF	2	1: Low	AF21	010 010 (18)
					2: Medium	AF22	010 100 (20)
					3: High	AF23	010 110 (22)

Table 14-4 *Mapping of IP Precedence and DSCP Fields (Continued)*

IP Precedence (3 Bits)			DSCP (6 Bits)				
Name	Value	Bits	Per-Hop Behavior	Class Selector	Drop Precedence	Codepoint Name	DSCP Bits (Decimal)
Flash	3	011	AF	3	1: Low	AF31	011 010 (26)
					2: Medium	AF32	011 100 (28)
					3: High	AF33	011 110 (30)
Flash Override	4	100	AF	4	1: Low	AF41	100 010 (34)
					2: Medium	AF42	100 100 (36)
					3: High	AF43	100 110 (38)
Critical	5	101	EF			EF	101 110 (46)*
Internetwork Control	6	110					(48–55)
Network Control	7	111					(56–63)

*IP precedence value 5 (DSCP EF) corresponds to the range of DSCP bits 101000 through 101111, or 40–47. However, only the value 101110 or 46 is commonly used and is given the EF designation.

The three class selector bits (DS5 through DS3) coarsely classify packets into one of seven classes:

- Class 0, the default class, offers only best-effort forwarding.

- Classes 1 through 4 are called *Assured Forwarding (AF)* service levels. Higher AF class numbers indicate the presence of higher-priority traffic.

Packets in the AF classes can be dropped, if necessary, with the lower-class numbers the most likely to be dropped. For example, packets with AF Class 4 will be delivered in preference to packets with AF Class 3.

- Class 5 is known as *Expedited Forwarding (EF)*, with those packets given premium service. EF is the least likely to be dropped, so it always is reserved for time-critical data such as voice traffic.

- Classes 6 and 7 are called *Internetwork Control* and *Network Control*, respectively, and are set aside for network control traffic. Usually, routers and switches use these classes for things such as the Spanning Tree Protocol and routing protocols. This ensures timely delivery of the packets that keep the network stable and operational.

Each class represented in the DSCP also has three levels of drop precedence, contained in bits DS2 through DS0 (DS0 is always zero):

■ Low (1)

■ Medium (2)

■ High (3)

Within a class, packets marked with a higher drop precedence have the potential for being dropped before those with a lower value. In other words, a lower drop precedence value gives better service. This gives finer granularity to the decision of what packets to drop when necessary.

> **TIP**   The DSCP value can be given as a codepoint name, with the class selector providing the two letters and a number followed by the drop precedence number. For example, class AF Level 2 with drop precedence 1 (low) is written as AF21. The DSCP commonly is given as a decimal value. For AF21, the decimal value is 18. The relationship is confusing, and Table 14-2 should be a handy aid.
>
> You should try to remember a few codepoint names and numbers. Some common values are EF (46) and most of the classes with low drop precedences: AF41 (34), AF31 (26), AF21 (18), and AF11 (10). Naturally, the default DSCP has no name (0).

Implementing QoS for Voice

To manipulate packets according to QoS policies, a switch somehow must identify which level of service each packet should receive. This process is known as *classification*. Each packet is classified according to the type of traffic (UDP or TCP port number, for example), according to parameters matched by an access list or something more complex, such as by stateful inspection of a traffic flow.

Recall that IP packets carry a ToS or DSCP value within their headers as they travel around a network. Frames on a trunk also can have CoS values associated with them. A switch then can decide whether to trust the ToS, DSCP, or CoS values already assigned to inbound packets. If it trusts any of these values, the values are carried over and used to make QoS decisions inside the switch.

If the QoS values are not trusted, they can be reassigned or overruled. This way, a switch can set the values to something known and trusted, and something that falls within the QoS policies that must be met. This prevents nonpriority users in the network from falsely setting the ToS or DSCP values of their packets to inflated levels so that they receive priority service.

Every switch must decide whether to trust incoming QoS values. Generally, an organization should be able to trust QoS parameters anywhere inside its own network. At the boundary with another organization or service provider, QoS typically should not be trusted. It is also prudent to trust only QoS values that have been assigned by the network devices themselves. Therefore, the QoS values produced by the end users should not be trusted until the network can verify or override them.

The perimeter formed by switches that do not trust incoming QoS is called the *trust boundary*. Usually, the trust boundary exists at the farthest reaches of the enterprise network (access-layer switches and WAN or ISP demarcation points). When the trust boundary has been identified and the switches there are configured with untrusted ports, everything else inside the perimeter can be configured to blindly trust incoming QoS values.

> **TIP**   Every switch and router within a network must be configured with the appropriate QoS features and policies, so that a trust boundary is completely formed. The BCMSN course and exam limit QoS coverage to the switches at the access layer, where the trust boundary is configured and enforced. Other more involved QoS topics are dealt with in the "Implementing Cisco Quality of Service (QoS)" course, as well as these Cisco Press books: *Cisco Catalyst QoS: Quality of Service in Campus Networks* (ISBN 1587051206) and *Cisco DQOS Exam Certification Guide* (ISBN 1587200589).

Figure 14-4 shows a simple network in which the trust boundary is defined at the edges, where the network connects to end users and public networks. On Catalyst A, port GigabitEthernet2/1 is configured to consider inbound data as untrusted. Catalyst B's port FastEthernet0/2 connects to a PC that also is untrusted. The Cisco IP Phone on Catalyst B port FastEthernet0/1 is a special case because it supports its own voice traffic and an end user's PC. Therefore, the trust boundary can't be clearly defined on that switch port.

Figure 14-4   *A QoS Trust Boundary Example*

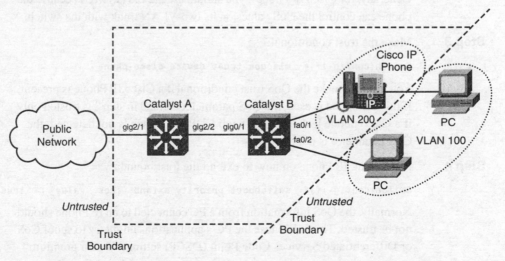

Configuring a Trust Boundary

When a Cisco IP Phone is connected to a switch port, think of the phone as another switch (which it is). If you install the phone as a part of your network, you probably can trust the QoS information relayed by the phone.

However, remember that the phone also has two sources of data:

■ **The VoIP packets native to the phone**—The phone can control precisely what QoS information is included in the voice packets because it produces those packets.

■ **The user PC data switch port**—Packets from the PC data port are generated elsewhere, so the QoS information cannot necessarily be trusted to be correct or fair.

A switch instructs an attached IP Phone through CDP messages on how it should extend QoS trust to its own user data switch port. To configure the trust extension, use the following configuration steps:

Step 1   Enable QoS on the switch:

```
Switch(config)# mls qos
```

By default, QoS is disabled globally on a switch and all QoS information is allowed to pass from one switch port to another. When you enable QoS, all switch ports are configured as untrusted, by default.

Step 2   Define the QoS parameter that will be trusted:

```
Switch(config)# interface type mod/num
Switch(config-if)# mls qos trust {cos | ip-precedence | dscp}
```

You can choose to trust the CoS, IP precedence, or DSCP values of incoming packets on the switch port. Only one of these parameters can be selected. Generally, for Cisco IP Phones, you should use the **cos** keyword because the phone can control the CoS values on its two-VLAN trunk with the switch.

Step 3   Make the trust conditional:

```
Switch(config-if)# mls qos trust device cisco-phone
```

You also can make the QoS trust conditional if a Cisco IP Phone is present. If this command is used, the QoS parameter defined in step 2 is trusted only if a Cisco phone is detected through CDP. If a phone is not detected, the QoS parameter is not trusted.

Step 4   Instruct the IP Phone on how to extend the trust boundary:

```
Switch(config-if)# switchport priority extend {cos value | trust}
```

Normally, the QoS information from a PC connected to an IP Phone should not be trusted. This is because the PC's applications might try to spoof CoS or Differentiated Services Code Point (DSCP) settings to gain premium network service. In this case, use the **cos** keyword so that the CoS bits are overwritten to *value* by the IP Phone as packets are forwarded to the switch. If CoS values from the PC cannot be trusted, they should be overwritten to a value of 0.

In some cases, the PC might be running trusted applications that are allowed to request specific QoS or levels of service. Here, the IP Phone can extend complete QoS trust to the PC, allowing the CoS bits to be forwarded through the phone unmodified. This is done with the **trust** keyword.

By default, a switch instructs an attached IP Phone to consider the PC port as untrusted. The phone will overwrite the CoS values to 0.

What about switch ports that don't connect to end-user or phone devices? Switch uplinks always should be considered as trusted ports—as long as they connect to other trusted devices that are within the QoS boundary. QoS parameters are trusted or overwritten at the network edge, as packets enter the trusted domain. After that, every switch inside the trusted boundary can implicitly trust and use the QoS parameters in any packet passing through.

You can configure a switch uplink port to be trusted with the following commands:

```
Switch(config)# interface type mod/num
Switch(config-if)# mls qos trust cos
```

Here, the trust is not conditional. The switch will trust only the CoS values that are found in the incoming packets.

> **TIP**   A Cisco switch also has a CoS-to-DSCP map that is used to convert inbound CoS values to DSCP values. The CoS information is useful only on trunk interfaces because it can be carried within the trunk encapsulation. CoS must be converted to DSCP or IP precedence, which can be carried along in the IP packet headers on any type of connection.
>
> Switches use a default CoS-to-DSCP mapping, which can be configured or changed. However, this is beyond the scope of the BCMSN course and exam.

Using Auto-QoS to Simplify a Configuration

You can also configure Cisco switches to support a variety of other QoS mechanisms and parameters. The list of features and configuration commands can be overwhelming, and the actual configuration can be quite complex. This is one reason why the bulk of QoS topics are no longer covered in the BCMSN course and exam.

Courses and testing aside, you will sometimes need to configure some advanced QoS features on a switch. To reduce the complexity, Cisco introduced the Auto-QoS feature on most switch platforms. By entering only a couple of configuration commands, you can enable the switch to automatically configure a variety of QoS parameters.

Auto-QoS is actually handled by a macro command, which in turn enters many other configuration commands as if they were entered from the command-line interface. Because of this, Auto-QoS is best used on a switch that still has the default QoS configuration. Otherwise, any existing QoS commands could be overwritten or could interfere with the commands produced by the Auto-QoS macro.

> **TIP** The Auto-QoS feature is designed to automatically configure many more advanced QoS parameters, in specific applications. For example, Auto-QoS can be used on switch interfaces where Cisco IP Phones are connected. Auto-QoS is not meant to be used on all switches in a network. Therefore, you should consider using it in access layer switches and not necessarily the network core.

The configuration commands resulting from Auto-QoS were developed from rigorous testing and Cisco best practices. Auto-QoS handles the following types of QoS configuration:

- Enabling QoS

- CoS-to-DSCP mapping for QoS marking

- Ingress and egress queue tuning

- Strict priority queues for egress voice traffic

- Establishing an interface QoS trust boundary

Use the following steps to configure Auto-QoS:

Step 1   Select an interface at the QoS boundary:

```
Switch(config)# interface type mod/num
```

Step 2   Enable Auto-QoS with the appropriate trust:

```
Switch(config-if)# auto qos voip {cisco-phone | cisco-softphone | trust}
```

If the switch port is connected to a Cisco IP Phone, you should use the **cisco-phone** keyword. Once that is enabled, the switch will trust the class of service information presented by the phone, if a phone is detected by CDP. If no phone is connected, the port is considered untrusted.

If a PC running the Cisco SoftPhone application is connected, choose the **cisco-softphone** keyword. Packets that are received with DSCP values of 24, 26, or 46 will be trusted; packets with any other value will have their DSCP values set to zero.

On a switch port acting as an uplink to another switch or router, you should use the **trust** keyword. All packets received on that port will be trusted, and the QoS information will be left intact.

> **TIP** If you have already configured Auto-QoS on an interface by using the **cisco-phone**, **cisco-softphone**, or **trust** keyword, you won't be allowed to use the **auto qos voip** command again on the same interface. Instead, first remove any existing Auto-QoS by entering the **no auto qos voip** command. Then use the **auto qos voip** command with the desired keyword to enable Auto-QoS.

Remember that the **auto qos voip** command is actually a macro that executes many other configuration commands for you. The **auto qos voip** command will appear in the switch configuration, along with the other commands it enters. You won't see the additional commands until you show the running configuration. However, using the **debug auto qos** EXEC command displays the additional commands in the resulting debug messages. (Don't forget to disable the debugging with **no debug auto qos** when you're finished with it.)

Example 14-5 shows what Auto-QoS is doing behind the scenes. By entering one interface configuration command, you can effectively configure many QoS parameters—even if you don't understand their functions. The commands are shown here as a demonstration; the BCMSN course and exam don't cover their meaning or use.

Interface fastethernet 0/37 normally has a Cisco IP Phone connected to it. Therefore, the **auto qos voip cisco-phone** command is used. Notice that among the many **mls qos** and **wrr-queue** QoS-related commands are two shaded commands that enable trust for CoS values coming from a Cisco phone. Interface gigabitethernet 0/1 is an uplink to another trusted switch, so the **auto qos voip trust** command is used on it. The shaded **mls qos trust cos** command causes the CoS information to be implicitly trusted.

Example 14-5 *Auto-QoS Commands Revealed*

```
Switch#debug auto qos
AutoQoS debugging is on

Switch# config term
Enter configuration commands, one per line.  End with CNTL/Z.

Switch(config)# interface fastethernet 0/37
Switch(config-if)# auto qos voip cisco-phone
Switch(config-if)#
*Sep  7 04:14:41.618 EDT: mls qos map cos-dscp 0 8 16 26 32 46 48 56
*Sep  7 04:14:41.622 EDT: mls qos min-reserve 5 170
*Sep  7 04:14:41.622 EDT: mls qos min-reserve 6 85
*Sep  7 04:14:41.622 EDT: mls qos min-reserve 7 51
```

continues

Example 14-5 *Auto-QoS Commands Revealed (Continued)*

```
*Sep  7 04:14:41.626 EDT: mls qos min-reserve 8 34
*Sep  7 04:14:41.626 EDT: mls qos
*Sep  7 04:14:42.598 EDT: interface FastEthernet0/37
*Sep  7 04:14:42.598 EDT:   mls qos trust device cisco-phone
*Sep  7 04:14:42.602 EDT:   mls qos trust cos
*Sep  7 04:14:42.606 EDT: wrr-queue bandwidth 10 20 70 1
*Sep  7 04:14:42.610 EDT: wrr-queue min-reserve 1 5
*Sep  7 04:14:42.618 EDT: wrr-queue min-reserve 2 6
*Sep  7 04:14:42.626 EDT: wrr-queue min-reserve 3 7
*Sep  7 04:14:42.634 EDT: wrr-queue min-reserve 4 8
*Sep  7 04:14:42.642 EDT: no wrr-queue cos-map
*Sep  7 04:14:42.646 EDT: wrr-queue cos-map 1  0 1
*Sep  7 04:14:42.650 EDT: wrr-queue cos-map 2  2 4
*Sep  7 04:14:42.654 EDT: wrr-queue cos-map 3  3 6 7
*Sep  7 04:14:42.658 EDT: wrr-queue cos-map 4  5
*Sep  7 04:14:42.662 EDT: priority-queue out

Switch(config-if)# interface gigabitethernet 0/1
Switch(config-if)# auto qos voip trust
Switch(config-if)#
*Sep  7 15:05:50.943 EDT: interface GigabitEthernet0/1
*Sep  7 15:05:50.947 EDT:   mls qos trust cos
*Sep  7 15:05:50.951 EDT: wrr-queue bandwidth 10 20 70 1
*Sep  7 15:05:50.955 EDT: wrr-queue queue-limit 50 25 15 10
*Sep  7 15:05:50.959 EDT: no wrr-queue cos-map
*Sep  7 15:05:50.963 EDT: wrr-queue cos-map 1  0 1
*Sep  7 15:05:50.967 EDT: wrr-queue cos-map 2  2 4
*Sep  7 15:05:50.971 EDT: wrr-queue cos-map 3  3 6 7
*Sep  7 15:05:50.975 EDT: wrr-queue cos-map 4  5
*Sep  7 15:05:50.979 EDT: priority-queue out
```

Verifying Voice QoS

A switch port can be configured with a QoS trust state with the connected device. If that device is an IP Phone, the switch can instruct the phone on whether to extend QoS trust to an attached PC.

To verify how QoS trust has been extended to the IP Phone itself, use the following EXEC command:

```
Switch#show mls qos interface type mod/num
```

If the port is trusted, all traffic forwarded by the IP Phone is accepted with the QoS information left intact. If the port is not trusted, even the voice packets can have their QoS information overwritten by the switch. Example 14-6 demonstrates some sample output from the **show mls**

qos interface command, where the switch port is trusting CoS information from the attached IP Phone.

Example 14-6 *Verifying QoS Trust to the IP Phone*

```
Switch# show mls qos interface fastethernet 0/1
FastEthernet0/1
trust state: trust cos
trust mode: trust cos
trust enabled flag: ena
COS override: dis
default COS: 0
DSCP Mutation Map: Default DSCP Mutation Map
Trust device: none
```

Next, you can verify how the IP Phone has been instructed to treat incoming QoS information from its attached PC or other device. This is shown in the **trust device:** line in Example 14-6, where the device is the IP Phone's device. You also can use the following EXEC command:

```
Switch# show interface type mod/num switchport
```

Here, the device trust is called *appliance trust*, as shown in Example 14-7.

Example 14-7 *An Alternative Method for Verifying QoS Trust to an IP Phone*

```
Switch# show interface fastethernet 0/1 switchport
Name: Fa0/1
Switchport: Enabled
[output deleted...]
Voice VLAN: 2 (VLAN0002)
Appliance trust: none
```

Again, the IP Phone's device is not being trusted. If the switch port was configured with the **switchport priority extend trust** command, the appliance trust would show *trusted*. Example 14-8 shows the configuration commands that have been added to a switch interface where a Cisco IP Phone is connected.

Example 14-8 *Switch Port Configuration Commands to Support a Cisco IP Phone*

```
Switch# show running-config interface fastethernet 0/47
Building configuration...
Current configuration : 219 bytes
!
interface FastEthernet0/47
 switchport access vlan 10
 switchport trunk encapsulation dot1q
 switchport mode access
```

continues

Example 14-8 *Switch Port Configuration Commands to Support a Cisco IP Phone (Continued)*

```
 switchport voice vlan 100
 mls qos trust device cisco-phone
 mls qos trust cos
 no mdix auto
end
Switch#
```

If the IP Phone is not connected to the switch port, it is not detected and the trust parameter is not enabled, as Example 14-9 demonstrates.

Example 14-9 *Displaying IP Phone Connection and Trust Status*

```
Switch# show mls qos interface fastethernet 0/1
FastEthernet0/1
trust state: not trusted
trust mode: trust cos
trust enabled flag: dis
COS override: dis
default COS: 0
DSCP Mutation Map: Default DSCP Mutation Map
Trust device: cisco-phone
Switch#
```

When a Cisco IP Phone is connected, power is applied and the phone is detected. Then the conditional QoS trust (CoS, in this case) is enabled, as demonstrated in Example 14-10.

Example 14-10 *Conditional Trust (CoS) Enabled on a Cisco IP Phone*

```
6d18h: %ILPOWER-7-DETECT: Interface Fa1/0/1: Power Device detected: Cisco PD
6d18h: %ILPOWER-5-POWER_GRANTED: Interface Fa1/0/1: Power granted
6d18h: %LINK-3-UPDOWN: Interface FastEthernet1/0/1, changed state to up
6d18h: %LINEPROTO-5-UPDOWN: Line protocol on Interface FastEthernet1/0/1, changed state
   to up
6d18h: %SWITCH_QOS_TB-5-TRUST_DEVICE_DETECTED: cisco-phone detected on port Fa1/
   0/1, port trust enabled.
Switch# show mls qos interface fastethernet 1/0/1
FastEthernet1/0/1
trust state: trust cos
trust mode: trust cos
trust enabled flag: ena
COS override: dis
default COS: 0
DSCP Mutation Map: Default DSCP Mutation Map
Trust device: cisco-phone
Switch#
```

If you have used Auto-QoS to configure an interface, you can use the **show auto qos** [**interface** *type mod/num*] command to view the configuration status as demonstrated in Example 14-11.

Example 14-11 *Verifying Auto-Qos Interface Configuration*

```
Switch# show auto qos interface fastethernet 0/37
FastEthernet0/37
auto qos voip cisco-phone
```

Foundation Summary

The Foundation Summary is a collection of information that provides a convenient review of many key concepts in this chapter. If you are already comfortable with the topics in this chapter, this summary could help you recall a few details. If you just read this chapter, this review should help solidify some key facts. If you are doing your final preparation before the exam, this summarized information is a convenient way to review the day before the exam.

Table 14-5 *Commands for Configuring IP Telephony on a Catalyst Switch*

Task	Command Syntax
Set power over Ethernet behavior	**power inline** {**auto** I **never**} .
Enable QoS globally	**mls qos**
Define QoS parameter that will be trusted on an interface	**mls qos trust** {**cos** I **ip-precedence** I **dscp**}
Conditionally trust a Cisco IP Phone	**mls qos trust device cisco-phone**
Define the trunking on a port to a Cisco IP Phone	**switchport voice vlan** {*vlan-id* I **dot1p** I **untagged** I **none**}
Define the trust relationship of the IP Phone	**switchport priority extend** {**cos** *value* I **trust**}
Enable Auto-QoS on an interface	**auto qos voip** {**cisco-phone** I **cisco-softphone** I **trust**}

You can use the commands in Table 14-6 to verify or troubleshoot IP telephony on a Catalyst switch.

Table 14-6 *Commands for Troubleshooting IP Telephony on a Catalyst Switch*

Task	Command Syntax
Display Power over Ethernet status	**show power inline** [*type mod/num*]
Verify the voice VLAN	**show interface** *type mod/num* **switchport**
Display how QoS trust is extended to the phone	**show mls qos interface** *type mod/num*
Verify Auto-QoS settings	**show auto qos** [**interface** *type mod/num*]

Q&A

The questions and scenarios in this book are more difficult than what you should experience on the actual exam. The questions do not attempt to cover more breadth or depth than the exam; however, they are designed to make sure that you know the answers. Rather than allowing you to derive the answers from clues hidden inside the questions themselves, the questions challenge your understanding and recall of the subject. Hopefully, these questions will help limit the number of exam questions on which you narrow your choices to two options and then guess.

The answers to these questions can be found in Appendix A.

1. How does a Catalyst switch detect that a connected device is capable of using Power over Ethernet?

2. What type of trunk can be used between a Catalyst switch port and a Cisco IP Phone?

3. When a trunk is used on an IP Phone, on which VLAN is the data from an attached PC carried?

4. What is the difference between the VVID and the PVID?

5. Can the CoS information from the voice traffic be passed when the **switchport voice vlan untagged** command is used? If so, how?

6. What is the advantage of using the **switchport voice vlan dot1p** command?

7. By default, does a Cisco IP Phone trust QoS information from an attached PC?

8. The command **switchport priority extend cos 5** is entered for a switch port. Is this a good decision? Why or why not?

9. What commands can be used to enable Auto-Qos on interface FastEthernet 0/1, where a Cisco IP phone is connected?

10. The **show power inline** command is used to check the power status on each switch port. If the output is as shown here, what can you assume about interface fastethernet 0/1?

```
Interface Admin   Oper    Power    Device
                          (Watts)
---------- -----  ------- -------  -------------------
Fa0/1      auto   off      0  n/a
Fa0/2      auto   on       6.3 Cisco IP Phone 7960
```

11. What command can verify the QoS trust relationship between an IP Phone and its attached PC?

This chapter covers the following topics that you need to master for the CCNP BCMSN exam:

- **Port Security Using MAC Addresses**—This section explains how to configure switch ports to allow network access to only hosts with specific or learned MAC addresses.

- **Port-Based Security Using IEEE 802.1x**—This section discusses a method you can use to require user authentication before network access is offered to a client host.

- **Mitigating Spoofing Attacks**—This section covers several types of attacks in which a malicious user generates spoofed information to become a man-in-the-middle. When an attacker is wedged between other hosts and a router or gateway, for example, he can examine and exploit all traffic. DHCP snooping, IP source guard, and dynamic ARP inspection are three features that can be used to prevent these attacks.

- **Best Practices for Securing Switches**—This section provides several guidelines for tightening control over Catalyst switches and the protocols they use for switch communication and maintenance.

CHAPTER 15

Securing Switch Access

Traditionally, users have been able to connect a PC to a switched network and gain immediate access to enterprise resources. As networks grow and as more confidential data and restricted resources become available, it is important to limit the access that users receive.

Catalyst switches have a variety of methods that can secure or control user access. Users can be authenticated as they connect to or through a switch, and can be authorized to perform certain actions on a switch. User access can be recorded as switch accounting information. The physical switch port access also can be controlled based on the user's MAC address or authentication.

In addition, Catalyst switches can detect and prevent certain types of attacks. Several features can be used to validate information passing through a switch so that spoofed addresses can't be used to compromise hosts.

"Do I Know This Already?" Quiz

The purpose of the "Do I Know This Already?" quiz is to help you decide what parts of this chapter to use. If you already intend to read the entire chapter, you do not necessarily need to answer these questions now.

The quiz, derived from the major sections in the "Foundation Topics" portion of the chapter, helps you determine how to spend your limited study time.

Table 15-1 outlines the major topics discussed in this chapter and the "Do I Know This Already?" quiz questions that correspond to those topics.

Table 15-1   *"Do I Know This Already?" Foundation Topics Section-to-Question Mapping*

Foundation Topics Section	Questions Covered in This Section	Score
Port Security	1–4	
Port-Based Authentication	5–9	
Mitigating Spoofing Attacks	10–12	
Total Score		

CAUTION The goal of self-assessment is to gauge your mastery of the topics in this chapter. If you do not know the answer to a question or are only partially sure of the answer, you should mark this question wrong. Giving yourself credit for an answer you correctly guess skews your self-assessment results and might provide you with a false sense of security.

---

1. Which switch feature can grant access through a port only if the host with MAC address 0005.0004.0003 is connected?

   a. SPAN

   b. MAC address ACL

   c. Port security

   d. Port-based authentication

2. Port security is being used to control access to a switch port. Which one of these commands will put the port into the errdisable state if an unauthorized station connects?

   a. **switchport port-security violation protect**

   b. **switchport port-security violation restrict**

   c. **switchport port-security violation errdisable**

   d. **switchport port-security violation shutdown**

3. If port security is left to its default configuration, how many different MAC addresses can be learned at one time on a switch port?

   a. 0

   b. 1

   c. 16

   d. 256

4. The following commands are configured on a Catalyst switch port. What happens when the host with MAC address 0001.0002.0003 tries to connect?

   ```
   switchport port-security
   switchport port-security maximum 3
   switchport port-security mac-address 0002.0002.0002
   switchport port-security violation shutdown
   ```

   a. The port shuts down.

   b. The host is allowed to connect.

   c. The host is denied a connection.

   d. The host can connect only when 0002.0002.0002 is not connected.

5. What protocol is used for port-based authentication?

   a. 802.1D

   b. 802.1Q

   c. 802.1x

   d. 802.1w

6. When 802.1x is used for a switch port, where must it be configured?

   a. Switch port and client PC

   b. Switch port only

   c. Client PC only

   d. Switch port and a RADIUS server

7. When port-based authentication is enabled globally, what is the default behavior for all switch ports?

   a. Authenticate users before enabling the port.

   b. Allow all connections without authentication.

   c. Do not allow any connections.

   d. There is no default behavior.

8. When port-based authentication is enabled, what method is available for a user to authenticate?

   a. Web browser

   b. Telnet session

   c. 802.1x client

   d. DHCP

9. The users in a department are using a variety of host platforms, some old and some new. All of them have been approved with a user ID in a RADIUS server database. Which one of these features should be used to restrict access to the switch ports in the building?

   a. AAA authentication

   b. AAA authorization

   c. Port security

   d. Port-based authentication

10. With DHCP snooping, an untrusted port filters out which one of the following?

   a. DHCP replies from legitimate DHCP servers

   b. DHCP replies from rogue DHCP servers

   c. DHCP requests from legitimate clients

   d. DHCP requests from rogue clients

11. Which two of the following methods does a switch use to detect spoofed addresses when IP source guard is enabled?

   a. ARP entries

   b. DHCP database

   c. DHCP snooping database

   d. Static IP source binding entries

   e. Reverse path forwarding entries

12. Which one of the following should be configured as a trusted port for dynamic ARP inspection?

   a. The port where the ARP server is located

   b. The port where an end-user host is located

   c. The port where another switch is located

   d. None; all ports are untrusted

The answers to the "Do I Know This Already?" quiz are found in Appendix A, "Answers to Chapter 'Do I Know This Already?' Quizzes and Q&A Sections." The suggested choices for your next step are as follows:

■ **11 or less overall score**—Read the entire chapter. This includes the "Foundation Topics," "Foundation Summary," and "Q&A" sections.

■ **12 score**—If you want more review on these topics, skip to the "Foundation Summary" section and then go to the "Q&A" section at the end of the chapter. Otherwise, move to Chapter 16, "Securing with VLANs."

Foundation Topics

Port Security

In some environments, a network must be secured by controlling what stations can gain access to the network itself. Where user workstations are stationary, their MAC addresses always can be expected to connect to the same access-layer switch ports. If stations are mobile, their MAC addresses can be learned dynamically or added to a list of addresses to expect on a switch port.

Catalyst switches offer the port security feature to control port access based on MAC addresses. To configure port security on an access-layer switch port, begin by enabling it with the following interface-configuration command:

```
Switch(config-if)#switchport port-security
```

Next, you must identify a set of allowed MAC addresses so that the port can grant them access. You can explicitly configure addresses or they can be learned dynamically from port traffic. On each interface that uses port security, specify the maximum number of MAC addresses that will be allowed access using the following interface configuration command:

```
Switch(config-if)#switchport port-security maximum max-addr
```

By default, only one MAC address will be allowed access on each switch port. You can set the maximum number of addresses in the range of 1 to 1,024.

Each interface using port security dynamically learns MAC addresses by default and expects those addresses to appear on that interface in the future. These are called *sticky MAC addresses*. MAC addresses are learned as hosts transmit frames on an interface. The interface learns up to the maximum number of addresses allowed. Learned addresses also can be aged out of the table if those hosts are silent for a period of time. By default, no aging occurs.

For example, to set the maximum number of MAC addresses that can be active on a switch port at any time to two, you could use the following command:

```
Switch(config-if)#switchport port-security maximum 2
```

You also can statically define one or more MAC addresses on an interface. Any of these addresses are allowed to access the network through the port. Use the following interface configuration command to define a static address:

```
Switch(config-if)#switchport port-security mac-address mac-addr
```

The MAC address is given in dotted-triplet format. If the number of static addresses configured is less than the maximum number of addresses secured on a port, the remaining addresses are learned dynamically. Be sure to set the maximum number appropriately.

You can use the following command to configure a static address entry on an interface:

```
Switch(config-if)#switchport port-security mac-address 0006.5b02.a841
```

Finally, you must define how each interface using port security should react if a MAC address is in violation by using the following interface-configuration command:

```
Switch(config-if)# switchport port-security violation {shutdown | restrict |
    protect}
```

A violation occurs if more than the maximum number of MAC addresses are learned or if an unknown (not statically defined) MAC address attempts to transmit on the port. The switch port takes one of the following configured actions when a violation is detected:

- **shutdown**—The port immediately is put into the errdisable state, which effectively shuts it down. It must be re-enabled manually or through errdisable recovery to be used again.

- **restrict**—The port is allowed to stay up, but all packets from violating MAC addresses are dropped. The switch keeps a running count of the number of violating packets and can send an SNMP trap and a syslog message as an alert of the violation.

- **protect**—The port is allowed to stay up, as in the **restrict** mode. Although packets from violating addresses are dropped, no record of the violation is kept.

As an example of the **restrict** mode, a switch interface has received the following configuration commands:

```
interface GigabitEthernet0/11
 switchport access vlan 991
 switchport mode access
 switchport port-security
 switchport port-security violation restrict
 spanning-tree portfast
```

When the default maximum of one MAC address is exceeded on this interface, the condition is logged but the interface stays up. This is shown by the following syslog message:

```
Jun  3 17:18:41.888 EDT: %PORT_SECURITY-2-PSECURE_VIOLATION: Security violation
    occurred, caused by MAC address 0000.5e00.0101 on port GigabitEthernet0/11.
```

TIP If an interface is undergoing the **restrict** or **protect** condition, you might need to clear the learned MAC addresses so that a specific host can use the switch port. You can clear a MAC address or the complete port cache with the following command:

```
Switch#clear port-security dynamic [address mac-addr | interface type mod/num]
```

In the **shutdown** mode, the port security action is much more drastic. When the maximum number of MAC addresses is exceeded, the following syslog messages indicate that the port has been shut down in the errdisable state:

```
Jun  3 17:14:19.018 EDT: %PM-4-ERR_DISABLE: psecure-violation error detected on
Gi0/11, putting Gi0/11 in err-disable state
Jun  3 17:14:19.022 EDT: %PORT_SECURITY-2-PSECURE_VIOLATION: Security violation
  occurred, caused by MAC address 0003.a089.efc5 on port GigabitEthernet0/11.
Jun  3 17:14:20.022 EDT: %LINEPROTO-5-UPDOWN: Line protocol on Interface Gigabit
Ethernet0/11, changed state to down
Jun  3 17:14:21.023 EDT: %LINK-3-UPDOWN: Interface GigabitEthernet0/11, changed state
  to down
```

You also can show the port status with the **show port-security interface** command, as demonstrated in Example 15-1.

Example 15-1 *Displaying Port Security Port Status*

```
Switch#show port-security interface gigabitethernet 0/11
Port Security              : Enabled
Port Status                : Secure-shutdown
Violation Mode             : Shutdown
Aging Time                 : 0 mins
Aging Type                 : Absolute
SecureStatic Address Aging : Disabled
Maximum MAC Addresses      : 1
Total MAC Addresses        : 0
Configured MAC Addresses   : 0
Sticky MAC Addresses       : 0
Last Source Address        : 0003.a089.efc5
Security Violation Count   : 1
Switch#
```

To see a quick summary of only ports in the errdisable state, along with the reason for errdisable, you can use the **show interfaces status err-disabled** command, as demonstrated in Example 15-2.

Example 15-2 *Displaying Summary Information for Ports in the Errdisable State*

```
Switch#show interfaces status err-disabled
Port     Name            Status       Reason
Gi0/11   Test port       err-disabled psecure-violation
Switch#
```

TIP   When a port is moved to the errdisable state, you must either manually cycle it or configure the switch to automatically re-enable ports after a prescribed delay. To manually cycle a port and return it to service, use the following commands:

```
Switch(config)#interface type mod/num
Switch(config-if)#shutdown
Switch(config-if)#no shutdown
```

Finally, you can display a summary of the port-security status with the **show port-security** command, as demonstrated in Example 15-3.

Example 15-3 *Displaying Port Security Status Summary Information*

```
Switch#show port-security
Secure Port  MaxSecureAddr  CurrentAddr  SecurityViolation  Security Action
             (Count)        (Count)      (Count)
---------------------------------------------------------------------------
    Gi0/11          5             1              0           Restrict
    Gi0/12          1             0              0           Shutdown
---------------------------------------------------------------------------
Total Addresses in System (excluding one mac per port)    : 0
Max Addresses limit in System (excluding one mac per port) : 6176
Switch#
```

Port-Based Authentication

Catalyst switches can support port-based authentication, a combination of AAA authentication and port security. This feature is based on the IEEE 802.1x standard. When it is enabled, a switch port will not pass any traffic until a user has authenticated with the switch. If the authentication is successful, the user can use the port normally.

For port-based authentication, both the switch and the end user's PC must support the 802.1x standard, using the Extensible Authentication Protocol over LANs (EAPOL). The 802.1x standard is a cooperative effort between the client and the switch offering network service. If the client PC is configured to use 802.lx but the switch does not support it, the PC abandons the protocol and communicates normally. However, if the switch is configured for 802.1x but the PC does not support it, the switch port remains in the unauthorized state so that it will not forward any traffic to the client PC.

> **NOTE** 802.1x EAPOL is a Layer 2 protocol. At the point that a switch detects the presence of a device on a port, the port remains in the unauthorized state. Therefore, the client PC cannot communicate with anything other than the switch by using EAPOL. If the PC does not already have an IP address, it cannot request one. The PC also has no knowledge of the switch or its IP address, so any means other than a Layer 2 protocol is not possible. This is why the PC must also have an 802.1x-capable application or client software.

An 802.1x switch port begins in the unauthorized state so that no data other than the 802.1x protocol itself is allowed through the port. Either the client or the switch can initiate an 802.1x session. The authorized state of the port ends when the user logs out, causing the 802.1x client to inform the switch to revert back to the unauthorized state. The switch can also time out the user's authorized session. If this happens, the client must reauthenticate to continue using the switch port.

802.1x Configuration

Port-based authentication can be handled by one or more external Remote Authentication Dial-In User Service (RADIUS) servers. Although many Cisco switch platforms will allow other authentication methods to be configured, only RADIUS is supported for 802.1x.

The actual RADIUS authentication method must be configured first, followed by 802.1x, as shown in the following steps:

Step 1   Enable AAA on the switch.

By default, AAA is disabled. You can enable AAA for port-based authentication by using the following global configuration command:

```
Switch(config)#aaa new-model
```

The **new-model** keyword refers to the use of method lists, by which authentication methods and sources can be grouped or organized. The new model is much more scalable than the "old model," in which the authentication source was explicitly configured.

Step 2   Define external RADIUS servers.

First, define each server along with its secret shared password. This string is known only to the switch and the server, and provides a key for encrypting the authentication session. Use the following global configuration command:

```
Switch(config)#radius-server host {hostname | ip-address} [key string]
```

This command can be repeated to define additional RADIUS servers.

Step 3   Define the authentication method for 802.1x.

Using the following command causes all RADIUS authentication servers that are defined on the switch to be used for 802.1x authentication:

```
Switch(config)#aaa authentication dot1x default group radius
```

Step 4   Enable 802.1x on the switch:

```
Switch(config)#dot1x system-auth-control
```

Step 5   Configure each switch port that will use 802.1x:

```
Switch(config)# interface type mod/num
Switch(config-if)#dot1x  port-control {force-authorized | force-
    unauthorized  |  auto}
```

Here, the 802.1x state is one of the following:

- **force-authorized**—The port is forced to always authorize any connected client. No authentication is necessary. This is the default state for all switch ports when 802.1x is enabled.

- **force-unauthorized**—The port is forced to never authorize any connected client. As a result, the port cannot move to the authorized state to pass traffic to a connected client.

- **auto**—The port uses an 802.1x exchange to move from the unauthorized to the authorized state, if successful. This requires an 802.1x-capable application on the client PC.

TIP   After 802.1x is globally enabled on a switch, all switch ports default to the **force-authorized** state. This means that any PC connected to a switch port can immediately start accessing the network. Ideally, you should explicitly configure each port to use the **auto** state so that connected PCs are forced to authenticate through the 802.1x exchange.

Step 6   Allow multiple hosts on a switch port.

It might be obvious that port-based authentication is tailored to controlling access to a single host PC that is connected to a switch port. However, 802.1x also supports cases in which multiple hosts are attached to a single switch port through an Ethernet hub or another access-layer switch.

If the switch should expect to find multiple hosts present on the switch port, use the following interface configuration command:

```
Switch(config-if)#dot1x host-mode multi-host
```

TIP   You can use the **show dot1x all** command to verify the 802.1x operation on each switch port that is configured to use port-based authentication.

802.1x Port-Based Authentication Example

In Example 15-4, two RADIUS servers are located at 10.1.1.1 and 10.1.1.2. Switch ports FastEthernet 0/1 through 0/40 will use 802.1x for port-based authentication. Once authenticated, the end users will be associated with VLAN 10.

Example 15-4   *Configuring 802.1x Port-Based Authentication*

```
Switch(config)#aaa new-model
Switch(config)#radius-server host 10.1.1.1 key BigSecret
Switch(config)#radius-server host 10.1.1.2 key AnotherBigSecret
Switch(config)#aaa authentication dot1x default group radius
Switch(config)#dot1x system-auth-control
Switch(config)#interface range FastEthernet0/1 - 40
Switch(config-if)#switchport access vlan 10
Switch(config-if)#switchport mode access
Switch(config-if)#dot1x port-control auto
```

Mitigating Spoofing Attacks

Malicious users sometimes can send spoofed information to trick switches or other hosts into using a rogue machine as a gateway. The attacker's goal is to become the "man-in-the-middle," with a naïve user sending packets to the attacker as if it were a router. The attacker can glean information from the packets sent to it before it forwards them normally. This section describes three Cisco Catalyst features—DHCP snooping, IP source guard, and dynamic ARP inspection— that prevent certain types of spoofing attack.

DHCP Snooping

A DHCP server normally provides all the basic information a client PC needs to operate on a network. For example, the client might receive an IP address, a subnet mask, a default gateway address, DNS addresses, and so on.

Suppose that an attacker could bring up a rogue DHCP server on a machine in the same subnet as that same client PC. Now when the client broadcasts its DHCP request, the rogue server could send a carefully crafted DHCP reply with its own IP address substituted as the default gateway.

When the client receives the reply, it begins using the spoofed gateway address. Packets destined for addresses outside the local subnet then go to the attacker's machine first. The attacker can forward the packets to the correct destination, but in the meantime, it can examine every packet that it intercepts. In effect, this becomes a type of man-in-the-middle attack; the attacker is wedged into the path and the client doesn't realize it.

Cisco Catalyst switches can use the DHCP snooping feature to help mitigate this type of attack. When DHCP snooping is enabled, switch ports are categorized as trusted or untrusted. Legitimate DHCP servers can be found on trusted ports, whereas all other hosts sit behind untrusted ports.

A switch intercepts all DHCP requests coming from untrusted ports before flooding them throughout the VLAN. Any DHCP replies coming from an untrusted port are discarded because they must have come from a rogue DHCP server. In addition, the offending switch port automatically is shut down in the errdisable state.

DHCP snooping also keeps track of the completed DHCP bindings as clients receive legitimate replies. This database contains the client MAC address, IP address offered, lease time, and so on.

You can configure DHCP snooping first by enabling it globally on a switch with the following configuration command:

```
Switch(config)#ip dhcp snooping
```

Next identify the VLANs where DHCP snooping should be implemented with the following command:

```
Switch(config)#ip dhcp snooping vlan vlan-id [vlan-id]
```

You can give a single VLAN number as *vlan-id* or a range of VLAN numbers by giving the start and end VLAN IDs of the range.

By default, all switch ports are assumed to be untrusted so that DHCP replies are not expected or permitted. Only trusted ports are allowed to send DHCP replies. Therefore, you should identify only the ports where known, trusted DHCP servers are located. You can do this with the following interface configuration command:

```
Switch(config)#interface type mod/num
Switch(config-if)#ip dhcp snooping trust
```

For untrusted ports, an unlimited rate of DHCP requests is accepted. If you want to rate-limit DHCP traffic on an untrusted port, use the following interface configuration command:

```
Switch(config)#interface type mod/num
Switch(config-if)#ip dhcp snooping limit rate rate
```

The *rate* can be 1 to 2048 DHCP packets per second.

You also can configure the switch to use DHCP option-82, the DHCP Relay Agent Information option, which is described in RFC 3046. When a DHCP request is intercepted on an untrusted port, the switch adds its own MAC address and the switch port identifier into the option-82 field of the request. The request then is forwarded normally so that it can reach a trusted DHCP server.

Adding option-82 provides more information about the actual client that generated the DHCP request. In addition, the DHCP reply (if any) echoes back the option-82 information. The switch intercepts the reply and compares the option-82 data to confirm that the request came from a valid port on itself. This feature is enabled by default. You can enable or disable option-82 globally with the following configuration command:

```
Switch(config)#[no] ip dhcp snooping information option
```

When DHCP snooping is configured, you can display its status with the following command:

```
Switch#show ip dhcp snooping [binding]
```

You can use the **binding** keyword to display all the known DHCP bindings that have been overheard. The switch maintains these in its own database. Otherwise, only the switch ports that are trusted or that have rate limiting applied are listed. All other ports are considered to be untrusted with an unlimited DHCP request rate.

As an example, interfaces FastEthernet 0/35 and 0/36 use access VLAN 104, are considered untrusted, and have DHCP rate limiting applied at three per second. A known DHCP server is located on the GigabitEthernet 0/1 uplink. Example 15-5 shows the configuration for this scenario.

Example 15-5 *DHCP Snooping Configuration*

```
Switch(config)#ip dhcp snooping
Switch(config)#ip dhcp snooping vlan 104
Switch(config)#interface range fastethernet 0/35 - 36
Switch(config-if)#ip dhcp snooping limit rate 3
Switch(config-if)#interface gigabitethernet 0/1
Switch(config-if)#ip dhcp snooping trust
```

Example 15-6 shows the resulting DHCP snooping status.

Example 15-6 *DHCP Snooping Status Display*

```
Switch#show ip dhcp snooping
Switch DHCP snooping is enabled
DHCP snooping is configured on following VLANs:
104
Insertion of option 82 is enabled
Interface                  Trusted      Rate limit (pps)
----------------------     -------      ----------------
FastEthernet0/35           no           3
FastEthernet0/36           no           3
GigabitEthernet0/1         yes          unlimited
Switch#
```

IP Source Guard

Address spoofing is one type of attack that can be difficult to mitigate. Normally, a host is assigned an IP address and is expected to use that address in all the traffic it sends out. IP addresses are effectively used on the honor system, where hosts are trusted to behave themselves and use their own legitimate source addresses.

A rogue or compromised host PC doesn't necessarily play by those rules. It can use its legitimate address, or it can begin to use spoofed addresses—borrowed from other hosts or used at random. Spoofed addresses are often used to disguise the origin of denial-of-service attacks. If the source address doesn't really exist, no return traffic will find its way back to the originator.

Routers or Layer 3 devices can perform some simple tests to detect spoofed source addresses in packets passing through. For example, if the 10.10.0.0 network is known to exist on VLAN 10, packets entering from VLAN 20 should never have source addresses in that subnet.

However, it is difficult to detect spoofed addresses when they are used *inside* the VLAN or subnet where they should already exist. For example, within the 10.10.0.0 network on VLAN 10, as shown in Figure 15-1, a rogue host begins to send packets with a spoofed source address of 10.10.10.10. The 10.10.10.10 address is certainly within the 10.10.0.0/16 subnet, so it doesn't stand out as an obvious spoof. Therefore, the rogue host might be very successful in attacking other hosts in its own subnet or VLAN.

Figure 15-1 *Using a Spoofed Address Within a Subnet*

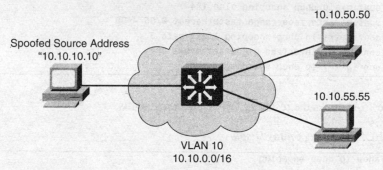

Cisco Catalyst switches can use the IP source guard feature to detect and suppress address spoofing attacks—even if they occur within the same subnet. A Layer 2 switch, and a Layer 2 port in turn, normally learns and stores MAC addresses. The switch must have a way to look up MAC addresses and find out what IP address are associated with them.

IP source guard does this by making use of the DHCP snooping database, as well as static IP source binding entries. If DHCP snooping is configured and enabled, the switch learns the MAC and IP addresses of hosts that use DHCP. Packets arriving on a switch port can be tested for one of the following conditions:

■ The source IP address must be identical to the IP address learned by DHCP snooping or a static entry. A dynamic port ACL is used to filter traffic. The switch automatically creates this ACL, adds the learned source IP address to the ACL, and applies the ACL to the interface where the address is learned.

■ The source MAC address must be identical to the MAC address learned on the switch port and by DHCP snooping. Port security is used to filter traffic.

If the address is something other than the one learned or statically configured, the switch will drop the packet.

To configure IP source guard, first configure and enable DHCP snooping, as presented in the previous section. If you want IP source guard to detect spoofed MAC addresses, you will also need to configure and enable port security.

For the hosts that don't use DHCP, you can configure a static IP source binding with the following configuration command:

```
Switch(config)#ip source binding mac-address vlan vlan-id ip-address interface type
    mod/num
```

Here, the host's MAC address is bound to a specific VLAN and IP address, and is expected to be found on a specific switch interface.

Next, enable IP source guard on one or more switch interfaces with the following configuration commands:

```
Switch(config)#interface type mod/num
Switch(config-if)#ip verify source [port-security]
```

The **ip verify source** command will inspect the source IP address only. You can add the **port-security** keyword to inspect the source MAC address, too.

To verify the IP source guard status, you can use the following EXEC command:

```
Switch#show ip verify source [interface type mod/num]
```

If you need to verify the information contained in the IP source binding database, either learned or statically configured, you can use the following EXEC command:

```
Switch#show ip source bindng [ip-address] [mac-address] [dhcp-snooping | static]
    [interface type mod/num] [vlan vlan-id]
```

Dynamic ARP Inspection

Hosts normally use the Address Resolution Protocol (ARP) to resolve an unknown MAC address when the IP address is known. If a MAC address is needed so that a packet can be forwarded at Layer 2, a host broadcasts an ARP request that contains the IP address of the target in question. If any other host is using that IP address, it responds with an ARP reply containing its MAC address.

The ARP process works well among trusted and well-behaved users. However, suppose that an attacker could send its own crafted ARP reply when it overhears an ARP request being broadcast. The reply could contain its own MAC address, causing the original requester to think that it is bound to the IP address in question. The requester would add the bogus ARP entry into its own ARP cache, only to begin forwarding packets to the spoofed MAC address.

In effect, this scheme places the attacker's machine right in the middle of an otherwise legitimate path. Packets will be sent to the attacker instead of another host or the default gateway. The attacker will be able to intercept packets and (perhaps) will forward them on only after examining the packets' contents.

This attack is known as *ARP poisoning* or *ARP spoofing*, and it is considered to be a type of man-in-the-middle attack. The attacker wedges into the normal forwarding path, transparent to the end users. Cisco Catalyst switches can use the dynamic ARP inspection (DAI) feature to help mitigate this type of attack.

DAI works much like DHCP snooping. All switch ports are classified as trusted or untrusted. The switch intercepts and inspects all ARP packets that arrive on an untrusted port; no inspection is done on trusted ports.

When an ARP reply is received on an untrusted port, the switch checks the MAC and IP addresses reported in the reply packet against known and trusted values. A switch can gather trusted ARP information from statically configured entries or from dynamic entries in the DHCP snooping database. In the latter case, DHCP snooping must be enabled in addition to DAI.

If an ARP reply contains invalid information or values that conflict with entries in the trusted database, it is dropped and a log message is generated. This action prevents invalid or spoofed ARP entries from being sent and added to other machines' ARP caches.

You can configure DAI by first enabling it on one or more client VLANs with the following configuration command:

```
Switch(config)#ip arp inspection vlan vlan-range
```

The VLAN range can be a single VLAN ID, a range of VLAN IDs separated by a hyphen, or a list of VLAN IDs separated by commas.

By default, all switch ports associated with the VLAN range are considered to be untrusted. You should identify trusted ports as those that connect to other switches. In other words, the local switch will not inspect ARP packets arriving on trusted ports; it will assume that the neighboring switch also is performing DAI on all of its ports in that VLAN. Configure a trusted port with the following interface configuration command:

```
Switch(config)#interface type mod/num
Switch(config-if)#ip arp inspection trust
```

If you have hosts with statically configured IP address information, there will be no DHCP message exchange that can be inspected. Instead, you can configure an ARP access list that defines static MAC-IP address bindings that are permitted. Use the following configuration commands to define the ARP access list and one or more static entries:

```
Switch(config)#arp access-list acl-name
Switch(config-acl)#permit ip host sender-ip mac host sender-mac [log]
[Repeat the previous command as needed]
Switch(config-acl)#exit
```

Now the ARP access list must be applied to DAI with the following configuration command:

```
Switch(config)#ip arp inspection filter arp-acl-name vlan vlan-range [static]
```

When ARP replies are intercepted, their contents are matched against the access list entries first. If no match is found, the DHCP snooping bindings database is checked next. You can give the **static** keyword to prevent the DHCP bindings database from being checked at all. In effect, this creates an implicit deny statement at the end of the ARP access list; if no match is found in the access list, the ARP reply is considered to be invalid.

Finally, you can specify further validations on the contents of ARP reply packets. By default, only the MAC and IP addresses contained within the ARP reply are validated. This doesn't take the actual MAC addresses contained in the Ethernet header of the ARP reply.

To validate that an ARP reply packet is really coming from the address listed inside it, you can enable DAI validation with the following configuration command:

```
Switch(config)#ip arp inspection validate {[src-mac] [dst-mac] [ip]}
```

Be sure to specify at least one of the options:

- **src-mac**—Check the source MAC address in the Ethernet header against the sender MAC address in the ARP reply.

- **dst-mac**—Check the destination MAC address in the Ethernet header against the target MAC address in the ARP reply.

- **ip**—Check the sender's IP address in all ARP requests; check the sender's IP address against the target IP address in all ARP replies.

Example 15-7 demonstrates where DAI is enabled for all switch ports associated with VLAN 104 on an access-layer switch. The uplink to a distribution switch is considered to be trusted.

Example 15-7 *Configuring DAI to Validate ARP Replies*

```
Switch(config)#ip arp inspection vlan 104
Switch(config)#arp access-list StaticARP
Switch(config-acl)#permit ip host 192.168.1.10 mac host 0006.5b02.a841
Switch(config-acl)#exit
Switch(config)#ip arp inspection filter StaticARP vlan 104
Switch(config)#interface gigabitethernet 0/1
Switch(config-if)#ip arp inspection trust
```

You can display DAI status information with the **show ip arp inspection** command.

Best Practices for Securing Switches

You can configure and use many different features on Cisco Catalyst switches. You should be aware of some common weaknesses that can be exploited. In other words, don't become complacent and assume that everyone connected to your network will be good citizens and play by the rules. Think ahead and try to prevent as many things as possible that might be leveraged to assist an attacker.

This section presents a brief overview of many best-practice suggestions that will help secure your switched network.

- **Configure secure passwords**—Whenever possible, you should use the **enable secret** command to set the privileged-level password on a switch. This command uses a stronger encryption than the normal **enable password** command and stores the password in a secure location in NVRAM.

  You also should use external AAA servers to authenticate administrative users whenever possible. The usernames and passwords are maintained externally, so they are not stored or managed directly on the switch. In addition, having a centralized user management is much more scalable than configuring and changing user credentials on many individual switches and routers.

  Finally, you always should use the **service password-encryption** configuration command to automatically encrypt password strings that are stored in the switch configuration. Although the encryption is not strong, it can prevent casual observers from seeing passwords in the clear.

- **Use system banners**—When users successfully access a switch, they should be aware of any specific access or acceptable use policies that are pertinent to your organization. You should configure system banners so that this type of information is displayed when users log in to a switch. The idea is to warn unauthorized users (if they gain access) that their activities could be grounds for prosecution—or that they are unwelcome, at the very least.

  You should use the **banner motd** command to define the text that is displayed to authenticated users. Try to avoid using other banner types that display information about your organization or the switch before users actually log in. Never divulge any extra information about your network that malicious users could use.

- **Disable unnecessary or insecure services**—Cisco devices sometimes have unused or unnecessary services enabled by default. To tighten security, you should allow only the services, features, and protocols that are needed for your infrastructure. Anything more than that can become a potential weakness that could be exploited.

  For example, you should strongly consider disabling the HTTP server on a Catalyst switch. This often is used for a web-based switch-management tool but is usually unneeded in a production environment. You can disable it with the **no ip http server** configuration command.

  Although Cisco IOS Software releases have begun to disable other uncommon services as the default, you should make sure that none of the following commands is present in your switch configuration:

  ```
  service tcp-small-servers
  service udp-small-servers
  service finger
  service config
  ```

  If any of these commands are present, disable them by preceding them with the **no** keyword.

- **Secure the switch console**—In many environments, switches are locked away in wiring closets where physical security is used to keep people from connecting to the switch console. Even so, you always should configure authentication on any switch console. It is usually appropriate to use the same authentication configuration on the console as the virtual terminal (vty) lines.

- **Secure virtual terminal access**—You always should configure user authentication on *all* of the vty lines on a switch. In addition, you should use access lists to limit the source IP addresses of potential administrative users who try to use Telnet or Secure Shell (SSH) to access a switch.

  You can use a simple IP access list to permit inbound connections only from known source addresses, as in the following example:

  ```
  Switch(config)#access-list 10 permit 192.168.199.10
  Switch(config)#access-list 10 permit 192.168.201.100
  Switch(config)#line vty 0 15
  Switch(config-line)#access-class 10 in
  ```

  Be sure you apply the access list to all the **line vty** entries in the switch configuration. Many times, the vty lines are separated into groups in the configuration. You can use the **show user all** command to see every possible line that can be used to access a switch.

- **Use SSH whenever possible**—Although Telnet access is easy to configure and use, Telnet is not secure. Every character you type in a Telnet session is sent to and echoed from a switch in the clear, with no encryption. Therefore, it is very easy to eavesdrop on Telnet sessions to overhear usernames and passwords.

  Instead, you should use SSH whenever possible. SSH uses strong encryption to secure session data. Therefore, you need a strong-encryption IOS image running on a switch before SSH can be configured and used. You should use the highest SSH version that is available on a switch. The early SSHv1 and SSHv1.5 have some weaknesses. SSHv2 is better yet but is available only in more recent IOS releases, such as 12.2(25)SEB1 on the Catalyst 3750.

- **Secure SNMP access**—To prevent unauthorized users from making changes to a switch configuration, you should disable any read-write SNMP access. These are commands of the form **snmp-server community** *string* **RW**.

  Instead, you should have only read-only commands in the configuration. In addition, you should use access lists to limit the source addresses that have read-only access. Don't depend on the SNMP community strings for security because these are passed in the clear in SNMP packets.

- **Secure unused switch ports**—Every unused switch port should be disabled so that unexpected users can't connect and use them without your knowledge. You can do this with the **shutdown** interface configuration command.

  In addition, you should configure every user port as an access port with the **switchport mode access** interface configuration command. Otherwise, a malicious user might connect and attempt to negotiate trunking mode on a port. You also should consider associating every unused access port with a bogus or isolated VLAN. If an unexpected user does gain access to a port, he will have access only to a VLAN that is isolated from every other resource on your network.

TIP You might consider using the **switchport host** interface configuration command as a quick way to force a port to support only a single PC. This command is actually a macro, as shown in the following example:

```
Switch(config)#interface fastethernet 1/0/1
Switch(config-if)#switchport host
switchport mode will be set to access
spanning-tree portfast will be enabled
channel group will be disabled
Switch(config-if)#
```

- **Secure STP operation**—A malicious user can inject STP bridge protocol data units (BPDUs) into switch ports or VLANs, and can disrupt a stable, loop-free topology. You always should enable the BPDU guard feature so that access switch ports automatically are disabled if unexpected BPDUs are received.

- **Secure the use of CDP**—By default, CDP advertisements are sent on *every* switch port at 60-second intervals. Although CDP is a very handy tool for discovering neighboring Cisco devices, you shouldn't allow CDP to advertise unnecessary information about your switch to listening attackers.

  For example, the following information is sent in a CDP advertisement in the clear. An attacker might be able to use the device ID to physically locate the switch, its IP address to target Telnet or SNMP attacks, or the native VLAN and switch port ID to attempt a VLAN hopping attack.

```
CDP - Cisco Discovery Protocol
  Version:            2
  Time to live:       180  seconds
  Checksum:           0xD0AE
  Device ID:          BldgA-Rm110
Version:              Cisco Internetwork Operating System Software .IOS
(tm) C3750 Software (C3750-I9-M), Version 12.2(20)SE4, RELEASE SOFTWARE
(fc1).Copyright  1986-2005 by cisco Systems, Inc..Compiled Sun 09-Jan-05
00:09 by antonino
  Platform:           cisco WS-C3750-48P
  IP Address:         192.168.100.85
  Port ID:            FastEthernet1/0/48
  Capabilities:       0x00000028  Switch  IGMP
  VTP Domain:         MyCompany
  Native VLAN:    101
  Duplex:      0x01Full
```

CDP should be enabled only on switch ports that connect to other trusted Cisco devices. Don't forget that CDP must be enabled on access switch ports where Cisco IP Phones are connected. When the CDP messages reach the IP Phone, they won't be relayed on to a PC connected to the phone's data port. You can disable CDP on a port-by-port basis with the **no cdp enable** interface configuration command.

Foundation Summary

The Foundation Summary is a collection of tables that provides a convenient review of many key concepts in this chapter. If you are already comfortable with the topics in this chapter, this summary can help you recall a few details. If you just read this chapter, this review should help solidify some key facts. If you are doing your final preparation before the exam, these tables and figures are a convenient way to review the day before the exam.

Table 15-2 *Port Security Configuration Commands*

Task	Command Syntax
Enable port security on an interface	**switchport port-security**
Set the maximum number of learned addresses	**switchport port-security maximum** *max-addr*
Define a static MAC address	**switchport port-security mac-address** *mac-addr*
Define an action to take	**switchport port-security violation** {**shutdown**	**restrict**	**protect**}

Table 15-3 *Port-Based Authentication Configuration Commands*

Task	Command Syntax
Define a method list for 802.1x	**aaa authentication dot1x default group radius**
Globally enable 802.1x	**dot1x system-auth-control**
Define the 802.1x behavior on a port	**dot1x port-control** {**force-authorized**	**force-unauthorized**	**auto**}
Support more than one host on a port	**dot1x host-mode multi-host**

Table 15-4 *DHCP Snooping Configuration Commands*

Task	Command Syntax
Globally enable DHCP snooping	**ip dhcp snooping**
Define a trusted interface	**ip dhcp snooping trust**
Limit the interface DHCP packet rate	**ip dhcp snooping limit rate** *rate*

Table 15-5 *IP Source Guard Configuration Commands*

Task	Command Syntax
Define a static IP source binding entry	**ip source binding** *mac-address* **vlan** *vlan-id ip-address* **interface** *type mod/num*
Enable IP source guard on an interface	**ip verify source** [**port-security**]

Table 15-6 *Dynamic ARP Inspection Configuration Commands*

Task	Command Syntax
Enable DAI on a VLAN	**ip arp inspection vlan** *vlan-range*
Define a trusted interface	**ip arp inspection trust**
Define a static ARP inspection binding	**arp access-list** *acl-name* **permit ip host** *sender-ip* **mac host** *sender-mac* [**log**]
Apply static ARP inspection bindings	**ip arp inspection filter** *arp-acl-name* **vlan** *vlan-range* [**static**]
Validate addresses within ARP replies	**ip arp inspection validate** {[**src-mac**] [**dst-mac**] [**ip**]}

Q&A

The questions and scenarios in this book are more difficult than what you should experience on the actual exam. The questions do not attempt to cover more breadth or depth than the exam; however, they are designed to make sure that you know the answers. Rather than allowing you to derive the answers from clues hidden inside the questions themselves, the questions challenge your understanding and recall of the subject. Hopefully, these questions will help limit the number of exam questions on which you narrow your choices to two options and then guess.

The answers to these questions can be found in Appendix A.

1. When might the command **switchport port-security maximum 2** be used?

2. After port-based authentication is configured and enabled, can any host connect as long as the user can authenticate?

3. When the 802.1x **force-authorized** keyword is used, how does the switch react to users attempting to connect?

4. Can more than one host be authenticated on a single switch port with port-based authentication?

5. In DHCP spoofing and ARP poisoning attacks, what is the goal of the attacker? What Catalyst features can be used to mitigate the risk of these attacks?

6. Which switch ports should be configured as trusted for DHCP snooping?

7. What Catalyst feature can be used to mitigate an address spoofing attack? Can the feature be used to detect a spoofed MAC address? A spoofed IP address?

8. What is the function of a trusted port in DAI?

9. To inspect ARP information from a host that has received its IP address from a DHCP server, what must be enabled in addition to DAI?

This chapter covers the following topics that you need to master for the CCNP BCMSN exam:

- **VLAN Access Lists**—This section discusses how traffic can be controlled within a VLAN. You can use VLAN access control lists (ACL) to filter packets even as they are bridged or switched.

- **Private VLANs**—This section explains the mechanisms that you can use to provide isolation within a single VLAN. Private VLANs have a unidirectional nature; several of them can be isolated yet share a common subnet and gateway.

- **Securing VLAN Trunks**—This section covers two types of attacks that can be leveraged against a VLAN trunk link. If a trunk link is extended to or accessible from an attacker, any VLAN carried over the trunk can be compromised in turn.

CHAPTER 16

Securing with VLANs

Traditionally, traffic has been filtered only at router boundaries, where packets naturally are inspected before forwarding. This is true within Catalyst switches because access lists can be applied as a part of multilayer switching. Catalysts also can filter packets even if they stay within the same VLAN; VLAN access control lists, or VACLs, provide this capability.

Catalyst switches also have the capability to logically divide a single VLAN into multiple partitions. Each partition can be isolated from others, with all of them sharing a common IP subnet and a common gateway address. Private VLANs make it possible to offer up a single VLAN to many disparate customers or organizations without any interaction between them.

VLAN trunks are commonly used on links between switches to carry data from multiple VLANs. If the switches are all under the same administrative control, it is easy to become complacent about the security of the trunks. A few known attacks can be used to gain access to the VLANs that are carried over trunk links. Therefore, network administrators should be aware of the steps that can be taken to prevent any attacks.

"Do I Know This Already?" Quiz

The purpose of the "Do I Know This Already?" quiz is to help you decide what parts of this chapter to use. If you already intend to read the entire chapter, you do not necessarily need to answer these questions now.

The quiz, derived from the major sections in the "Foundation Topics" portion of the chapter, helps you determine how to spend your limited study time.

Table 16-1 outlines the major topics discussed in this chapter and the "Do I Know This Already?" quiz questions that correspond to those topics.

Table 16-1 *"Do I Know This Already?" Foundation Topics Section-to-Question Mapping*

Foundation Topics Section	Questions Covered in This Section	Score
VLAN ACLs	1–4	
Private VLANs	5–8	
Securing VLAN Trunks	9–12	
Total Score		

> **CAUTION** The goal of self-assessment is to gauge your mastery of the topics in this chapter. If you do not know the answer to a question or are only partially sure of the answer, you should mark this question wrong. Giving yourself credit for an answer you correctly guess skews your self-assessment results and might give you a false sense of security.

1. Which one of the following can filter packets even if they are not routed to another Layer 3 interface?

    a. IP extended access lists

    b. MAC address access lists

    c. VLAN access lists

    d. Port-based access lists

2. In what part of a Catalyst switch are VLAN ACLs implemented?

    a. NVRAM

    b. CAM

    c. RAM

    d. TCAM

3. Which one of the following commands can implement a VLAN ACL called *test*?

    a. **access-list vlan test**

    b. **vacl test**

    c. **switchport vacl test**

    d. **vlan access-map test**

4. After a VACL is configured, where is it applied?

   a. Globally on a VLAN

   b. On the VLAN interface

   c. In the VLAN configuration

   d. On all ports or interfaces mapped to a VLAN

5. Which of the following private VLANs is the most restrictive?

   a. Community VLAN

   b. Isolated VLAN

   c. Restricted VLAN

   d. Promiscuous VLAN

6. The **vlan 100** command has just been entered. What is the next command needed to configure VLAN 100 as a secondary isolated VLAN?

   a. **private-vlan isolated**

   b. **private-vlan isolated 100**

   c. **pvlan secondary isolated**

   d. No further configuration is necessary.

7. What type of port configuration should you use for private VLAN interfaces that connect to a router?

   a. Host

   b. Gateway

   c. Promiscuous

   d. Transparent

8. Promiscuous ports must be _____ to primary and secondary VLANs, and host ports must be _____.

   a. mapped, associated

   b. mapped, mapped

   c. associated, mapped

   d. associated, associated

9. In a switch spoofing attack, an attacker makes use of which one of the following?

    a. The switch-management IP address

    b. CDP message exchanges

    c. Spanning Tree Protocol

    d. DTP to negotiate a trunk

10. Which one of the following commands can be used to prevent a switch spoofing attack on an end-user port?

    a. **switchport mode access**

    a. **switchport mode trunk**

    a. **no switchport spoof**

    b. **spanning-tree spoof-guard**

11. Which one of the following represents the spoofed information an attacker sends in a VLAN hopping attack?

    a. 802.1Q tags

    b. DTP information

    c. VTP information

    d. 802.1x information

12. Which one of the following methods can be used to prevent a VLAN hopping attack?

    a. Use VTP throughout the network

    a. Set the native VLAN to the user access VLAN

    a. Prune the native VLAN off a trunk link

    b. Avoid using EtherChannel link bundling

The answers to the "Do I Know This Already?" quiz are found in Appendix A, "Answers to Chapter 'Do I Know This Already?' Quizzes and Q&A Sections." The suggested choices for your next step are as follows:

■ **10 or less overall score**—Read the entire chapter. This includes the "Foundation Topics," "Foundation Summary," and "Q&A" sections.

■ **11 or more overall score**—If you want more review on these topics, skip to the "Foundation Summary" section and then go to the "Q&A" section at the end of the chapter. Otherwise, move to Chapter 17, "Wireless LAN Overview."

Foundation Topics

VLAN Access Lists

Access lists can manage or control traffic as it passes through a switch. When normal access lists are configured on a Catalyst switch, they filter traffic through the use of the Ternary Content Addressable Memory (TCAM). Recall from Chapter 3, "Switch Operation," that access lists (also known as *router access lists*, or *RACLs*) are merged or compiled into the TCAM. Each ACL is applied to an interface according to the direction of traffic—inbound or outbound. Packets then can be filtered in hardware with no switching performance penalty. However, only packets that pass *between* VLANs can be filtered this way.

Packets that stay in the same VLAN do not cross a VLAN or interface boundary and do not necessarily have a direction in relation to an interface. These packets also might be non-IP, non-IPX, or completely bridged; therefore, they never pass through the multilayer switching mechanism. VLAN access lists (VACLs) are filters that directly can affect how packets are handled *within* a VLAN.

VACLs are somewhat different from RACLs or traditional access control lists. Although they, too, are merged into the TCAM, they can permit, deny, or redirect packets as they are matched. VACLs also are configured in a route map fashion, with a series of matching conditions and actions to take.

VACL Configuration

VACLs are configured as a VLAN access map, in much the same format as a route map. A VLAN access map consists of one or more statements, each having a common map name. First, you define the VACL with the following global configuration command:

```
Switch(config)# vlan access-map map-name [sequence-number]
```

Access map statements are evaluated in sequence, according to the *sequence-number*. Each statement can contain one or more matching conditions, followed by an action.

Next, define the matching conditions that identify the traffic to be filtered. Matching is performed by access lists (IP, IPX, or MAC address ACLs), which you must configure independently. Configure a matching condition with one of the following access map configuration commands:

```
Switch(config-access-map)# match ip  address {acl-number | acl-name}
Switch(config-access-map)# match ipx address {acl-number | acl-name}
Switch(config-access-map)# match mac address acl-name
```

You can repeat these commands to define several matching conditions; the first match encountered triggers an action to take. Define the action with the following access map configuration command:

```
Switch(config-access-map)# action {drop | forward [capture] | redirect type
    mod/num}
```

A VACL can either **drop** a matching packet, **forward** it, or **redirect** it to another interface. The TCAM performs the entire VACL match and action, as packets are switched or bridged within a VLAN, or routed into or out of a VLAN.

Finally, you must apply the VACL to a VLAN using the following global configuration command:

```
Switch(config)# vlan filter map-name vlan-list vlan-list
```

Notice that the VACL is applied globally to one or more VLANs listed and not to a VLAN interface (SVI). Recall that VLANs can be present in a switch as explicit interfaces or as inherent Layer 2 entities. The VLAN interface is the point where packets enter or leave a VLAN, so it does not make sense to apply a VACL there. Instead, the VACL needs to function *within* the VLAN itself, where there is no inbound or outbound direction.

For example, suppose that you need to filter traffic within VLAN 99 so that host 192.168.99.17 is not allowed to contact any other host on its local subnet. Access list **local-17** is created to identify traffic between this host and anything else on its local subnet. Then a VLAN access map is defined: If the **local-17** access list permits the IP address, the packet is dropped; otherwise, the packet is forwarded. Example 16-1 shows the commands necessary for this example.

Example 16-1 *Filtering Traffic Within the Local Subnet*

```
Switch(config)# ip access-list extended local-17
Switch(config-acl)# permit ip host 192.168.99.17 192.168.99.0 0.0.0.255
Switch(config-acl)# exit
Switch(config)# vlan access-map block-17 10
Switch(config-access-map)# match ip address local-17
Switch(config-access-map)# action drop
Switch(config-access-map)# vlan access-map block-17 20
Switch(config-access-map)# action forward
Switch(config-access-map)# exit
Switch(config)# vlan filter block-17 vlan-list 99
```

Private VLANs

Normally, traffic is allowed to move unrestricted within a VLAN. Packets sent from one host to another normally are heard only by the destination host because of the nature of Layer 2 switching.

However, if one host broadcasts a packet, all hosts on the VLAN must listen. You can use a VACL to filter packets between a source and destination in a VLAN if both connect to the local switch.

Sometimes it would be nice to have the capability to segment traffic within a single VLAN, without having to use multiple VLANs and a router. For example, in a single-VLAN server farm, all servers should be capable of communicating with the router or gateway, but the servers should not have to listen to each other's broadcast traffic. Taking this a step further, suppose that each server belongs to a separate organization. Now each server should be isolated from the others but still be capable of reaching the gateway to find clients not on the local network.

Another application is a service provider network. Here, the provider might want to use a single VLAN to connect to several customer networks. Each customer needs to be able to contact the provider's gateway on the VLAN. Clearly, the customer sites do not need to interact with each other.

Private VLANs (PVLANs) solve this problem on Catalyst switches. In a nutshell, a normal, or *primary,* VLAN can be logically associated with special unidirectional, or *secondary,* VLANs. Hosts associated with a secondary VLAN can communicate with ports on the primary VLAN (a router, for example), but not with another secondary VLAN. A secondary VLAN is configured as one of the following types:

- **Isolated**—Any switch ports associated with an isolated VLAN can reach the primary VLAN but not any other secondary VLAN. In addition, hosts associated with the same isolated VLAN cannot reach each other. They are, in effect, isolated from everything except the primary VLAN.

- **Community**—Any switch ports associated with a common community VLAN can communicate with each other and with the primary VLAN but not with any other secondary VLAN. This provides the basis for server farms and workgroups within an organization, while giving isolation between organizations.

All secondary VLANs must be associated with one primary VLAN to set up the uni-directional relationship. Private VLANs are configured using special cases of regular VLANs. However, the VLAN Trunking Protocol (VTP) does not pass any information about the private VLAN configuration. Therefore, private VLANs are only locally significant to a switch. Each of the private VLANs must be configured locally on each switch that interconnects them.

You must configure each physical switch port that uses a private VLAN with a VLAN association. You also must define the port with one of the following modes:

■ **Promiscuous**—The switch port connects to a router, firewall, or other common gateway device. This port can communicate with anything else connected to the primary or any secondary VLAN. In other words, the port is in promiscuous mode, in which the rules of private VLANs are ignored.

■ **Host**—The switch port connects to a regular host that resides on an isolated or community VLAN. The port communicates only with a promiscuous port or ports on the same community VLAN.

Figure 16-1 shows the basic private VLAN operation. Some host PCs connect to a secondary community VLAN. The two community VLANs associate with a primary VLAN, where the router connects. The router connects to a promiscuous port on the primary VLAN. A single host PC connects to a secondary isolated VLAN, so it can communicate only with the router's promiscuous port.

Figure 16-1 *Private VLAN Functionality Within a Switch*

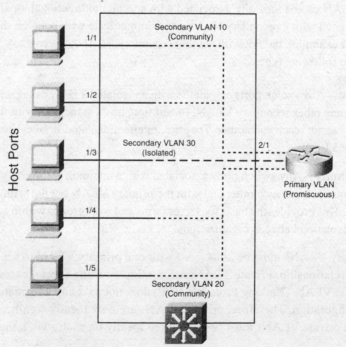

Private VLAN Configuration

Defining a private VLAN involves several configuration steps. These steps are described in the sections that follow so you can use them.

Configure the Private VLANs

To configure a private VLAN, begin by defining any secondary VLANs that are needed for isolation using the following configuration commands:

```
Switch(config)# vlan vlan-id
Switch(config-vlan)# private-vlan {isolated | community}
```

The secondary VLAN can be an isolated VLAN (no connectivity between isolated ports) or a community VLAN (connectivity between member ports).

Now define the primary VLAN that will provide the underlying private VLAN connectivity using the following configuration commands:

```
Switch(config)# vlan vlan-id
Switch(config-vlan)# private-vlan primary
Switch(config-vlan)# private-vlan association {secondary-vlan-list | add
   secondary-vlan-list | remove secondary-vlan-list}
```

Be sure to associate the primary VLAN with all its component secondary VLANs using the **association** keyword. If the primary VLAN already has been configured, you can add (**add**) or remove (**remove**) secondary VLAN associations individually.

These VLAN configuration commands set up only the mechanisms for unidirectional connectivity from the secondary VLANs to the primary VLAN. You also must associate the individual switch ports with their respective private VLANs.

Associate Ports with Private VLANs

First, define the function of the port that will participate on a private VLAN using the following configuration command:

```
Switch(config-if)# switchport mode private-vlan {host | promiscuous}
```

If the host connected to this port is a router, firewall, or common gateway for the VLAN, use the **promiscuous** keyword. This allows the host to reach all other promiscuous, isolated, or community ports associated with the primary VLAN. Otherwise, any isolated or community port must receive the **host** keyword.

For a nonpromiscuous port (using the **switchport mode private-vlan host** command), you must associate the switch port with the appropriate primary and secondary VLANs. Remember, only the private VLANs themselves have been configured until now. The switch port must know how to interact with the various VLANs using the following interface configuration command:

```
Switch(config-if)# switchport private-vlan host-association primary-vlan-id
   secondary-vlan-id
```

> **NOTE**   When a switch port is associated with private VLANs, you don't have to configure a static access VLAN. Instead, the port takes on membership in the primary and secondary VLANs simultaneously. This does not mean that the port has a fully functional assignment to multiple VLANs. Instead, it takes on only the unidirectional behavior between the secondary and primary VLANs.

For a promiscuous port (using the **switchport mode private-vlan promiscuous** command), you must map the port to primary and secondary VLANs. Notice that promiscuous mode ports, or ports that can communicate with any other private VLAN device, are mapped, while other secondary VLAN ports are associated. One (promiscuous mode port) exhibits bidirectional behavior, whereas the other (secondary VLAN ports) exhibits unidirectional or logical behavior.

Use the following interface configuration command to map promiscuous mode ports to primary and secondary VLANs:

```
Switch(config-if)# switchport private-vlan mapping primary-vlan-id secondary-
     vlan-list | {add secondary-vlan-list} | {remove secondary-vlan-list}
```

As an example, assume that the switch in Figure 16-1 is configured as in Example 16-2. Host PCs on ports FastEthernet 1/1 and 1/2 are in community VLAN 10, hosts on ports FastEthernet 1/4 and 1/5 are in community VLAN 20, and the host on port FastEthernet 1/3 is in isolated VLAN 30. The router on port FastEthernet 2/1 is in promiscuous mode on primary VLAN 100. Each VLAN is assigned a role, and the primary VLAN is associated with its secondary VLANs. Then each interface is associated with a primary and secondary VLAN (if a host is attached) or mapped to the primary and secondary VLANs (if a promiscuous host is attached).

Example 16-2   *Configuring Ports with Private VLANs*

```
Switch(config)# vlan 10
Switch(config-vlan)# private-vlan community
Switch(config)# vlan 20
Switch(config-vlan)# private-vlan community
Switch(config)# vlan 30
Switch(config-vlan)# private-vlan isolated
Switch(config)# vlan 100
Switch(config-vlan)# private-vlan primary
Switch(config-vlan)# private-vlan association 10,20,30
Switch(config-vlan)# exit
Switch(config)# interface range fastethernet 1/1 - 1/2
Switchconfig# switchport private-vlan host
Switch(config-if)# switchport private-vlan host-association 100 10
Switch(config)# interface range fastethernet 1/4 - 1/5
```

Example 16-2 *Configuring Ports with Private VLANs (Continued)*

```
Switchconfig# switchport private-vlan host
Switch(config-if)# switchport private-vlan host-association 100 20
Switch(config)# interface fastethernet 1/3
Switchconfig# switchport private-vlan host
Switch(config-if)# switchport private-vlan host-association 100 30

Switch(config)# interface fastethernet 2/1
Switch(config-if)# switchport mode private-vlan promiscuous
Switch(config-if)# switchport private-vlan mapping 100 10,20,30
```

Associate Secondary VLANs to a Primary VLAN SVI

On switched virtual interfaces, or VLAN interfaces configured with Layer 3 addresses, you must configure some additional private VLAN mapping. Consider the SVI for the primary VLAN, VLAN 100, that has an IP address and participates in routing traffic. Secondary VLANs 40 (an isolated VLAN) and 50 (a community VLAN) are associated at Layer 2 with primary VLAN 100 using the configuration in Example 16-3.

Example 16-3 *Associating Secondary VLANs to a Primary VLAN*

```
Switch(config)# vlan 40
Switch(config-vlan)# private-vlan isolated vlan 50
Switch(config-vlan)# private-vlan community vlan 200
Switch(config-vlan)# private-vlan primary
Switch(config-vlan)# private-vlan association 40,50
Switch(config-vlan)# exit
Switch(config)# interface vlan 200
Switch(config-if)# ip address 192.168.199.1 255.255.255.0
```

Primary VLAN 200 can forward traffic at Layer 3, but the secondary VLAN associations with it are good at only Layer 2. To allow Layer 3 traffic switching coming from the secondary VLANs as well, you must add a private VLAN mapping to the primary VLAN (SVI) interface, using the following interface configuration command:

```
Switch(config-if)# private-vlan mapping {secondary-vlan-list | add secondary-
    vlan-list | remove secondary-vlan-list}
```

The primary VLAN SVI function is extended to the secondary VLANs instead of requiring SVIs for each of them. If some mapping already has been configured for the primary VLAN SVI, you can add (**add**) or remove (**remove**) secondary VLAN mappings individually.

For the example, you would map the private VLAN with the following command:

```
Switch(config)# interface  vlan  200
Switch(config-iff)# private-vlan  mapping  40,50
```

Securing VLAN Trunks

Because trunk links usually are bounded between two switches, you might think that they are more or less secure. Each end of the trunk is connected to a device that is under your control, VLANs carried over the trunk remain isolated, and so on.

Some attacks or exploits can be leveraged to gain access to a trunk or to the VLANs carried over a trunk. Therefore, you should become familiar with how the attacks work and what steps you can take to prevent them in the first place.

Switch Spoofing

Recall from Chapter 5, "VLANs and Trunks," that two switches can be connected by a common trunk link that can carry traffic from multiple VLANs. The trunk doesn't have to exist all the time. The switches dynamically can negotiate its use and its encapsulation mode by exchanging Dynamic Trunking Protocol (DTP) messages.

Although DTP can make switch administration easier, it also can expose switch ports to be compromised. Suppose that a switch port is left to its default configuration, in which the trunking mode is **auto**. Normally, the switch port would wait to be asked by another switch in the **auto** or **on** mode to become a trunk.

Now suppose that an end user's PC is connected to that port. A well-behaved end user would not use DTP at all, so the port would come up in access mode with a single-access VLAN. A malicious user, however, might exploit the use of DTP and attempt to negotiate a trunk with the switch port. This makes the PC appear to be another switch; in effect, the PC is spoofing a switch.

After the trunk is negotiated, the attacker has access to any VLAN that is permitted to pass over the trunk. If the switch port has been left to its default configuration, *all* VLANs configured on the switch are allowed onto the trunk. This scenario is shown in Figure 16-2. The attacker can receive any traffic being sent over the trunk on any VLAN. In addition, he can send traffic into any VLAN of his choice.

Figure 16-2 *An Example of Switch Spoofing to Gain Access to a Trunk*

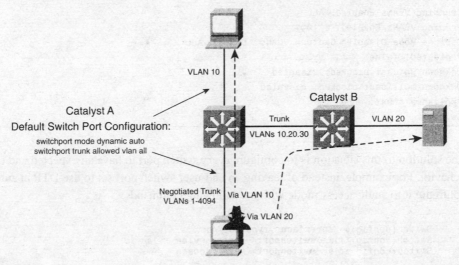

To demonstrate this further, consider the output in Example 16-4, which shows the default access switch port configuration. Notice that trunking is possible because the port is set to dynamic auto mode, awaiting DTP negotiation from a connected device. If a trunk is negotiated, all VLANs are permitted to be carried over it.

Example 16-4 *Displaying the Default Switch Port Configuration*

```
Switch# show interfaces fastethernet 1/0/46 switchport
Name: Fa1/0/46
Switchport: Enabled
Administrative Mode: dynamic auto
Operational Mode: trunk
Administrative Trunking Encapsulation: negotiate
Negotiation of Trunking: On
Access Mode VLAN: 1 (default)
Trunking Native Mode VLAN: 1 (default)
Administrative Native VLAN tagging: enabled
Voice VLAN: none
Administrative private-vlan host-association: none
Administrative private-vlan mapping: none
Administrative private-vlan trunk native VLAN: none
Administrative private-vlan trunk Native VLAN tagging: enabled
Administrative private-vlan trunk encapsulation: dot1q
Administrative private-vlan trunk normal VLANs: none
Administrative private-vlan trunk private VLANs: none
Operational private-vlan: none
```

continues

Example 16-4 *Displaying the Default Switch Port Configuration (Continued)*

```
Trunking VLANs Enabled: ALL
Pruning VLANs Enabled: 2-1001
Capture Mode Disabled Capture VLANs Allowed: ALL
Protected: false
Unknown unicast blocked: disabled
Unknown multicast blocked: disabled
Appliance trust: none
Switch#
```

The solution to this situation is to configure *every* switch port to have an expected and controlled behavior. For example, instead of leaving an end-user switch port set to use DTP in auto mode, configure it to static access mode with the following commands:

```
Switch(config)# interface type mod/num
Switch(config-if)# switchport access vlan vlan-id
Switch(config-if)# switchport mode access
```

This way, an end user never will be able to send any type of spoofed traffic that will make the switch port begin trunking.

In addition, you might be wise to disable any unused switch ports to prevent someone from discovering a live port that might be exploited.

VLAN Hopping

When securing VLAN trunks, also consider the potential for an exploit called *VLAN hopping*. Here, an attacker positioned on one access VLAN can craft and send frames with spoofed 802.1Q tags so that the packet payloads ultimately appear on a totally different VLAN, all without the use of a router.

For this exploit to work, the following conditions must exist in the network configuration:

■ The attacker is connected to an access switch port.

■ The same switch must have an 802.1Q trunk.

■ The trunk must have the attacker's access VLAN as its native VLAN.

Figure 16-3 shows how VLAN hopping works. The attacker, situated on VLAN 10, sends frames that are doubly tagged as if an 802.1Q trunk were being used. Naturally, the attacker is not connected to a trunk; he is spoofing the trunk encapsulation to trick the switch into making the frames hop over to another VLAN.

Figure 16-3 *VLAN Hopping Attack Process*

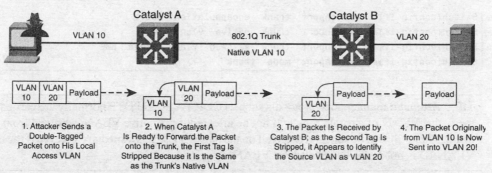

1. Attacker Sends a Double-Tagged Packet onto His Local Access VLAN

2. When Catalyst A Is Ready to Forward the Packet onto the Trunk, the First Tag Is Stripped Because it Is the Same as the Trunk's Native VLAN

3. The Packet Is Received by Catalyst B; as the Second Tag Is Stripped, it Appears to Identify the Source VLAN as VLAN 20

4. The Packet Originally from VLAN 10 Is Now Sent into VLAN 20!

The regular frame—or malicious payload, in this case—is first given an 802.1Q tag with the VLAN ID of the target VLAN. Then a second bogus 802.1Q tag is added with the attacker's access VLAN ID.

When the local switch Catalyst A receives a doubly tagged frame, it decides to forward it out the trunk interface. Because the first (outermost) tag has the same VLAN ID as the trunk's native VLAN, that tag is removed as the frame is sent on the trunk. The switch believes that the native VLAN should be untagged, as it should. Now the second (innermost) tag is exposed on the trunk.

When Catalyst B receives the frame, it examines any 802.1Q tag it finds. The spoofed tag for VLAN 20 is found, so the tag is removed and the frame is forwarded onto VLAN 20. Now the attacker successfully has sent a frame on VLAN 10 and gotten the frame injected onto VLAN 20—all through Layer 2 switching.

Clearly, the key to this type of attack revolves around the use of untagged native VLANs. Therefore, to thwart VLAN hopping, you always should carefully configure trunk links with the following steps:

Step 1   Set the native VLAN of a trunk to a bogus or unused VLAN ID.

Step 2   Prune the native VLAN off both ends of the trunk.

For example, suppose that an 802.1Q trunk should carry only VLANs 10 and 20. You should set the native VLAN to an unused value, such as 800. Then you should remove VLAN 800 from the trunk so that it is confined to the trunk link itself. Example 16-5 demonstrates how to accomplish this.

Example 16-5 *Configuring the 802.1Q Trunk to Carry Only VLANs 10 and 20*

```
Switch(config)# vlan 800
Switch(config-vlan)# name bogus_native
Switch(config-vlan)# exit
Switch(config)# interface gigabitethernet 1/1
```

continues

Example 16-5 *Configuring the 802.1Q Trunk to Carry Only VLANs 10 and 20 (Continued)*

```
Switch(config-if)#  switchport  trunk  encapsulation  dot1q
Switch(config-if)#  switchport  trunk  native  vlan  800
Switch(config-if)#  switchport  trunk  allowed  vlan  remove  800
Switch(config-if)#  switchport  mode  trunk
```

TIP   Although maintenance protocols such as CDP, PAgP, and DTP normally are carried over the native VLAN of a trunk, they will not be affected if the native VLAN is pruned from the trunk. They still will be sent and received on the native VLAN as a special case even if the native VLAN ID is not in the list of allowed VLANs.

One alternative is to force all 802.1Q trunks to add tags to frames for the native VLAN, too. The double-tagged VLAN hopping attack won't work because the switch won't remove the first tag with the native VLAN ID (VLAN 10 in the example). Instead, that tag will remain on the spoofed frame as it enters the trunk. At the far end of the trunk, the same tag will be examined, and the frame will stay on the original access VLAN (VLAN 10).

To force a switch to tag the native VLAN on all its 802.1Q trunks, you can use the following command:

```
Switch(config)#  vlan  dot1q  tag  native
```

Foundation Summary

The Foundation Summary is a collection of information that provides a convenient review of many key concepts in this chapter. If you are already comfortable with the topics in this chapter, this summary can help you recall a few details. If you just read this chapter, this review should help solidify some key facts. If you are doing your final preparation before the exam, this information will hopefully be a convenient way to review the day before the exam.

■ VLAN Access Lists (VACLs) can control packets that are bridged, switched, or routed. VACLs are effective on packets that stay *within* a single VLAN.

Table 16-2 *VLAN ACL Configuration Commands*

Task	Command Syntax
Define a VACL	**vlan access-map** *map-name* [*sequence-number*]
Define a matching condition	**match** {**ip address** {*acl-number* | *acl-name*}} | {**ipx address** {*acl- number* | *acl-name*} | {**mac address** *acl-name*}}
Define an action	**action** {**drop** | **forward** [**capture**] | **redirect** *type mod/num*}
Apply the VACL to VLANs	**vlan filter** *map-name* **vlan-list** *vlan-list*

■ Private VLANs provide special unidirectional relationships between entities on a single VLAN.

■ Private VLANs are implemented as primary and secondary VLANs.

■ Primary VLANs allow hosts to communicate with any other type of private (secondary) VLAN.

■ Secondary VLANs allow hosts to communicate with ports on a primary VLAN but not with other secondary VLANs.

■ Secondary VLANs are categorized as follows:

— **Isolated VLAN**—Hosts can communicate only with the primary VLAN, not any other isolated port or secondary VLAN.

— **Community VLAN**—Hosts can communicate with the primary VLAN and other hosts in the community VLAN but not with any other isolated or community VLAN.

■ Secondary VLANs must be associated with one primary VLAN.

You can configure switch ports using private VLANs, as follows:

— **Promiscuous**—Usually connects to a router, firewall, or gateway device; this type of port can communicate with any other type of private VLAN.

— **Host**—Usually connects to regular hosts; this type of port can communicate with a promiscuous port or ports on the same community VLAN.

Table 16-3 *Private VLAN Configuration Commands*

Task	Command Syntax
Define a secondary VLAN	**vlan** *vlan-id* **private-vlan** {**isolated** ǀ **community**}
Define a primary VLAN; associate it with secondary VLANs	**vlan** *vlan-id* **private-vlan primary** **private-vlan association** {*secondary-vlan-list* ǀ **add** *secondary-vlan-list* ǀ **remove** *secondary-vlan-list*}
Associate ports with private VLANs	**switchport mode private-vlan** {**host** ǀ **promiscuous**}
Associate nonpromiscuous ports with private VLANs	**switchport private-vlan host-association** *primary-vlan-id* *secondary-vlan-id*
Associate promiscuous ports with private VLANs	**switchport private-vlan mapping** {*primary-vlan-id*} {*secondary-vlan-list*} ǀ {**add** *secondary-vlan-list*} ǀ {**remove** *secondary-vlan-list*}
Associate secondary VLANs with a primary VLAN Layer 3 SVI	**private-vlan mapping** {*secondary-vlan-list* ǀ **add** *secondary-vlan-list* ǀ **remove** *secondary-vlan-list*}

Q&A

The questions and scenarios in this book are more difficult than what you should experience on the actual exam. The questions do not attempt to cover more breadth or depth than the exam; however, they are designed to make sure that you know the answers. Rather than allowing you to derive the answers from clues hidden inside the questions themselves, the questions challenge your understanding and recall of the subject. Hopefully, these questions will help limit the number of exam questions on which you narrow your choices to two options and then guess.

You can find the answers to these questions in Appendix A.

1. When a VACL is implemented on a switch, how is the switching speed affected?

2. What actions can be taken on packets matching a VACL?

3. After a VACL is applied using the **vlan filter** command, how is the traffic direction (inbound or outbound) specified?

4. A secondary community VLAN is associated with a primary VLAN on a switch. Can hosts assigned to the community VLAN communicate with each other?

5. A secondary isolated VLAN is associated with a primary VLAN on a switch. Can hosts assigned to the isolated VLAN communicate with each other?

6. What command is needed to configure a promiscuous VLAN?

7. A router is identified as the central gateway for a private VLAN. What command is needed to configure the switch port where a router is connected?

8. How many actual VLANs must be configured to implement a common router with two community VLANs?

9. In a switch spoofing attack, what is the attacker's goal?

10. What should be configured to prevent a switch spoofing attack?

11. Describe some methods that can be used to prevent a VLAN hopping attack.

This part of the book covers the following BCMSN exam topics:

■ Describe the components and operations of WLAN topologies (i.e., AP and Bridge)

■ Describe the features of Client Devices, Network Unification, and Mobility Platforms (i.e., CCX, LWAPP)

■ Configure a wireless client (i.e., ADU)

Part V: Wireless LANs

Part V: Wireless LANs

This chapter covers the following topics that you need to master for the CCNP BCMSN exam:

- **Wireless LAN Basics**—This section discusses wireless networks as they compare to wired Ethernet networks.

- **WLAN Building Blocks**—This section covers wireless service sets in addition to wireless access points and their coverage areas.

- **An Introduction to Wireless LAN RF**—Wireless networks use radio frequency (RF) transmissions as their communications medium. This section covers basic RF theory and the terminology that is used to define and describe wireless operation. This section also discusses wireless LAN antennas and their applications.

- **WLAN Standards**—This section describes the IEEE standards; specifically, the 802.11b, 802.11g, and 802.11a standards that are used in wireless LAN environments.

CHAPTER 17

Wireless LAN Overview

Switched networks generally form the foundation of an enterprise network. Connectivity is offered from the core layer downward to reach end users located at the access layer. Traditionally, these end users have used wires to connect to the access layer.

Wireless networks allow the access layer to be extended to end users without wires. By designing and placing wireless LAN devices across an entire area of the network, end users can even become mobile and move around without losing their network connections.

This chapter presents an overview of the technologies used in wireless LANs. By becoming familiar with some basic wireless theory, you will be able to understand, design, and use wireless LAN devices to expand your switched network to reach wireless users.

"Do I Know This Already?" Quiz

The purpose of the "Do I Know This Already?" quiz is to help you decide what parts of this chapter to use. If you already intend to read the entire chapter, you do not necessarily need to answer these questions now.

The quiz, derived from the major sections in the "Foundation Topics" portion of the chapter, helps you determine how to spend your limited study time.

Table 17-1 outlines the major topics discussed in this chapter and the "Do I Know This Already?" quiz questions that correspond to those topics.

Table 17-1 *"Do I Know This Already?" Foundation Topics Section-to-Question Mapping*

Foundation Topics Section	Questions Covered in This Section	Score
Wireless LAN Basics	1–2	
WLAN Building Blocks	3–4	
Wireless LAN RF	5–9	
WLAN Standards	10–12	
Total Score		

> **CAUTION** The goal of self-assessment is to gauge your mastery of the topics in this chapter. If you do not know the answer to a question or are only partially sure of the answer, you should mark this question wrong. Giving yourself credit for an answer you correctly guess skews your self-assessment results and might give you a false sense of security.

1. Which one of the following standard sets is used in wireless LANs?

    a. IEEE 802.1

    b. IEEE 802.3

    c. IEEE 802.5

    d. IEEE 802.11

2. Which one of the following methods is used to minimize collisions in a wireless LAN?

    a. CSMA/CD

    b. CSMA/CA

    c. LWAPP

    d. LACP

3. A wireless scenario is made up of five wireless clients and two APs connected by a switch. Which one of the following correctly describes the wireless network?

    a. BSS

    b. ESS

    c. IBSS

    d. CBS

4. If a wireless access point is connected to a switch by a trunk port, which one of the following is mapped to a VLAN?

    a. Channel

    b. Frequency

    c. BSS

    d. SSID

5. If an RF signal meets a large metal filing cabinet, which one of the following effects is likely to occur?

    a. Reflection

    b. Refraction

    c. Absorption

    d. Scattering

6. Suppose that a wireless access point transmits at 100 mW, and then it is reconfigured to transmit at 50 mW. What is the change in dBm?

    a. −50

    b. 0.5

    c. −3

    d. +3

7. Antenna gain is usually measured in which one of the following units?

    a. dBm

    b. dBi

    c. mW

    d. W

8. A wireless access point transmits at 100 mW or 20 dBm. A cable with a loss of 5 dB connects the AP to its antenna. The antenna is a dish model with a gain of 22. The receiving access point is located 1 mile away and uses an identical antenna and cable. What is the EIRP value?

    a. 0 dBm

    b. 20 dBm

    c. 37 dBm

    d. 74 dBm

9. A wireless AP with a built-in dipole antenna would be best suited for which one of the following, based on its capability to cover the area?

    a. Building-to-building link

    b. Rooms located down a long hallway

    c. An office made up of cubicles

    d. A four-story office building

10. The IEEE 802.11g standard is backward compatible with which other standard?

    a. IEEE 802.11a

    b. IEEE 802.11b

    c. IEEE 802.11c

    d. IEEE 802.11e

11.   Which nonoverlapping channels are commonly used in wireless LANs?

   a. 1, 2, 3

   b. 1, 3, 6

   c. 1, 6, 11

   d. 1, 11, 22

12.   Which one of the following represents the correct combination of frequency band and IEEE standard?

   a. 2.4 GHz, 802.11g

   b. 5 GHz, 802.11g

   c. 2.4 GHz, 802.11a

   d. 5 GHz, 802.11b

The answers to the "Do I Know This Already?" quiz are found in Appendix A, "Answers to Chapter 'Do I Know This Already?' Quizzes and Q&A Sections." The suggested choices for your next step are as follows:

■   **10 or less overall score**—Read the entire chapter. This includes the "Foundation Topics," "Foundation Summary," and "Q&A" sections.

■   **11 or more overall score**—If you want more review on these topics, skip to the "Foundation Summary" section and then go to the "Q&A" section at the end of the chapter. Otherwise, move to Chapter 18, "Wireless Architecture and Design."

Foundation Topics

Wireless LAN Basics

This chapter presents wireless LAN (WLAN) operation from a practical viewpoint, building on the knowledge you've gained from the switched LAN topics. After all, this is a book (and exam) about switching technology, so you should know enough about wireless LANs to be able to integrate them into your switched network.

Comparing Wireless and Wired LANs

How exactly does a wireless LAN get integrated with a wired LAN? Where does switching fit into a wireless LAN? Before answering these questions, it might be helpful to see how the two technologies compare.

At the most basic level, switched networks involve wires, and wireless networks don't. That might seem silly, but it points out some major differences in the physical layer.

A traditional Ethernet network is defined by the IEEE 802.3 standards. Every Ethernet connection must operate under tightly controlled conditions, especially regarding the physical link itself. For example, the link status, link speed, and duplex mode must all operate like the standards describe. Wireless LANs have a similar arrangement, but are defined by the IEEE 802.11 standards.

Wired Ethernet devices have to transmit and receive Ethernet frames according to the Carrier Sense Multiple Access/Collision Detect (CSMA/CD) method. On a shared Ethernet segment, where PCs communicate in half-duplex mode, each PC can freely "talk" first, and then listen for collisions with other devices that are also talking. The whole process of detecting collisions is based on having wired connections of a certain maximum length, with a certain maximum latency as a frame travels from one end of the segment to another before being detected at the far end.

Full-duplex or switched Ethernet links are not plagued with collisions or contention for the bandwidth. They do have to abide by the same specifications, though. For example, Ethernet frames must still be transmitted and received within an expected amount of time on a full-duplex link. This forces the maximum length of full-duplex, twisted-pair cabling to be the same as that of a half-duplex link.

Even though wireless LANs are also based on a set of stringent standards, the wireless medium itself is challenging to control. Generally speaking, when a PC attaches to a wired Ethernet network, it shares that network connection with a known number of other devices that are also connected. When the same PC uses a wireless network, it does so over the air. No wires or outlets exist at the access layer, as other end users are free to use the same air.

A wireless LAN then becomes a shared network, where a varying number of hosts contend for the use of the "air" at any time. Collisions are a fact of life in a wireless LAN because every wireless connection is in half-duplex mode.

> **TIP** IEEE 802.11 WLANs are always half-duplex because transmitting and receiving stations use the same frequency. Only one station can transmit at any time; otherwise, collisions occur. To achieve full-duplex mode, all transmitting would have to occur on one frequency and all receiving would occur over a different frequency—much like full-duplex Ethernet links work. Although this is certainly possible and practical, the 802.11 standards don't permit full-duplex operation.

Avoiding Collisions in a WLAN

When two or more wireless stations transmit at the same time, their signals become mixed. Receiving stations can see the result only as garbled data, noise, or errors.

No clear-cut way exists to determine whether a collision has occurred. Even the transmitting stations won't realize it because their receivers must be turned off while they are transmitting. As a basic feedback mechanism, whenever a wireless station transmits a frame, the receiving wireless station must send an acknowledgement back to confirm that the frame was received error-free.

Acknowledgement frames serve as a rudimentary collision detection tool; however, it doesn't work to prevent collisions from occurring in the first place.

The IEEE 802.11 standards use a method called Carrier Sense Multiple Access Collision *Avoidance* (CSMA/CA). Notice that wired 802.3 networks *detect* collisions, whereas 802.11 networks try to *avoid* collisions.

Collision avoidance works by requiring all stations to listen before they transmit a frame. When a station has a frame that needs to be sent, one of the two following conditions occurs:

■ **No other device is transmitting**—The station can transmit its frame immediately. The intended receiving station must send an acknowledgement frame to confirm that the original frame arrived intact and collision-free.

- **Another device is already transmitting a frame**—The station must wait until the frame in progress has completed, then it must wait a random amount of time before transmitting its own frame.

Wireless frames can vary in size. When a frame is transmitted, how can other stations know when the frame will be completed and the wireless medium is available for others to use? Obviously, stations could simply listen for silence, but doing so isn't always efficient. Other stations can listen, too, and would likely decide to transmit at the same time. The 802.11 standards require all stations to wait a short amount of time, called the *DCF interframe space (DIFS)*, before transmitting anything at all.

Transmitting stations can provide an estimate of the amount of time needed to send a frame by including a duration value within the 802.11 header. The duration contains the number of timeslots (typically in microseconds) needed for the size of frame being sent. Other wireless stations must look at the duration value and wait that length of time before considering their own transmissions.

Because every listening station receives and follows the same duration value found in a transmitted frame, every one of them might decide to transmit their own frames once the duration time has elapsed. This would result in a collision—the very condition that should be avoided.

In addition to the duration timer, every wireless station must also implement a random backoff timer. Before transmitting a frame, a station must select a random number of timeslots to wait. This number lies between zero and a maximum contention window value. The idea here is that stations ready to transmit will each wait a random amount of time, minimizing the number of stations that will try to transmit immediately.

This whole process is called the *Distributed Coordination Function (DCF)*, and is illustrated in Figure 17-1. Three wireless users have a frame to send at varying times. The following sequence of events occurs:

1. User A listens and determines that no other users are transmitting. User A transmits his frame and advertises the frame duration.

2. User B has a frame to transmit. He must wait until user A's frame is completed, and then wait until the DIFS period has expired.

3. User B waits a random backoff time before attempting to transmit.

4. While user B is waiting, user C has a frame to transmit. He listens and detects that no one is transmitting. User C waits a random time, which is shorter than User B's random time.

5. User B transmits a frame and advertises the frame duration.

6. User C must now wait the duration of user B's frame plus the DIFS time before attempting to transmit again.

Figure 17-1 *Avoiding Collisions with the DCF Process*

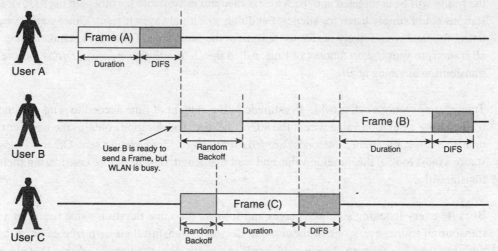

Because the backoff timer is random, a chance still exists that two or more stations will choose the same value. Nothing else will prevent these stations from transmitting at the same time and causing a collision. This will simply be seen as an error over the wireless network; no acknowledgements will be returned, and the stations will have to reconsider sending their frames again.

Finally, what if a station waits until its random backoff timer expires and is ready to transmit, only to find that someone else is already transmitting? The waiting station must now wait the duration of the newly transmitted frame, followed by the DIFS time, and then the random backoff time.

WLAN Building Blocks

At the most basic level, a wireless medium has no inherent organization. For example, a PC with wireless capability can simply bring up its wireless adapter anywhere at any time. Naturally, there must be something else that can also send and receive over the wireless media before the PC can communicate.

TIP In IEEE 802.11 terminology, any group of wireless devices is known as a *service set*. The devices must share a common *service set identifier (SSID)*, which is a text string included in every frame sent. If the SSIDs match across the sender and receiver, the two devices can communicate.

The PC, as an end-user station, becomes a client of the wireless network. It must have a wireless network adapter and a *supplicant*, or software that interacts with the wireless protocols.

The 802.11 standards allow two or more wireless clients to communicate directly with each other, with no other means of network connectivity. This is known as an *ad-hoc* wireless network, or an *Independent Basic Service Set (IBSS)*, as shown in part A of Figure 17-2.

Figure 17-2 *A Comparison of Wireless Service Sets*

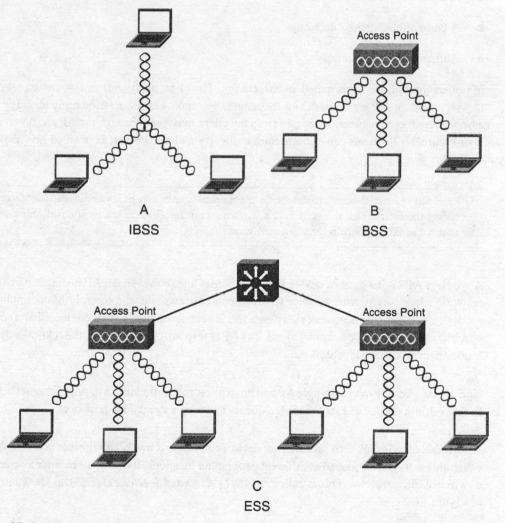

No inherent control exists over the number of devices that can transmit and receive frames over a wireless medium. As well, many variables exist that can affect whether a wireless station can receive from or transmit to other stations. This makes providing reliable wireless access to all stations difficult.

An 802.11 Basic Service Set (BSS) centralizes access and control over a group of wireless devices by placing an access point (AP) as the hub of the service set. Any wireless client attempting to use the wireless network must first arrange a membership with the AP. The AP can require any of the following criteria before allowing a client to join:

■ A matching SSID

■ A compatible wireless data rate

◢ Authentication credentials

Membership with the AP is called an *association*. The client must send an association request message, and the AP grants or denies the request by sending an association reply message. Once associated, all communications to and from the client must pass through the AP, as shown in part B of Figure 17-2. Clients can't communicate directly with each other, as in an ad-hoc network or IBSS.

TIP   Keep in mind that regardless of the association status, any PC is capable of listening to or receiving the frames that are sent over a wireless medium. Frames are freely available over the air to anyone who is within range to receive them.

A wireless AP isn't a passive device like an Ethernet hub, however. An AP manages its wireless network, advertises its own existence so that clients can associate, and controls the communication process. For example, recall that every data frame sent successfully (without a collision) over a wireless medium must be acknowledged. The AP is responsible for sending the acknowledgement frames back to the sending stations.

Notice that a BSS involves a single AP and no explicit connection into a regular Ethernet network. In that setting, the AP and its associated clients make up a standalone network.

An AP can also uplink into an Ethernet network because it has both wireless and wired capabilities. If APs are placed at different geographic locations, they can all be interconnected by a switched infrastructure. This is called an 802.11 *Extended Service Set (ESS)*, as shown in part C of Figure 17-2.

In an ESS, a wireless client can associate with one AP while it is physically located near that AP. If the client later moves to a different location, it can associate with a different nearby AP. The

802.11 standards also define a method to allow the client to roam or to be passed from one AP to another as its location changes.

Access Point Operation

An AP's primary function is to bridge wireless data from the air to a normal wired network. An AP can accept "connections" from a number of wireless clients so that they become members of the LAN, as if the same clients were using wired connections.

An AP can also act as a bridge to form a single wireless link from one LAN to another over a long distance. In that case, an AP is needed on each end of the wireless link. AP-to-AP or line-of-sight links are commonly used for connectivity between buildings or between cities.

Cisco has developed an AP platform that can even bridge wireless LAN traffic from AP to AP, in a daisy chain fashion. This allows a large open outdoor area to be covered with a wireless LAN but without the use of network cabling. The APs form a mesh topology, much like an ESS where APs are interconnected by other wireless connections.

APs act as the central point of access (hence the AP name), controlling client access to the wireless LAN. Any client attempting to use the WLAN must first establish an association with an AP. The AP can allow open access, so that any client can associate, or it can tighten control by requiring authentication credentials, or other criteria before allowing associations.

The WLAN operation is tightly coupled to feedback from the far end of a wireless connection. For example, clients must handshake with an AP before they can associate and use the WLAN. At the most basic level, this assures a working two-way wireless connection because both client and AP must be able to send and receive frames successfully. This process removes the possibility of one-way communication, where the client can hear the AP, but the AP can't hear the client.

As well, the AP can control many aspects of its WLAN by requiring conditions to be met before clients can associate. For example, the AP can require that clients support specific data rates, specific security measures, and specific credentials during client association.

You can think of an AP as a translational bridge, where frames from two dissimilar media are translated and then bridged at Layer 2. In simple terms, the AP is in charge of mapping a VLAN to an SSID. This is shown in the left portion of Figure 17-3, where VLAN 10 on the wired network is being extended to the AP over a switch port in access mode. The AP maps VLAN 10 to the wireless LAN using SSID "Marketing." Users associated with the "Marketing" SSID will appear to be connected to VLAN 10.

Figure 17-3 *Mapping VLANs to SSIDs*

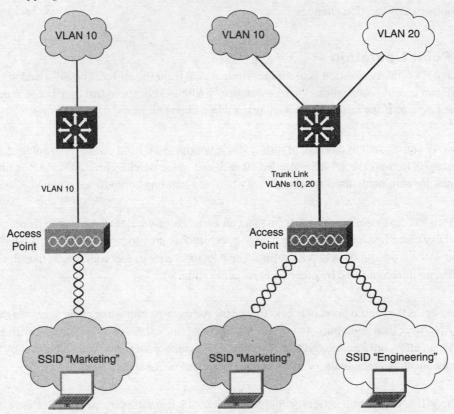

This concept can be extended so that multiple VLANs are mapped to multiple SSIDs. To do this, the AP must be connected to the switch by a trunk link that carries the VLANs. In the right portion of Figure 17-3, VLAN 10 and VLAN 20 are both trunked to the AP. The AP uses the 802.1Q tag to map the VLAN numbers to SSIDs. For example, VLAN 10 is mapped to SSID "Marketing," while VLAN 20 is mapped to SSID "Engineering."

In effect, when an AP uses multiple SSIDs, it is trunking VLANs over the air to end users. The end users must use the appropriate SSID that has been mapped to their respective VLAN.

Wireless LAN Cells

An AP can provide WLAN connectivity to only the clients within its range. The signal range is roughly defined by the AP's antenna pattern. In an open-air setting, this might be a circular shape surrounding an omnidirectional antenna. At least the pattern will appear as a circle on a floorplan—keep in mind that the pattern is three-dimensional, also affecting floors above and below, in a multilevel building.

The AP's location must be carefully planned so that its range matches up with the coverage area that is needed. Even though you might design the AP's location according to a floorplan or an outdoor layout, the WLAN will operate under changing conditions. Remember that although the AP's location will remain fixed, the wireless clients will change location quite frequently.

Mobile clients can make the AP's coverage turn out to be much different than you expect. After all, clients can move around and behind objects in a room, walls and doorways in a building, and so on. People will also be moving about, sometimes blocking the wireless signal.

The best approach to designing an AP's location and range or coverage area is to perform a *site survey*. A test AP is placed in a desirable spot while a test client moves about, taking live measurements of the signal strength and quality. The idea is to plot the AP's range using the actual environment it will be placed into, with the actual obstacles that might interfere with the client's operation. Obstacles and their effects on RF signals are covered in more detail in the "Signal Loss" section, later in this chapter.

An AP's coverage area is called a *cell*. Clients within that cell can associate with the AP and use the wireless LAN. This concept is shown in Figure 17-4. One client is located outside the cell because it is beyond the AP's signal range.

Figure 17-4 *Wireless Clients in an AP Cell*

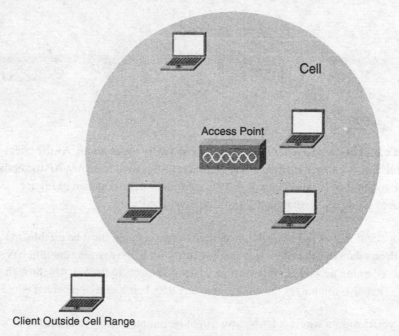

Suppose that a typical indoor AP cell has a radius of 100 feet, covering several rooms or part of a hallway. Clients can move around within that cell area and use the WLAN from any location.

However, that one cell is rather limiting because clients might need to operate in other surrounding rooms or on other floors without losing their connectivity.

To expand the overall WLAN coverage area, other cells can be placed in surrounding areas simply by distributing other APs throughout the area. The idea is to place the APs so that their cells cover every area where a client is likely to be located. In fact, their cell areas should overlap each other by a small percentage, as shown in Figure 17-5.

TIP   Once AP cells overlap, adjacent APs cannot use identical frequencies. If two neighboring APs did use the same frequency, they would only interfere with each other. Instead, AP frequencies must be alternated or staggered across the whole coverage area. This concept is covered in greater detail in Chapter 18, "Wireless Architecture and Design."

Figure 17-5   *AP Cells Arranged for Seamless Coverage*

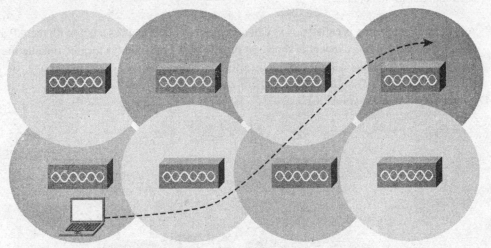

Once a client has associated with one AP, it can freely move about. As the client moves from one AP's cell into another, the client's association is also passed from one AP to another. Moving from one AP to another is called *roaming*. This movement is also shown in Figure 17-5, as the laptop PC moves along a path that passes through several AP cells.

When a client moves from one AP to another, its association must be established with the new AP. As well, any data that the client was sending just prior to the roaming condition is also relayed from the old AP to the new AP. In this way, any client connects to the WLAN through only one AP at a time. This also minimizes the chance that any data being sent or received while roaming is lost.

When you design a wireless LAN, you might be tempted to try to cover the most area possible with each AP. You could run each AP at its maximum transmit power to make the most of its range. Doing so would also reduce the number of APs necessary to cover an area, which would in turn reduce the overall cost. However, you should consider some other factors.

When an AP is configured to provide a large coverage area, it also opens the potential for overcrowding. Remember that an AP cell is essentially a half-duplex shared medium that all clients must share. As the number of clients goes up, the amount of available bandwidth and airtime goes down.

Instead, consider reducing the cell size (by reducing the transmit power) so that only clients in close proximity to the AP can associate and use bandwidth. The AP can also assist in controlling the number of clients that associate at any given time. This becomes important for time-critical or bandwidth-intensive traffic like voice, video, and medical applications.

When cell sizes are reduced, they are often called *microcells*. This concept can be further extended for extremely controlled environments like stock exchanges. In those cases, the AP power and cell size are minimized, and the cells are called *picocells*.

An Introduction to Wireless LAN RF

Radio frequency transmissions and reception are integral to WLAN operation. You should understand the basic theory behind RF so that you can be effective at designing and troubleshooting your WLAN network. However, RF theory can involve complex mathematics and physics principles. This section presents RF information in a practical sense, without all the equations.

Basic RF Operation

Radio frequency (RF) communication begins with an oscillating signal transmitted from one device to be received on one or more other devices. This oscillating signal is based around a constant, known frequency. Because the transmitter uses a set frequency, a receiver can tune to the same frequency and receive the same signal. You have probably had this experience by tuning a radio receiver in a car.

Basically, the transmitting station has a transmitter that generates the RF signal, an antenna, and a transmission line or cable that joins the two. The receiving station is identical, except that it receives the RF signal through its antenna and cable.

For simplicity, assume that wireless stations use a very small antenna that sends or receives an RF signal equally in all directions, as illustrated in the top portion of Figure 17-6, where each circle represents one portion of the wave that is produced by the transmitter. Each circle is actually a sphere because the wave moves through three-dimensional space. This can also be shown with a much simpler oscillating waveform representing the RF signal, as in the bottom portion of Figure 17-6. Although this illustration isn't technically correct, it serves only to show how an RF signal is sent between two devices.

Figure 17-6 *Representing Wireless Signals*

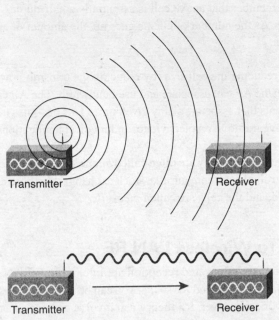

A broad range of frequencies used for similar functions is known as a *band*. For example, the AM radio band consists of the frequency range 550 MHz through 1720 MHz.

Some wireless LAN communication occurs in the 2.4 GHz band, whereas other wireless LANs use the 5 GHz band. Here, the bands are described by a rough estimate of the ranges—2.4 GHz represents more exact frequencies from 2.412 to 2.484 GHz, whereas 5 GHz represents the range 5.150 to 5.825 GHz.

The signal transmitted by a wireless station is usually called a *carrier signal*. A radio station broadcasting on a frequency of 840 MHz has its carrier oscillating at 840 MHz. However, if only the carrier signal is received, nothing else can be extracted from it. It is just a steady signal at a constant frequency. No audio, video, or data is present in the carrier signal itself, because it is meant to "carry" something else.

To transmit other information, the transmitter must *modulate* the carrier signal by inserting or encoding the information in a unique fashion. Receiving stations must reverse the process by demodulating the signal to recover the original information.

Some modulation techniques are simple—AM radio uses amplitude modulation (AM), where the strength of the carrier signal changes in proportion to the audio information. FM radio uses frequency modulation (FM), where the level of the audio causes the carrier signal to shift its frequency. WLANs use much more complex modulation techniques because their data rates are much greater than that of audio signals.

The idea behind WLAN modulation is to pack as much data as possible into the wireless signal, and to minimize the amount of data that might be lost due to interference or noise. When data is lost, it must be retransmitted, using more of the wireless resources.

Modulation schemes usually cause the carrier signal to be changed slightly over time. Because of that, both the transmitter and receiver must expect the carrier to appear on a fixed frequency, but vary within a certain range. This range is called a *channel*, although channels are usually referenced by a channel number or index, rather than a frequency. WLAN channels are defined according to which 802.11 standard is in use. The "WLAN Channels and Layout" section discusses channels in greater detail.

Figure 17-7 shows the relationship between the center or carrier frequency, the modulation, channels, and a band.

Figure 17-7 *RF Signal Terminology*

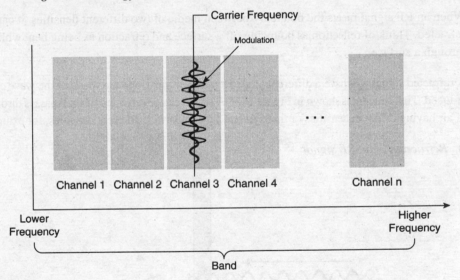

RF Characteristics

RF signals travel through the air as electromagnetic waves. In an ideal setting, a signal would arrive at the receiver exactly as it was sent by the transmitter. In the real world, this isn't always the case.

RF signals are affected by the objects and materials they meet as they travel from the transmitter to the receiver. This section briefly explores the conditions that can affect wireless signal propagation.

Reflection

If an RF signal traveling through the air as a wave meets a dense reflective material, the signal can be reflected. Think of the light emitted from a light bulb—though most of the light is traveling in all directions away from the bulb, some might be reflected from objects in a room. The reflected light might travel back toward the bulb or toward another area of the room, making that area even brighter.

Figure 17-8 depicts a reflected RF signal. Indoor objects such as metal furniture, filing cabinets, and metal doors can cause reflection. An outdoor wireless signal can be reflected by objects such as a body of water or a layer of the atmosphere.

Figure 17-8   *Reflection of an RF Signal*

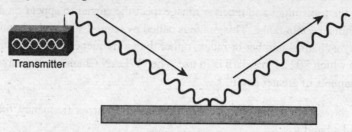

Refraction

When an RF signal meets the boundary between media of two different densities, it can also be refracted. Think of reflection as bouncing off a surface and refraction as being bent while passing through a surface.

A refracted signal will have a different angle from the original, and the speed of the wave can also be reduced. This concept is shown in Figure 17-9. A signal can be refracted when it passes through layers of air having different densities or through building walls with different densities, for example.

Figure 17-9   *Refraction of an RF Signal*

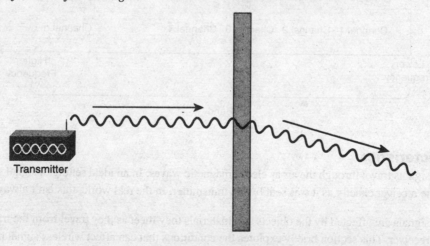

Absorption

If an RF signal passes into a material that can absorb its energy, the signal will be attenuated. The more dense the material, the more the signal will be attenuated. Figure 17-10 shows how a signal is affected by absorption, and how a receiver might be affected by the lower signal strength.

Figure 17-10 *Absorption of an RF Signal*

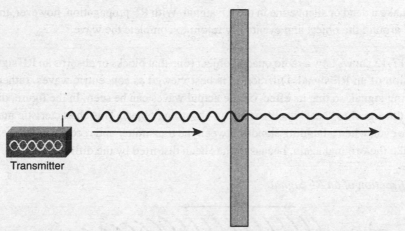

The most common example of absorption is when a wireless signal passes through water, which might be contained in tree leaves positioned along the wireless path, or in a human body that is positioned near a wireless device.

Scattering

When an RF signal passes into a medium that is rough, uneven, or made up of very small particles, the signal can be scattered into many different directions. This scattering happens because the tiny irregular surfaces of the medium can reflect the signal, as shown in Figure 17-11. Scattering can occur when a wireless signal passes through a dusty or sandy environment.

Figure 17-11 *Scattering an RF Signal*

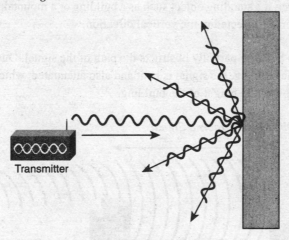

Diffraction

Suppose that an RF signal approaches an opaque object, or one that is able to absorb the energy that strikes it. You might think that the object would produce a shadow where the signal is absorbed, much like an object might make a shadow as light shines on it. If a shadow formed, it might make a dead or silent zone in the RF signal. With RF propagation, however, the signal tends to bend around the object and eventually rejoin to complete the wave.

Figure 17-12 shows how a radio opaque object (one that blocks or absorbs an RF signal) can cause diffraction of an RF signal. Diffraction is best viewed as concentric waves, rather than an oscillating signal, so that its effect on the actual waves can be seen. In the figure, diffraction has caused the signal to "heal" itself around an absorbing object. This characteristic makes reception possible even when a building stands between the transmitter and receiver. However, the signal is never like the original again, because it has been distorted by the diffraction.

Figure 17-12 *Diffraction of an RF Signal*

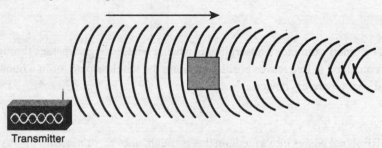

Fresnel Zones

If an object is standing free, so that an RF signal traveling parallel with the ground is diffracted around it on both sides, the signal will often fill in the object's "shadow" as it continues to propagate. However, if a standing object such as a building or a mountain obstructs the signal, the signal can be adversely affected in the vertical direction.

In Figure 17-13, a building partially obstructs the path of the signal. Due to diffraction along the front and top of the building, the signal is bent and also attenuated, which causes the signal to be masked behind most of the height of the building.

Figure 17-13 *A Standing Obstacle Diffracts a Signal*

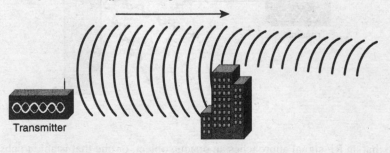

Taking this diffraction into account is especially important in narrow line-of-sight wireless transmission, which is suited for very long distances. These signals don't propagate in all directions; rather, they are focused as a beam, as shown in Figure 17-14. For a line-of-sight path, the signal must be clear of any obstructions between the transmitter's antenna and the receiver's antenna. Paths between buildings or between cities commonly have other buildings, trees, or other objects that might block the signal. In those cases, the antennas must be raised higher than the obstructions to get a clear path.

Figure 17-14 *A Line-of-Sight Wireless Signal*

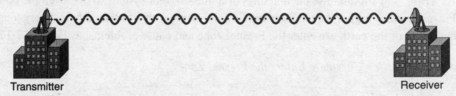

Transmitter   Receiver

Over a very long distance, the curvature of the earth actually becomes an obstacle that can affect the signal. Beyond a distance of about two miles, the far end can't be seen because it lies slightly below the horizon. Nevertheless, a wireless signal tends to propagate along the same curve, following the atmosphere around the earth's curvature.

Even narrow line-of-sight signals can be affected by diffraction, even if an object doesn't directly block the signal. An elliptical-shaped volume exists around the line of sight that must also remain free of obstructions. This area is called the *Fresnel zone*, as shown in Figure 17-15. If an object penetrates the Fresnel zone anywhere along the path, some portion of the RF signal can be diffracted by it. That portion of the signal gets bent, causing it to be delayed or altered so that it affects the overall signal arriving at the receiver.

TIP   The radius of the Fresnel zone, R1, can be calculated anywhere along the path. In practice, objects must stay below the bulk of the Fresnel zone—some sources recommend staying below 60% of the downward radius, whereas others recommend 50%.

Figure 17-15 *The Fresnel Zone*

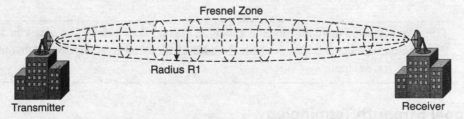

Fresnel Zone

Radius R1

Transmitter   Receiver

In Figure 17-16, a building lies along the signal's path, but doesn't obstruct the beam of the signal; however, it does penetrate the Fresnel zone, so the received signal will be negatively affected.

Figure 17-16 *Signal Degradation Due to a Fresnel Zone Obstruction*

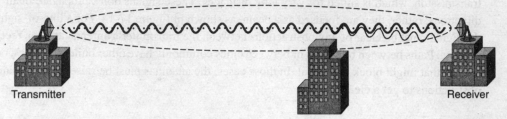

Transmitter   Receiver

As a rule, you should raise the antennas of a line-of-sight system so that even the bottom of the Fresnel zone is higher than any obstruction. Remember that as the path gets very long, even the curvature of the earth can enter the Fresnel zone and cause problems, as Figure 17-17 shows.

Figure 17-17 *The Earth's Curvature Enters the Fresnel Zone*

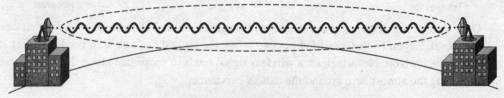

The radius of the Fresnel zone can be calculated according to a complex formula. However, you should only be concerned with the idea that the Fresnel zone exists and should remain clear. Table 17-2 gives some sample values of the Fresnel zone radius at the midpoint of some line-of-sight path lengths for wireless frequencies in the 2.4 GHz band.

Table 17-2 *Fresnel Zone Radius Values*

Path Length	Fresnel Zone Radius R1 at Path Midpoint
0.5 miles	16 feet
1.0 miles	23 feet
2.0 miles	33 feet
5.0 miles	52 feet
10.0 miles	72 feet

TIP You can find more information about the Fresnel Zone calculation at wikipedia.org. A Fresnel Zone calculator is also available from First Mile Wireless at http://www.firstmilewireless.com/calc_fresnel.html.

RF Signal Strength Terminology

Because so many variables exist in a wireless environment, being able to quantify an RF signal as it is transmitted and received is handy. Other factors that affect the signal strength can be taken into account, too.

An RF signal can be measured as a function of its power or energy in units of Watts (W) or milliWatts (mW)—one milliWatt is one-thousandth of one Watt. To put signal power into perspective, Table 17-3 shows typical power output from a variety of sources.

Table 17-3 *Sample RF Power Output*

Source	Power Output
Shortwave radio station	500,000 W
AM radio station	50,000 W
Microwave oven (2.4 GHz)	600–1000 W
Cell phone	200 mW
Wireless LAN AP (2.4 GHz)	1–100 mW

Power values can vary over such a wide range that making comparisons or computations is difficult. The *decibel (dB)* is a more flexible way to deal with power quantities for two reasons:

■ dB measures a *ratio* of actual power to a known reference power

■ dB is logarithmic, representing a wide range of values on a linear scale

To compute a power ratio in dB, use the following formula:

$$dB = 10\log_{10}\left(\frac{P_{sig}}{P_{ref}}\right)$$

Here, P_{sig} is the actual signal power and P_{ref} is the reference power. Most often, a reference power of 1.0 mW or 1.0 W is used. In those cases, the decibel abbreviation also changes to reflect the reference power:

■ **dBm**—The signal power is compared to 1 mW (the "m" in dBm reflects the "m" in milliWatt)

■ **dBw**—The signal power is compared to 1 W

You will commonly see dBm used with wireless LANs because the power used is around 100 mW or less. As an example, suppose that a wireless AP transmits at 100 mW. In dB, the output power would be represented as $10\log_{10}(100 \text{ mW}/1 \text{ mW})$ or 20 dBm.

If the output power was decreased to 1 mW, the result would be $10\log_{10}(1 \text{ mW}/1 \text{ mW})$ or 0 dBm. Therefore, 0 dBm always represents an output power that is equal to the reference power.

So far in this discussion, dB values have all been positive numbers. Positive dB values result from power values that are *greater than* the reference power. Most often, transmitter power levels will have positive dBm values because they are stronger than the reference.

dB values can also be negative. This doesn't mean that a negative amount of power is produced—rather, it means a power level that is less than the reference. For example, a signal power of 0.5 mW would result in $10\log_{10}(0.5 \text{ mW}/1 \text{ mW})$ or -3 dBm.

> **TIP** Notice that the sample power of 0.5 mW is half of the previous example, 1.0 mW. The dB value changed from 0 to approximately -3 dB, respectively. This change is significant because it demonstrates an important rule of thumb:
>
> ■ *Whenever a power value is halved, the dB change is approximately -3.*
>
> ■ *Whenever the power doubles, the dB change is approximately $+3$.*

Negative dBm values are often given for receivers, rather than transmitters. This is because receivers must be very sensitive to low signal levels (much lower than the 1 mW reference power) so that poor signals can be received with clarity. Receiver power levels are referred to as receiver sensitivity.

Signal Loss

Whenever an RF signal leaves the transmitter, even before it reaches the antenna, it is subject to outside influences that will reduce its strength. This is known as *signal loss*.

Signal loss can come from any of the following:

■ Cable loss from the transmitter to the antenna

■ Free space loss as the signal travels through the air

■ External obstacles

■ External noise or interference

■ Cable loss from the receiver's antenna to the receiver

Notice that this list covers conditions as they are encountered along the signal path from transmitter to receiver. The losses are actually cumulative, working together to degrade the signal. The total loss end-to-end is known as the *path loss*.

In an indoor wireless LAN environment, the antenna cabling distances are so short they are negligible. Typically, the antennas are built right onto the wireless adapters or within a portable PC, or directly connected to the RF electronics in an AP. The majority of path loss is due to physical objects in a room or building and the distance between the AP and a wireless client.

Outdoor environments can experience losses with components from all the factors listed. In a line-of-sight wireless path, the cables between APs and their antennas can be quite long. External objects might not be an issue if the path has been carefully selected. External interference can be a problem due to other nearby wireless installations, conflicts over channel use, or antennas that aren't aligned carefully.

In any environment, free-space loss is significant. The power of any RF transmission is inversely proportional to the square of the distance from the source. This simply means that the level of the received signal falls off rapidly as the receiver moves away from the transmitter.

For example, Table 17-4 shows how the dB level decreases as the distance increases. The dBm values shown are relative   you should notice that as the distance increases by 10 times, the signal drops by 20 dBm. As the distance increases by 100 times, the signal drops by 40 dBm.

Table 17-4 *Relative Signal Loss Due to Distance*

Distance	Relative Power	Relative Level (dBm)
1 m	100 mW	+20 dBm
5 m	4.0 mW	+6 dBm
10 m	1.0 mW	0 dBm
25 m	0.16 mW	–8 dBm
50 m	0.04 mW	–14 dBm
100 m	0.01 mW	–20 dBm

A receiver can be located too far from the transmitter to receive an intelligible signal. It can also be located behind too many objects that absorb or distort the signal. For example, even ordinary building materials such as drywall, block or concrete walls, wooden or metal doors, door frames, and windows can contribute to signal loss. Some sources estimate that within 100 meters from an AP in an office environment, a wireless signal can have a loss of 100 dBm! Because of this, performing a site survey that is based on a live WLAN signal in the actual physical environment is always a good idea.

Signal Gain

An RF signal can also be influenced by factors that actually increase its strength over a path. Signal gain can be produced by any of the following:

- Antenna gain at the transmitter

- Antenna gain at the receiver

An antenna can't create or add power to a signal by itself. How can it have gain? First, consider a transmitter antenna. Its gain is just a measure of how well the antenna can take the RF signal and project it in a specific direction.

However, antennas can be designed to favor different directions or patterns. Is one antenna better than another simply because it focuses a signal in one direction over another? Not necessarily. Typically, one antenna has more gain than another if it can focus the RF energy into a narrower pattern. As a result, antennas with higher gains are usually able to operate over longer distances.

The antenna gain is just a way to gauge how well the signal energy is focused, in comparison to an antenna that can't focus energy at all. An *isotropic* antenna is such an antenna—a theoretical model that is shaped like a small dot. It propagates a signal in all directions equally, in a spherical pattern. Its inability to focus the RF energy makes it the standard for comparison.

Antenna gain is usually given in dBi, which is computed exactly like dBm. The only difference is that the reference power comes from an isotropic antenna (hence the "i").

Wireless Path Performance

Often you will see settings or ratings of transmit power on an AP. This rating is usually the power measured at the output of the transmitter, without an antenna or cabling. The actual power of the transmitted signal will depend on the type of antenna used and the length of the antenna cable.

A much more realistic rating is the *Effective Isotropic Radiated Power (EIRP)*. To compute the EIRP, add the transmitter power (in dBm) to the transmit antenna gain (in dBi) and subtract any cabling loss (in dB).

For example, a transmitter power of 100 mW (20 dBm) connects to an antenna with a 16 dBi gain using a cable that has 3 dB loss. The EIRP of the transmitter system is 20 dBm + 16 dBi – 3 dB = 33 dBm.

To design a complete wireless system, you have to consider more than the power of the transmitter or AP. Instead, you need to account for every component that will add gain or subtract loss, from one end of the wireless link to the other.

The simplest way to determine the path performance or overall gain is to add all the gain or loss dB values. You can use the following formula as a rule of thumb:

System Gain = Transmit Power (dBm)
              + Transmit Antenna Gain (dBi)
              + Receive Antenna Gain (dBi)
              – Transmit Cable Loss (dB)
              – Receive Cable Loss (dB)
              – Receiver Sensitivity (dB)

Notice here that the receiver sensitivity is considered to be a loss and is subtracted. The receiver sensitivity represents the minimum threshold that must be overcome in order to have a usable signal. Therefore, that threshold must be subtracted to see the remaining gain that is available.

The range of a wireless link is determined by the overall path performance. When the total path loss becomes equal or greater than the total path gain, the receiver will be out of range.

WLAN Antennas

A variety of antennas suited for wireless LANs are available. Each type of antenna is designed for a specific application, either due to its ability to cover a certain area or pattern, or its capability to add gain to the signal.

Omnidirectional Antennas

Omnidirectional antennas, such as the one shown in Figure 17-18, can be made in the shape of a thin cylinder. The "rubber duckie"-style antenna that is pictured can be folded up or down, depending on how the AP is mounted. Other omnidirectional antennas include the dipole, which is also a slender cylinder, found embedded in several AP models.

Figure 17-18 *An Omnidirectional Antenna and Its Coverage Pattern*

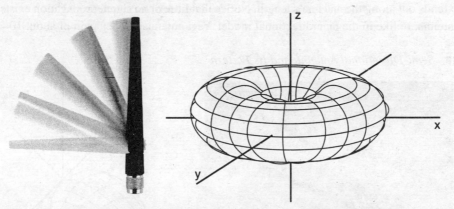

An omnidirectional antenna tends to propagate a signal equally in all directions in one plane, but not along the antenna's length. The result is a donut-shaped pattern as shown on the right portion of Figure 17-18. This type of antenna is well suited for broad coverage of a large room or floor area where the AP or its antenna is located in the center.

Because the omnidirectional antenna distributes the RF energy along a broad area, it has a low gain of about 2 dBi.

> **TIP** Sometimes an RF signal will be delayed or distorted due to reflection, refraction, or diffraction. When the affected signal arrives along with the original signal at the receiver, the two signals can tend to cancel each other. As a result, the receiver has a drop in signal level or no signal at all. When a signal competes with other copies of itself that have taken different paths, *multipath interference* results.
>
> To fix this problem, the receiver's antenna can simply be moved a short distance (about a one-half wavelength) to receive a better signal. Many APs have two omnidirectional antennas by default—these are correctly spaced so that one antenna or the other will always receive the best signal. The use of two antennas simultaneously is referred to as *diversity*.

Semi-Directional Antennas

Semi-directional antennas cover a broad elongated area, and are well suited to cover rooms along a long hallway, where the antenna is located at one end of the area. They can also be used to cover broad outdoor areas out away from a building.

Wall-mounted patch antennas have a flat rectangular shape, so that they can be mounted on a wall at the end of a hallway. Patch antennas produce a broad egg-shaped pattern that extends away from the flat patch. These antennas have a gain of about 6–8 dBi.

The wall or mast-mounted Yagi antenna shown in Figure 17-19 is shaped like a thick cylinder, but is made up of several parallel elements. It produces a more focused egg-shaped pattern that extends out along the antenna's length. Notice that little or no signal propagation exists behind the antenna, unlike in the omnidirectional model. Yagi antennas have a gain of about 10–14 dBi.

Figure 17-19 *Semi-Directional Antenna and Its Pattern*

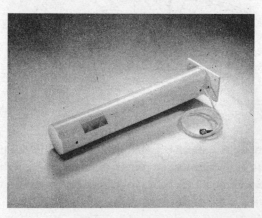
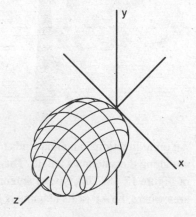

Highly Directional Antennas

In a line-of-sight wireless path, an RF signal must be propagated a long distance using a narrow beam. Highly directional antennas are tailored for that use, but focus the RF energy along one narrow elliptical pattern. Because the target is only one receiver location, the antenna doesn't have to cover any area outside of the line of sight. This type of antenna is well suited for building-to-building or site-to-site links, where the two AP or antenna locations are separated by a long distance.

Dish antennas, such as the one shown in Figure 17-20, use a parabolic dish to focus received signals onto an antenna mounted at the center. Notice how the antenna's coverage pattern is long and narrow, extending out away from the dish. The focused pattern gives the antenna a gain of around 22 dBi—the highest gain of all the wireless LAN antennas.

Figure 17-20 *A Highly Directional Dish Antenna and Its Coverage Pattern*

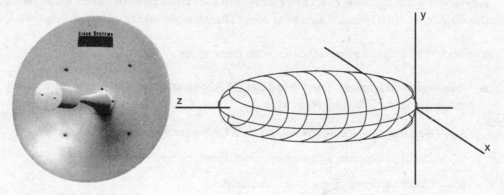

WLAN Standards

All the wireless LAN standards are collected in the IEEE 802.11 series. Every wireless device must adhere to one or more of these standards so that it can work with other wireless devices.

The 802.11 standards define wireless LAN operation at Layers 1 and 2. This includes the wireless frequencies and channels, as well as throughput, security, and mobility. Several of the basic standards are covered in the sections that follow.

Regulatory Agencies

The wireless LAN frequency bands are unlicensed, allowing anyone to use them without applying for a license. However, they are still regulated by various agencies that establish rules about which frequencies are available and how much signal power can be used.

For example, in the U.S., the Federal Communications Commission (FCC, http://www.fcc.gov) regulates wireless frequency use.

Other agencies are responsible for developing wireless standards that are accepted internationally. These include the Institute of Electrical and Electronics Engineers (IEEE, http://www.ieee.org), which developed the 802.11 standards, and the European Telecommunications Standard Institute (ETSI, http://www.etsi.org).

Still other organizations work to provide helpful information for wireless developers and users. The Wi-Fi Alliance (http://www.wi-fi.com), formerly named the Wireless Ethernet Compatibility Alliance (WECA), focuses on interoperability testing across vendors and platforms. The WLAN Association (WLANA, http://www.wlana.org) is a nonprofit educational trade association that provides information about Wireless LANs and applications to the public.

WLAN Frame Types and Sizes

Any device adhering to the 802.11 standards must use certain types of frames to communicate on the WLAN. Some frames are used by wireless clients, while others are suited only for AP use.

You should be acquainted with the following frame types:

■ **Management frames**—Used to manage WLAN advertisement and client membership; these can include the following frame types:

— Beacons announcing the AP and its WLAN parameters

— Client association, reassociation, and disassociation

— Client authentication and deauthentication

■ **Control frames**—Used to control client associations with the AP; these can include the following frame types:

— Probe request and response, when a client requests information about an AP

— RTS and CTS messages when the AP must intervene on behalf of clients announcing frame duration values

■ **Data frames**—Sent from any wireless device; contains general data or payload information

WLAN frames have a 32-byte header and a 4-byte frame check sequence (FCS) trailer. Source and destination addresses contained in the frames are always 48-bit MAC addresses, just as 802.3 Ethernet uses.

When management frames are sent, they always include a 48-bit Basic Service Set Identifier (BSSID) field. Recall that a BSS must have an AP as the central hub, connecting all the clients. The BSSID is simply the AP's MAC address, which uniquely identifies the collection of devices serviced by that AP.

802.11b

The 802.11b standard defines WLAN use in the 2.4-GHz band (2.4 to 2.5 GHz). The FCC has permitted WLAN use only in the specific range of 2.4000 to 2.4835 GHz.

TIP   It is interesting to note that the FCC considers the primary users in the 2.4-GHz band to be devices such as microwave ovens. WLAN devices are considered secondary users, and must always allow a primary user to overpower them whenever necessary. You might have experienced this when the WLAN in your office became unusable while someone cooked their popcorn.

The 2.4-GHz band is known as an Industrial, Scientific, and Medical (ISM) band. It consists of 14 channels, each 22 MHz wide. How do wireless APs and clients separate the channels?

802.11b Channels

The 802.11b standard defines a *spectral mask*, or a template that is used to filter out a single channel based around a center frequency. As shown in Figure 17-21, at 11 MHz on either side of the center, the signal must drop off to –30 dBr. This forms the basis of the 22 MHz-wide channel. The signal is also allowed to extend further, but must drop off to –50 dB at 22 MHz on each side of the center.

Figure 17-21   *802.11 Channel Spectral Mask*

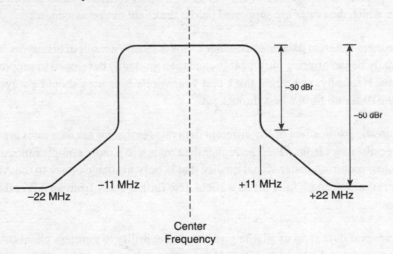

Notice that the entire band covers 2.4000 to 2.4835 GHz, and is 0.0835 GHz or 83.5 MHz wide. That leaves room for only 83.5/22 MHz or approximately 3.8 entire channels. How then are there 14 channels in the band?

The channels are actually centered on 5 MHz intervals, not on 22 MHz as you might expect. This causes the channels to overlap each other almost completely. A problem arises if two wireless stations try to use adjacent channels—their signals will bleed over into each other's channel, disrupting both channels.

The solution is to use as many channels as possible that don't overlap each other at all. This leaves only channels 1, 6, and 11 as illustrated in Figure 17-22.

Figure 17-22 *Three Non-Overlapping Channels: 1, 6, and 11*

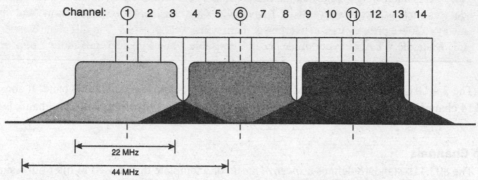

802.11b Data Rates

Devices operating on 802.11b typically use Direct Sequence Spread Spectrum (DSSS) modulation. The data rates on a channel can vary according to client capabilities and conditions. However, the only possible data rates are 1, 2, 5.5, and 11 Mbps. A wireless client and the AP must both agree on which data rates are supported before the client can be associated.

Why are there different data rates available? This is mostly a result of history, as 802.11b evolved. It originally began offering only 1 Mbps, and then gradually developed to support the increasing data rates. Naturally, you might think that your wireless devices should always operate at the maximum data rate for the best throughput.

One interesting side effect of the different data rates is that higher data rates are only successful at shorter distances from APs. The higher data rates use a more complex modulation than the lower rates, requiring better signal quality that is only available closer to the AP. As you might imagine, signal strength falls off as a client gets further away from an AP, and the noise level increases.

Having several data rates available gives some flexibility to wireless clients. As a portable client moves around in an AP cell, its data rate can change based on the current signal conditions. This is known as *dynamic data rate scaling*. When the client moves away from the AP and the signal quality drops below a certain threshold, it can "downshift" from 11 Mbps to 5.5 Mbps, 2 Mbps, or even 1 Mbps—as long as the AP will allow those data rates to be used within the cell.

> **TIP**   If an AP offers 1, 2, 5.5, and 11 Mbps, can only one data rate be used for an entire AP cell? With 802.11b, the answer is no; any of the data rates can be used with a mix of clients. Remember that only one station can transmit over the channel at any given time. However, the data rates can shift on a per-frame basis, based on the needs of the transmitting or receiving client.

802.11g

The 802.11g standard builds upon the 802.11b foundation by offering much higher data rates, with much more complex modulation techniques. It is also backward compatible with 802.11b, allowing devices using either standard to work together.

Devices using 802.11g operate on the same 2.4-GHz band as 802.11b. As well, the same three nonoverlapping 22-MHz channels (1, 6, and 11) are used.

Native 802.11g uses a modulation technique called *Orthogonal Frequency Division Multiplexing (OFDM)*. Devices can support data rates of 6, 9, 12, 18, 24, 36, 48, and 54 Mbps—quite an improvement over that of 802.11b.

However, to be backward compatible with a device that can use only 802.11b, the 802.11b modulation and data rates of 1, 2, 5.5, and 11 Mbps can be used instead.

> **TIP** You should be aware that backward compatibility with 802.11b has a downside. The 802.11g and 802.11b modulations can't be used simultaneously within an AP cell. If a mix of clients is present, the modulation that is common across them will be used.
>
> This means if even one 802.11b client associates to an 802.11g AP, and the AP permits 802.11b operation, the *entire* AP cell must shift to 802.11b mode! Even though the 802.11g cell could be using up to the 54-Mbps data rate, it will be limited to 11 Mbps.

The 802.11g standard also allows dynamic data rate scaling. Clients can use the 54-Mbps data rate when they are at close range to an AP, and can shift down to lower data rates as they move further away.

802.11a

The 802.11a standard defines WLAN use in the 5-GHz Unlicensed National Information Infrastructure (U-NII) band. Actually the FCC has broken that band up into three separate smaller bands for specific uses:

- **Lower band: 5.15 to 5.25 GHz**—Indoor use

- **Middle band: 5.25 to 5.35 GHz**—Indoor and outdoor use

- **Upper band: 5.725 to 5.825 GHz**—Outdoor use

Within each of these bands, 802.11a uses four nonoverlapping channels of 20-MHz each. This means it is possible to use 4, 8, or even 12 nonoverlapping channels in a WLAN environment. You might need more channels at your disposal if you need a high density of APs, for example.

The 802.11a standard allows dynamic data rate scaling, using 6, 9, 12, 18, 24, 36, 48, and 54 Mbps. Even at the 54-Mbps data rate, the typical maximum throughput is 28 Mbps. As with 802.11b and

802.11g, the higher data rates are possible at a close range to the AP. As a client moves away from the AP, successively slower data rates must be used.

> **TIP**   Even though 802.11a shares the same data rates and modulation techniques with 802.11g, the two standards are not compatible. In fact, 802.11a is not compatible with either 802.11b or 802.11g because the frequency bands are completely different.
>
> Both 802.11a and 802.11b/g devices can coexist in the same area as long as there are APs that serve each standard independently.

Additional 802.11 Standards

The IEEE has developed additional standards under the 802.11 wireless LAN umbrella. Although they are not covered in the BCMSN course or exam, you should be aware that the following standards exist:

- **802.11e**—Covers quality of service (QoS) for WLANs

- **802.11i**—Covers security enhancements

- **802.11n**—Covers improvements for higher throughput

Foundation Summary

The Foundation Summary is a collection of information that provides a convenient review of many key concepts in this chapter. If you are already comfortable with the topics in this chapter, this summary can help you recall a few details. If you just read this chapter, this review should help solidify some key facts. If you are doing your final preparation before the exam, this information will hopefully be a convenient way to review the day before the exam.

Table 17-5 *Quick Comparison of Wireless and Wired LANs*

Attribute	Wireless	Wired
IEEE standard set	802.11	802.3
Shared medium management	CSMA/CA (collision avoidance)	CSMA/CD (collision detection)
Duplex modes supported	Half	Half or full

Table 17-6 *Wireless LAN Service Set Acronyms*

Acronym	Description
IBSS	Independent basic service set; wireless devices communicating directly, without an AP; also known as *ad-hoc mode*
BSS	Basic service set; wireless clients communicating by way of a single AP
ESS	Extended service set; multiple BSSs that are interconnected to form a larger network
SSID	Service set identifier; a string identifying the AP(s) and clients belonging to a common logical WLAN

Table 17-7 *AP Coverage Terminology*

Term	Description
Cell	The general area or range covered by a single AP
Microcell	Relatively small cell size used to control client density
Picocell	Special application where every AP has a very small cell size; used to offer high bandwidth and low client density

Table 17-8 *RF Signal Terminology*

Term	Description
Carrier or center frequency	The constant, principal frequency at which the signal oscillates
Modulation	Additional changes to the carrier frequency that encodes information
Band	The entire frequency range that is set aside for a specific use
Channel	A small frequency range that is used for a single transmission; channels always have a numbered index

Table 17-9 *RF Signal Characteristics*

Cause	Effect
Reflection	Signal bounces or reflects off an object at the same angle as it began
Refraction	Signal passes through an object, but at a different angle
Absorption	Signal is absorbed or attenuated by an object, reducing its strength or power
Scattering	Signal is scattered into many different directions by a rough or irregular object surface
Diffraction	Signal bends around an object
Fresnel zone	Elliptical shaped volume around a line-of-sight path that must remain clear of objects; otherwise, signal can be diffracted and adversely affected

Table 17-10 *RF Power Terminology*

Term	Description
Power	Amount of energy present in an RF signal
W or mW	Watt or milliWatt, units of power
dB	Decibel, a ratio of actual to reference power: $dB = 10*\log(P_{actual}/P_{reference})$
dBm	Signal power as compared to a 1 mW reference signal
dBi	Antenna power gain as compared to an isotropic antenna
−3 dB	Rule of thumb: Signal is reduced by 3 dB when its power is cut in half
+3 dB	Rule of thumb: Signal is increased by 3 dB when its power is doubled
EIRP	Effective isotropic radiated power, or the net power provided at the transmitter antenna; add transmitter power (dBm) to the transmit antenna gain (dBi) and subtract transmit cabling loss (dB)

Table 17-11 *RF Signal Path Performance or Power Budget Calculation*

System Gain =	Transmit Power (dBm)
	+ Transmit Antenna Gain (dBi)
	+ Receive Antenna Gain (dBi)
	– Transmit Cable Loss (dB)
	– Receive Cable Loss (dB)
	– Receiver Sensitivity (dB)

Table 17-12 *Antenna Types and Attributes*

Antenna	Typical Gain	Pattern and Use
Omnidirectional (dipole or AP internal)	2 dBi	Round, centered about the antenna; used to cover area around an AP
Semi-directional (patch or Yagi)	6–8 dBi	Elongated, starting at the antenna; used to cover long area down a hallway or away from a wall
Highly directional (dish)	22 dBi	Narrow beam, starting at the antenna; used in line-of-sight signal paths

Table 17-13 *IEEE 802.11 Standards Used in WLANs*

	802.11b	802.11g	802.11a
Band	2.4 GHz	2.4 GHz	5 GHz in 3 bands
Channel Width	22 MHz	22 MHz	20 MHz
Number of Channels	14 (3 non-overlapping)	14 (3 non-overlapping)	4 nonoverlapping in each of 3 bands
Modulation	DSSS	DSSS and OFDM	OFDM
Data Rates	1, 2, 5.5, 11 Mbps	802.11g mode: 6, 9, 12, 18, 24, 36, 48, and 54 Mbps 802.11b mode: 1, 2, 5.5, and 11 Mbps	6, 9, 12, 18, 24, 36, 48, and 54 Mbps
Maximum Actual Throughput	6 Mbps	22 Mbps	28 Mbps

Q&A

The questions and scenarios in this book are more difficult than what you should experience on the actual exam. The questions do not attempt to cover more breadth or depth than the exam; however, they are designed to make sure that you know the answers. Rather than allowing you to derive the answers from clues hidden inside the questions themselves, the questions challenge your understanding and recall of the subject. Hopefully, these questions will help limit the number of exam questions on which you narrow your choices to two options and then guess.

You can find the answers to these questions in Appendix A.

1. What duplex modes can be used when a wireless client joins the wireless LAN?

2. How many nonoverlapping channels are available in 802.1g networks? Why?

3. Can a wireless network experience collisions? If so, how do the wireless devices handle them?

4. How does a wireless client know how long to wait before trying to transmit a frame?

5. Name three types of wireless service set and their functions.

6. Suppose that a wireless client just arrives within range of an access point. Can the client begin using the wireless LAN?

7. An AP can bridge a VLAN to a wireless LAN. How can it bridge more than one VLAN to the wireless LAN?

8. What is implied by saying that two wireless devices use the same channel?

9. Name two standards that operate in the same band. Then name two wireless LAN standards that operate in different bands.

10. Suppose that a wireless client is associated to a nearby AP. If a person came and stood between the client's antenna and the AP, what effect might this have on the signal?

11. Suppose that you are designing a wireless LAN and you need to choose the location of an AP for a group of wireless clients. The AP will be using an omnidirectional antenna. Should you consider the Fresnel zone in your decision?

12. What transmit power would an AP be delivering if it had a power level of 0 dBm?

13. Name some things that can cause RF signal loss.

14.   Briefly describe antenna gain. What is different about a dish antenna versus an omnidirectional antenna?

15.   What data rates are supported by the IEEE 802.11b standard?

16.   What is the maximum supported data rates in IEEE 802.11b and 802.11g?

17.   What is the maximum data rate available in an 802.11g wireless LAN when there is a mix of 802.11g and 802.11b clients?

This chapter covers the following topics that you need to master for the CCNP BCMSN exam:

- **WLAN Security**—This section presents an overview of the various methods for protecting a WLAN. These methods can be used to authenticate potential wireless clients and users, as well as to secure the data passing over the wireless medium.

- **Wireless Client Operation**—This section explains the Cisco Compatible Extensions program and how it is used to find wireless hardware with compatible feature sets.

- **AP Association and Roaming**—This section covers the process that wireless clients and access points use to form associations or logical connections. As wireless clients become mobile, their associations can be moved to other access points. This forms the basis of client roaming.

- **Cell Layout and Channel Usage**—This section discusses the theory behind sizing and positioning access points so that they can work together to cover a large area. Part of this layout process is the assignment of RF channels and their distribution over the access point population.

Wireless Architecture and Design

"Do I Know This Already?" Quiz

The purpose of the "Do I Know This Already?" quiz is to help you decide what parts of this chapter to use. If you already intend to read the entire chapter, you do not necessarily need to answer these questions now.

The quiz, derived from the major sections in the "Foundation Topics" portion of the chapter, helps you determine how to spend your limited study time.

Table 18-1 outlines the major topics discussed in this chapter and the "Do I Know This Already?" quiz questions that correspond to those topics.

Table 18-1 *"Do I Know This Already?" Foundation Topics Section-to-Question Mapping*

Foundation Topics Section	Questions Covered in This Section	Score
WLAN Security	1–5	
Wireless Client Operation	6	
AP Association and Roaming	7–10	
Cell Layout and Channel Usage	11–12	
Total Score		

CAUTION The goal of self-assessment is to gauge your mastery of the topics in this chapter. If you do not know the answer to a question or are only partially sure of the answer, you should mark this question wrong. Giving yourself credit for an answer you correctly guess skews your self-assessment results and might give you a false sense of security.

1. If WPA or WPA2 is used as a wireless security suite, which one of the following represents a feature that is not offered in other wireless security methods?

    a. Virus mitigation

    b. Packet authentication

    c. Strong password policy

    d. Session time limits

2. If WPA is used, how often can the encryption keys be generated?

    a. One key per AP association

    b. One key per client session

    c. One key per packet

    d. One key per minute

3. TKIP is a protocol that is used with WPA to do which one of the following functions?

    a. Negotiate static WEP keys

    b. Generate per-packet encryption keys

    c. Authenticate a wireless user

    d. Authenticate wireless packets

4. Most wireless security methods use which one of the following as the authentication mechanism?

    a. 802.1D

    b. 802.11x

    c. RADIUS

    d. 802.1X

5. Which one of the following is a security feature that is unique to WPA2?

    a. AES encryption

    b. 3DES encryption

    c. WEP encryption

    d. Token-based encryption

6. Which one of the following can be used to verify feature compatibility between wireless devices?

    a. IEEE 802.11b

    b. IEEE 802.11e

    c. CCX

    d. CCO

7. Which one of the following determines when a wireless client will roam from one AP to another?

    a. The current AP has a weak signal from the client and asks it to roam

    b. The next AP overhears the client and asks it to roam

    c. The client's roaming algorithm reaches a threshold

    d. The client loses its IP address

8. Which one of the following is moved when a wireless client roams to a new AP?

    a. Association

    b. Certificate

    c. Beacon

    d. Channel

9. When a wireless client is actively roaming, which one of the following actions does it take?

    a. It listens for 802.11 beacons

    b. It listens for 802.11 Roam advertisements

    c. It sends an 802.11 Roam Request

    d. It sends an 802.11 Probe Request

10. Wireless client roaming from AP to AP normally occurs at what layer of the OSI model?

    a. Layer 1

    b. Layer 2

    c. Layer 3

    d. Layer 4

11. Which channels should be used across the 802.11b APs that are covering a floor of a building?

    a. 1, 2, 3

    b. 1, 3, 6

    c. 1, 3, 6, 11

    d. 1, 6, 11

    e. Any channel is fine

12. When you are designing the AP channel layout for an area, which one of the following is the most important consideration?

    a. The number of channels is conserved

    b. APs in different areas use different channels

    c. Adjacent APs use nonoverlapping channels

    d. Clients are grouped into common channels

The answers to the "Do I Know This Already?" quiz are found in Appendix A, "Answers to Chapter 'Do I Know This Already?' Quizzes and Q&A Sections." The suggested choices for your next step are as follows:

- **10 or less overall score**—Read the entire chapter. This includes the "Foundation Topics," "Foundation Summary," and "Q&A" sections.

- **11 or more overall score**—If you want more review on these topics, skip to the "Foundation Summary" section and then go to the "Q&A" section at the end of the chapter. Otherwise, move to Chapter 19, "Cisco Unified Wireless Network."

Foundation Topics

WLAN Security

As the central hub of a Basic Service Set (BSS), an AP effectively manages the WLAN for all clients within its range. Remember that all traffic going to or from a wireless client must go *through* the AP to reach other WLAN clients in the BSS or wired clients located elsewhere as illustrated in Figure 18-1. Clients cannot communicate directly with each other.

Figure 18-1 *An AP Serving as the Central Point of Contact in a WLAN*

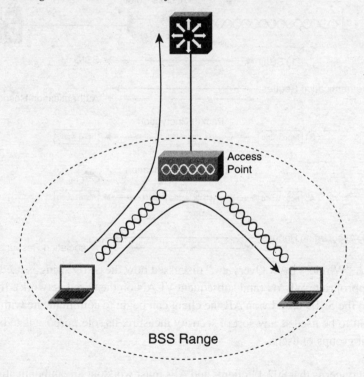

The AP is a natural place to implement various forms of security. For instance, an AP can control WLAN membership by authenticating clients. If a client fails to authenticate itself successfully, it won't be allowed to use the wireless network. As well, the AP and its clients can work together to secure the data that is passed between them. Otherwise, data sent over the air might be intercepted and exploited.

As a client brings up its wireless connection, it must find an AP that is reachable and that will approve its membership. The client must negotiate its membership and security measures in the following sequence, as shown in Figure 18-2:

1. Use an SSID that matches the AP

2. Authenticate with the AP

3. *(optional)* Use a packet encryption method (data privacy)

4. *(optional)* Use a packet authentication method (data integrity)

5. Build an association with the AP

Figure 18-2 *Basic Processes of Securing a Wireless LAN Connection*

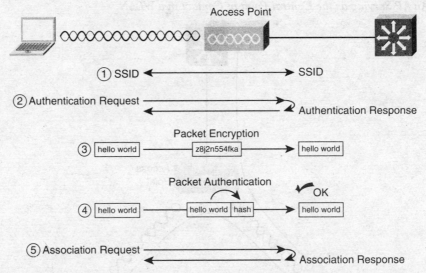

Chapter 17, "Wireless LAN Overview," discussed how the SSID string is used to match clients with the appropriate WLAN (and subsequent VLAN on the wired network). If a client's SSID is identical to the SSID used by an AP, the client can begin to communicate with the AP. The SSID is not meant to be used as any sort of security measure; its sole purpose is to break up a WLAN into logical groups of users.

Two basic concerns that 802.11 clients and APs must work out are authentication and encryption. Many different methods are available for authentication, encryption, and a combination of the two. The sections that follow briefly describe these methods.

Legacy Security

In 802.11 networks, clients can authenticate with an AP using one of the following methods:

■ **Open authentication**—No authentication method is used; any client is offered open access to the AP.

- **Pre-shared key (PSK)**—The same secret key is statically defined on the client and the AP. If the keys match, the client is permitted to have access.

Notice that the authentication process in these two methods stops at the AP. In other words, the AP has enough information on its own to independently determine which clients can or can't have access. Open authentication and PSK are considered to be legacy methods because they are not scalable and are not necessarily secure.

Open authentication is usually the default, and offers no client screening whatsoever. Any client is permitted to join the network without presenting any credentials. In effect, the SSID is the only credential that is required! Although this makes life easier, it doesn't do much to control access to the WLAN. In addition, open authentication doesn't provide a means to encrypt data sent over the WLAN.

Pre-shared key authentication uses a long Wireless Equivalence Protocol (WEP) key that is stored on the client and the AP. When a client wants to join the WLAN, the AP presents it with a challenge phrase. The client must use the challenge phrase and the WEP key to compute a value that can be shared publicly. That value is sent back to the AP. The AP uses its own WEP key to compute a similar value; if the two values are identical, the client is authenticated.

When pre-shared key authentication (commonly called *static WEP keys*) is used, the WEP key also serves as an encryption key. As each packet is sent over the WLAN, its contents and the WEP key are fed into a cryptographic process. When the packet is received at the far end, the contents are unencrypted using the same WEP key.

Pre-shared key authentication is more secure than open authentication, but it has two shortcomings:

- It doesn't scale well because a long key string must be configured into every device.

- It isn't very secure.

As you might expect, a static key persists for a very long time, until someone manually reconfigures a new key. The longer a key remains in use, the longer malicious users can gather data derived from it and eventually reverse-engineer the key. It is commonly known that static WEP keys can be broken, so this method is not recommended.

EAP-Based Security Methods

Fortunately, wireless security has evolved to use other more robust methods. APs can use a variety of authentication methods that leverage external authentication and authorization servers and their user databases.

The Extensible Authentication Protocol (EAP) forms the basis for many wireless security methods—most of which have similar acronyms that rhyme, such as EAP, PEAP, and LEAP. EAP is defined in RFC 3748, and was originally designed to handle user authentication for PPP users.

Because it is extensible, it is well suited for a variety of security environments. RFC 4017 covers the EAP variants that are used in WLANs.

EAP has its history in PPP communication—not in wireless authentication. Chapter 15, "Securing Switch Access," described the IEEE 802.1x protocol as port-based authentication, or the means to authenticate users to use switch ports. Through 802.1x, users can authenticate even at Layer 2, before gaining further network connectivity. WLANs can leverage 802.1x as the means to implement EAP at Layer 2 for wireless clients.

In a wireless LAN, you can find some of the following security method names: LEAP, PEAP, EAP-TLS, and EAP-FAST. So many different methods exist that becoming confused about what they are and what they do is easy. Just remember that each one is based on EAP and uses a different type of credentials to authenticate wireless users.

Some of the EAP-based methods go beyond authentication by adding extra security features, as you will see as each method is discussed in the following sections.

LEAP

Cisco developed a protocol called Lightweight EAP (LEAP or EAP-Cisco) to address some shortcomings in 802.11 security. With LEAP, an AP uses an external Remote Authentication Dial-In User Server/Service (RADIUS) server to handle the actual client authentication. In fact, the AP and wireless client authenticate each other using a challenge and response exchange through the RADIUS server. Usernames and passwords are used as credentials.

LEAP also addresses wireless data privacy by assisting with WEP key assignment. A unique WEP key is dynamically generated by the RADIUS server for each wireless client. This process provides fresh encryption key material on a per-client basis, each time the client authenticates, and eliminates the need to manually configure static WEP keys altogether.

EAP-TLS

The EAP-TLS method, defined in RFC 2716, uses the Transport Layer Security (TLS) protocol to secure client authentication. TLS is based on Secure Socket Layer (SSL), which is commonly used in secure web browser sessions. EAP-TLS uses digital certificates as authentication credentials, which means that every AP and wireless client must have a certificate generated and signed by a common certificate authority (CA).

EAP-TLS also addresses wireless data privacy by generating WEP keys automatically, each time the authentication server forces the client to reauthenticate. The TLS session key, unique to each wireless client that is authenticating, is used to derive a unique WEP key. The WEP key is then used to encrypt the wireless data.

PEAP

Protected EAP (PEAP or EAP-PEAP) is similar to EAP-TLS in that a TLS session is used to secure the authentication. PEAP requires a digital certificate only on the authentication server so that the server itself can be authenticated to the client. The wireless clients are authenticated using Microsoft Challenge Handshake Authentication Protocol version 2 (MSCHAPv2).

As with EAP-TLS, the TLS session key is used to derive a WEP key for encrypting the wireless data stream. The keys change periodically as the authentication server forces the client to reauthenticate.

EAP-FAST

EAP Flexible Authentication via Secure Tunneling (EAP-FAST) is a wireless security method developed by Cisco. EAP-FAST is not named for its speed; rather, it is named for its flexibility to reduce the administrative complexity. Clients aren't required to use digital certificates, and they aren't required to follow strict or strong password policies.

EAP-FAST works by building a secure tunnel between the client and the authentication server. A Protected Access Credential (PAC) is used as the only client credential to build the tunnel. The PAC can be assigned from a PAC server or it can be created dynamically during a phase of EAP-FAST negotiations. Once the tunnel is built, the client is authenticated using familiar username and password credentials.

EAP-FAST can derive a WEP key dynamically so that the wireless data stream can be encrypted.

WPA

The IEEE 802.11i standard focuses on addressing all aspects of wireless security—even beyond client authentication and data privacy using WEP keys. As the 802.11i standard was being developed, wireless LAN vendors have moved ahead to implement as many of its features as possible. As a result, the Wi-Fi Alliance developed *Wi-Fi Protected Access (WPA)* based on some of the 802.11 draft components.

WPA offers the following wireless LAN security measures:

- Client authentication using 802.1x or a pre-shared key

- Mutual client-server authentication

- Data privacy using Temporal Key Integrity Protocol (TKIP)

- Data integrity using Message Integrity Check (MIC)

TKIP leverages existing WEP encryption hardware that is embedded in wireless clients and APs. The WEP encryption process remains the same, but the WEP keys are generated much more frequently than the periodic reauthentications that occur with EAP-based authentication methods.

In fact, TKIP generates new WEP keys on a *per-packet* basis! An initial key is built as a client authenticates (or reauthenticates) with the EAP-based method. That key is formed by mixing the MAC address of the transmitter (the client or the AP) with a sequence number. Each time a packet is sent, the WEP key is incrementally updated. Once the client is forced to reauthenticate, an entirely new WEP key is built and the per-packet process repeats.

WPA can use a pre-shared key for authentication if external authentication servers aren't used or required. In that case, the pre-shared key is used only during the mutual authentication between the client and the AP. Data privacy or encryption doesn't use that pre-shared key at all. Instead, TKIP takes care of the rapid encryption key rotation for WEP encryption.

The MIC process is used to generate a "fingerprint" for each packet sent over the wireless network. If the fingerprint is made just before the packet is sent, the same fingerprint should match the packet contents once the packet is received. Why bother fingerprinting packets in the first place? When packets are sent over the air, they can be intercepted, modified, and re-sent—something that should never be allowed to happen. Fingerprinting is a way to protect the integrity of the data as it travels across a network.

For each packet, MIC generates a hash code (key), or a complex calculation that can only be generated in one direction. The MIC key uses the original unencrypted packet contents and the source and destination MAC addresses in its calculation, so that these values can't be tampered with along the way. As shown in Figure 18-2 under "Packet Authentication," the MIC hash key is added to the original packet so that the receiving end can examine the key and detect any tampering.

WPA2

Wi-Fi Protected Access version 2 (WPA2) is based on the final 802.11i standard. WPA2 goes several steps beyond WPA with its security measures.

For data encryption, the Advanced Encryption Standard (AES) is used. AES is a robust and scalable method that has been adopted by the National Institute of Standards and Technology (NIST, www.nist.gov) for use in the U.S. government organizations. TKIP is still supported for data encryption, for backward compatibility with WPA.

With WPA and other EAP-based authentication methods, a wireless client has to authenticate at each AP it visits. If a client is mobile, moving from AP to AP, the continuing authentication process can become cumbersome. WPA2 solves this problem by using proactive key caching (PKC). A client authenticates just once, at the first AP it encounters. As long as other APs visited support WPA2 and are configured as one logical group, the cached authentication and keys are passed automatically.

Wireless Client Operation

Wireless devices can be purchased from a variety of vendors, each with its own set of features and requirements. As well, wireless clients can exist as internal or external adapters installed in PC platforms. They can also be embedded in other devices such as cell phones, wireless phones, PDAs, medical devices, and tags used for location tracking. These are usually called *application-specific devices (ASDs)*.

If you use Cisco APs in your network, knowing whether each wireless device is indeed compatible with the features you plan to use would be nice. Cisco has developed the Cisco Compatible Extensions (CCX) program to address this need. Before a device can be CCX-compatible, it must be fully tested and verified to be compatible, which is especially handy when a pre-standard feature needs to be used, and you have no other guarantee that various vendors have implemented the feature in the same way.

As wireless LAN features have been introduced over time, the CCX program has evolved to include them. CCX is broken down into different versions, with each higher version containing all the features listed in lower versions. At press time, CCX version 4 was the most recent.

Table 18-2 breaks down the basic groups of features of the various CCX versions.

Table 18-2 *CCX Features*

CCX Version	Features Covered
CCXv1	Basic 802.11 and Wi-Fi compatibility 802.1X authentication for LEAP Multiple SSID use
CCXv2	WPA 802.1X authentication for PEAP Fast roaming with CCKM RF scanning for WLAN site survey and interference monitoring
CCXv3	WPA2, including AES encryption 802.1X authentication for EAP-FAST Wi-Fi Multimedia (WMM) as part of the 802.11e QoS standard
CCXv4	Cisco Network Admission Control (NAC) Call admission control for Voice over IP (VoIP) Reporting VoIP metrics Enhanced roaming 802.11 location tag functionality (radio frequency identification [RFID])

> **NOTE** You can find the latest CCX program details in the "Cisco Compatible Extensions Program for Wireless LAN (WLAN) Client Devices" document, at www.cisco.com/web/partners/pr46/pr147/partners_pgm_concept_home.html. The most current information on CCX versions can be found in "Cisco Compatible Extensions: Versions and Features" at www.cisco.com/web/partners/pr46/pr147/program_additional_information_new_release_features.html.

AP Association and Roaming

When a wireless client is associated with an AP, all data going to and from the client must pass through that AP. Recall from Chapter 17 that a client forms an association by sending an association request message to the AP. If the client is compatible with the WLAN by having the correct SSID, supporting the same data rates, and authenticating correctly, the AP responds with an association reply.

An association is maintained with the AP as long as the client stays within range of the AP. Consider the AP cell shown in Figure 18-3. As long as the client stays within points A and B, it is able to receive the AP's signal at an acceptable level. As soon as the client goes outside the cell range at point C, the signal strength falls below the acceptable threshold and the client loses the association.

Figure 18-3 *A Mobile Client Moves Within an AP Cell*

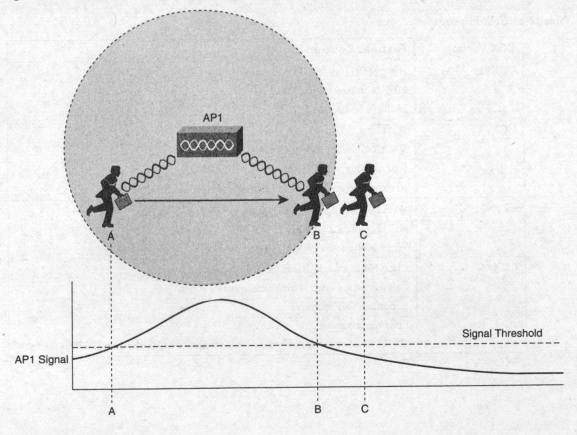

Other APs can be added so that the client can move within a larger area. However, the APs must be carefully deployed to allow the client to roam from AP to AP. *Roaming* is the process of moving an association from one AP to the next so that the wireless connection is maintained as the client moves.

In Figure 18-4, two APs are located side by side, each using the same channel. Building a large coverage area using a single channel might seem intuitive, but it turns out to be a bad idea because the client isn't able to decide when it has roamed away from one AP into the cell of another.

Figure 18-4 *Pitfalls of Reusing Channels in Adjacent APs*

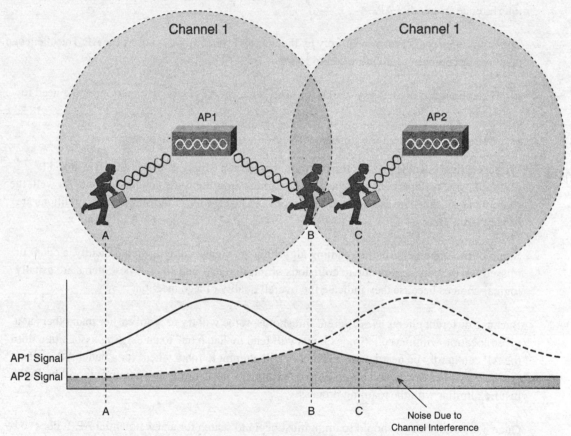

Remember that the signal from an AP doesn't actually stop at the edge of the cell—rather, it continues to propagate as it eventually dies off. This is shown by the signal strength graph of each AP. The client is able to form an association with AP1 at point A. Even at that location, some portion of AP2's signal can be received. Because AP2 is using the same channel as AP1, the two APs essentially interfere with each other.

Ideally, when the client in Figure 18-4 moves to location B, it should begin to anticipate the need to roam or transfer its association from AP1 to AP2. With channel interference from the two APs, it might never be able to roam cleanly. In fact, the client might never be able to operate cleanly in either cell.

The Roaming Process

What enables a client to roam in the first place? First, adjacent APs *must* be configured to use different nonoverlapping channels. For example, APs operating under 802.11b or 802.11g must use only channels 1, 6, and 11. An AP using channel 1 must not be adjacent to other APs using channel 1. This ensures that clients will be able to receive signals from a nearby AP without interference from other APs.

The roaming process is driven entirely by the wireless client driver—not by the AP. The client can take two approaches to decide when to roam:

■ The client can proactively search for other adjacent APs *before* it experiences the need to roam.

■ The client can search for adjacent APs *after* it realizes that it needs to roam.

Wireless clients decide that it's time to roam based on a variety of conditions. The 802.11 standards don't address this issue at all, so roaming algorithms are vendor-specific. As well, the roaming algorithms are usually "secret recipes" so that the exact thresholds and conditions are hidden from view.

Some of the ingredients in the roaming algorithm are signal strength, signal quality, a count of missed AP beacons, errors due to collisions or interference, and so on. These items are usually logical choices because they indicate the overall quality of a connection.

Because different clients use different thresholds, some will try to roam earlier than others at a given location within a cell. Some clients will tend to "latch on" to an existing association until the AP can hardly be heard, whereas others will attempt to roam whenever a better AP can be reached. In other words, don't worry too much about what controls the roaming algorithm. Rather, just be familiar with the roaming process.

Once a client decides it should roam, it must begin to search for a new potential AP. It does so by scanning the other channels to find other active APs. The client can take two approaches to the scanning process:

■ **Passive scanning**—The client takes time to scan other channels, but only listens for 802.11 beacons from available APs.

■ **Active scanning**—The client takes time to scan other channels, but sends 802.11 Probe Request frames to query available APs.

When a client passively scans, it has to only wait to receive beacons. Therefore, it is well suited for low-power and embedded wireless clients. Active scanning puts the client in control because it must send probes and wait to receive probe replies. Active scanning usually results in more efficient roaming than passive scanning because APs can be queried and identified on-demand.

In Figure 18-5, two APs have been correctly configured with nonoverlapping channels 1 and 6. The two AP signal strengths are also shown as a graph corresponding to the client's location. At location A, the client has a clear signal from AP1, so it maintains an association with that AP.

Figure 18-5 *A Client Roaming Between Two APs*

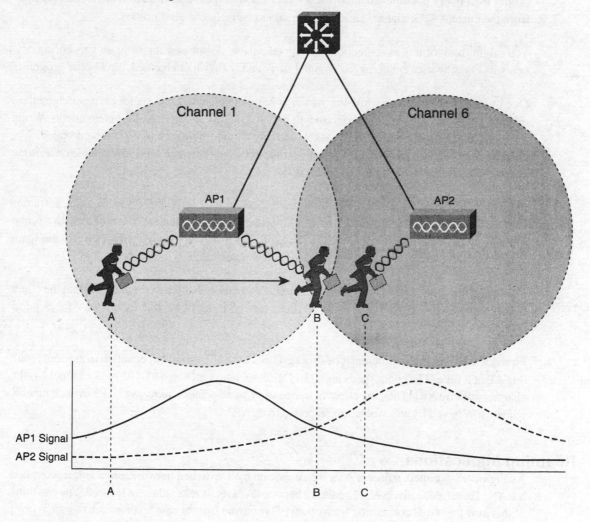

As the client moves toward location B, it decides that AP1's signal is no longer optimal. Somewhere along the way, the client begins to seek out a better AP where it can move its association. A wireless client does this in a two-step fashion:

Step 1   The client sends 802.11 *probe request* management frames to any listening AP.

Step 2   Any listening AP answers the client with 802.11 *probe response* frames, advertising the AP's existence.

The client doesn't know what channel is used on the next AP it encounters, so it must send the probes over every possible channel. Therefore, the client must take time to tune its radio away from the current AP's channel so it can scan other channels and send probes.

You might think of this as someone watching television. As the current program gets boring or nears its end, the viewer begins to "channel surf" and scans other channels for a better program.

One thing to keep in mind: while the viewer is scanning channels, he cannot keep watching the original program. Some of that program will be missed. This is also true of wireless clients. While a radio is scanning other channels, packets arriving on the original channel will be dropped because they can't be received. Therefore, a trade-off exists between staying available on a single channel and attempting to roam to other APs.

Returning to Figure 18-5, when the client nears location B, it sends 802.11 probe request frames on a variety of channels. When AP2 receives a probe request on channel 6, it replies with a probe reply on channel 6. After the client is satisfied with any probe replies it receives, it evaluates them to see which AP offers the most potential for a new association.

Now the client must roam and actually move its association. Notice in Figure 18-5 that the client is still associated with AP1 at location B, even though it might be able to receive AP2 as good or better.

First, the existing association must be dropped because a client is only permitted to associate with one AP at a time. The client sends an 802.11 disassociation message to AP1 over channel 1—the channel used by AP1. Then the client is free to send an association request to AP2 over channel 6, which is followed by an association response from AP2.

Roaming Implications

As Figure 18-5 hinted, adjacent APs are connected by a switched network and a single, common VLAN. Therefore, native 802.11 roaming between APs really takes place at Layer 2. You can think of this as if the wired connection for a client PC is moved from access layer switch to access layer switch—all within the same VLAN.

The implication here is that the client's IP address stays the same, even while roaming. This is handy because the client doesn't have to spend time acquiring a new IP address when it associates with a different AP.

During the roaming process, the client must release one association before negotiating the next association. There is a brief time when the client has no association with any AP. This is actual dead time when the client isn't able to send or receive data. However, the goal for Layer 2 roaming is to keep this dead time to a minimum so that delay-sensitive applications aren't adversely affected.

At some point, once the WLAN reaches a large size, it is better to start over with a new IP subnet and VLAN. From the earlier chapters in this book, you should recall that large campus networks should be broken down into switch blocks so that there aren't any end-to-end or campus VLANs. This is also important with WLANs, as they are really just an extension of the switched infrastructure.

If the WLAN is broken up into multiple VLANs and subnets, wireless clients might have to cross Layer 3 boundaries when they roam. At those locations, the client IP addresses will change from one AP to another. This involves more than simple 802.11 probes and association requests—it also requires additional dead time while the client requests and receives a new IP address.

Layer 3 roaming is not native to standard APs. It requires the leverage of other tools that can be overlaid on the 802.11 network. This problem can be solved with the wireless infrastructure that is described in Chapter 19, "Cisco Unified Wireless Network."

Cell Layout and Channel Usage

The previous section laid the foundation for roaming by describing movement between two AP cells. Most scenarios require more than two APs to cover the appropriate area within a building. Therefore, you need to consider the layout and configuration of more and more APs to scale the design to fit your wireless environment.

For example, to cover the entire area of a warehouse or one floor of a building, APs must be placed at regular intervals throughout that space. A site survey is a vital step toward deciding on AP placement, as actual live measurements are taken with an AP staged at various points in the actual space.

The two basic goals when designing a WLAN are

- Sizing the AP cells

- Selecting channels for the AP cells

The sections that follow describe these goals.

Sizing AP Cells

The size of AP cells determines the number of APs that must be purchased and deployed to cover an area; however, your design should not be driven by the cost alone. AP cell size can also affect the performance of the APs as clients move around or gather in one place.

Remember that a WLAN is a shared medium. Within a single AP cell, all the clients associated with that AP must share the bandwidth and contend for access. If the cell is large, a large number of clients could potentially gather and use that AP. If the cell size is reduced, the number of simultaneous clients can also be reduced.

> **TIP**   No clear rule of thumb exists for sizing AP cells for a specific number of clients. As with switched networks, the limiting factor is really the type of applications the clients will use, as well as the volume of data moving over the medium at any given time.
>
> As a very loose guideline, you can consider the maximum peak throughput of a wireless cell divided by the number of simultaneous clients to get a maximum data rate per user. Factoring in the overhead of 802.11 encapsulation and bandwidth contention, 802.11b generally offers up to 6.8 Mbps through an AP, whereas 802.11g and 802.11a offer up to 32 Mbps.
>
> This means, for example, in an 802.11b cell with 25 clients, each client would have a maximum throughput of 6.8 Mbps / 25, or 272 kbps. In an 802.11a or 802.11g cell, those same 25 users would have 32 Mbps / 25, or 1.28 Mbps.

You should also keep in mind that large cells can allow clients to step their data rates down as they move farther away from the APs. For example, when an 802.11b client is near an AP, it can use the highest data rate (11 Mbps). As the client moves out away from the AP, the data rate can be reduced to 5.5, 2, and finally 1 Mbps. You might want your clients to use only the highest data rates in a cell, which can be accomplished by reducing the cell size.

Generally, the AP cell size is driven by the AP's transmit power. Higher power equates to greater range, so the power must be adjusted so that the AP's signal doesn't propagate into nearby AP cells operating on the same channel.

> **TIP**   For more detailed information about AP cell size and wireless LAN site surveys, refer to the Cisco Airespace Installation, Administration, and Maintenance (CAIAM) or Cisco Aironet Wireless Site Survey (CAWSS) course.

Once the AP cells have been sized and pinpointed, clients should be able to associate and roam at any location within the coverage area. If one AP should fail, the area it originally covered will be left silent.

Naturally, this "hole" in the coverage can be fixed by simply replacing the failed AP—assuming that you could discover the failed AP radio in the first place. In the meantime, you could also configure adjacent APs to increase their output power to expand their coverage area over the hole. However, tweaking the AP power is a tricky task that can affect many other AP cells as well.

WLAN Channel Layout

To minimize channel overlap and interference, AP cells should be designed so that adjacent APs use different channels. With 802.11b and 802.11g, you are limited to using channels 1, 6, and 11. The cells could be laid out in a regular, alternating pattern, as Figure 18-6 illustrates.

Figure 18-6   *Holes in an Alternating Channel Pattern in 802.11b/g*

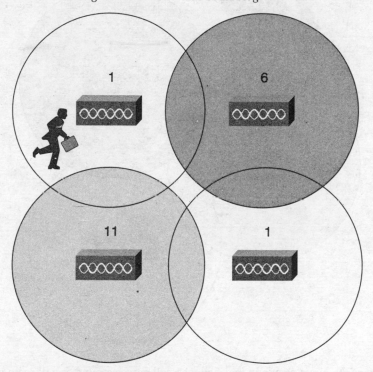

However, notice what is happening in the center where the cells meet—there is a small hole in RF coverage. If a client roams through that hole, his wireless signal will probably drop completely. As well, if the cells were brought closer together to close this hole, the two cells using channel 1 would overlap and begin interfering with each other.

Instead, you should lay out the cells in a "honeycomb" fashion as illustrated in Figure 18-7. This pattern is seamless, leaving no holes in coverage. In addition, notice how the two cells using channel 1 are well separated, providing isolation from interference. As far as ordering channels in the pattern, several different variations are available using combinations of the three channels, but the result is basically the same.

Figure 18-7 *An Alternating Channel Pattern in 802.11b/g*

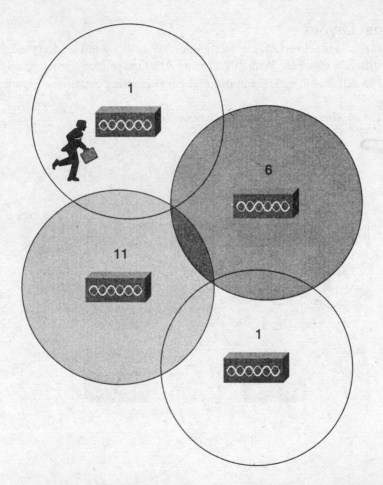

Notice that as the client shown in the channel 1 cell moves around, it will roam into adjacent cells on different channels. In order for roaming to work properly, a client must be able to move from one channel into a completely different channel.

Alternating channels to avoid overlap is commonly called *channel reuse*. The basic pattern shown in Figure 18-7 can be repeated to expand over a larger area, as Figure 18-8 illustrates.

Figure 18-8 *802.11b/g Channel Reuse over a Large Area*

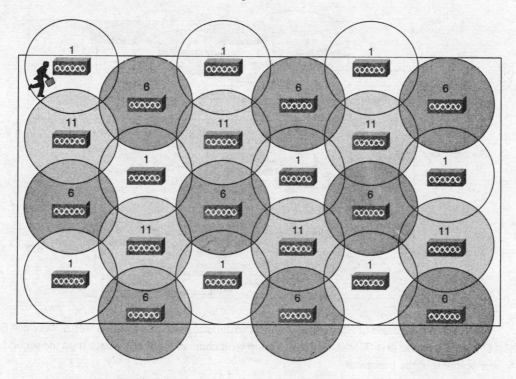

With 802.11a, the design is quite different. It has 4, 8, or even 12 nonoverlapping channels available, so the likelihood of adjacent cells using the same channel is very low. The FCC has added 11 additional channels in the U.S., for a total of 23 nonoverlapping choices.

So far, only the channel layout of a two-dimensional area has been discussed. For example, Figure 18-8 might represent only one floor of a building. What happens when you need to design a wireless LAN for multiple floors in the same building?

Recall that an RF signal propagating from an antenna actually takes on a three-dimensional shape. With an omnidirectional antenna, the pattern is somewhat like a donut shape with the antenna at the center. The signal extends outward, giving the cell a circular shape along the floor. The signal also extends upward and downward to a lesser extent—affecting AP cells on adjacent floors as well.

Consider the building with three floors shown in Figure 18-9. The same two-dimensional channel layout from Figure 18-8 is being used on the first floor. The floors in the figure are shown greatly separated, so that you can see the channel patterns and numbers. In reality, the cells on adjacent floors would touch or overlap, just as adjacent cells on the same floor do.

Figure 18-9 *Channel Layout in Three Dimensions*

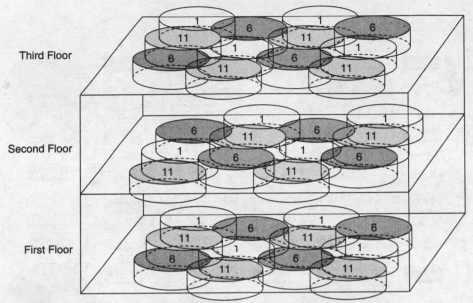

Now comes the puzzle of alternating channels within the plane of a floor, as well as between floors. Channel 1 on the first floor should not overlap with channel 1 directly above it on the second floor or below it in the basement.

When you consider each of the tasks involved in designing and maintaining a wireless LAN, it can really become a puzzle to solve! The cell size, AP transmit power, and channel assignment all have to be coordinated on each and every AP. Roaming also becomes an issue on a large scale, if clients are permitted to roam across the entire campus wireless network

The good news is that Chapter 19, "Cisco Unified Wireless Network," explains how to solve many of these puzzles.

Foundation Summary

The Foundation Summary is a collection of information that provides a convenient review of many key concepts in this chapter. If you are already comfortable with the topics in this chapter, this summary can help you recall a few details. If you just read this chapter, this review should help solidify some key facts. If you are doing your final preparation before the exam, this information will be a convenient way to review the day before the exam.

Table 18-3 *Comparison of Wireless LAN Security Methods*

Method	Credentials Used	Data Security
Open Authentication	None	None
Pre-Shared Key (static WEP)	Static WEP key	WEP encryption (static key)
LEAP	Username/password	WEP encryption (dynamic keys)
EAP-TLS	Digital certificate	WEP encryption (dynamic keys)
PEAP	Server: Digital certificate Client: Any EAP method	WEP encryption (dynamic keys)
EAP-FAST	PAC to build tunnel; Username/password	WEP encryption (dynamic keys)
WPA	Any EAP-based method or pre-shared key	WEP encryption, per-packet keys generated by TKIP MIC performs packet authentication for integrity
WPA2	Any EAP-based method Pre-shared key Proactive key caching (authenticate once while roaming across APs)	AES encryption or TKIP MIC performs packet authentication for integrity

In this table, the darker shading indicates increasing levels of security.

Table 18-4 *Client Roaming Methods*

Roaming Method	Description
Passive roaming	Client scans other channels to listen for beacons from candidate APs
Active roaming	Client scans other channels and sends 802.11 probe requests to find candidate APs

Table 18-5 *Best Practice AP Cell Size Guidelines*

AP Radio	Typical Maximum Throughput Per Cell
802.11b	6.8 Mbps
802.11g	32 Mbps
802.11a	32 Mbps

Q&A

The questions and scenarios in this book are more difficult than what you should experience on the actual exam. The questions do not attempt to cover more breadth or depth than the exam; however, they are designed to make sure that you know the answers. Rather than allowing you to derive the answers from clues hidden inside the questions themselves, the questions challenge your understanding and recall of the subject. Hopefully, these questions will help limit the number of exam questions on which you narrow your choices to two options and then guess.

You can find the answers to these questions in Appendix A.

1. Consider the following wireless security methods. Based on encryption alone, which could be considered the most secure?

    a. Open authentication

    b. Pre-shared key

    c. LEAP

    d. WPA

    e. WPA2

2. Describe the weakness of using static WEP keys.

3. When is it considered appropriate to secure a WLAN with only open authentication, assuming that the SSID is kept secret?

4. What things should you consider when sizing an AP cell?

5. Should adjacent AP cells be configured to operate on the same channel? Why or why not?

6. Suppose that a set of 802.11b APs are configured to use channels 1, 6, and 11 in an alternating fashion. What channels should you choose when the 802.11g portion of the same APs are configured?

7. Suppose that 802.11a clients and APs are introduced into an area already using 802.11b or 802.11g. What effect will this have?

8. Suppose that an office area has wireless coverage from several APs, each using a very small cell size. Should you be concerned about the power output (and therefore the cell size) of client devices?

This chapter covers the following topics that you need to master for the CCNP BCMSN exam:

- **Traditional WLAN Architecture**—This section discusses how traditional autonomous wireless access points are used in a network.

- **Cisco Unified Wireless Network Architecture**—This section covers the Cisco components that are used to build a wireless network that is both scalable and centrally managed.

- **Lightweight AP Operation**—This section explains the bootstrap procedure that a lightweight access point uses to join with a wireless LAN controller. In addition, traffic paths through a lightweight AP are compared to those of an autonomous AP.

- **Lightweight AP Association and Roaming**—This section discusses how wireless clients can negotiate associations with lightweight APs. As clients move around, they must also move their associations to other lightweight APs so that they may roam throughout the network.

- **Basic Wireless LAN Configuration**—In this section you will find information on how to configure wireless LAN controllers and lightweight access points for their initial, basic operation.

CHAPTER 19

Cisco Unified Wireless Network

Wireless networks have traditionally consisted of individually configured and individually operating access points, scattered about. Monitoring and maintaining such a diverse network has become too much of an administrative chore.

This chapter presents the Cisco technologies used to provide a unified and centrally managed wireless network.

"Do I Know This Already?" Quiz

The purpose of the "Do I Know This Already?" quiz is to help you decide what parts of this chapter to use. If you already intend to read the entire chapter, you do not necessarily need to answer these questions now.

The quiz, derived from the major sections in the "Foundation Topics" portion of the chapter, helps you determine how to spend your limited study time.

Table 19-1 outlines the major topics discussed in this chapter and the "Do I Know This Already?" quiz questions that correspond to those topics.

Table 19-1 *"Do I Know This Already?" Foundation Topics Section-to-Question Mapping*

Foundation Topics Section	Questions Covered in This Section	Score
Traditional WLAN Architecture	1–2	
Cisco Unified Wireless Network Architecture	3–6	
Lightweight AP Association and Roaming	7–8	
Basic Wireless LAN Configuration	9–12	
Total Score		

CAUTION   The goal of self-assessment is to gauge your mastery of the topics in this chapter. If you do not know the answer to a question or are only partially sure of the answer, you should mark this question wrong. Giving yourself credit for an answer you correctly guess skews your self-assessment results and might give you a false sense of security.

1.   Which of the following terms represents a Cisco wireless access point that cannot operate independently?

   a.   Autonomous AP

   b.   Roaming AP

   c.   Lightweight AP

   d.   Dependent AP

2.   Suppose that an autonomous AP is used to support wireless clients. Which one of the following answers lists the devices that traffic must take when passing from one wireless client to another?

   a.   Through the AP only

   b.   Through the AP and its controller

   c.   Through the controller only

   d.   None of these answers is correct; traffic can go directly over the air

3.   Suppose that a lightweight AP is used to support wireless clients. Which one of the following answers lists the device path that traffic must take when passing from one wireless client to another?

   a.   Through the AP only

   b.   Through the AP and its controller

   c.   Through the controller only

   d.   None of these answers is correct; traffic can go directly over the air

4.   A lightweight access point is said to have which one of the following architectures?

   a.   Proxy MAC

   b.   Tunnel MAC

   c.   Split-MAC

   d.   Fat MAC

5.   How does a lightweight access point communicate with a wireless LAN controller? Choose one correct answer.

   a.   Through an IPsec tunnel

   b.   Through an LWAPP tunnel

   c.   Through a GRE tunnel

   d.   Directly over Layer 2

6. Which one of the following types of traffic is sent securely over an LWAPP tunnel?

    a. Control messages

    b. User data

    c. DHCP requests

    d. 802.11 beacons

7. Which one of the following must be consistent in order for a wireless client to roam between lightweight APs that are managed by the same WLC?

    a. SSID

    b. Mobility group

    c. VLAN ID

    d. AP management VLAN

8. Which one of the following must be consistent in order for a wireless client to roam between lightweight APs that are managed by two different WLCs?

    a. VLAN ID

    b. SSID

    c. AP management VLAN

    d. Mobility group

9. Which WLC interface should be configured with an IP address that is located on the wireless client VLAN?

    a. Service port

    b. Distribution system port

    c. AP manager interface

    d. Dynamic interface

10. When a lightweight AP boots up, from which one of the following sources does it learn the WLC addresses?

    a. CDP

    b. Router's IP helper-address

    c. DHCP option 43

    d. Multicast announcement

11. Which one of the following describes the correct use of the virtual interface on a WLC?

   a. Used to relay DHCP messages

   b. Used to bring up LWAPP tunnels

   c. Used to extend into a wireless client VLAN

   d. Used to communicate with LAPs

12. Which one of the following WLC interfaces is used to connect to the switched network?

   a. Virtual interface

   b. Distribution system port

   c. Dynamic interface

   d. Service port

The answers to the "Do I Know This Already?" quiz are found in Appendix A, "Answers to Chapter 'Do I Know This Already?' Quizzes and Q&A Sections." The suggested choices for your next step are as follows:

■ **10 or less overall score**—Read the entire chapter. This includes the "Foundation Topics," "Foundation Summary," and "Q&A" sections.

■ **11 or more overall score**—If you want more review on these topics, skip to the "Foundation Summary" section and then go to the "Q&A" section at the end of the chapter. Otherwise, move to Chapter 20, "Scenarios for Final Preparation."

Foundation Topics

Traditional WLAN Architecture

In Chapter 17, "Wireless LAN Overview," and Chapter 18, "Wireless Architecture and Design," the wireless LAN (WLAN) architecture centered around the wireless access point (AP). Each AP served as the central hub of its own BSS, where clients located with the AP cell gained an association. The traffic to and from each client had to pass through the AP in order to reach any other part of the network.

Notice that even though an AP is centrally positioned to support its clients, it is quite isolated and self-sufficient. Each AP must be configured individually, although many APs might be configured with identical network policies. Each AP also operates independently—the AP handles its own use of radio frequency (RF) channels, clients associate with the AP directly, the AP enforces any security policies unassisted, and so on.

In a nutshell, each AP is autonomous within the larger network. Cisco calls this an *autonomous mode AP* to distinguish it from a more evolved mode.

Because each AP is autonomous, managing security over the wireless network can be difficult. Each autonomous AP handles its own security policies, with no central point of entry between the wireless and wired networks. That means no convenient place exists for monitoring traffic for things like intrusion detection and prevention, quality of service, bandwidth policing, and so on.

Finally, managing the RF operation of many autonomous APs can be quite difficult. As the network administrator, you are in charge of selecting and configuring AP channels, as well as detecting and resolving rogue APs that might be interfering. You must also manage things like AP output power, ensuring the wireless coverage is sufficient, that it doesn't overlap too much, and that no coverage holes exist—even when an AP's radio fails.

Cisco has realized the autonomous AP shortcomings and has offered a more unified approach. You should understand some important concepts about WLANs that are based on autonomous APs so that you can compare the traditional architecture to the unified architecture, as it is presented in the next section.

First, consider the traffic patterns in an autonomous AP architecture. Figure 19-1 shows two wireless clients associated with an autonomous AP. All traffic to and from the clients must pass through the AP. Notice how traffic from Client A to some other part of the network passes through the AP, where it is bridged onto the switched network. Even traffic between two wireless clients can't travel directly over the air—it must first pass through the AP and back out to the other client.

Figure 19-1 *Traffic Patterns Through an Autonomous AP*

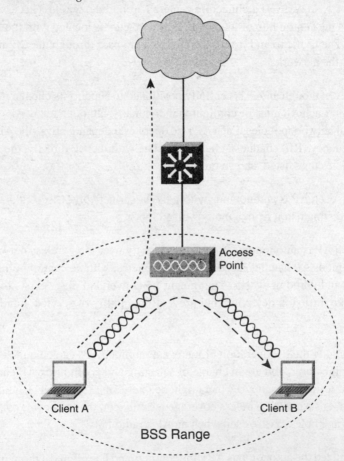

Recall from Chapter 18 that an AP can support multiple service set identifiers (SSIDs), if multiple virtual local area networks (VLANs) are extended to it over a trunk link. If you want to offer the same SSIDs from several autonomous APs, the VLANs must be extended to the APs in a contiguous fashion. This means that the switched network must carry the VLANs to each and every AP that needs them, as shown in Figure 19-2.

Figure 19-2   *The Extent of an SSID and Its VLAN over Multiple Autonomous APs*

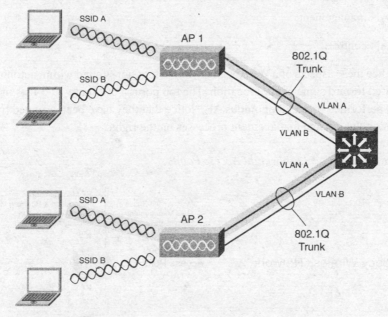

In the figure, SSID A and SSID B are offered on two APs. The two SSIDs correspond to VLAN A and VLAN B, respectively. The APs must be connected to a common switched network that extends VLANs A and B at Layer 2. This is done by carrying VLANs A and B over an 802.1Q trunk link to each AP.

Because SSIDs and their VLANs must be extended at Layer 2, you should consider how they are extended throughout the switched network. In Figure 19-2, SSID A and VLAN A have been shaded everywhere they appear. Naturally, they form a contiguous path that appears on both APs so that wireless clients can use SSID A in either location or while roaming between the two.

This concept becomes important when you think about extending SSIDs to many APs over a larger network. Perhaps you would like to offer an SSID on any AP served by your infrastructure, so that wireless clients can roam anywhere in the area. To do that, the SSID and its VLAN would have to be extended everywhere that the user could possibly roam. This has the potential to look like an end-to-end or campuswide VLAN—something that goes against good network design practice, as presented in the early chapters of this book.

Cisco Unified Wireless Network Architecture

Cisco has collected a complete set of functions that are integral to wireless LANs and called them the *Cisco Unified Wireless Network*. This new architecture offers the following capabilities, which are centralized so that they affect wireless LAN devices located anywhere in the network:

■   WLAN security

- WLAN deployment

- WLAN management

- WLAN control

To centralize these aspects of a WLAN, many of the functions found within autonomous APs have to be shifted toward some central location. The top portion of Figure 19-3 lists most of the activities performed by an autonomous AP. Notice that they have been grouped by real-time processes on the left and management processes on the right.

Figure 19-3 *Autonomous Versus Lightweight Access Points*

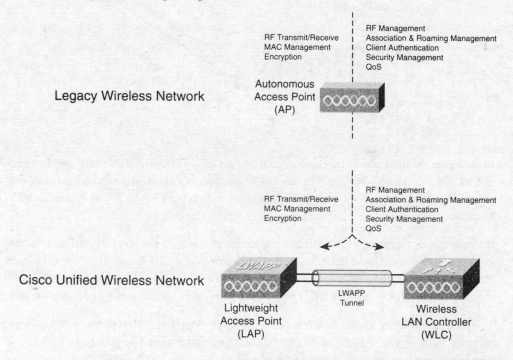

The real-time processes involve actually sending and receiving 802.11 frames, AP beacons, and probe messages. Data encryption is also handled in a real-time, per-packet basis. The AP must interact with wireless clients at the media access control (MAC) layer. These functions must stay with the AP hardware, closest to the clients.

The management functions are not integral to handling frames over the RF channels, but are things that should be centrally administered. Therefore, those functions are moved to a centrally located platform away from the AP.

In the Cisco unified wireless network, a lightweight access point (LAP) performs only the real-time 802.11 operation. The LAP gets its name because the code image and the local intelligence are stripped down, or lightweight, compared to the traditional autonomous AP.

The management functions are all performed on a wireless LAN controller (WLC), which is common to many LAPs. This is shown in the bottom portion of Figure 19-3. Notice that the LAP is left with duties in Layers 1 and 2, where frames are moved into and out of the RF domain. The LAP becomes totally dependent on the WLC for every other WLAN function, such as authenticating users, managing security policies, and even selecting RF channels and output power!

This division of labor is known as a *split-MAC architecture*, where the normal MAC operations are pulled apart into two distinct locations. This occurs for every LAP in the network—each one must bind itself to a WLC in order to boot up and support wireless clients. The WLC becomes the central hub that supports a number of LAPs scattered about in the switched network.

How does an LAP bind with a WLC to form a complete working access point? The two devices must bring up a tunnel between them to carry 802.11-related messages and also client data. Remember that the LAP and WLC can be located on the same VLAN or IP subnet, but they don't have to be. Instead, they can be located on two entirely different IP subnets in two entirely different locations.

The tunnel makes this all possible by encapsulating the data between the LAP and WLC within new IP packets. The tunneled data can then be switched or routed across the campus network. This concept is shown in Figure 19-4.

Figure 19-4 *Linking an LAP and WLC with LWAPP*

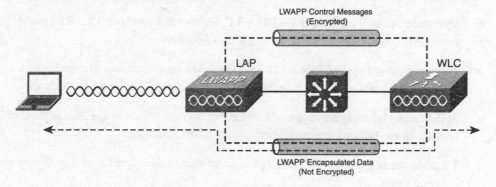

The LAP and WLC pair use the lightweight access point protocol (LWAPP) as the tunneling mechanism. Actually, LWAPP consists of the two tunnels shown in Figure 19-4:

■ **LWAPP control messages**—Exchanges that are used to configure the LAP and manage its operation. The control messages are authenticated and encrypted so that the LAP is securely controlled by only the WLC.

■ **LWAPP data**—Packets to and from wireless clients associated with the LAP. The data is encapsulated within LWAPP, but is not encrypted or otherwise secured between the LAP and WLC.

> **TIP** Although Cisco developed LWAPP, it submitted the protocol as an IETF draft. You can find the most current draft at the IETF Capwap working group's site: http://www1.tools.ietf.org/wg/capwap/draft-ohara-capwap-lwapp/
>
> LWAPP uses UDP destination ports 12222 and 12223 on the WLC end.

Every LAP and WLC must also authenticate each other with digital certificates. An X.509 certificate is pre-installed in each device when it is purchased. By using certificates behind the scenes, every device is properly authenticated before becoming part of the Cisco Unified Wireless Network. This process helps ensure that no rogue LAP or WLC (or devices posing as an LAP or WLC) can be introduced into the network.

WLC Functions

Once LWAPP tunnels are built from a WLC to one or more lightweight APs, the WLC can begin offering a variety of additional functions. Think of all the puzzles and shortcomings that were discussed for the traditional WLAN architecture as you read over the following list of WLC activities:

■ **Dynamic channel assignment**—The WLC chooses and configures the RF channel used by each LAP, based on other active access points in the area.

■ **Transmit power optimization**—The WLC sets the transmit power of each LAP based on the coverage area needed. Transmit power is also automatically adjusted periodically.

■ **Self-healing wireless coverage**—If an LAP radio dies, the coverage hole is "healed" by turning up the transmit power of surrounding LAPs automatically.

■ **Flexible client roaming**—Clients can roam at either Layer 2 or Layer 3 with very fast roaming times.

■ **Dynamic client load balancing**—If two or more LAPs are positioned to cover the same geographic area, the WLC can associate clients with the least used LAP. This distributes the client load across the LAPs.

- **RF monitoring**—The WLC manages each LAP so that it scans channels to monitor the RF usage. By listening to a channel, the WLC can remotely gather information about RF interference, noise, signals from surrounding LAPs, and signals from rogue APs or ad-hoc clients.

- **Security management**—The WLC can require wireless clients to obtain an IP address from a trusted DHCP server before allowing them to associate and access the WLAN.

Cisco WLCs are available in several platforms, differing mainly in the number of managed LAPs. Table 19-2 lists the WLC platforms.

Table 19-2 *Cisco WLC Platforms and Capabilities*

Model	Interfaces	Attributes
2006	4 10/100TX	Handles up to 6 LAPs
4402	2 GigE	Handles up to 12, 25, or 50 LAPs
4404	4 GigE	Handles up to 100 LAPs
WiSM	4 GigE bundled in an EtherChannel for each controller	Catalyst 6500 module with two WLC 4404s; handles up to 300 LAPs (150 per 4404 controller); up to 5 WiSMs in a single chassis
WLC module for ISR routers	Can be integrated in 2800, 3700, and 3800 routers	Handles up to 6 LAPs
Catalyst 3750G integrated WLC	N/A (integrated in 24-port 10/100/1000TX switch)	Handles up to 25 LAPs per switch, up to 100 LAPs per switch stack

You can also deploy several WLCs in a network to handle a large number of LAPs. As well, multiple WLCs offer some redundancy so that LAPs can recover from a WLC failure.

Managing several WLCs can require a significant effort, due to the number of LAPs and clients to be managed and monitored. The Cisco Wireless Control System (WCS) is an optional server platform that can be used as a single GUI front-end to all the WLCs in a network. From the WCS, you can perform any WLAN management or configuration task, as well as RF planning and wireless user tracking.

The WCS uses building floorplans to display dynamic representations of wireless coverage. It can also be fed information about the building construction to improve its concept of RF signal propagation. Once this is done, the WCS can locate a wireless client to within a few meters by triangulating the client's signal as received by multiple LAPs.

The WCS can be teamed with the Cisco Wireless Location Appliance to track the location of thousands of wireless clients. You can even deploy active 802.11 RFID tags to track objects as they move around in the wireless coverage area. Tracking objects by their MAC addresses can be handy when you need to locate a rogue or malicious wireless client, or when you need to track corporate assets that tend to move around within a building or complex.

Lightweight AP Operation

The lightweight AP is designed to be a "zero-touch" configuration. The LAP must find a WLC and obtain all of its configuration parameters, so you never have to actually configure it through its console port or over the network.

The following sequence of steps detail the bootstrap process that an LAP must complete before it becomes active:

Step 1   The LAP obtains an IP address from a DHCP server.

Step 2   The LAP learns the IP addresses of any available WLCs.

Step 3   The LAP sends a join request to the first WLC in its list of addresses. If that one fails to answer, the next WLC is tried. When a WLC accepts the LAP, it sends a join reply back to the LAP, effectively binding the two devices.

Step 4   The WLC compares the LAP's code image release to the code release stored locally. If they differ, the LAP downloads the code image stored on the WLC and reboots itself.

Step 5   The WLC and LAP build a secure LWAPP tunnel for management traffic and an LWAPP tunnel (not secured) for wireless client data.

You should notice a couple of things from this list. In step 2, the LAP can find the WLC IP addresses using any of these methods:

■   A DHCP server that adds option 43 to its reply containing a list of WLC addresses

■   With the IP subnet broadcast option, the LAP broadcasts a join request message, hoping that a WLC is also connected to the local subnet or VLAN. This method works only if the LAP and WLC are Layer 2 adjacent.

An LAP is always joined or bound to one WLC at any time. However, the LAP can maintain a list of up to three WLCs (primary, secondary, and tertiary). As an LAP boots up, it tries to contact each WLC address in sequential order. If it can't find a responding WLC at all, the LAP will try an IP subnet broadcast to find any available WLC.

Suppose that an LAP has booted up and has successfully joined a WLC. If that WLC fails for some reason, the LAP will no longer be able to forward traffic or to maintain client associations. Therefore, once the LAP realizes its WLC is no longer responding, it reboots and begins the process of searching for live WLCs again. This means any client associations will be dropped while the LAP reboots and joins a different controller.

> **TIP**   When an LAP is cut off from a WLC, client associations are normally dropped and no
> data can pass over the WLAN between clients. Cisco Remote Edge Access Point (REAP) is a
> special case for remote sites where the LAPs are separated from the WLC by a WAN link. With
> REAP, the remote LAPs can keep operating even while the WAN link is down and their WLC
> is not available. This allows wireless users to keep communicating within the remote site until
> the link (and WLC) is restored.

Traffic Patterns in a Cisco Unified Wireless Network

Because the lightweight APs connect to the wired network through logical LWAPP tunnels, the
traffic patterns into and out of the WLAN are different than traditional WLANs.

Consider the network shown in Figure 19-5. Two wireless clients are associated with the WLAN
that is formed by the LAP and WLC combination. Traffic from Client A to a host somewhere on
the network travels through the LAP, through the LWAPP tunnel to the WLC, and then out onto
the switched campus network.

Figure 19-5 *Traffic Patterns Through a Lightweight AP*

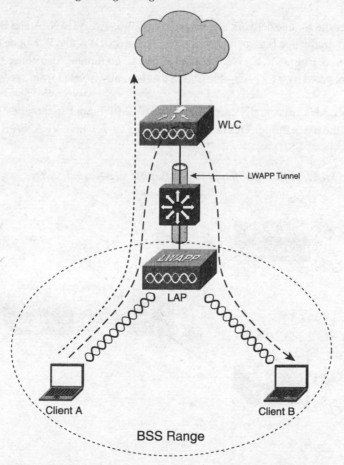

Traffic between the two wireless clients, however, takes an interesting path. That traffic must go from Client A through the LAP, through the LWAPP tunnel, into the WLC, back through the LWAPP tunnel, through the LAP and on to Client B. This further illustrates what a vital role the WLC plays in the unified infrastructure.

> **TIP** Even though all traffic into and out of the WLAN must pass through the LWAPP tunnel and the WLC, not all traffic operations are applied end-to-end across the tunnel.
>
> For example, wireless encryption can still be used to secure data over the air, as with traditional WLANs. However, the encrypted data does not pass through the LWAPP tunnel at all. Packets are encrypted as they leave the wireless client and unencrypted when they arrive on the LAP. The same is true for packet authentication, if it is used.
>
> All the packet authentication and encryption functions remain within the LAP hardware and are not distributed to the WLC at all.

When autonomous APs are used in a network, the access VLANs serving the wireless clients must be extended or trunked all the way out to touch the APs. This is not true for lightweight APs.

First, consider the sample network shown in Figure 19-6. Two VLANs A and B are used to carry wireless client traffic that is associated to the respective SSIDs A and B. Notice that VLANs A and B exist on the trunk from switch SW2 to the WLC, but go no further. Also notice that the WLC and the LAPs are connected by VLAN Z—something that is totally isolated from access VLANs A and B.

The access VLANs are actually carried over the LWAPP tunnel so that they logically touch the LAPs where the users reside. This is shown in Figure 19-7, where VLAN A is shaded as it extends to the two LAPs as SSID A.

Figure 19-6 *A Unified Wireless Network Supporting Multiple VLANs and SSIDs*

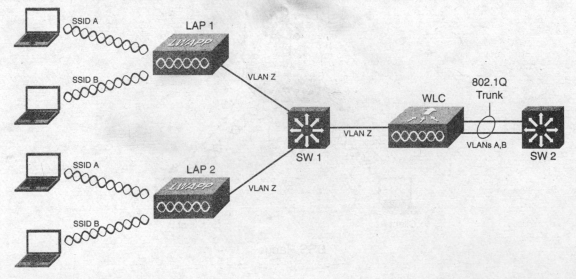

Figure 19-7 *VLAN A Extending over LWAPP Tunnels*

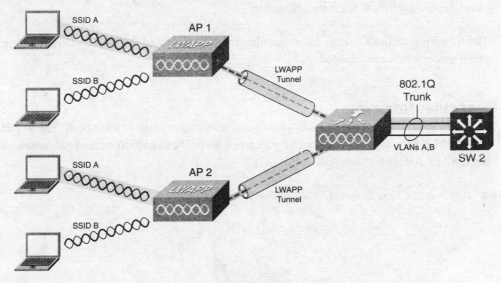

Lightweight AP Association and Roaming

Wireless clients must negotiate an association with lightweight APs, as with any 802.11 wireless network. However, the split-MAC architecture has an interesting effect on client associations.

Remember that an LAP handles mostly real-time wireless duties, so it will just pass the client's association requests on up to the WLC. In effect, the wireless clients negotiate their associations with the WLC directly. This is important for two reasons:

■ All client associations can be managed in a central location.

■ Client roaming becomes faster and easier; associations can be maintained or handed off at the controller level.

With autonomous APs, a client roams by moving its association from one AP to another. The client must negotiate the move with each AP independently, and the APs must also make sure any buffered data from the client is passed along to follow the association. Autonomous roaming occurs only at Layer 2; some other means must be added to support Layer 3 roaming.

With lightweight APs, a client still roams by moving its association. From the client's point of view, the association moves from AP to AP; actually it moves from WLC to WLC, according to the AP-WLC bindings.

Through the WLCs, lightweight APs can support both Layer 2 and Layer 3 roaming. Remember that the client's association is always contained within an LWAPP tunnel. Moving to a new AP also moves the association into a new tunnel—the tunnel that connects the new AP to its WLC.

The client's IP address can remain the same while roaming, no matter which LWAPP tunnel the client passes through to reach the controllers.

The following sections discuss client roaming from the aspect of the WLC, where roaming and client associations are managed.

Intra-Controller Roaming

In Figure 19-8, a wireless client has an active wireless association at location A. The association is with WLC1 through AP1. As you might expect, all traffic to and from the client passes through the LWAPP tunnel between AP1 and WLC1.

Figure 19-8   *A Wireless Client in an LAP Cell Before Roaming*

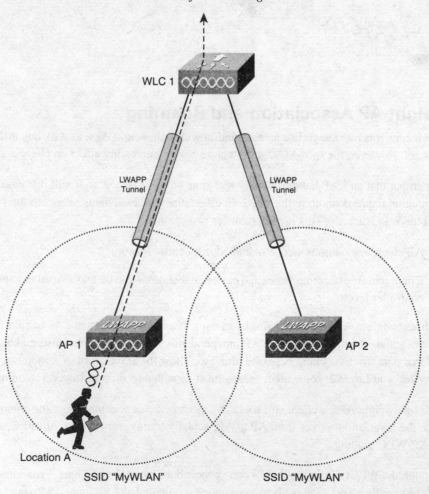

The client begins moving in Figure 19-9 and roams into the area covered by AP2. For this example, notice two things: The cells provided by AP1 and AP2 both use the SSID "MyWLAN," which enables the client to roam between them. In addition, both AP1 and AP2 are joined to a single controller, WC1.

Figure 19-9 *A Wireless Client After Roaming to a New LAP Cell*

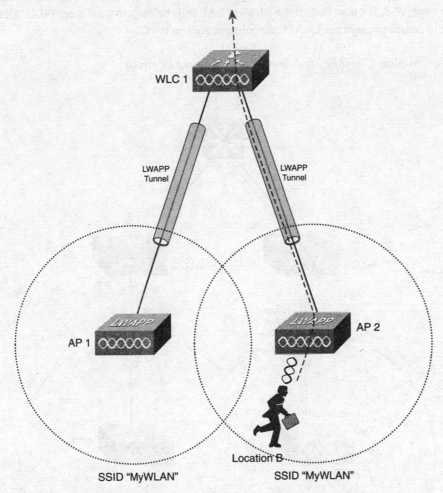

In the figure, the client has moved its association to WLC1 through AP2. Although the AP has changed, the same controller is providing the association and the LWAPP tunnel. This is known as an *intra-controller roam*, where the client's association stays within the same controller.

This type of roam is straightforward because controller WLC1 simply updates its tables to begin using the LWAPP tunnel to AP2 to find the client. Any leftover data that was buffered from the old association is easily shifted over to the new association within the controller.

Inter-Controller Roaming

In some cases, a client might roam from one controller to another. For example, a large wireless network might consist of too many LAPs to be supported by a single WLC. The LAPs could also be distributed over several controllers for load balancing or redundancy purposes.

In Figure 19-10, a wireless client is using an association with WLC1 through AP1. This is similar to Figure 19-8, but now each of the adjacent LAP cells belongs to a different WLC. All the client's traffic passes through the LWAPP tunnel from AP1 to WLC1.

Figure 19-10 *A Wireless Client Before Roaming to a Different Controller*

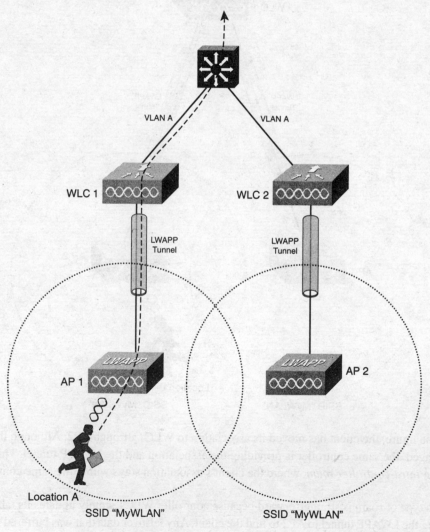

When the client moves into AP2's cell, the same SSID is found, and the client can move its association to WLC2. As long as the two controllers (WLC1 and WLC2) are located in the same IP subnet, they can easily hand off the client's association. This is done through a mobility message exchange where information about the client is transferred from one WLC to the other, as shown in Figure 19-11.

Figure 19-11 *After an Inter-Controller Roam, Controllers Are on the Same Subnet*

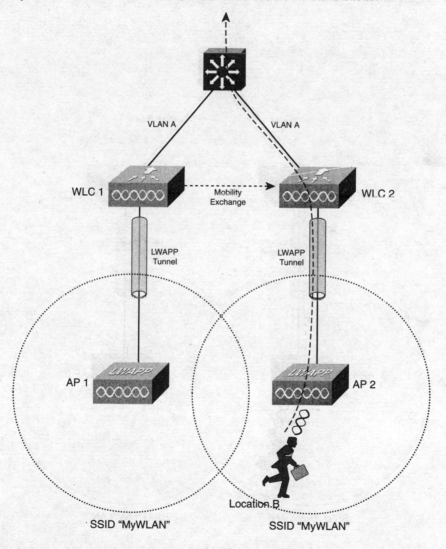

Once the mobility exchange occurs, the client begins using the LWAPP tunnel between AP2 and WLC2. The client's IP address has not changed; in fact, the roaming process was completely transparent to the client.

Now consider the scenario shown in Figure 19-12. The two controllers WLC1 and WLC2 are located in *different* IP subnets, shown as VLAN A and VLAN B. The wireless client begins in AP1's cell with an association to WLC1. The client obtains an IP address within VLAN A because AP1 offers VLAN A on its SSID. All the client's traffic passes through the LWAPP tunnel between AP1 and WLC1 and onto VLAN A.

Figure 19-12 *Before an Inter-Controller Roam, Controllers Are on Different Subnets*

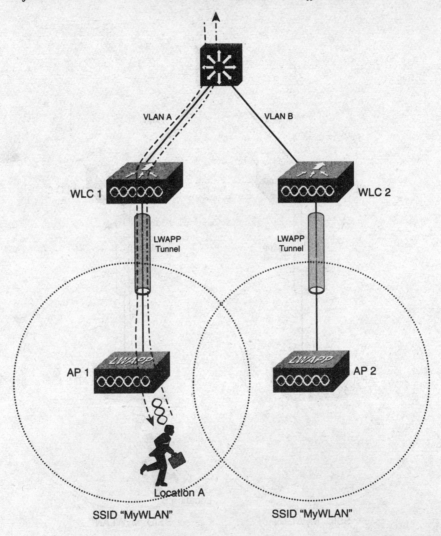

Once the client travels into the cell provided by AP2, something interesting happens. In Figure 19-13, the client moves its association over to WLC2, through AP2, which offers access to VLAN B. The client's IP address has remained constant, but WLC1 and WLC2 are not located on the same subnet or VLAN. Therefore, the client's IP address has moved into a foreign subnet.

The two controllers must begin working together to provide continuing service for the client, without requiring the client to obtain a new address. The two controllers bring up an Ether-IP tunnel between them for the specific purpose of carrying some of the client's traffic. The Ether-IP tunnel is simply a way that the controllers can encapsulate MAC-layer data inside an IP packet, using IP protocol 97. To move packets to and from the client, one controller encapsulates packets and sends them to the other controller. Packets received over the tunnel are unencapsulated by the other controller, where they reappear in their original form. (Ether-IP tunnels are defined in RFC 3378.)

Figure 19-13 *After an Inter-Controller Roam; Controllers Are on Different Subnets*

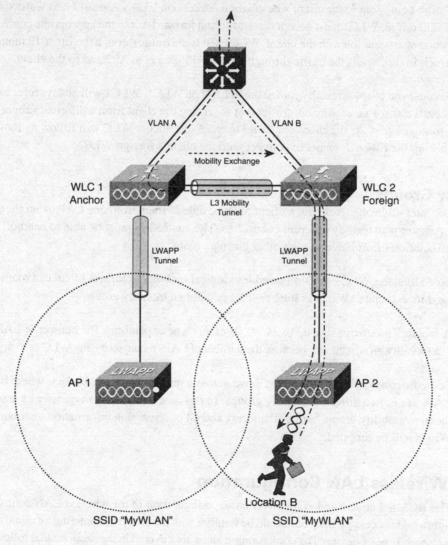

All the client's traffic will not be able to travel over the same path. Traffic *leaving* the client travels over the LWAPP tunnel from AP2 to WLC2 and onto VLAN B, as you might expect. Even though the client has an IP address that is foreign to its new VLAN, it can still send packets onto the foreign VLAN.

Traffic coming *toward* the client takes a different path. In Figure 19-13, traffic enters the switch on VLAN A and is forwarded to WLC1. Why does it enter VLAN A and not VLAN B, where the client is now located? Remember that the client is still using an IP address it obtained on VLAN A, so it will continue to appear in VLAN A—no matter where it roams within the wireless network.

Traffic being sent to the client's destination address on VLAN A must be forwarded onto VLAN A. Therefore, WLC1 must accept that traffic and forward it onto the appropriate controller that has a current association with the client. WLC1 sends the traffic through the Ether-IP tunnel to WLC2, which in turn sends the traffic through the LWAPP tunnel to AP2 and to the client.

Because the client originally joined the WLAN on WLC1, WLC1 will always refer to itself as the client's *anchor point*. Any controller that is serving the client from a different subnet is known as a *foreign agent*. As the client continues to roam, the anchor WLC will follow its movement by shifting the Ether-IP tunnel to connect with the client's foreign WLC.

Mobility Groups

For inter-controller roaming, a client must be able to roam from one LAP to another, where the LAPs are managed by different controllers. The controllers must be able to hand off a client's association information to each other during a roam.

To do this, the WLCs are configured into logical mobility groups. A client can roam to any LAP (and its associated WLC) as long as it stays within a mobility group.

A mobility group can have up to 24 WLCs of any type or platform. The number of LAPs contained in a mobility group can vary because the number of LAPs managed by any WLC can vary by platform.

Sometimes a wireless client might move across a mobility group boundary, where two adjacent LAPs are in two different mobility groups. In this case, the client can transfer its association into the new mobility group, but its IP address and all of its session information maintained in the WLCs will be dropped.

Basic Wireless LAN Configuration

The BCMSN course and exam cover basic configuration of the wireless LAN controller and lightweight access points. You should be familiar with the process of entering an initial configuration into each type of device. The configuration steps are covered in the sections that follow.

WLC Configuration

A Cisco WLC has several types of interfaces that are used for various purposes. Perhaps the most difficult part of configuring a WLC is deciding how to lay out and connect the interfaces.

Regardless of the hardware model, a WLC has the following interface types. Refer to Figure 19-14, which depicts the interfaces as they are commonly used in a network.

- **Management**—An interface with a static IP address used for in-band management traffic; you connect to this interface for web, Secure Shell (SSH), or Telnet sessions with the WLC.

- **AP Manager**—An interface with a static IP address that all LAPs use to terminate their LWAPP tunnels; the WLC also listens on this interface for subnet broadcasts from LAPs trying to discover controllers.

- **Virtual**—A logical interface used to relay DHCP requests from wireless clients.

  A bogus (but unique) static IP address is assigned to this interface, so that clients will see the virtual address as their DHCP server. All WLCs within a mobility group must use the same virtual interface address.

- **Service port**—An out-of-band Ethernet interface used on Cisco 4100 and 4400 series WLCs, only when the controller is booting or a network problem is preventing other types of access; the Catalyst 6500 Wireless Services Module (WiSM) has an internal service port that connects to the chassis supervisor.

- **Distribution system port**—An interface that connects the WLC to a switch in the campus network; this interface is usually a trunk that carries the VLANs that will appear on LAPs for wireless clients.

- **Dynamic**—An interface that is automatically created, as needed, for VLANs that are extended to LAPs through the LWAPP tunnels. A dynamic interface is sometimes called a *user interface*.

  Dynamic interfaces have IP addresses that belong to the subnets used on the wireless client VLANs or SSIDs.

Normally, you can set aside a management VLAN and subnet for WLC and LWAPP use. You can assign an address to the management interface and to the AP management interface from the same management subnet. All management traffic (web-based, Telnet, SSH, or AAA) and LWAPP tunnel traffic will come to these addresses from external sources. Remember that LAPs will be positioned in various places in the network—even in different switch blocks, so you should consider the LAP traffic to be external.

The LAPs will receive IP addresses that are not necessarily on the AP manager subnet. In a small network, you might have LAPs and WLCs located on the same subnet so that they are Layer 2 adjacent. In larger networks, LAPs will be distributed across switch blocks. Their IP addresses will vary because they are not Layer 2 adjacent, and they will not be located in the AP management subnet.

Figure 19-14 shows a sample scenario, with each type of WLC interface, along with the respective VLANs and IP addresses. The WLC's distribution system port is actually a trunk link carrying both the WLC and AP management subnet (VLAN 10) and the wireless client subnet (VLAN 100). Notice that the APs are located on access layer switch ports elsewhere in the network, and that they use a unique subnet (VLAN 200) that is set aside for APs within a switch block.

Figure 19-14 *Sample WLC Interface Layout*

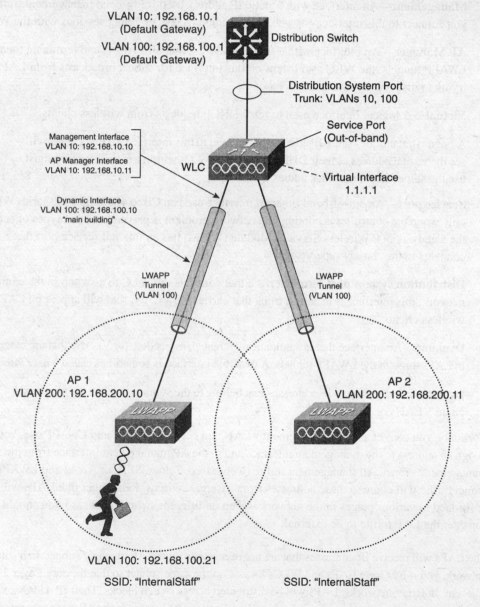

VLAN 10: 192.168.10.1
(Default Gateway)

VLAN 100: 192.168.100.1
(Default Gateway)

Distribution Switch

Distribution System Port
Trunk: VLANs 10, 100

Service Port
(Out-of-band)

Management Interface
VLAN 10: 192.168.10.10

AP Manager Interface
VLAN 10: 192.168.10.11

WLC

Virtual Interface
1.1.1.1

Dynamic Interface
VLAN 100: 192.168.100.10
"main building"

LWAPP
Tunnel
(VLAN 100)

LWAPP
Tunnel
(VLAN 100)

AP 1
VLAN 200: 192.168.200.10

AP 2
VLAN 200: 192.168.200.11

VLAN 100: 192.168.100.21

SSID: "InternalStaff"

SSID: "InternalStaff"

Initial WLC Configuration

The WLC must be configured with some initial information so that it can join the network. You can connect to the WLC's console port and use the Startup Wizard to enter parameters through the CLI. Once the WLC boots up and runs its code image, the CLI will begin interactively prompting for the following information:

1. The system name, consisting of a text string that identifies the WLC (up to 32 characters).

2. Administrative username and password (the default is *admin* and *admin*, respectively).

3. Service port IP address (DHCP or static address).

    If a static address is selected, you are prompted for the IP address, subnet mask, default gateway, and the VLAN number for the management interface. If the management VLAN is untagged (the native VLAN on a trunk), enter VLAN number **0**.

4. DHCP server address, from which wireless clients will receive their IP addresses.

5. IP address of the AP Manager interface.

6. IP address of the virtual interface (a bogus address, usually 1.1.1.1).

7. Mobility group name (must be identical on all WLCs in a mobility group).

8. Default SSID which is used for LAPs when they join a controller; the WLC will push other SSIDs down to the LAPs after they join.

9. Require clients to obtain IP addresses from a DHCP server?

    Enter **yes** to force clients to use a DHCP server; otherwise, enter **no** to allow clients to have statically configured addresses.

10. Configure a RADIUS server? (You can enter **no** and configure any RADIUS server from the web front-end.)

11. Country code. (Type **help** to see a list.)

12. Enable or disable 802.11a, 802.11b, and 802.11g on all APs managed by the WLC. (As you are prompted for each WLAN type, enter **yes** to enable it or **no** to disable it.)

13. Enable or disable radio resource management (RRM) auto-RF feature. (Enter **yes** to enable automatic RF parameter adjustments, or **no** to disable it.)

After this information has been entered, the WLC saves its configuration and reboots. From this point on, you can manage the WLC from its web interface.

Further WLC Configuration

The WLC uses dynamic interfaces to extend VLANs on the distribution system ports to the SSIDs on wireless LANs. You can use the following steps to configure the WLC for each WLAN:

Step 1   Create a dynamic interface for wireless clients.

Step 2   Create a WLAN that is bound to the dynamic interface.

Using the sample interface locations and address assignments from Figure 19-14, you would first create a dynamic interface for the client VLAN 100. You can do this by selecting the **Controller** tab on the WLC task bar. Then click on the **Interfaces** category in the left column. Clicking on the **New** button takes you to the screen shown in Figure 19-15. Here, you can give the dynamic interface a descriptive name ("Main Building") and bind it to a specific VLAN ID (VLAN 100).

Figure 19-15   *Creating a Dynamic Interface on the WLC*

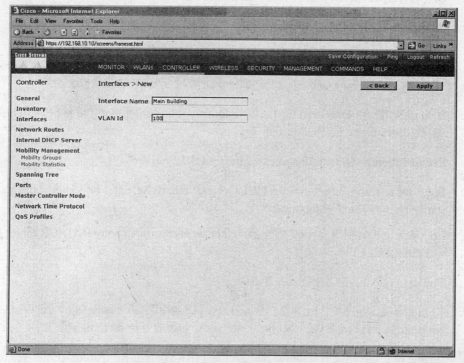

Next, you have to provide addressing information for the new dynamic interface. The WLC presents the screen shown in Figure 19-16. The WLC must also have the DHCP addresses for the wireless client subnet because it acts as a DHCP relay for clients that broadcast DHCP requests.

Figure 19-16   *Assigning Address Information to the Dynamic Interface*

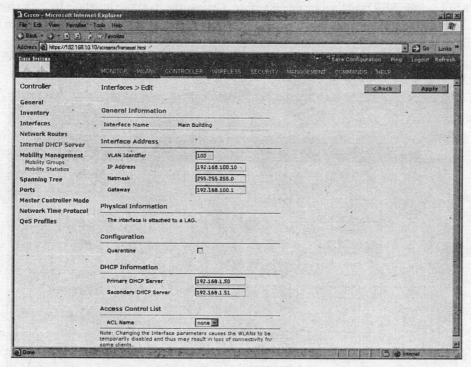

Finally, you define a WLAN that will actually serve wireless clients that are associated with LAPs that are joined to the WLC. Select the **WLANs** tab on the WLC task bar, and then click the **New** button. On the WLANs>New screen, as shown in Figure 19-17, enter the SSID string that will be used on the WLAN.

Figure 19-17   *Defining a New WLAN*

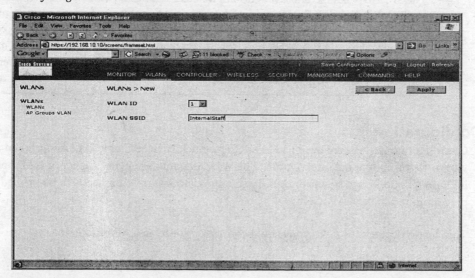

Finally, the WLC will present the WLANs>Edit screen shown in Figure 19-18. In this step, you will bind the SSID with a dynamic interface. Choose the dynamic interface from the list next to the **Interface Name** field. In the example, the SSID **InternalStaff** is bound to the **main building** interface.

Figure 19-18 *Binding a WLAN to a Dynamic Interface*

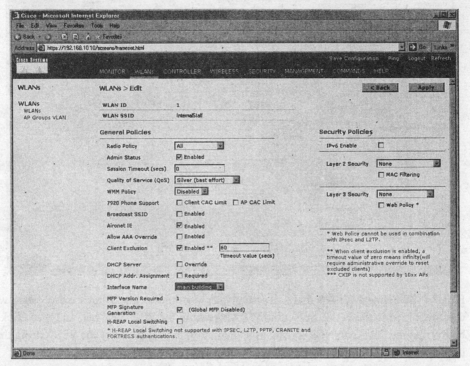

> **TIP.** The BCMSN course and exam do not discuss setting the clock or date and time parameters on WLCs or LAPs. However, when you configure these devices, you should remember to set the clocks and use a Network Time Protocol (NTP) server if at all possible. The WLCs and LAPs have embedded digital certificates that are used to authenticate the devices. Digital certificates are very dependent upon accurate date and time values—NTP offers the best accuracy and scalability across a network.

LAP Configuration

Cisco lightweight APs are designed to be "zero-touch" devices, which can be installed and used with little or no manual intervention. The WLC can manage every aspect of LAP operation, including code image synchronization, so almost no information needs to be primed or preconfigured in the LAP itself.

This section covers the tasks you should consider prior to an LAP installation.

Supplying Power to an LAP

A lightweight AP can require up to 15 W of power at 48 VDC. The exact amount of power depends upon the model and the types of radio that will be used. For example, a Cisco Aironet 1130AG requires a maximum of 12.2 W if both 802.11a and 802.11b/g radios are enabled at maximum transmit power.

Power can be supplied to an LAP through one of the following means:

- **AC adapter**—The power supply can be plugged directly into the LAP if an AC power source is located near the LAP unit.

- **Power over Ethernet (PoE)**—Power can be supplied over the switch port and Ethernet cable using either the Cisco inline power or the IEEE 802.3af method. Power can be supplied over Ethernet cable pairs 1,2 and 3,6 or over pairs 4,5 and 7,8.

- **Power injector**—A small box is inserted somewhere between the switch port and the LAP's Ethernet connection. The AC adapter plugs directly into the power injector, supplying LAP power over Ethernet cable pairs 4,5 and 7,8. This method is useful when PoE is not available on the switch where the LAP connects.

If power is supplied over the Ethernet cable, the length of the powered portion of the cable can increase the LAP power requirements. For example, if a full-length 100-meter cable is used, the maximum power needed by an LAP can increase by about 2.5 W, going from 12.2 W to 14.7 W.

> **TIP**   When PoE is used to power an LAP from a switch interface, it is no different than using it to power a Cisco IP Phone. Refer to Chapter 14, "IP Telephony," for PoE switch configuration information.

Switch Port Configuration for LAP

Before you connect an LAP to a switch port, you should make sure that the port is properly configured. The LAP requires an access mode port—not a trunking port. You can place the LAP on any VLAN that is convenient in a switch block. For example, the LAP can sit on the user access VLAN along with other end users in the area.

Usually the best practice is to set aside a VLAN strictly for LAP management traffic. This VLAN contains one IP subnet reserved only for LAPs.

You can also enable Spanning-Tree PortFast on the access mode ports where LAPs connect. The LAP VLAN terminates on the LAPs and doesn't get extended any further. Therefore, no danger exists of that VLAN forming a loop somewhere in the wireless cloud.

You can use the following Catalyst IOS commands to configure LAP switch ports:

```
! Define the LAP access VLAN
Switch(config)# vlan lap-vlan-num
Switch(config-vlan)# name lap-vlan-name
Switch(config-vlan)# exit
! Configure the LAP switch port
Switch(config)# interface type mod/num
Switch(config-if)# switchport
Switch(config-if)# switchport access vlan lap-vlan-num
Switch(config-if)# switchport host
Switch(config-if)# power inline auto
Switch(config-if)# no shutdown
Switch(config-if)# exit
```

Initial LAP Configuration

Once a WLC has been configured and is operational, a new LAP can be introduced on the network without any configuration—right out of the box! This is known as a "zero-touch" installation.

The LAP only needs two pieces of information to be able to boot up and start communicating with the WLC:

- An IP address

- Addresses of one or more WLCs

You can power up an LAP, connect to its console port, and preconfigure this information. However, that introduces some administrative tasks that you don't usually need. Instead, you can use a DHCP server that is located somewhere on the network to provide IP addresses to your LAPs.

An LAP needs an IP address so that it can exchange messages with a WLC and bring up an LWAPP tunnel. Think of this address as a management address—most likely located on a management subnet or VLAN within a switchblock. Any addresses or subnets needed for the end users or wireless clients will be brought down to the LAP through the LWAPP tunnel.

If the WLCs and LAPs have their management interfaces connected to the same Layer 2 VLAN and IP subnet, an LAP can find the WLCs by sending a subnet broadcast. Any WLCs present on the subnet will reply, allowing the LAP to build a list of addresses.

If the WLCs are located on different IP subnets than the LAPs, the WLC addresses can be obtained in the contents of DHCP option 43 when the LAP receives a DHCP reply. The format of option 43 varies according to the LAP model. Cisco 1000 and 1500 series LAPs use a comma-separated list of WLC management interface addresses.

All other LAP models use a string of hex digits that represent a TLV (Type, Length, Value) field. The field is made up of the following values:

- **Type**—One byte, hex 0xf1

- **Length**—Number of WLC addresses times 4 (4 bytes are in each WLC IP address)

- **Value**—WLC management interface IP addresses

As an example, suppose that an IOS-based switch is used as the DHCP server to supply LAP IP addresses. The following configuration commands can be used:

```
Switch(config)# ip dhcp pool pool-name
Switch (dhcp-config)# network ip-address subnet-mask
Switch (dhcp-config)# default-router ip-address
Switch (dhcp-config0# dns-server ip-address
Switch (dhcp-config)# option 43 {ascii | hex} string
Switch (dhcp-config)# exit
```

Suppose that the LAP management subnet is 192.168.10.0/24, the default router is 192.168.10.1, and the DNS server is 192.168.100.100. Three WLCs are present, and the LAP should try them in this order: 192.168.1.10, 192.168.1.11, and 192.168.1.12.

The IOS DHCP pool configuration would begin with the following commands:

```
Switch (config)# ip dhcp pool lap-pool
Switch (dhcp-config)# network 192.168.10.0 255.255.255.0
Switch (dhcp-config)# default-router 192.168.10.1
Switch (dhcp-config)# dns-server 192.168.100.100
```

For Cisco 1000 and 1500 series LAPs, DHCP option 43 would look like the following:

```
Switch (dhcp-config)# option 43 ascii "192.168.1,10,192.168.1.11,192.168.1.12"
```

whereas all other Cisco LAP models would have DHCP option 43 configured as follows:

```
Switch (dhcp-config)# option 43 hex 0xf10cc0a8010ac0a8010bc0a8010c
```

Here, the hex string is encoded as follows, from left to right:

- 0xf1 is the field type.

- 0c is the number of bytes in the list of WLC addresses; there are three IP addresses, for a total of 12 bytes (0c in hex).

- c0a8010a is 192.168.1.10 represented in hex.

- c0a8010b is 192.168.1.11.

- c0a8010c is 192.168.1.12.

> **TIP** LWAPP uses UDP ports 12222 and 12223. You should make sure that these ports are permitted to pass between an LAP and any WLCs.

Using the WLC web interface, you can verify the state of the LAPs. From the **Monitor Summary** screen, look under the **Access Point Summary** section and click on the **Detail** link that is next to **All APs**. Figure 19-19 shows an example of the LAP status screen. If the **Operational Status** field is shown as **REG**, the LAP is booted, has brought up an LWAPP tunnel with the WLC, and is fully functional.

Figure 19-19 *Displaying LAP Status Information*

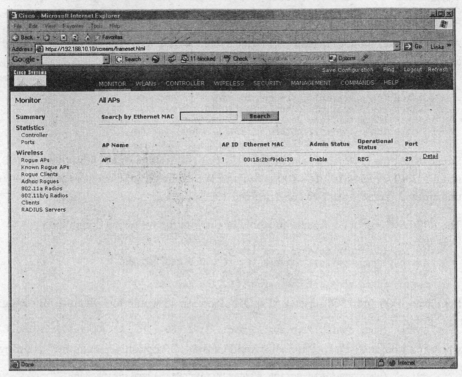

TIP   Several Cisco access point models can run in either autonomous or lightweight mode. The mode is determined by the IOS code release that is running on the AP. If you need to know which mode your AP is currently running, connect to its console port and use the **show version** command.

If the Cisco IOS Software release name ends with a "JX" suffix, the lightweight mode is being used. Otherwise, it is running in autonomous mode. In the following two examples, the first AP is running in autonomous mode, whereas the second AP is running in lightweight mode:

```
ap#show version
Cisco IOS Software, C1130 Software (C1130-K9W7-M), Version 12.3(7)JA1, RELEASE
  SOFTWARE (fc1)
Technical Support: http://www.cisco.com/techsupport
Copyright (c) 1986-2005 by Cisco Systems, Inc.
Compiled Thu 06-Oct-05 09:36 by evmiller
```

```
ap#show version
Cisco IOS Software, C1130 Software (C1130-K9W8-M), Version 12.3(7)JX3, RELEASE
  SOFTWARE (fc1)
Technical Support: http://www.cisco.com/techsupport
Copyright (c) 1986-2006 by Cisco Systems, Inc.
Compiled Tue 28-Feb-06 21:14 by kellythw
```

Foundation Summary

The Foundation Summary is a collection of information that provides a convenient review of many key concepts in this chapter. If you are already comfortable with the topics in this chapter, this summary can help you recall a few details. If you just read this chapter, this review should help solidify some key facts. If you are doing your final preparation before the exam, this information will hopefully be a convenient way to review the day before the exam.

Table 19-3 *AP Functions Divided as a Split-MAC Architecture*

Function	LAP	WLC
Transmit and receive 802.11 frames	Y	N
Frame buffering and MAC management	Y	N
802.11 encryption	Y	N
RF management	N	Y
Manage associations and roaming	N	Y
Authenticate clients	N	Y
Manage security policies	N	Y
Handle quality of service	N	Y

Table 19-4 *LWAPP Tunnel Contents*

LWAPP Tunnel Contents	Comments
Control messages	Messages between LAP and WLC; encrypted and authenticated
Client data	Packets between wireless clients and other hosts; not encrypted or protected

Table 19-5 *WLC Interfaces and Their Functions*

Interface Type	Function	IP Address
Management	In-band management, Web sessions, AAA servers	Static, from a management subnet
AP Management	LWAPP tunnel endpoint address	Static, from a management subnet
Virtual	Logical interface for DHCP relay	Bogus but unique address, can exist elsewhere in the network; 1.1.1.1 is commonly used
Service Port	Out-of-band management during network outage	Static, on a special out-of-band subnet
Distribution System Port	Connects WLC to switched network; usually a trunk link carrying wireless client VLANs	N/A
Dynamic	Extended through LWAPP tunnels to LAPs for wireless clients	Static, on the VLANs that will be extended to clients through LWAPP tunnels

Q&A

The questions and scenarios in this book are more difficult than what you should experience on the actual exam. The questions do not attempt to cover more breadth or depth than the exam; however, they are designed to make sure that you know the answers. Rather than allowing you to derive the answers from clues hidden inside the questions themselves, the questions challenge your understanding and recall of the subject. Hopefully, these questions will help limit the number of exam questions on which you narrow your choices to two options and then guess.

You can find the answers to these questions in Appendix A.

1. LWAPP is integral to operating a lightweight access point. What is so special about LWAPP?

2. How does a wireless client roam between two LAPs managed by the same WLC?

3. Can a client roam across two LAPs that are managed by two different WLCs? Explain why or why not.

4. Describe some of the functions that are divided between LAP and WLC in a "split-MAC" architecture.

5. List some of the advanced functions that can be performed by a WLC.

Part VI: Scenarios for Final Preparation

CHAPTER 20

Scenarios for Final Preparation

This chapter presents scenarios that you can use to review most of the concepts contained in this book. The scenarios are designed to assist you in final preparation for the BCMSN exam. Case studies are presented with network diagrams and questions covering many switching topics. This chapter emphasizes an overall understanding of switching concepts, configuration commands, and network operation. Although the Cisco BCMSN exam might not contain scenarios of this type, you can become better prepared by thinking about the "bigger picture" of a network and how you can apply each switching topic.

Scenario 1: Trunking and DTP

This scenario is built around a network of switches connected by trunking links. You need to think about how DTP operates and how trunks are negotiated (or not) between switches.

Consider the network shown in Figure 20-1 and answer the questions that follow. Assume that all switches shown support DTP.

Figure 20-1 *Diagram for Scenario 1*

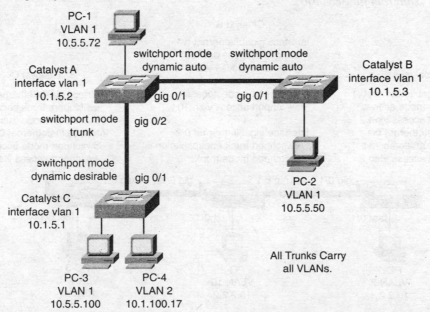

1. What is the mode of the link between Catalyst A and Catalyst B?

2. Suppose that the network administrator types these commands for interface GigabitEthernet 0/1 on Catalyst B:

   ```
   Switch(config)# interface gigabitethernet 0/1
   Switch(config-if)# switchport mode trunk
   Switch(config-if)# switchport nonegotiate
   ```

   What will the link mode be now?

3. Catalyst B has been given the command **no switchport nonegotiate** for interface GigabitEthernet 0/1. What is the link mode now?

4. What is the mode of the link between Catalyst A and Catalyst C?

5. Assume that all links between Catalyst switches are in trunking mode, transporting VLANs 1 through 1005. Can PC-2 ping PC-4?

6. Suppose that PC-1 begins to generate a broadcast storm. Where would the effects of this storm be experienced in this network? Consider both devices and links. Will PC-4 receive the broadcasts?

Scenario 2: VLANs, Trunking, and VTP

This scenario is designed to stir your thinking about VLAN and trunking connectivity. You also need to examine switch configurations and apply them to a network diagram. See the diagram shown in Figure 20-2 and answer the questions that follow. Portions of the configurations of the three Catalyst switches are shown above them.

Figure 20-2 *Diagram for Scenario 2*

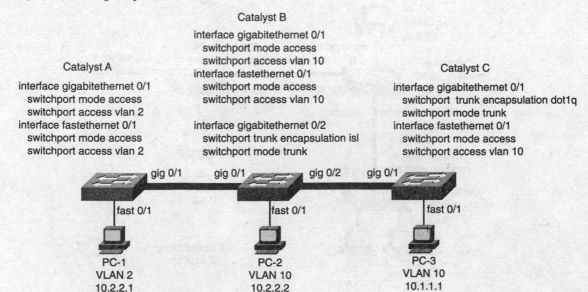

1. PC-1 and PC-2 both are configured with IP addresses on the same subnet. Notice that each PC connects to a different VLAN number. Given the switch configurations shown, can PC-1 ping PC-2?

2. PC-2 and PC-3 are assigned to the same IP subnet (using subnet mask 255.0.0.0) and the same VLAN. Can PC-2 and PC-3 ping each other?

3. Will the trunk link between Catalyst B and Catalyst C come up successfully?

4. Suppose that the trunk between Catalyst B and Catalyst C is configured properly. Where will VLAN1 be pruned? Why?

5. Suppose that Catalyst A is a VTP server, Catalyst C is a VTP client, and Catalyst B is configured for VTP transparent mode. All switches are in the Bermuda management domain. If VLAN14 is created on Catalyst A, which switches also will create VLAN 14 using VTP?

6. If VLAN 15 is created on Catalyst B, what other switches also will create VLAN 15 through VTP?

7. If VLAN 16 is created on Catalyst C, what will happen?

Scenario 3: EtherChannels

This scenario focuses on EtherChannel links between switches. See the diagram shown in Figure 20-3 and answer the questions that follow.

Figure 20-3 *Diagram for Scenario 3*

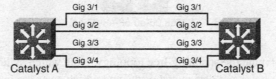

1. Four GigabitEthernet interfaces on Catalyst A are to be bundled into a Gigabit EtherChannel with Catalyst B. If each of these interfaces also is configured as a trunk, what must be similar about them on both switches?

2. Catalyst A should actively initiate an EtherChannel with Catalyst B. PAgP negotiation should be used. What commands should be used on each of Catalyst A's ports to configure negotiation of EtherChannel 1?

3. What is the default load-distribution algorithm, assuming that the switches are Catalyst 6500s?

4. Suppose that the EtherChannel is a Layer 3 interface on both switches so that each switch uses one MAC and one IP address. Should you choose the **src-dst-mac** or **src-dst-ip** algorithm to maximize the load distribution across all the links?

Scenario 4: Traditional STP

This scenario exercises your ability to think through the Spanning Tree Protocol operation. You are presented with a simple network of two switches. This keeps the STP complexity to a minimum while forcing you to think through the STP convergence process on a live network. Given the network diagram shown in Figure 20-4, complete the following exercises.

Figure 20-4 *Network Diagram for Scenario 4*

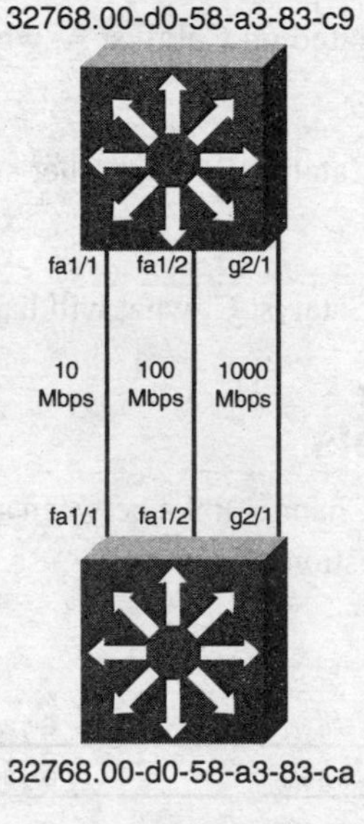

1. Manually compute the spanning-tree topology. Note which switch is the root bridge, which ports are root ports and designated ports, and which ports are in the Blocking state.

2. If the 100-Mbps link (port FastEthernet 1/2) is disconnected, what happens with the STP?

3. If the 1000-Mbps link (port GigabitEthernet 2/1) is disconnected, how much time will elapse before the two switches can communicate again? (Assume that both switches use the default STP timer values and no additional features for faster convergence.)

4. Assume that the physical 1000-Mbps link (port GigabitEthernet 2/1) stays up and active, but BPDUs are not allowed to pass (that is, an access list filter is blocking BPDUs). What happens and when?

Scenario 5: Advanced STP

A small network consists of two core switches, Catalyst C1 and C2, and an access switch, A1, as shown in Figure 20-5. Advanced Spanning Tree Protocol features will improve the convergence times and reduce the number of STP instances. Answer these questions.

Figure 20-5 *Network Diagram for Scenario 5*

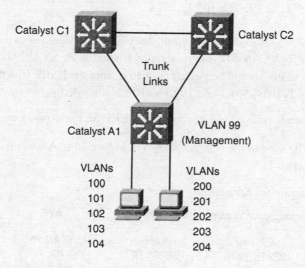

1. To prevent the possibility of a unidirectional link occurring on switch A1's uplinks, what switch feature can be used? What commands are necessary to enable this feature? Assume that the links should be disabled if a unidirectional condition is found. Which switches need to be configured this way?

2. On Catalyst A1, what feature and command should be used to prevent unexpected STP BPDUs from being received on the ports connected to end users?

3. For the links between switch A1 and the user PCs, what command is needed to configure these as RSTP edge ports?

4. By default, the traditional PVST+ mode is enabled on a switch. What command can be used to enable RSTP to be used with PVST+?

5. Suppose that MST is to be configured to reduce the number of STP instances because 12 unique VLANs are being used across the network. How many MST instances are needed for the three switches shown in Figure 20-5, assuming that traffic should be load-balanced across the two uplinks of switch A1?

6. What commands are needed to configure switch C1 for MST?

7. Now make sure that C1 is configured as the root bridge for one MST instance. What commands are needed?

Scenario 6: Router Redundancy with HSRP, VRRP, and GLBP

This scenario covers two methods by which you can configure multilayer switches to provide redundant router or gateway functionality: HSRP, VRRP, and GLBP.

A network consists of two VLANs: 101 and 102. Suppose that the PCs in VLAN 101 (192.168.101.0/24) use address 192.168.101.1 as their default gateway. The PCs in VLAN 102 (192.168.102.0/24) use 192.168.102.1.

1. What commands are necessary to configure HSRP on a Catalyst switch so that it becomes the active router for VLAN 101 and the standby router for VLAN 102? If a failed router interface is restored, control should be passed back to it from the HSRP standby router. (You can use IP addresses 192.168.101.2 and 192.168.102.2, if needed.)

2. What commands can you use to configure VRRP for the network described in question 1?

3. GLBP is to be used in the network shown in Figure 20-6. Answer the following questions about this network.

Figure 20-6 *Network Diagram for Scenario 6*

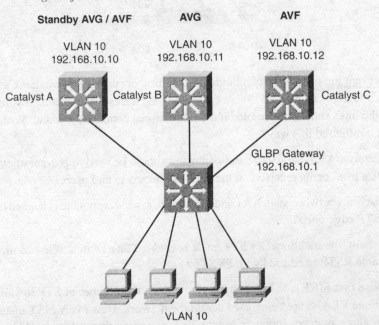

d. What command should you use to make Catalyst B become the active virtual gateway (AVG) for GLBP group 10?

b. The virtual gateway address is 192.168.10.1. Which switches should be configured for this, and with what command?

c. Give the command needed on the AVG to implement round-robin load balancing, evenly distributing the virtual gateway MAC addresses across the set of AVFs.

    d. Each of the AVF switches must be configured to become members of GLBP group 10. How can this be accomplished?

Scenario 7: IP Telephony in a Switched Network

This scenario uses a simple two-switch network to reinforce the concepts needed to properly implement IP telephony. Think about supplying power to the Cisco IP Phone, as well as how to implement QoS trust within this network. Use Figure 20-7 as a reference for the following questions.

Figure 20-7 *Network Diagram for Scenario 7*

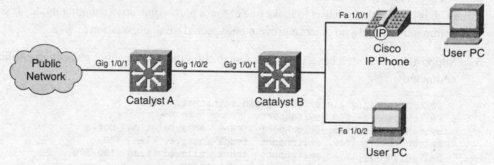

1. Assume that Catalyst B supports Power over Ethernet. If interface Fa1/0/1 has its default configuration, will power be supplied to the IP Phone? Now suppose that someone has entered the **power inline never** command for that interface. What command could you use to begin supplying power to the phone dynamically?

2. Where should a QoS trust boundary be implemented? In other words, which switches should trust incoming QoS information and which ones should not?

3. On Catalyst B, configure interface FastEthernet 3/1 to inform the IP Phone to use VLAN 17 for voice traffic. Also add a configuration command to ensure that no QoS trust is extended to the IP Phone's PC data port.

4. What configuration commands would be necessary to enable QoS trust on Catalyst B's Gig 1/0/1 uplink and to disable trust on port Fa1/0/2 where the user PC is connected?

Scenario 8: Securing Access and Managing Traffic in a Switched Network

This scenario is designed to stir your thinking about how to control access to switched networks, how to control traffic within a VLAN, and how to monitor traffic.

1. Network administrators want to have tight control over hosts moving around within their network. A Catalyst 3750 needs to have port-level security enabled on all 48 of its FastEthernet access-layer ports. Only one host should be connected per port, so the default behavior of shutting down the port is acceptable. What commands are necessary to do this?

2. Port-level security is desired on a Catalyst 3750 interface FastEthernet 1/0/18, where 24 users are connected through an Ethernet hub. Rather than have the switch port shut down on a security violation, network administrators want only the hosts in violation to be rejected. What command can accomplish this?

3. Configure a VLAN access control list that can perform packet filtering within a VLAN. Users in the 192.168.191.0 255.255.255.0 network should be allowed to use only HTTP (www) traffic to the web server 192.168.191.199/24, on VLAN 180. How can you configure the VACL to accomplish this?

4. An access-layer switch has ports FastEthernet 1/0/1 through 1/0/48 connected to end-user PCs. Is it possible for a user to make one of these ports come up in trunking mode? If so, what commands should you enter to prevent unexpected trunk negotiation?

5. Suppose that a switch has a trunk link GigabitEthernet 1/0/1 configured with the following commands:

```
Switch(config)# interface gigabitethernet 1/0/1
Switch(config-if)# switchport
Switch(config-if)# switchport trunk encapsulation dot1q
Switch(config-if)# switchport trunk native vlan 100
Switch(config-if)# switchport trunk allowed vlan 100-300
Switch(config-if)# switchport mode trunk
```

VLANs 100, 200, and 300 all are used for user traffic. What, if anything, should be done to the trunk configuration to prevent a VLAN hopping attack from occurring?

6. A Catalyst switch has users connected to ports FastEthernet 1/0/1 through 1/0/30. These users are associated with VLAN 50. Two production DHCP servers are connected to ports FastEthernet 1/0/40 and 1/0/41. What commands should be entered to enable DHCP snooping so that DHCP spoofing attacks can be detected and prevented?

Scenario 9: Implementing a Wireless LAN

This scenario is designed to stir your thinking about how to add WLAN components to an existing switched campus network, and how to extend network connectivity to wireless users. In this scenario, a Cisco Wireless LAN Controller (WLC) is positioned at the network core, and Cisco Lightweight Access Points (LAPs) are positioned at the access layer switches. Use Figure 20-8 as a reference for the questions that follow.

1. Suppose that LAP1 is configured to use 802.11g channel 1. What channel should be configured on LAP2?

2. Wireless users in the LAP1 cell use SSID "InMotion" to associate with their WLAN. What considerations should you make on LAP2 to allow users to roam between the cells?

Figure 20-8 *Network Diagram for Scenario 8*

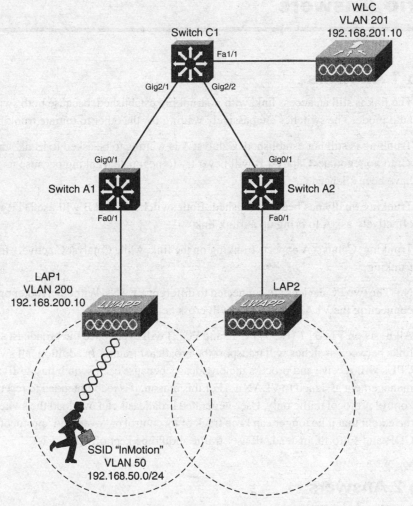

3. LAP1's wired Ethernet connection will belong to VLAN 200, using IP address 192.168.200.10. The LAP will also need to provide VLAN 50 to its wireless clients. What commands could you use to configure Switch A1's FastEthernet 0/1 interface, where LAP1 connects?

4. The WLC will use IP address 192.168.201.10 on VLAN 201 to form the LWAPP tunnels with the LAPs. On which WLC interface should you configure this address?

5. LAP1 is located on VLAN 200 in the 192.168.200.0/24 subnet. Both LAPs need to join the same WLC and both need to offer VLAN 50 to their wireless clients. Would you have to place LAP2 on VLAN 200 in the 192.168.200.0/24 subnet? Why or why not?

6. What two things must be configured on the WLC so that wireless clients using SSID "InMotion" can begin communicating on the 192.168.50.0/24 subnet?

Scenario Answers

Scenario 1 Answers

1. The link is still an access link, with no trunking established, because both switches are set to auto mode. The switches are passively waiting for the other to initiate trunking.

2. Trunking is still not established. Catalyst A is waiting to be asked to trunk, and Catalyst B is set to nonegotiate. Catalyst B will never try to negotiate trunking because its DTP packets have been silenced.

3. Trunking finally has been established. Both switches A and B will use DTP, and B will effectively ask A to bring up a trunk link.

4. Trunking. Catalyst A expects trunking on the link, while Catalyst C actively tries to negotiate trunking.

5. No. The two PC devices are connected to different VLANs. Without a router or Layer 3 device connecting the VLANs, no traffic will cross between them.

6. All hosts on VLAN 1 (PC-1, PC-2, and PC-3) will experience the broadcast storm. All trunk links between switches will transport the broadcast frames. In addition, all switch supervisor CPUs will receive and process the broadcasts because each switch has an IP address for management assigned to VLAN 1. (For this reason, it is recommended to reserve VLAN 1 for control protocol traffic only. User-generated broadcasts can overload the switch supervisor to the extent that it no longer can keep track of its control or "overhead" protocols, such as VTP, CDP, and so forth. Instead, all user traffic should be kept off VLAN 1.)

Scenario 2 Answers

1. Yes. PC-1 and PC-2 are connected to access VLAN switch ports, VLAN 2 and VLAN 10, respectively. Normally, if these were assigned to different VLANs, they could not ping each other unless a Layer 3 device were present to route between the Layer 2 VLANs. In this case, however, the link between Catalyst A and B is the key. On one switch, the link is an access VLAN port on VLAN 2; on the other end, it is an access VLAN port on VLAN 10. These are physically connected, and each switch has no knowledge of what VLAN the other has assigned to the link. Therefore, data can pass across the link freely, connecting the two VLANs.

2. No. Again, the key is the link between Catalyst B and C. Catalyst B has the link configured as an ISL trunk, whereas Catalyst C has it configured as an 802.1Q trunk. Because the trunk encapsulations are different, no data will pass between them.

3. Yes, the trunk link on each switch will come up successfully, even though the trunk will not work end to end because of the encapsulation mismatch. This is because DTP packets will be exchanged, but both ends of the link are configured to trunk unconditionally.

   As a side note, DTP and CDP packets will be exchanged between the switches. Both of these protocols are sent over VLAN 1 in ISL encapsulation and over the native VLAN (VLAN 1, by default) in dot1Q encapsulation. Because the trunk encapsulation is different on each end of the link, each switch will tag VLAN 1 differently. Therefore, VLAN 1 will not be contiguous across the link, and these protocols will not pass successfully.

4. VLAN 1 will not be pruned. Although VLAN 1 is present on all switches, it is not pruned because VLAN 1 is ineligible for pruning by definition.

5. Only Catalyst C creates VLAN 14 in response to VTP advertisements. Catalyst B in transparent mode relays only the VTP information, without interpreting the information.

6. Only Catalyst B creates VLAN 15. Because it is in transparent mode, no VLAN activity will be advertised to other neighboring switches. However, Catalyst B is allowed to create, delete, and rename VLANs freely. These VLANs are significant only to the local switch.

7. Catalyst C will not allow any VLANs to be created unless they are learned from a VTP server in the Bermuda domain. Because it is in VTP client mode, no VLAN changes can be performed from the console.

Scenario 3 Answers

1. All bundled ports must have the same set of allowed VLANs, the same native VLAN, the same trunk encapsulation, and the same trunk mode. (In addition, the switch ports all must have identical speed and duplex settings.)

2. You can use the following configuration commands:

   ```
   CatalystA(config)# interface range gigabitethernet 3/1 - 4
   CatalystA(config-if)# channel-protocol pagp
   CatalystA(config-if)# channel-group 1 mode desirable
   ```

3. The Catalyst 6500 default algorithm is the XOR of the source and destination IP addresses, using the **port-channel load-balance src-dst-ip** command.

4. Most of the traffic crossing the EtherChannel will have the same two MAC addresses as source or destination—that of the two Layer 3 interfaces. Therefore, the **src-dst-mac** algorithm will always use only one of the four links within the EtherChannel. The source and destination IP addresses, however, probably will be varied and will yield the best distribution.

Scenario 4 Answers

1. The spanning-tree topology should look like the diagram in Figure 20-9. Catalyst A is the root bridge, and only the 1000-Mbps link is forwarding. The root ports (RP) and designated ports (DP) are labeled on the diagram.

Figure 20-9   *Resulting Spanning-Tree Topology for Scenario 4*

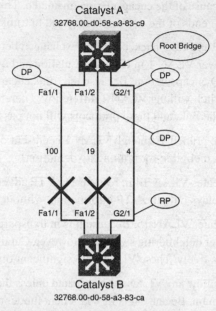

2. Because the 100-Mbps link is in the Blocking state on Catalyst B, no major change in the topology occurs. Effectively, this link already was "disconnected." However, after the physical link status goes down, both Catalyst A and Catalyst B sense the change and begin sending TCN BPDUs to notify each other of the topology change. Because Catalyst A is the root bridge, it acknowledges the TCN to Catalyst B. Both switches age out their MAC address tables in Forward Delay seconds.

3. Disconnecting the 1000-Mbps link causes Catalyst B to immediately find another root port. Ports 1/1 and 1/2 go into the Listening state, waiting to receive BPDUs. Port 1/2, with a cost of 19, becomes the next root port as soon as Catalyst B computes the root path cost (0 +19) for it. Port 1/2 stays in the Listening state for Forward Delay (15 seconds), and then in the Learning state for Forward Delay (15 seconds). Port 1/2 moves into the Forwarding state, restoring connectivity in 30 seconds. (If PAgP is operating on the port, an additional delay of 20 seconds occurs.)

4. Because the 1000-Mbps link's status stays up, neither Catalyst detects a link failure. Therefore, no immediate attempt to find another root port occurs. Instead, Catalyst B will not receive BPDUs from Catalyst A over link GigabitEthernet 2/1 because they are being filtered out. After the MaxAge Timer expires (20 seconds), Catalyst B ages out the stored BPDU for Catalyst A on port GigabitEthernet 2/1. Catalyst B moves ports FastEthernet 1/1 and 1/2 into the Listening state to determine a new root port. As in step 3, port FastEthernet 1/2 becomes the root port with a lower root path cost than port FastEthernet 1/1. The port moves through the Listening (15 seconds) and Learning (15 seconds) states and into the Forwarding state. The total time that has elapsed before connectivity restores is 20 + 15 + 15 = 50 seconds. (Again, if PAgP is active on the port, an additional 20 seconds can be added to the delay.)

Scenario 5 Answers

1. The Unidirectional Link Detection (UDLD) feature can be used. You can use the **udld aggressive** global-configuration command to enable UDLD on all fiber-optic ports. UDLD must be enabled on *both ends* of a link, so it should be enabled on switches A1 and also C1 and C2.

2. The BPDU Guard feature can be used to detect and stop unexpected BPDUs from being received on access layer ports. You can use the following interface-configuration command to enable this feature:

   ```
   Switch(config-if)# spanning-tree bpduguard enable
   ```

3. The **spanning-tree portfast** interface-configuration command defines an edge port.

4. You can use the following global configuration command to enable rapid PVST+:

   ```
   Switch(config)# spanning-tree mode rapid-pvst
   ```

5. A minimum of two MST instances are needed so that traffic can be load-balanced. One instance can support VLANs 100 through 104; the other can support VLANs 200 through 204. To load-balance, traffic from one instance must be carried over one uplink while the other instance is carried over the second uplink.

6. You can use these configuration commands:

   ```
   Switch(config)# spanning-tree mode mst
   Switch(config)# spanning-tree mst configuration
   Switch(config-mst)# name NorthWestDivision
   Switch(config-mst)# revision 1
   Switch(config-mst)# instance 1 vlan 100,101,102,103,104,99
   Switch(config-mst)# instance 2 vlan 200,201,202,203,204
   Switch(config-mst)# exit
   ```

   Notice that VLAN 99, used for switch-management traffic, also is mapped to an MST instance. It is sometimes easy to forget about nonuser or nonaccess VLANs.

7. This command makes C1 become the MST root bridge for instance 1:

   ```
   Switch(config)# spanning-tree mst 1 root primary
   ```

   This causes the uplink from C1 to A1 to be used for instance 1 by keeping it in the Forwarding state. Switch C2 also should be configured as the root for MST instance 2 so that the other uplink can be used for those VLANs.

Scenario 6 Answers

1. You can configure HSRP load balancing with the following Catalyst configuration commands:

   ```
   Switch(config)# interface vlan 101
   Switch(config-if)# ip address 192.168.101.2 255.255.255.0
   Switch(config-if)# standby 101 priority 110
   Switch(config-if)# standby 101 preempt
   ```

```
Switch(config-if)#  standby  101  ip  192.168.101.1
Switch(config-if)#  interface  vlan  102
Switch(config-if)#  ip  address  192.168.102.2  255.255.255.0
Switch(config-if)#  standby  102  priority  100
Switch(config-if)#  standby  102  preempt
Switch(config-if)#  standby  102  ip  192.168.102.1
```

The default gateway address that is shared between the switches is configured as
192.168.101.1 for VLAN 101 and 192.168.102.1 for VLAN 102. In VLAN 101, the virtual
interface has an IP address of 192.168.101.2. Two HSRP groups are defined, one for
each VLAN. Interface VLAN 101 will be the active router for VLAN 101 because of its
higher priority of 110 (over a default of 100 on the other Catalyst). If control is passed to the
standby router, this router can assume control again through the use of the **preempt**
command. For VLAN 102, the roles are reversed. This router becomes the standby router in
Group 102, with its lower priority of 100. (The other switch will be configured with priority
110 for VLAN 102 to take the active router role.)

2. Functionally, VRRP is very similar to HSRP. The following commands can be used to
    configure VRRP. No commands are necessary to enable the router to preempt for VRRP;
    preemption is the default.

    ```
    Switch(config)#  interface  vlan  101
    Switch(config-if)#  ip  address  192.168.101.2  255.255.255.0
    Switch(config-if)#  vrrp  101  priority  110
    Switch(config-if)#  vrrp  101  ip  192.168.101.1
    Switch(config-if)#  interface  vlan  102
    Switch(config-if)#  ip  address  192.168.102.2  255.255.255.0
    Switch(config-if)#  vrrp  102  priority  100
    Switch(config-if)#  vrrp  102  ip  192.168.102.1
    ```

3. The four-part answers to question 2 are as follows:

    a. By default, all switches have a GLBP priority of 100. Catalyst B's priority can be raised
        with the **glbp 10 priority 200** command.

    b. Only the AVG switch, Catalyst B, needs to be configured with the gateway address. It
        will inform all other members of the group. You should use the **glbp 10 ip 192.168.10.1**
        command.

    c. **glbp 10 load-balancing round-robin**

    d. Each AVF switch should receive the **glbp 10 ip** interface-configuration command. No IP
        address is needed here because the virtual gateway address is learned from the
        group's AVG.

Scenario 7 Answers

1. In the default configuration, PoE will automatically be supplied if a powered device is
    detected. If someone has disabled PoE on that interface, you can re-enable it by using the
    power inline auto interface configuration command.

2. The QoS domain should consist of the two Catalyst switches, A and B. QoS trust should be extended to the IP Phone connected to Catalyst B. QoS information should be trusted on the ports connecting switches A and B.

   QoS information should not be trusted on Catalyst A port Gig1/0/1 (the public network), Catalyst B port Fa1/0/2 (PC), or the IP Phone's PC data port. At these locations, incoming QoS information should be overwritten to known and trusted values, such as COS 0 or DSCP 0.

3. The following commands define VLAN 17 as the voice VLAN (VVID) and the IP Phone's data port as untrusted:

   ```
   Switch(config)# interface fastethernet 3/1
   Switch(config-if)# switchport voice vlan 17
   Switch(config-if)# switchport priority extend cos 0
   ```

4. To enable trust on the uplink, you can use the following commands:

   ```
   CatalystB(config)# interface gigabitethernet 1/0/1
   CatalystB(config-if)# mls qos trust cos
   ```

   Then to disable trust on Fa 1/0/2, you can use these commands:

   ```
   CatalystB(config)# interface fastethernet 1/0/2
   CatalystB(config-if)# no mls qos trust
   ```

Scenario 8 Answers

1. On a Catalyst 3750, you can use the following commands:

   ```
   Switch(config)# interface range fastethernet 1/0/1 - 48
   Switch(config-if)# switchport port-security
   ```

2. On a Catalyst 3750, you can use the following commands:

   ```
   Switch(config)# interface fastethernet 1/0/18
   Switch(config-if)# switchport port-security
   Switch(config-if)# switchport port-security maximum 24
   Switch(config-if)# switchport port-security violation restrict
   ```

   The first command line enables port-level security on the switch port. The second line configures port security to learn up to 24 MAC addresses dynamically on that port. The last line configures the switch to restrict any MAC addresses found to be in violation (any additional addresses learned beyond the 24). The port stays up, allowing the other users to communicate.

3. You can use the following commands:

   ```
   Switch(config)# access-list 101 permit tcp 192.168.191.0 0.0.0.255 host
     192.168.191.199 eq www
   Switch(config)# vlan access-map myfilter
   Switch(config-access-map)# match ip address 101
   Switch(config-access-map)# action forward
   Switch(config-access-map)# match
   Switch(config-access-map)# action drop
   Switch(config-access-map)# exit
   Switch(config)# vlan filter myfilter vlan-list 180
   ```

The first line configures an access list that will be used only to match against traffic being forwarded on a VLAN. The **permit** keyword causes matching traffic only to be eligible for an action by the VACL; it does not cause the matching traffic to be forwarded or not. The VACL is configured to first match traffic with access list 101; this traffic is forwarded as normal. Then a simple **match** statement is given so that all other traffic is matched; this remaining traffic is dropped so that it does not reach its destination. The VACL then is applied to VLAN 180.

4. In the default configuration, a switch port uses the **switchport mode dynamic auto** command. Therefore, it passively waits for a switch on the far end to initiate DTP negotiation to enter trunking mode. A malicious user could spoof the DTP exchange, causing the switch to bring the port into trunking mode.

   You can use the following commands to prevent unexpected trunk negotiation:

   ```
   Switch(config)# interface range fastethernet 1/0/1 - 48
   Switch(config-if)# switchport mode access
   ```

   In addition, you should disable any unused access ports and set the access VLAN to an unused or isolated VLAN ID.

5. The trunk configuration does have a weakness that could allow attackers to inject packets that essentially "hop" from one VLAN to another. The trunk has VLAN 100 as its native VLAN—a VLAN that also is used for user traffic elsewhere in the network.

   The solution is to configure the trunk to have an unused VLAN ID for its native VLAN. Then the native VLAN should be manually pruned or disallowed from entering the trunk. By adding the shaded command to the following interface configuration, the native VLAN becomes VLAN 9, which is not allowed on the trunk:

   ```
   Switch(config)# interface gigabitethernet 1/0/1
   Switch(config-if)# switchport
   Switch(config-if)# switchport trunk encapsulation dot1q
   Switch(config-if)# switchport trunk native vlan 9
   Switch(config-if)# switchport trunk allowed vlan 100-300
   Switch(config-if)# switchport mode trunk
   ```

6. You can use the following commands to enable DHCP snooping on the switch:

   ```
   Switch(config)# ip dhcp snooping
   Switch(config)# ip dhcp snooping vlan 50
   Switch(config)# interface range fastethernet 1/0/40 - 41
   Switch(config-if)# ip dhcp snooping trust
   ```

   Only the two ports where legitimate DHCP servers are connected are configured as trusted ports. All other ports are considered to be untrusted, by default. If the switch has an uplink to other switches, you also should use the **ip dhcp snooping trust** command to configure the uplink as trusted. This assumes that the upstream switches have DHCP snooping configured also; it's wise to extend trust to an uplink only if the trusted domain also extends to the neighboring switches.

Scenario 9 Answers

1. The two LAP cells should operate on different, nonoverlapping channels. If channel 1 is used with LAP1, LAP2 should use either channel 6 or 11.

2. LAP2 should use the same SSID as LAP1 so that users can move their association as they roam between the cells.

3. An LAP needs only an access VLAN from the switch port. The wireless client VLAN is carried over the LWAPP tunnel between the LAP and the WLC. Therefore, you could use the following commands to configure the switch port:

   ```
   Switch(config)# interface fastethernet 0/1
   Switch(config-if)# switchport
   Switch(config-if)# switchport access vlan 200
   Switch(config-if)# switchport host
   ```

4. The WLC uses its AP-manager interface to communicate with LAPs. Therefore, the AP-manager interface will use 192.168.201.10. The WLC can also have its Management interface located on the same VLAN, if you choose to do so. The management interface is not used for LWAPP tunnels, however.

5. LAP2 can be located on any access VLAN—not necessarily on VLAN 200 with LAP1. The WLC can build an LWAPP tunnel to LAP2, regardless of its VLAN, provided IP traffic is routable between the two devices.

6. The WLC must be able to bridge a Layer 2 wired VLAN with a Layer 2 WLAN. First, you have to configure a dynamic interface assigned to VLAN 50. Then you have to configure a WLAN that uses SSID "InMotion" and assign it to the new dynamic interface.

Part VII: Appendix

Answers to Chapter 'Do I Know This Already?' Quizzes and Q&A Sections

Chapter 1

"Do I Know This Already?"

1. c
2. e
3. d
4. d
5. a
6. c
7. b
8. c
9. c
10. c
11. d
12. c

Q&A

1. *For each layer of the OSI model, match the forwarding criteria used by a switch:*

C Layer 1	A. IP address
D Layer 2	B. UDP/TCP port
A Layer 3	C. None
B Layer 4	D. MAC address

2. *What is multilayer switching (MLS)?*

   Answer: MLS forwards traffic using information from Layer 2, Layer 3, and Layer 4—all in hardware at wire speed.

3. *Fill in the blanks in the following statement:*

   In the 20/80 rule of networking, 20% of the traffic on a segment usually stays _____, whereas 80% travels _____.

   Answer: Local, travels across the network

4. *What is a collision domain, and where does it exist in a switched LAN?*

   Answer: A collision domain is a network segment where shared media access is supported. Devices on the shared media must compete for access when transmitting data. In a switched network, the collision domain is restricted to a single switch port and does not extend across the switch.

5. *What is a broadcast domain, and where does it exist in a switched LAN?*

   Answer: A broadcast domain is the extent of a network where broadcast frames propagate. Basically, a broadcast domain covers an area where Layer 2 devices are located and terminates at the boundary of a Layer 3 device. In a switched network, the broadcast domain extends to all switch ports assigned to a common VLAN. This is because a switch forwards broadcasts out all available ports in a VLAN.

6. *What is a VLAN, and why is it used?*

   Answer: A virtual LAN (VLAN) is a group of switch ports that communicate as if they were attached to a single shared-media LAN segment. VLANs can extend across buildings or backbones, as long as the VLAN is connected end to end through trunking or physical connections. A VLAN is a broadcast domain. VLANs segment networks for ease of management and better performance.

7. *At what OSI layers do devices in the distribution layer usually operate?*

   Answer: Layers 2, 3, and 4

8. *What is network segmentation? When is it necessary, and how is it done in a campus network design?*

Answer: Segmentation is the process of dividing a LAN into smaller, discrete collision domains. If a large percentage of collisions is observed on a LAN, segmentation is appropriate. In a campus network design, segmentation occurs at each switch port. A similar form of segmentation involves reducing the size of broadcast domains. Placing Layer 3 devices in the distribution and core layers terminates the broadcast domains at those layer boundaries.

9. *Is it possible to use Layer 2 switches in the distribution layer rather than Layer 3 switches? If so, what are the limitations?*

Answer: It is generally best practice to use Layer 3 or multilayer switches in the distribution layer, as outlined in this chapter. However, in some environments, this might not be possible because of cost or implementation logistics. Layer 2 switches will work fine in the distribution layer but will not provide a VLAN or broadcast domain boundary in that layer. As a result, broadcasts will propagate into the core layer, using unnecessary bandwidth.

Chapter 2

"Do I Know This Already?"

1. c
2. c, d, e
3. a, b
4. a, c
5. c
6. d
7. a, c
8. c, d, e
9. b
10. b, c
11. c, d
12. a, b, c
13. b
14. c

Q&A

1. *Where is the most appropriate place to connect a block of enterprise (internal) servers? Why?*

   Answer: You should connect a block of enterprise servers into the core, just as you would switch blocks. The server farm building block should have a layer of access and distribution switches, just as in any switch block. This maximizes connectivity from the servers to all other devices in the network. In effect, all users will see the same number of switch "hops" to access a server. Connecting into the core also provides maximum scalability because you can add more server blocks in the future.

2. *How can you provide redundancy at the switch and core block layers? (Consider physical means, as well as functional methods using protocols, algorithms, and so on.)*

   Answer: In a switch block, you can provide redundancy through two distribution switches. Each access switch can be linked to both distribution switches for fault tolerance. The Layer 3 distribution layer allows both uplinks to be used at the same time, with little or no failover time required. In the core layer, a dual core can be used with two core switches. Each distribution switch has dual uplinks, with one link to each core switch. Here, the redundant links can stay active for load sharing and redundancy, thanks to the Layer 3 routing protocols running in the distribution and core layers.

3. *What factors should you consider when sizing a switch block?*

   Answer: Consider traffic types, flows, and patterns, as well as the size and number of common workgroups. Additionally, the Layer 3 switching capacity in the distribution layer should be sized according to the amount of traffic crossing from one VLAN to another.

4. *What are the signs of an oversized switch block?*

   Answer: The distribution switches begin to become bottlenecks in handling the interVLAN traffic volume. Access list processing in the distribution layer also can become a rate-limiting factor. Broadcast and multicast traffic forwarding can slow the Layer 2 and Layer 3 switches in the block.

5. *What are the attributes and issues of having a collapsed core block?*

   Answer: Attributes: Cost savings (no separate high-end core switches) and design simplicity. Issues: Scalability becomes limited.

6. *How many switches are sufficient in a core block design?*

   Answer: Two switches are usually sufficient in a core block, offering load sharing and redundancy. However, you can add core switches as the size of the network and core traffic flow dictates.

7. *What building blocks are used to build a scalable campus network?*

   Answer: The switch block is the template used to group access-layer switches and their respective distribution-layer switches. Switch blocks then are connected into the core block to build a scalable network. Depending on the other resources that are present in a campus network, other building blocks can include a server farm block, a network management block, and an enterprise edge block. The service provider edge block exists outside the campus network, although it does interface with the enterprise edge block.

8. *What are two types of core, or backbone, designs?*

   Answer: Collapsed core and dual core.

9. *Why should links and services provided to remote sites be grouped in a distinct building block?*

   Answer: Remote sites and roaming VPN users should be considered corporate users, as if they were connected directly inside the enterprise network. These users should enjoy the same efficient access to any enterprise resource that internal users have. Additionally, VPN tunnels should terminate in a secure area of the enterprise network. Connections into the Internet (through service providers) are just the inverse—users from all parts of the enterprise need equal and efficient access to resources located out on the Internet. Therefore, a separate building block connected into the core is justified.

10. *Why should network-management applications and servers be placed in a distinct building block?*

    Answer: Network-management applications must be capable of polling, querying, or accessing devices anywhere in the campus network. Moving these resources into a distinct building block provides redundant and efficient access into the network core so that all devices can be managed with equal access.

Chapter 3

"Do I Know This Already?"

1. b
2. b
3. b
4. c
5. d
6. b

7. c

8. d

9. b

10. c

11. d

12. b

Q&A

1. *By default, how long are CAM table entries kept before they are aged out?*

    Answer: 300 seconds

2. *A TCAM lookup involves which values?*

    Answer: Mask, Value, Result

3. *How many table lookups are required to find a MAC address in the CAM table?*

    Answer: 1

4. *How many table lookups are required to match a packet against an access list that has been compiled into 10 TCAM entries?*

    Answer: 1

5. *How many value patterns can a TCAM store for each mask?*

    Answer: 8

6. *Can all packets be switched in hardware by a multilayer switch?*

    Answer: No; some must be flagged for process switching by the switch CPU.

7. *Multilayer switches must rewrite which portions of an Ethernet frame?*

    Answer:

    Source and destination MAC addresses
    IP Time-To-Live
    Checksums

8. *If a station receives only Ethernet frames and doesn't transmit anything, how will a switch learn of its location?*

    Answer: You must configure a static CAM entry with the station's MAC address and the switch port where it is located. Otherwise, the switch must flood every frame destined for that host out every switch port in an effort to find it.

9. *What is a TCAM's main purpose?*

    Answer: To process access lists as a single table lookup.

10. *Why do the TCAM mask and pattern fields consist of so many bits?*

    Answer: So that a combination of several address fields in a frame can be inspected at once.

11. *In a multilayer switch with a TCAM, a longer access list (more ACEs or statements) takes longer to process for each frame. True or false?*

    Answer: False

12. *A multilayer switch receives a packet with a certain destination IP address. Suppose that the switch has that IP address in its Layer 3 forwarding table but has no corresponding Layer 2 address. What happens to the packet next?*

    Answer: The switch CPU sends an ARP request.

13. *Suppose that a multilayer switch can't support a protocol with CEF, and it relies on fallback bridging. Can the switch still route that traffic?*

    Answer: No. That traffic is transparently bridged. An external multilayer switch or router is required to route the bridged packets.

14. *To configure a static CAM table entry, the **mac address-table static** mac-address command is used. Which two other parameters also must be given?*

    Answer:

    vlan *vlan-id*
    interface *type mod/num*

15. *As a network administrator, what aspects of a switch TCAM should you be concerned with?*

    Answer: The size of the TCAM resources

16. *What portion of the TCAM is used to evaluate port number comparisons in an access list?*

    Answer: LOU

17. *Someone has asked you where the host with MAC address 00-10-20-30-40-50 is located. Assuming that you already know the switch it is connected to, what command can you use to find it?*

    Answer: **show mac address-table dynamic address 0010.2030.4050**

18. *Complete this command to display the size of the CAM table:* **show mac** _____.

    Answer: **address-table count**

19. *What protocol is used to advertise CAM table entries among neighboring switches?*

    Answer: None; the entries are not advertised.

20. *Suppose that a host uses one MAC address to send frames and another to receive them. In other words, one address will always be the source address sent in frames, and the other is used only as a destination address in incoming frames. Is it possible for that host to communicate with others through a Layer 2 switch? If so, how?*

    Answer: Yes, but not very efficiently. The Layer 2 switch will learn one of the host's MAC addresses as the host sends frames. That address will be seen as the source address on frames arriving at the switch. However, because the second MAC address never is used to send frames, the switch will never be capable of learning of its existence. When frames are sent to the host using that second MAC address, the switch is forced to flood the frames out all relevant switch ports. The host receives those frames only because it is connected to a port where the frames were flooded. All other hosts on the same VLAN also receive the flooded frames, even though they have no interest in that traffic.

Chapter 4

"Do I Know This Already?"

1. c
2. b
3. a
4. b
5. b
6. b
7. c
8. c

9. c

10. d

11. e

Q&A

1. *Put the following Ethernet standards in order of increasing bandwidth:*

    a. *802.3z*

    b. *802.3ae*

    c. *802.3*

    d. *802.3u*

    Answer: c, d, a, b

2. *What benefits does switched Ethernet have over shared Ethernet?*

    Answer: Switched Ethernet ports receive dedicated bandwidth, have a reduced collision domain, and show increased performance because of segmentation or fewer users per port.

3. *When a 10/100 Ethernet link is autonegotiating, which will be chosen if both stations can support the same capabilities—10BASE-T full duplex, 100BASE-TX half duplex, or 100BASE-TX full duplex?*

    Answer: 100BASE-TX full duplex will be chosen because it has the highest autonegotiation priority and is common to both end stations.

4. *How many pairs of copper wires does a 1000BASE-T connection need?*

    Answer: Four pairs

5. *A switch port is being configured as shown here. What command is needed next to set the port to full-duplex mode?*

    ```
    Switch(config)# interface fastethernet 0/13
    Switch(config-if)#
    ```

    Answer: Enter the command **duplex full** at the prompt.

6. *If a full-duplex Gigabit Ethernet connection offers 2 Gbps throughput, can a single host send data at 2 Gbps?*

    Answer: No, a full-duplex Gigabit Ethernet connection allows only 1 Gbps simultaneously in each direction across the link.

7. *Which GBIC would you use for a connection over multimode fiber (MMF)?*

Answer: You could use either a 1000BASE-SX or a 1000BASE-LX/LH.

8. *A Category 5 cable having only pins 1, 2 and 3, 6 has been installed and used for a Fast Ethernet link. Can this same cable be used for a migration to Gigabit Ethernet using 1000BASE-T GBICs, assuming that the length is less than 100 m?*

Answer: No. 1000BASE-T requires all four pairs of wires to be present.

9. *A Catalyst 3560 switch port has been configured for 100 Mbps full-duplex mode, but a link cannot be established. What are some commands that you could use to investigate and correct the problem?*

Answer: To see the current state of one or more ports, you could use the **show interface** command. This would show the ports' speed and duplex modes, and whether a link has been established. One reason the link is not established could be that the port is shut down or disabled. To enable the port, use the **no shutdown** interface-configuration command. Because the port has been set to 100 Mbps full-duplex mode, it is possible that the end station can support only 10 Mbps at half duplex. Therefore, set the port for autonegotiate mode with the **speed auto** and **duplex auto** commands. Otherwise, you could set the port to a fixed speed and mode that would match that of the end station.

10. *The 10-Gigabit Ethernet is backward-compatible with other forms of Ethernet at Layer _____ but not at Layer _____.*

Answer: 10-Gigabit Ethernet is backward compatible with other forms of Ethernet at Layer 2 but not at Layer 1.

11. *What one switch command will select Fast Ethernet interfaces 4/1 through 48 for a common configuration?*

Answer: **interface range fastethernet 4/1 – 48**

12. *What is the purpose of a GBIC?*

Answer: A GBIC is used as a modular medium-independent connection for Gigabit Ethernet. A switch with a GBIC port will accept GBIC modules that support various network media types. Changing network media cabling requires only a low-cost GBIC module change.

13. *Suppose that you need to apply several different common configurations to Fast Ethernet interfaces 3/1 through 12, 3/34, 3/48, and 5/14 through 48. What commands are needed to create an interface macro to accomplish this, and what command would apply the macro?*

Answer:

```
define interface-range mymacro fastethernet 3/1 - 12, fastethernet 3/34 -
48 , fastethernet 5/14 - 48
interface range macro mymacro
```

14. *If a switch port is configured with the **speed 100** and **duplex full** commands, what will happen if the PC connected to it is set for autonegotiated speed and duplex? Now reverse the roles. (The switch will autonegotiate, but the PC won't.) What will happen?*

Answer: When the PC attempts to autonegotiate the link settings, it will detect the switch port's speed of 100 Mbps. However, the duplex cannot be detected without a two-way information exchange, so the PC probably will fall back to half duplex. The results are similar when the roles are reversed because the switch will decide on 100 Mbps half duplex. In either case, a duplex mismatch will occur.

15. *By default, what will a switch do if one of its ports has a serious error condition, and how can you tell when this has happened?*

Answer: By default, every possible error condition is detected on every port. If any one of these conditions occurs, the port automatically will be shut down in the errdisable state. The **show interface status err-disabled** command shows a brief summary of all ports in the errdisable state.

16. *What port speeds can you assign to a UTP Gigabit Ethernet switch port? Consider both 1000BASE-T GBIC and native RJ-45 copper switch module ports.*

Answer: A 1000BASE-T GBIC is fixed at 1 Gbps, whereas switch modules with UTP Gigabit Ethernet ports can be 10 Mbps, 100 Mbps, or 1000 Mbps.

17. *What command can you use to make sure that no switch ports automatically are shut down in an errdisable state for any reason?*

Answer: Use the **no errdisable detect cause all** interface configuration command. Remember that all causes are enabled by default, so you must disable all causes first.

18. *Suppose that you commonly find that switch ports are being shut down in errdisable because users are making their connections go up and down too often. Thinking that this might be the result of odd PC behavior, you would like to visit each user to troubleshoot the problem; however, this is a minor error and you don't want to inconvenience the end users too much. What commands can you use to have the switch automatically re-enable the ports after 10 minutes? Make sure a flapping link will be recovered automatically in this time frame.*

Answer:

```
errdisable recovery interval 600
errdisable recovery cause link-flap
```

19. *Look at the following **show interfaces** output. Does the high number of collisions indicate a problem? Why or why not?*

```
FastEthernet0/6 is up, line protocol is up
Hardware is Fast Ethernet, address is 000a.f4d2.5506 (bia 000a.f4d2.5506)
  Description: Front Office PC
  MTU 1500 bytes, BW 10000 Kbit, DLY 1000 usec,
     reliability 255/255, txload 1/255, rxload 1/255
  Encapsulation ARPA, loopback not set
  Keepalive set (10 sec)
  Half-duplex, 10Mb/s
  input flow-control is off, output flow-control is off
  ARP type: ARPA, ARP Timeout 04:00:00
  Last input never, output 00:00:00, output hang never
  Last clearing of "show interface" counters never
  Input queue: 0/75/0/0 (size/max/drops/flushes); Total output drops: 0
  Queueing strategy: fifo
  Output queue :0/40 (size/max)
  5 minute input rate 0 bits/sec, 0 packets/sec
  5 minute output rate 0 bits/sec, 0 packets/sec
     1321140 packets input, 227738894 bytes, 0 no buffer
     Received 13786 broadcasts, 0 runts, 0 giants, 0 throttles
     1 input errors, 1 CRC, 0 frame, 0 overrun, 0 ignored
     0 watchdog, 42 multicast, 0 pause input
     0 input packets with dribble condition detected
     87798820 packets output, 2662785561 bytes, 1316 underruns
     6 output errors, 406870 collisions, 3 interface resets
     0 babbles, 0 late collision, 19458 deferred
     0 lost carrier, 0 no carrier, 0 PAUSE output
  1316  output  buffer  failures,  0  output  buffers  swapped  out
```

Answer: Yes, this probably would be normal, considering that the interface is set for 10 Mbps half duplex. Collisions are to be expected on a link with shared bandwidth; in this case, the link is part of a collision domain. If the link were showing full duplex at any speed, collisions never should be detected.

Chapter 5

"Do I Know This Already?"

1. c
2. b
3. b
4. b
5. b
6. c
7. d
8. c
9. b
10. a
11. c
12. a

Q&A

1. *What is a VLAN? When is it used?*

   Answer: A VLAN is a group of devices on the same broadcast domain, such as a logical subnet or segment. VLANs can span switch ports, switches within a switch block, or closets and buildings. VLANs group users and devices into common workgroups across geographical areas. VLANs help provide segmentation, security, and problem isolation.

2. *When a VLAN is configured on a Catalyst switch port, in how much of the campus network will the VLAN number be unique and significant?*

   Answer: The VLAN number will be significant in the local switch. If trunking is enabled, the VLAN number will be significant across the entire trunking domain. In other words, the VLAN will be transported to every switch that has a trunk link supporting that VLAN.

3. *Name two types of VLANs in terms of spanning areas of the campus network.*

   Answer:

   Local VLAN
   End-to-end VLAN

4. *What switch commands configure Fast Ethernet port 4/11 for VLAN 2?*

Answer:

```
interface fastethernet 4/11
switchport mode access
switchport access vlan 2
```

5. *Generally, what must be configured (both switch and end-user device) for a port-based VLAN?*

Answer: The switch port

6. *What is the default VLAN on all ports of a Catalyst switch?*

Answer: VLAN 1

7. *What is a trunk link?*

Answer: A trunk link is a connection between two switches that transports traffic from multiple VLANs. Each frame is identified with its source VLAN during its trip across the trunk link.

8. *What methods of Ethernet VLAN frame identification can be used on a Catalyst switch trunk?*

Answer:

802.1Q
ISL

9. *What is the difference between the two trunking methods? How many bytes are added to trunked frames for VLAN identification in each method?*

Answer: ISL uses encapsulation and adds a 26-byte header and a 4-byte trailer. 802.1Q adds a 4-byte tag field within existing frames, without encapsulation.

10. *What is the purpose of the Dynamic Trunking Protocol (DTP)?*

Answer: DTP allows negotiation of a common trunking method between endpoints of a trunk link.

11. *What commands are needed to configure a Catalyst switch trunk port GigabitEthernet 3/1 to transport only VLANs 100, 200 through 205, and 300 using IEEE 802.1Q? (Assume that trunking is enabled and active on the port already. Also assume that the **interface gigabit 3/1** command already has been entered.)*

Answer: **switchport trunk allowed vlan 100, 200-205, 300**

12. *Two neighboring switch trunk ports are set to the auto mode with ISL trunking encapsulation mode. What will the resulting trunk mode become?*

Answer: Trunking will not be established. Both switches are in the passive auto state and are waiting to be asked to start the trunking mode. The link will remain an access link on both switches.

13. *Complete the following command to configure the switch port to use DTP to actively ask the other end to become a trunk:*

```
switchport mode _____
```

Answer: `switchport mode dynamic desirable`

14. *Which command can set the native VLAN of a trunk port to VLAN 100 after the interface has been selected?*

Answer: `switchport trunk native vlan 100`

15. *What command can configure a trunk port to stop sending and receiving DTP packets completely?*

Answer: `switchport nonegotiate`

16. *What command can be used on a Catalyst switch to verify exactly what VLANs will be transported over trunk link gigabitethernet 4/4?*

Answer:

```
show interface gigabitethernet 4/4 switchport
```
or
```
show interface gigabitethernet 4/4 trunk
```

17. *Suppose that a switch port is configured with the following commands. A PC with a nontrunking NIC card then is connected to that port. What, if any, traffic will the PC successfully send and receive?*

```
interface fastethernet 0/12
switchport trunk encapsulation dot1q
switchport trunk native vlan 10
switchport trunk allowed vlan 1-1005
switchport mode trunk
```

Answer: The PC expects only a single network connection, using a single VLAN. In other words, the PC can't participate in any form of trunking. Only untagged or unencapsulated frames will be understood. Recall that an 802.1Q trunk's native VLAN is the only VLAN that has untagged frames. Therefore, the PC will be capable of exchanging frames only on VLAN 10, the native VLAN.

Chapter 6

"Do I Know This Already?"

1. c
2. a
3. c
4. b
5. b
6. b, c
7. a
8. c
9. c
10. b
11. d
12. b

Q&A

1. *True or false: You can use VTP domains to separate broadcast domains.*

    Answer: False. Broadcast domains can be separated only with VLANs because a VLAN defines a broadcast domain's boundaries. A VTP domain is a different concept; it defines the management domain where a set of switches can exchange information about VLAN configuration.

2. *What VTP modes can a Catalyst switch be configured for? Can VLANs be created in each of the modes?*

    Answer: Server, client, and transparent modes. VLANs can be created in server mode. VLANs cannot be created in client mode. In transparent mode, VLANs can be created, but only on the local switch; they are not advertised to other switches.

3. *How many VTP management domains can a Catalyst switch participate in? How many VTP servers can a management domain have?*

    Answer: A switch can be a member of only one VTP management domain. A domain must have at least one server for VLAN changes to be propagated throughout the domain. There can be more than one server, for redundancy.

4. *What conditions must exist for two Catalyst switches to be in the same VTP management domain?*

Answer: Both switches must have the same VTP domain name defined and enabled, both switches must be adjacent on a trunk link, and trunking must be enabled and active between them.

Two switches also can operate in the same VTP domain if one of them is new and has the default NULL domain name. That switch will listen and pick up the first VTP domain name it hears in VTP advertisements.

5. *On a VTP server switch, identify what you can do to reset the VTP configuration revision number to 0.*

Answer: Set the VTP domain name to a bogus value and change it back.

Configure the switch for VTP transparent mode and then configure the switch back to server mode.

6. *How can you clear the configuration revision number on a VTP client?*

Answer: You can't. The VTP client bases all VLAN and VTP information on advertisements from a VTP server. Therefore, the configuration revision number on the client comes directly from the same number on the server.

7. *Complete this command to make all VLANs other than 30 and 100 eligible for pruning on the trunk interface:*

```
switchport  trunk  pruning  vlan  _____
```
Answer: `switchport trunk pruning vlan except 30,100`

8. *Which VLAN numbers are never eligible for VTP pruning? Why?*

Answer: VLAN numbers 1 and 1001 to 1005. VLAN 1 is reserved as a VLAN for control protocol traffic, and VLANs 1002 to 1005 are reserved as the default FDDI and Token Ring function VLANs.

9. *What does the acronym VTP stand for?*

Answer: VLAN Trunking Protocol

10. *What VTP domain name is defined on a new switch with no configuration?*

Answer: A NULL or empty string. The switch defaults to server mode and learns a VTP domain name from the first VTP server heard on a trunk link. Otherwise, you manually must configure the domain name.

11. *In a network of switches, VTP domain Engineering has been configured with VLANs 1, 10 through 30, and 100. The VTP configuration revision number is currently at 23. Suppose a new switch is connected to the network, and it has the following configuration: VTP domain Engineering, VTP server mode, only VLANs 1 and 2 defined, and configuration revision number of 30.*

    What happens when the switch is connected to the network?

    Answer: Because the new switch has a higher configuration revision number, the other switches in the VTP domain Engineering will learn all its VLAN and VTP configuration information. The new switch has two VLANs configured on itself: VLAN 1 and 2. The other switches will assume that they should delete all VLANs except for VLAN 1, and VLAN 2 will be created. Obviously, this will cause a major outage on the network because active VLANs 10 through 30 and 100 will be deleted and will go inactive. A network administrator will have to manually restore the configurations of those VLANs.

12. *A VTP client switch has VLANs 1, 2, 3, 10, and 30 configured as part of a VTP domain; however, the switch has users connected only to access switch ports defined on VLANs 3 and 30. If VTP pruning is enabled and all VLANs are eligible, which VLANs will be pruned on the upstream switch?*

    Answer: 2, 10

13. *The VTP domain Area3 consists of one server and several clients. The server's VTP configuration revision number is at 11. A new switch is added to the network. It has VTP domain name Area5 and a configuration revision number of 10. What happens when the new switch is added to the network? What happens when the VTP domain name is changed to Area3 on the new switch?*

    Answer: Domain Area5 will experience no change when the switch is added. The two domains, Area3 and Area5, will coexist on the same network with different sets of clients. The configuration revision numbers on both servers will stay unchanged. When the domain is changed to Area3, that domain then will have two VTP servers. The switch that has the newly configured domain name has a lower configuration revision number, so it will learn all VTP information from the existing server. The new switch's revision number will become 11, and its list of defined VLANs will change to match the existing server.

14. *What command shows information about the VTP configuration on a Catalyst 3560?*

    Answer: **show vtp status**

Chapter 7

"Do I Know This Already?"

1. e
2. c
3. c
4. d
5. c
6. c
7. a
8. d
9. b
10. c
11. c
12. c
13. c

Q&A

1. *What are some benefits of an EtherChannel?*

   Answer: Increased bandwidth

   Link redundancy

2. *How many links can be aggregated into an EtherChannel?*

   Answer: 2 to 8

3. *Traffic between two hosts will be distributed across all links in an EtherChannel. True or false?*

   Answer: False. Packets are distributed onto the EtherChannel links based on the load distribution method or algorithm that is configured. It is entirely possible that traffic passing between two hosts will end up on just one link within the bundle if a method involving source or destination addresses is used.

4. *Which methods can you use to distribute traffic in an EtherChannel?*

   Answer:

   MAC address
   IP address
   Layer 4 port

5. *How does an EtherChannel distribute broadcasts and multicasts?*

   Answer: Broadcasts and multicasts are distributed across the links within an EtherChannel, just like any other traffic. The broadcast or multicast addresses are used in the hash or load balancing algorithm to determine the link index.

6. *When load balancing, what hashing functions choose a link for a frame?*

   Answer: If the hashing function is based on a single address (MAC, IP, or port), the low-order bits of that address are used as a link index. If two addresses or port numbers are used, the exclusive-OR (XOR) of those two values is used to derive the low-order bits that form a link index.

7. *What protocols can negotiate an EtherChannel between two switches?*

   Answer: PAgP and LACP

8. *Suppose that a switch at one end of an EtherChannel is configured to use source MAC addresses for load balancing. The switch on the other end is configured to use both source and destination IP addresses. What happens?*

   Answer: The EtherChannel successfully will transport traffic between the two switches. However, the traffic load will not be distributed evenly or symmetrically across the links in the channel.

9. *Two switches have a four-port EtherChannel between them. Both switches are load balancing using source and destination IP addresses. If a packet has the source address 192.168.15.10 and destination address 192.168.100.31, what is the EtherChannel link index?*

   Answer: The link index is computed by an XOR of the source and destination IP addresses. Because this is a four-port link, only the 2 low-order bits are needed. 10 XOR 31 can be computed by using binary values: 00001010 XOR 00011111 = 00010101. The lowest 2 bits (01) give a link index of 1.

10. *What does the acronym PAgP stand for?*

    Answer: Port Aggregation Protocol

11. *Two switches should be configured to negotiate an EtherChannel. If one switch is using PagP auto mode, what should the other switch use?*

Answer: PAgP desirable mode

12. *What is the LACP system priority value used for?*

Answer: The switch with the lowest system ID (system priority + MAC address) is allowed to make decisions regarding which ports actively will participate in an EtherChannel and which ones will be held in a standby state.

13. *Complete the following command to put an interface into EtherChannel group 3 and to use PAgP to ask the far-end switch to participate in the EtherChannel. This switch port also should require PAgP packets back from the far-end switch.*

```
Switch(config-if)#  channel-group _____
```

Answer: Switch(config-if)#channel-group 3 mode desirable non-silent

14. *What interface configuration command is needed to select LACP as the EtherChannel negotiation protocol?*

Answer: **channel-protocol lacp**

15. *What command could you use to see the status of every port in an EtherChannel?*

Answer: **show etherchannel summary**

16. *What command could you use to verify the hashing algorithm used for EtherChannel load balancing?*

Answer: **show etherchannel load-balance**

17. *Suppose that a switch is used in a small data center where one server offers an IP-based application to many clients throughout the campus. An EtherChannel connects the data-center switch to a Layer 3 core switch, which routes traffic to all clients. What EtherChannel load-balancing method might be most appropriate at the data-center switch?*

   a. *Source MAC address*

   b. *Source IP address*

   c. *Destination MAC address*

   d. *Destination IP address*

   e. *Source and destination MAC address*

   f. *Source and destination IP address*

Answer: d. Remember that the EtherChannel will load-balance only outbound traffic, or that from the server toward the clients. Here are brief explanations of each of the choices, to help clarify the answer.

a. **Source MAC address**—Not very useful. The source MAC address (the server) always is the same. One link in the channel always would be selected.

b. **Source IP address**—Not very useful. Again, the source IP address (the server) is constant.

c. **Destination MAC address**—Not very useful. Because a Layer 3 switch is positioned in the core layer, it always appears as the destination MAC address for all client destinations.

d. **Destination IP address**—This is the best choice because the destination IP addresses of the clients are diverse and are not modified along the path.

e. **Source and destination MAC address**—Not very useful. Because the destination MAC address always is the Layer 3 switch, only one link will be used.

f. **Source and destination IP address**—This would make a good choice, although the combination of addresses doesn't add anything. The source IP address (the server) always is constant. Therefore, source XOR destination always yields something similar to the destination address itself.

18. *Suppose that a mainframe is connected to a switch that has an EtherChannel uplink to a campus network. The EtherChannel has been configured with the **port-channel load- balance src-dst-ip** command. Most of the mainframe traffic is SNA (non-IP). What will happen to the SNA frames when they are switched? Would it be better to reconfigure the channel with **port-channel load-balance src-dst-mac**?*

Answer: The SNA frames are non-IP, so only MAC addresses are relevant. The switch has been configured to load-balance according to the XOR of the source and destination IP addresses. Obviously, the SNA frames will have neither of these values present. The switch will realize this and fall back to the "lower" method of src-dst-mac (XOR of the source and destination MAC addresses) for each SNA frame. No configuration changes are necessary for this to occur.

There really isn't a good reason to reconfigure for src-dst-mac because the switch can forward the SNA frames already. However, if it were reconfigured, any IP packets would be encapsulated in Ethernet frames, providing MAC addresses within the frames.

19. *What attributes of a set of switch ports must match to form an EtherChannel?*

Answer:

Port speed
Port duplex
Trunking mode
Trunking encapsulation
Access or native VLAN

20. *What happens if one port of an EtherChannel is unplugged or goes dead? What happens when that port is reconnected?*

Answer: Traffic on the disconnected port is moved to the next available link in the EtherChannel bundle. When the port is reconnected, traffic does not automatically move back to the bundle's original port. Instead, new traffic is learned and applied to the restored link.

Chapter 8

"Do I Know This Already?"

1. c
2. c
3. b
4. b
5. c
6. c
7. a
8. b
9. d
10. b
11. b
12. c

Q&A

1. *What is a bridging loop? Why is it bad?*

Answer: A bridging loop is a path through a bridged or switched network that provides connectivity in an endless loop. Unknown unicast, broadcast, or multicast frames introduced into the loop are propagated by each switch, causing the frames to circulate around and around the loop. Network bandwidth and CPU resources can be absorbed completely by the increasing amount of broadcast traffic. Breaking the loop connectivity can end bridging loops.

2.   *Put the following STP port states in chronological order:*

   a. *Learning*

   b. *Forwarding*

   c. *Listening*

   d. *Blocking*

   Answer: d, c, a, b

3.   *Choose two types of STP messages used to communicate between bridges:*

   a. *Advertisement BPDU*

   b. *Configuration BPDU*

   c. *ACK BPDU*

   d. *TCN BPDU*

   Answer: b, d

4.   *What criteria are used to select the following?*

   a. *Root Bridge*

   b. *Root Port*

   c. *Designated Port*

   d. *Redundant (or secondary) Root Bridges*

   Answer:

   a. Lowest Bridge ID (Bridge priority, MAC address)
   b. Lowest Root Path Cost
   c. Lowest Root Path Cost on a shared segment
   d. Next-to-lowest Bridge ID

   If a tie occurs, these parameters are used to decide:

   1. Lowest Bridge ID
   2. Lowest Root Path Cost
   3. Lowest Sender Bridge ID
   4. Lowest Sender Port ID

5. *Which of the following switches becomes the Root Bridge, given the information in the following table? Which switch becomes the secondary Root Bridge if the Root Bridge fails?*

Switch Name	Bridge Priority	MAC Address	Port Costs
Catalyst A	32,768	00-d0-10-34-26-a0	All are 19
Catalyst B	32,768	00-d0-10-34-24-a0	All are 4
Catalyst C	32,767	00-d0-10-34-27-a0	All are 19
Catalyst D	32,769	00-d0-10-34-24-a1	All are 19

Answer: Catalyst C will become the primary Root because of its lower Bridge Priority value. (Bridge Priority has a greater weight on the election than a lower MAC address.) The secondary Root will be Catalyst B; both A and B have the next-lowest Bridge Priorities, but B also has a lower MAC address.

6. *What conditions cause an STP topology change? What effect does this have on STP and the network?*

Answer: A topology change occurs when a port moves to the Forwarding state, or from Forwarding or Learning to the Blocking state. During a topology change, addresses are aged out in Forward Delay seconds, whereas active stations are not aged out of the bridging table.

The STP is not recomputed; TCN BPDUs are sent throughout the network, notifying other switches of the topology change. Only the port where the topology change is occurring is affected, by moving through the STP states.

7. *A Root Bridge has been elected in a switched network. Suppose that a new switch is installed with a lower Bridge ID than the existing Root Bridge. What will happen?*

Answer: The new switch will begin life by advertising itself as the Root Bridge, thinking it is the only bridge on the network. Because it has a lower Bridge ID than the current Root, it will win the election after the BPDUs converge and when all switches have a knowledge of the new, better choice.

8. *Suppose that a switch receives Configuration BPDUs on two of its ports. Both ports are assigned to the same VLAN. Each of the BPDUs announces Catalyst A as the Root Bridge. Can the switch use both of these ports as Root Ports? Why?*

Answer: The STP doesn't allow more than one Root Port per switch (bridge). Because of this, both ports cannot become Root Ports. Only the port with the lowest Root Path Cost (or one of the successive STP tie-breaker decisions) will become the Root Port.

9. *How is the Root Path Cost calculated for a switch port?*

    Answer: The Root Path cost is a cumulative value that is incremented as Configuration BPDUs are passed from switch to switch. A switch adds the Port Cost of the local port to the current Root Path Cost value as a BPDU is received.

10. *What conditions can cause ports on a network's Root Bridge to move into the Blocking state?*

    (Assume that all switch connections are to other switches. No crossover cables are used to connect two ports on the same switch.)

    Answer: By definition, all ports on the Root Bridge are Designated Ports because they are in the closest possible location to the Root Bridge. Therefore, those ports never can be put into the Blocking state. The only exception to this is if two of the Root Bridge switch's ports are connected, a situation that could but shouldn't occur.

11. *What parameters can be tuned to influence the selection of a port as a Root or Designated Port?*

    Answer: Port Cost

12. *After a bridging loop forms, how can you stop the endless flow of traffic?*

    Answer: Turn off the switch or unplug a cable on a port that is part of the loop. Turning off the switch is obviously a drastic measure, but it does help to clear the loop. Any method might be used, as long as the loop manually is broken or disconnected. In some cases, the traffic volume caused by the loop can overwhelm the switch CPU. If that happens, you won't be able to connect to the switch CLI to shut down an interface or reload the switch.

13. *In a BPDU, when can the Root Bridge ID have the same value as the Sender Bridge ID?*

    Answer: When the switch that is sending the BPDU is also the Root Bridge

14. *Which of these is true about the Root Path Cost?*

    a. It is a value sent by the Root Bridge that cannot be changed along the way.

    b. It is incremented as a switch receives a BPDU.

    c. It is incremented as a switch sends a BPDU.

    d. It is incremented by the Path Cost of a port.

    Answer: b, d

15. *Suppose that two switches are connected by a common link. Each must decide which one will have the Designated Port on the link. Which switch takes on this role if these STP advertisements occur?*

    a. *The link is on switch A's port number 12 and on switch B's port number 5.*

    b. *Switch A has a Bridge ID of 32,768:0000.1111.2222, and switch B has 8192:0000.5555.6666.*

    c. *Switch A advertises a Root Path Cost of 8, while B advertises 12.*

Answer: Switch A will have the Designated Port. The STP tie-breaking sequence must be used for the decision. The first relevant decision is that of the lowest Root Path Cost, advertised by switch A. If both switches advertised an identical Root Path Cost, the lowest Sender Bridge ID (that of switch B) would be used.

16. *Using the default STP timers, how long does it take for a port to move from the Blocking state to the Forwarding state?*

Answer: 30 seconds

17. *If the Root Bridge sets the Topology Change flag in the BPDU, what must the other switches in the network do?*

Answer: Shorten their bridge table aging times

18. *Over what VLANs does the CST form of STP run?*

Answer: The native VLAN

19. *What is the major difference between PVST and PVST+?*

Answer: PVST+ interoperates with CST and PVST.

20. *Two switches are connected by a common active link. When might neither switch have a Designated Port on the link?*

Answer: Never; this can't happen

Chapter 9

"Do I Know This Already?"

    1. c

    2. c

    3. d

4. c

5. c

6. c

7. b

8. d

9. c

10. a

11. a

12. d

Q&A

1. *What commands can configure a Catalyst 4500 switch as the Root Bridge on VLAN 10, assuming that the other switches are using the default STP values?*

   Answer: **spanning-tree vlan 10 root primary**

2. *Using your Root Bridge answer from question 1, what commands can configure a Catalyst 3560 switch as a secondary or backup Root Bridge on VLAN 10?*

   Answer: **spanning-tree vlan 10 root secondary**

3. *Which of the following switches will become the Root Bridge, given the information in the following table? Which switch will become the secondary Root Bridge if the Root Bridge fails?*

Switch Name	Bridge Priority	MAC Address	Port Costs
Catalyst A	32,768	00-d0-10-34-26-a0	All are 19.
Catalyst B	32,768	00-d0-10-34-24-a0	All are 4.
Catalyst C	32,767	00-d0-10-34-27-a0	All are 19.
Catalyst D	32,769	00-d0-10-34-24-a1	All are 19.

   Answer: The root bridge will be Catalyst C because its bridge priority has the lowest value. The bridge priority is more significant because it is stored in the upper bits of the Bridge ID field. If Catalyst C fails in its duty as root bridge, Catalyst B will take over as the secondary root bridge. Because Catalyst B has the default bridge priority (32,768), along with another switch, the lowest MAC address will be the deciding factor.

Questions 4 through 7 are based on a network that contains two switches, Catalyst A and B. Their bridge priorities and MAC addresses are 32,768:0000.aaaa.aaaa and 32,768:0000.bbbb.bbbb, respectively.

4. *Which switch will become the Root Bridge?*

   Answer: Catalyst A. The bridge priorities are equal, so the lowest MAC address is the deciding factor.

5. *If switch B's bridge priority is changed to 10,000, which one will be root?*

   Answer: Catalyst B will become the new root bridge because its new priority is the lowest.

6. *If switch B's bridge priority is changed to 32,769, which one will be root?*

   Answer: Catalyst A will become the root again because B's priority is slightly higher.

7. *If switch C is introduced with 40000:0000.0000.cccc, which will be the secondary root?*

   Answer: Catalyst B was previously the secondary root, with the second-highest bridge priority. It will remain the secondary root because Catalyst C has a higher bridge priority.

8. *Suppose that a switch is configured with the **spanning-tree vlan 10 root primary** command. Then, another switch is connected to the network. The new switch has a bridge priority of 8,192. Which one of the following happens?*

   a. *When the new switch advertises itself, the original Root Bridge detects it and lower its bridge priority to 4,096 less than the new switch.*

   b. *The new switch becomes and stays the Root Bridge (bridge priority 8,192).*

   c. *No change; both switches keep their current bridge priorities.*

   d. *The new switch detects that a Root Bridge already exists and raises its own bridge priority to 32,768.*

   Answer: b

9. *Three switches in a network have the following bridge priorities: 32,768, 16,384, and 8,192. If a fourth switch is configured with **spanning-tree vlan 1 root secondary**, what is the bridge priority of the switches that become the primary and secondary Root Bridges?*

   Answer: Primary root: 8,192; secondary root: 16,384. (The switch configured with the **root** secondary keywords can't detect any other potential secondary roots, so it can set its priority only to 28,672.)

10. *What STP timer values automatically can be modified by setting the network diameter?*

Answer:

Hello timer
Forward Delay timer
Max Age timer

11. *Which STP timer determines how long a port stays in the Listening state? What is its default value?*

Answer: The Forward Delay timer; default 15 seconds

12. *What is the purpose of the Max Age timer?*

Answer: It sets the length of time received BPDUs are held if a neighboring switch is not heard from on a nondesignated port. After the Max Age timer expires, the BPDU for the neighbor is flushed and that port enters the Listening state, eventually becoming the new designated port on the segment.

13. *Three switches are connected to each other, forming a triangle shape. STP prevents a loop from forming. What is the most accurate value that could be used for the network diameter?*

Answer: 3

14. *Which of the following will not benefit from STP UplinkFast?*

  a. *An access-layer switch with one uplink port*

  b. *An access-layer switch with two uplink ports*

  c. *An access-layer switch with three uplink ports*

  d. *An access-layer switch with four uplink ports*

Answer: a

15. *What command can enable the STP PortFast feature on a switch? What configuration mode must you enter first?*

Answer: **spanning-tree portfast**, in interface configuration mode

16. *What happens if the STP Hello Time is decreased to 1 second in an effort to speed up STP convergence? What happens if the Hello Time is increased to 10 seconds?*

Answer: Setting the Hello timer to 1 second doubles the number of configuration BPDUs that a switch sends, as compared to the default 2-second timer. Although this does share BPDU information more often, it doesn't help the long convergence delay when a port comes up. The significant delays come from the Forward Delay timer, which is used to move a port through the Listening and Learning states. By default, this process takes 30 seconds and is unaffected by the Hello timer.

17. *What switch command safely can adjust the STP timers on the Root Bridge in VLAN 7?*
Assume that the network consists of Catalysts A, B, and C, all connected to each other in a
triangle fashion.

Answer: Because the three switches form a triangle loop, one link eventually will be
placed in the Blocking state. Therefore, the maximum distance across the network is
three switch hops.

This value can be used to define the network diameter to safely adjust the STP timers for faster
convergence:

spanning-tree vlan 7 root primary diameter 3

For questions 18 and 19, refer to the following output:

```
Switch# show spanning-tree vlan 50
VLAN50
  Spanning tree enabled protocol ieee
  Root ID    Priority    8000
             Address     00d0.0457.3831
             Cost        12
             Port        49 (GigabitEthernet0/1)
             Hello Time   2 sec  Max Age 20 sec  Forward Delay 15 sec
  Bridge ID  Priority    32818  (priority 32768 sys-id-ext 50)
             Address     0009.b7ee.9800
             Hello Time   2 sec  Max Age 20 sec  Forward Delay 15 sec
             Aging Time 300

Interface                                        Designated
Name             Port ID Prio  Cost Sts  Cost Bridge ID           Port ID
---------------- ------- ---  ------ ---  ---- -------------------- --
FastEthernet0/1    128.1   128    19 FWD   12  328180009.b7ee.9800128.1
FastEthernet0/2    128.2   128    19 FWD   12  328180009.b7ee.9800128.2
FastEthernet0/4    128.4   128   100 FWD   12  328180009.b7ee.9800128.4
FastEthernet0/7    128.7   128    19 FWD   12  328180009.b7ee.9800128.7
FastEthernet0/8    128.8   128    19 FWD   12  328180009.b7ee.9800128.8
FastEthernet0/9    128.9   128    19 FWD   12  328180009.b7ee.9800128.9
FastEthernet0/10   128.10  128    19 FWD   12  328180009.b7ee.9800128.10
FastEthernet0/11   128.11  128    19 FWD   12  328180009.b7ee.9800128.11
FastEthernet0/12   128.12  128    19 FWD   12  328180009.b7ee.9800128.12
FastEthernet0/17   128.13  128    19 FWD   12  328180009.b7ee.9800128.13
FastEthernet0/20   128.16  128    19 FWD   12  328180009.b7ee.9800128.16
FastEthernet0/21   128.17  128    19 FWD   12  328180009.b7ee.9800128.17
FastEthernet0/23   128.19  128    19 FWD   12  328180009.b7ee.9800128.19
FastEthernet0/24   128.20  128    19 FWD   12  328180009.b7ee.9800128.20
```

18. *What is the Bridge ID for the current Root Bridge? Is the switch that produced this output the*
actual Root Bridge?

Answer: The root Bridge ID is 8000:00d0.0457.3831. The local switch is not the root bridge
because its Bridge ID (32818:0009.b7ee.9800) is different from the root.

19. *What is the path cost of interface FastEthernet 0/4, and why is it different from the others?*

Answer: The path cost is 100. This is because that interface currently is operating at 10Mbps
(STP cost 100), whereas the others are operating at 100Mbps (STP cost 19).

20. *Why does the column marked "Designated Bridge ID" have the same value for every switch port?*

    Answer: Each of the switch ports shown has won the election to become the designated port for its local segment. Each designated port must identify its own Bridge ID, which is 32818:0009.b7ee.9800. Naturally, the Bridge ID is the same for all ports on VLAN 50.

21. *Suppose that you need to troubleshoot your spanning-tree topology and operation. What commands and information can you use on a switch to find information about the current STP topology in VLAN 39?*

    Answer: The **show spanning-tree vlan 39 root** command displays the current root bridge and the root port for VLAN 39. The **show spanning-tree vlan 39 brief** command shows a listing of every switch port on VLAN 39, along with its path cost and STP state. The designated Bridge ID is also shown on every switch port segment. For a quick summary of the total number of ports participating in each active VLAN, use the **show spanning-tree summary** command.

Chapter 10

"Do I Know This Already?"

1. b
2. c
3. c
4. b
5. b
6. a
7. b
8. b
9. c
10. c
11. c
12. b

Q&A

1. *Why would a unidirectional link be bad?*

Answer: Switches must exchange BPDUs in both directions across a link. If one side of the link is disrupted and the switches think the link is still operational, one of the switches will not receive BPDUs. If that switch had its end of the link in the Blocking state to prevent a bridging loop, the absence of BPDUs will cause it to promote the link toward the Forwarding state. At that point, the loop will form.

2. *What condition must be met to keep a switch port in the Blocking state?*

Answer: A constant flow of BPDUs. Without them, the switch thinks there is no need to block the port any longer.

3. *If a switch port is shown to be in the root-inconsistent state, what has happened on it?*

Answer: Root guard has detected someone advertising a BPDU that is superior to the current Root Bridge.

4. *When root guard has been triggered on a switch port, what must be done to enable the port for use again?*

Answer: Root guard automatically allows the port to be moved through the STP states as soon as the superior BPDUs no longer are received.

5. *When BPDU guard is enabled on a switch port, what state will the port be put in if a BPDU is received on it?*

Answer: errdisable

6. *When BPDU guard has been triggered on a switch port, what must be done to enable the port for use again?*

Answer: If the errdisable timeout feature has been enabled, the switch automatically puts the switch port back into service after a set amount of time. Otherwise, the port remains disabled until you manually enable it again.

7. *When loop guard is enabled on a switch port, what state will the port be put in if BPDUs are noted to be missing?*

Answer: loop-inconsistent

8. *Can STP loop guard be enabled on all switch ports?*

Answer: Yes. Only the nondesignated ports are affected by loop guard.

9. *When UDLD is enabled on a switch port, what else must be done to detect a unidirectional link on the port?*

   Answer: Enable UDLD on the far-end switch on the same link.

10. *What is the difference between the UDLD normal and aggressive modes?*

    Answer: Normal mode detects and reports a unidirectional link condition. Aggressive mode detects the condition, reports it, and moves the port to the errdisable state so that it can't be used.

11. *What command enables UDLD aggressive mode on a switch interface?*

    Answer: **udld aggressive**

12. *If two switches enable UDLD on the ports that have a common link, do their UDLD message times have to agree?*

    Answer: No. The UDLD messages are just echoed back, so the message times are only locally significant.

13. *UDLD should be used on switch ports with what type of media?*

    Answer: Fiber-optic media

14. *Can UDLD be used on all switch ports without causing problems?*

    Answer: Yes, although it is needed only on all fiber-based ports. The device on the far end of the port connection also must support UDLD so that UDLD messages can be echoed back to the switch.

15. *Is it possible to disable STP on a single switch port without disabling the whole STP instance? If so, how can you do that?*

    Answer: Yes, you can use BPDU filtering to effectively disable STP on a switch port. BPDUs are neither processed when they arrive nor sent on the switch port. You can use the **spanningtree bpdufilter enable** interface-configuration command to enable BPDU filtering.

    Otherwise, the whole STP instance for a VLAN must be disabled.

16. *Complete the following command to display all ports that are disabled because of STP protection features:*

    ```
    show  spanning-tree  _____
    ```
    Answer: **show spanning-tree inconsistentports**

Chapter 11

"Do I Know This Already?"

1. b
2. c
3. a
4. c
5. a
6. b
7. c
8. d
9. c
10. d
11. b
12. c

Q&A

1. *What is synchronization in RSTP?*

   Answer: Because RSTP works to converge a switched network, each switch effectively isolates itself from the next layer of neighbors until an agreement can be reached about who will have the designated port on each segment.

2. *What is an alternate port?*

   Answer: A port with an alternative path to the root. The path is less desirable than the one through the root port but is flagged for immediate use if the root port path fails.

3. *What is the difference between an alternate port and a backup port?*

   Answer: An alternate port connects to a different segment than the root port to provide an alternate path to the root. A backup port connects to the same segment as another port on the local switch to provide another path out of the switch, but not necessarily another path back to the root.

4. *Can a switch port be a designated port and be in the Discarding state?*

    Answer: Yes. RSTP removes the link between a port's role and its state. In 802.1D, a designated port must be forwarding, but RSTP doesn't have the same requirement.

5. *Which port type cannot participate in RSTP synchronization?*

    Answer: Edge port

6. *What two messages must be exchanged during RSTP synchronization?*

    Answer: Proposal and agreement

7. *After an agreement message is received from a neighboring switch, how much time elapses before the port can begin forwarding? (Consider any timers that must expire or other conditions that must be met.)*

    Answer: The port is moved to the Forwarding state immediately after the agreement message is received. With RSTP, no other conditions are necessary because two switches have completed a quick handshake by exchanging proposal and agreement messages.

8. *After a switch receives news of a topology change, how long does it wait to ush entries from its CAM table?*

    Answer: The switch flushes entries immediately instead of employing the timer reduction that 802.1D uses.

9. *What command configures a port as an RSTP edge port?*

    Answer: **spanning-tree portfast**

10. *Suppose that interface FastEthernet 0/1 is in half-duplex mode, but you want it to be considered a point-to-point link for RSTP. What command can accomplish this?*

    Answer: **spanning-tree link-type point-to-point**

11. *Put the following in order of the number of supported STP instances, from lowest to highest:*

    a. *MST*

    b. *PVST+*

    c. *CST*

    d. *802.1D*

    Answer: d, c, a, b (d and c both have a single instance.)

12. *What three parameters must be configured to uniquely define an MST region?*

Answer: The region name, configuration revision number, and instance-to-VLAN mappings

13. *What parameter does a switch examine to see if its neighbors have the same VLAN-to-MST instance mappings? How is that information passed among switches?*

Answer: The VLAN-to-instance mapping is kept in a table of 4,096 entries. This information is passed along in the MST BPDUs. Instead of passing the entire table, switches include only a digest of their current table contents.

14. *Which MST instance in a region corresponds to the CST of 802.1Q?*

Answer: The Internal Spanning Tree (IST) instance

15. *Which MST instance is the IST?*

Answer: IST is instance 0. Instances 1 through 15 are available for other use.

16. *When an MST region meets a PVST+ domain, how is each MST instance propagated into PVST+?*

Answer: The BPDUs from each instance are replicated and sent into all the appropriate VLANs in the PVST+ switch.

17. *Is it wise to assign VLANs to MST instance 0? Why or why not?*

Answer: No. By default, all VLANs are mapped to instance 0, the IST. You should select the number of instances needed and map all active VLANs to them. Otherwise, you can't have full control over the topologies independent of IST and CST.

18. *The commands have just been entered to define an MST region on a switch. You are still at the MST configuration prompt. What command must you enter to commit the MST changes on the switch?*

Answer: **exit** (When the MST configuration mode is exited, the changes are committed immediately.)

19. *How can MST configuration information be propagated to other Cisco switches?*

Answer: The MST information must be configured manually in each switch within the MST region. Currently, no method or protocol automatically can propagate the MST configuration.

20. *A switch can interact with both 802.1D and RSTP. Can it run both PVST+ and MST simultaneously?*

Answer: No. A switch can run either PVST+ or MST. If a switch is running MST, it can interact and interoperate with PVST+, 802.1D, and RSTP.

Chapter 12

"Do I Know This Already?"

1. d
2. a
3. a
4. b
5. c
6. c
7. c
8. d
9. c
10. c
11. d
12. c

Q&A

1. *What might you need to implement interVLAN routing?*

Answer:

One or more Layer 3 interfaces
One or more SVIs
Static routes
A dynamic routing protocol

2. *Can interVLAN routing be performed over a single trunk link?*

Answer: Yes. Packets can be forwarded between the VLANs carried over the trunk.

3. *To configure an SVI, what commands are needed?*

Answer: First, make sure the VLAN is defined on the switch.

```
interface vlan vlan-id
ip address ip-address mask
no shutdown
```

4. *What command can verify the VLAN assignments on a Layer 2 port?*

Answer:

show interface *type mod/num* **switchport**
or
show interface status

5. *A switch has the following interface configurations in its running configuration:*

```
interface  fastethernet  0/1
switchport  access  vlan  5
!
interface  vlan  5
ip  address  192.168.10.1  255.255.255.0
no  shutdown
```

What is necessary for packets to get from the FastEthernet interface to the VLAN 5 SVI?

Answer: Nothing. Both are assigned to VLAN 5, so normal Layer 2 transparent bridging will take care of all forwarding between the two.

6. *What is the source of FIB information?*

Answer: The routing table, as computed by the Layer 3 engine portion of a switch.

7. *How often is the FIB updated?*

Answer: As needed. It is downloaded or updated dynamically by the Layer 3 engine whenever the routing topology changes or an ARP entry changes.

8. *What is meant by the term "CEF punt"?*

Answer: A packet can't be forwarded or switched by CEF directly because it needs further processing. The packet is "punted" to the Layer 3 engine, effectively bypassing CEF for a more involved resolution.

9. *What happens to the FIB when distributed CEF (dCEF) is used?*

Answer: It is simply replicated to each of the independent CEF engines. The FIB itself remains intact so that each engine receives a duplicate copy.

10.   *What happens during a "CEF glean" process?*

Answer: The MAC address (ARP reply) for a next-hop FIB entry is not yet known. The Layer 3 engine must generate an ARP request and wait for a reply before CEF forwarding can continue to that destination.

11.   *What does a multilayer switch do to the IP TTL value just before a packet is forwarded?*

Answer: The TTL is decremented by one, as if a router had forwarded the packet.

12.   *What is fallback bridging?*

Answer: On switch platforms that cannot multilayer-switch (route) all routable protocols, those protocols can be bridged transparently between VLANs instead.

13.   *Is it possible for an SVI to go down? If so, for what reasons?*

Answer: Yes. The SVI can be shut down administratively with the shutdown command, as with any other interface. Also, if the VLAN associated with the SVI is not defined or active, the SVI will appear to be down.

Chapter 13

"Do I Know This Already?"

1.   d

2.   d

3.   c

4.   b

5.   b

6.   b

7.   c

8.   c

9.   c

10.   b

11.   b

12.   b

Q&A

1. *A multilayer switch has been configured with the command* **standby 5 priority 120**. *What router-redundancy protocol is being used?*

    Answer: HSRP

2. *What feature can you use to prevent other routers from accidentally participating in an HSRP group?*

    Answer: HSRP authentication

3. *What command can configure an HSRP group to use a virtual router address of 192.168.222.100?*

    Answer: **standby 1 ip 192.168.222.100**

4. *The* **show standby vlan 271** *command produces the following output:*

    ```
    Vlan271 - Group 1
      Local state is Active, priority 210, may preempt
      Hellotime 3 holdtime 40 configured hellotime 3 sec holdtime 40 sec
      Next hello sent in 00:00:00.594
      Virtual IP address is 192.168.111.1 configured
        Secondary virtual IP address 10.1.111.1
        Secondary virtual IP address 172.21.111.1
      Active router is local
      Standby router is unknown expires in 00:00:37
      Standby virtual mac address is 0000.0c07.ac01
      2 state changes, last state change 5d17h
    ```

    If the local router fails, which router takes over the active role for the virtual router address 192.168.111.1?

    Answer: None. There is no known standby router, so it also has failed.

5. *What is meant by pre-empting in HSRP?*

    Answer: Normally, if the active router (highest priority) fails, another router takes over its active role. The original active router is not allowed to resume the active role when it is restored until the new active router fails. Pre-empting allows a higher-priority router to take over the active role immediately or after a configurable delay.

6. *What protocols discussed in this chapter support interface tracking?*

    Answer: HSRP, GLBP

7. *The **show standby brief** command has been used to check the status of all HSRP groups on the local router. The output from this command is as follows:*

```
Switch# show standby brief
                     P indicates configured to preempt.
                     |
Interface  Grp Prio P State    Activeaddr   Standbyaddr    Groupaddr
Vl100        1  210 P Active   local        192.168.75.2   192.168.75.1
Vl101        1  210 P Active   local        192.168.107.2  192.168.107.1
Vl102        1  210 P Active   local        192.168.71.2   192.168.71.1
```

Each interface is shown to have Group 1. Is this a problem?

Answer: No, as long as there is no bridging between VLANs. The HSRP group number can be repeated because each group is isolated on its own VLAN.

8. *How many HSRP groups are needed to load-balance traffic over two routers?*

Answer: Two

9. *What load-balancing methods can GLBP use?*

Answer: Round robin, weighted, host dependent

10. *What command can you use to see the status of the active and standby routers on the VLAN 171 interface?*

Answer: **show standby vlan 171**

11. *How many GLBP groups are needed to load-balance traffic over four routers?*

Answer: One

12. *To use NSF on a multilayer switch with redundant supervisor modules, what must be configured in addition to the redundancy mode? What else must be present in the network?*

Answer: First, the SSO redundancy mode must be enabled with the **redundancy** and **mode sso** configuration commands. NSF can be enabled only when it is configured within the respective routing protocol configurations. When NSF is configured on a switch, there must be other neighboring switches or routers that are NSF-aware. The local switch depends on these devices to provide it with routing information during a failover.

13. *How is SSO different from SRM with SSO redundancy mode?*

Answer: There is no difference. SRM refers to Single Router Mode, in which only one of the two route processors can be active at any time. Only one route processor can be active for the Stateful Switchover (SSO) mode, so SRM is used inherently with SSO.

14. *If two Catalyst 6500 power supplies are configured with the **power redundancy-mode combined** command, what will happen if one of them fails?*

Answer: In combined mode, both power supplies actively share the total power load of the chassis. As long as the total power budget is less than the maximum capacity of one power supply, the one working power supply can continue to power the switch. Otherwise, the supervisor will begin removing power from switch modules until the power load becomes less than the power supply capacity.

Chapter 14

"Do I Know This Already?"

1. b

2. d

3. c

4. b

5. a

6. d

7. a

8. d

9. c

10. b

11. b

12. d

Q&A

1. *How does a Catalyst switch detect that a connected device is capable of using Power over Ethernet?*

Answer: The device first must loop the Ethernet connection's transmit and receive pairs. The switch then can hear its own test tone, confirming that the device does need inline power. When the power is enabled on the port, the switch and the device can exchange CDP messages so that the amount of power can be adjusted.

2. *What type of trunk can be used between a Catalyst switch port and a Cisco IP Phone?*

Answer: A special-case 802.1Q trunk with only two VLANs

3. *When a trunk is used on an IP Phone, on which VLAN is the data from an attached PC carried?*

Answer: PC data always is carried over the native (untagged) VLAN in the trunk. Voice packets can be carried over the native VLAN, too, or over a unique voice VLAN.

4. *What is the difference between the VVID and the PVID?*

Answer: VVID refers to the voice VLAN ID, whereas PVID refers to the port VLAN ID.

5. *Can the CoS information from the voice traffic be passed when the **switchport voice vlan untagged** command is used? If so, how?*

Answer: Yes, CoS information is passed within the 802.1p portion of the 802.1Q trunk encapsulation.

6. *What is the advantage of using the **switchport voice vlan dot1p** command?*

Answer: Voice traffic is carried over VLAN 0 on the IP Phone trunk, so a unique voice VLAN is not necessary. This can be an advantage when a new VLAN can't be added to a network or switch. CoS information still is carried over the trunk in the 802.1p field.

7. *By default, does a Cisco IP Phone trust QoS information from an attached PC?*

Answer: No. The phone will overwrite all QoS information (both CoS and DSCP) to 0, considering the PC an untrusted source.

8. *The command **switchport priority extend cos 5** is entered for a switch port. Is this a good decision? Why or why not?*

Answer: Probably not. After that is done, all packets from an attached PC will be marked with CoS 5, the same value the phone gives to its voice-bearer packets. Any upstream switches will be incapable of distinguishing the two types of traffic just by examining the CoS value.

9. *What commands can be used to enable Auto-Qos on interface FastEthernet 0/1, where a Cisco IP phone is connected?*

Answer:

interface fastethernet 0/1
auto qos voip cisco-phone

10. *The **show power inline** command is used to check the power status on each switch port. If the output is as shown here, what can you assume about interface fastethernet 0/1?*

```
Interface  Admin  Oper    Power     Device
                          (Watts)
---------  -----  ------  -------   ------------------
Fa0/1      auto   off           0   n/a
Fa0/2      auto   on          6.3   Cisco  IP  Phone  7960
```

Answer: Interface fastethernet 0/1 shows an operational inline power state of "off," with 0W of power. This could mean that nothing is plugged into that switch port. It also could mean that an IP Phone is connected to the port but that the port has inline power set to the "off" state.

11. *What command can verify the QoS trust relationship between an IP Phone and its attached PC?*

Answer:

show mls qos interface
or
show interface switchport

Chapter 15

"Do I Know This Already?"

1. c

2. d

3. b

4. b The trick is in the **maximum 3** keywords. This sets the maximum number of addresses that can be learned on a port. If only one static address is configured, two more addresses can be learned dynamically.

5. c

6. a

7. b

8. c

9. c Because of the variety of user host platforms, port-based authentication (802.1x) cannot be used. The problem also states that the goal is to restrict access to physical switch ports, so AAA is of no benefit. Port security can do the job by restricting access according to the end users' MAC addresses.

10. b

11. c, d

12. c

Q&A

1. *When might the command **switchport port-security maximum 2** be used?*

Answer: The **switchport port-security maximum 2** command might be used if it is too much trouble to manually configure MAC addresses into the port security feature. Up to two MAC addresses then would be learned dynamically. The network administrator also might want to control what is connected to that switch port. If another switch or a hub were connected, the total number of active stations easily could rise above two.

2. *After port-based authentication is configured and enabled, can any host connect as long as the user can authenticate?*

Answer: No, only hosts that have 802.1x-capable applications can communicate with the switch port to properly authenticate.

3. *When the 802.1x **force-authorized** keyword is used, how does the switch react to users attempting to connect?*

Answer: The switch always authorizes any connecting user, without any authentication.

4. *Can more than one host be authenticated on a single switch port with port-based authentication?*

Answer: Yes, if the **dot1x multi-hosts** command is configured on the switch port interface.

5. *In DHCP spoofing and ARP poisoning attacks, what is the goal of the attacker? What Catalyst features can be used to mitigate the risk of these attacks?*

Answer: In both types of attacks, the attacker is attempting to be positioned as a man-in-the-middle, to be used as the default gateway address by unsuspecting clients. Sitting between a client and other resources, the attacker then can intercept and inspect packets coming from the client. The DHCP snooping and dynamic ARP inspection (DAI) Catalyst switch features can be used to detect and prevent these attacks when they are attempted.

6. *Which switch ports should be configured as trusted for DHCP snooping?*

Answer: You should configure a port as trusted only if it connects to a known, trusted DHCP server. In addition, you can make a port trusted if it connects to another switch that also is performing DHCP snooping.

7. *What Catalyst feature can be used to mitigate an address spoofing attack? Can the feature be used to detect a spoofed MAC address? A spoofed IP address?*

    Answer: IP source guard can be used to mitigate an address spoofing attack. IP source guard can detect a spoofed source MAC address or a spoofed source IP address.

8. *What is the function of a trusted port in DAI?*

    Answer: No ARP inspection is performed on a trusted port; the inspection process is reserved for ARP replies on untrusted ports only. You can configure a port as trusted if it connects a neighboring switch that also has DAI enabled or if it connects to a trusted host.

9. *To inspect ARP information from a host that has received its IP address from a DHCP server, what must be enabled in addition to DAI?*

    Answer: DHCP snooping must be enabled, too. The DHCP snooping feature maintains a database of dynamic MAC–to–IP address mappings. This information is used by DAI to validate the ARP responses it inspects.

Chapter 16

"Do I Know This Already?"
1. c
2. d
3. d
4. a
5. b
6. a
7. c
8. a
9. d
10. a
11. a
12. c

Q&A

1.   *When a VACL is implemented on a switch, how is the switching speed affected?*

     Answer: It isn't; VACLs are implemented in hardware, so packets can be inspected as they are being switched, with no performance penalty.

2.   *What actions can be taken on packets matching a VACL?*

     Answer: Packets can be forwarded, dropped, marked for capture, or redirected to a different Layer 2 switch port.

3.   *After a VACL is applied using the **vlan filter** command, how is the traffic direction (inbound or outbound) specified?*

     Answer: It isn't; VACLs operate on packets as they are being forwarded within a VLAN. Therefore, there is no concept of direction within the VLAN. A direction can't be specified.

4.   *A secondary community VLAN is associated with a primary VLAN on a switch. Can hosts assigned to the community VLAN communicate with each other?*

     Answer: Yes, they can. However, they can't communicate with any other community or isolated VLAN.

5.   *A secondary isolated VLAN is associated with a primary VLAN on a switch. Can hosts assigned to the isolated VLAN communicate with each other?*

     Answer: No, hosts on an isolated VLAN can't communicate even among themselves. They can reach only the promiscuous host on the primary VLAN.

6.   *What command is needed to configure a promiscuous VLAN?*

     Answer: This isn't possible. The primary VLAN can communicate with all the secondary VLANs that are associated with it. The only promiscuous objects that can be configured are promiscuous hosts, located on the primary VLAN.

7.   *A router is identified as the central gateway for a private VLAN. What command is needed to configure the switch port where a router is connected?*

     Answer: **switchport mode private-vlan promiscuous**

8.   *How many actual VLANs must be configured to implement a common router with two community VLANs?*

     Answer: Three VLANs must be used: one for the primary VLAN where the router is connected and two more for the secondary community VLANs. The primary VLAN will be logically associated with the two community VLANs, but all three must be configured.

9. *In a switch spoofing attack, what is the attacker's goal?*

Answer: An attacker spoofs DTP messages on a normal access-layer switch port, hoping that the switch responds and will negotiate trunking mode. If that happens, the attacker can spoof VLAN ID tags to inject traffic onto any VLAN that is carried over the trunk.

10. *What should be configured to prevent a switch spoofing attack?*

Answer: You always should configure every access-layer switch port to a fixed mode so that DTP is disabled, preventing the possibility of trunk negotiation with an attacker. Switch ports default to the **switchport mode dynamic auto** mode, allowing a connected device to actively negotiate the port into the trunking mode. You can use the **switchport mode access** command to force static access mode, thereby disabling DTP negotiation completely.

11. *Describe some methods that can be used to prevent a VLAN hopping attack.*

Answer: You always should configure a trunk's native VLAN to an unused VLAN number and prune the native VLAN from each end of the trunk. This isolates the native VLAN completely so that no traffic can be injected onto it.

In addition, you can configure Catalyst switches to require a tag on *all* VLANs carried over a trunk, including the native VLAN.

Chapter 17

"Do I Know This Already?"

1. d

2. b

3. b

4. d

5. a

6. c

7. b

8. c

9. c

10. b

11. c

12. a

Q&A

1. *What duplex modes can be used when a wireless client joins the wireless LAN?*

    Answer: Only half-duplex mode is supported. Every wireless client associated with an AP shares the same frequency for both transmitting and receiving. The AP also uses the same frequency. Therefore, only one device should transmit at any given time. To achieve full-duplex operation, separate frequencies would have to be used for transmitting and receiving.

2. *How many nonoverlapping channels are available in 802.1g networks? Why?*

    Answer: Three. Although the 802.1b and 802.1g standards define up to 14 separate channels, only three of them are nonoverlapping. Each channel has 22 MHz reserved for it, but the channels are spaced only 5 MHz apart. Therefore, only channels 1, 6, and 11 are spaced appropriately so no overlap occurs.

3. *Can a wireless network experience collisions? If so, how do the wireless devices handle them?*

    Answer: Yes, wireless LANs can experience collisions. All wireless devices are required to use the CSMA/CA method to avoid or minimize the possibility of creating collisions. Wireless stations must listen first, transmitting only if the channel is idle and clear. A random backoff timer is used to introduce some randomness as stations begin to transmit.

4. *How does a wireless client know how long to wait before trying to transmit a frame?*

    Answer: If another device is transmitting, all other devices must first wait until that frame is completed. The duration of a frame is recorded in the frame header itself, so other stations can gauge the initial wait time. After that, stations must wait until the DIFS, a small amount of time between frames, expires. Further, stations waiting to transmit must wait a brief random time before using the channel.

5. *Name three types of wireless service set and their functions.*

    Answer:

    IBSS: An ad-hoc network consisting only of wireless clients communicating directly.
    BSS: A group of wireless clients associated to one central access point.
    ESS: Multiple access points (and their respective groups of clients) interconnected by a switched network.

6. *Suppose a wireless client just arrives within range of an access point. Can the client begin using the wireless LAN?*

    Answer: No, the client must meet all the conditions required by the AP before using the WLAN. The client must use the same channel, SSID, and data rates that the AP is configured to use. Also, the client must request an association with the AP and might be required to authenticate itself before any data will be accepted from the client.

7. *An AP can bridge a VLAN to a wireless LAN. How can it bridge more than one VLAN to the wireless LAN?*

    Answer: The AP bridges each VLAN onto a separate SSID. The SSIDs then become like the tags used to encapsulate frames on an Ethernet trunk. Any wireless clients using a common SSID will appear to be connected to the VLAN that is mapped to that SSID.

8. *What is implied by saying that two wireless devices use the same channel?*

    Answer: Both devices are tuned to the same carrier or center frequency. Also, both use the same modulation technique to encode or decode information that is found within the channel's frequency range surrounding the carrier frequency.

9. *Name two standards that operate in the same band. Then name two wireless LAN standards that operate in different bands.*

    Answer: IEEE 802.1b and 802.1g both operate in the 2.4-GHz band. IEEE 802.1a operates in the 5-GHz band, which is different than either 802.1b or 802.1g.

10. *Suppose a wireless client is associated to a nearby AP. If a person came and stood between the client's antenna and the AP, what effect might this have on the signal?*

    Answer: The signal between the client and the AP might be absorbed by the person's body, reducing the signal strength.

11. *Suppose you are designing a wireless LAN and you need to choose the location of an AP for a group of wireless clients. The AP will be using an omnidirectional antenna. Should you consider the Fresnel zone in your decision?*

    Answer: No, the Fresnel zone really only comes into play with line-of-sight RF signal paths. An AP using an omnidirectional antenna transmits its signal in all directions. Besides, clearing a broad signal path area of all obstacles would be impractical.

12. *What transmit power would an AP be delivering if it had a power level of 0 dBm?*

    Answer: With dBm, the actual power is compared to a reference of 1 mW. Therefore, 10*log of the power ratio must be 0 dBm—a condition that is met only when the ratio is one. Therefore, the power output must be 1 mW, the same as the reference power.

13. *Name some things that can cause RF signal loss.*

    Answer: Transmitter or receiver antenna cabling, free space loss, external obstacles, and signal interference

14.   *Briefly describe antenna gain. What is different about a dish antenna versus an omnidirectional antenna?*

Answer: Antenna gain is a gauge of how well the antenna can focus RF signal energy over that of an isotropic antenna (no focusing at all). For example, a dish antenna has a much higher gain than an omnidirectional simply because it does a much better job of focusing the signal into a narrow beam.

15.   *What data rates are supported by the IEEE 802.11b standard?*

Answer: 1, 2, 5.5, and 11 Mbps.

16.   *What is the maximum supported data rates in IEEE 802.11b and 802.11g?*

Answer: The maximum in 802.11b is 11 Mbps, while 802.11g supports up to 54 Mbps.

17.   *What is the maximum data rate available in an 802.11g wireless LAN when there is a mix of 802.11g and 802.11b clients?*

Answer: Although 802.11g supports up to 54 Mbps, the wireless devices will fall back into 802.11b mode if even one 802.11b client is present, which reduces the maximum data rate to 11 Mbps.

Chapter 18

"Do I Know This Already?"

1.   b

2.   c

3.   b

4.   d

5.   a

6.   c

7.   c

8.   a

9.   d

10.   b

11.   d

12.   c

Q&A

1. *Consider the following wireless security methods. Based on encryption alone, which could be considered the most secure?*

    a. *Open authentication*

    b. *Pre-shared key*

    c. *LEAP*

    d. *WPA*

    e. *WPA2*

    Answer: WPA2 offers the most encryption security with its use of AES.

2. *Describe the weakness of using static WEP keys.*

    Answer: A static WEP key must be manually configured, requiring administrative overhead to install and update keys on many APs. Static WEP keys also have an indefinite lifetime, allowing attackers to gather enough information to reverse-engineer the encryption process.

3. *When is it considered appropriate to secure a WLAN with only open authentication, assuming the SSID is kept secret?*

    Answer: By using only open authentication, potential clients are not challenged to present any credentials. As long as a client knows the correct SSID, that client can associate. The SSID is simply a string in cleartext that is used to logically bind wireless clients with the appropriate wireless LAN. SSIDs were never meant to be used as a security measure.

4. *What things should you consider when sizing an AP cell?*

    Answer: Probably the most important consideration is the number of clients that can associate to a single AP. Every client associated with an AP has to contend with every other client for the shared bandwidth. Smaller cell sizes tend to limit the number of clients simply because wireless clients aren't usually congregated in a small area.

    Smaller cell sizes also assure that clients are within the range of the greatest data rate and have a good quality signal to and from the AP.

    You should also consider what might happen if an AP fails. If the cell size is large, the large hole of lost coverage could affect a large number of clients. Smaller cells reduce the number of clients left in a coverage hole.

5. *Should adjacent AP cells be configured to operate on the same channel? Why or why not?*

    Answer: No, adjacent APs should always be configured to use nonoverlapping channels. If they use the same channel, the signals from the two APs will interfere with each other. This will make it difficult for clients in either cell to communicate with their respective APs. Roaming will also become difficult, as no distinct point exists where one AP is more reachable than another due to the interference.

608   Appendix A: Answers to Chapter 'Do I Know This Already?' Quizzes and Q&A Sections

6. *Suppose that a set of 802.11b APs are configured to use channels 1, 6, and 11 in an alternating fashion. What channels should you choose when the 802.11g portion of the same APs are configured?*

   Answer: The 802.11g AP radios actually co-exist with the 802.11b radios, so the two can (and do) use the same channels.

7. *Suppose that 802.11a clients and APs are introduced into an area already using 802.11b or 802.11g. What effect will this have?*

   Answer: Devices using 802.11b and 802.11g operate within the same 2.4 GHz frequency band. Devices using 802.11a operate within the 5 GHz band, so there will be no interference with 802.11b/g. In fact, many APs and clients have radios that can work in 802.11b, 802.11g, and 802.11a simultaneously. For example, this means an AP can offer both 802.11b/g and 802.11a operations on their respective channels.

8. *Suppose that an office area has wireless coverage from several APs, each using a very small cell size. Should you be concerned about the power output (and therefore the cell size) of client devices?*

   Answer: Simply put, yes, you should be concerned about the clients' cell sizes, too. You might not think of a wireless client having a cell or cell size, as it represents only a single wireless connection to an external AP. However, a client does transmit with a set power level that usually propagates within a radius of itself. In effect, this forms a circular cell of transmissions on a specific channel.

   If the client's cell size is sufficiently larger than the AP cells, it can begin to interfere with other APs operating on the same channel. Therefore, you should keep in mind that it is better to have clients using cells that are roughly the same size as the APs.

Chapter 19

"Do I Know This Already?"

1. c
2. a
3. b
4. c
5. b
6. a
7. a

8. d

9. d

10. c

11. a

12. b

Q&A

1. *LWAPP is integral to operating a lightweight access point. What is so special about LWAPP?*

Answer: LWAPP is the protocol used to build a tunnel between a lightweight AP and a WLC. Through this protocol, the LAP can be centrally managed, can synchronize code images, and can transport wireless client traffic across a switched network from WLC to LAP.

2. *How does a wireless client roam between two LAPs managed by the same WLC?*

Answer: The client must move its association from one LAP to another in order to roam. Because the same WLC manages both LAPs, the client associations stay within the WLC. Therefore, the WLC updates its database and finds the client through the LWAPP tunnel to the second AP.

3. *Can a client roam across two LAPs that are managed by two different WLCs? Explain why or why not.*

Answer: Yes; as the client roams to the second LAP, the WLCs negotiate the association hand-off. The client is able to roam as long as both WLCs belong to the same mobility group.

4. *Describe some of the functions that are divided between LAP and WLC in a "split-MAC" architecture.*

Answer: The LAP retains the real-time wireless activities, while the WLC maintains all of the management functions. The two devices essentially perform as one complete device operating at the MAC layer.

5. *List some of the advanced functions that can be performed by a WLC.*

Answer: By managing a complete set of LAPs from one central location, a WLC can monitor and make adjustments to the wireless LAN as a whole. The WLC can manage dynamic channel assignment, make transmit power adjustments, heal coverage holes due to radio failures, and collect statistics about RF channel usage.

Index

Numerics

X-Y-Z